THE LITURGY DOCUMENTS
A PARISH RESOURCE

VOLUME ONE

THE LITURGY DOCUMENTS
A PARISH RESOURCE

Volume One

Fourth Edition

LITURGY
TRAINING
PUBLICATIONS

This book was edited by David Lysik, with assistance from Theresa Pincich, Lorraine Schmidt, Laura Goodman, and Audrey Novak Riley. The index was compiled by Mary Laur. Ana Aguilar-Islas designed the book and Mark Hollopeter set the type. Cover design by Barb Rohm and Lucy Smith. Cover art © 1997, Romare Bearden Foundation/Licensed by VAGA, New York, NY, *Farewell Eugene.*

10 09 08 07   6 5 4 3 2

ISBN 978-1-56854-468-7
LDOC1

CONTENTS

ABBREVIATIONS

Many texts listed here appear in *Documents on the Liturgy, 1963–1979: Conciliar, Papal and Curial Texts* (DOL) (Collegeville MN: The Liturgical Press, 1982).

AAS — *Acta Apostolicae Sedis,* (1909–)

AG — Vatican Council II, decree *Ad gentes divinitus* (on the church's missionary activity) (December 7, 1965)

BB — *Book of Blessings*

BCL — Bishops' Committee on the Liturgy, NCCB

BLS — BCL, *Built of Living Stones: Art, Architecture, and Worship* (2000)

c.; cc. — canon; canons

CB — *Ceremonial of Bishops* (1989)

CCC — *Catechism of the Catholic Church* (1992)

CCCB — Canadian Conference of Catholic Bishops

CCEC — Code of Canons of the Eastern Churches *(Codex canonum ecclesiarum orientalium)* (1990)

CCL — *Corpus christianorum, Series Latina* (Turnhout, 1953–)

CD — Vatican Council II, decree *Christus dominus* (on the pastoral office of bishops in the church) (October 28, 1965)

CDF — Congregation for the Doctrine of the Faith

CDW — Congregation for Divine Worship

CEILT — NCCB, *Criteria for the Evaluation of Inclusive Language Translations of Scriptural Texts Proposed for Liturgical Use* (1990)

CI — CDW, *Christian Initiation, General Introduction* (1969, 1974)

CIC — Code of Canon Law *(Codex iuris canonici)*

1917 CIC — 1917 Code of Canon Law *(Codex iuris canonici)*

CP — Consilium, instruction *Comme le prévoit* (on the translation of liturgical texts for celebrations with a congregation) (January 25, 1969)

CR — Congregation of Rites

CSEL — *Corpus scriptorum ecclesiasticorum latinorum* (Vienna, 1866–)

CT — John Paul II, apostolic exhortation *Catechesi tradendae* (October 16, 1979)

DD — John Paul II, apostolic letter *Dies domini* (on keeping the Lord's day holy) (May 31, 1998)

DE — Pontifical Council for Promoting Christian Unity, *Directory for the Application of Principles and Norms on Ecumenism* (1993)

DedCh — *Dedication of a Church and an Altar* (1978, rev. 1989)

DMC — CDW, *Directory for Masses with Children* (1973)

DV — Vatican Council II, dogmatic constitution *Dei verbum* (on divine revelation) (November 18, 1965)

EACW — BCL, *Environment and Art in Catholic Worship* (1978)

EM — CR, instruction *Eucharisticum mysterium* (on the worship of the eucharist) (May 25, 1967)

FYH — NCCB, Bishops' Committee on Priestly Life and Ministry, *Fulfilled in Your Hearing: The Homily in the Sunday Assembly* (1982)

GIapp   Appendix to the *General Instruction of the Roman Missal* for the Dioceses of the United States (rev. 1985)

GILOH   CDW, *General Instruction of the Liturgy of the Hours* (1971)

GIRM   CDW, *General Instruction of the Roman Missal* (1975, 2003)

GMEF   BCL, *God's Mercy Endures Forever: Guidelines on the Presentation of Jews and Judaism in Catholic Preaching* (1988)

GNLY   *General Norms for the Liturgical Year and the Calendar* (1969)

GS   Vatican Council II, pastoral constitution *Gaudium et spes*, (on the church in the modern world) (December 7, 1965)

GSPD   NCCB, *Guidelines for the Celebration of the Sacraments with Persons with Disabilities* (1995)

HLS   NCCB, *This Holy and Living Sacrifice: Directory for the Celebration and Reception of Communion under Both Kinds* (1984)

IRL   Congregation for Divine Worship and the Discipline of the Sacraments, *Inculturation and the Roman Liturgy: Fourth Instruction for the Right Application of the Conciliar Constitution on the Liturgy*, nn. 37–40 (1994)

IST   BCL, *In Spirit and Truth: Black Catholic Reflections on the Order of Mass* (1987)

LG   Vatican Council II, dogmatic constitution *Lumen gentium* (on the church) (November 21, 1964)

LM   *Lectionary for Mass*, second *editio typica* (1981)

LMT   BCL, *Liturgical Music Today* (1982)

MCW   BCL, *Music in Catholic Worship* (1972, 1983)

MS   CR, instruction *Musicam sacram* (1967)

n.; nn.   number; numbers

NCCB   National Conference of Catholic Bishops

NDR   USCCB, *Norms for the Distribution and Holy Reception of Holy Communion Under Both Kinds in the Dioceses of the United States of America* (2001)

OCF   *Order of Christian Funerals.*

OE   Vatican Council II, decree *Orientalium ecclesiarum* (on the Catholic Eastern churches) (November 21, 1965)

OT   Vatican Council II, decree *Optatam totius* (on the training of priests) (October 28, 1965)

par.   parallel passages in the synoptic gospels

PCS   *Pastoral Care of the Sick: Rites of Anointing and Viaticum* (1983)

PG   J.P. Migne, *Patrologiae cursus completus: Series Graeca*

PGR   NCCB, Secretariat for the Liturgy and Secretariat for Black Catholics, *Plenty Good Room: The Spirit and Truth of African American Catholic Worship* (1990)

PL   J.P. Migne, *Patrologiae cursus completus: Series Latina*

PO   Vatican Council II, decree *Presbyterorum ordinis* (on the life and ministry of priests) (December 7, 1965)

PS   CDW, circular letter *Paschale solemnitatis* (on preparing and celebrating the paschal feasts) (January 16, 1988)

RBaptC   *Rite of Baptism for Children*

RCIA   *Rite of Christian Initiation of Adults*

RConf   *Rite of Confirmation*

RM   John Paul II, encyclical *Redemptoris missio* (on the permanent validity of the church's missionary mandate) (December 7, 1990)

RMarr	*Rite of Marriage*
RomM	*Roman Missal*
RP	*Roman Pontifical*
RPen	*Rite of Penance*
SC	Vatican Council II, constitution *Sacrosanctum concilium* (on the sacred liturgy) (December 4, 1963)
SCC	CCCB, *To Speak as a Christian Community: Pastoral Message on Inclusive Language* (1989)
SCh	*Sources chrétiennes* (Paris, 1941–)
UR	Vatican Council II, decree *Unitatis redintegratio* (on ecumenism) (November 21, 1964)
USCCB	United States Conference of Catholic Bishops
VQA	John Paul II, apostolic letter *Vicesimus quintus annus*
WWHSH	*What We Have Seen and Heard: A Pastoral Letter on Evangelization from the Black Bishops of the United States* (1984)

GENERAL INTRODUCTION

Kevin W. Irwin

The documents in this collection span four decades and reflect the most comprehensive revision of the liturgy ever undertaken at one time in the history of the Roman Catholic Church. When the bishops of the Second Vatican Council decided that all "the liturgical books are to be revised as soon as possible" (*Constitution on the Sacred Liturgy*, n. 25) they inaugurated a project that was to affect every Catholic because these revisions would change how the sacred liturgy is celebrated. To appreciate the breadth of these changes and the meaning of the liturgy as it was revised, it is crucially important to understand what these documents say about what liturgy means as well as about the way it is celebrated. Therefore a study of the documents in this collection will be of benefit to every Catholic who seeks to appreciate as fully as possible what it means to participate in the liturgical prayer of the church.

From the outset, it is important to recall that within and among church documents some bear greater weight than others, and that some are written for the whole church while some are written for a particular country. Hence, in what follows, the first document—the *Constitution on the Sacred Liturgy* from Vatican II—may be regarded as the *magna carta* that led to the rest of the documents because it was decreed by the highest authority in the church for the whole church. Nine of the documents reprinted in this collection were originally published as introductions to the revised liturgical books for the whole church. Six were published by the United States Conference of Catholic Bishops to guide and help in the implementation of the reformed liturgy in our country. Each in its own way should be regarded as normative for the celebration of the liturgy. That some specifically emphasize canon law (for example, *National Statutes for the Catechumenate*) will be clear. Each should be respected as binding on dioceses in the United States for the proper implementation of the liturgy as revised after Vatican II.

As we begin this guided tour through these documents, it is important to realize that the liturgy is an action comprising at least two things. It is a public act of the whole church, in which God is revealed and worshiped. Liturgy is also that privileged kind of prayer in which the church is always renewed and sanctified. We come to the liturgy—this public prayer of the church—at God's gracious invitation to become ever more faithful disciples. One of the great benefits of the way the reformed liturgy is celebrated is that we can appreciate directly what is said and done in the liturgy for our salvation and sanctification. A careful study of these fifteen church documents on the liturgy can be an important tool guiding our appreciation and understanding of the liturgy.

CONSTITUTION ON THE SACRED LITURGY

In January 1959, Pope John XXIII announced his intention to assemble the world's bishops for the most solemn and authoritative kind of church meeting possible—an ecumenical council. The world's bishops have met only twenty-one times for such an ecumenical council (as opposed to regional meetings and other kinds of meetings such as synods), and the decisions that they reached through debate and discussion have affected the church's teachings on matters of faith and morals and the church's discipline and structures. The title "Second Vatican Council" recalls that in 1869–70 the world's Catholic bishops met at the Vatican, which meeting is now termed the "First Vatican Council."

After almost four years of preparatory meetings and drafting of documents to be discussed, the bishops met to open the Second Vatican Council in October 1962. The period from October 1962 through December 1965 will be remembered as the time when the bishops met in council to make a number of decisions and to usher in dramatic developments in many areas of church life. The first document approved by the bishops at the Second Vatican Council was the *Constitution on the Sacred Liturgy.* By calling it a "constitution" (as opposed to other "declarations" and "decrees"), the bishops were saying that this document should receive the highest priority, along with the other three constitutions from the Council (one on divine revelation and two on the church). Since the *Constitution on the Sacred Liturgy* was the first document approved and promulgated (on December 4, 1963) it is not surprising that its opening paragraph deals with the intentions of the Council in general. It states: "It is the goal of this most sacred Council to intensify the daily growth of Catholics in Christian living; to make more responsive to the signs of our times those Church observances which are open to adaptation; to nurture whatever can contribute to the unity of all who believe in Christ; and to strengthen those aspects of the Church which can help summon all mankind into her embrace" (n. 1). Clearly the reform of the liturgy was seen as serving these wider purposes. The reform of the liturgy was viewed as one of the tools the church would use to carry out these stated goals of the Council.

The Constitution is divided into seven unequal chapters. The first chapter is clearly the most important; it sets forth the "general principles for the restoration and promotion of the Sacred Liturgy." This part of the Constitution includes a succinct description of what the liturgy is (nn. 1–11) and the need for its reform so that one of the repeated goals of the liturgical reform can be accomplished, namely the "full, conscious and active participation . . . demanded by the very nature of the liturgy" (n. 14). Succeeding paragraphs of this chapter indicate the importance of studying the liturgy (nn. 17–19) and give the guiding principles for the work of liturgical revision (nn. 21–46). The rest of the Constitution discusses specific liturgies and related matters, namely the eucharist (chapter 2), other sacraments and sacramentals (chapter 3), the divine office (chapter 4), the liturgical year (chapter 5), sacred music (chapter 6) and sacred art and furnishings (chapter 7).

It is important to understand that the Constitution decreed that all liturgical rites should be revised and gives an overview of what should be looked at. It is thus the most important "first word" on the project that occupied the church for the four decades to follow (and which will occupy our attention for years to come). The Constitution is *not* the "last word" in what should be undertaken in reforming the liturgy. After the Constitution was promulgated, the Vatican congregation dealing with the liturgy (formerly called the Congregation for Rites and subsequently renamed the Sacred Congregation for Divine Worship) established a number of committees comprising bishops and experts in liturgy and allied disciplines to work on the revision of the liturgical rites themselves. In some cases, there were several committees dealing with the revision of a given rite, for example, the eucharist. These committees took the vision of the *Constitution on the Sacred Liturgy* (for example, Chapter Two, on the eucharist) and determined the scope of the work required to implement that vision. In each and every case, what resulted from several years' work after 1963 was the promulgation of a revised liturgical rite (prayers, rites, readings, and the protocols for conducting the liturgy). These occurred at various times from 1969 through the present. Each of these revised liturgical rites is introduced by a document that helps to explain the scope of the liturgical revision and the theological and spiritual meaning of that revision. Again, these introductory documents are important to study in order to appreciate what those responsible for the revisions understood to be the theological meaning of what they were presenting for the church's prayer and belief. It is to a number of these introductory documents that we now turn.

GENERAL INSTRUCTION OF THE ROMAN MISSAL

Like all the other liturgical rites revised since Vatican II, the revised *Roman Missal* (book containing the prayers for Mass) contains an explanatory introductory document, its "General Instruction." What this document shares in common with all the other introductions to the revised rites is a thorough description of the rite at hand as well as some theological, liturgical, and canonical explanations of that rite. Despite the word "Instruction," what is contained here is less a "how to do it" description of the Mass than an explanation of what we are doing at the various parts of the Mass and why. This text was first published in 1969 and printed in the revised Missal in 1970 (first in Latin, subsequently in the various vernacular translations). A newly revised edition was printed in 2002 (again in Latin) when Pope John Paul II issued the third edition of the *Roman Missal.*

From the perspective of the theology of what the Eucharist enacts and the liturgical principles that undergird the revision of the structures and prayers of the Mass, the Introduction (nn. 1–15), Chapter One, and at least the first part of Chapter Two are extremely important. This part of the Instruction reminds us that the Mass is understood as "the action of Christ himself" (n.11) in which the church takes part. The first paragraphs of Chapter One emphasize "the ecclesial nature of the celebration" and that the Mass "is the action of Christ and the Church, in which the priest fulfills his own principal office and always acts for the people's salvation" (n. 19). The copious references to the documents of Vatican II help to underscore how what is enshrined here draws out the conciliar teaching on liturgy and applies them to the celebration of the eucharist. Chapter Two can be divided into two parts. The first part contains a helpful description of the different elements of the Mass: the proclamation of the word of God, prayers assigned to the priest for proclamation, the importance of singing, movements and postures at Mass, and the value of silence (nn. 27–45). The balance of the chapter discusses each of the parts of the Mass in some detail, always with an eye toward offering a theological explanation for what occurs (nn. 46–90). Chapter Three explains "Duties and Ministries at Mass" (nn. 91–111) including "the functions of the people of God" (nn. 95–96). Here, the people's presumed participation and its theological and spiritual value is underscored. Chapter Four describes (in nn. 115–272) the "different forms of celebrating Mass," that is, "with a congregation," "concelebrated Masses," and "Mass at which only one minister participates" (a shift from the former terminology of "the private Mass"). The last part of this chapter contains some helpful information about venerating the altar, the Book of the Gospels, incensation, and Holy Communion under both kinds (nn. 273–285). Chapter Five concerns the "Arrangement and Furnishing of Churches for the Celebration of the Eucharist" (nn. 288–318) including how the sanctuary is arranged, the location of the altar, the ambo, the chair for the priest celebrant, the places for the faithful, the place for the choir and musicians, the place for the reservation of the Most Holy Eucharist, and sacred images. This is followed in the Chapter Six with additional explanations of "Requisites for the Celebration of Mass" (nn. 319–351) including the bread and wine, "sacred furnishings in general," "sacred vessels," "sacred vestments," and other things required for Mass. Chapters Seven and Eight deal with the scriptural and prayer texts used at Mass and offers norms about how they are chosen (nn. 352–385). The last chapter, Chapter Nine, is an entirely new addition to this Instruction. It explains a number of things in terms of the competence and responsibility of the conference of bishops in the celebration of Mass (for example, translations of liturgical texts into the vernacular, regulation of concelebration, nn. 386–392). It also emphasizes participation through singing (n. 393) and notes in a summary fashion how the Roman rite has adopted and adapted features from other cultures into its rites (n. 397). In connection with this last chapter, it is important to realize that the Roman rite is celebrated in various countries and cultures and that some aspects of the way the liturgy is conducted will vary from place to place (for example, color of vestments for certain occasions, type of music to be sung). This ICEL English translation of the GIRM (2002) contains both the Roman original and the specific adaptations made by the United States bishops for the liturgy in this country.

It is important to emphasize the Introduction and Chapter One of this document. They remind us that any act of liturgy is less about "how to do the rite" than it is an action of God in which we take part to glorify God and to grow in holiness.

LECTIONARY FOR MASS: INTRODUCTION

One of the most important features of every liturgy is the proclamation of the word of God. The *Lectionary for Mass* (the book containing the scripture readings for Mass and an Introduction) was first published in 1969 in Latin and in 1970 in English. Most of the Introduction to this first edition of this important liturgical book concerned the rationale for the arrangement of the scripture readings for proclamation at Mass. In 1981 a revised edition of this Introduction was published containing a much expanded explanation of the importance of the proclamation of the word at Mass (see chapters one, two, and three, specifically paragraphs 1–48). Chapters four to six of this revised document explain the structure of the lectionary, that is to say, why certain scripture texts are assigned to be read at certain times of the church year, that is, for particular feasts, seasons, and the like.

This document helps to unpack the assertion in the *Constitution on the Sacred Liturgy* that the word and eucharist are so closely joined together that they form one act of worship (n. 48). It also helps to draw out the traditional maxim that at Mass we are fed spiritually from the table of the word of God and the altar table of the Lord.

GENERAL NORMS FOR THE LITURGICAL YEAR AND THE CALENDAR

This relatively short document was first published in 1969 to accompany the publication of the revised *Roman Missal*. It contains brief descriptions of the importance of Sunday (nn. 4–7) and the various gradations of feast days (now specifically named "solemnities," "feasts," and "memorials" in nn. 8–16). In describing the overall content of the church year, these general norms emphasize that the Easter triduum of Holy Thursday, Good Friday, and the Easter Vigil and Easter day encompass the most important celebrations of the entire church year (nn. 18–26) and how Lent leads to that triduum (nn. 27–31). The document then describes how the celebration of Christmas is second only to Easter in theological importance (nn. 32–38) with Advent leading up to it (nn. 39–42). The other seasons and feasts of the year are treated in the balance of the document (nn. 43–59) followed by a helpful summary, the "Table of Liturgical Days."

CHRISTIAN INITIATION: GENERAL INTRODUCTION

This succinct document contains a wealth of theology about the sacraments of baptism, confirmation, and eucharist (as summarized in n. 2). Its title is important—"Christian Initiation"—because a main emphasis in the liturgical reforms since Vatican II has been the appreciation of how these sacraments bring one into the life of God in the church and that these sacraments should be understood in relation to each other.

The document was originally written in 1969 to introduce the revised rite of infant baptism. Therefore most of the document concerns baptism: its dignity and implication (nn. 3–6), those who are involved in administering baptism (nn. 7–17), what is required for baptism (nn. 18–29, including water, the font, the baptistry), and brief indications of adaptations of the universal ritual by local conferences of bishops (nn. 30–33) and by individual ministers of baptism (nn. 34–35). The emphasis on communal celebrations of baptism is notable here (n. 27), as is the preference for immersing the persons to be baptized (n. 22). With regard to the theology of baptism, the document's emphases on how the baptized come to share in the paschal mystery of Christ (nn. 6, 28) and in the life of the Trinity (n. 5, 23) are significant. These emphases are also seen in the introductory documents for infant baptism, adult baptism, and confirmation.

Much of what is summarized in the previous document is fleshed out in this introductory document to the rite for the Christian initiation of adults. The word "initiation" in the name of this rite presumes that adults will celebrate baptism, confirmation, and eucharist at the same celebration (most often at the Easter Vigil). The emphasis on being drawn into the life of the Trinity (nn. 1, 28, 29, 31, 34) and into the paschal mystery (nn. 4, 8,19, 21, 32, 37) in the community of the church (nn. 4, 7, 14, 18, 19, 20, 22,27, 30, 33, 37, 39, 41, 43) is significant. These theological premises help ground the structure of adult initiation in terms of the rite's vision of four stages: evangelization and precatechumenate (nn. 9–13), the catechumenate itself (nn. 14–20), period of purification and enlightenment (during Lent, nn. 21–26), the celebration of the sacraments of initiation (nn. 27–36), and the period of postbaptismal catechesis (mystagogy, nn. 37–40). Because some terms often used in reference to the sacraments of initiation may still be unfamiliar and their meaning unclear (for example, "mystagogy"), a careful study of this document will be helpful. It also helps explain what happens in most parishes and dioceses during Lent (the rite of election as Lent begins, the scrutinies on the Third, Fourth, and Fifth Sundays in Lent), and the initiation of adults at the Easter Vigil.

Like all the revised liturgical rites since Vatican II, this one specifically mentions "adaptations by episcopal conferences" (nn. 64–65, followed by adaptations by the United States bishops).

NATIONAL STATUTES FOR THE CATECHUMENATE

This document was drafted by the United States Conference of Catholic Bishops to help guide and implement the liturgical revisions of Vatican II. The use of the word "statutes" in the title indicates that the directives contained therein are to be implemented as widely and as fully as possible in parishes and dioceses in the United States. Specific areas of interest concern the Christian initiation of children of catechetical age (nn. 18–19), adult Catholics who were baptized but who have received little or no formation in the faith (nn. 26–29), those baptized in another religion who want to become Catholic (nn. 30–37).

The document's appendices are worth serious study and reflection. The first collects a number of statements from recent church teachings about initiation (Appendix A), offering a great deal of theological insight. The second collects a number of statements from canon law about adult initiation (Appendix B).

ORDER FOR CHRISTIAN FUNERALS: GENERAL INTRODUCTION

The principle of adapting the universal Roman liturgy of the whole church for a specific country is reflected in the fact that this introduction was first published in 1985 and then adapted and reissued for dioceses in the United States in 1989 (see the foreword and nn. 21–22). Like other introductory documents, this introduction begins by emphasizing the theology of Christian death as the culmination of Christian initiation into the paschal mystery of Christ (n. 1). In general the rite envisions that the liturgy comprise not only the celebration of Mass but also a vigil for the deceased the night before the Mass and a liturgical rite at the site of burial (n. 4–8). While this introduction envisions that a conference of bishops may decide not to observe all three stages for funeral rites (nn. 9, 19, which notes that the lack of ordained priests and deacons may require that burials be presided over by laypersons), it remains clear that prayer for the deceased should not be limited to the celebration of the eucharist. Also notable is the emphasis given to the involvement and participation of all the people of God engaged in their respective ministries (n. 16).

This introduction also points out the importance of "preparing and planning the celebration" (nn. 23–25), in which the priest or other minister presiding over these liturgies should consider the specific circumstances and the wishes of the family (n. 23), and strive to balance these with the legitimate demands of the liturgy. In addition, while this introduction presumes the presence of the body of the deceased, it also allows for cremation (n. 15). The American bishops voted to permit cremation and more recently have decreed that a memorial Mass may be celebrated with the ashes present.

DIRECTORY FOR MASSES WITH CHILDREN

This document is among the most pastoral and practical of the post–Vatican II liturgical documents. It makes clear the importance of the liturgy itself as something that instructs and catechizes all who participate (nn. 9, 12), and allows for certain adaptations in the way the Mass is celebrated so that children may participate in the liturgy more easily and readily (n. 3). The possibility of adaptation is built into the revisions of the rites after Vatican II (see *Constitution on the Sacred Liturgy* nn. 37–40, as well as the last sections of almost all the introductory documents for the revised liturgical rites), and the 1967 Synod of Bishops addressed the adaptation of the revised liturgy to the needs of children in a formal way. This shows the church's concern for children of all ages (n. 1), especially those from the age of reason to preadolescence (n. 6) for whom even the revised rites may not be conducive to full, conscious, and active participation. This directory focuses on this segment of the Catholic population and seeks to enable their participation in the liturgy as effectively as possible (n. 8).

The directory envisions two circumstances in which children are present at the liturgy. The first is at the usual Sunday liturgy, where the children are not to be ignored. Rather the priest is encouraged to speak to them directly in the introductory rites and in the homily (n. 17). If it seems wise, the children may be dismissed from the eucharistic assembly and sent to a separate place to celebrate the liturgy of the word of God (n. 17). Then the children reassemble with the rest of the congregation at the presentation of the gifts. Some might well bring forward the gifts (n. 18). The other circumstance is when children celebrate Mass with only a few adults present. The directory envisions that these Masses normally take place during the week (nn. 20–21).

The liturgical principle is that the liturgy (especially on Sundays) should be appreciated as being celebrated with and for the whole church, and that people of all ages and nationalities feel welcome (n. 24). In addition, it is presumed that children who participate at liturgy with adults learn by doing, imitating how adults participate in gestures, postures, singing, processing, silence, and so on. Therefore, for liturgies with children and only a few adults, this directory envisions some specific adaptations (nn. 22–24). These include children assuming the roles of cantor, reader, or server (n. 22, 34). The priest is encouraged to make generous use of introductory comments at various parts of the Mass to help children appreciate what is taking place and participate in it more fully (for example, in the introductory rites, before the readings, before the eucharistic prayer, at the dismissal). In addition, the directory understands the value of the homily as a central way that children can understand and appropriate the scriptures proclaimed at Mass, so much so that it states: "with the consent of the pastor . . . one of the adults may speak to the children after the gospel, especially if the priest finds it difficult to adapt himself to the mentality of the children" (n. 24). These general recommendations are followed in the last part of the document with notes about specific aspects of the liturgy that can be adjusted in these situations (nn. 40–54).

The next section of the directory discusses liturgical participation in general, offering insight into the value of singing acclamations and prayers (nn. 30–32), the importance of gestures for all who participate (nn. 33–34), visual elements in the liturgy (n. 35, for example, the paschal candle, veneration of the cross, lighting of candles, and so on), and silence in the liturgy (n. 37). These paragraphs are worthy of thoughtful reflection by all who participate in the liturgy. They are helpful explanations of what the liturgy comprises and how it always an experience in which people participate in a variety of ways—visual, vocal, gestural, and so on.

CEREMONIAL OF BISHOPS

The sections of the *Ceremonial of Bishops* reproduced here are from a larger text published in 1984 that describes a number of things related to the role of the bishop at liturgy. Various liturgies and the bishop's role in them are described in great detail in Parts Two through Eight of this ceremonial. But what lays the groundwork for these specific applications is found in Part One (fully reproduced here). Chapter One of this foundational section discusses the importance of liturgies at which the bishop presides (nn. 1–17), providing valuable insights about what it means to belong to the church and the role of the bishop as one who presides, preaches, and teaches. The second chapter concerns offices and ministries in the liturgy (nn. 18–41) and includes significant descriptions of the role of presbyters, deacons, acolytes, readers, cantors, masters of ceremonies, sacristans, and musicians. Most of what is contained here can be applied to almost all other celebrations of the liturgy. In effect, the restoration of liturgical roles as envisioned in the *Constitution on the Sacred Liturgy*, n. 28, is fleshed out here in detail.

That the bishop normally presides at liturgy in the diocesan cathedral church is reflected in the useful description of the cathedral church in Chapter Three (nn. 42–54). The description of the *cathedra* or chair—from which the cathedral takes its name—is particularly notable (n. 47). The balance of this chapter, entitled "General Norms" (nn. 55–118), offers succinct descriptions of elements found in many other acts of liturgy. Those that describe the role of the human body in liturgy (nn. 68–109) serve to remind us that we use our bodies in liturgy because we are enfleshed human beings.

Most of the rest of the *Ceremonial* reproduced here describe particular liturgies, feasts, and seasons when bishops normally preside at the cathedral. Again what is said about particular seasons and ceremonies (for example, the Easter triduum, nn. 295–317, excerpts) summarizes theological aspects of these liturgies which deserve reflection even by those who do not ordinarily celebrate them with the bishop at the diocesan cathedral.

MUSIC IN CATHOLIC WORSHIP

Beginning with this document on music, we turn our attention to texts prepared by various offices and committees of the United States Conference of Catholic Bishops to assist in the pastoral implementation of the reformed liturgy.

Clearly, one of the most important ways that people participate in the liturgy is by singing. This document makes clear that liturgical participation through music means singing the texts that are intrinsic to the liturgy (that is, acclamations, responsorial psalm, and so on) rather than other music added to what is envisioned in the liturgical rites.

Beginning as early as 1903, the teaching of the popes and the magisterium of the church has emphasized liturgical participation through singing. In 1967, the United States Conference of Catholic Bishops published "The Place of Music in Liturgical Celebrations." Once the revised rites after Vatican II began to appear it became clear that a new document was needed to suit the shape and content of these new rituals. *Music in Catholic Worship* was published in 1972 and slightly revised in 1983. Its purpose was to outline how American Catholics could participate in the new Order of Mass. (The next document reprinted in this book, *Liturgical Music Today*, concerns the Liturgy of the Hours and sacramental liturgies other than the eucharist.)

Significantly more than half of this document outlines general principles about the liturgy in general and about liturgical participation. It opens with a "theology of [liturgical] celebration" (nn. 1–9), a description of "pastoral planning for celebration" (nn. 10–22) emphasizing the role of the "congregation" in the liturgy (n.15–18). The next section concerns "the place of music in the celebration" (nn.23–41). These paragraphs help those who prepare and celebrate liturgy to understand that choosing appropriate music for the liturgy requires the careful exercise of three judgments—musical, liturgical, and pastoral. Musical judgment means that that the music to be used should be evaluated and found to be "technically, aesthetically, and expressively good" (n. 26). The description of liturgical judgment states that "the nature of the liturgy itself will help to determine what kind of music is called for, what parts are to be preferred for singing, and who is to sing them" (n. 30). (The following paragraphs, nn. 31–38, include important consideration of the structure of the liturgy, the requirements of the texts of the liturgy, and the various roles in liturgical participation through music, specifically congregation, cantor, choir, and instrumentalists.) The last judgment to be exercised is "pastoral," concerning the choice and role of music "in this particular situation, in these concrete circumstances" (n. 39). For example, what might serve a monastic community might not be useful for parish community, or what might be useful for a solemnity like Pentecost might not be suitable for a weekday.)

The next section of the document outlines the structure and constitutive parts of the revised Order of Mass (for example, introductory rites, n. 44). These succinct assertions about what a particular part of the liturgy is and the way it is meant to function in the whole of the eucharistic liturgy are very helpful. This document has proven to be of enormous pastoral value. Its scope is limited, however, with scant attention to other sacramental celebrations (nn. 79–83). Therefore, the United States Bishops' Committee on the Liturgy drafted a complementary document, *Liturgical Music Today*, a decade later.

LITURGICAL MUSIC TODAY

This document begins, as does *Music in Catholic Worship*, by setting forth principles about the liturgy and liturgical participation (nn. 1–14). These are followed by some comments that supplement what the former document said about music at the eucharist (nn. 16–21). These lead to the two major concerns in this text: music for other sacraments and rites (nn. 22–33) and music in the Liturgy of the Hours (nn. 34–45). The document concludes with rather general assertions about other aspects of liturgical music (nn. 46–70), including music ministry, music from the past, cultural heritage, as well as recorded and instrumental music.

FULFILLED IN YOUR HEARING: THE HOMILY IN THE SUNDAY ASSEMBLY

This document arose from concerns raised in the United States Bishops' Committee on Priestly Life about the increased demands on priests as a result of the implementation of the revised liturgies, in particular in terms of preaching homilies. The text is divided into four parts: the assembly, the preacher, the homily, and homiletic method, that is, homily preparation.

That the document begins by focusing on the assembly is significant. From the outset the authors of the document assert that every particular homily is addressed to and should meet the needs of a particular liturgical assembly. The next section, on the preacher, discusses his role as a "mediator of meaning" for a congregation that he knows. The section on the homily itself is particularly attuned to the challenges which the liturgical proclamation of the word places on the preacher. It the preacher's need to be faithful to the scriptures as assigned by the *Lectionary for Mass* for that particular Sunday and to the needs of the particular assembly celebrating the liturgy. The final section has proven to be very helpful for many preachers in the method it sets forth for homily preparation. Reading, listening, and praying over the word are highlighted, leading to suggestions about drafting a homily, revising, and delivering it. The document recommends that the preacher meet with a "homily preparation group" from the community where he preaches, a very helpful practice that many priests follow. (One of the most valuable things about such meetings is that parishioners who participate help the preacher make connections between the scriptures and the life of the parish community.)

Undoubtedly an important aspect of celebrating the reformed liturgy is the setting in which it takes place—the church. In 1978, the Bishops' Committee on the Liturgy published *Environment and Art in Catholic Worship* to help parish communities appreciate the importance of renovating existing churches and building new ones that would be suitable for celebrating the reformed liturgy. Twenty-two years later, the United States Conference of Catholic Bishops approved *Built of Living Stones,* which reflects a more mature appreciation of the reformed liturgy and the church documents published after 1978 that come to bear on building and renovating churches.

The structure of the text is important to note. Chapter One, "The Living Church," develops a general theology of liturgy as it is celebrated in church buildings. Chapter Two complements these general observations by an expansive consideration of "The Church Building and the Sacred Rites Celebrated There." The chapter focuses on the eucharist (celebration and reservation) and also includes considerations of baptism, other sacraments, and the Liturgy of the Hours. Particularly helpful observations here concern the assembly's postures and gestures during the liturgy and specific celebrations, from the liturgies of Holy Week to Sunday celebrations in the absence of a priest. This chapter also includes important comments about sacred images and the stations of the cross.

Chapter Three briefly describes the work of artists and the crafting of suitable art for the liturgy. Chapter Four, "Building a Church: Practical Considerations," gives detailed suggestions about the process of building a church in relation to a number of factors, including the importance of parish education and the role of professionals (architects, liturgical consultants, contractors). The chapter ends with some comments about the renovation of existing church buildings in light of the rest of the document.

NORMS FOR THE CELEBRATION AND RECEPTION OF HOLY COMMUNION UNDER BOTH KINDS IN THE DIOCESES OF THE UNITED STATES OF AMERICA

In 1984, the United States Conference of Catholic Bishops published *This Holy and Living Sacrifice,* subtitled "Directory for the Celebration and Reception of Communion under Both Kinds." This document was both instructional for what it set forth about the church's teaching on the eucharist and prescriptive for what it set forth as the protocols to be followed when the eucharist was distributed under both species. Eighteen years later, the United States Conference of Catholic Bishops approved this new document on the same subject, *Norms for the Celebration and Reception of Holy Communion Under Both Kinds in the Dioceses of the United States of America.* This revised document has been published in conjunction with the *General Instruction of the Roman Missal* and serves as normative for dioceses in the United States in the way the eucharist is distributed. Like its predecessor, this text offers ample and important catechesis in Part One about "Holy Communion: The Body and Blood of the Lord Jesus." This part ends with specific reference to the sign value and importance of receiving under both kinds (nn. 17–21).

The second part concerns the specific norms for distribution of communion (nn. 22–57), underscoring the value of catechesis about the eucharist (n. 25) as well as outlining specific requirements for preparation, planning, and distributing Holy Communion. The sections on planning and preparation (nn. 30–36) make clear the importance of consecrating sufficient amounts of bread and wine for the particular liturgy in vessels of appropriate size and number.

It is clear that while we can gain much information from the documents about the liturgy, it is not until they are implemented in local parishes and other churches that they really take on the life and vitality they are meant to have. Liturgy is less about words on a page than it is about the spoken and sung words, symbols, signs, and gestures in which human beings engage for the glory of God and their sanctification. The documents collected here are meant to serve and foster a proper appreciation of liturgy. They should help us in worshiping God and in appropriating the gifts of salvation, redemption, and sanctification that the liturgy uniquely offers us.

CONSTITUTION
ON THE
SACRED LITURGY

SACROSANCTUM CONCILIUM

SECOND VATICAN COUNCIL
4 DECEMBER 1963

OUTLINE

CONSTITUTION ON THE SACRED LITURGY

1.   This Sacred Council has several aims in view: it desires to impart an ever increasing vigor to the Christian life of the faithful; to adapt more suitably to the needs of our own times those institutions that are subject to change; to foster whatever can promote union among all who believe in Christ; to strengthen whatever can help to call the whole of humanity into the household of the Church. The Council therefore sees particularly cogent reasons for undertaking the reform and promotion of the liturgy.

2.   For the liturgy, "making the work of our redemption a present actuality,"[1] most of all in the divine sacrifice of the eucharist, is the outstanding means whereby the faithful may express in their lives and manifest to others the mystery of Christ and the real nature of the true Church. It is of the essence of the Church to be both human and divine, visible yet endowed with invisible resources, eager to act yet intent on contemplation, present in this world yet not at home in it; and the Church is all these things in such wise that in it the human is directed and subordinated to the divine, the visible likewise to the invisible, action to contemplation, and this present world to that city yet to come which we seek.[2] While the liturgy daily builds up those who are within into a holy temple of the Lord, into a dwelling place for God in the Spirit,[3] to the mature measure of the fullness of Christ,[4] at the same time it marvelously strengthens their power to preach Christ and thus shows forth the Church to those who are outside as a sign lifted up among the nations,[5] under which the scattered children of God may be gathered together,[6] until there is one sheepfold and one shepherd.[7]

3.   Wherefore the Council judges that the following principles concerning the promotion and reform of the liturgy should be called to mind and practical norms established.

Among these principles and norms there are some that can and should be applied both to the Roman Rite and also to all the other rites. The practical norms that follow, however, should be taken as applying only to the Roman Rite, except for those that, in the very nature of things, affect other rites as well.

4.   Lastly, in faithful obedience to tradition, the Council declares that the Church holds all lawfully acknowledged rites to be of equal right and dignity and wishes to preserve them in the future and to foster them in every way. The Council also desires that, where necessary, the rites be revised carefully in the light of sound tradition and that they be given new vigor to meet the circumstances and needs of modern times.

CHAPTER I
GENERAL PRINCIPLES FOR THE REFORM AND PROMOTION OF THE SACRED LITURGY
I. NATURE OF THE LITURGY AND ITS IMPORTANCE IN THE CHURCH'S LIFE

5.　　God who "wills that all be saved and come to the knowledge of the truth" (1 Tm 2:4), "who in many and various ways spoke in times past to the fathers by the prophets" (Heb 1:1), when the fullness of time had come sent his Son, the Word made flesh, anointed by the Holy Spirit, to preach the Gospel to the poor, to heal the contrite of heart;[1] he is "the physician, being both flesh and of the Spirit,"[2] the mediator between God and us.[3] For his humanity, united with the person of the Word, was the instrument of our salvation. Therefore in Christ "the perfect achievement of our reconciliation came forth and the fullness of divine worship was given to us.[4]

The wonderful works of God among the people of the Old Testament were a prelude to the work of Christ the Lord. He achieved his task of redeeming humanity and giving perfect glory to God, principally by the paschal mystery of his blessed passion, resurrection from the dead, and glorious ascension, whereby "dying, he destroyed our death and, rising, he restored our life."[5] For it was from the side of Christ as he slept the sleep of death upon the cross that there came forth the sublime sacrament of the whole Church.[6]

6.　　As Christ was sent by the Father, he himself also sent the apostles, filled with the Holy Spirit. Their mission was, first, by preaching the Gospel to every creature,[7] to proclaim that by his death and resurrection Christ has freed us from Satan's grip[8] and brought us into the Father's kingdom. But the work they preached they were also to bring into effect through the sacrifice and the sacraments, the center of the whole liturgical life. Thus by baptism all are plunged into the paschal mystery of Christ: they die with him, are buried with him, and rise with him;[9] they receive the spirit of adoption as children "in which we cry: Abba, Father" (Rom 8:15), and thus become true adorers whom the Father seeks.[10] In like manner, as often as they eat the supper of the Lord they proclaim the death of the Lord until he comes.[11] For that reason, on the very day of Pentecost when the Church appeared before the world, "those who received the word" of Peter "were baptized." And "they continued steadfastly in the teaching of the apostles and in the communion of the breaking of bread and in prayers . . . praising God and being in favor with all the people" (Acts 2:41–47). From that time onward the Church has never failed to come together to celebrate the paschal mystery: reading those things "which were in all the Scriptures concerning him" (Lk 24:27); celebrating the eucharist, in which "the victory and triumph of his death are again made present";[12] and at the same time giving thanks "to God for his inexpressible gift" (2 Cor 9:15) in Christ Jesus, "in praise of his glory" (Eph 1:12), through the power of the Holy Spirit.

7.　　To accomplish so great a work, Christ is always present in his Church, especially in its liturgical celebrations. He is present in the sacrifice of the

Mass, not only in the person of his minister, "the same now offering, through the ministry of priests, who formerly offered himself on the cross,"[13] but especially under the eucharistic elements. By his power he is present in the sacraments, so that when a man baptizes it is really Christ himself who baptizes.[14] He is present in his word, since it is he himself who speaks when the holy Scriptures are read in the Church. He is present, lastly, when the Church prays and sings, for he promised: "Where two or three are gathered together in my name, there am I in the midst of them" (Mt 18:20).

Christ always truly associates the Church with himself in this great work wherein God is perfectly glorified and the recipients made holy. The Church is the Lord's beloved Bride who calls to him and through him offers worship to the eternal Father.

Rightly, then, the liturgy is considered as an exercise of the priestly office of Jesus Christ. In the liturgy, by means of signs perceptible to the senses, human sanctification is signified and brought about in ways proper to each of these signs; in the liturgy the whole public worship is performed by the Mystical Body of Jesus Christ, that is, by the Head and his members.

From this it follows that every liturgical celebration, because it is an action of Christ the Priest and of his Body which is the Church, is a sacred action surpassing all others; no other action of the Church can equal its effectiveness by the same title and to the same degree.

8. In the earthly liturgy we take part in a foretaste of that heavenly liturgy celebrated in the holy city of Jerusalem toward which we journey as pilgrims, where Christ is sitting at the right hand of God, a minister of the holies and of the true tabernacle;[15] we sing a hymn to the Lord's glory with the whole company of heaven; venerating the memory of the saints, we hope for some part and fellowship with them; we eagerly await the Savior, our Lord Jesus Christ, until he, our life, shall appear and we too will appear with him in glory.[16]

9. The liturgy does not exhaust the entire activity of the Church. Before people can come to the liturgy they must be called to faith and to conversion: "How then are they to call upon him in whom they have not yet believed? But how are they to believe him whom they have not heard? And how are they to hear if no one preaches? And how are men to preach unless they be sent?" (Rom 10:14–15).

Therefore the Church announces the good tidings of salvation to those who do not believe, so that all may know the true God and Jesus Christ whom he has sent and may be converted from their ways, doing penance.[17] To believers, also, the Church must ever preach faith and penance, prepare them for the sacraments, teach them to observe all that Christ has commanded,[18] and invite them to all the works of charity, worship, and the apostolate. For all these works make it clear that Christ's faithful, though not of this world, are to be the light of the world and to glorify the Father in the eyes of all.

10. Still, the liturgy is the summit toward which the activity of the Church is directed; at the same time it is the fount from which all the Church's power

flows. For the aim and object of apostolic works is that all who are made children of God by faith and baptism should come together to praise God in the midst of his Church, to take part in the sacrifice, and to eat the Lord's Supper.

The liturgy in its turn moves the faithful, filled with "the paschal sacraments," to be "one in holiness";[19] it prays that "they may hold fast in their lives to what they have grasped by their faith";[20] the renewal in the eucharist of the covenant between the Lord and his people draws the faithful into the compelling love of Christ and sets them on fire. From the liturgy, therefore, particularly the eucharist, grace is poured forth upon us as from a fountain; the liturgy is the source for achieving in the most effective way possible human sanctification and God's glorification, the end to which all the Church's other activities are directed.

11.   But in order that the liturgy may possess its full effectiveness, it is necessary that the faithful come to it with proper dispositions, that their minds be attuned to their voices, and that they cooperate with divine grace, lest they receive it in vain.[21] Pastors must therefore realize that when the liturgy is celebrated something more is required than the mere observance of the laws governing valid and lawful celebration; it is also their duty to ensure that the faithful take part fully aware of what they are doing, actively engaged in the rite, and enriched by its effects.

12.   The spiritual life, however, is not limited solely to participation in the liturgy. Christians are indeed called to pray in union with each other, but they must also enter into their chamber to pray to the Father in secret;[22] further, according to the teaching of the Apostle, they should pray without ceasing.[23] We learn from the same Apostle that we must always bear about in our body the dying of Jesus, so that the life also of Jesus may be made manifest in our bodily frame.[24] This is why we ask the Lord in the sacrifice of the Mass that "receiving the offering of the spiritual victim," he may fashion us for himself "as an eternal gift."[25]

13.   Popular devotions of the Christian people are to be highly endorsed, provided they accord with the laws and norms of the Church, above all when they are ordered by the Apostolic See.

Devotions proper to particular Churches also have a special dignity if they are undertaken by mandate of the bishops according to customs or books lawfully approved.

But these devotions should be so fashioned that they harmonize with the liturgical seasons, accord with the sacred liturgy, are in some way derived from it, and lead the people to it, since, in fact, the liturgy, by its very nature far surpasses any of them.

II. PROMOTION OF LITURGICAL INSTRUCTION AND ACTIVE PARTICIPATION

14.   The Church earnestly desires that all the faithful be led to that full, conscious, and active participation in liturgical celebrations called for by the very nature of the liturgy. Such participation by the Christian people as "a chosen

race, a royal priesthood, a holy nation, God's own people" (1 Pt 2:9; see 2:4–5) is their right and duty by reason of their baptism.

In the reform and promotion of the liturgy, this full and active participation by all the people is the aim to be considered before all else. For it is the primary and indispensable source from which the faithful are to derive the true Christian spirit and therefore pastors must zealously strive in all their pastoral work to achieve such participation by means of the necessary instruction.

Yet it would be futile to entertain any hopes of realizing this unless, in the first place, the pastors themselves become thoroughly imbued with the spirit and power of the liturgy and make themselves its teachers. A prime need, therefore, is that attention be directed, first of all, to the liturgical formation of the clergy. Wherefore the Council has decided to enact what follows.

15. Professors appointed to teach liturgy in seminaries, religious houses of study, and theological faculties must be thoroughly trained for their work in institutes specializing in this subject.

16. The study of liturgy is to be ranked among the compulsory and major courses in seminaries and religious houses of studies; in theological faculties it is to rank among the principal courses. It is to be taught under its theological, historical, spiritual, pastoral, and canonical aspects. Moreover, other professors, while striving to expound the mystery of Christ and the history of salvation from the angle proper to each of their own subjects, must nevertheless do so in a way that will clearly bring out the connection between their subjects and the liturgy, as also the underlying unity of all priestly training. This consideration is especially important for professors of dogmatic, spiritual, and pastoral theology and for professors of holy Scripture.

17. In seminaries and houses of religious, clerics shall be given a liturgical formation in their spiritual life. The means for this are: proper guidance so that they may be able to understand the sacred rites and take part in them wholeheartedly; the actual celebration of the sacred mysteries and of other, popular devotions imbued with the spirit of the liturgy. In addition they must learn how to observe the liturgical laws, so that life in seminaries and houses of religious may be thoroughly permeated by the spirit of the liturgy.

18. Priests, both secular and religious, who are already working in the Lord's vineyard are to be helped by every suitable means to understand ever more fully what it is they are doing in their liturgical functions; they are to be aided to live the liturgical life and to share it with the faithful entrusted to their care.

19. With zeal and patience pastors must promote the liturgical instruction of the faithful and also their active participation in the liturgy both internally and externally, taking into account their age and condition, their way of life, and their stage of religious development. By doing so, pastors will be fulfilling one of their chief duties as faithful stewards of the mysteries of God; and in this matter they must lead their flock not only by word but also by example.

20.   Radio and television broadcasts of sacred rites must be marked by discretion and dignity, under the leadership and direction of a competent person appointed for this office by the bishops. This is especially important when the service to be broadcast is the Mass.

III. THE REFORM OF THE SACRED LITURGY

21.   In order that the Christian people may more surely derive an abundance of graces from the liturgy, the Church desires to undertake with great care a general reform of the liturgy itself. For the liturgy is made up of immutable elements, divinely instituted, and of elements subject to change. These not only may but ought to be changed with the passage of time if they have suffered from the intrusion of anything out of harmony with the inner nature of the liturgy or have become pointless.

In this reform both texts and rites should be so drawn up that they express more clearly the holy things they signify and that the Christian people, as far as possible, are able to understand them with ease and to take part in the rites fully, actively, and as befits a community.

Wherefore the Council establishes tbe general norms that follow.

A. General Norms

22.   § 1. Regulation of the liturgy depends solely on the authority of the Church, that is, on the Apostolic See and, accordingly as the law determines, on the bishop.

§ 2. In virtue of power conceded by the law, the regulation of the liturgy within certain defined limits belongs also to various kinds of competent territorial bodies of bishops lawfully established.

§ 3. Therefore, no other person, not even if he is a priest, may on his own add, remove, or change anything in the liturgy.

23.   That sound tradition may be retained and yet the way remain open to legitimate progress, a careful investigation is always to be made into each part of the liturgy to be revised. This investigation should be theological, historical, and pastoral. Also the general laws governing the structure and meaning of the liturgy must be studied in conjunction with the experience derived from recent liturgical reforms and from the indults conceded to various places. Finally, there must be no innovations unless the good of the Church genuinely and certainly requires them; care must be taken that any new forms adopted should in some way grow organically from forms already existing.

As far as possible, marked differences between the rites used in neighboring regions must be carefully avoided.

24.   Sacred Scripture is of the greatest importance in the celebration of the liturgy. For it is from Scripture that the readings are given and explained in the homily and that psalms are sung; the prayers, collects, and liturgical songs are scriptural in their inspiration; it is from the Scriptures that actions and signs

derive their meaning. Thus to achieve the reform, progress, and adaptation of the liturgy, it is essential to promote that warm and living love for Scripture to which the venerable tradition of both Eastern and Western rites gives testimony.

25. The liturgical books are to be revised as soon as possible; experts are to be employed in this task and bishops from various parts of the world are to be consulted.

B. Norms Drawn from the Hierarchic and Communal Nature of the Liturgy

26. Liturgical services are not private functions, but are celebrations belonging to the Church, which is the "sacrament of unity," namely, the holy people united and ordered under their bishops.[26]

Therefore liturgical services involve the whole Body of the Church; they manifest it and have effects upon it; but they also concern the individual members of the Church in different ways, according to their different orders, offices, and actual participation.

27. Whenever rites, according to their specific nature, make provision for communal celebration involving the presence and active participation of the faithful, it is to be stressed that this way of celebrating them is to be preferred, as far as possible, to a celebration that is individual and, so to speak, private.

This applies with special force to the celebration of Mass and the administration of the sacraments, even though every Mass has of itself a public and social character.

28. In liturgical celebrations each one, minister or layperson, who has an office to perform, should do all of, but only, those parts which pertain to that office by the nature of the rite and the principles of liturgy.

29. Servers, readers, commentators, and members of the choir also exercise a genuine liturgical function. They ought to discharge their office, therefore, with the sincere devotion and decorum demanded by so exalted a ministry and rightly expected of them by God's people.

Consequently, they must all be deeply imbued with the spirit of the liturgy, in the measure proper to each one, and they must be trained to perform their functions in a correct and orderly manner.

30. To promote active participation, the people should be encouraged to take part by means of acclamations, responses, psalmody, antiphons, and songs, as well as by actions, gestures, and bearing. And at the proper times all should observe a reverent silence.

31. The revision of the liturgical books must ensure that the rubrics make provision for the parts belonging to the people.

32.   The liturgy makes distinctions between persons according to their liturgical function and sacred orders and there are liturgical laws providing for due honors to be given to civil authorities. Apart from these instances, no special honors are to be paid in the liturgy to any private persons or classes of persons, whether in the ceremonies or by external display.

C. Norms Based on the Teaching and
Pastoral Character of the Liturgy

33.   Although the liturgy is above all things the worship of the divine majesty, it likewise contains rich instruction for the faithful.[27] For in the liturgy God is speaking to his people and Christ is still proclaiming his gospel. And the people are responding to God by both song and prayer.

Moreover, the prayers addressed to God by the priest, who presides over the assembly in the person of Christ, are said in the name of the entire holy people and of all present. And the visible signs used by the liturgy to signify invisible divine realities have been chosen by Christ or the Church. Thus not only when things are read "that were written for our instruction" (Rom 15:4), but also when the Church prays or sings or acts, the faith of those taking part is nourished and their minds are raised to God, so that they may offer him their worship as intelligent beings and receive his grace more abundantly.

In the reform of the liturgy, therefore, the following general norms are to be observed.

34.   The rites should be marked by a noble simplicity; they should be short, clear, and unencumbered by useless repetitions; they should be within the people's powers of comprehension and as a rule not require much explanation.

35.   That the intimate connection between words and rites may stand out clearly in the liturgy:

1. In sacred celebrations there is to be more reading from holy Scripture and it is to be more varied and apposite.

2. Because the spoken word is part of the liturgical service, the best place for it, consistent with the nature of the rite, is to be indicated even in the rubrics; the ministry of preaching is to be fulfilled with exactitude and fidelity. Preaching should draw its content mainly from scriptural and liturgical sources, being a proclamation of God's wonderful works in the history of salvation, the mystery of Christ, ever present and active within us, especially in the celebration of the liturgy.

3. A more explicitly liturgical catechesis should also be given in a variety of ways. Within the rites themselves provision is to be made for brief comments, when needed, by the priest or a qualified minister; they should occur only at the more suitable moments and use a set formula or something similar.

4. Bible services should be encouraged, especially on the vigils of the more solemn feasts, on some weekdays in Advent and Lent, and on Sundays and holy

days. They are particularly to be recommended in places where no priest is available; when this is the case, a deacon or some other person authorized by the bishop is to preside over the celebration.

(36) § 1. Particular law remaining in force, the use of the Latin language is to be preserved in the Latin rites.

§ 2. But since the use of the mother tongue, whether in the Mass, the administration of the sacraments, or other parts of the liturgy, frequently may be of great advantage to the people, the limits of its use may be extended. This will apply in the first place to the readings and instructions and to some prayers and chants, according to the regulations on this matter to be laid down for each case in subsequent chapters.

§ 3. Respecting such norms and also, where applicable, consulting the bishops of nearby territories of the same language, the competent, territorial ecclesiastical authority mentioned in art. 22, §2 is empowered to decide whether and to what extent the vernacular is to be used. The enactments of the competent authority are to be approved, that is, confirmed by the Holy See.

§ 4. Translations from the Latin text into the mother tongue intended for use in the liturgy must be approved by the competent, territorial ecclesiastical authority already mentioned.

D. Norms for Adapting the Liturgy to the Culture and Traditions of Peoples

37. Even in the liturgy the Church has no wish to impose a rigid uniformity in matters that do not affect the faith or the good of the whole community; rather, the Church respects and fosters the genius and talents of the various races and peoples. The Church considers with sympathy and, if possible, preserves intact the elements in these peoples' way of life that are not indissolubly bound up with superstition and error. Sometimes in fact the Church admits such elements into the liturgy itself, provided they are in keeping with the true and authentic spirit of the liturgy.

38. Provisions shall also be made, even in the revision of liturgical books, for legitimate variations and adaptations to different groups, regions, and peoples, especially in mission lands, provided the substantial unity of the Roman Rite is preserved; this should be borne in mind when rites are drawn up and rubrics devised.

39. Within the limits set by the *editio typica* of the liturgical books, it shall be for the competent, territorial ecclesiastical authority mentioned in art. 22, §2 to specify adaptations, especially in the case of the administration of the sacraments, the sacramentals, processions, liturgical language, sacred music, and the arts. This, however, is to be done in accord with the fundamental norms laid down in this Constitution.

(40.) In some places and circumstances, however, an even more radical adaptation of the liturgy is needed and this entails greater difficulties. Wherefore:

1. The competent, territorial ecclesiastical authority mentioned in art. 22, §2, must, in this matter, carefully and prudently weigh what elements from the traditions and culture of individual peoples may be appropriately admitted into divine worship. They are to propose to the Apostolic See adaptations considered useful or necessary that will be introduced with its consent.

2. To ensure that adaptations are made with all the circumspection they demand, the Apostolic See will grant power to this same territorial ecclesiastical authority to permit and to direct, as the case requires, the necessary preliminary experiments within certain groups suited for the purpose and for a fixed time.

3. Because liturgical laws often involve special difficulties with respect to adaptation, particularly in mission lands, experts in these matters must be employed to formulate them.

IV. PROMOTION OF LITURGICAL LIFE IN DIOCESE AND PARISH

41. The bishop is to be looked on as the high priest of his flock, the faithful's life in Christ in some way deriving from and depending on him.

Therefore all should hold in great esteem the liturgical life of the diocese centered around the bishop, especially in his cathedral church; they must be convinced that the preeminent manifestation of the Church is present in the full, active participation of all God's holy people in these liturgical celebrations, especially in the same eucharist, in a single prayer, at one altar at which the bishop presides, surrounded by his college of priests and by his ministers.[28]

42. But because it is impossible for the bishop always and everywhere to preside over the whole flock in his Church, he cannot do otherwise than establish lesser groupings of the faithful. Among these the parishes, set up locally under a pastor taking the place of the bishop, are the most important: in some manner they represent the visible Church established throughout the world.

And therefore both in attitude and in practice the liturgical life of the parish and its relationship to the bishop must be fostered among the faithful and clergy; efforts must also be made toward a lively sense of community within the parish, above all in the shared celebration of the Sunday Mass.

V. PROMOTION OF PASTORAL-LITURGICAL ACTION

43. Zeal for the promotion and restoration of the liturgy is rightly held to be a sign of the providential dispositions of God in our time, a movement of the Holy Spirit in his Church. Today it is a distinguishing mark of the Church's life, indeed of the whole tenor of contemporary religious thought and action.

So that this pastoral-liturgical action may become even more vigorous in the Church, the Council decrees what follows.

44.   It is advisable that the competent, territorial ecclesiastical authority mentioned in art. 22, §2 set up a liturgical commission, to be assisted by experts in liturgical science, music, art, and pastoral practice. As far as possible the commission should be aided by some kind of institute for pastoral liturgy, consisting of persons eminent in these matters and including the laity as circumstances suggest. Under the direction of the aforementioned territorial ecclesiastical authority, the commission is to regulate pastoral-liturgical action throughout the territory and to promote studies and necessary experiments whenever there is question of adaptations to be proposed to the Apostolic See.

45.   For the same reason every diocese is to have a commission on the liturgy, under the direction of the bishop, for promoting the liturgical apostolate.

Sometimes it may be advisable for several dioceses to form among themselves one single commission, in order to promote the liturgy by means of shared consultation.

46.   Besides the commission on the liturgy, every diocese, as far as possible, should have commissions for music and art.

These three commissions must work in closest collaboration; indeed it will often be best to fuse the three of them into one single commission.

CHAPTER II
THE MOST SACRED MYSTERY OF THE EUCHARIST

47.   At the Last Supper, on the night when he was betrayed, our Savior instituted the eucharistic sacrifice of his body and blood. He did this in order to perpetuate the sacrifice of the cross throughout the centuries until he should come again and in this way to entrust to his beloved Bride, the Church, a memorial of his death and resurrection: a sacrament of love, a sign of unity, a bond of charity,[1] a paschal banquet "in which Christ is eaten, the heart is filled with grace, and a pledge of future glory given to us."[2]

48.   The Church, therefore, earnestly desires that Christ's faithful, when present at this mystery of faith, should not be there as strangers or silent spectators; on the contrary, through a good understanding of the rites and prayers they should take part in the sacred service conscious of what they are doing, with devotion and full involvement. They should be instructed by God's word and be nourished at the table of the Lord's body; they should give thanks to God; by offering the immaculate Victim, not only through the hands of the priest, but also with him, they should learn to offer themselves as well; through Christ the Mediator,[3] they should be formed day by day into an ever more perfect unity with God and with each other, so that finally God may be all in all.

49.   Thus, mindful of those Masses celebrated with the assistance of the faithful, especially on Sundays and holy days of obligation, the Council makes the following decrees in order that the sacrifice of the Mass, even in its ritual forms, may become pastorally effective to the utmost degree.

50. The Order of Mass is to be revised in a way that will bring out more clearly the intrinsic nature and purpose of its several parts, as also the connection between them, and will more readily achieve the devout, active participation of the faithful.

For this purpose the rites are to be simplified, due care being taken to preserve their substance; elements that, with the passage of time, came to be duplicated or were added with but little advantage are now to be discarded; other elements that have suffered injury through accident of history are now, as may seem useful or necessary, to be restored to the vigor they had in the traditions of the Fathers.

51. The treasures of the Bible are to be opened up more lavishly, so that a richer share in God's word may be provided for the faithful. In this way a more representative portion of holy Scripture will be read to the people in the course of a prescribed number of years.

52. By means of the homily the mysteries of the faith and the guiding principles of the Christian life are expounded from the sacred text during the course of the liturgical year; as part of the liturgy itself therefore, the homily is strongly recommended; in fact, at Masses celebrated with the assistance of the people on Sundays and holy days of obligation it is not to be omitted except for a serious reason.

53. Especially on Sundays and holy days of obligation there is to be restored, after the gospel and the homily, "the universal prayer" or "the prayer of the faithful." By this prayer, in which the people are to take part, intercession shall be made for holy Church, for the civil authorities, for those oppressed by various needs, for all people, and for the salvation of the entire world.[4]

54. With art. 36 of this Constitution as the norm, in Masses celebrated with the people a suitable place may be allotted to their mother tongue. This is to apply in the first place to the readings and "the universal prayer," but also, as local conditions may warrant, to those parts belonging to the people.

Nevertheless steps should be taken enabling the faithful to say or to sing together in Latin those parts of the Ordinary of the Mass belonging to them.

Wherever a more extended use of the mother tongue within the Mass appears desirable, the regulation laid down in art. 40 of this Constitution is to be observed.

55. That more complete form of participation in the Mass by which the faithful, after the priest's communion, receive the Lord's body from the sacrifice, is strongly endorsed.

The dogmatic principles laid down by the Council of Trent remain intact.[5] In instances to be specified by the Apostolic See, however, communion under both kinds may be granted both to clerics and religious and to the laity at the discretion of the bishops, for example, to the ordained at the Mass of their ordination, to the professed at the Mass of their religious profession, to the newly baptized at the Mass following their baptism.

56. The two parts that, in a certain sense, go to make up the Mass, namely, the liturgy of the word and the liturgy of the eucharist, are so closely connected with each other that they form but one single act of worship. Accordingly this Council strongly urges pastors that in their catechesis they insistently teach the faithful to take part in the entire Mass, especially on Sundays and holy days of obligation.

57. § 1. Concelebration, which aptly expresses the unity of the priesthood, has continued to this day as a practice in the Church of both East and West. For this reason it has seemed good to the Council to extend permission for concelebration to the following cases:

    1. a. on Holy Thursday, both the chrism Mass and the evening Mass;

       b. Masses during councils, bishops' conferences, and synods;

       c. the Mass at the blessing of an abbot.

    2. Also, with permission of the Ordinary, who is the one to decide whether concelebration is opportune, to:

       a. the conventual Mass and the principal Mass in churches, when the needs of the faithful do not require that all the priests on hand celebrate individually;

       b. Masses celebrated at any kind of meeting of priests, whether secular or religious.

    § 2. 1. The regulation, however, of the discipline of concelebration in the diocese pertains to the bishop.

    2. This, however, does not take away the option of every priest to celebrate Mass individually, not, however, at the same time and in the same church as a concelebrated Mass or on Holy Thursday.

58. A new rite for concelebration is to be drawn up and inserted into the Roman Pontifical and Roman Missal.

CHAPTER III
THE OTHER SACRAMENTS AND THE SACRAMENTALS

59. The purpose of the sacraments is to make people holy, to build up the Body of Christ, and, finally, to give worship to God; but being signs they also have a teaching function. They not only presuppose faith, but by words and objects they also nourish, strengthen, and express it; that is why they are called "sacraments of faith." They do indeed impart grace, but, in addition, the very act of celebrating them disposes the faithful most effectively to receive this grace in a fruitful manner, to worship God rightly, and to practice charity.

It is therefore of the highest importance that the faithful should readily understand the sacramental signs and should with great eagerness frequent those sacraments that were instituted to nourish the Christian life.

60. The Church has, in addition, instituted sacramentals. These are sacred signs bearing a kind of resemblance to the sacraments: they signify effects, particularly of a spiritual kind, that are obtained through the Church's intercession. They dispose people to receive the chief effect of the sacraments and they make holy various occasions in human life.

61. Thus, for well-disposed members of the faithful, the effect of the liturgy of the sacraments and sacramentals is that almost every event in their lives is made holy by divine grace that flows from the paschal mystery of Christ's passion, death, and resurrection, the fount from which all sacraments and sacramentals draw their power. The liturgy means also that there is hardly any proper use of material things that cannot thus be directed toward human sanctification and the praise of God.

62. With the passage of time, however, certain features have crept into the rites of the sacraments and sacramentals that have made their nature and purpose less clear to the people of today; hence some changes have become necessary as adaptations to the needs of our own times. For this reason the Council decrees what follows concerning the revision of these rites.

63. Because the use of the mother tongue in the administration of the sacraments and sacramentals can often be of considerable help for the people, this use is to be extended according to the following norms:

a. With art. 36 as the norm, the vernacular may be used in administering the sacraments and sacramentals.

b. Particular rituals in harmony with the new edition of the Roman Ritual shall be prepared without delay by the competent, territorial ecclesiastical authority mentioned in art. 22, §2 of this Constitution. These rituals are to be adapted, even in regard to the language employed, to the needs of the different regions. Once they have been reviewed by the Apostolic See, they are to be used in the regions for which they have been prepared. But those who draw up these rituals or particular collections of rites must not leave out the prefatory instructions for the individual rites in the Roman Ritual, whether the instructions are pastoral and rubrical or have some special social bearing.

64. The catechumenate for adults, divided into several stages, is to be restored and put into use at the discretion of the local Ordinary. By this means the time of the catechumenate, which is intended as a period of well-suited instruction, may be sanctified by sacred rites to be celebrated at successive intervals of time.

65. With art. 37–40 of this Constitution as the norm, it is lawful in mission lands to allow, besides what is part of Christian tradition, those initiation elements in use among individual peoples, to the extent that such elements are compatible with the Christian rite of initiation.

66.   Both of the rites for the baptism of adults are to be revised: not only the simpler rite, but also the more solemn one, with proper attention to the restored catechumenate. A special Mass "On the Occasion of a Baptism" is to be incorporated into the Roman Missal.

67.   The rite for the baptism of infants is to be revised and it should be suited to the fact that those to be baptized are infants. The roles as well as the obligations of parents and godparents should be brought out more clearly in the rite itself.

68.   The baptismal rite should contain alternatives, to be used at the discretion of the local Ordinary, for occasions when a very large number are to be baptized together. Moreover, a shorter rite is to be drawn up, especially in mission lands, for use by catechists, but also by the faithful in general, when there is danger of death and neither a priest nor a deacon is available.

69.   In place of the rite called the "Order of Supplying What Was Omitted in the Baptism of an Infant," a new rite is to be drawn up. This should manifest more clearly and fittingly that an infant who was baptized by the short rite has already been received into the Church.

Similarly, a new rite is to be drawn up for converts who have already been validly baptized; it should express that they are being received into the communion of the Church.

70.   Except during the Easter season, baptismal water may be blessed within the rite of baptism itself by use of an approved, shorter formulary.

71.   The rite of confirmation is also to be revised in order that the intimate connection of this sacrament with the whole of Christian initiation may stand out more clearly; for this reason it is fitting for candidates to renew their baptismal promises just before they are confirmed.

Confirmation may be conferred within Mass when convenient; as for the rite outside Mass, a formulary is to be composed for use as an introduction.

72.   The rite and formularies for the sacrament of penance are to be revised so that they more clearly express both the nature and effect of the sacrament.

73.   "Extreme unction," which may also and more properly be called "anointing of the sick," is not a sacrament for those only who are at the point of death. Hence, as soon as any one of the faithful begins to be in danger of death from sickness or old age, the fitting time for that person to receive this sacrament has certainly already arrived.

74.   In addition to the separate rites for anointing of the sick and for viaticum, a continuous rite shall be drawn up, structured so that the sick person is anointed after confessing and before receiving viaticum.

75.   The number of the anointings is to be adapted to the circumstances; the prayers that belong to the rite of anointing are to be so revised that they correspond to the varying conditions of the sick who receive the sacrament.

76.   Both the ceremonies and texts of the ordination rites are to be revised. The address given by the bishop at the beginning of each ordination or consecration may be in the vernacular.

When a bishop is consecrated, all the bishops present may take part in the laying on of hands.

77.   The marriage rite now found in the Roman Ritual is to be revised and enriched in such a way that it more clearly signifies the grace of the sacrament and imparts a knowledge of the obligations of spouses.

"If any regions follow other praiseworthy customs and ceremonies when celebrating the sacrament of marriage, the Council earnestly desires that by all means these be retained."[1]

Moreover, the competent, territorial ecclesiastical authority mentioned in art. 22, §2 of this Constitution is free to draw up, in accord with art. 63, its own rite, suited to the usages of place and people. But the rite must always conform to the law that the priest assisting at the marriage must ask for and obtain the consent of the contracting parties.

78.   Marriage is normally to be celebrated within Mass, after the reading of the gospel and the homily and before "the prayer of the faithful." The prayer for the bride, duly emended to remind both spouses of their equal obligation to remain faithful to each other, may be said in the vernacular.

But if the sacrament of marriage is celebrated apart from Mass, the epistle and gospel from the nuptial Mass are to be read at the beginning of the rite and the blessing is always to be given to the spouses.

79.   The sacramentals are to be reviewed in the light of the primary criterion that the faithful participate intelligently, actively, and easily; the conditions of our own days must also be considered. When rituals are revised, in accord with art. 63, new sacramentals may also be added as the need for them becomes apparent.

Reserved blessings shall be very few; reservations shall be in favor only of bishops and Ordinaries.

Let provision be made that some sacramentals, at least in special circumstances and at the discretion of the Ordinary, may be administered by qualified laypersons.

80.   The rite for the consecration to a life of virginity as it exists in the Roman Pontifical is to be revised.

A rite of religious profession and renewal of vows shall be drawn up with a view to achieving greater unity, simplicity, and dignity. Apart from exceptions in particular law, this rite should be adopted by those who make their profession or renewal of vows within Mass.

Religious profession should preferably be made within Mass.

81. The rite of funerals should express more clearly the paschal character of Christian death and should correspond more closely to the circumstances and traditions of various regions. This applies also to the liturgical color to be used.

82. The rite for the burial of infants is to be revised and a special Mass for the occasion provided.

CHAPTER IV
DIVINE OFFICE

83. Christ Jesus, High Priest of the new and eternal covenant, taking human nature, introduced into this earthly exile the hymn that is sung throughout all ages in the halls of heaven. He joins the entire human community to himself, associating it with his own singing of this canticle of divine praise.

For he continues his priestly work through the agency of his Church, which is unceasingly engaged in praising the Lord and interceding for the salvation of the whole world. The Church does this not only by celebrating the eucharist, but also in other ways, especially by praying the divine office.

84. By tradition going back to early Christian times, the divine office is so arranged that the whole course of the day and night is made holy by the praises of God. Therefore, when this wonderful song of praise is rightly performed by priests and others who are deputed for this purpose by the Church's ordinance or by the faithful praying together with the priest in the approved form, then it is truly the voice of a bride addressing her bridegroom; it is the very prayer that Christ himself, together with his Body, addresses to the Father.

85. Hence all who render this service are not only fulfilling a duty of the Church, but also are sharing in the greatest honor of Christ's Bride, for by offering these praises to God they are standing before God's throne in the name of the Church, their Mother.

86. Priests engaged in the sacred pastoral ministry will offer the praises of the hours with greater fervor the more vividly they realize that they must heed St. Paul's exhortation: "Pray without ceasing" (1 Thes 5:17). For the work in which they labor will effect nothing and bring forth no fruit except by the power of the Lord who said: "Without me you can do nothing" (Jn 15:5). That is why the apostles, instituting deacons, said: "We will devote ourselves to prayer and to the ministry of the word" (Acts 6:4).

87. In order that the divine office may be better and more completely carried out in existing circumstances, whether by priests or by other members of the Church, the Council, carrying further the restoration already so happily begun

by the Apostolic See, has seen fit to decree what follows concerning the office of the Roman Rite.

88.   Because the purpose of the office is to sanctify the day, the traditional sequence of the hours is to be restored so that once again they may be genuinely related to the hour of the day when they are prayed, as far as it is possible. Moreover, it will be necessary to take into account the modern conditions in which daily life has to be lived, especially by those who are called to labor in apostolic works.

89.   Therefore, when the office is revised, these norms are to be observed:

a. By the venerable tradition of the universal Church, lauds as morning prayer and vespers as evening prayer are the two hinges on which the daily office turns; hence they are to be considered as the chief hours and celebrated as such.

b. Compline is to be so composed that it will be a suitable prayer for the end of the day.

c. The hour known as matins, although it should retain the character of nocturnal praise when celebrated in choir, shall be adapted so that it may be recited at any hour of the day; it shall be made up of fewer psalms and longer readings.

d. The hour of prime is to be suppressed.

e. In choir the minor hours of terce, sext, and none are to be observed. But outside choir it will be lawful to choose whichever of the three best suits the hour of the day.

90.   The divine office, because it is the public prayer of the Church, is a source of devotion and nourishment also for personal prayer. Therefore priests and all others who take part in the divine office are earnestly exhorted in the Lord to attune their minds to their voices when praying it. The better to achieve this, let them take steps to improve their understanding of the liturgy and of the Bible, especially the psalms.

In revising the Roman office, its ancient and venerable treasures are to be so adapted that all those to whom they are handed on may more fully and readily draw profit from them.

91.   So that it may really be possible in practice to observe the course of the hours proposed in art. 89, the psalms are no longer to be distributed over just one week, but over some longer period of time.

The work of revising the psalter, already happily begun, is to be finished as soon as possible and is to take into account the style of Christian Latin, the liturgical use of psalms, including their being sung, and the entire tradition of the Latin Church.

92. As regards the readings, the following shall be observed:

a. Readings from sacred Scripture shall be arranged so that the riches of God's word may be easily accessible in more abundant measure.

b. Readings excerpted from the works of the Fathers, doctors, and ecclesiastical writers shall be better selected.

c. The accounts of the martyrdom or lives of the saints are to be made to accord with the historical facts.

93. To whatever extent may seem advisable, the hymns are to be restored to their original form and any allusion to mythology or anything that conflicts with Christian piety is to be dropped or changed. Also, as occasion arises, let other selections from the treasury of hymns be incorporated.

94. That the day may be truly sanctified and the hours themselves recited with spiritual advantage, it is best that each of them be prayed at a time most closely corresponding to the true time of each canonical hour.

95. In addition to the conventual Mass, communities obliged to choral office are bound to celebrate the office in choir every day. In particular:

a. Orders of canons, of monks and of nuns, and of other regulars bound by law or constitutions to choral office must celebrate the entire office.

b. Cathedral or collegiate chapters are bound to recite those parts of the office imposed on them by general or particular law.

c. All members of the above communities who are in major orders or are solemnly professed, except for lay brothers, are bound individually to recite those canonical hours which they do not pray in choir.

96. Clerics not bound to office in choir, if they are in major orders, are bound to pray the entire office every day, either in common or individually, following the norms in art. 89.

97. Appropriate instances are to be defined by the rubrics in which a liturgical service may be substituted for the divine office.

In particular cases and for a just reason Ordinaries may dispense their subjects wholly or in part from the obligation of reciting the divine office or may commute it.

98. Members of any institute dedicated to acquiring perfection who, according to their constitutions, are to recite any parts of the divine office are thereby performing the public prayer of the Church.

They too perform the public prayer of the Church who, in virtue of their constitutions, recite any little office, provided this has been drawn up after the pattern of the divine office and duly approved.

99. Since the divine office is the voice of the Church, that is, of the whole Mystical Body publicly praising God, those clerics who are not obliged to office in choir, especially priests who live together or who meet together for any purpose, are urged to pray at least some part of the divine office in common.

All who pray the divine office, whether in choir or in common, should fulfill the task entrusted to them as perfectly as possible: this refers not only to the internal devotion of their minds but also to their external manner of celebration.

It is advantageous, moreover, that the office in choir and in common be sung when there is an opportunity to do so.

100. Pastors should see to it that the chief hours, especially vespers, are celebrated in common in church on Sundays and the more solemn feasts. The laity, too, are encouraged to recite the divine office either with the priests, or among themselves, or even individually.

101. § 1. In accordance with the centuries-old tradition of the Latin rite, clerics are to retain the Latin language in the divine office. But in individual cases the Ordinary has the power of granting the use of a vernacular translation, prepared in accord with art. 36, to those clerics for whom the use of Latin constitutes a grave obstacle to their praying the office properly.

§ 2. The competent superior has the power to grant the use of the vernacular in the celebration of the divine office, even in choir, to nuns and to members of institutes dedicated to acquiring perfection, both men who are not clerics and women. The version, however, must be one that has been approved.

§ 3. Any cleric bound to the divine office fulfills his obligation if he prays the office in the vernacular together with a group of the faithful or with those mentioned in §2, provided the text of the translation has been approved.

CHAPTER V
THE LITURGICAL YEAR

102. The Church is conscious that it must celebrate the saving work of the divine Bridegroom by devoutly recalling it on certain days throughout the course of the year. Every week, on the day which the Church has called the Lord's Day, it keeps the memory of the Lord's resurrection, which it also celebrates once in the year, together with his blessed passion, in the most solemn festival of Easter.

Within the cycle of a year, moreover, the Church unfolds the whole mystery of Christ, from his incarnation and birth until his ascension, the day of Pentecost, and the expectation of blessed hope and of the Lord's return.

Recalling thus the mysteries of redemption, the Church opens to the faithful the riches of the Lord's powers and merits, so that these are in some way made present in every age in order that the faithful may lay hold on them and be filled with saving grace.

103. In celebrating this annual cycle of Christ's mysteries, the Church honors with special love Mary, the Mother of God, who is joined by an inseparable bond to the saving work of her Son. In her the Church holds up and admires the most excellent effect of the redemption and joyfully contemplates, as in a flawless image, that which the Church itself desires and hopes wholly to be.

104. The Church has also included in the annual cycle days devoted to the memory of the martyrs and the other saints. Raised up to perfection by the manifold grace of God and already in possession of eternal salvation, they sing God's perfect praise in heaven and offer prayers for us. By celebrating their passage from earth to heaven the Church proclaims the paschal mystery achieved in the saints, who have suffered and been glorified with Christ; it proposes them to the faithful as examples drawing all to the Father through Christ and pleads through their merits for God's favors.

105. Finally, in the various seasons of the year and according to its traditional discipline, the Church completes the formation of the faithful by means of devout practices for soul and body, by instruction, prayer, and works of penance and of mercy.

Accordingly the sacred Council has seen fit to decree what follows.

106. By a tradition handed down from the apostles and having its origin from the very day of Christ's resurrection, the Church celebrates the paschal mystery every eighth day, which, with good reason, bears the name of the Lord's Day or Sunday. For on this day Christ's faithful must gather together so that, by hearing the word of God and taking part in the eucharist, they may call to mind the passion, the resurrection, and the glorification of the Lord Jesus and may thank God, who "has begotten them again unto a living hope through the resurrection of Jesus Christ from the dead" (1 Pt 1:3). Hence the Lord's Day is the first holy day of all and should be proposed to the devotion of the faithful and taught to them in such a way that it may become in fact a day of joy and of freedom from work. Other celebrations, unless they be truly of greatest importance, shall not have precedence over the Sunday, the foundation and core of the whole liturgical year.

107. The liturgical year is to be so revised that the traditional customs and usages of the sacred seasons are preserved or restored to suit the conditions of modern times; their specific character is to be retained, so that they duly nourish the devotion of the faithful who celebrate the mysteries of Christian redemption and above all the paschal mystery. If certain adaptations are considered necessary on account of local conditions, they are to be made in accordance with the provisions of art. 39 and 40.

108. The minds of the faithful must be directed primarily toward those feasts of the Lord on which the mysteries of salvation are celebrated in the course of the year. Therefore, the Proper of Seasons shall be given the precedence due to it over the feasts of the saints, in order that the entire cycle of the mysteries of salvation may be celebrated in the measure due to them.

109. Lent is marked by two themes, the baptismal and the penitential. By recalling or preparing for baptism and by repentance, this season disposes the faithful, as they more diligently listen to the word of God and devote themselves to prayer, to celebrate the paschal mystery. The baptismal and penitential aspects of Lent are to be given greater prominence in both the liturgy and liturgical catechesis. Hence:

a. More use is to be made of the baptismal features proper to the Lenten liturgy; some of those from an earlier era are to be restored as may seem advisable.

b. The same is to apply to the penitential elements. As regards catechesis, it is important to impress on the minds of the faithful not only the social consequences of sin but also the essence of the virtue of penance, namely, detestation of sin as an offense against God; the role of the Church in penitential practices is not to be neglected and the people are to be exhorted to pray for sinners.

110. During Lent penance should be not only inward and individual, but also outward and social. The practice of penance should be fostered, however, in ways that are possible in our own times and in different regions and according to the circumstances of the faithful; it should be encouraged by the authorities mentioned in art. 22.

Nevertheless, let the paschal fast be kept sacred. Let it be observed everywhere on Good Friday and, where possible, prolonged throughout Holy Saturday, as a way of coming to the joys of the Sunday of the resurrection with uplifted and welcoming heart.

111. The saints have been traditionally honored in the Church and their authentic relics and images held in veneration. For the feasts of the saints proclaim the wonderful works of Christ in his servants and display to the faithful fitting examples for their imitation.

Lest the feasts of the saints take precedence over the feasts commemorating the very mysteries of salvation, many of them should be left to be celebrated by a particular Church or nation or religious family; those only should be extended to the universal Church that commemorate saints of truly universal significance.

CHAPTER VI
SACRED MUSIC

112. The musical tradition of the universal Church is a treasure of inestimable value, greater even than that of any other art. The main reason for this preeminence is that, as sacred song closely bound to the text, it forms a necessary or integral part of the solemn liturgy.

Holy Scripture itself has bestowed praise upon sacred song[1] and the same may be said of the Fathers of the Church and of the Roman pontiffs, who in recent times, led by St. Pius X, have explained more precisely the ministerial function supplied by sacred music in the service of the Lord.

Therefore sacred music will be the more holy the more closely it is joined to the liturgical rite, whether by adding delight to prayer, fostering oneness of spirit, or investing the rites with greater solemnity. But the Church approves of all forms of genuine art possessing the qualities required and admits them into divine worship.

Accordingly, the Council, keeping the norms and precepts of ecclesiastical tradition and discipline and having regard to the purpose of sacred music, which is the glory of God and the sanctification of the faithful, decrees what follows.

113. A liturgical service takes on a nobler aspect when the rites are celebrated with singing, the sacred ministers take their parts in them, and the faithful actively participate.

As regards the language to be used, the provisions of art. 36 are to be observed; for the Mass, those of art. 54; for the sacraments, those of art. 63; for the divine office, those of art. 101.

114. The treasure of sacred music is to be preserved and fostered with great care. Choirs must be diligently developed, especially in cathedral churches; but bishops and other pastors of souls must be at pains to ensure that whenever a liturgical service is to be celebrated with song, the whole assembly of the faithful is enabled, in keeping with art. 28 and 30, to contribute the active participation that rightly belongs to it.

s to be attached to the teaching and practice of music in ...ates and houses of study of religious of both sexes, and ...stitutions and schools. To impart this instruction, those sacred music are to receive thorough training.

It is rec... led also that higher institutes of sacred music be established whenever possible.

Musicians and singers, especially young boys, must also be given a genuine liturgical training.

116. The Church acknowledges Gregorian chant as distinctive of the Roman liturgy; therefore, other things being equal, it should be given pride of place in liturgical services.

But other kinds of sacred music, especially polyphony, are by no means excluded from liturgical celebrations, provided they accord with the spirit of the liturgical service, in the way laid down in art. 30.

117. The *editio typica* of the books of Gregorian chant is to be completed and a more critical edition is to be prepared of those books already published since the reform of St. Pius X.

It is desirable also that an edition be prepared containing the simpler melodies for use in small churches.

118. The people's own religious songs are to be encouraged with care so that in sacred devotions as well as during services of the liturgy itself, in keeping with rubrical norms and requirements, the faithful may raise their voices in song.

119. In certain parts of the world, especially mission lands, people have their own musical traditions and these play a great part in their religious and social life. Thus, in keeping with art. 39 and 40, due importance is to be attached to their music and a suitable place given to it, not only in forming their attitude toward religion, but also in adapting worship to their native genius.

Therefore, when missionaries are being given training in music, every effort should be made to see that they become competent in promoting the traditional music of the people, both in schools and in sacred services, as far as may be practicable.

120. In the Latin Church the pipe organ is to be held in high esteem, for it is the traditional musical instrument that adds a wonderful splendor to the Church's ceremonies and powerfully lifts up the spirit to God and to higher things.

But other instruments also may be admitted for use in divine worship, with the knowledge and consent of the competent territorial authority and in conformity with art. 22, §2, art. 37 and art. 40. This applies, however, only on condition that the instruments are suitable, or can be made suitable, for sacred use, are in accord with the dignity of the place of worship, and truly contribute to the uplifting of the faithful.

121. Composers, filled with the Christian spirit, should feel that their vocation is to develop sacred music and to increase its store of treasures.

Let them produce compositions having the qualities proper to genuine sacred music, not confining themselves to works that can be sung only by large choirs, but providing also for the needs of small choirs and for the active participation of the entire assembly of the faithful.

The texts intended to be sung must always be consistent with Catholic teaching; indeed they should be drawn chiefly from holy Scripture and from liturgical sources.

CHAPTER VII
SACRED ART AND SACRED FURNISHINGS

122. The fine arts are deservedly ranked among the noblest activities of human genius and this applies especially to religious art and to its highest achievement, sacred art. These arts, by their very nature, are oriented toward the infinite beauty of God, which they attempt in some way to portray by the work of human hands. They are dedicated to advancing God's praise and glory to the degree that they center on the single aim of turning the human spirit devoutly toward God.

The Church has therefore always been the friend of the fine arts, has ever sought their noble help, and has trained artists with the special aim that all things

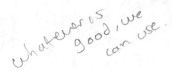
Whatever is good, we can use.

set apart for use in divine worship are truly worthy, becoming, and beautiful, signs and symbols of the supernatural world. The Church has always regarded itself as the rightful arbiter of the arts, deciding which of the works of artists are in accordance with faith, with reverence, and with honored traditional laws and are thereby suited for sacred use.

The Church has been particularly careful to see that sacred furnishings worthily and beautifully serve the dignity of worship and has admitted changes in materials, design, or ornamentation prompted by the progress of the technical arts with the passage of time.

Wherefore it has pleased the Fathers to issue the following decrees on these matters.

123. The Church has not adopted any particular style of art as its very own but has admitted styles from every period, according to the proper genius and circumstances of peoples and the requirements of the many different rites in the Church. Thus, in the course of the centuries, the Church has brought into being a treasury of art that must be very carefully preserved. The art of our own days, coming from every race and region, shall also be given free scope in the Church, on condition that it serves the places of worship and sacred rites with the reverence and honor due to them. In this way contemporary art can add its own voice to that wonderful chorus of praise sung by the great masters of past ages of Catholic faith.

124. In encouraging and favoring art that is truly sacred, Ordinaries should strive after noble beauty rather than mere sumptuous display. This principle is to apply also in the matter of sacred vestments and appointments.

Let bishops carefully remove from the house of God and from other places of worship those works of artists that are repugnant to faith and morals and to Christian devotion and that offend true religious sense either by their grotesqueness or by the deficiency, mediocrity, or sham in their artistic quality.

When churches are to be built, let great care be taken that they are well suited to celebrating liturgical services and to bringing about the active participation of the faithful.

125. The practice of placing sacred images in churches so that they may be venerated by the faithful is to be maintained. Nevertheless there is to be restraint regarding their number and prominence so that they do not create confusion among the Christian people or foster religious practices of doubtful orthodoxy.

126. When deciding on works of art, local Ordinaries shall give hearing to the diocesan commission on sacred art, and if need be, to others who are especially expert, as well as to the commissions referred to in art. 44, 45, and 46. Ordinaries must be very careful to see that sacred furnishings and valuable works of art are not disposed of or damaged, for they are the adornment of the house of God.

127. Bishops should have a special concern for artists, so as to imbue them with the spirit of sacred art and liturgy. This they may do in person or through competent priests who are gifted with a knowledge and love of art.

It is also recommended that schools or academies of sacred art to train artists be founded in those parts of the world where they seem useful.

All artists who, prompted by their talents, desire to serve God's glory in holy Church, should ever bear in mind that they are engaged in a kind of sacred imitation of God the Creator and are concerned with works intended to be used in Catholic worship, to uplift the faithful, and to foster their devotion and religious formation.

128. Along with the revision of the liturgical books, as laid down in art. 25, there is to be an early revision of the canons and ecclesiastical statutes regulating the supplying of material things involved in sacred worship. This applies in particular to the worthy and well-planned construction of places of worship, the design and construction of altars, the nobility, placement, and security of the eucharistic tabernacle, the practicality and dignity of the baptistry, the appropriate arrangement of sacred images and church decorations and appointments. Laws that seem less suited to the reformed liturgy are to be brought into harmony with it or else abolished; laws that are helpful are to be retained if already in use or introduced where they are lacking.

With art. 22 of this Constitution as the norm, the territorial bodies of bishops are empowered to make adaptations to the needs and customs of their different regions; this applies especially to the material and design of sacred furnishings and vestments.

129. During their philosophical and theological studies, clerics are to be taught about the history and development of sacred art and about the sound principles on which the production of its works must be grounded. In consequence they will be able to appreciate and preserve the Church's treasured monuments and be in a position to offer good advice to artists who are engaged in producing works of art.

130. It is fitting that the use of pontifical insignia be reserved to those ecclesiastical persons who have either episcopal rank or some definite jurisdiction.

APPENDIX
DECLARATION OF THE SECOND VATICAN ECUMENICAL COUNCIL ON REVISION OF THE CALENDAR

131. The Second Vatican Ecumenical Council recognizes the importance of the wishes expressed by many on assigning the feast of Easter to a fixed Sunday and on an unchanging calendar and has considered the effects that could result from the introduction of a new calendar. Accordingly the Council issues the following declaration:

1. The Council is not opposed to the assignment of the feast of Easter to a particular Sunday of the Gregorian Calendar, provided those whom it may concern, especially other Christians who are not in communion with the Apostolic See, give their assent.

2. The Council likewise declares that it does not oppose measures designed to introduce a perpetual calendar into civil society.

Among the various systems being suggested to establish a perpetual calendar and to introduce it into civil life, only those systems are acceptable to the Church that retain and safeguard a seven-day week with Sunday and introduce no days outside the week, so that the present sequence of weeks is left intact, unless the most serious reasons arise. Concerning these the Apostolic See will make its own judgment.

The Fathers of the Council have given assent to all and to each part of the matters set forth in this Constitution. And together with the venerable Fathers, we, by the apostolic power given to us by Christ, approve, enact, and establish in the Holy Spirit each and all the decrees in this Constitution and command that what has been thus established in the Council be promulgated for the glory of God.

NOTES

1. RomM, prayer over the gifts, Holy Thursday and 2d Sunday in Ordinary Time.

2. See Heb 13:14.

3. See Eph 2:21–22.

4. See Eph 4:13.

5. See Is 11:12.

6. See Jn 11:52.

7. See Jn 10:16.

CHAPTER I

1. See Is 61:1; Lk 4:18.

2. Ignatius of Antioch, *To the Ephesians* 7, 2.

3. See 1 Tm 2:5.

4. *Sacramentarium Veronense* (ed. Mohlberg), no. 1265.

5. RomM, preface I of Easter.

6. RomM, prayer after the seventh reading, Easter Vigil.

7. See Mk 16:15.

8. See Acts 26:18.

9. See Rom 6:4; Eph 2:6; Col 3:1.

10. See Jn 4:23.

11. See 1 Cor 11:26.

12. Council of Trent, sess. 13, 11 Oct 1551, *Decree on the Holy Eucharist*, chap. 5.

13. Council of Trent, sess. 22, 17 Sept 1562, *Doctrine on the Holy Sacrifice of the Mass*, chap. 2.

14. See Augustine, *In Ioannis Evangelium Tractatus 6*, chap. 1, n. 7.

15. See Rv. 21:2; Col 3:1; Heb 8:2.

16. See Phil 3:20; Col 3:4.

17. See Jn 17:3; Lk 24:47; Acts 2:38.

18. See Mt 28:20.

19. RomM, prayer after communion, Easter Vigil.

20. RomM, opening prayer, Mass for Monday of Easter Week.

21. See 2 Cor 6:1.

22. See Mt 6:6.

23. See 1 Thes 5:17.

24. See 2 Cor 4:10–11.

25. RomM, prayer over the gifts, Saturday after the 2d, 4th, and 6th Sundays of Easter.

26. Cyprian, *On the Unity of the Catholic Church 7;* see *Letter 66*, n. 8, 3.

27. See Council of Trent, sess. 22, 17 Sept 1562, *Doctrine on the Holy Sacrifice of the Mass*, chap. 8.

28. See Ignatius of Antioch, *To the Magnesians*, 7; *To the Philadelphians*, 4; *To the Smyrnians*, 8.

CHAPTER II

1. See Augustine, *In Ioannis Evangelium Tractatus 36*, chap. 6, n. 13.

2. Liturgy of the Hours, antiphon for Canticle of Mary, evening prayer II, feast of Corpus Christi.

3. See Cyril of Alexandria, *Commentary on the Gospel of John*, book 11, chap. 11–12.

4. See 1 Tm 2:1–2.

5. Council of Trent, sess. 21, *Doctrine on Communion under Both Species*, chap. 1–3.

CHAPTER III

1. Council of Trent, sess. 24, *Decree on Reform*, chap. 1. See also RomR, title 8, chap. 2, n. 6.

CHAPTER VI

1. See Eph 5:19; Col 3:16.

GENERAL INSTRUCTION
OF THE
ROMAN MISSAL

INCLUDING ADAPTATIONS FOR THE DIOCESES OF
THE UNITED STATES OF AMERICA

CONGREGATION FOR DIVINE WORSHIP AND
THE DISCIPLINE OF THE SACRAMENTS

LATIN
17 MARCH 2002

ENGLISH
17 MARCH 2003

Lat: Instituto Generalis
(General Establishment)

OUTLINE

GENERAL INSTRUCTION OF THE ROMAN MISSAL

PREAMBLE

1.   When he was about to celebrate with his disciples the Passover meal in which he instituted the sacrifice of his Body and Blood, Christ the Lord gave instructions that a large, furnished upper room should be prepared (Lk 22:12). The Church has always regarded this command as applying also to herself when she gives directions about the preparation of people's hearts and minds, and of the places, rites, and texts for the celebration of the Most Holy Eucharist. The current norms, prescribed in keeping with the will of the Second Vatican Ecumenical Council, and the new Missal that the Church of the Roman Rite is to use from now on in the celebration of Mass are also evidence of the great concern of the Church, of her faith, and of her unchanged love for the great mystery of the Eucharist. They likewise bear witness to the Church's continuous and unbroken tradition, irrespective of the introduction of certain new features.

A WITNESS TO UNCHANGED FAITH

2.   The sacrificial nature of the Mass, solemnly asserted by the Council of Trent in accordance with the Church's universal tradition,[1] was reaffirmed by the Second Vatican Council, which offered these significant words about the Mass: "At the Last Supper our Savior instituted the Eucharistic Sacrifice of his Body and Blood, by which he would perpetuate the Sacrifice of the Cross throughout the centuries until he should come again, thus entrusting to the Church, his beloved Bride, the memorial of his death and resurrection."[2]

What the Council thus teaches is expressed constantly in the formulas of the Mass. This teaching, which is concisely expressed in the statement already contained in the ancient Sacramentary commonly known as the Leonine—"As often as the commemoration of this sacrifice is celebrated, the work of our redemption is carried out"[3]—is aptly and accurately developed in the Eucharistic Prayers. For in these prayers the priest, while he performs the commemoration, turns towards God, even in the name of the whole people, renders him thanks, and offers the living and holy Sacrifice, namely, the Church's offering and the Victim by whose immolation God willed to be appeased;[4] and he prays that the Body and Blood of Christ may be a sacrifice acceptable to the Father and salvific for the whole world.[5]

In this new Missal, then, the Church's rule of prayer (*lex orandi*) corresponds to her perennial rule of belief (*lex credendi*), by which namely we are taught that the Sacrifice of the Cross and its sacramental renewal in the Mass, which Christ the Lord instituted at the Last Supper and commanded the Apostles to do in his memory, are one and the same, differing only in the manner of offering, and that consequently the Mass is at once a sacrifice of praise and thanksgiving, of propitiation and satisfaction.

3.   Moreover, the wondrous mystery of the Lord's real presence under the eucharistic species, reaffirmed by the Second Vatican Council[6] and other documents of the Church's Magisterium[7] in the same sense and with the same words that the Council of Trent had proposed as a matter of faith,[8] is proclaimed in the celebration of Mass not only by means of the very words of consecration, by which Christ becomes present through transubstantiation, but also by that interior disposition and outward expression of supreme reverence and adoration in which the Eucharistic Liturgy is carried out. For the same reason the Christian people is drawn on Holy Thursday of the Lord's Supper, and on the solemnity of the Most Holy Body and Blood of Christ, to venerate this wonderful Sacrament by a special form of adoration.

4.   Further, the nature of the ministerial priesthood proper to a Bishop and a priest, who offer the Sacrifice in the person of Christ and who preside over the gathering of the holy people, is evident in the form of the rite itself, by reason of the more prominent place and office of the priest. The meaning of this office is enunciated and explained clearly and at greater length, in the Preface for the Chrism Mass on Holy Thursday, the day commemorating the institution of the priesthood. The Preface brings to light the conferral of the priestly power accomplished through the laying on of hands; and, by listing the various duties, it describes that power, which is the continuation of the power of Christ the High Priest of the New Testament.

5.   In addition, the nature of the ministerial priesthood also puts into its proper light another reality, which must indeed be highly regarded, namely, the royal priesthood of the faithful, whose spiritual sacrifice is brought to completeness through the ministry of the Bishop and the priests in union with the sacrifice of Christ, the one and only Mediator.[9] For the celebration of the Eucharist is an action of the whole Church, and in it each one should carry out solely but completely that which pertains to him or her, in virtue of the rank of each within the People of God. In this way greater consideration will also be given to some aspects of the celebration that have sometimes been accorded less attention in the course of time. For this people is the People of God, purchased by Christ's Blood, gathered together by the Lord, nourished by his word. It is a people called to bring to God the prayers of the entire human family, a people giving thanks in Christ for the mystery of salvation by offering his Sacrifice. Finally, it is a people made one by by sharing in the Communion of Christ's Body and Blood. Though holy in its origin, this people nevertheless grows continually in holiness by its conscious, active, and fruitful participation in the mystery of the Eucharist.[10]

6.   In setting forth its instructions for the revision of the Order of Mass, the Second Vatican Council, using the same words as did Saint Pius V in the Apostolic Constitution *Quo primum*, by which the Missal of Trent was promulgated in 1570, also ordered, among other things, that some rites be restored "to the original norm of the holy Fathers."[11] From the fact that the same words are used it can be seen how both *Roman Missals*, although separated by four centuries, embrace one and the same tradition. Furthermore, if the inner elements of this tradition are reflected upon, it also becomes clear how outstandingly and felicitously the older *Roman Missal* is brought to fulfillment in the new.

7.   In a difficult period when the Catholic faith on the sacrificial nature of the Mass, the ministerial priesthood, and the real and permanent presence of Christ under the eucharistic species were placed at risk, Saint Pius V was especially concerned with preserving the more recent tradition, then unjustly being assailed, introducing only very slight changes into the sacred rite. In fact, the Missal of 1570 differs very little from the very first printed edition of 1474, which in turn faithfully follows the Missal used at the time of Pope Innocent III. Moreover, even though manuscripts in the Vatican Library provided material for the emendation of some expressions, they by no means made it possible to inquire into "ancient and approved authors" farther back than the liturgical commentaries of the Middle Ages.

8.   Today, on the other hand, countless learned studies have shed light on the "norm of the holy Fathers" which the revisers of the Missal of Saint Pius V followed. For following the publication first of the Sacramentary known as the Gregorian in 1571, critical editions of other ancient Roman and Ambrosian Sacramentaries were published, often in book form, as were ancient Hispanic and Gallican liturgical books which brought to light numerous prayers of no slight spiritual excellence that had previously been unknown.

In a similar fashion, traditions dating back to the first centuries, before the formation of the rites of East and West, are better known today because of the discovery of so many liturgical documents.

Moreover, continuing progress in the study of the holy Fathers has also shed light upon the theology of the mystery of the Eucharist through the teachings of such illustrious Fathers of Christian antiquity as Saint Irenaeus, Saint Ambrose, Saint Cyril of Jerusalem, and Saint John Chrysostom.

9.   For this reason, the "norm of the holy Fathers" requires not only the preservation of what our immediate forebears have passed on to us, but also an understanding and a more profound study of the Church's entire past and of all the ways in which her one and only faith has been set forth in the quite diverse human and social forms prevailing in the Semitic, Greek, and Latin areas. Moreover, this broader view allows us to see how the Holy Spirit endows the People of God with a marvelous fidelity in preserving the unalterable deposit of faith, even amid a very great variety of prayers and rites.

10.   The new Missal, therefore, while bearing witness to the Roman Church's rule of prayer (*lex orandi*), also safeguards the deposit of faith handed down by the more recent Councils, and marks in its own right a step of great importance in liturgical tradition.

Indeed, when the Fathers of the Second Vatican Council reaffirmed the dogmatic pronouncements of the Council of Trent, they spoke at a far different time in world history, so that they were able to bring forward proposals and measures of a pastoral nature that could not have even been foreseen four centuries earlier.

11.   The Council of Trent already recognized the great catechetical value contained in the celebration of Mass but was unable to bring out all its consequences in regard to actual practice. In fact, many were pressing for permission to use the vernacular in celebrating the eucharistic Sacrifice; but the Council, weighing the conditions of that age, considered it a duty to answer this request with a reaffirmation of the Church's traditional teaching, according to which the Eucharistic Sacrifice is, first and foremost, the action of Christ himself, and therefore that its proper efficacy is unaffected by the manner in which the faithful take part in it. The Council for this reason stated in firm but measured words, "Although the Mass contains much instruction for people of faith, nevertheless it did not seem expedient to the Fathers that it be celebrated everywhere in the vernacular."[12] The Council accordingly anathematized anyone maintaining that "the rite of the Roman Church, in which part of the Canon and the words of consecration are spoken in a low voice, is to be condemned, or that the Mass must be celebrated only in the vernacular."[13] Although on the one hand it prohibited the use of the vernacular in the Mass, nevertheless, on the other hand, the Council did direct pastors of souls to put appropriate catechesis in its place: "Lest Christ's flock go hungry . . . the Holy Synod commands pastors and all others having the care of souls to give frequent instructions during the celebration of Mass, either personally or through others, concerning what is read at Mass; among other things, they should include some explanation of the mystery of this most holy Sacrifice, especially on Sundays and holy days."[14]

12.   Therefore, when the Second Vatican Council convened in order to accommodate the Church to the requirements of her proper apostolic office precisely in these times, it examined thoroughly, as had Trent, the instructive and pastoral character of the Sacred Liturgy.[15] Since no Catholic would now deny the lawfulness and efficacy of a sacred rite celebrated in Latin, the Council was also able to grant that "the use of the vernacular language may frequently be of great advantage to the people" and gave the faculty for its use.[16] The enthusiasm in response to this measure has been so great everywhere that it has led, under the leadership of the Bishops and the Apostolic See itself, to permission for all liturgical celebrations in which the people participate to be in the vernacular, for the sake of a better comprehension of the mystery being celebrated.

13.   Indeed, since the use of the vernacular in the Sacred Liturgy may certainly be considered an important means for presenting more clearly the catechesis

regarding the mystery that is inherent in the celebration itself, the Second Vatican Council also ordered that certain prescriptions of the Council of Trent that had not been followed everywhere be brought to fruition, such as the homily to be given on Sundays and holy days[17] and the faculty to interject certain explanations during the sacred rites themselves.[18]

Above all, the Second Vatican Council, which urged "that more perfect form of participation in the Mass by which the faithful, after the priest's Communion, receive the Lord's Body from the same Sacrifice,"[19] called for another desire of the Fathers of Trent to be realized, namely that for the sake of a fuller participation in the holy Eucharist "the faithful present at each Mass should communicate not only by spiritual desire but also by sacramental reception of the Eucharist."[20]

14. Moved by the same desire and pastoral concern, the Second Vatican Council was able to give renewed consideration to what was established by Trent on Communion under both kinds. And indeed, since no one today calls into doubt in any way the doctrinal principles on the complete efficacy of Eucharistic Communion under the species of bread alone, the Council thus gave permission for the reception of Communion under both kinds on some occasions, because this clearer form of the sacramental sign offers a particular opportunity of deepening the understanding of the mystery in which the faithful take part.[21]

15. In this manner the Church, while remaining faithful to her office as teacher of truth safeguarding "things old," that is, the deposit of tradition, fulfills at the same time another duty, that of examining and prudently bringing forth "things new" (cf. Mt 13:52).

Accordingly, a part of the new Missal directs the prayers of the Church in a more open way to the needs of our times, which is above all true of the Ritual Masses and the Masses for Various Needs, in which tradition and new elements are appropriately harmonized. Thus, while many expressions, drawn from the Church's most ancient tradition and familiar through the many editions of the Roman Missal, have remained unchanged, many other expressions have been accommodated to today's needs and circumstances. Still others, such as the prayers for the Church, the laity, the sanctification of human work, the community of all peoples, and certain needs proper to our era, have been newly composed, drawing on the thoughts and often the very phrasing of the recent documents of the Council.

Moreover, on account of the same attitude toward the new state of the present world, it seemed that in the use of texts from the most ancient tradition, so revered a treasure would in no way be harmed if some phrases were changed so that the style of language would be more in accord with the language of modern theology and would truly reflect the current discipline of the Church. Thus, not a few expressions bearing on the evaluation and use of the goods of the earth have been changed, as have also not a few allusions to a certain form of outward penance belonging to past ages of the Church.

Finally, in this manner the liturgical norms of the Council of Trent have certainly been completed and perfected in many respects by those of the Second Vatican Council, which has brought to realization the efforts of the last four hundred years to bring the faithful closer to the Sacred Liturgy especially in recent times, and above all the zeal for the Liturgy promoted by Saint Pius X and his successors.

CHAPTER I
THE IMPORTANCE AND DIGNITY OF
THE EUCHARISTIC CELEBRATION

16.   The celebration of Mass, as the action of Christ and the People of God arrayed hierarchically, is the center of the whole Christian life for the Church both universal and local, as well as for each of the faithful individually.[22] In it is found the high point both of the action by which God sanctifies the world in Christ and of the worship that the human race offers to the Father, adoring him through Christ, the Son of God, in the Holy Spirit.[23] In it, moreover, during the course of the year, the mysteries of redemption are recalled so as in some way to be made present.[24] Furthermore, the other sacred actions and all the activities of the Christian life are bound up with it, flow from it, and are ordered to it.[25]

17.   It is therefore of the greatest importance that the celebration of the Mass—that is, the Lord's Supper—be so arranged that the sacred ministers and the faithful taking part in it, according to the proper state of each, may derive from it more abundantly[26] those fruits for the sake of which Christ the Lord instituted the Eucharistic Sacrifice of his Body and Blood and entrusted it to the Church, his beloved Bride, as the memorial of his Passion and Resurrection.[27]

18.   This will best be accomplished if, with due regard for the nature and the particular circumstances of each liturgical assembly, the entire celebration is planned in such a way that it leads to a conscious, active, and full participation of the faithful both in body and in mind, a participation burning with faith, hope, and charity, of the sort which is desired by the Church and demanded by the very nature of the celebration, and to which the Christian people have a right and duty by reason of their Baptism.[28]

19.   Even if it is sometimes not possible to have the presence and active participation of the faithful, which bring out more plainly the ecclesial nature of the celebration,[29] the Eucharistic Celebration always retains its efficacy and dignity because it is the action of Christ and the Church, in which the priest fulfills his own principal office and always acts for the people's salvation.

It is therefore recommended that the priest celebrate the Eucharistic Sacrifice even daily, if possible.[30]

20.   Because, however, the celebration of the Eucharist, like the entire Liturgy, is carried out through perceptible signs that nourish, strengthen, and express faith,[31] the utmost care must be taken to choose and to arrange those forms and

. elements set forth by the Church that, in view of the circumstances of the people and the place, will more effectively foster active and full participation and more properly respond to the spiritual needs of the faithful.

21.   This Instruction aims both to offer general guidelines for properly arranging the Celebration of the Eucharist and to set forth rules for ordering the various forms of celebration.[32]

22.   The celebration of the Eucharist in a particular Church is of utmost importance.

For the diocesan Bishop, the chief steward of the mysteries of God in the particular Church entrusted to his care, is the moderator, promoter, and guardian of the whole of its liturgical life.[33] In celebrations at which the Bishop presides, and especially in the celebration of the Eucharist led by the Bishop himself with the presbyterate, the deacons, and the people taking part, the mystery of the Church is revealed. For this reason, the solemn celebration of Masses of this sort must be an example for the entire diocese.

The Bishop should therefore be determined that the priests, the deacons, and the lay Christian faithful grasp ever more deeply the genuine meaning of the rites and liturgical texts and thereby be led to an active and fruitful celebration of the Eucharist. To the same end, he should also be vigilant that the dignity of these celebrations be enhanced. In promoting this dignity, the beauty of the sacred place, of music, and of art should contribute as greatly as possible.

23.   Moreover, in order that such a celebration may correspond more fully to the prescriptions and spirit of the Sacred Liturgy, and also in order to increase its pastoral effectiveness, certain accommodations and adaptations are specified in this General Instruction and in the Order of Mass.

24.   These adaptations consist for the most part in the choice of certain rites or texts, that is, of the chants, readings, prayers, explanations, and gestures that may respond better to the needs, preparation, and culture of the participants and that are entrusted to the priest celebrant. Nevertheless, the priest must remember that he is the servant of the Sacred Liturgy and that he himself is not permitted, on his own initiative, to add, to remove, or to change anything in the celebration of Mass.[34]

25.   In addition, certain adaptations are indicated in the proper place in the Missal and pertain respectively to the diocesan Bishop or to the Conference of Bishops, in accord with the *Constitution on the Sacred Liturgy*[35] (cf. below, nos. 387, 388–393).

26.   As for variations and the more substantial adaptations in view of the traditions and culture of peoples and regions, to be introduced in accordance with article 40 of the *Constitution on the Sacred Liturgy* because of benefit or need, the norms set forth in the Instruction *On the Roman Liturgy and Inculturation*[36] and below (nos. 395–399) are to be observed.

CHAPTER II
THE STRUCTURE OF THE MASS, ITS ELEMENTS AND ITS PARTS

I. THE GENERAL STRUCTURE OF THE MASS

27. At Mass—that is, the Lord's Supper—the People of God is called together, with a priest presiding and acting in the person of Christ, to celebrate the memorial of the Lord, the Eucharistic Sacrifice.[37] For this reason Christ's promise applies in an outstanding way to such a local gathering of the holy Church: "Where two or three are gathered in my name, there am I in their midst" (Mt 18:20). For in the celebration of Mass, in which the Sacrifice of the Cross is perpetuated,[38] Christ is really present in the very liturgical assembly gathered in his name, in the person of the minister, in his word, and indeed substantially and continuously under the Eucharistic species.[39]

28. The Mass is made up, as it were, of two parts: the Liturgy of the Word and the Liturgy of the Eucharist. These, however, are so closely interconnected that they form but one single act of worship.[40] For in the Mass the table both of God's word and of Christ's Body is prepared, from which the faithful may be instructed and refreshed.[41] There are also certain rites that open and conclude the celebration.

II. THE DIFFERENT ELEMENTS OF THE MASS

READING AND EXPLAINING THE WORD OF GOD

29. When the Sacred Scriptures are read in the Church, God himself speaks to his people, and Christ, present in his own word, proclaims the Gospel.

Therefore, all must listen with reverence to the readings from God's word, for they make up an element of greatest importance in the Liturgy. Although in the readings from Sacred Scripture God's word is addressed to all people of every era and is understandable to them, nevertheless, a fuller understanding and a greater effectiveness of the word is fostered by a living commentary on the word, that is, the homily, as part of the liturgical action.[42]

THE PRAYERS AND OTHER PARTS PERTAINING TO THE PRIEST

30. Among the parts assigned to the priest, the foremost is the Eucharistic Prayer, which is the high point of the entire celebration. Next are the orations: that is to say, the collect, the prayer over the offerings, and the prayer after Communion. These prayers are addressed to God in the name of the entire holy people and all present, by the priest who presides over the assembly in the person of Christ.[43] It is with good reason, therefore, that they are called the "presidential prayers."

31. It is also up to the priest, in the exercise of his office of presiding over the gathered assembly, to offer certain explanations that are foreseen in the rite

itself. Where it is indicated in the rubrics, the celebrant is permitted to adapt them somewhat in order that they respond to the understanding of those participating. However, he should always take care to keep to the sense of the text given in the Missal and to express them succinctly. The presiding priest is also to direct the word of God and to impart the final blessing. In addition, he may give the faithful a very brief introduction to the Mass of the day (after the initial Greeting and before the Act of Penitence), to the Liturgy of the Word (before the readings), and to the Eucharistic Prayer (before the Preface), though never during the Eucharistic Prayer itself; he may also make concluding comments to the entire sacred action before the dismissal.

32. The nature of the "presidential" texts demands that they be spoken in a loud and clear voice and that everyone listen with attention.[44] Thus, while the priest is speaking these texts, there should be no other prayers or singing, and the organ or other musical instruments should be silent.

33. The priest, in fact, as the one who presides, prays in the name of the Church and of the assembled community; but at times he prays only in his own name, asking that he may exercise his ministry with greater attention and devotion. Prayers of this kind, which occur before the reading of the Gospel, at the Preparation of the Gifts, and also before and after the Communion of the priest, are said quietly.

THE OTHER FORMULAS IN THE CELEBRATION

34. Since the celebration of Mass by its nature has a "communitarian" character,[45] both the dialogues between the priest and the faithful gathered together and the acclamations are of great significance;[46] in fact, they are not simply outward signs of communal celebration but foster and bring about communion between priest and people.

35. The acclamations and the responses of the faithful to the priest's greetings and prayers constitute that level of active participation that the gathered faithful are to contribute in every form of the Mass, so that the action of the entire community may be clearly expressed and fostered.[47]

36. Other parts, very useful for expressing and fostering the faithful's active participation, that are assigned to the whole assembly that is called together include especially the Act of Penitence, the Profession of Faith, the Prayer of the Faithful, and the Lord's Prayer.

37. Finally, concerning the other formulas,

   a. Some constitute an independent rite or act, such as the *Gloria*, the responsorial Psalm, the Alleluia and verse before the Gospel, the *Sanctus*, the Memorial Acclamation, and the *cantus post communionem*;

   b. Others accompany another rite, such as the chants at the Entrance, at the Offertory, at the fraction (*Agnus Dei*), and at Communion.

38.   In texts that are to be spoken in a loud and clear voice, whether by the priest or the deacon, or by the lector, or by all, the tone of voice should correspond to the genre of the text itself, that is, depending upon whether it is a reading, a prayer, a commentary, an acclamation, or a sung text; the tone should also be suited to the form of celebration and to the solemnity of the gathering. Consideration should also be given to the idiom of different languages and the culture of different peoples.

In the rubrics and in the norms that follow, words such as "say" and "proclaim" are to be understood of both singing and reciting, according to the principles just stated above.

THE IMPORTANCE OF SINGING

39.   The Christian faithful who gather together as one to await the Lord's coming are instructed by the Apostle Paul to sing together psalms, hymns, and spiritual songs (cf. Col 3:16). Singing is the sign of the heart's joy (cf. Acts 2:46). Thus Saint Augustine says rightly, "Singing is for one who loves."[48] There is also the ancient proverb: "One who sings well prays twice."

40.   Great importance should therefore be attached to the use of singing in the celebration of the Mass, with due consideration for the culture of the people and abilities of each liturgical assembly. Although it is not always necessary (e.g., in weekday Masses) to sing all the texts that are of themselves meant to be sung, every care should be taken that singing by the ministers and the people is not absent in celebrations that occur on Sundays and on holy days of obligation.

In the choosing of the parts actually to be sung, however, preference should be given to those that are of greater importance and especially to those to be sung by the priest or the deacon or the lector, with the people responding, or by the priest and people together.[49]

41.   All other things being equal, Gregorian chant holds pride of place because it is proper to the Roman Liturgy. Other types of sacred music, in particular polyphony, are in no way excluded, provided that they correspond to the spirit of the liturgical action and that they foster the participation of all the faithful.[50]

Since faithful from different countries come together ever more frequently, it is fitting that they know how to sing together at least some parts of the Ordinary of the Mass in Latin, especially the Creed and the Lord's Prayer, set to the simpler melodies.[51]

MOVEMENTS AND POSTURE

42.   The gestures and posture of the priest, the deacon, and the ministers, as well as those of the people, ought to contribute to making the entire celebration resplendent with beauty and noble simplicity, so that the true and full meaning of the different parts of the celebration is evident and that the participation of all is fostered.[52] Therefore, attention should be paid to what is determined by

this General Instruction and the traditional practice of the Roman Rite and to what serves the common spiritual good of the People of God, rather than private inclination or arbitrary choice.

A common posture, to be observed by all participants, is a sign of the unity of the members of the Christian community gathered for the Sacred Liturgy: it both expresses and fosters the intention and spiritual attitude of the participants.

43. The faithful should stand from the beginning of the Entrance chant, or while the priest approaches the altar, until the end of the Collect; for the *Alleluia* chant before the Gospel; while the Gospel itself is proclaimed; during the Profession of Faith and the Prayer of the Faithful; from the invitation, *Orate, fraters* (*Pray, brethren*), before the prayer over the offerings until the end of Mass, except at the places indicated below.

They should, however, sit while the readings before the Gospel and the responsorial Psalm are proclaimed and for the homily and while the Preparation of the Gifts at the Offertory is taking place; and, as circumstances allow, they may sit or kneel while the period of sacred silence after Communion is observed.

In the dioceses of the United States of America, they should kneel beginning after the singing or recitation of the *Sanctus* until after the *Amen* of the Eucharistic Prayer, except when prevented on occasion by reasons of health, lack of space, the large number of people present, or some other good reason. Those who do not kneel ought to make a profound bow when the priest genuflects after the consecration. The faithful kneel after the *Agnus Dei* unless the diocesan Bishop determines otherwise.[53]

With a view to a uniformity in gestures and postures during one and the same celebration, the faithful should follow the directions which the deacon, lay minister, or priest gives according to whatever is indicated in the Missal.

44. Among gestures included are also actions and processions: of the priest going with the deacon and ministers to the altar; of the deacon carrying the Evangeliary or *Book of the Gospels* to the ambo before the proclamation of the Gospel; of the faithful presenting the gifts and coming forward to receive Communion. It is appropriate that actions and processions of this sort be carried out with decorum while the chants proper to them occur, in keeping with the norms prescribed for each.

SILENCE

45. Sacred silence also, as part of the celebration, is to be observed at the designated times.[54] Its purpose, however, depends on the time it occurs in each part of the celebration. Thus within the Act of Penitence and again after the invitation to pray, all recollect themselves; but at the conclusion of a reading or the homily, all meditate briefly on what they have heard; then after Communion, they praise and pray to God in their hearts.

Even before the celebration itself, it is commendable that silence to be observed in the church, in the sacristy, in the vesting room, and in adjacent areas, so that all may dispose themselves to carry out the sacred action in a devout and fitting manner.

III. THE INDIVIDUAL PARTS OF THE MASS

A. The Introductory Rites

46.　The rites preceding the Liturgy of the Word, namely the Entrance, Greeting, Act of Penitence, *Kyrie, Gloria,* and Collect, have the character of a beginning, introduction, and preparation.

Their purpose is to ensure that the faithful who come together as one establish communion and dispose themselves to listen properly to God's word and to celebrate the Eucharist worthily.

In certain celebrations that are combined with Mass according to the norms of the liturgical books, the Introductory Rites are omitted or performed in a particular way.

THE ENTRANCE

47.　After the people have gathered, the Entrance chant begins as the priest enters with the deacon and ministers. The purpose of this chant is to open the celebration, foster the unity of those who have been gathered, introduce their thoughts to the mystery of the liturgical season or festivity, and accompany the procession of the priest and ministers.

48. The singing at this time is done either alternately by the choir and the people or in a similar way by the cantor and the people, or entirely by the people, or by the choir alone. In the dioceses of the United States of America there are four options for the Entrance Chant: (1) the antiphon from the *Roman Missal* or the Psalm from the *Roman Gradual* as set to music there or in another musical setting; (2) the seasonal antiphon and Psalm of the *Simple Gradual;* (3) a song from another collection of psalms and antiphons, approved by the Conference of Bishops or the diocesan Bishop, including psalms arranged in responsorial or metrical forms; (4) a suitable liturgical song similarly approved by the Conference of Bishops or the diocesan Bishop.[55]

If there is no singing at the entrance, the antiphon in the Missal is recited either by the faithful, or by some of them, or by a lector; otherwise, it is recited by the priest himself, who may even adapt it as an introductory explanation (cf. above, no. 31).

GREETING OF THE ALTAR AND OF THE PEOPLE GATHERED TOGETHER

49.　When they reach the sanctuary, the priest, the deacon, and the ministers reverence the altar with a profound bow.

As an expression of veneration, moreover, the priest and deacon then kiss the altar itself; as the occasion suggests, the priest also incenses the cross and the altar.

50. When the Entrance chant is concluded, the priest stands at the chair and, together with the whole gathering, makes the Sign of the Cross. Then he signifies the presence of the Lord to the community gathered there by means of the Greeting. By this Greeting and the people's response, the mystery of the Church gathered together is made manifest.

After the greeting of the people, the priest, the deacon, or a lay minister may very briefly introduce the faithful to the Mass of the day.

THE ACT OF PENITENCE

51. Then the priest invites those present to take part in the Act of Penitence, which, after a brief pause for silence, the entire community carries out through a formula of general confession. The rite concludes with the priest's absolution, which, however, lacks the efficacy of the Sacrament of Penance.

On Sundays, especially in the Season of Easter, in place of the customary Act of Penitence, from time to time the blessing and sprinkling of water to recall Baptism may take place.[56]

THE *KYRIE ELEISON*

52. After the Act of Penitence, the *Kyrie* is always begun, unless it has already been included as part of the Act of Penitence. Since it is a chant by which the faithful acclaim the Lord and implore his mercy, it is ordinarily done by all, that is, by the people and with the choir or cantor having a part in it.

As a rule, each acclamation is sung or said twice, though it may be repeated several times, by reason of the character of the various languages, as well as of the artistry of the music or of other circumstances. When the *Kyrie* is sung as a part of the Act of Penitence, a trope may precede each acclamation.

THE *GLORIA*

53. The *Gloria* is a very ancient and venerable hymn in which the Church, gathered together in the Holy Spirit, glorifies and entreats God the Father and the Lamb. The text of this hymn may not be replaced by any other text. The *Gloria* is intoned by the priest or, if appropriate, by a cantor or by the choir; but it is sung either by everyone together, or by the people alternately with the choir, or by the choir alone. If not sung, it is to be recited either by all together or by two parts of the congregation responding one to the other.

It is sung or said on Sundays outside the Seasons of Advent and Lent, on solemnities and feasts, and at special celebrations of a more solemn character.

THE COLLECT

54. Next the priest invites the people to pray. All, together with the priest, observe a brief silence so that they may be conscious of the fact that they are in God's presence and may formulate their petitions mentally. Then the priest says the prayer which is customarily known as the Collect and through which the character of the celebration is expressed. In accordance with the ancient

tradition of the Church, the collect prayer is usually addressed to God the Father, through Christ, in the Holy Spirit,[57] and is concluded with a trinitarian, that is to say the longer ending, in the following manner:

> If the prayer is directed to the Father: *Per Dominum nostrum Iesum Christum Filium tuum, qui tecum vivit et regnat in unitate Spiritus Sancti, Deus, per omnia saecula saeculorum* (*Through our Lord, Jesus Christ, your Son, who lives and reigns with you and the Holy Spirit, one God, forever and ever*);

> If it is directed to the Father, but the Son is mentioned at the end: *Qui tecum vivit et regnat in unitate Spiritus Sancti, Deus, per omnia saecula saeculorum* (*Who lives and reigns with you and the Holy Spirit, one God, forever and ever*);

> If it is directed to the Son: *Qui vivis et regnas cum Deo Patre in unitate Spiritus Sancti, Deus, per omnia saecula saeculorum* (*You live and reign with God the Father in the unity of the Holy Spirit, one God, forever and ever*).

The people, uniting themselves to this entreaty, make the prayer their own with the acclamation, *Amen.*

There is always only one collect used in a Mass.

B. The Liturgy of the Word

55. The main part of the Liturgy of the Word is made up of the readings from Sacred Scripture together with the chants occurring between them. The homily, Profession of Faith, and Prayer of the Faithful, however, develop and conclude this part of the Mass. For in the readings, as explained by the homily, God speaks to his people,[58] opening up to them the mystery of redemption and salvation and offering them spiritual nourishment; and Christ himself is present in the midst of the faithful through his word.[59] By their silence and singing the people make God's word their own, and they also affirm their adherence to it by means of the Profession of Faith. Finally, having been nourished by it, they pour out their petitions in the Prayer of the Faithful for the needs of the entire Church and for the salvation of the whole world.

SILENCE

56. The Liturgy of the Word is to be celebrated in such a way as to promote meditation, and so any sort of haste that hinders recollection must clearly be avoided. During the Liturgy of the Word, it is also appropriate to include brief periods of silence, accommodated to the gathered assembly, in which, at the prompting of the Holy Spirit, the word of God may be grasped by the heart and a response through prayer may be prepared. It may be appropriate to observe such periods of silence, for example, before the Liturgy of the Word itself begins, after the first and second reading, and lastly at the conclusion of the homily.[60]

THE BIBLICAL READINGS

57. In the readings, the table of God's word is prepared for the faithful, and the riches of the Bible are opened to them.[61] Hence, it is preferable to maintain

the arrangement of the biblical readings, by which light is shed on the unity of both Testaments and of salvation history. Moreover, it is unlawful to substitute other, non-biblical texts for the readings and responsorial Psalm, which contain the word of God.[62]

58.   In the celebration of the Mass with a congregation, the readings are always proclaimed from the ambo.

59.   By tradition, the function of proclaiming the readings is ministerial, not presidential. The readings, therefore, should be proclaimed by a lector, and the Gospel by a deacon or, in his absence, a priest other than the celebrant. If, however, a deacon or another priest is not present, the priest celebrant himself should read the Gospel. Further, if another suitable lector is also not present, then the priest celebrant should also proclaim the other readings.

After each reading, whoever reads gives the acclamation, to which the gathered people reply, honoring the word of God that they have received in faith and with grateful hearts.

60.   The reading of the Gospel is the high point of the Liturgy of the Word. The Liturgy itself teaches that great reverence is to be shown to it by setting it off from the other readings with special marks of honor: whether the minister appointed to proclaim it prepares himself by a blessing or prayer; or the faithful, standing as they listen to it being read, through their acclamations acknowledge and confess Christ present and speaking to them; or the very marks of reverence are given to the *Book of the Gospels.*

THE RESPONSORIAL PSALM

61.   After the first reading comes the responsorial Psalm, which is an integral part of the Liturgy of the Word and holds great liturgical and pastoral importance, because it fosters meditation on the word of God.

The responsorial Psalm should correspond to each reading and should, as a rule, be taken from the Lectionary.

It is preferable that the responsorial Psalm be sung, at least as far as the people's response is concerned. Hence, the psalmist, or the cantor of the Psalm, sings the verses of the Psalm from the ambo or another suitable place. The entire congregation remains seated and listens but, as a rule, takes part by singing the response, except when the Psalm is sung straight through without a response. In order, however, that the people may be able to sing the Psalm response more readily, texts of some responses and Psalms have been chosen for the various seasons of the year or for the various categories of Saints. These may be used in place of the text corresponding to the reading whenever the Psalm is sung. If the Psalm cannot be sung, then it should be recited in such a way that it is particularly suited to fostering meditation on the word of God.

In the dioceses of the United States of America, the following may also be sung in place of the Psalm assigned in the *Lectionary for Mass:* either the proper or seasonal antiphon and Psalm from the *Lectionary,* as found either in the

Roman Gradual or *Simple Gradual* or in another musical setting; or an antiphon and Psalm from another collection of the psalms and antiphons, including psalms arranged in metrical form, providing that they have been approved by the United States Conference of Catholic Bishops or the diocesan Bishop. Songs or hymns may not be used in place of the responsorial Psalm.

62.   After the reading that immediately precedes the Gospel, the *Alleluia* or another chant indicated by the rubrics is sung, as required by the liturgical season. An acclamation of this kind constitutes a rite or act in itself, by which the assembly of the faithful welcomes and greets the Lord who is about to speak to them in the Gospel and professes their faith by means of the chant. It is sung by all while standing and is led by the choir or a cantor, being repeated if this is appropriate. The verse, however, is sung either by the choir or by the cantor.

> a. The *Alleluia* is sung in every season other than Lent. The verses are taken from the Lectionary or the *Graduale.*
>
> b. During Lent, in place of the *Alleluia,* the verse before the Gospel is sung, as indicated in the Lectionary. It is also permissible to sing another psalm or tract, as found in the *Graduale.*

63.   When there is only one reading before the Gospel,

> a. During a season when the *Alleluia* is to be said, either the *Alleluia* Psalm or the responsorial Psalm followed by the *Alleluia* with its verse may be used;
>
> b. During the season when the *Alleluia* is not to be said, either the psalm and the verse before the Gospel or the psalm alone may be used;
>
> c. The *Alleluia* or verse before the Gospel may be omitted if they are not sung.

64.   The Sequence, which is optional except on Easter Sunday and on Pentecost Day, is sung before the *Alleluia.*

THE HOMILY

65.   The homily is part of the Liturgy and is strongly recommended,[63] for it is necessary for the nurturing of the Christian life. It should be an exposition of some aspect of the readings from Sacred Scripture or of another text from the Ordinary or from the Proper of the Mass of the day and should take into account both the mystery being celebrated and the particular needs of the listeners.[64]

66.   The homily should ordinarily be given by the priest celebrant himself. He may entrust it to a concelebrating priest or occasionally, according to circumstances, to the deacon, but never to a lay person.[65] In particular cases and for a just cause, the homily may even be given by a Bishop or a priest who is present at the celebration but cannot concelebrate.

There is to be a homily on Sundays and holy days of obligation at all Masses that are celebrated with the participation of a congregation; it may not be omitted without a serious reason. It is recommended on other days, especially on the weekdays of Advent, Lent, and the Easter Season, as well as on other festive days and occasions when the people come to church in greater numbers.[66]

After the homily a brief period of silence is appropriately observed.

THE PROFESSION OF FAITH

67.   The purpose of the *Symbolum* or Profession of Faith, or Creed, is that the whole gathered people may respond to the word of God proclaimed in the readings taken from Sacred Scripture and explained in the homily and that they may also call to mind and confess the great mysteries of the faith by reciting the rule of faith in a formula approved for liturgical use, before these mysteries are celebrated in the Eucharist.

68.   The Creed is to be sung or said by the priest together with the people on Sundays and Solemnities. It may be said also at particular celebrations of a more solemn character.

If it is sung, it is begun by the priest or, if this is appropriate, by a cantor or by the choir. It is sung, however, either by all together or by the people alternating with the choir.

If not sung, it is to be recited by all together or by two parts of the assembly responding one to the other.

THE PRAYER OF THE FAITHFUL

69.   In the Prayer of the Faithful, the people respond in a certain way to the word of God which they have welcomed in faith and, exercising the office of their baptismal priesthood, offer prayers to God for the salvation of all. It is fitting that such a prayer be included, as a rule, in Masses celebrated with a congregation, so that petitions will be offered for the holy Church, for civil authorities, for those weighed down by various needs, for all men and women, and for the salvation of the whole world.[67]

70.   As a rule, the series of intentions is to be

    a. For the needs of the Church;

    b. For public authorities and the salvation of the whole world;

    c. For those burdened by any kind of difficulty;

    d. For the local community.

Nevertheless, in a particular celebration, such as Confirmation, Marriage, or a Funeral, the series of intentions may reflect more closely the particular occasion.

71.   It is for the priest celebrant to direct this prayer from the chair. He himself begins it with a brief introduction, by which he invites the faithful to pray, and likewise he concludes it with a prayer. The intentions announced should be

sober, be composed freely but prudently, and be succinct, and they should express the prayer of the entire community.

The intentions are announced from the ambo or from another suitable place, by the deacon or by a cantor, a lector, or one of the lay faithful.[68]

The people, however, stand and give expression to their prayer either by an invocation said together after each intention or by praying in silence.

C. The Liturgy of the Eucharist

72.   At the Last Supper Christ instituted the Paschal Sacrifice and banquet by which the Sacrifice of the Cross is continuously made present in the Church whenever the priest, representing Christ the Lord, carries out what the Lord himself did and handed over to his disciples to be done in his memory.[69]

For Christ took the bread and the chalice and gave thanks; he broke the bread and gave it to his disciples, saying, "Take, eat, and drink: this is my Body; this is the cup of my Blood. Do this in memory of me." Accordingly, the Church has arranged the entire celebration of the Liturgy of the Eucharist in parts corresponding to precisely these words and actions of Christ:

1. At the Preparation of the Gifts, the bread and the wine with water are brought to the altar, the same elements that Christ took into his hands.

2. In the Eucharistic Prayer, thanks is given to God for the whole work of salvation, and the offerings become the Body and Blood of Christ.

3. Through the fraction and through Communion, the faithful, though they are many, receive from the one bread the Lord's Body and from the one chalice the Lord's Blood in the same way the Apostles received them from Christ's own hands.

THE PREPARATION OF THE GIFTS

73.   At the beginning of the Liturgy of the Eucharist the gifts, which will become Christ's Body and Blood, are brought to the altar.

First, the altar, the Lord's table, which is the center of the whole Liturgy of the Eucharist,[70] is prepared by placing on it the corporal, purificator, Missal, and chalice (unless the chalice is prepared at the credence table).

The offerings are then brought forward. It is praiseworthy for the bread and wine to be presented by the faithful. They are then accepted at an appropriate place by the priest or the deacon and carried to the altar. Even though the faithful no longer bring from their own possessions the bread and wine intended for the liturgy as in the past, nevertheless the rite of carrying up the offerings still retains its force and its spiritual significance.

It is well also that money or other gifts for the poor or for the Church, brought by the faithful or collected in the church, should be received. These are to be put in a suitable place but away from the eucharistic table.

74. The procession bringing the gifts is accompanied by the Offertory chant (cf. above, no. 37b), which continues at least until the gifts have been placed on the altar. The norms on the manner of singing are the same as for the Entrance chant (cf. above, no. 48). Singing may always accompany the rite at the offertory, even when there is no procession with the gifts.

75. The bread and wine are placed on the altar by the priest to the accompaniment of the prescribed formulas. The priest may incense the gifts placed upon the altar and then incense the cross and the altar itself, so as to signify the Church's offering and prayer rising like incense in the sight of God. Next, the priest, because of his sacred ministry, and the people, by reason of their baptismal dignity, may be incensed by the deacon or another minister.

76. The priest then washes his hands at the side of the altar, a rite that is an expression of his desire for interior purification.

THE PRAYER OVER THE OFFERINGS

77. Once the offerings have been placed on the altar and the accompanying rites completed, the invitation to pray with the priest and the prayer over the offerings conclude the preparation of the gifts and prepare for the Eucharistic Prayer.

In the Mass, only one Prayer over the Offerings is said, and it ends with the shorter conclusion: *Per Christum Dominum nostrum (Through Christ our Lord).* If, however, the Son is mentioned at the end of this prayer, the conclusion is, *Qui vivit et regnat in saecula saeculorum (Who lives and reigns forever and ever).*

The people, uniting themselves to this entreaty, make the prayer their own with the acclamation, *Amen.*

THE EUCHARISTIC PRAYER

78. Now the center and summit of the entire celebration begins: namely, the Eucharistic Prayer, that is, the prayer of thanksgiving and sanctification. The priest invites the people to lift up their hearts to the Lord in prayer and thanksgiving; he unites the congregation with himself in the prayer that he addresses in the name of the entire community to God the Father through Jesus Christ in the Holy Spirit. Furthermore, the meaning of the Prayer is that the entire congregation of the faithful should join itself with Christ in confessing the great deeds of God and in the offering of Sacrifice. The Eucharistic Prayer demands that all listen to it with reverence and in silence.

79. The chief elements making up the Eucharistic Prayer may be distinguished in this way:

   a. *Thanksgiving* (expressed especially in the Preface): In which the priest, in the name of the entire holy people, glorifies God the Father and gives thanks for the whole work of salvation or for some special aspect of it that corresponds to the day, festivity, or season.

b. *Acclamation:* In which the whole congregation, joining with the heavenly powers, sings the *Sanctus.* This acclamation, which is part of the Eucharistic Prayer itself, is sung or said by all the people with the priest.

c. *Epiclesis:* In which, by means of particular invocations, the Church implores the power of the Holy Spirit that the gifts offered by human hands be consecrated, that is, become Christ's Body and Blood, and that the spotless Victim to be received in Communion be for the salvation of those who will partake of it.

d. *Institution narrative and consecration:* In which, by means of words and actions of Christ, the Sacrifice is carried out which Christ himself instituted at the Last Supper, when he offered his Body and Blood under the species of bread and wine, gave them to his Apostles to eat and drink, and left them the command to perpetuate this same mystery.

e. *Anamnesis:* In which the Church, fulfilling the command that she received from Christ the Lord through the Apostles, keeps the memorial of Christ, recalling especially his blessed Passion, glorious Resurrection, and Ascension into heaven.

f. *Offering:* By which, in this very memorial, the Church—and in particular the Church here and now gathered—offers in the Holy Spirit the spotless Victim to the Father. The Church's intention, however, is that the faithful not only offer this spotless Victim but also learn to offer themselves,[71] and so day by day to be consummated, through Christ the Mediator, into unity with God and with each other, so that at last God may be all in all.[72]

g. *Intercessions:* By which expression is given to the fact that the Eucharist is celebrated in communion with the entire Church, of heaven as well as of earth, and that the offering is made for her and for all her members, living and dead, who have been called to participate in the redemption and the salvation purchased by Christ's Body and Blood.

h. *Final doxology:* By which the glorification of God is expressed and is confirmed and concluded by the people's acclamation, *Amen.*

THE COMMUNION RITE

80.   Since the Eucharistic Celebration is the Paschal Banquet, it is desirable that in keeping with the Lord's command, his Body and Blood should be received by the faithful who are properly disposed as spiritual food. This is the sense of the fraction and the other preparatory rites by which the faithful are led directly to Communion.

THE LORD'S PRAYER

81.   In the Lord's Prayer a petition is made for daily food, which for Christians means preeminently the Eucharistic bread, and also for purification from sin, so that what is holy may, in fact, be given to those who are holy. The priest says the invitation to the prayer, and all the faithful say it with him; the priest alone

adds the embolism, which the people conclude with a doxology. The embolism, enlarging upon the last petition of the Lord's Prayer itself, begs deliverance from the power of evil for the entire community of the faithful.

The invitation, the Prayer itself, the embolism, and the doxology by which the people conclude these things are sung or said aloud.

THE RITE OF PEACE

82. The Rite of Peace follows, by which the Church asks for peace and unity for herself and for the whole human family, and the faithful express to each other their ecclesial communion and mutual charity before communicating in the Sacrament.

As for the sign of peace to be given, the manner is to be established by Conferences of Bishops in accordance with the culture and customs of the peoples. It is, however, appropriate that each person offer the sign of peace only to those who are nearest and in a sober manner.

THE FRACTION

83. The priest breaks the Eucharistic Bread, assisted, if the case calls for it, by the deacon or a concelebrant. Christ's gesture of breaking bread at the Last Supper, which gave the entire Eucharistic Action its name in apostolic times, signifies that the many faithful are made one body (1 Cor 10:17) by receiving Communion from the one Bread of Life which is Christ, who died and rose for the salvation of the world. The fraction or breaking of bread is begun after the sign of peace and is carried out with proper reverence, though it should not be unnecessarily prolonged, nor should it be accorded undue importance. This rite is reserved to the priest and the deacon.

The priest breaks the Bread and puts a piece of the host into the chalice to signify the unity of the Body and Blood of the Lord in the work of salvation, namely, of the living and glorious Body of Jesus Christ. The supplication *Agnus Dei*, is, as a rule, sung by the choir or cantor with the congregation responding; or it is, at least, recited aloud. This invocation accompanies the fraction and, for this reason, may be repeated as many times as necessary until the rite has reached its conclusion, the last time ending with the words *dona nobis pacem* (*grant us peace*).

COMMUNION

84. The priest prepares himself by a prayer, said quietly, that he may fruitfully receive Christ's Body and Blood. The faithful do the same, praying silently.

The priest next shows the faithful the Eucharistic Bread, holding it above the paten or above the chalice, and invites them to the banquet of Christ. Along with the faithful, he then makes an act of humility using the prescribed words taken from the Gospels.

85. It is most desirable that the faithful, just as the priest himself is bound to do, receive the Lord's Body from hosts consecrated at the same Mass and that,

in the instances when it is permitted, they partake of the chalice (cf. below, no. 283), so that even by means of the signs Communion will stand out more clearly as a participation in the sacrifice actually being celebrated.[73]

86. While the priest is receiving the Sacrament, the Communion chant is begun. Its purpose is to express the communicants' union in spirit by means of the unity of their voices, to show joy of heart, and to highlight more clearly the "communitarian" nature of the procession to receive Communion. The singing is continued for as long as the Sacrament is being administered to the faithful.[74] If, however, there is to be a hymn after Communion, the Communion chant should be ended in a timely manner.

Care should be taken that singers, too, can receive Communion with ease.

87. In the dioceses of the United States of America there are four options for the Communion chant: (1) the antiphon from the *Roman Missal* or the Psalm from the *Roman Gradual* as set to music there or in another musical setting; (2) the seasonal antiphon and Psalm of the *Simple Gradual*; (3) a song from another collection of psalms and antiphons, approved by the United States Conference of Catholic Bishops or the Diocesan Bishop, including psalms arranged in responsorial or metrical forms; (4) a suitable liturgical song chosen in accordance with no. 86 above. This is sung either by the choir alone or by the choir or cantor with the people.

If there is no singing, however, the Communion antiphon found in the Missal may be recited either by the faithful, or by some of them, or by a lector. Otherwise the priest himself says it after he has received Communion and before he distributes Communion to the faithful.

88. When the distribution of Communion is finished, as circumstances suggest, the priest and faithful spend some time praying privately. If desired, a psalm or other canticle of praise or a hymn may also be sung by the entire congregation.

89. To bring to completion the prayer of the People of God, and also to conclude the entire Communion Rite, the priest says the Prayer after Communion, in which he prays for the fruits of the mystery just celebrated.

In the Mass only one prayer after Communion is said, which ends with a shorter conclusion; that is,

—If the prayer is directed to the Father: *Per Christum Dominum nostrum* (*Through Christ our Lord*);

—If it is directed to the Father, but the Son is mentioned at the end: *Qui vivit et regnat in saecula saeculorum* (*Who lives and reigns forever and ever*);

—If it is directed to the Son: *Qui vivis et regnas in saecula saeculorum* (*You live and reign forever and ever*).

The people make the prayer their own by the acclamation, *Amen.*

90. The concluding rites consist of

    a. Brief announcements, if they are necessary;

    b. The priest's greeting and blessing, which on certain days and occasions is enriched and expressed in the prayer over the People or another more solemn formula;

    c. The dismissal of the people by the deacon or the priest, so that each may go out to do good works, praising and blessing God;

    d. The kissing of the altar by the priest and the deacon, followed by a profound bow to the altar by the priest, the deacon, and the other ministers.

CHAPTER III
THE DUTIES AND MINISTRIES IN THE MASS

91. The Eucharistic celebration is an action of Christ and the Church, namely, the holy people united and ordered under the Bishop. It therefore pertains to the whole Body of the Church, manifests it, and has its effect upon it. It also affects the individual members of the Church in different ways, according to their different orders, offices, and actual participation.[75] In this way, the Christian people, "a chosen race, a royal priesthood, a holy nation, God's own people," expresses its cohesion and its hierarchical ordering.[76] All, therefore, whether they are ordained ministers or lay Christian faithful, in fulfilling their office or their duty should carry out solely but completely that which pertains to them.[77]

I. THE DUTIES OF THOSE IN HOLY ORDERS

92. Every legitimate celebration of the Eucharist is directed by the Bishop, either in person or through priests who are his helpers.[78]

Whenever the Bishop is present at a Mass where the people are gathered, it is most fitting that he himself celebrate the Eucharist and associate priests with himself as concelebrants in the sacred action. This is done not to add external solemnity to the rite but to express in a clearer light the mystery of the Church, "the sacrament of unity."[79]

Even if the Bishop does not celebrate the Eucharist but has assigned someone else to do this, it is appropriate that he should preside over the Liturgy of the Word, wearing the pectoral cross, stole, and cope over an alb, and that he give the blessing at the end of Mass.[80]

93. A priest also, who possesses within the Church the power of Holy Orders to offer sacrifice in the person of Christ,[81] stands for this reason at the head of the faithful people gathered together here and now, presides over their prayer, proclaims the message of salvation to them, associates the people with himself in the offering of sacrifice through Christ in the Holy Spirit to God the Father, gives his brothers and sisters the Bread of eternal life, and partakes of it with

them. When he celebrates the Eucharist, therefore, he must serve God and the people with dignity and humility, and by his bearing and by the way he says the divine words he must convey to the faithful the living presence of Christ.

94. After the priest, the deacon, in virtue of the sacred ordination he has received, holds first place among those who minister in the Eucharistic Celebration. For the sacred Order of the diaconate has been held in high honor in the Church even from the time of the Apostles.[82] At Mass the deacon has his own part in proclaiming the Gospel, in preaching God's word from time to time, in announcing the intentions of the Prayer of the Faithful, in ministering to the priest, in preparing the altar and serving the celebration of the Sacrifice, in distributing the Eucharist to the faithful, especially under the species of wine, and sometimes in giving directions regarding the people's gestures and posture.

II. THE DUTIES OF THE PEOPLE OF GOD

95. In the celebration of Mass the faithful form a holy people, a people whom God has made his own, a royal priesthood, so that they may give thanks to God and offer the spotless Victim not only through the hands of the priest but also together with him, and so that they may learn to offer themselves.[83] They should, moreover, endeavor to make this clear by their deep religious sense and their charity toward brothers and sisters who participate with them in the same celebration.

Thus, they are to shun any appearance of individualism or division, keeping before their eyes that they have only one Father in heaven and accordingly are all brothers and sisters to each other.

96. Indeed, they form one body, whether by hearing the word of God, or by joining in the prayers and the singing, or above all by the common offering of Sacrifice and by a common partaking at the Lord's table. This unity is beautifully apparent from the gestures and postures observed in common by the faithful.

97. The faithful, moreover, should not refuse to serve the People of God gladly whenever they are asked to perform some particular ministry or function in the celebration.

III. PARTICULAR MINISTRIES

THE MINISTRY OF THE INSTITUTED ACOLYTE AND LECTOR

98. The acolyte is instituted to serve at the altar and to assist the priest and deacon. In particular, it is his responsibility to prepare the altar and the sacred vessels and, if it is necessary, as an extraordinary minister, to distribute the Eucharist to the faithful.[84]

In the ministry of the altar, the acolyte has his own functions (cf. below, nos. 187–193), which he must perform personally.

99. The lector is instituted to proclaim the readings from Sacred Scripture, with the exception of the Gospel. He may also announce the intentions for the

Prayer of the Faithful and, in the absence of a psalmist, proclaim the Psalm between the readings.

In the Eucharistic Celebration, the lector has his own proper office (cf. below, nos. 194–198), which he must exercise personally.

OTHER MINISTRIES

100. In the absence of an instituted acolyte, lay ministers may be deputed to serve at the altar and assist the priest and the deacon; they may carry the cross, the candles, the thurible, the bread, the wine, and the water, and they may also be deputed to distribute Holy Communion as extraordinary ministers.[85]

101. In the absence of an instituted lector, other laypersons may be commissioned to proclaim the readings from Sacred Scripture. They should be truly suited to perform this function and should receive careful preparation, so that the faithful by listening to the readings from the sacred texts may develop in their hearts a warm and living love for Sacred Scripture.[86]

102. The psalmist's role is to sing the Psalm or other biblical canticle that comes between the readings. To fulfill this function correctly, it is necessary that the psalmist have the ability for singing and a facility in correct pronunciation and diction.

103. Among the faithful, the *schola cantorum* or choir exercises its own liturgical function, ensuring that the parts proper to it, in keeping with the different types of chants, are properly carried out and fostering the active participation of the faithful through the singing.[87] What is said about the choir also applies, in accordance with the relevant norms, to other musicians, especially the organist.

104. It is fitting that there be a cantor or a choir director to lead and sustain the people's singing. When in fact there is no choir, it is up to the cantor to lead the different chants, with the people taking part.[88]

105. The following also exercise a liturgical function:

    a. The sacristan, who carefully arranges the liturgical books, the vestments, and other things necessary in the celebration of Mass.

    b. The commentator, who provides the faithful, when appropriate, with brief explanations and commentaries with the purpose of introducing them to the celebration and preparing them to understand it better. The commentator's remarks must be meticulously prepared and clear though brief. In performing this function the commentator stands in an appropriate place facing the faithful, but not at the ambo.

    c. Those who take up the collection in the church.

    d. Those who, in some places, meet the faithful at the church entrance, lead them to appropriate places, and direct processions.

106. It is appropriate, at least in cathedrals and in larger churches, to have some competent minister, that is to say a master of ceremonies, to oversee the proper planning of sacred actions and their being carried out by the sacred ministers and the lay faithful with decorum, order, and devotion.

107. The liturgical duties that are not proper to the priest or the deacon and are listed above (cf. nos. 100–106) may also be entrusted by a liturgical blessing or a temporary deputation to suitable lay persons chosen by the pastor or rector of the church.[89] All should observe the norms established by the Bishop for his diocese regarding the office of those who serve the priest at the altar.

IV. THE DISTRIBUTION OF DUTIES AND THE PREPARATION OF THE CELEBRATION

108. One and the same priest celebrant must always exercise the presidential office in all of its parts, except for those parts which are proper to a Mass at which the Bishop is present (cf. above, no. 92).

109. If there are several persons present who are able to exercise the same ministry, nothing forbids their distributing among themselves and performing different parts of the same ministry or duty. For example, one deacon may be assigned to take the sung parts, another to serve at the altar; if there are several readings, it is well to distribute them among a number of lectors. The same applies for the other ministries. But it is not at all appropriate that several persons divide a single element of the celebration among themselves, e.g., that the same reading be proclaimed by two lectors, one after the other, except as far as the Passion of the Lord is concerned.

110. If only one minister is present at a Mass with a congregation, that minister may exercise several different duties.

111. Among all who are involved with regard to the rites, pastoral aspects, and music there should be harmony and diligence in the effective preparation of each liturgical celebration in accord with the Missal and other liturgical books. This should take place under the direction of the rector of the church and after the consultation with the faithful about things that directly pertain to them. The priest who presides at the celebration, however, always retains the right of arranging those things that are his own responsibility.[90]

CHAPTER IV
THE DIFFERENT FORMS OF CELEBRATING MASS

112. In the local Church, first place should certainly be given, because of its significance, to the Mass at which the Bishop presides, surrounded by his presbyterate, deacons, and lay ministers,[91] and in which the holy people of God participate fully and actively, for it is there that the preeminent expression of the Church is found.

At a Mass celebrated by the Bishop or at which he presides without celebrating the Eucharist, the norms found in the *Caeremoniale Episcoporum* should be observed.[92]

113. Great importance should also be attached to a Mass celebrated with any community, but especially with the parish community, inasmuch as it represents the universal Church gathered at a given time and place. This is particularly true in the communal Sunday celebration.[93]

114. Among those Masses celebrated by some communities, moreover, the conventual Mass, which is a part of the daily Office, or the community Mass has a particular place. Although such Masses do not have a special form of celebration, it is nevertheless most proper that they be celebrated with singing, especially with the full participation of all members of the community, whether of religious or of canons. In these Masses, therefore, individuals should exercise the office proper to the Order or ministry they have received. It is appropriate, therefore, that all the priests who are not bound to celebrate individually for the pastoral benefit of the faithful concelebrate at the conventual or community Mass in so far as it is possible. In addition, all priests belonging to the community who are obliged, as a matter of duty, to celebrate individually for the pastoral benefit of the faithful may also on the same day concelebrate at the conventual or community Mass.[94] For it is preferable that priests who are present at a Eucharistic Celebration, unless excused for a good reason, should as a rule exercise the office proper to their Order and hence take part as concelebrants, wearing the sacred vestments. Otherwise, they wear their proper choir dress or a surplice over a cassock.

I. MASS WITH A CONGREGATION

115. By "Mass with a congregation" is meant a Mass celebrated with the participation of the faithful. It is moreover appropriate, whenever possible and especially on Sundays and holy days of obligation, that the celebration of this Mass take place with singing and with a suitable number of ministers.[95] It may, however, also be celebrated without singing and with only one minister.

116. If a deacon is present at any celebration of Mass, he should exercise his office. Furthermore, it is desirable that, as a rule, an acolyte, a lector, and a cantor should be there to assist the priest celebrant. In fact, the rite to be described below foresees a greater number of ministers.

THE ARTICLES TO BE PREPARED

117. The altar is to be covered with at least one white cloth. In addition, on or next to the altar are to be placed candlesticks with lighted candles: at least two in any celebration, or even four or six, especially for a Sunday Mass or a holy day of obligation. If the diocesan Bishop celebrates, then seven candles should be used. Also on or close to the altar, there is to be a cross with a figure of Christ crucified. The candles and the cross adorned with a figure of Christ crucified may also be carried in the Entrance Procession. On the altar itself may be placed

the *Book of the Gospels,* distinct from the book of other readings, unless it is carried in the Entrance Procession.

118. The following are also to be prepared:

a. Next to the priest's chair: the Missal and, as needed, a hymnal;

b. At the ambo: the Lectionary;

c. On the credence table: the chalice, a corporal, a purificator, and, if appropriate, the pall; the paten and, if needed, ciboria; bread for the Communion of the priest who presides, the deacon, the ministers, and the people; cruets containing the wine and the water, unless all of these are presented by the faithful in procession at the Offertory; the vessel of water to be blessed, if the *asperges* occurs; the Communion-plate for the Communion of the faithful; and whatever is needed for the washing of hands.

It is a praiseworthy practice to cover the chalice with a veil, which may be either the color of the day or white.

119. In the sacristy, the sacred vestments (cf. below, nos. 337–341) for the priest, the deacon, and other ministers are to be prepared according to the various forms of celebration:

a. For the priest: the alb, the stole, and the chasuble;

b. For the deacon: the alb, the stole, and the dalmatic; the dalmatic may be omitted, however, either out of necessity or on account of a lesser degree of solemnity;

c. For the other ministers: albs or other lawfully approved attire.[96]

All who wear an alb should use a cincture and an amice unless, due to the form of the alb, they are not needed.

When there is an Entrance Procession, the following are also to be prepared: the *Book of the Gospels;* on Sundays and festive days, the thurible and the boat with incense, if incense is used; the cross to be carried in procession; and candlesticks with lighted candles.

A. Mass Without a Deacon

THE INTRODUCTORY RITES

120. Once the people have gathered, the priest and ministers, clad in the sacred vestments, go in procession to the altar in this order:

a. The thurifer carrying a thurible with burning incense, if incense is used;

b. The ministers who carry lighted candles, and between them an acolyte or other minister with the cross;

c. The acolytes and the other ministers;

d. A lector, who may carry the *Book of the Gospels* (though not the Lectionary), which should be slightly elevated;

e. The priest who is to celebrate the Mass.

If incense is used, before the procession begins, the priest puts some in the thurible and blesses it with the Sign of the Cross without saying anything.

121. During the procession to the altar, the Entrance chant takes place (cf. above, nos. 47–48).

122. On reaching the altar, the priest and ministers make a profound bow.

The cross adorned with a figure of Christ crucified and perhaps carried in procession may be placed next to the altar to serve as the altar cross, in which case it ought to be the only cross used; otherwise it is put away in a dignified place. In addition, the candlesticks are placed on the altar or near it. It is a praiseworthy practice that the *Book of the Gospels* be placed upon the altar.

123. The priest goes up to the altar and venerates it with a kiss. Then, as the occasion suggests, he incenses the cross and the altar, walking around the latter.

124. After doing these things, the priest goes to the chair. Once the Entrance chant is concluded, the priest and faithful, all standing, make the Sign of the Cross. The priest says, *In nomine Patris et Filii et Spiritus Sancti (In the name of the Father, and of the Son, and of the Holy Spirit)*. The people answer, *Amen.*

Then, facing the people and extending his hands, the priest greets the people, using one of the formulas indicated. The priest himself or some other minister may also very briefly introduce the faithful to the Mass of the day.

125. The Act of Penitence follows. Afterwards, the *Kyrie* is sung or said, in keeping with the rubrics (cf. above, no. 52).

126. For celebrations where it is prescribed, the *Gloria* is either sung or said (cf. above, no. 53).

127. The priest then invites the people to pray, saying, with hands joined, *Oremus (Let us pray)*. All pray silently with the priest for a brief time. Then the priest, with hands extended, says the Collect, at the end of which the people make the acclamation, *Amen.*

THE LITURGY OF THE WORD

128. After the Collect, all sit. The priest may, very briefly, introduce the faithful to the Liturgy of the Word. Then the lector goes to the ambo and, from the Lectionary already placed there before Mass, proclaims the first reading, to which all listen. At the end, the lector says the acclamation *Verbum Domini (The word of the Lord)*, and all respond, *Deo gratias (Thanks be to God)*.

Then, as appropriate, a few moments of silence may be observed so that all may meditate on what they have heard.

129. Then the psalmist or even a lector proclaims the verses of the Psalm and the people sing or say the response as usual.

130. If there is to be a second reading before the Gospel, the lector proclaims it from the ambo. All listen and at the end respond to the acclamation, as noted above (cf. no. 128). Then, as appropriate, a few moments of silence may be observed.

131. Afterwards, all rise, and the *Alleluia* or other chant is sung as required by the liturgical season (cf. above, nos. 62–64).

132. During the singing of the *Alleluia* or other chant, if incense is used, the priest puts some into the thurible and blesses it. Then, with hands joined, he bows profoundly before the altar and quietly says, *Munda cor meum* (*Almighty God, cleanse my heart*).

133. If the *Book of the Gospels* is on the altar, the priest then takes it and goes to the ambo, carrying the *Book of the Gospels* slightly elevated and preceded by the lay ministers, who may carry the thurible and the candles. Those present turn towards the ambo as a sign of special reverence to the Gospel of Christ.

134. At the ambo, the priest opens the book and, with hands joined, says, *Dominus vobiscum* (*The Lord be with you*), and the people respond, *Et cum spiritu tuo* (*And also with you*). Then he says, *Lectio sancti Evangelii* (*A reading from the holy Gospel*), making the sign of the cross with his thumb on the book and on his forehead, mouth, and breast, which everyone else does as well. The people say the acclamation *Gloria tibi, Domine* (*Glory to you, Lord*). The priest incenses the book, if incense is used (cf. below, nos. 276–277). Then he proclaims the Gospel and at the end says the acclamation *Verbum Domini* (*The Gospel of the Lord*), to which all respond, *Laus tibi, Christe* (*Praise to you, Lord Jesus Christ*). The priest kisses the book, saying quietly, *Per evangelica dicta* (*May the words of the gospel*).

135. If no lector is present, the priest himself proclaims all the readings and the Psalm, standing at the ambo. If incense is used, remaining at the ambo he puts some into the thurible, blesses it, and, bowing profoundly, says, *Munda cor meum* (*Almighty God, cleanse my heart*).

136. The priest, standing at the chair or at the ambo itself or, when appropriate, in another suitable place, gives the homily. When the homily is completed, a period of silence may be observed.

137. The Creed is sung or recited by the priest together with the people (cf. above, no. 68) with everyone standing. At the words *et incarnatus est* (*by the power of the Holy Spirit . . . became man*) all make a profound bow; but on the solemnities of the Annunciation and of the Nativity of the Lord, all genuflect.

138. After the recitation of the Creed, the priest, standing at the chair with hands joined, by means of a brief introduction invites the faithful to participate in the Prayer of the Faithful. Then the cantor, the lector, or another person announces

the intentions from the ambo or from some other suitable place while facing the people, who take their part by responding in supplication. After the intentions, the priest, with hands extended, concludes the petitions with a prayer.

139. When the Prayer of the Faithful is completed, all sit, and the Offertory chant begins (cf. above, no. 74).

An acolyte or other lay minister arranges the corporal, the purificator, the chalice, the pall, and the Missal upon the altar.

140. It is appropriate for the faithful's participation to be expressed by an offering, whether of the bread and wine for the celebration of the Eucharist or of other gifts for the relief of the needs of the Church and of the poor.

The offerings of the faithful are received by the priest, assisted by the acolyte or other minister. The bread and wine for the Eucharist are carried to the celebrant, who places them upon the altar, while other gifts are put in another appropriate place (cf. above, no. 73).

141. At the altar the priest accepts the paten with the bread. With both hands he holds it slightly raised above the altar and says quietly, *Benedictus es, Domine* (*Blessed are you, Lord*). Then he places the paten with the bread on the corporal.

142. After this, as the minister presents the cruets, the priest stands at the side of the altar and pours wine and a little water into the chalice, saying quietly, *Per huius aquae* (*By the mystery of this water*). He returns to the middle of the altar, takes the chalice with both hands, raises it a little, and says quietly, *Benedictus es, Domine* (*Blessed are you, Lord*). Then he places the chalice on the corporal and covers it with a pall, as appropriate.

If, however, there is no Offertory chant and the organ is not played, in the presentation of the bread and wine the priest may say the formulas of blessing aloud, to which the people make the acclamation, *Benedictus Deus in saecula* (*Blessed be God for ever*).

143. After placing the chalice upon the altar, the priest bows profoundly and says quietly, *In spiritu humilitatis* (*Lord God, we ask you to receive us*).

144. If incense is used, the priest then puts some in the thurible, blesses it without saying anything, and incenses the offerings, the cross, and the altar. A minister, while standing at the side of the altar, incenses the priest and then the people.

145. After the prayer *In spiritu humilitatis* (*Lord God, we ask you to receive us*) or after the incensation, the priest washes his hands standing at the side of the altar and, as the minister pours the water, says quietly, *Lava me, Domine* (*Lord, wash away my iniquity*).

146. Upon returning to the middle of the altar, the priest, facing the people and extending and then joining his hands, invites the people to pray, saying, *Orate,*

fraters (*Pray, brethren*). The people rise and make their response: *Suscipiat Dominus* (*May the Lord accept*). Then the priest, with hands extended, says the prayer over the offerings. At the end the people make the acclamation, *Amen*.

147. Then the priest begins the Eucharistic Prayer. In accordance with the rubrics (cf. below, no. 365), he selects a Eucharistic Prayer from those found in the *Roman Missal* or approved by the Apostolic See. The Eucharistic Prayer demands, by its very nature, that the priest say it in virtue of his ordination. The people, for their part, should associate themselves with the priest in faith and in silence, as well as through their parts as prescribed in the course of the Eucharistic Prayer: namely the responses in the Preface dialogue, the *Sanctus*, the acclamation after the consecration, the acclamatory *Amen* after the final doxology, as well as other acclamations approved by the Conference of Bishops and recognized by the Holy See.

It is very appropriate that the priest sing those parts of the Eucharistic Prayer for which musical notation is provided.

148. As he begins the Eucharistic Prayer, the priest extends his hands and sings or says, *Dominus vobiscum* (*The Lord be with you*). The people respond, *Et cum spiritu tuo* (*And also with you*). As he continues, *Sursum corda* (*Lift up your hearts*), he raises his hands. The people respond, *Habemus ad Dominum* (*We lift them up to the Lord*). Then the priest, with hands outstretched, adds, *Gratias agamus Domino Deo nostro* (*Let us give thanks to the Lord, our God*), and the people respond, *Dignum et iustum est* (*It is right to give him thanks and praise*). Next, the priest, with hands extended, continues the Preface. At its conclusion, he joins his hands, and together with everyone present, sings or says aloud the *Sanctus* (cf. above, no. 79b).

149. The priest continues the Eucharistic Prayer in accordance with the rubrics that are set forth in each of the Prayers.

If the celebrant is a Bishop, in the Prayers, after the words *Papa nostro N.* (*N., our Pope*), he adds, *et me, indigno famulo tuo* (*and me, your unworthy servant*). If, however, the Bishop is celebrating outside his own diocese, after the words *Papa nostro N.* (*N., our Pope*), he adds, *et me indigno famulo tuo, et fratre meo N., Episcopo huius Ecclesiae N.* (*me, your unworthy servant, and my brother N., the Bishop of this Church of N.*).

The diocesan Bishop or anyone equivalent to him in law must be mentioned by means of this formula: *una cum famulo tuo Papa nostro N. et Episcopo* (or *Vicario, Prelato, Praefecto, Abbate*) (*together with your servant N., our Pope, and N., our Bishop* [or *Vicar, Prelate, Prefect, Abbot*]).

It is permitted to mention Coadjutor and Auxiliary Bishops in the Eucharistic Prayer, but not other Bishops who happen to be present. When several are to be named, this is done with the collective formula *et Episcopo nostro N. eiusque Episcopis adiutoribus* (*N., our Bishop and his assistant Bishops*).

In each of the Eucharistic Prayers, these formulas are to be modified according to the requirements of grammar.

150. A little before the consecration, when appropriate, a server rings a bell as a signal to the faithful. According to local custom, the server also rings the bell as the priest shows the host and then the chalice.

If incense is used, a server incenses the host and the chalice when each is shown to the people after the consecration.

151. After the consecration when the priest has said, *Mysterium fidei* (*Let us proclaim the mystery of faith*), the people sing or say an acclamation using one of the prescribed formulas.

At the end of the Eucharistic Prayer, the priest takes the paten with the host and the chalice and elevates them both while alone singing or saying the doxology, *Per ipsum* (*Through him*). At the end the people make the acclamation, *Amen.* Then the priest places the paten and the chalice on the corporal.

152. After the Eucharistic Prayer is concluded, the priest, with hands joined, says the introduction to the Lord's Prayer. With hands extended, he then says this prayer together with the people.

153. After the Lord's Prayer is concluded, the priest alone, with hands extended, says the *embolism Libera nos* (*Deliver us*). At the end, the people make the acclamation *Quia tuum est regnum* (*For yours is the kingdom*).

154. Then the priest, with hands extended, says aloud the prayer, *Domine Iesu Christe, qui dixisti* (*Lord Jesus Christ, you said*). After this prayer is concluded, extending and then joining his hands, he gives the greeting of peace while facing the people and saying, *Pax Domini sit simper vobiscum* (*The peace of the Lord be with you always*). The people answer, *Et cum spiritu tuo* (*And also with you*). Afterwards, when appropriate, the priest adds, *Offerte vobis pacem* (*Let us offer each other the sign of peace*).

The priest may give the sign of peace to the ministers but always remains within the sanctuary, so as not to disturb the celebration. In the dioceses of the United States of America, for a good reason, on special occasions (for example, in the case of a funeral, a wedding, or when civic leaders are present) the priest may offer the sign of peace to a few of the faithful near the sanctuary. At the same time, in accord with the decisions of the Conference of Bishops, all offer one another a sign that expresses peace, communion, and charity. While the sign of peace is being given, one may say, *Pax Domini sit semper tecum* (*The peace of the Lord be with you always*), to which the response is *Amen.*

155. The priest then takes the host and breaks it over the paten. He places a small piece in the chalice, saying quietly, *Haec commixtio* (*May the mingling*). Meanwhile the *Agnus Dei* is sung or said by the choir and congregation (cf. above, no. 83).

156. Then the priest, with hands joined, quietly says the preparatory prayer of Communion: *Domine Iesu Christe, Fili Dei vivi* (*Lord Jesus Christ, Son of the*

living God) or *Perceptio Corporis et Sanguinis* (*Lord Jesus Christ, with faith in your love and mercy*).

157. When the prayer is concluded, the priest genuflects, takes the host consecrated in the same Mass, and, holding it slightly raised above the paten or above the chalice, while facing the people, says, *Ecce Agnus Dei* (*This is the Lamb of God*). With the people he adds, *Domine, non sum dignus* (*Lord, I am not worthy*).

158. After this, standing and turned toward the altar, the priest says quietly, *Corpus Christi custodiat me in vitam aeternam* (*May the Body of Christ bring me to everlasting life*) and reverently receives the Body of Christ. Then he takes the chalice, saying quietly, *Sanguis Christi custodiat me in vitam aeternam* (*May the Blood of Christ bring me to everlasting life*), and reverently receives the Blood of Christ.

159. The Communion chant begins while the priest is receiving the Sacrament (cf. above, no. 86).

160. The priest then takes the paten or ciborium and goes to the communicants, who, as a rule, approach in a procession.

The faithful are not permitted to take the consecrated bread or the sacred chalice by themselves and, still less, to hand them from one to another. The norm for reception of Holy Communion in the dioceses of the United States is standing. Communicants should not be denied Holy Communion because they kneel. Rather, such instances should be addressed pastorally, by providing the faithful with proper catechesis on the reasons for this norm.

When receiving Holy Communion, the communicant bows his or her head before the Sacrament as a gesture of reverence and receives the Body of the Lord from the minister. The consecrated host may be received either on the tongue or in the hand, at the discretion of each communicant. When Holy Communion is received under both kinds, the sign of reverence is also made before receiving the Precious Blood.

161. If Communion is given only under the species of bread, the priest raises the host slightly and shows it to each, saying, *Corpus Christi* (*The Body of Christ*). The communicant replies, *Amen*, and receives the Sacrament either on the tongue or, where this is allowed and if the communicant so chooses, in the hand. As soon as the communicant receives the host, he or she consumes it entirely.

If, however, Communion is given under both kinds, the rite prescribed in nos. 284–287 is followed.

162. The priest may be assisted in the distribution of Communion by other priests who happen to be present. If such priests are not present and there is a very large number of communicants, the priest may call upon extraordinary ministers to assist him, e.g., duly instituted acolytes or even other faithful who have been deputed for this purpose.[97] In case of necessity, the priest may depute suitable faithful for this single occasion.[98]

These ministers should not approach the altar before the priest has received Communion, and they are always to receive from the hands of the priest celebrant the vessel containing either species of the Most Holy Eucharist for distribution to the faithful.

163. When the distribution of Communion is finished, the priest himself immediately and completely consumes at the altar any consecrated wine that happens to remain; as for any consecrated hosts that are left, he either consumes them at the altar or carries them to the place designated for the reservation of the Eucharist.

Upon returning to the altar, the priest collects any fragments that may remain. Then, standing at the altar or at the credence table, he purifies the paten or ciborium over the chalice then purifies the chalice, saying quietly, *Quod ore sumpsimus* (*Lord, may I receive*), and dries the chalice with a purificator. If the vessels are purified at the altar, they are carried to the credence table by a minister. Nevertheless, it is also permitted, especially if there are several vessels to be purified, to leave them suitably covered on a corporal, either at the altar or at the credence table, and to purify them immediately after Mass following the dismissal of the people.

164. Afterwards, the priest may return to the chair. A sacred silence may now be observed for some period of time, or a Psalm or another canticle of praise or a hymn may be sung (cf. above, no. 88).

165. Then, standing at the chair or at the altar and facing the people the priest, with hands joined says, *Oremus* (*Let us pray*); then, with hands extended, he recites the prayer after Communion. A brief period of silence may precede the prayer, unless this has been already observed immediately after Communion. At the end of the prayer the people say the acclamation, Amen.

THE CONCLUDING RITES

166. When the prayer after Communion is concluded, brief announcements to the people may be made, if they are needed.

167. Then the priest, extending his hands, greets the people, saying, *Dominus vobiscum* (*The Lord be with you*). They answer, *Et cum spiritu tuo* (*And also with you*). The priest, joining his hands again and then immediately placing his left hand on his breast, raises his right hand and adds, *Benedicat vos omnipotens Deus* (*May Almighty God Bless you*) and, as he makes the Sign of the Cross over the people, continues, *Pater, et Filius, et Spiritus Sanctus* (*the Father, and the Son, and the Holy Spirit*). All answer, *Amen.*

On certain days and occasions this blessing, in accordance with the rubrics, is expanded and expressed by a prayer over the People or another more solemn formula.

A Bishop blesses the people with the appropriate formula, making the Sign of the Cross three times over the people.[99]

168. Immediately after the blessing, with hands joined, the priest adds, *Ite, Missa est* (*The Mass is ended, go in peace*), and all answer, *Deo gratias* (*Thanks be to God*).

169. Then, as a rule, the priest venerates the altar with a kiss and, after making a profound bow with the lay ministers, departs with them.

170. If, however, another liturgical action follows the Mass, the concluding rites, that is, the greeting, the blessing, and the dismissal, are omitted.

B. Mass With a Deacon

171. When he is present at the Eucharistic Celebration, a deacon should exercise his ministry, wearing sacred vestments. For the deacon

   a. Assists the priest and remains at his side;

   b. Ministers at the altar, with the chalice as well as the book;

   c. Proclaims the Gospel and, at the direction of the priest celebrant, may preach the homily (cf. above, no. 66);

   d. Guides the faithful by appropriate introductions and explanations, and announces the intentions of the Prayer of the Faithful;

   e. Assists the priest celebrant in distributing Communion, and purifies and arranges the sacred vessels;

   f. As needed, fulfills the duties of other ministers himself if none of them is present.

THE INTRODUCTORY RITES

172. Carrying the *Book of the Gospels* slightly elevated, the deacon precedes the priest as he approaches the altar or else walks at the priest's side.

173. When he reaches the altar, if he is carrying the *Book of the Gospels*, he omits the sign of reverence and goes up to the altar. It is particularly appropriate that he should place the *Book of the Gospels* on the altar, after which, together with the priest, he venerates the altar with a kiss.

If, however, he is not carrying the *Book of the Gospels*, he makes a profound bow to the altar with the priest in the customary way and with him venerates the altar with a kiss.

Lastly, if incense is used, he assists the priest in putting some into the thurible and in incensing the cross and the altar.

174. After the incensation of the altar, he goes to the chair together with the priest, takes his place there at the side of the priest and assists him as necessary.

175. If incense is used, the deacon assists the priest when he puts incense in the thurible during the singing of the *Alleluia* or other chant. Then he makes a profound bow before the priest and asks for the blessing, saying in a low voice, *Iube, domine, benedicere* (*Father, give me your blessing*). The priest blesses him, saying, *Dominus sit in corde tuo* (*The Lord be in your heart*). The deacon signs himself with the Sign of the Cross and responds, *Amen*. Having bowed to the altar, he then takes up the *Book of the Gospels* which was placed upon it. He proceeds to the ambo, carrying the book slightly elevated. He is preceded by a thurifer, carrying a thurible with smoking incense, and by servers with lighted candles. There the deacon, with hands joined, greets the people, saying, *Dominus vobiscum* (*The Lord be with you*). Then, at the words *Lectio sancti Evangelii* (*A reading from the holy Gospel*), he signs the book with his thumb and, afterwards, himself on his forehead, mouth, and breast. He incenses the book and proclaims the Gospel reading. When the reading is concluded, he says the acclamation *Verbum Domini* (*The Gospel of the Lord*), and all respond, *Laus tibi, Christe* (*Praise to you, Lord Jesus Christ*). He then venerates the book with a kiss, saying privately, *Per evangelica dicta* (*May the words of the Gospel*), and returns to the priest's side.

When the deacon is assisting the Bishop, he carries the book to him to be kissed, or else kisses it himself, saying quietly, *Per evangelica dicta dicta* (*May the words of the Gospel*). In more solemn celebrations, as the occasion suggests, a Bishop may impart a blessing to the people with the *Book of the Gospels*.

Lastly, the deacon may carry the *Book of the Gospels* to the credence table or to another appropriate and dignified place.

176. If, in addition, there is no other suitable lector present, the deacon should proclaim the other readings as well.

177. After the introduction by the priest it is the deacon himself who normally announces the intentions of the Prayer of the Faithful, from the ambo.

THE LITURGY OF THE EUCHARIST

178. After the Prayer of the Faithful, while the priest remains at the chair, the deacon prepares the altar, assisted by the acolyte, but it is the deacon's place to take care of the sacred vessels himself. He also assists the priest in receiving the people's gifts. Next, he hands the priest the paten with the bread to be consecrated, pours wine and a little water into the chalice, saying quietly, *Per huius aquae* (*By the mystery of this water*), and after this presents the chalice to the priest. He may also carry out the preparation of the chalice at the credence table. If incense is used, the deacon assists the priest during the incensation of the gifts, the cross, and the altar; afterwards, the deacon himself or the acolyte incenses the priest and the people.

179. During the Eucharistic Prayer, the deacon stands near the priest but slightly behind him, so that when needed he may assist the priest with the chalice or the Missal.

From the epiclesis until the priest shows the chalice, the deacon normally remains kneeling. If several deacons are present, one of them may place incense in the thurible for the consecration and incense the host and the chalice as they are shown to the people.

180. At the final doxology of the Eucharistic Prayer, the deacon stands next to the priest, holding the chalice elevated while the priest elevates the paten with the host, until the people have responded with the acclamation, *Amen*.

181. After the priest has said the prayer at the Rite of Peace and the greeting *Pax Domini sit semper vobiscum* (*The peace of the Lord be with you always*) and the people have responded, *Et cum spiritu tuo* (*And also with you*), the deacon, if it is appropriate, invites all to exchange the sign of peace. He faces the people and, with hands joined, says, *Offerte vobis pacem pacem* (*Let us offer each other the sign of peace*). Then he himself receives the sign of peace from the priest and may offer it to those other ministers who are closer to him.

182. After the priest's Communion, the deacon receives Communion under both kinds from the priest himself and then assists the priest in distributing Communion to the people. If Communion is given under both kinds, the deacon himself administers the chalice to the communicants; and, when the distribution is completed, he immediately and reverently consumes at the altar all of the Blood of Christ that remains, assisted if necessary by other deacons and priests.

183. When the distribution of Communion is completed, the deacon returns to the altar with the priest and collects the fragments, if any remain, and then carries the chalice and other sacred vessels to the credence table, where he purifies them and arranges them in the usual way while the priest returns to the chair. It is also permissible to leave the vessels that need to be purified, suitably covered, at the credence table on a corporal and to purify them immediately after Mass following the dismissal of the people.

THE CONCLUDING RITES

184. Once the prayer after Communion has been said, the deacon makes brief announcements to the people, if indeed any need to be made, unless the priest prefers to do this himself.

185. If a prayer over the people or a solemn formula for the blessing is used, the deacon says, *Inclinate vos ad benedictionem* (*Bow your heads and pray for God's blessing*). After the priest's blessing, the deacon, with hands joined and facing the people, dismisses them, saying, *Ite, missa est* (*The Mass is ended, go in peace*).

186. Then, together with the priest, the deacon venerates the altar with a kiss, makes a profound bow, and departs in a manner similar to the procession beforehand.

C. The Duties of the Acolyte

187. The duties that the acolyte may carry out are of various kinds and several may coincide. Hence, it is desirable that these duties be suitably distributed among several acolytes. If, however, only one acolyte is present, he should perform the more important duties while the rest are to be distributed among several ministers.

THE INTRODUCTORY RITES

188. In the procession to the altar, the acolyte may carry the cross, walking between two ministers with lighted candles. Upon reaching the altar, the acolyte places the cross upright near the altar so that it may serve as the altar cross; otherwise, he puts it in a worthy place. Then he takes his place in the sanctuary.

189. Through the entire celebration, the acolyte is to approach the priest or the deacon, whenever necessary, in order to present the book to them and to assist them in any other way required. Thus it is appropriate, insofar as possible, that the acolyte occupy a place from which he can conveniently carry out his ministry either at the chair or at the altar.

THE LITURGY OF THE EUCHARIST

190. If no deacon is present, after the Prayer of the Faithful is concluded and while the priest remains at the chair, the acolyte places the corporal, the purificator, the chalice, the pall, and the Missal on the altar. Then, if necessary, the acolyte assists the priest in receiving the gifts of the people and, if appropriate, brings the bread and wine to the altar and hands them to the priest. If incense is used, the acolyte presents the thurible to the priest and assists him while he incenses the gifts, the cross, and the altar. Then the acolyte incenses the priest and the people.

191. A duly instituted acolyte, as an extraordinary minister, may, if necessary, assist the priest in giving Communion to the people.[100] If Communion is given under both kinds, when no deacon is present, the acolyte administers the chalice to the communicants or holds the chalice if Communion is given by intinction.

192. Likewise, when the distribution of Communion is completed, a duly instituted acolyte helps the priest or deacon to purify and arrange the sacred vessels. When no deacon is present, a duly instituted acolyte carries the sacred vessels to the credence table and there purifies, wipes, and arranges them in the usual way.

193. After the celebration of Mass, the acolyte and other ministers return in procession to the sacristy, together with the deacon and the priest in the same way and order in which they entered.

D. The Duties of the Lector

194. In coming to the altar, when no deacon is present, the lector, wearing approved attire, may carry the *Book of the Gospels*, which is to be slightly elevated. In that case, the lector walks in front of the priest but otherwise along with the other ministers.

195. Upon reaching the altar, the lector makes a profound bow with the others. If he is carrying the *Book of the Gospels*, he approaches the altar and places the *Book of the Gospels* upon it. Then the lector takes his own place in the sanctuary with the other ministers.

THE LITURGY OF THE WORD

196. The lector reads from the ambo the readings that precede the Gospel. If there is no psalmist, the lector may also proclaim the responsorial Psalm after the first reading.

197. When no deacon is present, the lector, after the introduction by the priest, may announce from the ambo the intentions of the Prayer of the Faithful.

198. If there is no singing at the Entrance or at Communion and the antiphons in the Missal are not recited by the faithful, the lector may read them at the appropriate time (cf. above, nos. 48, 87).

II. CONCELEBRATED MASS

199. Concelebration, which appropriately expresses the unity of the priesthood, of the Sacrifice, and also of the whole People of God, is prescribed by the rite itself for the Ordination of a Bishop and of priests, at the blessing of an abbot, and at the Chrism Mass.

Unless the good of the Christian faithful requires or suggests otherwise, concelebration is also recommended at

a. The Evening Mass of the Lord's Supper;

b. The Mass during Councils, meetings of Bishops, and synods;

c. The conventual Mass and the principal Mass in churches and oratories;

d. Masses at any kind of meeting of priests, either secular or religious.[101]

An individual priest is, however, permitted to celebrate the Eucharist individually, though not at the same time as a concelebration is taking place in the same church or oratory. On Holy Thursday, however, and for Mass of the Easter Vigil, it is not permitted to celebrate individually.

200. Visiting priests should be gladly welcomed to eucharistic concelebration, as long as their priestly standing is ascertained.

201. Where there is a large number of priests, concelebration may take place even several times on the same day, wherever necessity or pastoral benefit suggest it. Nevertheless, it must be held at different times or in distinct sacred places.[102]

202. It is for the Bishop, in accordance with the norm of law, to regulate the discipline for concelebration in all churches and oratories of his diocese.

203. To be held in high regard is that concelebration in which the priests of each diocese concelebrate with their own Bishop at a stational Mass, especially on the more solemn days of the liturgical year, at the Ordination Mass of a new Bishop of the diocese or of his Coadjutor or Auxiliary, at the Chrism Mass, at the Evening Mass of the Lord's Supper, at celebrations of the Founder Saint of a local Church or the Patron of the diocese, on anniversaries of the Bishop, and, lastly, on the occasion of a Synod or a pastoral visitation.

    For this same reason, concelebration is recommended whenever priests gather together with their own Bishop either on the occasion of a retreat or at any other meeting. In these instances the sign of the unity of the priesthood and also of the Church inherent in every concelebration is made more clearly manifest.[103]

204. For a particular reason, having to do either with the significance of the rite or of the festivity, the faculty is given to celebrate or concelebrate more than once on the same day in the following cases:

    a. A priest who has celebrated or concelebrated the Chrism Mass on Holy Thursday may also celebrate or concelebrate the Evening Mass of the Lord's Supper;

    b. A priest who has celebrated or concelebrated the Mass of the Easter Vigil may celebrate or concelebrate Mass during the day on Easter Sunday;

    c. On the Nativity of the Lord (Christmas Day), all priests may celebrate or concelebrate three Masses, provided the Masses are celebrated at their proper times of day;

    d. On the Commemoration of All the Faithful Departed (All Souls' Day), all priests may celebrate or concelebrate three Masses, provided that the celebrations take place at different times, and that the norms established regarding the application of second and third Masses are observed;[104]

    e. A priest who concelebrates with the Bishop or his delegate at a Synod or pastoral visitation, or concelebrates on the occasion of a meeting of priests, may celebrate Mass again for the benefit of the faithful. This holds also, with due regard for the prescriptions of law, for groups of religious.

205. A concelebrated Mass, whatever its form, is arranged in accordance with the norms commonly in force (cf. above, nos. 112–198), except for those matters that are to be observed, even with appropriate adaptation to circumstances, as set forth below.

206. No one is ever to enter into a concelebration or to be admitted as a concelebrant once the Mass has already begun.

207. In the sanctuary there should be prepared

    a. Seats and texts for the concelebrating priests;

    b. On the credence table: a chalice of sufficient size or else several chalices.

208. If a deacon is not present, his proper duties are to be carried out by some of the concelebrants.

In the absence also of other ministers, their proper parts may be entrusted to other suitable members of the faithful; otherwise, they are carried out by some of the concelebrants.

209. In the vesting room or other suitable place, the concelebrants put on the sacred vestments they customarily wear when celebrating Mass individually. Should, however, a good reason arise, (e.g., a large number of concelebrants or a lack of vestments), concelebrants other than the principal celebrant may omit the chasuble and simply wear the stole over the alb.

THE INTRODUCTORY RITES

210. When everything has been properly arranged, the procession moves as usual through the church to the altar, the concelebrating priests walking ahead of the principal celebrant.

211. On reaching the altar, the concelebrants and the principal celebrant, after making a profound bow, venerate the altar with a kiss, then go to their designated seats. The principal celebrant, if appropriate, also incenses the cross and the altar and then goes to the chair.

THE LITURGY OF THE WORD

212. During the Liturgy of the Word, the concelebrants remain at their places, sitting or standing whenever the principal celebrant does.

When the *Alleluia* is begun, all rise, except for a Bishop, who puts incense into the thurible without saying anything and blesses the deacon or, if there is no deacon, the concelebrant who is to proclaim the Gospel. In a concelebration where a priest presides, however, the concelebrant who in the absence of a deacon proclaims the Gospel neither requests nor receives the blessing of the principal celebrant.

213. The homily is usually given by the principal celebrant or by one of the concelebrants.

THE LITURGY OF THE EUCHARIST

214. The Preparation of the Gifts (cf. above, nos. 139–146) is carried out by the principal celebrant, while the other concelebrants remain at their places.

215. After the prayer over the offerings has been said by the principal celebrant, the concelebrants approach the altar and stand around it, but in such a way that they do not obstruct the execution of the rites and that the sacred action may be seen clearly by the faithful. They should not be in the deacon's way whenever he needs to go to the altar to perform his ministry.

The deacon exercises his ministry at the altar whenever he needs to assist with the chalice and the Missal. However, insofar as possible, he stands back slightly, behind the concelebrating priests standing around the principal celebrant.

THE MANNER OF SPEAKING THE EUCHARISTIC PRAYER

216. The Preface is sung or said by the principal priest celebrant alone; but the *Sanctus* is sung or recited by all the concelebrants, together with the congregation and the choir.

217. After the *Sanctus*, the priest concelebrants continue the Eucharistic Prayer in the way described below. Unless otherwise indicated, only the principal celebrant makes the gestures.

218. The parts spoken by all the concelebrants together and especially the words of consecration, which all are bound to say, are to be said in such a way that the concelebrants speak them in a very low voice and that the principal celebrant's voice be clearly heard. In this way the words can be better understood by the people.

It is a praiseworthy practice for the parts that are to be said by all the concelebrants together and for which musical notation is provided in the Missal to be sung.

EUCHARISTIC PRAYER I: THAT IS, THE ROMAN CANON

219. In Eucharistic Prayer I, that is, the Roman Canon, the prayer *Te igitur* (*We come to you, Father*) is said by the principal celebrant alone, with hands extended.

220. It is appropriate that the commemoration of the living (*the Memento*) and the *Communicantes* (*In union with the whole Church*) be assigned to one or other of the concelebrating priests, who then speaks these prayers aloud, with hands extended.

221. The *Hanc igitur* (*Father, accept this offering*) is likewise said by the principal celebrant alone, with hands extended.

222. From the *Quam oblationem* (*Bless and approve our offering*) up to and including the *Supplices* (*Almighty God, we pray that your angel*), the principal celebrant alone makes the gestures, while all the concelebrants speak everything together, in this manner:

   a. The *Quam oblationem* (*Bless and approve our offering*) with hands extended toward the offerings;

b. The *Qui pridie* (*The day before he suffered*) and the *Simili modo* (*When supper was ended*) with hands joined;

c. While speaking the words of the Lord, each extends his right hand toward the bread and toward the chalice, if this seems appropriate; as the host and the chalice are shown, however, they look toward them and afterwards bow profoundly;

d. The *Unde et memores* (*Father, we celebrate the memory*) and the *Supra quae* (*Look with favor*) with hands extended;

e. From the *Supplices* (*Almighty God, we pray that your angel*) up to and including the words *ex hac altaris participatione* (*as we receive from this altar*), they bow with hands joined; then they stand upright and cross themselves at the words *omni benedictione et gratia repleamur* (*let us be filled with every grace and blessing*).

223. The commemoration of the dead (*Memento*) and the *Nobis quoque peccatoribus* (*Though we are sinners*) are appropriately assigned to one or other of the concelebrants, who speaks them aloud alone, with hands extended.

224. At the words *Nobis quoque peccatoribus* (*Though we are sinners*) all the concelebrants strike their breast.

225. The *Per quem haec omnia* (*Through him you give us all these gifts*) is said by the principal celebrant alone.

EUCHARISTIC PRAYER II

226. In Eucharistic Prayer II the *Vere sanctus* (*Lord, you are holy indeed*) is spoken by the principal celebrant alone, with hands extended.

227. From the *Haec ergo dona* (*Let your Spirit come upon*) to the *Et supplices* (*May all of us who share*) inclusive, all the concelebrants speak all the following together:

a. The *Haec ergo dona* (*Let your Spirit come upon*) with hands extended toward the offerings;

b. The *Qui cum passioni* (*Before he was given up to death*) and the *Simili modo* (*When supper was ended*) with hands joined;

c. While speaking the words of the Lord, each extends his right hand toward the bread and toward the chalice, if this seems appropriate; as the host and the chalice are shown, however, they look toward them and afterwards bow profoundly;

d. The *Memores igitur* (*In memory of his death*) and the *Et supplices* (*May all of us who share*) with hands extended.

228. The intercessions for the living (*Recordare, Domine* [*Lord, remember your Church*]) and for the dead (*Memento etiam fratrum nostrorum* [*Remember our*

brothers and sisters]) are appropriately assigned to one or other of the concelebrants, who speaks them aloud alone, with hands extended.

229. In Eucharistic Prayer III, the *Vere sanctus* (*Father, you are holy indeed*) is spoken by the principal celebrant alone, with hands extended.

230. From the *Supplices ergo te, Domine* (*And so, Father, we bring you these gifts*) to the *Respice, quaesumus* (*Look with favor*) inclusive, all the concelebrants speak all the following together:

    a. The *Supplices ergo te, Domine* (*And so, Father, we bring you these gifts*) with hands extended toward the offerings;

    b. The *Ipse enim in qua nocte tradebatur* (*On the night he was betrayed*) and the *Simili modo* (*When supper was ended*) with hands joined;

    c. While speaking the words of the Lord, each extends his right hand toward the bread and toward the chalice, if this seems appropriate; as the host and the chalice are shown, however, they look at them and, afterwards, bow profoundly;

    d. The *Memores igitur* (*Father, calling to mind*) and the *Respice, quaesumus* (*Look with favor*) with hands outstretched.

231. The intercessions *Ipse nos* (*May he make us an everlasting gift*), *Haec hostia nostrae reconciliationis* (*Lord, may this sacrifice*), and *Fratres nostros* (*Welcome into your kingdom*) are appropriately assigned to one or other of the concelebrants, who speaks them aloud alone, with hands extended.

232. In Eucharistic Prayer IV, the *Confitemur tibi, Pater sancte* (*Father, we acknowledge*) up to and including the words *omnem sanctificationem compleret* (*bring us the fullness of grace*) is spoken by the principal celebrant alone, with hands extended.

233. From the *Quaesumus, igitur, Domine* (*Father, may this Holy Spirit*) to the *Respice, Domine* (*Lord, look upon the sacrifice*) inclusive, all the concelebrants speak all the following together:

    a. The *Quaesumus igitur, Domine* (*Father, may this Holy Spirit*) with hands extended toward the offerings;

    b. The *Ipse enim, cum hora venisset* (*He always loved those*) and the *Simili modo* (*When supper was ended*) with hands joined;

    c. While speaking the words of the Lord, each extends his right hand toward the bread and toward the chalice, if this seems appropriate; as the host and the chalice are shown, however, they look toward them and afterwards bow profoundly;

    d. The *Unde et nos (Father, we now celebrate)* and the *Respice, Domine (Lord, look upon this sacrifice)* with hands outstretched.

234. The intercessions *Nunc ergo, Domine, omnium recordare (Lord, remember those)* and *Nobis omnibus (Father, in your mercy)* are appropriately assigned to one or other of the concelebrants, who speaks them aloud alone, with hands extended.

235. As to other Eucharistic Prayers approved by the Apostolic See, the norms established for each one are to be observed.

236. The concluding doxology of the Eucharistic Prayer is spoken solely by the principal priest celebrant and, if this is desired, together with the other concelebrants, but not by the faithful.

THE COMMUNION RITE

237. Then the principal celebrant, with hands joined, says the introduction to the Lord's Prayer. Then, with hands extended, he says the prayer itself together with the other concelebrants, who also pray with hands extended and with the people.

238. *Libera nos (Deliver us)* is said by the principal celebrant alone, with hands extended. All the concelebrants, together with the people, sing or say the final acclamation *Quia tuum est regnum (For the kingdom)*.

239. After the deacon or, when no deacon is present, one of the concelebrants has said the invitation *Offerte vobis pacem pacem (Let us offer each other the sign of peace)*, all exchange the sign of peace with one another. The concelebrants who are nearer the principal celebrant receive the sign of peace from him before the deacon does.

240. While the *Agnus Dei* is sung or said, the deacons or some of the concelebrants may help the principal celebrant break the hosts for Communion, both of the concelebrants and of the people.

241. After the commingling, the principal celebrant alone, with hands joined, privately says the prayer *Domine Iesu Christe, Fili Dei vivi (Lord Jesus Christ, Son of the living God)* or *Perceptio Corporis et Sanguinis (Lord Jesus Christ, with faith in your love and mercy)*.

242. When this prayer before Communion is finished, the principal celebrant genuflects and steps back a little. Then one after another the concelebrants come to the middle of the altar, genuflect, and reverently take the Body of Christ from the altar. Then holding it in their right hand, with the left hand placed below, they return to their places. The concelebrants may, however, remain in their places and take the Body of Christ from the paten presented to them by the principal celebrant or by one or more of the concelebrants, or by passing the paten one to another.

243. Then the principal celebrant takes a host consecrated in the same Mass, holds it slightly raised above the paten or the chalice, and, facing the people, says the *Ecce Agnus Dei* (*This is the Lamb of God*). With the concelebrants and the people he continues, saying the *Domine, non sum dignus* (*Lord, I am not worthy*).

244. Then the principal celebrant, facing the altar, says quietly, *Corpus Christi custodiat me ad vitam aeternam* (*May the body of Christ bring me to everlasting life*), and reverently receives the Body of Christ. The concelebrants do likewise, communicating themselves. After them the deacon receives the Body and Blood of the Lord from the principal celebrant.

245. The Blood of the Lord may be received either by drinking from the chalice directly, or by intinction, or by means of a tube or a spoon.

246. If Communion is received by drinking directly from the chalice, one or other of two procedures may be followed:

    a. The principal celebrant, standing at the middle of the altar, takes the chalice and says quietly, *Sanguis Christi custodiat me in vitam aeternam* (*May the Blood of Christ bring me to everlasting life*). He consumes a little of the Blood of Christ and hands the chalice to the deacon or a concelebrant. He then distributes Communion to the faithful (cf. above, nos. 160–162).

        The concelebrants approach the altar one after another or, if two chalices are used, two by two. They genuflect, partake of the Blood of Christ, wipe the rim of the chalice, and return to their seats.

    b. The principal celebrant normally consumes the Blood of the Lord standing at the middle of the altar.

        The concelebrants may, however, partake of the Blood of the Lord while remaining in their places and drinking from the chalice presented to them by the deacon or by one of the concelebrants, or else passed from one to the other. The chalice is always wiped either by the one who drinks from it or by the one who presents it. After communicating, each returns to his seat.

247. The deacon reverently drinks at the altar all of the Blood of Christ that remains, assisted, if necessary, by some of the concelebrants. He then carries the chalice over to the credence table and there he or a duly instituted acolyte purifies, wipes, and arranges it in the usual way (cf. above, no. 183).

248. The Communion of the concelebrants may also be arranged so that each concelebrant communicates the Body of the Lord at the altar and, immediately afterwards, the Blood of the Lord.

    In this case the principal celebrant receives Communion under both kinds in the usual way (cf. above, no. 158), observing, however, the rite chosen in each particular instance for Communion from the chalice; and the other concelebrants should follow suit.

After the principal celebrant's Communion, the chalice is placed on another corporal at the side of the altar. The concelebrants approach the middle of the altar one after another, genuflect, and receive the Body of the Lord; then they go to the side of the altar and consume the Blood of the Lord, following the rite chosen for Communion from the chalice, as has just been said.

The Communion of the deacon and the purification of the chalice take place as already described.

249. If the concelebrants' Communion is by intinction, the principal celebrant receives the Body and Blood of the Lord in the usual way, but making sure that enough of the precious Blood remains in the chalice for the Communion of the concelebrants. Then the deacon, or one of the concelebrants, arranges the chalice as appropriate in the center of the altar or at the side on another corporal together with the paten containing particles of the host.

The concelebrants approach the altar one after another, genuflect, and take a particle, dip it partly into the chalice, and, holding a purificator under their chin, consume the intincted particle. They then return to their places as at the beginning of Mass.

The deacon also receives Communion by intinction and to the concelebrant's words *Corpus et Sanguis Christi* (*The Body and Blood of Christ*) makes the response *Amen*. The deacon, however, consumes at the altar all that remains of the Precious Blood, assisted, if necessary, by some of the concelebrants. He carries the chalice to the credence table and there he or a duly instituted acolyte purifies, wipes and arranges it in the usual way.

THE CONCLUDING RITES

250. Everything else is done by the principal celebrant in the usual way until the end of Mass (cf. above, nos. 166–168), while the other concelebrants remain at their seats.

251. Before leaving the altar, the concelebrants make a profound bow to the altar. For his part the principal celebrant, along with the deacon, venerates the altar with a kiss in the usual way.

III. MASS AT WHICH ONLY ONE MINISTER PARTICIPATES

252. At a Mass celebrated by a priest with only one minister to assist him and to make the responses, the rite of Mass with a congregation is followed (cf. above, nos. 120–169) the minister saying the people's parts as appropriate.

253. If, however, the minister is a deacon, he performs his proper duties (cf. above, nos. 171–186) and likewise carries out the other parts, that is, those of the people.

254. Mass should not be celebrated without a minister or at least one of the faithful, except for a just and reasonable cause. In this case, the greetings, the

introductory or explanatory remarks (*monitiones*), and the blessing at the end of Mass are omitted.

255. Before Mass, the necessary vessels are prepared either at the credence table or on the righthand side of the altar.

THE INTRODUCTORY RITES

256. The priest approaches the altar and, after making a profound bow along with the minister, venerates the altar with a kiss and goes to the chair. If he wishes, the priest may remain at the altar; in this case, the Missal is likewise prepared there. Then the minister or the priest says the Entrance Antiphon.

257. Then the priest, standing, makes with the minister the sign of the Cross as the priest says, *In nomine Patris* (*In the name of the Father*). Facing the minister, he greets the minister choosing one of the formulas of greeting.

258. Then the Act of Penitence takes place, and, if required by the rubrics, the *Kyrie* and *Gloria* are said.

259. Then, with hands joined, the priest says, *Oremus* (*Let us pray*). After a suitable pause, with hands extended he says the collect. At the end the minister makes the acclamation, *Amen*.

THE LITURGY OF THE WORD

260. The readings should whenever possible be proclaimed from the ambo or a lectern.

261. After the collect, the minister reads the first reading and Psalm, the second reading, when it is to be said, and the verse for the *Alleluia* or other chant.

262. Then the priest bows profoundly and says the *Munda cor meum* (*Almighty God, cleanse my heart*) and, afterwards, reads the Gospel. At the conclusion he says, *Verbum Domini* (*The Gospel of the Lord*), to which the minister responds, *Laus tibi, Christe* (*Praise to you, Lord Jesus Christ*). The priest then venerates the book with a kiss, saying quietly the *Per evangelica dicta* (*May the words of the Gospel*).

263. Afterwards, if required by the rubrics, the priest says the Creed together with the minister.

264. The Prayer of the Faithful follows, which may be said even in this form of Mass. The priest introduces and concludes it, with the minister announcing the intentions.

THE LITURGY OF THE EUCHARIST

265. In the Liturgy of the Eucharist, everything is done as in a Mass with a congregation, with the following exceptions.

266. After the acclamation at the end of the embolism that follows the Lord's Prayer, the priest says the prayer *Domine Iesu Christe, qui dixisti* (*Lord Jesus Christ, you said*). He then adds, *Pax Domini sit semper vobiscum* (*The peace of the Lord be with you always*), and the minister answers, *Et cum spiritu tuo* (*And also with you*). The priest gives the sign of peace to the minister, if appropriate.

267. Then, while he says the *Agnus Dei* (*Lamb of God*) with the minister, the priest breaks the host over the paten. After the *Agnus Dei*, he performs the commixtion, saying quietly the *Haec commixtio* (*May this mingling*).

268. After the commingling, the priest quietly says the prayer *Domine Iesu Christe, Fili Dei vivi* (*Lord Jesus Christ, Son of the living God*) or *Perceptio* (*Lord Jesus Christ, with faith in your love and mercy*). Then he genuflects, takes the host, and, if the minister is to receive Communion, turns to the minister and, holding the host a little above the paten or the chalice, says the *Ecce Agnus Dei* (*This is the Lamb of God*), adding with the minister the *Domine, non sum dignus* (*Lord, I am not worthy*). Facing the altar, the priest then partakes of the Body of Christ. If, however, the minister does not receive Communion, the priest, after genuflecting, takes the host and, facing the altar, says quietly the *Domine, non sum dignus* (*Lord, I am not worthy*) and the *Corpus Christi custodiat* (*May the Body of Christ bring*) and then receives the Body of Christ. Then he takes the chalice and says quietly, *Sanguis Christi custodiat* (*May the Blood of Christ bring*), and then consumes the Blood of Christ.

269. Before Communion is given to the minister, the Communion Antiphon is said by the minister or by the priest himself.

270. The priest purifies the chalice at the credence table or at the altar. If the chalice is purified at the altar, it may be carried to the credence table by the minister or may again be placed on the altar at the side.

271. After the purification of the chalice, the priest should observe some moments of silence, after which he says the prayer after Communion.

THE CONCLUDING RITES

272. The concluding rites are carried out as at a Mass with a congregation, but the dismissal formula is omitted. The priest venerates the altar in the usual way with a kiss and, after making a profound bow with the minister, departs.

IV. SOME GENERAL NORMS FOR ALL FORMS OF MASS

VENERATION OF THE ALTAR AND THE BOOK OF THE GOSPELS

273. According to traditional practice, the altar and the *Book of the Gospels* are venerated by means of a kiss. Where, however, a sign of this kind is not in harmony with the traditions or the culture of some region, it is for the Conference of Bishops to establish some other sign in its place, with the consent of the Apostolic See.

274. A genuflection, made by bending the right knee to the ground, signifies adoration, and therefore it is reserved for the Most Blessed Sacrament, as well as for the Holy Cross from the solemn adoration during the liturgical celebration on Good Friday until the beginning of the Easter Vigil.

During Mass, three genuflections are made by the priest celebrant: namely, after the showing of the host, after the showing of the chalice, and before Communion. Certain specific features to be observed in a concelebrated Mass are noted in their proper place (cf. above, nos. 210–251).

If, however, the tabernacle with the Most Blessed Sacrament is present in the sanctuary, the priest, the deacon, and the other ministers genuflect when they approach the altar and when they depart from it, but not during the celebration of Mass itself.

Otherwise all who pass before the Most Blessed Sacrament genuflect, unless they are moving in procession.

Ministers carrying the processional cross or candles bow their heads instead of genuflecting.

275. A bow signifies reverence and honor shown to the persons themselves or to the signs that represent them. There are two kinds of bows: a bow of the head and a bow of the body.

a. A bow of the head is made when the three Divine Persons are named together and at the names of Jesus, of the Blessed Virgin Mary, and of the Saint in whose honor Mass is being celebrated.

b. A bow of the body, that is to say a profound bow, is made to the altar; during the prayers *Munda cor meum* (*Almighty God, cleanse my heart*) and *In spiritu humilitatis* (*Lord God, we ask you to receive*); in the Creed at the words *Et incarnatus est* (*by the power of the Holy Spirit . . . made man*); in the Roman Canon at the words *Supplices te rogamus* (*Almighty God, we pray that your angel*). The same kind of bow is made by the deacon when he asks for a blessing before the proclamation of the Gospel. In addition, the priest bows slightly as he speaks the words of the Lord at the consecration.

INCENSATION

276. Thurification or incensation is an expression of reverence and of prayer, as is signified in Sacred Scripture (cf. Ps 141 [140]:2, Rev 8:3).

Incense may be used if desired in any form of Mass:

a. During the Entrance procession;

b. At the beginning of Mass, to incense the cross and the altar;

c. At the Gospel procession and the proclamation of the Gospel itself;

d. After the bread and the chalice have been placed upon the altar, to incense the offerings, the cross, and the altar, as well as the priest and the people;

e. At the showing of the host and the chalice after the consecration.

277. The priest, having put incense into the thurible, blesses it with the sign of the Cross, without saying anything.

Before and after an incensation, a profound bow is made to the person or object that is incensed, except for the incensation of the altar and the offerings for the Sacrifice of the Mass.

The following are incensed with three swings of the thurible: the Most Blessed Sacrament, a relic of the Holy Cross and images of the Lord exposed for public veneration, the offerings for the sacrifice of the Mass, the altar cross, the Book of the Gospels, the Paschal Candle, the priest, and the people.

The following are incensed with two swings of the thurible: relics and images of the Saints exposed for public veneration. This should be done, however, only at the beginning of the celebration, after the incensation of the altar.

The altar is incensed with single swings of the thurible in this way:

a. If the altar is freestanding with respect to the wall, the priest incenses walking around it;

b. If the altar is not freestanding, the priest incenses it while walking first to the righthand side, then to the left.

The cross, if situated on or near the altar, is incensed by the priest before he incenses the altar; otherwise, he incenses it when he passes in front of it.

The priest incenses the offerings with three swings of the thurible or by making the sign of the cross over the offerings with the thurible, then going on to incense the cross and the altar.

THE PURIFICATION

278. Whenever a fragment of the host adheres to his fingers, especially after the fraction or the Communion of the faithful, the priest is to wipe his fingers over the paten or, if necessary, wash them. Likewise, he should also gather any fragments that may have fallen outside the paten.

279. The sacred vessels are purified by the priest, the deacon, or an instituted acolyte after Communion or after Mass, insofar as possible at the credence table. The purification of the chalice is done with water alone or with wine and water, which is then drunk by whoever does the purification. The paten is usually wiped clean with the purificator.

Care must be taken that whatever may remain of the Blood of Christ after the distribution of Communion is consumed immediately and completely at the altar.

280. If a host or any particle should fall, it is to be picked up reverently. If any of the Precious Blood is spilled, the area where the spill occurred should be washed with water, and this water should then be poured into the sacrarium in the sacristy.

COMMUNION UNDER BOTH KINDS

281. Holy Communion has a fuller form as a sign when it is distributed under both kinds. For in this form the sign of the eucharistic banquet is more clearly evident and clear expression is given to the divine will by which the new and eternal Covenant is ratified in the Blood of the Lord, as also the relationship between the Eucharistic banquet and the eschatological banquet in the Father's Kingdom.[105]

282. Sacred pastors should take care to ensure that the faithful who participate in the rite or are present at it are as fully aware as possible of the Catholic teaching on the form of Holy Communion as set forth by the Ecumenical Council of Trent. Above all, they should instruct the Christian faithful that the Catholic faith teaches that Christ, whole and entire, and the true Sacrament, is received even under only one species, and consequently that as far as the effects are concerned, those who receive under only one species are not deprived of any of the grace that is necessary for salvation.[106]

They are to teach, furthermore, that the Church, in her stewardship of the Sacraments, has the power to set forth or alter whatever provisions, apart from the substance of the Sacraments, that she judges to be most conducive to the veneration of the Sacraments and the well-being of the recipients, in view of changing conditions, times, and places.[107] At the same time, the faithful should be encouraged to seek to participate more eagerly in this sacred rite, by which the sign of the Eucharistic banquet is made more fully evident.

283. In addition to those cases given in the ritual books, Communion under both kinds is permitted for

a. Priests who are not able to celebrate or concelebrate Mass;

b. The deacon and others who perform some duty at the Mass;

c. Members of communities at the conventual Mass or "community" Mass, along with seminarians, and all who are engaged in a retreat or are taking part in a spiritual or pastoral gathering.

The diocesan Bishop may establish norms for Communion under both kinds for his own diocese, which are also to be observed in churches of religious and at celebrations with small groups. The diocesan Bishop is also given the faculty to permit Communion under both kinds whenever it may seem appropriate to the priest to whom, as its own shepherd, a community has been entrusted, provided that the faithful have been well instructed and there is no danger of profanation of the Sacrament or of the rite's becoming difficult because of the large number of participants or some other reason.

In all that pertains to Communion under both kinds, the *Norms for the Distribution and Reception of Holy Communion under Both Kinds in the Dioceses of the United States of America* are to be followed (see nos. 27–54).

284. When Communion is distributed under both kinds,

    a. The chalice is usually administered by a deacon or, when no deacon is present, by a priest, or even by a duly instituted acolyte or another extraordinary minister of Holy Communion, or by a member of the faithful who in case of necessity has been entrusted with this duty for a single occasion;

    b. Whatever may remain of the Blood of Christ is consumed at the altar by the priest or the deacon or the duly instituted acolyte who ministered the chalice. The same then purifies, wipes, and arranges the sacred vessels in the usual way.

Any of the faithful who wish to receive Holy Communion under the species of bread alone should be granted their wish.

285. For Communion under both kinds the following should be prepared:

    a. If Communion from the chalice is carried out by communicants' drinking directly from the chalice, a chalice of a sufficiently large size or several chalices are prepared. Care should, however, be taken in planning lest beyond what is needed of the Blood of Christ remains to be consumed at the end of the celebration.

    b. If Communion is carried out by intinction, the hosts should be neither too thin nor too small, but rather a little thicker than usual, so that after being dipped partly into the Blood of Christ they can still easily be distributed to each communicant.

286. If Communion of the Blood of Christ is carried out by communicants' drinking from the chalice, each communicant, after receiving the Body of Christ, moves and stands facing the minister of the chalice. The minister says, *Sanguis Christi* (*The Blood of Christ*), the communicant responds, *Amen*, and the minister hands over the chalice, which the communicant raises to his or her mouth. Each communicant drinks a little from the chalice, hands it back to the minister, and then withdraws; the minister wipes the rim of the chalice with the purificator.

287. If Communion from the chalice is carried out by intinction, each communicant, holding a communion-plate under the chin, approaches the priest, who holds a vessel with the sacred particles, a minister standing at his side and holding the chalice. The priest takes a host, dips it partly into the chalice and, showing it, says, *Corpus et Sanguis Christi* (*The Body and Blood of Christ*). The communicant responds, *Amen*, receives the Sacrament in the mouth from the priest, and then withdraws.

CHAPTER V
THE ARRANGEMENT AND FURNISHING OF CHURCHES FOR THE CELEBRATION OF THE EUCHARIST

I. GENERAL PRINCIPLES

288. For the celebration of the Eucharist, the people of God normally are gathered together in a church or, if there is no church or if it is too small, then in another respectable place that is nonetheless worthy of so great a mystery. Churches, therefore, and other places should be suitable for carrying out the sacred action and for ensuring the active participation of the faithful. Sacred buildings and requisites for divine worship should, moreover, be truly worthy and beautiful and be signs and symbols of heavenly realities.[108]

289. Consequently, the Church constantly seeks the noble assistance of the arts and admits the artistic expressions of all peoples and regions.[109] In fact, just as she is intent on preserving the works of art and the artistic treasures handed down from past centuries[110] and, insofar as necessary, on adapting them to new needs, so also she strives to promote new works of art that are in harmony with the character of each successive age.[111]

On account of this, in commissioning artists and choosing works of art to be admitted into a church, what should be required is that true excellence in art which nourishes faith and devotion and accords authentically with both the meaning and the purpose for which it is intended.[112]

290. All churches should be dedicated or, at least, blessed. Cathedrals and parish churches, however, are to be dedicated with a solemn rite.

291. For the proper construction, restoration, and remodeling of sacred buildings, all who are involved in the work are to consult the diocesan commission on the Sacred Liturgy and sacred art. The diocesan Bishop, moreover, should use the counsel and help of this commission whenever it comes to laying down norms on this matter, approving plans for new buildings, and making decisions on the more important issues.[113]

292. Church decor should contribute toward the church's noble simplicity rather than ostentation. In the choice of materials for church appointments there should be a concern for genuineness of materials and an intent to foster the instruction of the faithful and the dignity of the entire sacred place.

293. A proper arrangement of a church and its surroundings that appropriately meets contemporary needs requires attention not only to the elements related more directly to the celebration of the sacred actions but also to those things conducive to the appropriate comfort of the faithful that are normally forthcoming in places where people regularly gather.

294. The People of God, gathered for Mass, has a coherent and hierarchical structure, which finds its expression in the variety of ministries and the variety

of actions according to the different parts of the celebration. The general ordering of the sacred building must be such that in some way it conveys the image of the gathered assembly and allows the appropriate ordering of all the participants, as well as facilitating each in the proper carrying out of his function.

The faithful and the choir should have a place that facilitates their active participation.[114]

The priest celebrant, the deacon, and the other ministers have places in the sanctuary. Seats for concelebrants should also be prepared there. If, however, their number is great, seats should be arranged in another part of the church, but near the altar.

All these elements, even though they must express the hierarchical structure and the diversity of ministries, should nevertheless bring about a close and coherent unity that is clearly expressive of the unity of the entire holy people. Indeed, the character and beauty of the place and all its furnishings should foster devotion and show forth the holiness of the mysteries celebrated there.

II. ARRANGEMENT OF THE SANCTUARY FOR THE SACRED SYNAXIS (EUCHARISTIC ASSEMBLY)

295. The sanctuary is the place where the altar stands, where the word of God is proclaimed, and where the priest, the deacon, and the other ministers exercise their offices. It should suitably be marked off from the body of the church either by its being somewhat elevated or by a particular structure and ornamentation. It should, however, be large enough to allow the Eucharist to be celebrated properly and easily seen.[115]

THE ALTAR AND ITS APPOINTMENTS

296. The altar on which the Sacrifice of the Cross is made present under sacramental signs is also the table of the Lord to which the People of God is called together to participate in the Mass, as well as the center of the thanksgiving that is accomplished through the Eucharist.

297. The celebration of the Eucharist in a sacred place is to be carried out on an altar; but outside a sacred place, it may be carried out on a suitable table, always with the use of a cloth, a corporal, a cross, and candles.

298. It is appropriate to have a fixed altar in every church, since it more clearly and permanently signifies Christ Jesus, the living stone (1 Pt 2:4; cf. Eph 2:20). In other places set aside for sacred celebrations, the altar may be movable.

An altar is called "fixed" if it is attached to the floor so as not to be irremoveable; otherwise it is called "moveable."

299. The altar should be built apart from the wall, in such a way that it is possible to walk around it easily and that Mass can be celebrated at it facing the people, which is desirable wherever possible. The altar should, moreover, be so

placed as to be truly the center toward which the attention of the whole congregation of the faithful naturally turns.[116] The altar is usually fixed and is dedicated.

300. An altar whether fixed or movable is dedicated according to the rite prescribed in the Roman Pontifical; but it is permissible for a movable altar simply to be blessed.

301. In keeping with the Church's traditional practice and the altar's symbolism, the table of a fixed altar is to be of stone and indeed of natural stone. In the dioceses of the United States of America, however, wood which is worthy, solid, and well-crafted may be used, provided that the altar is structurally immobile. The supports or base for upholding the table, however, may be made of any sort of material, provided it is worthy and solid.

A movable altar may be constructed of any noble and solid materials suited to liturgical use, according to the traditions and usages of the different regions.

302. The practice of placing relics of Saints, even those not Martyrs, under the altar to be dedicated is fittingly retained. Care should be taken, however, to ensure the authenticity of such relics.

303. In building new churches, it is preferable to erect a single altar which in the gathering of the faithful will signify the one Christ and the one Eucharist of the Church.

In already existing churches, however, when the old altar is positioned so that it makes the people's participation difficult but cannot be moved without damage to its artistic value, another fixed altar, of artistic merit and duly dedicated, should be erected and sacred rites celebrated on it alone. In order not to distract the attention of the faithful from the new altar, the old altar should not be decorated in any special way.

304. Out of reverence for the celebration of the memorial of the Lord and for the banquet in which the Body and Blood of the Lord are offered on an altar where this memorial is celebrated, there should be at least one white cloth, its shape, size, and decoration in keeping with the altar's design. When, in the dioceses of the United States of America, other cloths are used in addition to the altar cloth, then those cloths may be of other colors possessing Christian honorific or festive significance according to longstanding local usage, provided that the uppermost cloth covering the *mensa* (i.e., the altar cloth itself) is always white in color.

305. Moderation should be observed in the decoration of the altar.

During Advent the floral decoration of the altar should be marked by a moderation suited to the character of this season, without expressing prematurely the full joy of the Nativity of the Lord. During Lent it is forbidden for the altar to be decorated with flowers. *Laetare* Sunday (Fourth Sunday of Lent), Solemnities, and Feasts are exceptions.

Floral decorations should always be done with moderation and placed around the altar rather than on its *mensa*.

306. Only what is required for the celebration of the Mass may be placed on the *mensa* of the altar: namely, from the beginning of the celebration until the proclamation of the Gospel, the *Book of the Gospels;* then from the Presentation of the Gifts until the purification of the vessels, the chalice with the paten, a ciborium if necessary, and, finally, the corporal, the purificator, the pall, and the Missal.

In addition, microphones that may be needed to amplify the priest's voice should be arranged discreetly.

307. The candles, which are required at every liturgical service out of reverence and on account of the festiveness of the celebration (cf. above, no. 117), are to be appropriately placed either on or around the altar in a way suited to the design of the altar and the sanctuary so that the whole may be well balanced and not interfere with the faithful's clear view of what takes place at the altar or what is placed on it.

308. There is also to be a cross, with the figure of Christ crucified upon it, either on the altar or near it, where it is clearly visible to the assembled congregation. It is appropriate that such a cross, which calls to mind for the faithful the saving Passion of the Lord, remain near the altar even outside of liturgical celebrations.

THE AMBO

309. The dignity of the word of God requires that the church have a place that is suitable for the proclamation of the word and toward which the attention of the whole congregation of the faithful naturally turns during the Liturgy of the Word.[117]

It is appropriate that this place be ordinarily a stationary ambo and not simply a movable lectern. The ambo must be located in keeping with the design of each church in such a way that the ordained ministers and lectors may be clearly seen and heard by the faithful.

From the ambo only the readings, the responsorial Psalm, and the Easter Proclamation (*Exsultet*) are to be proclaimed; it may be used also for giving the homily and for announcing the intentions of the Prayer of the Faithful. The dignity of the ambo requires that only a minister of the word should go up to it.

It is appropriate that a new ambo be blessed according to the rite described in the Roman Ritual[118] before it is put into liturgical use.

THE CHAIR FOR THE PRIEST CELEBRANT AND OTHER SEATS

310. The chair of the priest celebrant must signify his office of presiding over the gathering and of directing the prayer. Thus the best place for the chair is in a position facing the people at the head of the sanctuary, unless the design of the building or other circumstances impede this: for example, if the great distance

would interfere with communication between the priest and the gathered assembly, or if the tabernacle is in the center behind the altar. Any appearance of a throne, however, is to be avoided.[119] It is appropriate that, before being put into liturgical use, the chair be blessed according to the rite described in the Roman Ritual.[120]

Likewise, seats should be arranged in the sanctuary for concelebrating priests as well as for priests who are present for the celebration in choir dress but who are not concelebrating.

The seat for the deacon should be placed near that of the celebrant. Seats for the other ministers are to be arranged so that they are clearly distinguishable from those for the clergy and so that the ministers are easily able to fulfill the function entrusted to them.[121]

III. THE ARRANGEMENT OF THE CHURCH

THE PLACES FOR THE FAITHFUL

311. Places should be arranged with appropriate care for the faithful so that they are able to participate in the sacred celebrations visually and spiritually, in the proper manner. It is expedient for benches or seats usually to be provided for their use. The custom of reserving seats for private persons, however, is reprehensible.[122] Moreover, benches or chairs should be arranged, especially in newly built churches, in such a way that the people can easily take up the postures required for the different parts of the celebration and can easily come forward to receive Holy Communion.

Care should be taken that the faithful be able not only to see the priest, the deacon, and the lectors but also, with the aid of modern technical means, to hear them without difficulty.

THE PLACE FOR THE CHOIR AND THE MUSICAL INSTRUMENTS

312. The choir should be positioned with respect to the design of each church so as to make clearly evident its character as a part of the gathered community of the faithful fulfilling a specific function. The location should also assist the choir to exercise its function more easily and conveniently allow each choir member full, sacramental participation in the Mass.[123]

313. The organ and other lawfully approved musical instruments are to be placed in an appropriate place so that they can sustain the singing of both the choir and the congregation and be heard with ease by all if they are played alone. It is appropriate that, before being put into liturgical use, the organ be blessed according to the rite described in the Roman Ritual.[124]

In Advent the organ and other musical instruments should be used with a moderation that is consistent with the season's character and does not anticipate the full joy of the Nativity of the Lord.

In Lent the playing of the organ and musical instruments is allowed only to support the singing. Exceptions are *Laetare* Sunday (Fourth Sunday of Lent), solemnities, and Feasts.

THE PLACE FOR THE RESERVATION OF THE MOST HOLY EUCHARIST

314. In accordance with the structure of each church and legitimate local customs, the Most Blessed Sacrament should be reserved in a tabernacle in a part of the church that is truly noble, prominent, readily visible, beautifully decorated, and suitable for prayer.[125]

The one tabernacle should be immovable, be made of solid and inviolable material that is not transparent, and be locked in such a way that the danger of profanation is prevented to the greatest extent possible.[126] Moreover, it is appropriate that, before it is put into liturgical use, it be blessed according to the rite described in the Roman Ritual.[127]

315. It is more in keeping with the meaning of the sign that the tabernacle in which the Most Holy Eucharist is reserved not be on an altar on which Mass is celebrated.[128]

Consequently, it is preferable that the tabernacle be located, according to the judgment of the diocesan Bishop,

  a. Either in the sanctuary, apart from the altar of celebration, in a form and place more appropriate, not excluding on an old altar no longer used for celebration (cf. above, no. 303);

  a. Or even in some chapel suitable for the faithful's private adoration and prayer[129] and which is organically connected to the church and readily visible to the Christian faithful.

316. In accordance with traditional custom, near the tabernacle a special lamp, fueled by oil or wax, should be kept alight to indicate and honor the presence of Christ.[130]

317. In no way should all the other things prescribed by law concerning the reservation of the Most Holy Eucharist be forgotten.[131]

SACRED IMAGES

318. In the earthly Liturgy, the Church participates, by a foretaste, in that heavenly Liturgy which is celebrated in the holy city of Jerusalem toward which she journeys as a pilgrim, and where Christ is sitting at the right hand of God; and by venerating the memory of the Saints, she hopes one day to have some part and fellowship with them.[132]

Thus, images of the Lord, the Blessed Virgin Mary, and the Saints, in accordance with the Church's most ancient tradition, should be displayed for veneration by the faithful in sacred buildings[133] and should be arranged so as to usher the faithful toward the mysteries of faith celebrated there. For this reason, care should be taken that their number not be increased indiscriminately, and that they be arranged in proper order so as not to distract the faithful's attention from the celebration itself.[134] There should usually be only one image of any given Saint. Generally speaking, in the ornamentation and arrangement of a church as far as images are concerned, provision should be made for the devotion of the entire community as well as for the beauty and dignity of the images.

CHAPTER VI
THE REQUISITES FOR THE CELEBRATION OF MASS

I. THE BREAD AND WINE FOR CELEBRATING THE EUCHARIST

319. Following the example of Christ, the Church has always used bread and wine with water to celebrate the Lord's Supper.

320. The bread for celebrating the Eucharist must be made only from wheat, must be recently baked, and, according to the ancient tradition of the Latin Church, must be unleavened.

321. The meaning of the sign demands that the material for the Eucharistic celebration truly have the appearance of food. It is therefore expedient that the eucharistic bread, even though unleavened and baked in the traditional shape, be made in such a way that the priest at Mass with a congregation is able in practice to break it into parts for distribution to at least some of the faithful. Small hosts are, however, in no way ruled out when the number of those receiving Holy Communion or other pastoral needs require it. The action of the fraction or breaking of bread, which gave its name to the Eucharist in apostolic times, will bring out more clearly the force and importance of the sign of unity of all in the one bread, and of the sign of charity by the fact that the one bread is distributed among the brothers and sisters.

322. The wine for the eucharistic celebration must be from the fruit of the grapevine (cf. Lk 22:18), natural, and unadulterated, that is, without admixture of extraneous substances.

323. Diligent care should be taken to ensure that the bread and wine intended for the Eucharist are kept in a perfect state of conservation: that is, that the wine does not turn to vinegar nor the bread spoil or become too hard to be broken easily.

324. If the priest notices after the consecration or as he receives Communion that not wine but only water was poured into the chalice, he pours the water into some container, then pours wine with water into the chalice and consecrates it. He says only the part of the institution narrative related to the consecration of the chalice, without being obliged to consecrate the bread again.

II. SACRED FURNISHINGS IN GENERAL

325. As in the case of the building of churches, so also regarding all sacred furnishings the Church admits the artistic style of each region and accepts those adaptations that are in keeping with the culture and traditions of each people, provided that all fit the purpose for which the sacred furnishings are intended.[135]

In this matter as well, a noble simplicity should be ensured such as is the best companion of genuine art.

326. In the choice of materials for sacred furnishings, besides those which are traditional, others are acceptable if by contemporary standards they are considered to be noble, are durable, and are well suited for sacred use. In the dioceses of the United States of America these materials may include wood, stone, or metal which are solid and appropriate to the purpose for which they are employed.

III. SACRED VESSELS

327. Among the requisites for the celebration of Mass, the sacred vessels are held in special honor, especially the chalice and paten, in which the bread and wine are offered and consecrated, and from which they are consumed.

328. Sacred vessels are to be made from precious metal. If they are made from metal that rusts or from a metal less precious than gold, then ordinarily they should be gilded on the inside.

329. In the dioceses of the United States of America, sacred vessels may also be made from other solid materials that, according to the common estimation in each region, are precious, for example, ebony or other hard woods, provided that such materials are suited to sacred use and do not easily break or deteriorate. This applies to all vessels which hold the hosts, such as the paten, the ciborium, the pyx, the monstrance, and other things of this kind.

330. As regards chalices and other vessels that are intended to serve as receptacles for the Blood of the Lord, they are to have bowls of nonabsorbent material. The base, on the other hand, may be made of other solid and worthy materials.

331. For the consecration of hosts, a large paten may appropriately be used; on it is placed the bread for the priest and the deacon as well as for the other ministers and for the faithful.

332. As to the form of the sacred vessels, the artist may fashion them in a manner that is more in keeping with the customs of each region, provided each vessel is suited to the intended liturgical use and is clearly distinguishable from those intended for everyday use.

333. For the blessing of sacred vessels, the rites prescribed in the liturgical books are to be followed.[136]

334. The practice is to be kept of building a sacrarium in the sacristy, into which are poured the water from the purification of sacred vessels and linens (cf. above, no. 280).

IV. SACRED VESTMENTS

335. In the Church, which is the Body of Christ, not all members have the same office. This variety of offices in the celebration of the Eucharist is shown outwardly by the diversity of sacred vestments, which should therefore be a sign of the office proper to each minister. At the same time, however, the sacred vestments should also contribute to the beauty of the sacred action itself. It is appropriate that the vestments to be worn by priests and deacons, as well as those garments to be worn by lay ministers, be blessed according to the rite described in the Roman Ritual[137] before they put into liturgical use.

336. The sacred garment common to ordained and instituted ministers of any rank is the alb, to be tied at the waist with a cincture unless it is made so as to fit even without such. Before the alb is put on, should this not completely cover the ordinary clothing at the neck, an amice should be put on. The alb may not be replaced by a surplice, not even over a cassock, on occasions when a chasuble or dalmatic is to be worn or when, according to the norms, only a stole is worn without a chasuble or dalmatic.

337. The vestment proper to the priest celebrant at Mass and other sacred actions directly connected with Mass is, unless otherwise indicated, the chasuble, worn over the alb and stole.

338. The vestment proper to the deacon is the dalmatic, worn over the alb and stole. The dalmatic may, however, be omitted out of necessity or on account of a lesser degree of solemnity.

339. In the dioceses of the United States of America, acolytes, altar servers, lectors, and other lay ministers may wear the alb or other suitable vesture or other appropriate and dignified clothing.

340. The stole is worn by the priest around his neck and hanging down in front. It is worn by the deacon over his left shoulder and drawn diagonally across the chest to the right side, where it is fastened.

341. The cope is worn by the priest in processions and other sacred actions, in keeping with the rubrics proper to each rite.

342. Regarding the design of sacred vestments, Conferences of Bishops may determine and propose to the Apostolic See adaptations that correspond to the needs and the usages of their regions.[138]

343. In addition to the traditional materials, natural fabrics proper to each region may be used for making sacred vestments; artificial fabrics that are in

keeping with the dignity of the sacred action and the person wearing them may also be used. The Conference of Bishops will be the judge in this matter.[139]

344. It is fitting that the beauty and nobility of each vestment derive not from abundance of overly lavish ornamentation, but rather from the material that is used and from the design. Ornamentation on vestments should, moreover, consist of figures, that is, of images or symbols, that evoke sacred use, avoiding thereby anything unbecoming.

345. The purpose of a variety in the color of the sacred vestments is to give effective expression even outwardly to the specific character of the mysteries of faith being celebrated and to a sense of Christian life's passage through the course of the liturgical year.

346. As to the color of sacred vestments, the traditional usage is to be retained: namely,

   a. White is used in the Offices and Masses during the Easter and Christmas seasons; also on celebrations of the Lord other than of his Passion, of the Blessed Virgin Mary, of the Holy Angels, and of Saints who were not Martyrs; on the Solemnities of All Saints (1 November) and of the Nativity of Saint John the Baptist (24 June); and on the Feasts of Saint John the Evangelist (27 December), of the Chair of Saint Peter (22 February), and of the Conversion of Saint Paul (25 January).

   b. Red is used on Palm Sunday of the Lord's Passion and on Good Friday, on Pentecost Sunday, on celebrations of the Lord's Passion, on the feasts of the Apostles and Evangelists, and on celebrations of Martyr Saints.

   c. Green is used in the Offices and Masses of Ordinary Time.

   d. Violet or purple is used in Advent and of Lent. It may also be worn in Offices and Masses for the Dead (cf. below).

   e. Besides violet, white or black vestments may be worn at funeral services and at other Offices and Masses for the Dead in the dioceses of the United States of America.

   f. Rose may be used, where it is the practice, on *Gaudete* Sunday (Third Sunday of Advent) and on *Laetare* Sunday (Fourth Sunday of Lent).

   g. On more solemn days, sacred vestments may be used that are festive, that is, more precious, even if not of the color of the day.

   h. Gold or silver colored vestments may be worn on more solemn occasions in the dioceses of the United States of America.

347. Ritual Masses are celebrated in their proper color, in white, or in a festive color; Masses for Various Needs, on the other hand, are celebrated in the color proper to the day or the season or in violet if they are of a penitential character, for example, in the *Roman Missal*, no. 31 (in Time of War or Conflict), no. 33 (in

Time of Famine), or no. 38 (for the Forgiveness of Sins); Votive Masses are celebrated in the color suited to the Mass itself or even in the color proper to the day or the season.

V. OTHER THINGS INTENDED FOR CHURCH USE

348. Besides sacred vessels and sacred vestments for which some special material is prescribed, other furnishings that either are intended for strictly liturgical use[140] or are in any other way admitted into a church should be worthy and suited to their particular purpose.

349. In a special way, care must be taken that the liturgical books, particularly the *Book of the Gospels* and the Lectionary, which are intended for the proclamation of the word of God and hence enjoy special veneration, really serve in a liturgical action as signs and symbols of heavenly realities and hence are truly worthy, dignified, and beautiful.

350. Furthermore, great attention is to be paid whatever is directly associated with the altar and the eucharistic celebration, e.g., the altar cross and the cross carried in procession.

351. Every effort should be made to ensure that even as regards objects of lesser importance the canons of art be appropriately taken into account and that noble simplicity come together with elegance.

CHAPTER VII
THE CHOICE OF THE MASS AND ITS PARTS

352. The pastoral effectiveness of a celebration will be greatly increased if the texts of the readings, the prayers, and the liturgical songs correspond as closely as possible to the needs, spiritual preparation, and culture of those taking part. This is achieved by appropriate use of the wide options described below.

The priest, therefore, in planning the celebration of Mass, should have in mind the common spiritual good of the people of God, rather than his own inclinations. He should, moreover, remember that the selection of different parts is to be made in agreement with those who have some role in the celebration, including the faithful, in regard to the parts that more directly pertain to each.

Since, indeed, a variety of options is provided for the different parts of the Mass, it is necessary for the deacon, the lectors, the psalmist, the cantor, the commentator, and the choir to be completely sure before the celebration which text for which each is responsible is to be used and that nothing be improvised. Harmonious planning and carrying out of the rites will great assistance in disposing the faithful to participate in the Eucharist.

I. THE CHOICE OF MASS

353. On solemnities the priest is bound to follow the calendar of the church where he is celebrating.

354. On Sundays, on the weekdays of the Advent, Christmas, Lenten, and Easter Seasons, on feasts, and on obligatory memorials:

a. If Mass is celebrated with a congregation, the priest should follow the calendar of the church where he is celebrating;

b. If Mass is celebrated with the participation of one minister only, the priest may choose either the calendar of the church or his own proper calendar.

355. On optional memorials,

a. On the weekdays of Advent from 17 December to 24 December, on days within the Octave of Christmas, and on the weekdays of Lent, except Ash Wednesday and during Holy Week, the Mass for the current liturgical day is to be used; but the Collect may be taken from a memorial which happens to be listed in the General Calendar for that day, except on Ash Wednesday and during Holy Week. On weekdays of the Easter Season, memorials of Saints may rightly be celebrated fully.

b. On the weekdays of Advent before 17 December, the weekdays of the Christmas Season from 2 January, and the weekdays of the Easter Season, it is possible to choose either the weekday Mass, or the Mass of the Saint, or the Mass of one of the Saints whose memorial is observed, or the Mass of any Saint listed in the Martyrology for that day.

c. On the weekdays in Ordinary Time, it is possible to choose either a weekday Mass, or the Mass of an optional memorial which happens to occur on that day, or the Mass of any Saint listed in the Martyrology for that day, or a Mass for Various Needs, or a Votive Mass.

If he celebrates with a congregation, the priest will take care not to omit the readings assigned for each day in the Lectionary for weekdays too frequently and without sufficient reason, since the Church desires that a richer portion at the table of God's word be provided for the faithful.[141]

For the same reason he should use Masses for the Dead in moderation, since every Mass is offered for both the living and the dead, and there is a commemoration of the dead in the Eucharistic Prayer.

Where, however, the optional memorials of the Blessed Virgin Mary or of the Saints are dear to the faithful, the priest should satisfy their legitimate devotion.

When, on the other hand, the option is given of choosing between a memorial found in the General Calendar and one found in a diocesan or religious calendar, preference should be given, all things being equal and in keeping with tradition, to the memorial inscribed in the particular calendar.

II. THE CHOICE OF MASS TEXTS

356. In the choice of texts for the several parts of the Mass, whether of the Season or of the Saints, the following norms should be observed.

THE READINGS

357. For Sundays and solemnities, three readings are assigned: that is, from a Prophet, an Apostle, and a Gospel. By these the Christian people are brought to know the continuity of the work of salvation according to the God's wonderful plan. These readings should be followed strictly. During the Easter Season, according to the tradition of the Church, instead of the reading from the Old Testament, the reading is taken from the Acts of the Apostles.

For Feasts, on the other hand, two readings are assigned. If, however, according to the norms a feast is raised to the rank of a solemnity, a third reading is added, taken from the Common.

For memorials of Saints, unless strictly proper readings are given, the readings assigned for the weekday are customarily used. In certain cases, readings are provided that highlight some particular aspect of the spiritual life or activity of the Saint. The use of such readings is not to be insisted upon, unless a pastoral reason suggests it.

358. In the Lectionary for weekdays, readings are provided for each day of every week throughout the entire year; as a result, these readings are for the most part to be used on the days to which they are assigned, unless there occurs a solemnity, feast, or memorial that has its own proper New Testament readings, that is to say, readings in which mention is made of the Saint being celebrated.

If, however, the continuous reading during the week is interrupted by the occurrence of some solemnity or feast, or some particular celebration, then the priest, taking into consideration the entire week's scheme of readings, is allowed either to combine parts omitted with other readings or to decide which readings are to be preferred over others.

In Masses with special groups, the priest is allowed to choose texts more suited to the particular celebration, provided they are taken from the texts of an approved lectionary.

359. In addition, the Lectionary has a special selection of texts from Sacred Scripture for Ritual Masses into which certain Sacraments or Sacramentals are incorporated, or for Masses that are celebrated for certain needs.

Selections of readings of this kind have been established in this way, so that through a more apt hearing of the word of God the faithful may be led to a fuller understanding of the mystery in which they are participating and may be brought to a more ardent love of the word of God.

As a result, texts spoken in the celebration are to be chosen keeping in mind both a suitable pastoral reason and the options allowed in this matter.

360. At times, a longer and shorter form of the same text is given. In choosing between these two forms, a pastoral criterion must be kept in mind. At such times, attention should be paid to the capacity of the faithful to listen with understanding to a reading of greater or lesser length, and to their capacity to hear a more complete text, which is then explained in the homily.[142]

361. When a choice is allowed between alternative texts, whether they are fixed or optional, attention must be paid to what is in the best interests of those taking part, whether it is a matter of using the easier text or one more appropriate in a given group or of repeating or setting aside a text that is assigned as proper to some particular celebration while being optional for another,[143] as pastoral advantage may suggest.

Such a situation may arise when the same text would have to be read again within a few days, as, for example, on a Sunday and on a following weekday, or when it is feared that a certain text might create some difficulties for a particular group of the Christian faithful. Care should, however, be taken that, when choosing scriptural passages, parts of Sacred Scripture are not permanently excluded.

362. The adaptations to the *Ordo Lectionum Missae* as contained in the Lectionary for Mass for use in the dioceses of the United States of America should be carefully observed.

THE ORATIONS

363. In any Mass the orations proper to that Mass are used, unless otherwise noted.

On memorials of Saints, the collect proper to the day is used or, if none is available, one from an appropriate Common. The prayer over the offerings, however, and the prayer after Communion, unless they are proper, may be taken either from the Common or from the weekdays of the current Season.

On the weekdays in Ordinary Time, however, besides the orations from the previous Sunday, orations from another Sunday in Ordinary Time may be used, or one of the prayers for various needs provided in the Missal. It is always permissible, however, to use the collect alone from these Masses.

In this way a richer collection of texts is available, by which the prayer life of the faithful is more abundantly nourished.

During the more important seasons of the year, however, the proper seasonal orations appointed for each weekday in the Missal already make provision for this.

364. The purpose of the many prefaces that enrich the *Roman Missal* is to bring out more fully the motives for thanksgiving within the Eucharistic Prayer and to set out more clearly the different facets of the mystery of salvation.

365. The choice among the Eucharistic Prayers found in the Order of Mass is suitably guided by the following norms:

a. Eucharistic Prayer I, that is, the Roman Canon, which may always be used, is especially suited to be sung or said on days when there is a proper text for the *Communicantes* (*In union with the whole Church*) or in Masses endowed with a proper form of the *Hanc igitur* (*Father, accept this offering*) and also in the celebrations of the Apostles and of the Saints mentioned in the Prayer itself; it is likewise especially appropriate for Sundays, unless for pastoral considerations Eucharistic Prayer III is preferred.

b. Eucharistic Prayer II, on account of its particular features, is more appropriately used on weekdays or in special circumstances. Although it has been provided with its own Preface, it may also be used with other Prefaces, especially those that summarize the mystery of salvation, such as the common Prefaces. When Mass is celebrated for a particular dead person, the special formula may be inserted in the place indicated, namely, before the *Memento etiam* (*Remember our brothers and sisters*).

c. Eucharistic Prayer III may be said with any Preface. Its use is preferred on Sundays and feast days. If, however, this Eucharistic Prayer is used in Masses for the Dead, the special formula for the dead may be used, to be included at the proper place, namely, after the *Omnes filios tuos ubique dispersos, tibi, clemens Pater, miseratus coniunge* (*In mercy and love unite all your children*).

d. Eucharistic Prayer IV has an invariable Preface and gives a fuller summary of salvation history. It may be used when a Mass has no Preface of its own and on Sundays in Ordinary Time. Because of its structure, no special formula for the dead may be inserted into this prayer.

THE CHANTS

366. It is not permitted to substitute other chants for those found in the Order of Mass, such as at the *Agnus Dei*.

367. The norms laid down in their proper places are to be observed for the choice of the chants between the readings, as well as of the chants at the entrance, at the offertory, and at Communion (cf. above, nos. 40–41, 47–48, 61–64, 74, 86–88).

CHAPTER VIII
MASSES AND PRAYERS FOR VARIOUS CIRCUMSTANCES AND MASSES FOR THE DEAD

I. MASSES AND PRAYERS FOR VARIOUS CIRCUMSTANCES

368. Since the liturgy of the Sacraments and Sacramentals causes, for the faithful who are properly disposed, almost every event in life to be sanctified by divine grace that flows from the paschal mystery,[144] and because the Eucharist is the Sacrament of Sacraments, the Missal provides formularies for Masses and orations that may be used in the various circumstances of Christian life, for the needs of the whole world or for the needs of the Church, whether universal or local.

369. In view of the rather broad range of choice among the readings and orations, it is best if Masses for various circumstances be used in moderation, that is, when the occasion truly requires.

370. In all the Masses for various circumstances, unless otherwise expressly indicated, it is permissible to use the weekday readings and also the chants between them, if they are suited to the celebration.

371. Among Masses of this kind are included Ritual Masses, Masses for Various Needs, Masses for Various Circumstances, and Votive Masses.

372. Ritual Masses are connected to the celebration of certain Sacraments or Sacramentals. They are prohibited on Sundays of Advent, Lent, and Easter, on solemnities, on the days within the Octave of Easter, on the Commemoration of All the Faithful Departed (All Souls' Day), on Ash Wednesday, and during Holy Week, taking due account of the norms given in the ritual books or in the Masses themselves.

373. Masses for Various Needs or Masses for Various Circumstances are used in certain situations either as matters arise or at fixed times.

Days or periods of prayer for the fruits of the earth, prayer for human rights and equality, prayer for world justice and peace, and penitential observances outside Lent are to be observed in the dioceses of the United States of America at times to be designated by the diocesan Bishop.

In all the dioceses of the United States of America, January 22 (or January 23, when January 22 falls on a Sunday) shall be observed as a particular day of penance for violations to the dignity of the human person committed through acts of abortion, and of prayer for the full restoration of the legal guarantee of the right to life. The Mass "For Peace and Justice" (no. 21 of the "Masses for Various Needs") should be celebrated with violet vestments as an appropriate liturgical observance for this day.

374. In cases of serious need or pastoral advantage, at the direction of the diocesan Bishop or with his permission, an appropriate Mass may be celebrated on any day except solemnities, the Sundays of Advent, Lent, and Easter, days within the Octave of Easter, the Commemoration of All the Faithful Departed (All Souls' Day), Ash Wednesday, and Holy Week.

375. Votive Masses of the mysteries of the Lord or in honor of the Blessed Virgin Mary or of the Angels or of any given Saint or of all the Saints may be said for the sake of the faithful's devotion on weekdays in Ordinary Time, even if an optional memorial occurs. It is not, however, allowed to celebrate as Votive Masses, those that refer to mysteries related to events in the life of the Lord or of the Blessed Virgin Mary, with the exception of the Mass of the Immaculate Conception, since their celebration is an integral part of the unfolding of the liturgical year.

376. On obligatory memorials, on the weekdays of Advent up to and including December 16, of the Christmas Season from January 2, and of the Easter Season after the Octave of Easter, Masses for Various Needs, Masses for Various Circumstances, and Votive Masses are as such forbidden. If, however, required by some real need or pastoral advantage, according to the judgment of the rector of the church or the priest celebrant himself, a Mass corresponding to such a need or advantage may be used in a celebration with a congregation.

377. On weekdays in Ordinary Time when there is an optional memorial or the Office is of the weekday, it is permissible to use any Mass or oration for various circumstances, though not from the Ritual Masses.

378. It is especially recommended to celebrate commemoration of the Blessed Virgin Mary on Saturday, because it is to the Mother of the Redeemer in the Liturgy of the Church that in the first place and before all the Saints veneration is given.[145]

II. MASSES FOR THE DEAD

379. The Church offers the Eucharistic Sacrifice of Christ's Passover for the dead so that, since all the members of Christ's body are in communion with each other, the petition for spiritual help on behalf of some may bring comforting hope to others.

380. Among the Masses for the Dead, the Funeral Mass holds first place. It may be celebrated on any day except for Solemnities that are holy days of obligation, Holy Thursday, the Easter Triduum, and the Sundays of Advent, Lent, and Easter, with due regard also for all the other requirements of the norm of the law.[146]

381. A Mass for the Dead may be celebrated on receiving the news of a death, for the final burial, or the first anniversary, even on days within the Octave of Christmas, on obligatory Memorials, and on weekdays, except for Ash Wednesday or weekdays during Holy Week.

Other Masses for the Dead, that is, "daily" Masses, may be celebrated on weekdays in Ordinary Time on which optional memorials occur or when the Office is of the weekday, provided such Masses are actually applied for the dead.

382. At the Funeral Mass there should, as a rule, be a short homily, but never a eulogy of any kind.

383. The faithful, and especially the family of the deceased, should be urged to participate in the Eucharistic Sacrifice offered for the deceased person also by receiving Holy Communion.

384. If the Funeral Mass is directly joined to the burial rite, once the prayer after Communion has been said and omitting the concluding rite, the rite of final commendation or farewell takes place. This rite is celebrated only if the body is present.

385. In the arranging and choosing of the variable parts of the Mass for the Dead, especially the Funeral Mass (e.g., orations, readings, Prayer of the Faithful), pastoral considerations bearing upon the deceased, the family, and those attending should rightly be taken into account.

Pastors should, moreover, take into special account those who are present at a liturgical celebration or who hear the Gospel on the occasion of the funeral and who may be non-Catholics or Catholics who never or rarely participate in the Eucharist or who seem even to have lost the faith. For priests are ministers of Christ's Gospel for all.

CHAPTER IX
ADAPTATIONS WITHIN THE COMPETENCE OF BISHOPS AND BISHOPS' CONFERENCES

386. The renewal of the *Roman Missal,* carried out in our time in accordance with the decrees of the Second Vatican Ecumenical Council, has taken great care that all the faithful may engage in the celebration of the Eucharist with that full, conscious, and active participation that is required by the nature of the Liturgy itself and to which the faithful, in virtue of their status as such, have a right and duty.[147]

In order, however, to enable such a celebration to correspond all the more fully to the norms and the spirit of the sacred Liturgy, certain further adaptations are set forth in this Instruction and in the Order of Mass and entrusted to the judgment either of the diocesan Bishop or of the Bishops' Conferences.

387. The diocesan Bishop, who is to be regarded as the high priest of his flock, and from whom the life in Christ of the faithful under his care in a certain sense derives and upon whom it depends,[148] must promote, regulate, and be vigilant over the liturgical life in his diocese. It is to him that in this Instruction is entrusted the regulating of the discipline of concelebration (cf. above, nos. 202, 374) and the establishing of norms regarding the function of serving the priest

at the altar (cf. above, no. 107), the distribution of Holy Communion under both kinds (cf. above, no. 283), and the construction and ordering of churches (cf. above, no. 291). With him lies responsibility above all for fostering the spirit of the sacred Liturgy in the priests, deacons, and faithful.

388. The adaptations spoken of below that call for a wider degree of coordination are to be decided, in accord with the norm of law, by the Conference of Bishops.

389. It is the competence of the Conferences of Bishops in the first place to prepare and approve an edition of this *Roman Missal* in the authorized vernacular languages, for use in the regions under their care, once their decisions have been accorded the recognitio of the Apostolic See.[149]

The *Roman Missal*, whether in Latin or in lawfully approved vernacular translations, is to be published in its entirety.

390. It is up to the Conferences of Bishops to decide on the adaptations indicated in this General Instruction and in the Order of Mass and, once their decisions have been accorded the recognitio of the Apostolic See, to introduce them into the Missal itself. These adaptations include

—The gestures and posture of the faithful (cf. no. 43 above);

—The gestures of veneration toward the altar and the *Book of the Gospels* (cf. no. 273 above);

—The texts of the chants at the entrance, at the presentation of the gifts, and at Communion (cf. nos. 48, 74, 87 above);

—The readings from Sacred Scripture to be used in special circumstances (cf. no. 362 above);

—The form of the gesture of peace (cf. no. 82 above);

—The manner of receiving Holy Communion (cf. nos. 160, 283 above);

—The materials for the altar and sacred furnishings, especially the sacred vessels, and also the materials, form, and color of the liturgical vestments (cf. nos. 301, 326, 329, 339, 342–346 above).

Directories or pastoral instructions that the Conferences of Bishops judge useful may, with the prior *recognitio* of the Apostolic See, be included in the *Roman Missal* at an appropriate place.

391. It is up to the Conferences of Bishops to provide for the translations of the biblical texts used in the celebration of Mass, exercising special care in this. For it is out of the Sacred Scripture that the readings are read and explained in the homily and that psalms are sung, and it is drawing upon the inspiration and spirit of Sacred Scripture that prayers, orations, and liturgical songs are fashioned in such a way that from them actions and signs derive their meaning.[150]

Language should be used that can be grasped by the faithful and that is suitable for public proclamation, while maintaining those characteristics that are proper to the different ways of speaking used in the biblical books.

392. It will also be up to the Conferences of Bishops to prepare, by means of careful study, a translation of the other texts, so that, even though the character of each language is respected, the meaning of the original Latin text is fully and faithfully rendered. In accomplishing this task, it is expedient to take account of the different literary genres used at Mass, such as the presidential prayers, the antiphons, the acclamations, the responses, the litanies of supplication, and so on.

It should be borne in mind that the primary purpose of the translation of the texts is not with a view to meditation, but rather that they be proclaimed or sung during an actual celebration.

Language should be used that is accommodated to the faithful of the region, but is noble and marked by literary quality, and there will always remain the need for some catechesis on the biblical and Christian meaning of certain words and expressions.

It is, indeed, of advantage that in regions using the same language, the same translation be used whenever possible for liturgical texts, especially for biblical texts and for the Order of Mass.[151]

393. Bearing in mind the important place that singing has in a celebration as a necessary or integral part of the Liturgy,[152] all musical settings of the texts for the people's responses and acclamations in the Order of Mass and for special rites that occur in the course of the liturgical year must be submitted to the Secretariat for the Liturgy of the United States Conference of Catholic Bishops for review and approval prior to publication.

While the organ is to be accorded pride of place, other wind, stringed, or percussion instruments may be used in liturgical services in the dioceses of the United States of America, according to longstanding local usage, provided they are truly apt for sacred use or can be rendered apt.

394. Each diocese should have its own Calendar and Proper of Masses. For its part, the of Bishops' Conference should draw up a proper calendar for the nation or, together with other Conferences, a calendar for a wider territory, to be approved by the Apostolic See.[153]

In carrying this out, to the greatest extent possible the Lord's Day is to be preserved and safeguarded, as the primordial holy day, and hence other celebrations, unless they be truly of the greatest importance, should not have precedence over it.[154] Care should likewise be taken that the liturgical year as revised by decree of the Second Vatican Council not be obscured by secondary elements.

In the drawing up of the calendar of a nation, the Rogation and Ember Days should be indicated (cf. above, no. 373), as well as the forms and texts for their celebration,[155] and other special measures should also be taken into consideration.

It is appropriate that in publishing the Missal, celebrations proper to an entire nation or territory be inserted at the correct place among the celebrations of the General Calendar, while those proper to a region or diocese be placed in a special appendix.

395. Finally, if the participation of the faithful and their spiritual welfare requires variations and more thoroughgoing adaptations in order that the sacred celebration respond to the culture and traditions of the different peoples, then Bishops' Conferences may propose such to the Apostolic See in accordance with article 40 of the *Constitution on the Sacred Liturgy* for introduction with the latter's consent, especially in the case of peoples to whom the Gospel has been more recently proclaimed.[156] The special norms given in the *Instruction On the Roman Liturgy and Inculturation*[157] should be carefully observed.

Regarding procedures to be followed in this matter, the following should be followed:

In the first place, a detailed preliminary proposal should be set before the Apostolic See, so that, after the necessary faculty has been granted, the detailed working out of the individual points of adaptation may proceed.

Once these proposals have been duly approved by the Apostolic See, experiments should be carried out for specified periods and at specified places. If need be, once the period of experimentation is concluded, the Bishops' Conference shall decide upon pursuing the adaptations and shall propose a mature formulation of the matter to the Apostolic See for its decision.[158]

396. Before, however, proceeding to new adaptations, especially those more thoroughgoing, great care should be taken to promote the proper instruction of clergy and faithful in a wise and orderly fashion, so as to take advantage of the faculties already foreseen and to implement fully the pastoral norms concerning the spirit of a celebration.

397. Furthermore, the principle shall be respected according to which each particular Church must be in accord with the universal Church not only regarding the doctrine of the faith and sacramental signs, but also as to the usages universally handed down by apostolic and unbroken tradition. These are to be maintained not only so that errors may be avoided, but also so that the faith may be passed on in its integrity, since the Church's rule of prayer (*lex orandi*) corresponds to her rule of belief (*lex credendi*).[159]

The Roman Rite constitutes a notable and precious part of the liturgical treasure and patrimony of the Catholic Church. Its riches are of benefit to the universal Church, so that were they to be lost, the Church would be seriously harmed.

Throughout the ages, the Roman Rite has not only preserved the liturgical usages that arose in the city of Rome but has also in a deep, organic, and harmonious way incorporated into itself certain other usages derived from the customs and culture of different peoples and of various particular Churches of both West and East, so that in this way, the Roman Rite has acquired a certain supraregional character. In our own times, on the other hand, the identity and unitary expression of this Rite is found in the typical editions of the liturgical books promulgated by authority of the Supreme Pontiff, and in those liturgical books corresponding to them approved by the Bishops' Conferences for their territories with the recognitio of the Apostolic See.[160]

398. The norm established by the Second Vatican Council—that in the liturgical reform there should be no innovations unless required in order to bring a genuine and certain benefit to the Church, and taking care that any new forms adopted should in some way grow organically from forms already existing[161]— must also be applied to efforts at the inculturation of the same Roman Rite.[162] Inculturation, moreover, requires a necessary length of time, lest the authentic liturgical tradition suffer contamination due to haste and a lack of caution.

Finally, the purpose of pursuing inculturation is not in any way the creation of new families of rites, but aims rather at meeting the needs of a particular culture in such a way that adaptations introduced either in the Missal or in combination with other liturgical books are not at variance with the distinctive character of the Roman Rite.[163]

399. And so, the *Roman Missal*, even if in different languages and with some variety of customs,[164] must be preserved in the future as an instrument and an outstanding sign of the integrity and unity of the Roman Rite.[164]

ENDNOTES

1. Ecumenical Council of Trent, Session 22, *Doctrina de ss. Missae sacrificio*, 17 September 1562: *Enchiridion Symbolorum*, H. Denzinger and A. Schönmetzer, editors (editio XXXIII, Freiburg: Herder, 1965; hereafter, Denz-Schön), 1738–1759.

2. Second Vatican Ecumenical Council, Constitution on the Sacred Liturgy, *Sacrosanctum Concilium*, no. 47; cf. Second Vatican Ecumenical Council, Dogmatic Constitution on the Church, *Lumen gentium,*, nos. 3, 28; Second Vatican Ecumenical Council, Decree on the Ministry and Life of Priests, *Presbyterorum ordinis*, nos. 2, 4, 5.

3. Evening Mass of the Lord's Supper, prayer over the offerings. Cf. *Sacramentarium Veronense*, L.C. Mohlberg et al., editors, (3rd edition, Rome, 1978), section I, no. 93.

4. Cf. Eucharistic Prayer III.

5. Cf. Eucharistic Prayer IV.

6. Second Vatican Ecumenical Council, Constitution on the Sacred Liturgy, *Sacrosanctum Concilium*, nos. 7, 47; Decree on the Ministry and Life of Priests, *Presbyterorum ordinis*, nos. 5, 18.

7. Cf. Pius XII, Encyclical Letter *Humani generis*, 12 August 1950: *Acta Apostolicae Sedis, Commentarium Officiale* (Vatican City; hereafter, AAS), 42 (1950), pp. 570–571; Paul VI, Encyclical Letter *Mysterium fidei*, On the doctrine and worship of the Eucharist, 3 September 1965: AAS 57 (1965), pp. 762–769; Paul VI, Solemn Profession of Faith, 30 June 1968, nos. 24–26: AAS 60 (1968), pp. 442–443; Sacred Congregation of Rites, Instruction *Eucharisticum mysterium*, On the worship of the Eucharist, 25 May 1967, nos. 3f, 9: AAS 59 (1967), pp. 543, 547.

8. Cf. Council of Trent, session 13, *Decretum de ss. Eucharistia*, 11 October 1551: Denz-Schön, 1635–1661.

9. Cf. Second Vatican Ecumenical Council, Decree on the Ministry and Life of Priests, *Presbyterorum ordinis*, no. 2.

10. Cf. Second Vatican Ecumenical Council, Constitution on the Sacred Liturgy, *Sacrosanctum Concilium*, no. 11.

11. Second Vatican Ecumenical Council, Constitution on the Sacred Liturgy, *Sacrosanctum Concilium*, no. 50.

12. Ecumenical Council of Trent, Session 22, *Doctrina de ss. Missae sacrificio*, 17 September 1562, chapter 8: Denz-Schön, 1749.

13. Ecumenical Council of Trent, Session 22, *Doctrina de ss. Missae sacrificio*, 17 September 1562, chapter 9: Denz-Schön, 1759.

14. Ecumenical Council of Trent, Session 22, *Doctrina de ss. Missae sacrificio*, 17 September 1562, chapter 8: Denz-Schön, 1749.

15. Cf. Second Vatican Ecumenical Council, Constitution on the Sacred Liturgy, *Sacrosanctum Concilium*, no. 33.

16. Cf. Second Vatican Ecumenical Council, Constitution on the Sacred Liturgy, *Sacrosanctum Concilium*, no. 36.

17. Cf. Second Vatican Ecumenical Council, Constitution on the Sacred Liturgy, *Sacrosanctum Concilium*, no. 52.

18. Cf. Second Vatican Ecumenical Council, Constitution on the Sacred Liturgy, *Sacrosanctum Concilium*, no. 35:3.

19. Second Vatican Ecumenical Council, Constitution on the Sacred Liturgy, *Sacrosanctum Concilium*, no. 55.

20. Ecumenical Council of Trent, Session 22, *Doctrina de ss. Missae sacrificio*, 17 September 1562, chapter 6: Denz-Schön, 1747.

21. Cf. Second Vatican Ecumenical Council, Constitution on the Sacred Liturgy, *Sacrosanctum Concilium*, no. 55.

22. Cf. Second Vatican Ecumenical Council, Constitution on the Sacred Liturgy, *Sacrosanctum Concilium*, no. 41; Dogmatic Constitution on the Church, *Lumen gentium*, no. 11; Decree on the Ministry and Life of Priests, *Presbyterorum ordinis*, nos. 2, 5, 6; Decree on the Pastoral Office of Bishops, *Christus Dominus*, 28 October 1965 , no. 30; Second Vatican Ecumenical

Council, Decree on Ecumenism, *Unitatis redintegratio*, 21 November 1964, no. 15; Sacred Congregation of Rites, Instruction *Eucharisticum mysterium*, On the worship of the Eucharist, 25 May 1967, nos. 3e, 6: AAS 59 (1967), pp. 542, 544–545.

23. Cf. Second Vatican Ecumenical Council, Constitution on the Sacred Liturgy, *Sacrosanctum Concilium*, no. 10.

24. Cf. Second Vatican Ecumenical Council, Constitution on the Sacred Liturgy, *Sacrosanctum Concilium*, no. 102.

25. Cf. Second Vatican Ecumenical Council, Constitution on the Sacred Liturgy, *Sacrosanctum Concilium*, no. 10; cf. Decree on the Ministry and Life of Priests, *Presbyterorum ordinis*, no. 5.

26. Cf. Second Vatican Ecumenical Council, Constitution on the Sacred Liturgy, *Sacrosanctum Concilium*, nos. 14, 19, 26, 28, 30.

27. Cf. Second Vatican Ecumenical Council, Constitution on the Sacred Liturgy, *Sacrosanctum Concilium*, no. 47.

28. Cf. Second Vatican Ecumenical Council, Constitution on the Sacred Liturgy, *Sacrosanctum Concilium*, no. 14.

29. Cf. Second Vatican Ecumenical Council, Constitution on the Sacred Liturgy, *Sacrosanctum Concilium*, no. 41.

30. Cf. Second Vatican Ecumenical Council, Decree on the Ministry and Life of Priests, *Presbyterorum ordinis*, no. 13; *Codex Iuris Canonici*, can. 904.

31. Cf. Second Vatican Ecumenical Council, Constitution on the Sacred Liturgy, *Sacrosanctum Concilium*, no. 59.

32. Special celebrations of Mass should observe the guidelines established for them: For Masses with special groups, cf. Sacred Congregation for Divine Worship, Instruction *Actio pastoralis*, on Masses with special groups, 15 May 1969: AAS 61 (1969), pp. 806–811; for Masses with children, cf. Sacred Congregation for Divine Worship, *Directory for Masses with Children*, 1 November 1973: AAS 66 (1974), pp. 30–46; for the manner of joining the Hours of the Office with the Mass, cf. Sacred Congregation for Divine Worship, General Instruction of the Liturgy of the Hours, *editio typica*, 11 April 1971, *editio typica altera*, 7 April

1985, nos. 93–98; for the manner of joining certain blessings and the crowning of an image of the Blessed Virgin Mary with the Mass, cf. The Roman Ritual, *Book of Blessings, editio typica*, 1984, Introduction, no. 28; *Order of Crowning an Image of the Blessed Virgin Mary, editio typica*, 1981, nos. 10 and 14.

33. Cf. Second Vatican Ecumenical Council, Decree on the Pastoral Office of Bishops, *Christus Dominus*, no. 15; cf. also Constitution on the Sacred Liturgy, *Sacrosanctum Concilium*, no. 41.

34. Cf. Second Vatican Ecumenical Council, Constitution on the Sacred Liturgy, *Sacrosanctum Concilium*, no. 22.

35. Cf. also Second Vatican Ecumenical Council, Constitution on the Sacred Liturgy, *Sacrosanctum Concilium*, nos 38, 40; Paul VI, Apostolic Constitution *Missale Romanum*, above.

36. Congregation for Divine Worship and the Discipline of the Sacraments, Instruction *Varietates legitimae*, 25 January 1994: AAS 87 (1995), pp. 288–314.

37. Cf. Second Vatican Ecumenical Council, Decree on the Ministry and Life of Priests, *Presbyterorum ordinis*, no. 5; Constitution on the Sacred Liturgy, *Sacrosanctum Concilium*, no. 33.

38. Cf. Ecumenical Council of Trent, Session 22, *Doctrina de ss. Missae sacrificio*, 17 September 1562, chapter 1: Denz-Schön, 1740; Paul VI, Solemn Profession of Faith, 30 June 1968, no. 24: AAS 60 (1968), p. 442.

39. Cf. Second Vatican Ecumenical Council, Constitution on the Sacred Liturgy, *Sacrosanctum Concilium*, no. 7; Paul VI, Encyclical Letter *Mysterium fidei*, On the doctrine and worship of the Eucharist, 3 September 1965: AAS 57 (1965), p. 764; Sacred Congregation of Rites, Instruction *Eucharisticum mysterium*, On the worship of the Eucharist, 25 May 1967, no. 9: AAS 59 (1967), p. 547.

40. Cf. Second Vatican Ecumenical Council, Constitution on the Sacred Liturgy, *Sacrosanctum Concilium*, no. 56; Sacred Congregation of Rites, Instruction *Eucharisticum mysterium*, On the worship of the Eucharist, 25 May 1967, no. 3: AAS 59 (1967), p. 542.

41. Cf. Second Vatican Ecumenical Council, Constitution on the Sacred Liturgy, *Sacrosanctum Concilium*, nos. 48, 51; Second Vatican Ecumenical Council, Dogmatic Constitution on Divine Revelation, *Dei Verbum*, 18 November 1965, no. 21; Decree on the Ministry and Life of Priests, *Presbyterorum ordinis*, no. 4.

42. Cf. Second Vatican Ecumenical Council, Constitution on the Sacred Liturgy, *Sacrosanctum Concilium*, nos. 7, 33, 52.

43. Cf. Second Vatican Ecumenical Council, Constitution on the Sacred Liturgy, *Sacrosanctum Concilium*, no. 33.

44. Cf. Sacred Congregation of Rites, Instruction *Musicam sacram*, On music in the Liturgy, 5 March 1967, no. 14: AAS 59 (1967), p. 304.

45. Cf. Second Vatican Ecumenical Council, Constitution on the Sacred Liturgy, *Sacrosanctum Concilium*, nos. 26–27; Sacred Congregation of Rites, Instruction *Eucharisticum mysterium*, On the worship of the Eucharist, 25 May 1967, no. 3d: AAS 59 (1967), p. 542.

46. Cf. Second Vatican Ecumenical Council, Constitution on the Sacred Liturgy, *Sacrosanctum Concilium*, no. 30.

47. Cf. Sacred Congregation of Rites, Instruction *Musicam sacram*, On music in the Liturgy, 5 March 1967, no. 16a: AAS 59 (1967), p. 305.

48. Saint Augustine of Hippo, Sermo 336, 1: *Patrologiae cursus completus: Series latina*, J. P. Migne, editor, Paris, 1844–1855, 38, 1472.

49. Cf. Sacred Congregation of Rites, Instruction *Musicam sacram*, On music in the Liturgy, 5 March 1967, nos. 7, 16: AAS 59 (1967), pp. 302, 305.

50. Cf. Second Vatican Ecumenical Council, Constitution on the Sacred Liturgy, *Sacrosanctum Concilium*, no. 116; cf. also Sacred Congregation of Rites, Instruction *Musicam sacram*, On music in the Liturgy, 5 March 1967, no. 30.

51. Cf. Second Vatican Ecumenical Council, Constitution on the Sacred Liturgy, *Sacrosanctum Concilium*, no. 54; Sacred Congregation of Rites, Instruction *Inter Oecumenici*, on the orderly carrying out of the Constitution on the Sacred Liturgy, 26 September 1964, no. 59: AAS 56 (1964), p. 891; Sacred Congregation of Rites, Instruction *Musicam sacram*, On music in the Liturgy, 5 March 1967, no. 47: AAS 59 (1967), p. 314.

52. Cf. Second Vatican Ecumenical Council, Constitution on the Sacred Liturgy, *Sacrosanctum Concilium*, nos. 30, 34; cf. also Sacred Congregation of Rites, Instruction *Musicam sacram*, On music in the Liturgy, 5 March 1967, no. 21.

53. Cf. Second Vatican Ecumenical Council, Constitution on the Sacred Liturgy, *Sacrosanctum Concilium*, no. 40; Congregation for Divine Worship and the Discipline of the Sacraments, Instruction *Varietates legitimae*, 25 January 1994, no. 41: AAS 87 (1995), p. 304.

54. Cf. Second Vatican Ecumenical Council, Constitution on the Sacred Liturgy, *Sacrosanctum Concilium*, no. 30; Sacred Congregation of Rites, Instruction *Musicam sacram*, On music in the Liturgy, 5 March 1967, no. 17: AAS 59 (1967), p. 305.

55. Cf. John Paul II, Apostolic Letter *Dies Domini*, 31 May 1998, no. 50: AAS 90 (1998), p. 745.

56. Cf. below, pp. 1249–1252.

57. Cf. Tertullian, *Adversus Marcionem*, IV, 9: *Corpus Christianorum, Series latina*, Turnhout, Belgium, 1953– (hereafter, CCSL), 1, p. 560. PL 2, 376A; Origen, *Disputatio cum Heracleida*, no. 4, 24: Sources chrétiennes, H. deLubac et al., ed. (Paris, 1941–), p. 62; *Statuta Concilii Hipponensis Breviata*, 21: CCSL 149, p. 39.

58. Cf. Second Vatican Ecumenical Council, Constitution on the Sacred Liturgy, *Sacrosanctum Concilium*, no. 33.

59. Cf. Second Vatican Ecumenical Council, Constitution on the Sacred Liturgy, *Sacrosanctum Concilium*, no. 7.

60. Cf. The Roman Missal, *Lectionary for Mass, editio typica altera*, 1981, Introduction, no. 28.

61. Cf. Second Vatican Ecumenical Council, Constitution on the Sacred Liturgy, *Sacrosanctum Concilium*, no. 51.

62. Cf. John Paul II, Apostolic Letter *Vicesimus quintus annus*, 4 December 1988, no. 13: AAS 81 (1989), p. 910.

63. Cf. Second Vatican Ecumenical Council, Constitution on the Sacred Liturgy, *Sacrosanctum Concilium*, no. 52; Codex Iuris Canonici, can. 767 § 1.

64. Cf. Sacred Congregation of Rites, Instruction *Inter Oecumenici*, on the orderly carrying out of the Constitution on the Sacred Liturgy, 26 September 1964, no. 54: AAS 56 (1964), p. 890.

65. Cf. *Codex Iuris Canonici*, can. 767 ? 1; Pontifical Commission for the Authentic Interpretation of the Code of Canon Law, response to *dubium* regarding can. 767 § 1: AAS 79 (1987), p. 1249; Interdicasterial Instruction on certain questions regarding the collaboration of the non-ordained faithful in the sacred ministry of priests, *Ecclesiae de mysterio*, 15 August 1997, art. 3: AAS 89 (1997), p. 864.

66. Cf. Sacred Congregation of Rites, Instruction *Inter Oecumenici*, on the orderly carrying out of the Constitution on the Sacred Liturgy, 26 September 1964, no. 53: AAS 56 (1964), p. 890.

67. Cf. Second Vatican Ecumenical Council, Constitution on the Sacred Liturgy, *Sacrosanctum Concilium*, no. 53.

68. Cf. Sacred Congregation of Rites, Instruction Inter Oecumenici, on the orderly carrying out of the Constitution on the Sacred Liturgy, 26 September 1964, no. 56: AAS 56 (1964), p. 890.

69. Cf. Second Vatican Ecumenical Council, Constitution on the Sacred Liturgy, *Sacrosanctum Concilium*, no. 47; Sacred Congregation of Rites, Instruction Eucharisticum mysterium, On the worship of the Eucharist, 25 May 1967, no. 3a, b: AAS 59 (1967), pp. 540–541.

70. Cf. Sacred Congregation of Rites, Instruction *Inter Oecumenici*, on the orderly carrying out of the Constitution on the Sacred Liturgy, 26 September 1964, no. 91: AAS 56 (1964), p. 898; Sacred Congregation of Rites, Instruction Eucharisticum mysterium, On the worship of the Eucharist, 25 May 1967, no. 24: AAS 59 (1967), p. 554.

71. Cf. Second Vatican Ecumenical Council, Constitution on the Sacred Liturgy, *Sacrosanctum Concilium*, no. 48; Sacred Congregation of Rites, Instruction Eucharisticum mysterium, On the worship of the Eucharist, 25 May 1967, no. 12: AAS 59 (1967), pp. 548–549.

72. Cf. Second Vatican Ecumenical Council, Constitution on the Sacred Liturgy, *Sacrosanctum Concilium*, no. 48; Decree on the Ministry and Life of Priests, *Presbyterorum ordinis*, no. 5; Sacred Congregation of Rites, Instruction *Eucharisticum mysterium*, On the worship of the Eucharist, 25 May 1967, no. 12: AAS 59 (1967), pp. 548–549.

73. Cf. Sacred Congregation of Rites, Instruction *Eucharisticum mysterium*, On the worship of the Eucharist, 25 May 1967, nos. 31, 32; Sacred Congregation for the Discipline of the Sacraments, Instruction *Immensae caritatis*, 29 January 1973, no. 2: AAS 65 (1973), pp. 267–268.

74. Cf. Sacred Congregation for the Sacraments and Divine Worship, Instruction *Inaestimabile donum*, 3 April 1980, no. 17: AAS 72 (1980), p. 338.

75. Cf. Second Vatican Ecumenical Council, Constitution on the Sacred Liturgy, *Sacrosanctum Concilium*, no. 26.

76. Cf. Second Vatican Ecumenical Council, Constitution on the Sacred Liturgy, *Sacrosanctum Concilium*, no. 14.

77. Cf. Second Vatican Ecumenical Council, Constitution on the Sacred Liturgy, *Sacrosanctum Concilium*, no. 28.

78. Cf. Second Vatican Ecumenical Council, Dogmatic Constitution on the Church, *Lumen gentium*, nos. 26, 28; Constitution on the Sacred Liturgy, *Sacrosanctum Concilium*, no. 42.

79. Cf. Second Vatican Ecumenical Council, Constitution on the Sacred Liturgy, *Sacrosanctum Concilium*, no. 26.

80. Cf. *Caeremoniale Episcoporum, editio typica*, 1984, nos. 175–186.

81. Cf. Second Vatican Ecumenical Council, Dogmatic Constitution on the Church, *Lumen gentium*, no. 28; Decree on the Ministry and Life of Priests, *Presbyterorum ordinis*, no. 2.

82. Cf. Paul VI, Apostolic Letter Sacrum *diaconatus ordinem*, 18 June 1967: AAS 59 (1967), pp. 697–704; The Roman Pontifical, Rites of Ordination of a Bishop, of Priests, and of Deacons, *editio typica altera*, 1989, no. 173.

83. Cf. Second Vatican Ecumenical Council, Constitution on the Sacred Liturgy, *Sacrosanctum Concilium*, no. 48; Sacred Congregation of Rites, Instruction *Eucharisticum mysterium*, On the worship of the Eucharist, 25 May 1967, no. 12: AAS 59 (1967), pp. 548–549.

84. Cf. *Codex Iuris Canonici*, can. 910 § 2; cf. also Interdicasterial Instruction on certain questions regarding the collaboration of the non-ordained faithful in the sacred ministry of priests, *Ecclesiae de mysterio*, 15 August 1997, art. 8: AAS 89 (1997), p. 871.

85. Cf. Sacred Congregation for the Discipline of the Sacraments, Instruction *Immensae caritatis*, 29 January 1973, no. 1: AAS 65 (1973), pp. 265–266; *Codex Iuris Canonici*, can. 230 § 3.

86. Cf. Second Vatican Ecumenical Council, Constitution on the Sacred Liturgy, *Sacrosanctum Concilium*, no. 24.

87. Cf. Sacred Congregation of Rites, Instruction *Musicam sacram*, On music in the Liturgy, 5 March 1967, no. 19: AAS 59 (1967), p. 306.

88. Cf. Sacred Congregation of Rites, Instruction *Musicam sacram*, On music in the Liturgy, 5 March 1967, no. 21: AAS 59 (1967), pp. 306–307.

89. Cf. Pontifical Commission for interpreting legal texts, response to *dubium* regarding can. 230 § 2: AAS 86 (1994), p. 541.

90. Cf. Second Vatican Ecumenical Council, Constitution on the Sacred Liturgy, *Sacrosanctum Concilium*, no. 22.

91. Cf. Second Vatican Ecumenical Council, Constitution on the Sacred Liturgy, *Sacrosanctum Concilium*, no. 41.

92. Cf. *Caeremoniale Episcoporum*, *editio typica*, 1984, nos. 119–186.

93. Cf. Second Vatican Ecumenical Council, Constitution on the Sacred Liturgy, *Sacrosanctum Concilium*, no. 42; Dogmatic Constitution on the Church, *Lumen gentium*, no. 28; Decree on the Ministry and Life of Priests, *Presbyterorum ordinis*, no. 5; Sacred Congregation of Rites, Instruction *Eucharisticum mysterium*, On the worship of the Eucharist, 25 May 1967, no. 26: AAS 59 (1967), p. 555.

94. Cf. Sacred Congregation of Rites, Instruction *Eucharisticum mysterium*, On the worship of the Eucharist, 25 May 1967, no. 47: AAS 59 (1967), p. 565.

95. Cf. Sacred Congregation of Rites, Instruction *Eucharisticum mysterium*, On the worship of the Eucharist, 25 May 1967, no. 26: AAS 59 (1967), p. 555; Sacred Congregation of Rites, Instruction *Musicam sacram*, On music in the Liturgy, 5 March 1967, nos. 16, 27: AAS 59 (1967), pp. 305, 308.

96. Cf. Interdicasterial Instruction on certain questions regarding the collaboration of the non-ordained faithful in the sacred ministry of priests, *Ecclesiae de mysterio*, 15 August 1997, art. 6: AAS 89 (1997), p. 869.

97. Cf. Sacred Congregation for the Sacraments and Divine Worship, Instruction *Inaestimabile donum*, 3 April 1980, no. 10: AAS 72 (1980), p. 336; Interdicasterial Instruction on certain questions regarding the collaboration of the non-ordained faithful in the sacred ministry of priests, *Ecclesiae de mysterio*, 15 August 1997, art. 8: AAS 89 (1997), p. 871.

98. Cf. *below*, Appendix, Order of Commissioning a Minister to Distribute Holy Communion on a Single Occasion, p. 1253.

99. Cf. *Caeremoniale Episcoporum*, *editio typica*, 1984, nos. 1118–1121.

100. Cf. Paul VI, Apostolic Letter *Ministeria quaedam*, 15 August 1972: AAS 64 (1972), p. 532.

101. Cf. Second Vatican Ecumenical Council, Constitution on the Sacred Liturgy, *Sacrosanctum Concilium*, no. 57; *Codex Iuris Canonici*, can. 902.

102. Cf. Sacred Congregation of Rites, Instruction *Eucharisticum mysterium*, On the worship of the Eucharist, 25 May 1967, no. 47: AAS 59 (1967), p. 566.

103. Cf. Sacred Congregation of Rites, Instruction *Eucharisticum mysterium*, On the worship of the Eucharist, 25 May 1967, no. 47: AAS 59 (1967), p. 565.

104. Cf. Benedict XV, Apostolic Constitution *Incruentum altaris sacrificium*, 10 August 1915: AAS 7 (1915), pp. 401–404.

105. Cf. Sacred Congregation of Rites, Instruction *Eucharisticum mysterium*, On the worship of the Eucharist, 25 May 1967, no. 32: AAS 59 (1967), p. 558.

106. Cf. Council of Trent, session 21, *Doctrina de communione sub utraque specie et parvulorum,* 16 July 1562, chapters 1–3: Denz-Schön, 1725–1729.

107. Cf. Council of Trent, session 21, *Doctrina de communione sub utraque specie et parvulorum,* chapter 2: Denz-Schön, 1728.

108. Cf. Second Vatican Ecumenical Council, Constitution on the Sacred Liturgy, *Sacrosanctum Concilium,* nos. 122–124; Decree on the Ministry and Life of Priests, *Presbyterorum ordinis,* no. 5; Sacred Congregation of Rites, Instruction *Inter Oecumenici,* on the orderly carrying out of the Constitution on the Sacred Liturgy, 26 September 1964, no. 90: AAS 56 (1964), p. 897; Sacred Congregation of Rites, Instruction *Eucharisticum mysterium,* On the worship of the Eucharist, 25 May 1967, no. 24: AAS 59 (1967), p. 554; Codex Iuris Canonici, can. 932 § 1.

109. Cf. Second Vatican Ecumenical Council, Constitution on the Sacred Liturgy, *Sacrosanctum Concilium,* no. 123.

110. Cf. Sacred Congregation of Rites, Instruction *Eucharisticum mysterium,* On the worship of the Eucharist, 25 May 1967, no. 24: AAS 59 (1967), p. 554.

111. Cf. Second Vatican Ecumenical Council, Constitution on the Sacred Liturgy, *Sacrosanctum Concilium,* nos. 123, 129; Sacred Congregation of Rites, Instruction *Inter Oecumenici,* on the orderly carrying out of the Constitution on the Sacred Liturgy, 26 September 1964, no. 13c: AAS 56 (1964), p. 880.

112. Cf. Second Vatican Ecumenical Council, Constitution on the Sacred Liturgy, *Sacrosanctum Concilium,* no. 123.

113. Cf. Second Vatican Ecumenical Council, Constitution on the Sacred Liturgy, *Sacrosanctum Concilium,* no. 126; Sacred Congregation of Rites, Instruction *Inter Oecumenici,* on the orderly carrying out of the Constitution on the Sacred Liturgy, 26 September 1964, no. 91: AAS 56 (1964), p. 898.

114. Cf. Sacred Congregation of Rites, Instruction *Inter Oecumenici,* on the orderly carrying out of the Constitution on the Sacred Liturgy, 26 September 1964, nos. 97–98: AAS 56 (1964), p. 899.

115. Cf. Sacred Congregation of Rites, Instruction *Inter Oecumenici,* on the orderly carrying out of the Constitution on the Sacred Liturgy, 26 September 1964, no. 91: AAS 56 (1964), p. 898.

116. Cf. Sacred Congregation of Rites, Instruction *Inter Oecumenici,* on the orderly carrying out of the Constitution on the Sacred Liturgy, 26 September 1964, no. 91: AAS 56 (1964), p. 898.

117. Cf. Sacred Congregation of Rites, Instruction *Inter Oecumenici,* on the orderly carrying out of the Constitution on the Sacred Liturgy, 26 September 1964, no. 92: AAS 56 (1964), p. 899.

118. Cf. The Roman Ritual, Book of Blessings, *editio typica,* 1984, Order for a Blessing on the Occasion of the Installation of a New Ambo, nos. 900–918.

119. Cf. Sacred Congregation of Rites, Instruction *Inter Oecumenici,* on the orderly carrying out of the Constitution on the Sacred Liturgy, 26 September 1964, no 92: AAS 56 (1964), p. 898.

120. Cf. The Roman Ritual, Book of Blessings, *editio typica,* 1984, Order for a Blessing on the Occasion of the Installation of a New Cathedra or Presidential Chair, nos. 880–899.

121. Cf. Sacred Congregation of Rites, Instruction *Inter Oecumenici,* on the orderly carrying out of the Constitution on the Sacred Liturgy, 26 September 1964, no. 92: AAS 56 (1964), p. 898.

122. Cf. Second Vatican Ecumenical Council, Constitution on the Sacred Liturgy, *Sacrosanctum Concilium,* no. 32.

123. Cf. Sacred Congregation of Rites, Instruction *Musicam sacram,* On music in the Liturgy, 5 March 1967, no. 23: AAS 59 (1967), p. 307.

124. Cf. The Roman Ritual, Book of Blessings, *editio typica,* 1984, Order for the Blessing of an Organ, nos. 1052–1067.

125. Cf. Sacred Congregation of Rites, Instruction *Eucharisticum mysterium,* On the worship of the Eucharist, 25 May 1967, no. 54: AAS 59 (1967), p. 568; cf. also Sacred Congregation of Rites, Instruction *Inter Oecumenici,* on the orderly carrying out of the Constitution on the Sacred Liturgy, 26 September 1964, no. 95: AAS 56 (1964), p. 898.

126. Cf. Sacred Congregation of Rites, Instruction *Eucharisticum mysterium*, On the worship of the Eucharist, 25 May 1967. no. 52: AAS 59 (1967), p. 568; Sacred Congregation of Rites, Instruction *Inter Oecumenici*, on the orderly carrying out of the Constitution on the Sacred Liturgy, 26 September 1964, no. 95: AAS 56 (1964), p. 898; Sacred Congregation for the Sacraments, Instruction *Nullo umquam tempore*, 28 May 1938, no. 4: AAS 30 (1938), pp. 199–200; The Roman Ritual, *Holy Communion and Worship of the Eucharist outside Mass, editio typica*, 1973, nos. 10–11; *Codex Iuris Canonici*, can. 938 § 3.

127. Cf. The Roman Ritual, Book of Blessings, *editio typica*, 1984, Order for a Blessing on the Occasion of the Installation of a New Tabernacle, nos. 919–929.

128. Cf. Sacred Congregation of Rites, Instruction *Eucharisticum mysterium*, On the worship of the Eucharist, 25 May 1967. no. 55: AAS 59 (1967), p. 569.

129. Cf. Sacred Congregation of Rites, Instruction *Eucharisticum mysterium*, On the worship of the Eucharist, 25 May 1967, no. 53: AAS 59 (1967), p. 568; The Roman Ritual, *Holy Communion and Worship of the Eucharist outside Mass, editio typica*, 1973, no. 9; *Codex Iuris Canonici* can. 938 § 2; John Paul II, Apostolic Letter *Dominicae Cenae*, 24 February 1980, no. 3: AAS 72 (1980), pp. 117–119.

130. Cf. *Codex Iuris Canonici*, can. 940; Sacred Congregation of Rites, Instruction *Eucharisticum mysterium*, On the worship of the Eucharist, 25 May 1967, no. 57: AAS 59 (1967), p. 569; The Roman Ritual, *Holy Communion and Worship of the Eucharist outside Mass, editio typica*, 1973, no. 11.

131. Cf. particularly in Sacred Congregation for the Sacraments, Instruction *Nullo umquam tempore*, 28 May 1938: AAS 30 (1938), pp. 198–207; *Codex Iuris Canonici*, cann. 934–944.

132. Cf. Second Vatican Ecumenical Council, Constitution on the Sacred Liturgy, *Sacrosanctum Concilium*, no. 8.

133. Cf. The Roman Pontifical: *Order of the Dedication of a Church and an Altar, editio typica*, 1984, Chapter 4, no. 10; The Roman Ritual, Book of Blessings, *editio typica*, 1984, Order for the Blessing of

Images for Public Veneration by the Faithful, nos. 984–1031.

134. Cf. Second Vatican Ecumenical Council, Constitution on the Sacred Liturgy, *Sacrosanctum Concilium*, no. 125.

135. Cf. Second Vatican Ecumenical Council, Constitution on the Sacred Liturgy, *Sacrosanctum Concilium*, no. 128.

136. Cf. The Roman Pontifical: *Order of the Dedication of a Church and an Altar, editio typica*, 1984, Chapter 7, Order of the Blessing of a Chalice and a Paten; The Roman Ritual, Book of Blessings, *editio typica*, 1984, Order for the Blessing of Articles for Liturgical Use, nos. 1068–1084.

137. Cf. The Roman Ritual, Book of Blessings, *editio typica*, 1984, Order for the Blessing of Articles for Liturgical Use, no 1070.

138. Cf. Second Vatican Ecumenical Council, Constitution on the Sacred Liturgy, *Sacrosanctum Concilium*, no. 128.

139. Cf. Second Vatican Ecumenical Council, Constitution on the Sacred Liturgy, *Sacrosanctum Concilium*, no. 128.

140. For blessing objects that are designed for liturgical use in churches, cf. The Roman Ritual, Book of Blessings, *editio typica*, 1984, part III.

141. Cf. Second Vatican Ecumenical Council, Constitution on the Sacred Liturgy, *Sacrosanctum Concilium*, no. 51.

142. The Roman Missal, Lectionary for Mass, *editio typica altera*, 1981, Introduction, no. 80

143. The Roman Missal, Lectionary for Mass, *editio typica altera*, 1981, Introduction, no. 81.

144. Cf. Second Vatican Ecumenical Council, Constitution on the Sacred Liturgy, *Sacrosanctum Concilium*, no. 61.

145. Cf. Second Vatican Ecumenical Council, Dogmatic Constitution on the Church, *Lumen gentium*, no. 54; Paul VI, Apostolic Exhortation *Marialis cultus*, 2 February 1974, no. 9: AAS 66 (1974), pp. 122–123.

146. Cf. particularly *Codex Iuris Canonici*, can. 1176–1185; The Roman Ritual, *Order of Christian Funerals, editio typica*, 1969.

147. Cf. Second Vatican Ecumenical Council, Constitution on the Sacred Liturgy, *Sacrosanctum Concilium*, no. 14.

148. Cf. Second Vatican Ecumenical Council, Constitution on the Sacred Liturgy, *Sacrosanctum Concilium*, no. 41.

149. Cf. *Codex Iuris Canonici*, can. 838 § 3.

150. Cf. Second Vatican Ecumenical Council, Constitution on the Sacred Liturgy, *Sacrosanctum Concilium*, no. 24.

151. Cf. Second Vatican Ecumenical Council, Constitution on the Sacred Liturgy, *Sacrosanctum Concilium*, no. 36 § 3.

152. Cf. Second Vatican Ecumenical Council, Constitution on the Sacred Liturgy, *Sacrosanctum Concilium*, no. 112.

153. Cf. *General Norms for the Liturgical Year and the Calendar* , nos. 48–51, below, p. 99; Sacred Congregation for Divine Worship, Instruction *Calendaria particularia*, 24 June 1970, nos. 4, 8: AAS 62 (1970), pp. 652–653.

154. Cf. Second Vatican Ecumenical Council, Constitution on the Sacred Liturgy, *Sacrosanctum Concilium*, no. 106.

155. Cf. *General Norms for the Liturgical Year and Calendar*, no. 46, below, p. 98; cf. also Sacred Congregation for Divine Worship, Instruction *Calendaria particularia*, 24 June 1970, no. 38: AAS 62 (1970), p. 660.

156. Cf. Second Vatican Ecumenical Council, Constitution on the Sacred Liturgy, *Sacrosanctum Concilium*, nos. 37–40.

157. Cf. Congregation for Divine Worship and the Discipline of the Sacraments, Instruction *Varietates legitimae*, 25 January 1994, nos. 54, 62–69: AAS 87 (1995), pp. 308–309, 311–313.

158. Cf. Congregation for Divine Worship and the Discipline of the Sacraments, Instruction *Varietates legitimae*, 25 January 1994, nos. 66–68: AAS 87 (1995), p. 313.

159. Cf. Congregation for Divine Worship and the Discipline of the Sacraments, Instruction *Varietates legitimae*, 25 January 1994, nos. 26–27: AAS 87 (1995), pp. 298–299.

160. Cf. John Paul II, Apostolic Letter *Vicesimus Quintus Annus*, 4 December 1988, no. 16: AAS 81 (1989), p. 912; Congregation for Divine Worship and the Discipline of the Sacraments, Instruction *Varietates legitimae*, 25 January 1994, nos. 2, 36: AAS 87 (1995), pp. 288, 302.

161. Cf. Second Vatican Ecumenical Council, Constitution on the Sacred Liturgy, *Sacrosanctum Concilium*, no. 23.

162. Cf. Congregation for Divine Worship and the Discipline of the Sacraments, Instruction *Varietates legitimae*, 25 January 1994, no. 46: AAS 87 (1995), p. 306.

163. Cf. Congregation for Divine Worship and the Discipline of the Sacraments, Instruction *Varietates legitimae*, 25 January 1994, no. 36: AAS 87 (1995), p. 302.

164. Cf. Congregation for Divine Worship and the Discipline of the Sacraments, Instruction *Varietates legitimae*, 25 January 1994, no. 54: AAS 87 (1995), pp. 308–309.

165. Cf. Second Vatican Ecumenical Council, Constitution on the Sacred Liturgy, *Sacrosanctum Concilium*, no. 38; Paul VI, Apostolic Constitution *Missale Romanum*, above, p. 14.

LECTIONARY FOR MASS: INTRODUCTION

CONGREGATION FOR DIVINE WORSHIP AND
THE DISCIPLINE OF THE SACRAMENTS
21 JANUARY 1981, 19 JUNE 1998

OUTLINE

SECOND PART: THE STRUCTURE OF THE ORDER
OF THE READINGS FOR MASS

CHAPTER IV: The General Arrangement of Readings for Mass

INTRODUCTION

PREAMBLE

CHAPTER I
GENERAL PRINCIPLES FOR THE LITURGICAL CELEBRATION
OF THE WORD OF GOD

1. Certain Preliminaries

A) THE IMPORTANCE OF THE WORD OF GOD IN LITURGICAL CELEBRATION

1.   The Second Vatican Council,[1] the magisterium of the Popes,[2] and various documents promulgated after the Council by the organisms of the Holy See[3] have already had many excellent things to say about the importance of the word of God and about reestablishing the use of Sacred Scripture in every celebration of the Liturgy. The Introduction to the 1969 edition of the Order of Readings for Mass has clearly stated and briefly explained some of the more important principles.[4]

On the occasion of this new edition of the Order of Readings for Mass, requests have come from many quarters for a more detailed exposition of the same principles. Hence, this expanded and more suitable arrangement of the Introduction first gives a general statement on the essential bond between the word of God and the liturgical celebration,[5] then deals in greater detail with the word of God in the celebration of Mass, and, finally explains the precise structure of the Order of Readings for Mass.

B) TERMS USED TO REFER TO THE WORD OF GOD

2.   For the sake of clear and precise language on this topic, a definition of terms might well be expected as a prerequisite. Nevertheless this Introduction will simply use the same terms employed in conciliar and postconciliar documents. Furthermore it will use "Sacred Scripture" and "word of God" interchangeably throughout when referring to the books written under the inspiration of the Holy Spirit, thus avoiding any confusion of language or meaning.[6]

C) THE SIGNIFICANCE OF THE WORD OF GOD IN THE LITURGY

3.   The many riches contained in the one word of God are admirably brought out in the different kinds of liturgical celebration and in the different gatherings of the faithful who take part in those celebrations. This takes place as the unfolding mystery of Christ is recalled during the course of the liturgical year,

as the Church's sacraments and sacramentals are celebrated, or as the faithful respond individually to the Holy Spirit working within them.[7] For then the liturgical celebration, founded primarily on the word of God and sustained by it, becomes a new event and enriches the word itself with new meaning and power. Thus in the Liturgy the Church faithfully adheres to the way Christ himself read and explained the Sacred Scriptures, beginning with the "today" of his coming forward in the synagogue and urging all to search the Scriptures.[8]

2. Liturgical Celebration of the Word of God

A) THE PROPER CHARACTER OF THE WORD OF GOD IN THE LITURGICAL CELEBRATION

4.   In the celebration of the Liturgy the word of God is not announced in only one way[9] nor does it always stir the hearts of the hearers with the same efficacy. Always, however, Christ is present in his word,[10] as he carries out the mystery of salvation, he sanctifies humanity and offers the Father perfect worship.[11]

Moreover, the word of God unceasingly calls to mind and extends the economy of salvation, which achieves its fullest expression in the Liturgy. The liturgical celebration becomes therefore the continuing, complete, and effective presentation of God's word.

The word of God constantly proclaimed in the Liturgy is always, then, a living and effective word[12] through the power of the Holy Spirit. It expresses the Father's love that never fails in its effectiveness toward us.

B) THE WORD OF GOD IN THE ECONOMY OF SALVATION

5.   When in celebrating the Liturgy the Church proclaims both the Old and New Testament, it is proclaiming one and the same mystery of Christ.

The New Testament lies hidden in the Old; the Old Testament comes fully to light in the New.[13] Christ himself is the center and fullness of the whole of Scripture, just as he is of all liturgical celebration.[14] Thus the Scriptures are the living waters from which all who seek life and salvation must drink.

The more profound our understanding of the celebration of the liturgy, the higher our appreciation of the importance of God's word. Whatever we say of the one, we can in turn say of the other, because each recalls the mystery of Christ and each in its own way causes the mystery to be carried forward.

C) THE WORD OF GOD IN THE LITURGICAL PARTICIPATION OF THE FAITHFUL

6.   In celebrating the Liturgy the Church faithfully echoes the "Amen" that Christ, the mediator between God and men and women, uttered once for all as he shed his blood to seal God's new covenant in the Holy Spirit.[15]

When God communicates his word, he expects a response, one that is, of listening and adoring "in Spirit and in truth" (John 4:23). The Holy Spirit makes that response effective, so that what is heard in the celebration of the Liturgy may be carried out in a way of life: "Be doers of the word and not hearers only" (James 1:22).

The liturgical celebration and the participation of the faithful receive outward expression in actions, gestures, and words. These derive their full meaning not simply from their origin in human experience but from the word of God and the economy of salvation, to which they refer. Accordingly, the participation of the faithful in the Liturgy increases to the degree that, as they listen to the word of God proclaimed in the Liturgy, they strive harder to commit themselves to the Word of God incarnate in Christ. Thus, they endeavor to conform their way of life to what they celebrate in the Liturgy, and then in turn to bring to the celebration of the Liturgy all that they do in life.[16]

3. The Word of God in the Life of the People of the Covenant

A) THE WORD OF GOD IN THE LIFE OF THE CHURCH

7. In the hearing of God's word the Church is built up and grows, and in the signs of the liturgical celebration God's wonderful, past works in the history of salvation are presented anew as mysterious realities. God in turn makes use of the congregation of the faithful that celebrates the Liturgy in order that his word may speed on and be glorified and that his name be exalted among the nations.[17]

Whenever, therefore, the Church, gathered by the Holy Spirit for liturgical celebration,[18] announces and proclaims the word of God, she is aware of being a new people in whom the covenant made in the past is perfected and fulfilled. Baptism and confirmation in the Spirit have made all Christ's faithful into messengers of God's word because of the grace of hearing they have received. They must therefore be the bearers of the same word in the Church and in the world, at least by the witness of their lives.

The word of God proclaimed in the celebration of God's mysteries does not only address present conditions but looks back to past events and forward to what is yet to come. Thus God's word shows us what we should hope for with such a longing that in this changing world our hearts will be set on the place where our true joys lie.[19]

B) THE CHURCH'S EXPLANATION OF THE WORD OF GOD

8. By Christ's own will there is a marvelous diversity of members in the new people of God and each has different duties and responsibilities with respect to the word of God. Accordingly, the faithful listen to God's word and meditate on it, but only those who have the office of teaching by virtue of sacred ordination or who have been entrusted with exercising that ministry expound the word of God.

This is how in doctrine, life, and worship the Church keeps alive and passes on to every generation all that she is, all that she believes. Thus with the passage of the centuries, the Church is ever to advance toward the fullness of divine truth until God's word is wholly accomplished in her.[20]

C) THE CONNECTION BETWEEN THE WORD OF GOD PROCLAIMED
AND THE WORKING OF THE HOLY SPIRIT

9   The working of the Holy Spirit is needed if the word of God is to make what we hear outwardly have its effect inwardly. Because of the Holy Spirit's inspiration and support, the word of God becomes the foundation of the liturgical celebration and the rule and support of all our life.

The working of the Holy Spirit precedes, accompanies, and brings to completion the whole celebration of the Liturgy. But the Spirit also brings home[21] to each person individually everything that in the proclamation of the word of God is spoken for the good of the whole gathering of the faithful. In strengthening the unity of all, the Holy Spirit at the same time fosters a diversity of gifts and furthers their multiform operation.

D) THE ESSENTIAL BOND BETWEEN THE WORD OF GOD
AND THE MYSTERY OF THE EUCHARIST

10.   The Church has honored the word of God and the Eucharistic mystery with the same reverence, although not with the same worship, and has always and everywhere insisted upon and sanctioned such honor. Moved by the example of its Founder, the Church has never ceased to celebrate his paschal mystery by coming together to read "what referred to him in all the Scriptures" (Luke 24:27) and to carry out the work of salvation through the celebration of the memorial of the Lord and through the sacraments. "The preaching of the word is necessary for the ministry of the sacraments, for these are sacraments of faith, which is born and nourished from the word."[22]

The Church is nourished spiritually at the twofold table of God's word and of the Eucharist:[23] from the one it grows in wisdom and from the other in holiness. In the word of God the divine covenant is announced; in the Eucharist the new and everlasting covenant is renewed. On the one hand the history of salvation is brought to mind by means of human sounds; on the other it is made manifest in the sacramental signs of the Liturgy.

It can never be forgotten, therefore, that the divine word read and proclaimed by the Church in the Liturgy has as its one purpose the sacrifice of the New Covenant and the banquet of grace, that is, the Eucharist. The celebration of Mass in which the word is heard and the Eucharist is offered and received forms but one single act of divine worship.[24] That act offers the sacrifice of praise to God and makes available to God's creatures the fullness of redemption.

FIRST PART
THE WORD OF GOD IN THE CELEBRATION OF MASS

CHAPTER II
THE CELEBRATION OF THE LITURGY OF THE WORD AT MASS

1. The Elements of the Liturgy of the Word and their Rites

11.　"Readings from Sacred Scripture and the chants between the readings form the main part of the liturgy of the word. The homily, the profession of faith, and the universal prayer or prayer of the faithful carry it forward and conclude it."[25]

A) THE BIBLICAL READINGS

12.　In the celebration of Mass the biblical readings with their accompanying chants from the Sacred Scriptures may not be omitted, shortened, or, worse still, replaced by nonbiblical readings.[26] For it is out of the word of God handed down in writing that even now "God speaks to his people"[27] and it is from the continued use of Sacred Scripture that the people of God, docile to the Holy Spirit under the light of faith, is enabled to bear witness to Christ before the world by its manner of life.

13.　The reading of the Gospel is the high point of the liturgy of the word. For this the other readings, in their established sequence from the Old to the New Testament, prepare the assembly.

14.　A speaking style on the part of the readers that is audible, clear, and intelligent is the first means of transmitting the word of God properly to the congregation. The readings, taken from the approved editions,[28] may be sung in a way suited to different languages. This singing, however, must serve to bring out the sense of the words, not obscure them. On occasions when the readings are in Latin, the manner given in the *Ordo cantus Missae* is to be maintained.[29]

15.　There may be concise introductions before the readings, especially the first. The style proper to such comments must be respected, that is, they must be simple, faithful to the text, brief, well prepared, and properly varied to suit the text they introduce.[30]

16.　In a Mass with the people the readings are always to be proclaimed at the ambo.[31]

17.　Of all the rites connected with the liturgy of the word, the reverence due to the Gospel reading must receive special attention.[32] Where there is an Evangeliary or Book of Gospels that has been carried in by the deacon or reader during the entry procession,[33] it is most fitting that the deacon or a priest, when there is no deacon, take the book from the altar[34] and carry it to the ambo. He is preceded by servers with candles and incense or other symbols of reverence that may be customary. As the faithful stand and acclaim the Lord, they show honor to the Book of Gospels. The deacon who is to read the Gospel, bowing in front of the one presiding, asks and receives the blessing. When no deacon is present, the priest, bowing before the altar, prays inaudibly, *Almighty God, cleanse my heart. . . .*[35]

At the ambo the one who proclaims the Gospel greets the people, who are standing, and announces the reading as he makes the sign of the cross on forehead, mouth, and breast. If incense is used, he next incenses the book, then reads the Gospel. When finished, he kisses the book, saying the appointed words inaudibly.

Even if the Gospel itself is not sung, it is appropriate for the greeting *The Lord be with you,* and *A reading from the holy Gospel according to . . . ,* and at the end *The Gospel of the Lord* to be sung, in order that the congregation may also sing its acclamations. This is a way both of bringing out the importance of the Gospel reading and of stirring up the faith of those who hear it.

18.   At the conclusion of the other readings, *The word of the Lord* may be sung, even by someone other than the reader; all respond with the acclamation. In this way the assembled congregation pays reverence to the word of God it has listened to in faith and gratitude.

B) THE RESPONSORIAL PSALM

19.   The responsorial psalm, also called the gradual, has great liturgical and pastoral significance because it is an "integral part of the liturgy of the word."[36] Accordingly, the faithful must be continually instructed on the way to perceive the word of God speaking in the psalms and to turn these psalms into the prayer of the Church. This, of course, "will be achieved more readily if a deeper understanding of the psalms, according to the meaning with which they are sung in the sacred Liturgy, is more diligently promoted among the clergy and communicated to all the faithful by means of appropriate catechesis."[37]

Brief remarks about the choice of the psalm and response as well as their correspondence to the readings may be helpful.

20.   As a rule the responsorial psalm should be sung. There are two established ways of singing the psalm after the first reading: responsorially and directly. In responsorial singing, which, as far as possible, is to be given preference, the psalmist, or cantor of the psalm, sings the psalm verse and the whole congregation joins in by singing the response. In direct singing of the psalm there is no intervening response by the community; either the psalmist, or cantor of the psalm, sings the psalm alone as the community listens or else all sing it together.

21.   The singing of the psalm, or even of the response alone, is a great help toward understanding and meditating on the psalm's spiritual meaning.

To foster the congregation's singing, every means available in each individual culture is to be employed. In particular, use is to be made of all the relevant options provided in the Order of Readings for Mass[38] regarding responses corresponding to the different liturgical seasons.

22.   When not sung, the psalm after the reading is to be recited in a manner conducive to meditation on the word of God.[39]

The responsorial psalm is sung or recited by the psalmist or cantor at the ambo.[40]

C) THE ACCLAMATION BEFORE THE READING OF THE GOSPEL

23.   The *Alleluia* or, as the liturgical season requires, the verse before the Gospel, is also a "rite or act standing by itself."[41] It serves as the greeting of welcome of the assembled faithful to the Lord who is about to speak to them and as an expression of their faith through song.

The *Alleluia* or the verse before the Gospel must be sung and during it all stand. It is not to be sung only by the cantor who intones it or by the choir, but by the whole of the people together.[42]

D) THE HOMILY

24.   Through the course of the liturgical year the homily sets forth the mysteries of faith and the standards of the Christian life on the basis of the sacred text. Beginning with the Constitution on the Liturgy, the homily as part of the liturgy of the word[43] has been repeatedly and strongly recommended and in some cases it is obligatory. As a rule it is to be given by the one presiding.[44] The purpose of the homily at Mass is that the spoken word of God and the liturgy of the Eucharist may together become "a proclamation of God's wonderful works in the history of salvation, the mystery of Christ."[45] Through the readings and homily Christ's paschal mystery is proclaimed; through the sacrifice of the Mass it becomes present.[46] Moreover Christ himself is always present and active in the preaching of his Church.[47]

Whether the homily explains the text of the Sacred Scriptures proclaimed in the readings or some other text of the Liturgy,[48] it must always lead the community of the faithful to celebrate the Eucharist actively, "so that they may hold fast in their lives to what they have grasped by faith."[49] From this living explanation, the word of God proclaimed in the readings and the Church's celebration of the day's Liturgy will have greater impact. But this demands that the homily be truly the fruit of meditation, carefully prepared, neither too long nor too short, and suited to all those present, even children and the uneducated.[50]

At a concelebration, the celebrant or one of the concelebrants as a rule gives the homily.[51]

25.   On the prescribed days, that is, Sundays and holydays of obligation, there must be a homily in all Masses celebrated with a congregation, even Masses on the preceding evening; the homily may not be omitted without a serious reason.[52] There is also to be a homily in Masses with children and with special groups[53]

A homily is strongly recommended on the weekdays of Advent, Lent, and the Easter season for the sake of the faithful who regularly take part in the celebration of Mass; also on other feasts and occasions when a large congregation is present.[54]

26.   The priest celebrant gives the homily, standing either at the chair or at the ambo.[55]

27.   Any necessary announcements are to be kept completely separate from the homily; they must take place following the prayer after Communion.[56]

E) SILENCE

28.   The liturgy of the word must be celebrated in a way that fosters meditation; clearly, any sort of haste that hinders recollection must be avoided. The dialogue between God and his people taking place through the Holy Spirit demands short intervals of silence, suited to the assembled congregation, as an opportunity to take the word of God to heart and to prepare a response to it in prayer.

Proper times for silence during the liturgy of the word are, for example, before this liturgy begins, after the first and the second reading, after the homily.[57]

F) THE PROFESSION OF FAITH

29.   The symbol, creed or profession of faith, said when the rubrics require, has as its purpose in the celebration of Mass that the assembled congregation may respond and give assent to the word of God heard in the readings and through the homily, and that before beginning to celebrate in the Eucharist the mystery of faith it may call to mind the rule of faith in a formulary approved by the Church.[58]

G) THE UNIVERSAL PRAYER OR PRAYER OF THE FAITHFUL

30.   In the light of God's word and in a sense in response to it, the congregation of the faithful prays in the universal prayer as a rule for the needs of the universal Church and the local community, for the salvation of the world and those oppressed by any burden, and for special categories of people.

The celebrant introduces the prayer; a deacon, another minister, or some of the faithful may propose intentions that are short and phrased with a measure of freedom. In these petitions "the people, exercising its priestly function, makes intercession for all men and women,"[59] with the result that, as the liturgy of the word has its full effects in the faithful, they are better prepared to proceed to the liturgy of the Eucharist.

31.   For the prayer of the faithful the celebrant presides at the chair and the intentions are announced at the ambo.[60]

The assembled congregation takes part in the prayer of the faithful while standing and by saying or singing a common response after each intention or by silent prayer.[61]

2. Aids to the Proper Celebration of the Liturgy of the Word

A) THE PLACE FOR THE PROCLAMATION OF THE WORD OF GOD

32.   There must be a place in the church that is somewhat elevated, fixed, and of a suitable design and nobility. It should reflect the dignity of God's word and

be a clear reminder to the people that in the Mass the table of God's word and of Christ's body is placed before them.[62] The place for the readings must also truly help the people's listening and attention during the liturgy of the word. Great pains must therefore be taken, in keeping with the design of each church, over the harmonious and close relationship of the ambo with the altar.

33.   Either permanently or at least on occasions of greater solemnity, the ambo should be decorated simply and in keeping with its design.

Since the ambo is the place from which the word of God is proclaimed by the ministers, it must of its nature be reserved for the readings, the responsorial psalm, and the Easter Proclamation (the *Exsultet*). The ambo may rightly be used for the homily and the prayer of the faithful, however, because of their close connection with the entire liturgy of the word. It is better for the commentator, cantor, or director of singing, for example, not to use the ambo.[63]

34.   In order that the ambo may properly serve its liturgical purpose, it is to be rather large, since on occasion several ministers must use it at the same time. Provision must also be made for the readers to have enough light to read the text and, as required, to have modern sound equipment enabling the faithful to hear them without difficulty.

B) THE BOOKS FOR PROCLAMATION OF THE WORD OF GOD IN THE LITURGY

35.   Along with the ministers, the actions, the allocated places, and other elements, the books containing the readings of the word of God remind the hearers of the presence of God speaking to his people. Since in liturgical celebrations the books too serve as signs and symbols of the higher realities, care must be taken to ensure that they truly are worthy, dignified and beautiful.[64]

36.   The proclamation of the Gospel always stands as the high point of the liturgy of the word. Thus the liturgical tradition of both West and East has consistently made a certain distinction between the books for the readings. The Book of Gospels was always fabricated and decorated with the utmost care and shown greater respect than any of the other books of readings. In our times also, then, it is very desirable that cathedrals and at least the larger, more populous parishes and the churches with a larger attendance possess a beautifully designed Book of Gospels, separate from any other book of readings. For good reason it is the Book of Gospels that is presented to a deacon at his ordination and that at an ordination to the episcopate is laid upon the head of the bishop-elect and held there.[65]

37.   Because of the dignity of the word of God, the books of readings used in the celebration are not to be replaced by other pastoral aids, for example, by leaflets printed for the preparation of the readings by the faithful or for their personal meditation.

No missalettes or bibles for liturgical books

CHAPTER III
OFFICES AND MINISTRIES IN THE CELEBRATION
OF THE LITURGY OF THE WORD WITHIN MASS

1. *The Function of the President at the Liturgy of the Word*

38. The one presiding at the liturgy of the word communicates the spiritual nourishment it contains to those present, especially in the homily. Even if he too is a listener to the word of God proclaimed by others, the duty of proclaiming it has been entrusted above all to him. Personally or through others he sees to it that the word of God is properly proclaimed. He then as a rule reserves to himself the tasks of composing comments to help the people listen more attentively and of preaching a homily that fosters in them a richer understanding of the word of God.

39. The first requirement for one who is to preside over the celebration is a thorough knowledge of the structure of the Order of Readings, so that he will know how to work a fruitful effect in the hearts of the faithful. Through study and prayer he must also develop a full understanding of the coordination and connection of the various texts in the liturgy of the word, so that the Order of Readings will become the source of a sound understanding of the mystery of Christ and his saving work.

40. The one presiding is to make ready use of the various options provided in the Lectionary regarding readings, responses, responsorial psalms, and Gospel acclamations;[66] but he is to do so in harmony[67] with all concerned and after listening to the opinions of the faithful in what concerns them.[68]

41. The one presiding exercises his proper office and the ministry of the word of God also as he preaches the homily.[69] In this way he leads his brothers and sisters to an affective knowledge of Scripture. He opens their minds to thanksgiving for the wonderful works of God. He strengthens the faith of those present in the word that in the celebration becomes sacrament through the Holy Spirit. Finally, he prepares them for a fruitful reception of Communion and invites them to take upon themselves the demands of the Christian life.

42. The president is responsible for preparing the faithful for the liturgy of the word on occasion by means of introductions before the readings.[70] These comments can help the assembled congregation toward a better hearing of the word of God, because they stir up an attitude of faith and good will. He may also carry out this responsibility through others, a deacon, for example, or a commentator.[71]

43. As he directs the prayer of the faithful and through their introduction and conclusion connects them, if possible, with the day's readings and the homily, the president leads the faithful toward the liturgy of the Eucharist.[72]

44.   Christ's word gathers the people of God as one and increases and sustains them. "This applies above all to the liturgy of the word in the celebration of Mass, where there are inseparably united the proclamation of the death of the Lord, the response of the people listening, and the very offering through which Christ has confirmed the New Covenant in his Blood, and in which the people share by their intentions and by reception of the sacrament."[73] For "not only when things are read 'that were written for our instruction' (Romans 15:4), but also when the Church prays or sings or acts, the faith of those taking part is nourished and their minds are raised to God, so that they may offer him rightful worship and receive his grace more abundantly."[74]

45.   In the liturgy of the word, the congregation of Christ's faithful even today receives from God the word of his covenant through the faith that comes by hearing, and must respond to that word in faith, so that they may become more and more truly the people of the New Covenant.

The people of God have a spiritual right to receive abundantly from the treasury of God's word. Its riches are presented to them through use of the Order of Readings, the homily, and pastoral efforts.

For their part, the faithful at the celebration of Mass are to listen to the word of God with an inward and outward reverence that will bring them continuous growth in the spiritual life and draw them more deeply into the mystery which is celebrated.[75]

46.   As a help toward celebrating the memorial of the Lord with eager devotion, the faithful should be keenly aware of the one presence of Christ in both the word of God—it is he himself "who speaks when the Sacred Scriptures are read in the Church"—and "above all under the Eucharistic species."[76]

47.   To be received and integrated into the life of Christ's faithful, the word of God demands a living faith.[77] Hearing the word of God unceasingly proclaimed arouses that faith.

The Sacred Scriptures, above all in their liturgical proclamation, are the source of life and strength. As the Apostle Paul attests, the Gospel is the saving power of God for everyone who believes.[78] Love of the Scriptures is therefore a force reinvigorating and renewing the entire people of God.[79] All the faithful without exception must therefore always be ready to listen gladly to God's word.[80] When this word is proclaimed in the Church and put into living practice, it enlightens the faithful through the working of the Holy Spirit and draws them into the entire mystery of the Lord as a reality to be lived.[81] The word of God reverently received moves the heart and its desires toward conversion and toward a life resplendent with both individual and community faith,[82] since God's word is the food of Christian life and the source of the prayer of the whole Church.[83]

48.   The intimate connection between the liturgy of the word and the liturgy of the Eucharist in the Mass should prompt the faithful to be present right from

the beginning of the celebration,[84] to take part attentively, and to prepare themselves in so far as possible to hear the word, especially by learning beforehand more about Sacred Scripture. That same connection should also awaken in them a desire for a liturgical understanding of the texts read and a readiness to respond through singing.[85]

When they hear the word of God and reflect deeply on it, Christ's faithful are enabled to respond to it actively with full faith, hope, and charity through prayer and self-giving, and not only during Mass but in their entire Christian life.

3. Ministries in the Liturgy of the Word

49.   Liturgical tradition assigns responsibility for the biblical readings in the celebration of Mass to ministers: to readers and the deacon. But when there is no deacon or no other priest present, the priest celebrant is to read the Gospel[86] and when there is no reader present, all the readings.[87]

50.   It pertains to the deacon in the liturgy of the word at Mass to proclaim the Gospel, sometimes to give the homily, as occasion suggests, and to propose to the people the intentions of the prayer of the faithful.[88]

51.   "The reader has his own proper function in the Eucharistic celebration and should exercise this even though ministers of a higher rank may be present."[89] The ministry of reader, conferred through a liturgical rite, must be held in respect. When there are instituted readers available, they are to carry out their office at least on Sundays and festive days, especially at the principal Mass of the day. These readers may also be given responsibility for assisting in the arrangement of the liturgy of the word, and, to the extent necessary, of seeing to the preparation of others of the faithful who may be appointed on a given occasion to read at Mass.[90]

52.   The liturgical assembly truly requires readers, even those not instituted. Proper measures must therefore be taken to ensure that there are certain suitable laypeople who have been trained to carry out this ministry.[91] Whenever there is more than one reading, it is better to assign the readings to different readers, if available.

53.   In Masses without a deacon, the function of announcing the intentions for the prayer of the faithful is to be assigned to the cantor, particularly when they are to be sung, to a reader, or to someone else.[92]

54.   During the celebration of Mass with a congregation a second priest, a deacon, and an instituted reader must wear the distinctive vestment of their office when they go up to the ambo to read the word of God. Those who carry out the ministry of reader just for the occasion or even regularly but without institution may go to the ambo in ordinary attire, but this should be in keeping with the customs of the different regions.

55.   "It is necessary that those who exercise the ministry of reader, even if they have not received institution, be truly suited and carefully prepared, so that the

faithful may develop a warm and living love for Sacred Scripture from listening to the sacred readings."[93]

Their preparation must above all be spiritual, but what may be called a technical preparation is also needed. The spiritual preparation presupposes at least a biblical and liturgical formation. The purpose of their biblical formation is to give readers the ability to understand the readings in context and to perceive by the light of faith the central point of the revealed message. The liturgical formation ought to equip the readers to have some grasp of the meaning and structure of the liturgy of the word and of the significance of its connection with the liturgy of the Eucharist. The technical preparation should make the readers more skilled in the art of reading publicly, either with the power of their own voice or with the help of sound equipment.

56. The psalmist, or cantor of the psalm, is responsible for singing, responsorially or directly, the chants between the readings—the psalm or other biblical canticle, the gradual and *Alleluia,* or other chant. The psalmist may, as occasion requires, intone the *Alleluia* and verse.[94]

For carrying out the function of psalmist it is advantageous to have in each ecclesial community laypeople with the ability to sing and read with correct diction. The points made about the formation of readers apply to cantors as well.

57. The commentator also fulfills a genuine liturgical ministry, which consists in presenting to the congregation of the faithful, from a suitable place, relevant explanations and comments that are clear, of marked sobriety, meticulously prepared, and as a rule written out and approved beforehand by the celebrant.[95]

SECOND PART
THE STRUCTURE OF THE ORDER OF READINGS FOR MASS

CHAPTER IV
THE GENERAL ARRANGEMENT OF READINGS FOR MASS

1. The Pastoral Purpose of the Order of Readings for Mass

58. On the basis of the intention of the Second Vatican Council, the Order of Readings provided by the Lectionary of the Roman Missal has been composed above all for a pastoral purpose. To achieve this aim, not only the principles underlying this new Order of Readings but also the lists of texts that it provides have been discussed and revised over and over again, with the cooperation of a great many experts in exegetical, liturgical, catechetical, and pastoral studies from all parts of the world. The Order of Readings is the fruit of this combined effort.

The prolonged use of this Order of Readings to proclaim and explain Sacred Scripture in the Eucharistic celebration will, it is hoped, prove to be an effective step toward achieving the objective stated repeatedly by the Second Vatican Council.[96]

59.   The decision on revising the Lectionary for Mass was to draw up and edit a single, rich, and full Order of Readings that would be in complete accord with the intent and prescriptions of the Second Vatican Council.[97] At the same time, however, the Order was meant to be of a kind that would meet the requirements and usages of particular Churches and celebrating congregations. For this reason, those responsible for the revision took pains to safeguard the liturgical tradition of the Roman Rite, but valued highly the merits of all the systems of selecting, arranging, and using the biblical readings in other liturgical families and in certain particular Churches. The revisers made use of those elements that experience has confirmed, but with an effort to avoid certain shortcomings found in the preceding form of the tradition.

60.   The present Order of Readings for Mass, then, is an arrangement of biblical readings that provides the faithful with a knowledge of the whole of God's word, in a pattern suited to the purpose. Throughout the liturgical year, but above all during the seasons of Easter, Lent, and Advent, the choice and sequence of readings are aimed at giving Christ's faithful an ever-deepening perception of the faith they profess and of the history of salvation.[98] Accordingly, the Order of Readings corresponds to the requirements and interests of the Christian people.

61.   The celebration of the Liturgy is not in itself simply a form of catechesis, but it does contain an element of teaching. The Lectionary of the Roman Missal brings this out[99] and therefore deserves to be regarded as a pedagogical resource aiding catechesis.

   This is so because the Order of Readings for Mass aptly presents from Sacred Scripture the principal deeds and words belonging to the history of salvation. As its many phases and events are recalled in the liturgy of the word, it will become clear to the faithful that the history of salvation is continued here and now in the representation of Christ's paschal mystery celebrated through the Eucharist.

62.   The pastoral advantage of having in the Roman Rite a single Order of Readings for the Lectionary is obvious on other grounds. All the faithful, particularly those who for various reasons do not always take part in Mass with the same assembly, will everywhere be able to hear the same readings on any given day or in any liturgical season and to meditate on the application of these readings to their own concrete circumstances. This is the case even in places that have no priest and where a deacon or someone else deputed by the bishop conducts a celebration of the word of God.[100]

63.   Pastors may wish to respond specifically from the word of God to the concerns of their own congregations. Although they must be mindful that they are above all to be heralds of the entire mystery of Christ and of the Gospel, they may rightfully use the options provided in the Order of Readings for Mass. This applies particularly to the celebration of a ritual or votive Mass, a Mass in honor of the Saints, or one of the Masses for various needs and occasions. With due regard for the general norms, special faculties are granted concerning the readings in Masses celebrated for particular groups.[101]

2. The Principles of Composition of the Order of Readings for Mass

64.   To achieve the purpose of the Order of Readings for Mass, the parts have been selected and arranged in such a way as to take into account the sequence of the liturgical seasons and the hermeneutical principles whose understanding and definition have been facilitated by modern biblical research.

It was judged helpful to state here the principles guiding the composition of the Order of Readings for Mass.

A) THE CHOICE OF TEXTS

65.   The course of readings in the Proper of Seasons is arranged as follows. Sundays and festive days present the more important biblical passages. In this way the more significant parts of God's revealed word can be read to the assembled faithful within an appropriate period of time. Weekdays present a second series of texts from Sacred Scripture and in a sense these complement the message of salvation explained on festive days. But neither series in these main parts of the Order of Readings—the series for Sundays and festive days and that for weekdays—is dependent on the other. The Order of Readings for Sundays and festive days extends over three years; for weekdays, over two. Thus each runs its course independently of the other.

The sequence of readings in other parts of the Order of Readings is governed by its own rules. This applies to the series of readings for celebrations of the Saints, ritual Masses, Masses for various needs and occasions, votive Masses, or Masses for the dead.

B) THE ARRANGEMENT OF THE READINGS FOR SUNDAYS AND FESTIVE DAYS

66.   The following are features proper to the readings for Sundays and festive days:

1. Each Mass has three readings: the first from the Old Testament, the second from an Apostle (that is, either from a Letter or from the Book of Revelation, depending on the season), and the third from the Gospels. This arrangement brings out the unity of the Old and New Testaments and of the history of salvation, in which Christ is the central figure, commemorated in his paschal mystery.

2. A more varied and richer reading of Sacred Scripture on Sundays and festive days results from the three-year cycle provided for these days, in that the same texts are read only every fourth year.[102]

3. The principles governing the Order of Reading for Sundays and festive days are called the principles of "harmony" and of "semicontinuous reading." One or the other applies according to the different seasons of the year and the distinctive character of the particular liturgical season.

67.   The best instance of harmony between the Old and New Testament readings occurs when it is one that Scripture itself suggests. This is the case when the doctrine and events recounted in texts of the New Testament bear a more or less explicit relationship to the doctrine and events of the Old Testament. The

present Order of Readings selects Old Testament texts mainly because of their correlation with New Testament texts read in the same Mass, and particularly with the Gospel text.

Harmony of another kind exists between texts of the readings for each Mass during Advent, Lent, and Easter, the seasons that have a distinctive importance or character.

In contrast, the Sundays in Ordinary Time do not have a distinctive character. Thus the text of both the apostolic and Gospel readings are arranged in order of semicontinuous reading, whereas the Old Testament reading is harmonized with the Gospel.

68. The decision was made not to extend to Sundays the arrangement suited to the liturgical seasons mentioned, that is, not to have an organic harmony of themes devised with a view to facilitating homiletic instruction. Such an arrangement would be in conflict with the genuine conception of liturgical celebration, which is always the celebration of the mystery of Christ and which by its own tradition makes use of the word of God not only at the prompting of logical or extrinsic concerns but spurred by the desire to proclaim the Gospel and to lead those who believe to the fullness of truth.

C) THE ARRANGEMENT OF THE READINGS FOR WEEKDAYS

69. The weekday readings have been arranged in the following way.

1. Each Mass has two readings: the first is from the Old Testament or from an Apostle (that is, either from a Letter or from the Book of Revelation), and during the Easter season from the Acts of the Apostles; the second, from the Gospels.

2. The yearly cycle for Lent has its own principles of arrangement, which take into account the baptismal and penitential character of this season.

3. The cycle for the weekdays of Advent, the Christmas season, and the Easter season is also yearly and the readings thus remain the same each year.

4. For the thirty-four weeks of Ordinary Time, the weekday Gospel readings are arranged in a single cycle, repeated each year. But the first reading is arranged in a two-year cycle and is thus read every other year. Year I is used during odd-numbered years; Year II, during even-numbered years.

Like the Order for Sundays and festive days, then, the weekday Order of Readings is governed by similar application of the principles of harmony and of semicontinuous reading, especially in the case of seasons with their own distinctive character.

D) THE READINGS FOR CELEBRATIONS OF THE SAINTS

70. Two series of readings are provided for celebrations of the Saints.

1. The Proper of Saints provides the first series, for solemnities, feasts, or memorials and particularly when there are proper texts for one or other

such celebration. Sometimes in the Proper, however, there is a reference to the most appropriate among the texts in the Commons as the one to be given preference.

2. The Commons of Saints provide the second, more extensive group of readings. There are, first, appropriate texts for the different classes of Saints (martyrs, pastors, virgins, etc.), then numerous texts that deal with holiness in general. These may be freely chosen whenever the Commons are indicated as the source for the choice of readings.

71. As to their sequence, all the texts in this part of the Order of Readings appear in the order in which they are to be read at Mass. Thus the Old Testament texts are first, then the texts from the Apostles, followed by the psalms and verses between the readings, and finally the texts from the Gospels. The rationale of this arrangement is that, unless otherwise noted, the celebrant may choose at will from such texts, in view of the pastoral needs of the congregation taking part in the celebration.

E) READINGS FOR RITUAL MASSES, MASSES FOR VARIOUS NEEDS AND OCCASIONS, VOTIVE MASSES, AND MASSES FOR THE DEAD

72. For ritual Masses, Masses for various needs and occasions, votive Masses, and Masses for the dead, the texts for the readings are arranged as just described, that is, numerous texts are grouped together in the order of their use, as in the Commons of Saints.

F) THE MAIN CRITERIA APPLIED IN CHOOSING AND ARRANGING THE READINGS

73. In addition to the guiding principles already given for the arrangement of readings in the individual parts of the Order of Readings, others of a more general nature follow.

1) The Reservation of Some Books to Particular Liturgical Seasons

74. In this Order of Readings, some biblical books are set aside for particular liturgical seasons on the basis both of the intrinsic importance of subject matter and of liturgical tradition. For example, the Western (Ambrosian and Hispanic) and Eastern tradition of reading the Acts of the Apostles during the Easter season is maintained. This usage results in a clear presentation of how the Church's entire life derives its beginning from the paschal mystery. The tradition of both West and East is also retained, namely the reading of the Gospel of John in the latter weeks of Lent and in the Easter season.

Tradition assigns the reading of Isaiah, especially the first part, to Advent. Some texts of this book, however, are read during the Christmas season, to which the First Letter of John is also assigned.

2) The Length of the Texts

75. A *middle way* is followed in regard to the length of texts. A distinction has been made between narratives, which require reading a fairly long passage

but which usually hold the attention of the faithful, and texts that should not be lengthy because of the profundity of their doctrine.

In the case of certain rather lengthy texts, longer and shorter versions are provided to suit different situations. The editing of the shorter version has been carried out with great caution.

3) Difficult Texts

76. In readings for Sundays and solemnities, texts that present real difficulties are avoided for pastoral reasons. The difficulties may be objective, in that the texts themselves raise profound literary, critical, or exegetical problems; or the difficulties may lie, at least to a certain extent, in the ability of the faithful to understand the texts. But there could be no justification for concealing from the faithful the spiritual riches of certain texts on the grounds of difficulty if the problem arises from the inadequacy either of the religious education that every Christian should have or of the biblical formation that every pastor of souls should have. Often a difficult reading is clarified by its correlation with another in the same Mass.

4) The Omission of Certain Verses

77. The omission of verses in readings from Scripture has at times been the tradition of many liturgies, including the Roman liturgy. Admittedly such omissions may not be made lightly, for fear of distorting the meaning of the text or the intent and style of Scripture. Yet on pastoral grounds it was decided to continue the traditional practice in the present Order of Readings, but at the same time to ensure that the essential meaning of the text remained intact. One reason for the decision is that otherwise some texts would have been unduly long. It would also have been necessary to omit completely certain readings of high spiritual value for the faithful because those readings include some verse that is pastorally less useful or that involves truly difficult questions.

3. Principles to be Followed in the Use of the Order of Readings

A) THE FREEDOM OF CHOICE REGARDING SOME TEXTS

78. The Order of Readings sometimes leaves it to the celebrant to choose between alternative texts or to choose one from the several listed together for the same reading. The option seldom exists on Sundays, solemnities, or feasts, in order not to obscure the character proper to the particular liturgical season or needlessly interrupt the semicontinuous reading of some biblical book. On the other hand, the option is given readily in celebrations of the Saints, in ritual Masses, Masses for various needs and occasions, votive Masses, and Masses for the dead.

These options, together with those indicated in the General Instruction of the Roman Missal and the *Ordo cantus Missae*,[103] have a pastoral purpose. In arranging the liturgy of the word, then, the priest should "consider the general spiritual good of the congregation rather than his personal outlook. He should be mindful that the choice of texts is to be made in harmony with the ministers and others who have any role in the celebration and should listen to the opinions of the faithful in what concerns them more directly."[104]

1) The Two Readings before the Gospel

79.   In Masses to which three readings are assigned, all three are to be used. If, however, for pastoral reasons the Conference of Bishops has given permission for two readings only to be used,[105] the choice between the two first readings is to be made in such a way as to safeguard the Church's intent to instruct the faithful more completely in the mystery of salvation. Thus, unless the contrary is indicated in the text of the Lectionary, the reading to be chosen as the first reading is the one that is more closely in harmony with the Gospel, or, in accord with the intent just mentioned, the one that is more helpful toward a coherent catechesis over an extended period, or that preserves the semicontinuous reading of some biblical book.[106]

2) The Longer and Shorter Forms of Texts

80.   A pastoral criterion must also guide the choice between the longer and shorter forms of the same text. The main consideration must be the capacity of the hearers to listen profitably either to the longer or to the shorter reading; or to listen to a more complete text that will be explained through the homily.

3) When Two Texts Are Provided

81.   When a choice is allowed between alternative texts, whether they are fixed or optional, the first consideration must be the best interest of those taking part. It may be a matter of using the easier texts or the one more relevant to the assembled congregation or, as pastoral advantage may suggest, of repeating or replacing a text that is assigned as proper to one celebration and optional to another.

The issue may arise when it is feared that some text will create difficulties for a particular congregation or when the same text would have to be repeated within a few days, as on a Sunday and on a day during the week following.

4) The Weekday Readings

82.   The arrangement of weekday readings provides texts for every day of the week throughout the year. In most cases, therefore, these readings are to be used on their assigned days, unless a solemnity, a feast, or else a memorial with proper readings occurs.[107]

In using the Order of Readings for weekdays attention must be paid to whether one reading or another from the same biblical book will have to be omitted because of some celebration occurring during the week. With the arrangement of readings for the entire week in mind, the priest in that case arranges to omit the less significant passages or combines in the most appropriate manner them with other readings, if they contribute to an integral view of a particular theme.

5) The Celebrations of the Saints

83.   When they exist, proper readings are given for celebrations of the Saints, that is, biblical passages about the Saint or the mystery that the Mass is celebrating. Even in the case of a memorial these readings must take the place of

the weekday readings for the same day. This Order of Readings makes explicit note of every case of proper readings on a memorial.

In some cases there are accommodated readings, those, namely, that bring out some particular aspect of a Saint's spiritual life or work. Use of such readings does not seem binding, except for compelling pastoral reasons. For the most part references are given to readings in the Commons in order to facilitate choice. But these are merely suggestions: in place of an accommodated reading or the particular reading proposed from a Common, any other reading from the Commons referred to may be selected.

The first concern of a priest celebrating with a congregation is the spiritual benefit of the faithful and he will be careful not to impose his personal preference on them. Above all he will make sure not to omit too often or without sufficient cause the readings assigned for each day in the weekday Lectionary: the Church's desire is that a more lavish table of the word of God be spread before the faithful.[108]

There are also common readings, that is, those placed in the Commons either for some determined class of Saints (martyrs, virgins, pastors) or for the Saints in general. Because in these cases several texts are listed for the same reading, it will be up to the priest to choose the one best suited to those listening.

In all celebrations of Saints the readings may be taken not only from the Commons to which the references are given in each case, but also from the Common of Men and Women Saints, whenever there is special reason for doing so.

84. For celebrations of the Saints the following should be observed:

1. On solemnities and feasts the readings must be those that are given in the Proper or in the Commons. For solemnities and feasts of the General Roman Calendar proper readings are always assigned.

2. On solemnities inscribed in particular calendars, three readings are to be assigned, unless the Conference of Bishops has decreed that there are to be only two readings.[109] The first reading is from the Old Testament (but during the Easter season, from the Acts of the Apostles or the Book of Revelation); the second, from an Apostle; the third, from the Gospels.

3. On feasts and memorials, which have only two readings, the first reading can be chosen from either the Old Testament or from an Apostle; the second is from the Gospels. Following the Church's traditional practice, however, the first reading during the Easter season is to be taken from an Apostle, the second, as far as possible, from the Gospel of John.

6) Other Parts of the Order of Readings

85. In the Order of Readings for ritual Masses the references given are to the texts already published for the individual rites. This obviously does not include the texts belonging to celebrations that must not be integrated with Mass.[110]

86. The Order of Readings for Masses for various needs and occasions, votive Masses, and Masses for the dead provides many texts that can be of assistance in adapting such celebrations to the situation, circumstances, and concerns of the particular groups taking part.[111]

87. In ritual Masses, Masses for various needs and occasions, votive Masses, and Masses for the dead, since many texts are given for the same reading, the choice of readings follows the criteria already indicated for the choice of readings from the Common of Saints.

88. On a day when some ritual Mass is not permitted and when the norms in the individual rite allow the choice of one reading from those provided for ritual Masses, the general spiritual welfare of the participants must be considered.[112]

B) THE RESPONSORIAL PSALM AND THE ACCLAMATION BEFORE THE GOSPEL READING

89. Among the chants between the readings, the psalm which follows the first reading is of great importance. As a rule the psalm to be used is the one assigned to the reading. But in the case of readings for the Common of Saints, ritual Masses, Masses for various needs and occasions, votive Masses, and Masses for the dead the choice is left up to the priest celebrating. He will base his choice on the principle of the pastoral benefit of those present.

But to make it easier for the people to join in the response to the psalm, the Order of Readings lists certain other texts of psalms and responses that have been chosen according to the various seasons or classes of Saints. Whenever the psalm is sung, these texts may replace the text corresponding to the reading.[113]

90. The chant between the second reading and the Gospel is either specified in each Mass and correlated with the Gospel or else it is left as a choice to be made from those in the series given for a liturgical season or one of the Commons.

91. During Lent one of the acclamations from those given in the Order of Readings may be used, depending on the occasion.[114] This acclamation precedes and follows the verse before the Gospel.

CHAPTER V
DESCRIPTION OF THE ORDER OF READINGS

92. It seems useful to provide here a brief description of the Order of Readings, at least for the principal celebrations and the different seasons of the liturgical year. With these in mind, readings were selected on the basis of the rules already stated. This description is meant to assist pastors of souls to understand the structure of the Order of Readings, so that their use of it will become more perceptive and the Order of Readings a source of good for Christ's faithful.

I. Advent

A) THE SUNDAYS

93.   Each Gospel reading has a distinctive theme: the Lord's coming at the end of time (First Sunday of Advent), John the Baptist (Second and Third Sunday), and the events that prepared immediately for the Lord's birth (Fourth Sunday).

The Old Testament readings are prophecies about the Messiah and the Messianic age, especially from the Book of Isaiah.

The readings from an Apostle contain exhortations and proclamations, in keeping with the different themes of Advent.

B) THE WEEKDAYS

94.   There are two series of readings: one to be used from the beginning of Advent until 16 December; the other from 17 to 24 December.

In the first part of Advent there are readings from the Book of Isaiah, distributed in accord with the sequence of the book itself and including the more important texts that are also read on the Sundays. For the choice of the weekday Gospel the first reading has been taken into consideration.

On Thursday of the second week the readings from the Gospel concerning John the Baptist begin. The first reading is either a continuation of Isaiah or a text chosen in view of the Gospel.

In the last week before Christmas the events that immediately prepared for the Lord's birth are presented from the Gospel of Matthew (chapter 1) and Luke (chapter 1). The texts in the first reading, chosen in view of the Gospel reading, are from different Old Testament books and include important Messianic prophecies.

2. The Christmas Season

A) THE SOLEMNITIES, FEASTS, AND SUNDAYS

95.   For the vigil and the three Masses of Christmas both the prophetic readings and the others have been chosen from the Roman tradition.

The Gospel on the Sunday within the Octave of Christmas, Feast of the Holy Family, is about Jesus' childhood and the other readings are about the virtues of family life.

On the Octave Day of Christmas, Solemnity of the Blessed Virgin Mary, the Mother of God, the readings are about the Virgin Mother of God and the giving of the holy Name of Jesus.

On the second Sunday after Christmas, the readings are about the mystery of the Incarnation.

On the Epiphany of the Lord, the Old Testament reading and the Gospel continue the Roman tradition; the text for the reading from the Letters of the Apostles is about the calling of the nations to salvation.

On the Feast of the Baptism of the Lord, the texts chosen are about this mystery.

B) THE WEEKDAYS

96.   From 29 December on, there is a continuous reading of the whole of the First Letter of John, which actually begins earlier, on 27 December, the Feast of St. John the Evangelist, and on 28 December, the Feast of the Holy Innocents. The Gospels relate manifestations of the Lord: events of Jesus' childhood from the Gospel of Luke (29–30 December); passages from the first chapter of the Gospel of John (31 December–5 January); other manifestations of the Lord from the four Gospels (7–12 January).

3. Lent

A) THE SUNDAYS

97.   The Gospel readings are arranged as follows:

The first and second Sundays maintain the accounts of the Temptation and Transfiguration of the Lord, with readings, however, from all three Synoptics.

On the next three Sundays, the Gospels about the Samaritan woman, the man born blind, and the raising of Lazarus have been restored in Year A. Because these Gospels are of major importance in regard to Christian initiation, they may also be read in Year B and Year C, especially in places where there are catechumens.

Other texts, however, are provided for Year B and Year C: for Year B, a text from John about Christ's coming glorification through his Cross and Resurrection and for Year C, a text from Luke about conversion.

On Palm Sunday of the Lord's Passion the texts for the procession are selections from the Synoptic Gospels concerning the Lord's solemn entry into Jerusalem. For the Mass the reading is the account of the Lord's Passion.

The Old Testament readings are about the history of salvation, which is one of the themes proper to the catechesis of Lent. The series of texts for each Year presents the main elements of salvation history from its beginning until the promise of the New Covenant.

The readings from the Letters of the Apostles have been selected to fit the Gospel and the Old Testament readings and, to the extent possible, to provide a connection between them.

B) THE WEEKDAYS

98.   The readings from the Gospels and the Old Testament were selected because they are related to each other. They treat various themes of the Lenten catechesis

that are suited to the spiritual significance of this season. Beginning with Monday of the Fourth week of Lent, there is a semicontinuous reading of the Gospel of John, made up of texts that correspond more closely to the themes proper to Lent.

Because the readings about the Samaritan woman, the man born blind, and the raising of Lazarus are now assigned to Sundays, but only for Year A (in Year B and Year C they are optional), provision has been made for their use on weekdays. Thus at the beginning of the Third, Fourth, and Fifth Weeks of Lent optional Masses with these texts for the Gospel have been inserted and may be used in place of the readings of the day on any weekday of the respective week.

In the first days of Holy Week the readings are about the mystery of Christ's passion. For the Chrism Mass the readings bring out both Christ's Messianic mission and its continuation in the Church by means of the sacraments.

4. The Sacred Triduum and the Easter Season

A) THE SACRED EASTER TRIDUUM

99. On Holy Thursday at the evening Mass the remembrance of the meal preceding the Exodus casts its own special light because of the Christ's example in washing the feet of his disciples and Paul's account of the institution of the Christian Passover in the Eucharist.

On Good Friday the liturgical service has as its center John's narrative of the Passion of he who was proclaimed in Isaiah as the Servant of the Lord and who became the one High Priest by offering himself to the Father.

At the Vigil on the holy night of Easter there are seven Old Testament readings which recall the wonderful works of God in the history of salvation. There are two New Testament readings, the announcement of the Resurrection according to one of the Synoptic Gospels and a reading from St. Paul on Christian baptism as the sacrament of Christ's Resurrection.

The Gospel reading for the Mass on Easter day is from John on the finding of the empty tomb. There is also, however, the option to use the Gospel texts from the Easter Vigil or, when there is an evening Mass on Easter Sunday, to use the account in Luke of the Lord's appearance to the disciples on the road to Emmaus. The first reading is from the Acts of the Apostles, which throughout the Easter season replaces the Old Testament reading. The reading from the Apostle Paul concerns the living out of the paschal mystery in the Church.

B) THE SUNDAYS

100. The Gospel readings for the first three Sundays recount the appearances of the risen Christ. The readings about the Good Shepherd are assigned to the Fourth Sunday. On the Fifth, Sixth, and Seventh Sundays, there are excerpts from the Lord's discourse and prayer at the end of the Last Supper.

The first reading is from the Acts of the Apostles, in a three-year cycle of parallel and progressive selections: material is presented on the life of the early Church, its witness, and its growth.

For the reading from the Apostles, the First Letter of Peter is in Year A, the First Letter of John in Year B, the Book of Revelation in Year C. These are the texts that seem to fit in especially well with the spirit of joyous faith and sure hope proper to this season.

C) THE WEEKDAYS

101. As on the Sundays, the first reading is a semicontinuous reading from the Acts of the Apostles. The Gospel readings during the Easter octave are accounts of the Lord's appearances. After that there is a semicontinuous reading of the Gospel of John, but with texts that have a paschal character, in order to complete the reading from John during Lent. This paschal reading is made up in large part of the Lord's discourse and prayer at the end of the Last Supper.

D) THE SOLEMNITIES OF THE ASCENSION AND OF PENTECOST

102. For the first reading the Solemnity of the Ascension retains the account of the Ascension according to the Acts of the Apostles. This text is complemented by the second reading from the Apostle on Christ in exaltation at the right hand of the Father. For the Gospel reading, each of the three Years has its own text in accord with the differences in the Synoptic Gospels.

In the evening Mass celebrated on the Vigil of Pentecost four Old Testament texts are provided; any one of them may be used, in order to bring out the many aspects of Pentecost. The reading from the Apostles shows the actual working of the Holy Spirit in the Church. The Gospel reading recalls the promise of the Spirit made by Christ before his own glorification.

For the Mass on Pentecost day itself, in accord with received usage, the account in the Acts of the Apostles of the great occurrence on Pentecost day is taken as the first reading. The texts from the Apostle Paul bring out the effect of the action of the Spirit in the life of the Church. The Gospel reading is a remembrance of Jesus bestowing his Spirit on the disciples on the evening of Easter day; other optional texts describe the action of the Spirit on the disciples and on the Church.

5. Ordinary Time

A) THE ARRANGEMENT AND CHOICE OF TEXTS

103. Ordinary Time begins on the Monday after the Sunday following 6 January; it lasts until the Tuesday before Lent inclusive. It begins again on the Monday after Pentecost Sunday and finishes before evening prayer I of the First Sunday of Advent.

The Order of Readings provides readings for thirty-four Sundays and the weeks following them. In some years, however, there are only thirty-three weeks of Ordinary Time. Further, some Sundays either belong to another season (the Sunday on which the Feast of the Baptism of the Lord falls and Pentecost Sunday) or else are impeded by a solemnity that coincides with that Sunday (e.g. The Most Holy Trinity or Christ the King).

104. For the correct arrangement in the use of the readings for Ordinary Time, the following are to be respected.

1. The Sunday on which the Feast of the Baptism of the Lord falls replaces the First Sunday in Ordinary Time. Therefore the readings of the First Week in Ordinary Time begin on the Monday after the Sunday following 6 January. When the Feast of the Baptism of the Lord is celebrated on Monday because the Epiphany has been celebrated on the Sunday, the readings of the First Week begin on Tuesday.

2. The Sunday following the Feast of the Baptism of the Lord is the Second Sunday of Ordinary Time. The remaining Sundays are numbered consecutively up to the Sunday preceding the beginning of Lent. The readings for the week in which Ash Wednesday falls are interrupted after the Tuesday readings.

3. For the resumption of the readings of Ordinary Time after Pentecost Sunday:

—when there are thirty-four Sundays in Ordinary Time, the week to be used is the one that immediately follows the last week used before Lent;[115]

—when there are thirty-three Sundays in Ordinary Time, the first week that would have been used after Pentecost is omitted, in order to reserve for the end of the year the eschatological texts that are assigned to the last two weeks.[116]

B) THE SUNDAY READINGS

1) The Gospel Readings

105. On the Second Sunday in Ordinary Time the Gospel continues to center on the manifestation of the Lord, which is celebrated on the Solemnity of the Epiphany, through the traditional passage about the wedding feast at Cana and two other passages from the Gospel of John.

Beginning with the Third Sunday, there is a semicontinuous reading of the Synoptic Gospels. This reading is arranged in such a way that as the Lord's life and preaching unfold the doctrine proper to each of these Gospels is presented.

This distribution also provides a certain coordination between the meaning of each Gospel and the progress of the liturgical year. Thus after Epiphany the readings are on the beginning of the Lord's preaching and they fit in well with Christ's baptism and the first events in which he manifests himself. The liturgical year leads quite naturally to a conclusion in the eschatological theme proper to the last Sundays, since the chapters of the Synoptics that precede the account of the Passion treat this eschatological theme rather extensively.

After the Sixteenth Sunday in Year B, five readings are incorporated from John chapter 6 (the discourse on the bread of life). This is the natural place for these readings because the multiplication of the loaves from the Gospel of John takes the place of the same account in Mark. In the semicontinuous reading of Luke for Year C, the introduction of this Gospel has been prefixed to the first text (that is, on the Third Sunday). This passage expresses the author's intention very beautifully and there seemed to be no better place for it.

2) The Old Testament Readings

106. These readings have been chosen to correspond to the Gospel passages in order to avoid an excessive diversity between the readings of different Masses and above all to bring out the unity between the Old and the New Testament. The connection between the readings of the same Mass is shown by a precise choice of the readings prefixed to the individual readings.

To the degree possible, the readings were chosen in such a way that they would be short and easy to grasp. But care has been taken to ensure that many Old Testament texts of major significance would be read on Sundays. Such readings are distributed not according to a logical order but on the basis of what the Gospel reading requires. Still, the treasury of the word of God will be opened up in such a way that nearly all the principal pages of the Old Testament will become familiar to those taking part in the Mass on Sundays.

3) The Readings from the Apostles

107. There is a semicontinuous reading of the Letters of Paul and James (the Letters of Peter and John being read during the Easter and Christmas seasons).

Because it is quite long and deals with such diverse issues, the First Letter to the Corinthians has been spread over the three years of the cycle at the beginning of Ordinary Time. It also was thought best to divide the Letter to the Hebrews into two parts; the first part is read in Year B and the second in Year C.

Only readings that are short and readily grasped by the people have been chosen.

Table II at the end of this Introduction[117] indicates the distribution of Letters of the Apostles over the three-year cycle of the Sundays of Ordinary Time.

C) THE READINGS FOR SOLEMNITIES OF THE LORD DURING ORDINARY TIME

108. On the solemnities of Holy Trinity, Corpus Christi, and the Sacred Heart, the texts chosen correspond to the principal themes of these celebrations.

The readings of the Thirty-Fourth and last Sunday in Ordinary Time celebrate Christ the universal King. He was prefigured by David and proclaimed as king amid the humiliations of his Passion and Cross; he reigns in the Church and will come again at the end of time.

D) THE WEEKDAY READINGS

109. The *Gospels* are so arranged that Mark is read first (First to Ninth Week), then Matthew (Tenth to Twenty-First Week), then Luke (Twenty-Second to

Thirty-Fourth Week). Mark chapters 1–12 are read in their entirety, with the exception only of the two passages of Mark chapter 6 that are read on weekdays in other seasons. From Matthew and Luke the readings comprise all the material not contained in Mark. All the passages that either are distinctively presented in each Gospel or are needed for a proper understanding of its progression are read two or three times. Jesus' eschatological discourse as contained in its entirety in Luke is read at the end of the liturgical year.

110. The *first reading* is taken in periods of several weeks at a time first from one then from the other Testament; the number of weeks depends on the length of the biblical books read.

Rather large sections are read from the New Testament books in order to give the substance, as it were, of each of the Letters.

From the Old Testament there is room only for select passages that, as far as possible, bring out the character of the individual books. The historical texts have been chosen in such a way as to provide an overall view of the history of salvation before the Incarnation of the Lord. But lengthy narratives could hardly be presented; sometimes verses have been selected that make for a reading of moderate length. In addition, the religious significance of the historical events is sometimes brought out by means of certain texts from the wisdom books that are placed as prologues or conclusions to a series of historical readings.

Nearly all the Old Testament books have found a place in the Order of Readings for weekdays in the Proper of Seasons. The only omissions are the shortest of the prophetic books (Obadiah and Zephaniah) and a poetic book (the Song of Songs). Of those narratives of edification requiring a lengthy reading if they are to be understood, Tobit and Ruth are included, but the others (Esther and Judith) are omitted. Texts from these latter two books are assigned, however, to Sundays and weekdays at other times of the year.

Table III at the end of this Introduction[118] lists the way the books of the Old and the New Testament are distributed over the weekdays in Ordinary Time in the course of two years.

At the end of the liturgical year the readings are from the books that correspond to the eschatological character of this period, Daniel and the Book of Revelation.

CHAPTER VI
ADAPTATIONS, TRANSLATIONS AND FORMAT
OF THE ORDER OF READINGS

1. Adaptations and Translations

111. In the liturgical assembly the word of God must always be read either from the Latin texts prepared by the Holy See or from vernacular translations approved for liturgical use by the Conferences of Bishops, according to existing norms.[119]

112. The Lectionary for Mass must be translated integrally in all its parts, including the Introduction. If the Conference of Bishops has judged it necessary and useful to add certain adaptations, these are to be incorporated after their confirmation by the Holy See.[120]

113. The size of the Lectionary will necessitate editions in more than one volume; no particular division of the volumes is prescribed. But each volume is to contain the explanatory texts on the structure and purpose of the section it contains.

The ancient custom is recommended of having separate books, one for the Gospels and the other for the other readings for the Old and New Testament.

It may also be useful to publish separately a Sunday lectionary (which could also contain selected excerpts from the sanctoral cycle), and a weekday lectionary. A practical basis for dividing the Sunday lectionary is the three-year cycle, so that all the readings for each year are presented in sequence.

But there is freedom to adopt other arrangements that may be devised and seem to have pastoral advantages.

114. The texts for the chants are always to be adjoined to the readings, but separate books containing the chants alone are permitted. It is recommended that the texts be printed with divisions into stanzas.

115. Whenever a text consists of different parts, the typography must make this structure of the text clear. It is likewise recommended that even non-poetic texts be printed with division into sense lines to assist the proclamation of the readings.

116. Where there are longer and shorter forms of a text, they are to be printed separately, so that each can be read with ease. But if such a separation does not seem feasible, a way is to be found to ensure that each text can be proclaimed without mistakes.

117. In vernacular editions the texts are not to be printed without headings prefixed. If it seems advisable, an introductory note on the general meaning of the passage may be added to the heading. This note is to carry some distinctive symbol or is to be set in different type to show clearly that it is an optional text.[121]

118. It would be useful for every volume to have an index of the passages of the Bible, modeled on the biblical index of the present volume.[122] This will provide ready access to texts of the lectionaries for Mass that may be needed or helpful for specific occasions.

2. The Format of Individual Readings

For each reading the present volume carries the textual reference, the headings, and the *incipit*.

119. The text reference (that is, to chapter and verses) is always given according to the Neo-Vulgate edition for the psalms.[123] But a second reference according to the original text (Hebrew, Aramaic, or Greek) has been added wherever there is a discrepancy. Depending on the decrees of the competent Authorities for the individual languages, vernacular versions may retain the enumeration corresponding to the version of the Bible approved for liturgical use by the same Authorities. Exact references to chapter and verses, however, must always appear and may be given in the text or in the margin.

120. These references provide liturgical books with the basis of the "announcement" of the text that must be read in the celebration, but which is not printed in this volume. This "announcement" of the text will observe the following norms, but they may be altered by decree of the competent authorities on the basis of what is customary and useful for different places and languages.

121. The formula to be used is always: "A *reading* from the Book of . . . ," "A *reading* from the Letter of . . . ," or "A *reading* from the holy Gospel according to . . . ," and not: "The *beginning* of . . . ," (unless this seems advisable in particular instances) nor: "The *continuation* of. . . ."

122. The traditionally accepted titles for books are to be retained with the following exceptions.

1. Where there are two books with the same name, the title is to be: The first Book, The second Book (for example, of Kings, of Maccabees) or The first Letter, The second Letter.

2. The title more common in current usage is to be accepted for the following books:

—I and II Samuel instead of I and II Kings;

—I and II Kings instead of III and IV Kings;

—I and II Chronicles instead of I and II Paralipomenon;

—The Books of Ezra and Nehemiah instead of I and II Ezra.

3. The distinguishing titles for the wisdom books are: The Book of Job, Book of Proverbs, Book of Ecclesiastes, the Song of Songs, the Book of Wisdom, and the Book of Sirach.

4. For all the books that are included among the prophets in the Neo-Vulgate, the formula is to be: "A reading from the Book of the prophet Isaiah, or of the prophet Jeremiah or of the prophet Baruch" and: "A reading from the Book of the prophet Ezekiel, of the prophet Daniel, of the prophet Hosea, of the prophet Malachi," even in the case of books not regarded by some as being in actual fact prophetic.

5. The title is to be book of Lamentations and letter to the Hebrews, with no mention of Jeremiah or Paul.

B) THE HEADING

123. There is a *heading* prefixed to each text, chosen carefully (usually from the words of the text itself) in order to point out the main theme of the reading and, when necessary, to make the connection between the readings of the same Mass clear.

C) THE "INCIPIT"

124. In this Order of Readings the first element of the *incipit* is the customary introductory phrase: "At that time," "In those days," "Brothers and Sisters," "Beloved," "Dearly Beloved," "Dearest Brothers and Sisters," or "Thus says the Lord", "Thus says the Lord God." These words are not given when the text itself provides sufficient indication of the time or the persons involved or where such phrases would not fit in with the very nature of the text. For the individual languages, such phrases may be changed or omitted by decree of the competent Authorities.

After the first words of the *incipit* the Order of Readings gives the proper beginning of the reading, with some words deleted or supplied for intelligibility, inasmuch as the text is separated from its context. When the text for a reading is made up of non-consecutive verses and this has required changes in wording, these are appropriately indicated.

D) THE FINAL ACCLAMATION

125. In order to facilitate the congregation's acclamation, the words for the reader *The word of the Lord*, or similar words suited to local custom, are to be printed at the end of the reading for use by the reader.

TABLES

TABLE 1

Principal Celebrations of the Liturgical Year

YEAR	SUNDAY CYCLE	WEEKDAY CYCLE	ASH WEDNESDAY	EASTER	ASCENSION THURSDAY	PENTECOST
2003	B	I	5 March	20 April	29 May	8 June
2004	C	II	25 Feb.	11 April	20 May	30 May
2005	A	I	9 Feb.	27 March	5 May	15 May
2006	B	II	1 March	16 April	25 May	4 June
2007	C	I	21 Feb.	8 April	17 May	27 May
2008	A	II	6 Feb.	23 March	1 May	11 May
2009	B	I	25 Feb.	12 April	21 May	31 May
2010	C	II	17 Feb.	4 April	13 May	23 May
2011	A	I	9 March	24 April	2 June	12 June
2012	B	II	22 Feb.	8 April	17 May	27 May
2013	C	I	13 Feb.	31 March	9 May	19 May
2014	A	II	5 March	20 April	29 May	8 June
2015	B	I	18 Feb.	5 April	14 May	24 May
2016	C	II	10 Feb.	27 March	5 May	15 May
2017	A	I	1 March	16 April	25 May	4 June

WEEKS IN ORDINARY TIME				
BEFORE LENT		AFTER EASTER SEASON		
ENDING	IN WEEK NO.	BEGINNING	IN WEEK NO.	1ST SUNDAY OF ADVENT
4 March	8	9 June	10	30 Nov.
24 Feb.	7	31 May	9	28 Dec.
8 Feb.	5	16 May	7	27 Nov.
28 Feb.	8	5 June	9	3 Dec.
20 Feb.	7	28 May	8	2 Dec.
5 Feb.	4	12 May	6	30 Nov.
24 Feb.	7	1 June	9	29 Nov.
16 Feb.	6	24 May	8	28 Nov.
8 March	9	13 June	11	27 Nov.
21 Feb.	7	28 May	8	2 Dec.
12 Feb.	5	20 May	7	1 Dec.
4 March	8	9 June	10	30 Nov.
17 Feb.	6	25 May	8	29 Nov.
11 Feb.	5	16 May	7	27 Nov.
2 March	8	5 June	9	3 Dec.

TABLE II

Order of the Second Reading on the Sundays of Ordinary Time

SUNDAY	YEAR A	YEAR B	YEAR C
2	1 Corinthians 1–4	1 Corinthians 6–11	1 Corinthians 12–15
3	"	"	"
4	"	"	"
5	"	"	"
6	"	"	"
7	"	2 Corinthians	"
8	"	"	"
9	Romans	"	Galatians
10	"	"	"
11	"	"	"
12	"	"	"
13	"	"	"
14	"	"	"
15	"	Ephesians	Colossians
16	"	"	"
17	"	"	"
18	"	"	"
19	"	"	Hebrews 11–12
20	"	"	"
21	"	"	"
22	"	James	"
23	"	"	Philemon
24	"	"	1 Timothy
25	Philippians	"	"
26	"	"	"
27	"	Hebrews 2–10	2 Timothy
28	"	"	"
29	1 Thessalonians	"	"
30	"	"	"
31	"	"	2 Thessalonians
32	"	"	"
33	"	"	"

TABLE III

Order of the First Reading on the Weekdays of Ordinary Time

WEEK	YEAR I	YEAR II
1	Hebrews	1 Samuel
2	"	"
3	"	2 Samuel
4	"	2 Samuel; 1 Kings 1–16
5	Genesis 1–11	1 Kings 1–16
6	"	James
7	Sirach (Ecclesiasticus)	"
8	"	1 Peter; Jude
9	Tobit	2 Peter; 2 Timothy
10	2 Corinthians	1 Kings 17–22
11	"	1 Kings 17–22; 2 Kings
12	Genesis 12–50	2 Kings; Lamentations
13	"	Amos
14	"	Hosea; Isaiah
15	Exodus	Isaiah; Micah
16	"	Micah; Jeremiah
17	Exodus; Leviticus	Jeremiah
18	Numbers; Deuteronomy	Jeremiah; Nahum; Habakkuk
19	Deuteronomy; Joshua	Ezekiel
20	Judges; Ruth	"
21	1 Thessalonians	2 Thessalonians; 1 Corinthians
22	1 Thessalonians; Colossians	1 Corinthians
23	Colossians; 1 Timothy	"
24	1 Timothy	"
25	Ezra; Haggai; Zechariah	Proverbs, Qoheleth (Ecclesiastes)
26	Zechariah; Nehemiah; Baruch	Job
27	Jonah; Malachi; Joel	Galatians
28	Romans	Galatians; Ephesians
29	"	Ephesians
30	"	"
31	"	Ephesians; Philippians
32	Wisdom	Titus; Philemon; 2 and 3 John
33	1 and 2 Maccabees	Revelation
34	Daniel	"

NOTES

1. See SC, 7, 24, 33, 35, 48, 51, 52, 56; DV, 21, 25, 26; AG, 6; PO, 18.

2. See Paul VI, *motu proprio Ministeria quaedam*, V; apostolic exhortation *Evangelii nuntiandi* (EN), 28, 43, 47; apostolic exhortation *Marialis cultus* (MC), 12; John Paul II, apostolic constitution *Scripturarum thesaurus*, p. v–viii; apostolic exhortation *Catechesi tradendae* (CT), 23, 27, 48; letter *Dominicae cenae* (DC), 10.

3. See EM, 10; CDW, instruction *Liturgicae instaurationes* (LI) 2; GCD, 10–12, 25; GIRM, 9, 11, 24, 33, 60, 62, 316, 320; SDW, instruction *Inaestimabile donum*, (ID), 1, 2, 3.

4. See LMIn (1969), nos. 1–7; decree of promulgation: AAS 61 (1969) 548–549.

5. See SC, 35, 56; EN, 28, 47; DC, 10, 11, 12.

6. CDW, instruction *Liturgicae instaurantiones* (LI) 2, for example, the terms, *word of God, sacred Scripture, Old* and *New Testament, reading(s) of the word of God, reading(s) from sacred scripture, celebration(s) of the word of God,* etc.

7. Thus the same text may be read or used for various reasons on various occasions and celebrations of the church's liturgical year. This is to be recalled in the homily, in pastoral exegesis, and in catechesis.

8. See Luke 4:16–21; 24:25–35 and 44–49.

9. Thus, for example, in the celebration of the Mass there is proclamation, reading, etc. (see GIRM, 21, 23, 95, 131, 146, 234, 235). There are also other celebrations of the word of God in the Roman Pontifical, Ritual and Liturgy of the Hours as restored by decree of the Second Vatican Council.

10. See SC, 7, 33; Mark 16:19–20; Matthew 28:20.

11. See SC, 7.

12. See Hebrews 4:12.

13. See Augustine, *Quaestionum in Heptateuchum*, book 2; DV, 16.

14. See Jerome, "If, as St. Paul says (1 Cor 1:24), Christ is the power of God and the wisdom of God, anyone who does not know the Scriptures does not know the power of God or his wisdom. For not to know the Scriptures is not to know Christ" (*Commentarii in Isaiam prophetam*, prologue); DV, 25.

15. See 2 Corinthians 1:20–22.

16. See SC, 10.

17. See 2 Thessalonians 3:1.

18. See RomM, opening prayers A, B and C in Mass for the Universal Church.

19. See RomM, opening prayer for the Twenty-first Sunday in Ordinary Time.

20. See DV, 8.

21. See John 14:15–17, 25–26; 15:26—16:15.

22. See PO, 4.

23. See SC, 51; PO, 18; DV, 21; AG, 6; GIRM, 8.

24. SC, 56.

25. GIRM, 33.

26. See LI, 2; DC, 10; ID, 1.

27. SC, 33.

28. See LMIn, 111.

29. See RomM, *Ordo cantus Missae* (ed. typ., 1972), Praenotanda, 4, 6, 10.

30. See GIRM, 11.

31. See GIRM, 272; LMIn, 32–34.

32. See GIRM, 35, 95.

33. See GIRM, 82–84.

34. See GIRM, 94, 131.

35. See RomM, Order of Mass, "Liturgy of the Word: The Gospel."

36. See GIRM, 36.

37. Paul VI, apostolic constitution *Laudis canticum*, in *The Liturgy of the Hours*; see also SC, 24, 90; CR, instruction *Musicam Sacram* (MS) 39.

38. See LMIn, 89–90.

39. See GIRM, 18, 39.

40. See GIRM, 272; LMIn, 32ff.

41. See GIRM, 39.

42. See GIRM, 37—39; RomM, *Ordo cantus Missae*, Praenotanda, 7–9; *Graduale Romanum* (1974), Praenotanda, 7, *Graduale Simple* (2d ed. typ., 1975); Praenotanda, 16.

43. See SC, 52; CR, instruction *Inter oecumenici* (IOe) 54.

44. See GIRM, 42.

45. See SC, 35, 2.

46. See SC, 6, 47.

47. See Paul VI, encyclical, *Mysterium fidei*, 3 Sept 1965; AG, 9; EN, 43.

48. See SC, 35, 2; GIRM, 41.

49. SC, 10.

50. See CT, 48.

51. See GIRM, 165.

52. See GIRM, 42; EM, 28.

53. See AP, 6g; DMC, 48.

54. See GIRM, 42, 338; *Rite of Marriage* (1969), 22, 42, 57 and *Rite of Funerals* (1969), 41, 64.

55. See GIRM, 97.

56. See GIRM, 139.

57. See GIRM, 23.

58. See GIRM, 43.

59. See GIRM, 45.

60. See GIRM, 99.

61. See GIRM, 47.

62. See LMIn, note 23.

63. See GIRM, 272.

64. See SC, 122.

65. See Roman Pontifical, *Ordination of Deacons, Priests and Bishops* (1968): of deacons, 24; of deacons and priests, 21; of a deacon, 24; of a bishop, 25; of bishops, 25.

66. See LMIn, 78–91.

67. See GIRM, 318–320; 324–325.

68. See GIRM, 313.

69. See GIRM, 42; ID, 3.

70. See GIRM, 11.

71. See GIRM, 68.

72. See GIRM, 33, 47.

73. PO, 4.

74. SC, 33.

75. See GIRM, 9.

76. See SC, 7.

77. See SC, 9.

78. See Romans 1:16.

79. See DV, 21.

80. Ibid.

81. See John 14:15–26; 15:26—16:4, 5–15.

82. See AG, 6, 15; DV, 26.

83. See SC, 24; GCD, 25.

84. See SC, 56; ID, 1.

85. See SC, 24, 35.

86. See GIRM, 34.

87. See GIRM, 96.

88. See GIRM, 47, 61, 132; ID 3.

89. GIRM, 66.

90. See MQ, no. V.

91. See ID, 2, 18; DMC, 22, 24, 27.

92. See GIRM, 47, 66, 151.

93. GIRM, 66.

94. See GIRM, 37a, 67.

95. See GIRM, 68.

96. See Paul VI, apostolic constitution, *Missale Romanum*.

97. See SC, 35, 51.

98. See Paul VI, apostolic constitution, *Missale Romanum*: "This is meant to provide a fuller exposition of the continuing process of the mystery of salvation as shown in the words of divine revelation."

99. See SC, 9, 33; IOe, 7; CT, 23.

100. See SC, 35,4; IOe, 37–38.

101. See AP, 6; DMC, 41–47; MC, 12.

102. Each of the years is designated by the letter A, B or C. The following is the procedure to determine which year is A, B, or C. The letter C designates a year whose number is divisible into three equal parts, as though the cycle had taken its beginning from the first year of the Christian era. Thus the year 1 would have been Year A; year 2, Year B; year 3, Year C (as would years 6, 9 and 12). [Thus, year 1998 was Year C; 1999, Year A; 2000, Year B; and 2001, Year C again.] And so forth. Obviously, each cycle runs in accord with the plan of the liturgical year, that is, it begins with the first

week of Advent, which falls in the preceding year of the civil calendar.

The years in each cycle [are] marked in a sense by the principal charadcteristic of the synoptic gospel (Matthew, Mark or Luke) used for the semicontinuous reading of Ordinary Time. Thus the first Year of the cycle is the Year for the reading of the Gospel of Matthew and is so named; the second and third Years are the Year of Mark and the Year of Luke.

103. See GIRM, 36–40.

104. GIRM, 313.

105. See GIRM, 318; ID, 1.

106. For example: in Lent the continuity of the Old Testament readings corresponds to the unfolding of the history of salvation; the Sundays in Ordinary Time provide the semicontinuous reading of one of the letters of the apostles. In these cases it is right that the pastor of souls choose one or other of the readings in a systematic way over a series of Sundays, so that he may establish a coherent plan for catechesis. It is not right to read indiscriminately on one day from the Old Testament, on another from the letter of an apostle, without any orderly plan for the texts that follow.

107. See GIRM, 319.

108. See GIRM, 316c; SC, 51.

109. See GIRM, 318.

110. See *Rite of Penance* (1974), introduction, no. 13.

111. See GIRM, 320.

112. See GIRM, 313.

113. See Lectionary for Mass, nos. 173–174.

114. See Lectionary for Mass, no. 223.

115. So, for example, when there are six weeks before Lent, the seventh week begins on the Monday after Pentecost. The solemnity of the Most Holy Trinity replaces the Sunday of Ordinary Time.

116. When there are, for example, five weeks before Lent, the Monday after Pentecost begins with the Seventh Week of Ordinary Time and the Sixth Week is omitted.

117. See LMIn, Table II.

118. See LMIn, Table III.

119. See Consilium, instruction *De Popularibus interpretationibus conficiendis*, 25

Jan 1969: Notitiae 5 (1969) 3–12; CDW, *Epistola ad Praesides Conferentiarum Episcoporum de linguis vulgaribus in S. Liturgiam inducendis:* Notitiae 12 (1976) 300–302.

120. See LI, 11; GIRM, 325.

121. See GIRM, 11, 29, 68a, 139.

122. See Lectionary for Mass, index of readings.

123. The references for the psalms follow the order of the *Liber Psalmorum*, Pontifical Commission for the Neo-Vulgate.

GENERAL NORMS
FOR THE
LITURGICAL YEAR
AND THE
CALENDAR

SACRED CONGREGATION OF RITES
21 MARCH 1969

OUTLINE

GENERAL NORMS FOR THE LITURGICAL YEAR AND THE CALENDAR

CHAPTER I
THE LITURGICAL YEAR

1. Christ's saving work is celebrated in sacred memory by the Church on fixed days throughout the year. Each week on the day called the Lord's Day the Church commemorates the Lord's resurrection. Once a year at Easter the Church honors this resurrection and passion with the utmost solemnity. In fact through the yearly cycle the Church unfolds the entire mystery of Christ and keeps the anniversaries of the saints.

During the different seasons of the liturgical year, the Church, in accord with traditional discipline, carries out the formation of the faithful by means of devotional practices, both interior and exterior, instruction, and works of penance and mercy.[1]

2. The principles given here may and must be applied to both the Roman Rite and all others; but the practical rules are to be taken as pertaining solely to the Roman Rite, except in matters that of their nature also affect the other rites.[2]

TITLE I: LITURGICAL DAYS

I. The Liturgical Day in General

3. Each day is made holy through the liturgical celebrations of the people of God, especially through the eucharistic sacrifice and the divine office.

The liturgical day runs from midnight to midnight, but the observance of Sunday and solemnities begins with the evening of the preceding day.

II. Sunday

4. The Church celebrates the paschal mystery on the first day of the week, known as the Lord's Day or Sunday. This follows a tradition handed down from the apostles and having its origin from the day of Christ's resurrection. Thus Sunday must be ranked as the first holy day of all.[3]

5. Because of its special importance, the Sunday celebration gives way only to solemnities or feasts of the Lord. The Sundays of the seasons of Advent, Lent, and Easter, however, take precedence over all solemnities and feasts of the Lord. Solemnities occurring on these Sundays are observed on the Saturday preceding.

6.   By its nature, Sunday excludes any other celebration's being permanently assigned to that day, with these exceptions:

   a. Sunday within the octave of Christmas is the feast of the Holy Family;

   b. Sunday following 6 January is the feast of the Baptism of the Lord;

   c. Sunday after Pentecost is the solemnity of the Holy Trinity;

   d. The last Sunday in Ordinary Time is the solemnity of Christ the King.

7.   In those places where the solemnities of Epiphany, Ascension, and Corpus Christi are not observed as holy days of obligation, they are assigned to a Sunday, which is then considered their proper day in the calendar. Thus:

   a. Epiphany, to the Sunday falling between 2 January and 8 January;

   b. Ascension, to the Seventh Sunday of Easter;

   c. the solemnity of Corpus Christi, to the Sunday after Trinity Sunday.

III. Solemnities, Feasts, and Memorials

8.   As it celebrates the mystery of Christ in yearly cycle, the Church also venerates with a particular love Mary, the Mother of God, and sets before the devotion of the faithful the memory of the martyrs and other saints.[4]

9.   The saints of universal significance have celebrations obligatory throughout the entire Church. Other saints either are listed in the General Calendar for optional celebration or are left to the veneration of some particular Church, region, or religious family.[5]

10.   According to their importance, celebrations are distinguished from each other and named as follows: solemnities, feasts, memorials.

11.   Solemnities are counted as the principal days in the calendar and their observance begins with evening prayer I of the preceding day. Some also have their own vigil Mass for use when Mass is celebrated in the evening of the preceding day.

12.   The celebration of Easter and Christmas, the two greatest solemnities, continues for eight days, with each octave governed by its own rules.

13.   Feasts are celebrated within the limits of the natural day and accordingly do not have evening prayer I. Exceptions are feasts of the Lord that fall on a Sunday in Ordinary Time and in the Christmas season and that replace the Sunday office.

14.   Memorials are either obligatory or optional. Their observance is integrated into the celebration of the occurring weekday in accord with the norms set forth in the *General Instruction of the Roman Missal* and the *Liturgy of the Hours*.

Obligatory memorials occurring on Lenten weekdays may only be celebrated as optional memorials.

Should more than one optional memorial fall on the same day, only one may be celebrated; the others are omitted.

15.   On Saturdays in Ordinary Time when there is no obligatory memorial, an optional memorial of the Blessed Virgin Mary is allowed.

IV. Weekdays

16.   The days following Sunday are called weekdays. They are celebrated in different ways according to the importance each one has.

a. Ash Wednesday and the days of Holy Week, from Monday to Thursday inclusive, have precedence over all other celebrations.

b. The weekdays of Advent from 17 December to 24 December inclusive and all the weekdays of Lent have precedence over obligatory memorials.

c. All other weekdays give way to solemnities and feasts and are combined with memorials.

TITLE II: THE YEARLY CYCLE

17.   By means of the yearly cycle the Church celebrates the whole mystery of Christ, from his incarnation until the day of Pentecost and the expectation of his coming again.[6]

I. Easter Triduum

18.   Christ redeemed us all and gave perfect glory to God principally through his paschal mystery: dying he destroyed our death and rising he restored our life. Therefore the Easter triduum of the passion and resurrection of Christ is the culmination of the entire liturgical year.[7] Thus the solemnity of Easter has the same kind of preeminence in the liturgical year that Sunday has in the week.[8]

19.   The Easter triduum begins with the evening Mass of the Lord's Supper, reaches its high point in the Easter Vigil, and closes with evening prayer on Easter Sunday.

20.   On Good Friday[9] and, if possible, also on Holy Saturday until the Easter Vigil,[10] the Easter fast is observed everywhere.

21.   The Easter Vigil, during the holy night when Christ rose from the dead, ranks as the "mother of all vigils."[11] Keeping watch, the Church awaits Christ's resurrection and celebrates it in the sacraments. Accordingly, the entire celebration of this vigil should take place at night, that is, it should either begin after nightfall or end before the dawn of Sunday.

II. Easter Season

22. The fifty days from Easter Sunday to Pentecost are celebrated in joyful exultation as one feast day, or better as one "great Sunday."[12]

These above all others are the days for the singing of the *Alleluia*.

23. The Sundays of this season rank as the paschal Sundays and, after Easter Sunday itself, are called the Second, Third, Fourth, Fifth, Sixth, and Seventh Sundays of Easter. The period of fifty sacred days ends on Pentecost Sunday.

24. The first eight days of the Easter season make up the octave of Easter and are celebrated as solemnities of the Lord.

25. On the fortieth day after Easter the Ascension is celebrated, except in places where, not being a holy day of obligation, it has been transferred to the Seventh Sunday of Easter (see no. 7).

26. The weekdays after the Ascension until the Saturday before Pentecost inclusive are a preparation for the coming of the Holy Spirit.

III. Lent

27. Lent is a preparation for the celebration of Easter. For the Lenten liturgy disposes both catechumens and the faithful to celebrate the paschal mystery: catechumens, through the several stages of Christian initiation; the faithful, through reminders of their own baptism and through penitential practices.[13]

28. Lent runs from Ash Wednesday until the Mass of the Lord's Supper exclusive.

The *Alleluia* is not used from the beginning of Lent until the Easter Vigil.

29. On Ash Wednesday, a universal day of fast,[14] ashes are distributed.

30. The Sundays of this season are called the First, Second, Third, Fourth, and Fifth Sundays of Lent. The Sixth Sunday, which marks the beginning of Holy Week, is called Passion Sunday (Palm Sunday).

31. Holy Week has as its purpose the remembrance of Christ's passion, beginning with his Messianic entrance into Jerusalem.

At the chrism Mass on Holy Thursday morning the bishop, concelebrating Mass with his body of priests, blesses the oils and consecrates the chrism.

IV. Christmas Season

32. Next to the yearly celebration of the paschal mystery, the Church holds most sacred the memorial of Christ's birth and early manifestations. This is the purpose of the Christmas season.

33. The Christmas season runs from evening prayer I of Christmas until the Sunday after Epiphany or after 6 January, inclusive.

34.   The Mass of the vigil of Christmas is used in the evening of 24 December, either before or after evening prayer I.

On Christmas itself, following an ancient tradition of Rome, three Masses may be celebrated: namely, the Mass at Midnight, the Mass at Dawn, and the Mass during the Day.

35.   Christmas has its own octave, arranged as follows:

   a. Sunday within the octave is the feast of the Holy Family;

   b. 26 December is the feast of Saint Stephen, First Martyr;

   c. 27 December is the feast of Saint John, Apostle and Evangelist;

   d. 28 December is the feast of the Holy Innocents;

   e. 29, 30, and 31 December are days within the octave;

   f. 1 January, the octave day of Christmas, is the solemnity of Mary, Mother of God. It also recalls the conferral of the holy Name of Jesus.

36.   The Sunday falling between 2 January and 5 January is the Second Sunday after Christmas.

37.   Epiphany is celebrated on 6 January, unless (where it is not observed as a holy day of obligation) it has been assigned to the Sunday occurring between 2 January and 8 January (see no. 7).

38.   The Sunday falling after 6 January is the feast of the Baptism of the Lord.

V. Advent

39.   Advent has a twofold character: as a season to prepare for Christmas when Christ's first coming to us is remembered; as a season when that remembrance directs the mind and heart to await Christ's Second Coming at the end of time. Advent is thus a period for devout and joyful expectation.

40.   Advent begins with evening prayer I of the Sunday falling on or closest to 30 November and ends before evening prayer I of Christmas.

41.   The Sundays of this season are named the First, Second, Third, and Fourth Sundays of Advent.

42.   The weekdays from 17 December to 24 December inclusive serve to prepare more directly for the Lord's birth.

VI. Ordinary Time

43.   Apart from those seasons having their own distinctive character, thirty-three or thirty-four weeks remain in the yearly cycle that do not celebrate a specific aspect of the mystery of Christ. Rather, especially on the Sundays, they are devoted to the mystery of Christ in all its aspects. This period is known as Ordinary Time.

44. Ordinary Time begins on Monday after the Sunday following 6 January and continues until Tuesday before Ash Wednesday inclusive. It begins again on Monday after Pentecost and ends before evening prayer I of the First Sunday of Advent.

This is also the reason for the series of liturgical texts found in both the Roman Missal and *The Liturgy of the Hours* (vols. III–IV), for Sundays and weekdays in this season.

VII. Rogation and Ember Days

45. On rogation and ember days the practice of the Church is to offer prayers to the Lord for the needs of all people, especially for the productivity of the earth and for human labor, and to give him public thanks.

46. In order to adapt the rogation and ember days to various regions and the different needs of the people, the conference of bishops should arrange the time and plan of their celebration.

Consequently, the competent authority should lay down norms, in view of local conditions, on extending such celebrations over one or several days and on repeating them during the year.

47. On each day of these celebrations the Mass should be one of the votive Masses for various needs and occasions that is best suited to the intentions of the petitioners.

CHAPTER II
THE CALENDAR

TITLE I: CALENDAR AND CELEBRATIONS TO BE ENTERED

48. The arrangement for celebrating the liturgical year is governed by the calendar: the General Calendar, for use in the entire Roman Rite, or a particular calendar, for use in a particular Church or in families of religious.

49. In the General Calendar the entire cycle of celebrations is entered: celebrations of the mystery of salvation as found in the Proper of Seasons, of those saints having universal significance who must therefore be celebrated by everyone or of saints who show the universality and continuity of holiness within the people of God.

Particular calendars have more specialized celebrations, arranged to harmonize with the general cycle.[1] The individual Churches or families of religious should show a special honor to those saints who are properly their own.

Particular calendars, drawn up by the competent authority, must be approved by the Apostolic See.

50.   The drawing up of a particular calendar is to be guided by the following considerations:

a. The Proper of Seasons (that is, the cycle of seasons, solemnities, and feasts that unfold and honor the mystery of redemption during the liturgical year) must be kept intact and retain its rightful preeminence over particular celebrations.

b. Particular celebrations must be coordinated harmoniously with universal celebrations, with care for the rank and precedence indicated for each in the Table of Liturgical Days. Lest particular calendars be enlarged disproportionately, individual saints may have only one feast in the liturgical year. For persuasive pastoral reasons there may be another celebration in the form of an optional memorial marking the transfer or discovery of the bodies of patrons or founders of Churches or of families of religious.

c. Feasts granted by indult may not duplicate other celebrations already contained in the cycle of the mystery of salvation, nor may they be multiplied out of proportion.

51.   Although it is reasonable for each diocese to have its own calendar and propers for the Mass and office, there is no reason why entire provinces, regions, countries, or even larger areas may not have common calendars and propers, prepared with the cooperation of all the parties involved.

This principle may also be followed in the case of the calendars for several provinces of religious within the same civil territory.

52.   A particular calendar is prepared by inserting in the General Calendar special solemnities, feasts, and memorials proper to that calendar:

a. in a diocesan calendar, in addition to celebrations of its patrons and the dedication of the cathedral, the saints and the blessed who bear some special connection with that diocese, for example, as their birthplace, residence over a long period, or place of death;

b. in the calendar of religious, besides celebrations of their title, founder, or patron, those saints and blesseds who were members of that religious family or had some special relationship with it;

c. in a calendar for individual churches, celebrations proper to a diocese or religious community, those celebrations that are proper to that church and are listed in the Table of Liturgical Days and also the saints who are buried in that church. Members of religious communities should join with the community of the local Church in celebrating the anniversary of the dedication of the cathedral and the principal patrons of the place and of the larger region where they live.

53.   When a diocese or religious family has the distinction of having many saints and blessed, care must be taken not to overload the calendar of the entire diocese or institute. Consequently:

a. The first measure that can be taken is to have a common feast of all the saints and the blessed of a given diocese or religious family or of some category.

b. Only the saints and blessed of particular significance for an entire diocese or religious family may be entered in the calendar with an individual celebration.

c. The other saints or blessed are to be celebrated only in those places with which they have closer ties or where their bodies are buried.

54. Proper celebrations should be entered in the calendar as obligatory or optional memorials, unless other provisions have been made for them in the Table of Liturgical Days or there are special historical or pastoral reasons. But there is no reason why some celebrations may not be observed with greater solemnity in some places than in the rest of the diocese or religious community.

55. Celebrations entered in a particular calendar must be observed by all who are bound to follow that calendar. Only with the approval of the Apostolic See may celebrations be removed from a calendar or changed in rank.

TITLE II: THE PROPER DATE FOR CELEBRATIONS

56. The Church's practice has been to celebrate the saints on the date of their death ("birthday"), a practice it would be well to follow when entering proper celebrations in particular calendars.

Even though proper celebrations have special importance for individual local Churches or religious families, it is of great advantage that there be as much unity as possible in the observance of solemnities, feasts, and obligatory memorials listed in the General Calendar.

In entering proper celebrations in a particular calendar, therefore, the following are to be observed.

a. Celebrations listed in the General Calendar are to be entered on the same date in a particular calendar, with a change in rank of celebration if necessary.

This also applies to diocesan or religious calendars when celebrations proper to an individual church alone are added.

b. Celebrations for saints not included in the General Calendar should be assigned to the date of their death. If the date of death is not known, the celebrations should be assigned to a date associated with the saint on some other grounds, such as the date of ordination or of the discovery or transfer of the saint's body; otherwise it is celebrated on a date unimpeded by other celebrations in that particular calendar.

c. If the date of death or other appropriate date is impeded in the General Calendar or in a particular calendar by another obligatory celebration, even of lower rank, the celebration should be assigned to the closest date not so impeded.

d. If, however, it is a question of celebrations that cannot be transferred to another date because of pastoral reasons, the impeding celebration should itself be transferred.

e. Other celebrations, called feasts granted by indult, should be entered on a date more pastorally appropriate.

f. The cycle of the liturgical year should stand out with its full preeminence, but at the same time the celebration of the saints should not be permanently impeded. Therefore, dates that most of the time fall during Lent and the octave of Easter, as well as the weekdays between 17 December and 31 December, should remain free of any particular celebration, unless it is a question of optional memorials, feasts found in the Table of Liturgical Days under no. 8 a, b, c, d, or solemnities that cannot be transferred to another season.

The solemnity of Saint Joseph (19 March), except where it is observed as a holy day of obligation, may be transferred by the conference of bishops to another day outside Lent.

57. If some saints or blessed are listed in the calendar on the same date, they are always celebrated together whenever they are of equal rank, even though one or more of them may be more proper to that calendar. If one or other of these saints or blessed is to be celebrated with a higher rank, that office alone is observed and the others are omitted, unless it is appropriate to assign them to another date in the form of an obligatory memorial.

58. For the pastoral advantage of the people, it is permissible to observe on the Sundays in Ordinary Time those celebrations that fall during the week and have special appeal to the devotion of the faithful, provided the celebrations take precedence over these Sundays in the Table of Liturgical Days. The Mass for such celebrations may be used at all the Masses at which a congregation is present.

59. Precedence among liturgical days relative to the celebration is governed solely by the following table.

TABLE OF LITURGICAL DAYS
ACCORDING TO THEIR ORDER OF PRECEDENCE

I

1. Easter triduum of the Lord's passion and resurrection.

2. Christmas, Epiphany, Ascension, and Pentecost.
   Sundays of Advent, Lent, and the Easter season.
   Ash Wednesday.
   Weekdays of Holy Week from Monday to Thursday inclusive.
   Days within the octave of Easter.

3. Solemnities of the Lord, the Blessed Virgin Mary, and saints listed in the General Calendar.
   All Souls.

4. Proper solemnities, namely:

    a. Solemnity of the principal patron of the place, that is, the city or state.

    b. Solemnity of the dedication of a particular church and the anniversary.

    c. Solemnity of the title of a particular church.

    d. Solemnity of the title, or of the founder, or of the principal patron of a religious order or congregation.

II

5. Feasts of the Lord in the General Calendar.

6. Sundays of the Christmas season and Sundays in Ordinary Time.

7. Feasts of the Blessed Virgin Mary and of the saints in the General Calendar.

8. Proper feasts, namely:

    a. Feast of the principal patron of the diocese.

    b. Feast of the anniversary of the dedication of the cathedral.

    c. Feast of the principal patron of a region or province, or a country, or of a wider territory.

    d. Feast of the title, founder, or principal patron of an order or congregation and of a religious province, without prejudice to the directives in no. 4.

    e. Other feasts proper to an individual church.

    f. Other feasts listed in the calendar of a diocese or of a religious order or congregation.

9. Weekdays of Advent from 17 December to 24 December inclusive.
Days within the octave of Christmas.
Weekdays of Lent.

III

10. Obligatory memorials in the General Calendar.

11. Proper obligatory memorials, namely:

    a. Memorial of a secondary patron of the place, diocese, region, or province, country or wider territory, or of an order or congregation and of a religious province.

    b. Obligatory memorials listed in the calendar of a diocese, or of an order or congregation.

12. Optional memorials; but these may be celebrated even on the days listed in no. 9, in the special manner described by the General Instruction of the Roman Missal and of the Liturgy of the Hours.

In the same manner obligatory memorials may be celebrated as optional memorials if they happen to fall on the Lenten weekdays.

13. Weekdays of Advent up to 16 December inclusive.

Weekdays of the Christmas season from 2 January until the Saturday after Epiphany.

Weekdays of the Easter season from Monday after the octave of Easter until the Saturday before Pentecost inclusive.

Weekdays in Ordinary Time.

---

60. If several celebrations fall on the same day, the one that holds the highest rank according to the preceding Table of Liturgical Days is observed. But a solemnity impeded by a liturgical day that takes precedence over it should be transferred to the closest day not listed in nos. 1–8 in the table of the precedence; the rule of no. 5 remains in effect. Other celebrations are omitted that year.

61. If the same day were to call for celebration of evening prayer of that day's office and evening prayer I of the following day, evening prayer of the day with the higher rank in the Table of Liturgical Days takes precedence; in cases of equal rank, evening prayer of the actual day takes precedence.

NOTES

CHAPTER I

1. See SC 102–105.

2. See SC 5.

3. See SC 106.

4. See SC 103–104.

5. See SC 111 .

6. See SC 102.

7. See SC 5.

8. See SC 106.

9. See Paul VI, apostolic constitution, *Paeni-temini*, 17 Feb 1966, II, §3.

10. See SC 110.

11. Augustine, Sermo 219.

12. Athanasius, *Epist. fest.* 1.

13. See SC 109.

14. See *Paenitemini*, 11, §3.

CHAPTER II

1. See CDW, instruction, *Calendaria particularia*, 24 June 1970.

CHRISTIAN INITIATION
GENERAL INTRODUCTION

CONGREGATION FOR DIVINE WORSHIP
15 MAY 1969, 23 SEPTEMBER 1974

OUTLINE

CHRISTIAN INITIATION, GENERAL INTRODUCTION

1. In the sacraments of Christian initiation we are freed from the power of darkness and joined to Christ's death, burial, and resurrection. We receive the Spirit of filial adoption and are part of the entire people of God in the celebration of the memorial of the Lord's death and resurrection.[1]

2. Baptism incorporates us into Christ and forms us into God's people. This first sacrament pardons all our sins, rescues us from the power of darkness, and brings us to the dignity of adopted children,[2] a new creation through water and the Holy Spirit. Hence we are called and are indeed the children of God.[3]

By signing us with the gift of the Spirit, confirmation makes us more completely the image of the Lord and fills us with the Holy Spirit, so that we may bear witness to him before all the world and work to bring the Body of Christ to its fullness as soon as possible.[4]

Finally, coming to the table of the eucharist, we eat the flesh and drink the blood of the Son of Man so that we may have eternal life[5] and show forth the unity of God's people. By offering ourselves with Christ, we share in the universal sacrifice, that is, the entire community of the redeemed offered to God by their High Priest,[6] and we pray for a greater outpouring of the Holy Spirit, so that the whole human race can be brought into the unity of God's family.[7]

Thus the three sacraments of Christian initiation closely combine to bring us, the faithful of Christ, to his full stature and to enable us to carry out the mission of the entire people of God in the Church and in the world.[8]

DIGNITY OF BAPTISM

3. Baptism, the door to life and to the kingdom of God, is the first sacrament of the New Law, which Christ offered to all, that they might have eternal life.[9] He later entrusted this sacrament and the Gospel to his Church, when he told his apostles: "Go, make disciples of all nations, and baptize them in the name of the Father, and of the Son, and of the Holy Spirit."[10] Baptism is therefore, above all, the sacrament of that faith by which, enlightened by the grace of the Holy Spirit, we respond to the Gospel of Christ. That is why the Church believes that it is its most basic and necessary duty to inspire all, catechumens, parents of children still to be baptized, and godparents, to that true and living faith by which they hold fast to Christ and enter into or confirm their commitment to the New Covenant. In order to enliven such faith, the Church prescribes the pastoral instruction of catechumens, the preparation of the children's parents,

the celebration of God's word, and the profession of faith at the celebration of baptism.

4.   Further, baptism is the sacrament by which its recipients are incorporated into the Church and are built up together in the Spirit into a house where God lives,[11] into a holy nation and a royal priesthood.[12] Baptism is a sacramental bond of unity linking all who have been signed by it.[13] Because of that unchangeable effect (given expression in the Latin liturgy by the anointing of the baptized person with chrism in the presence of God's people), the rite of baptism is held in highest honor by all Christians. Once it has been validly celebrated, even if by Christians with whom we are not in full communion, it may never lawfully be repeated.

5.   Baptism, the cleansing with water by the power of the living word,[14] washes away every stain of sin, original and personal, makes us sharers in God's own life[15] and his adopted children.[16] As proclaimed in the prayers for the blessing of the water, baptism is a cleansing water of rebirth[17] that makes us God's children born from on high. The blessed Trinity is invoked over those who are to be baptized, so that all who are signed in this name are consecrated to the Trinity and enter into communion with the Father, the Son, and the Holy Spirit. They are prepared for this high dignity and led to it by the scriptural readings, the prayer of the community, and their own profession in the belief in the Father, the Son, and the Holy Spirit.

6.   Far superior to the purifications of the Old Law, baptism produces these effects by the power of the mystery of the Lord's passion and resurrection. Those who are baptized are united to Christ in a death like his;[18] buried with him in death, they are given life again with him, and with him they rise again.[19] For baptism recalls and makes present the paschal mystery itself, because in baptism we pass from the death of sin into life. The celebration of baptism should therefore reflect the joy of the resurrection, especially when the celebration takes place during the Easter Vigil or on a Sunday.

OFFICES AND MINISTRIES OF BAPTISM

7.   The preparation for baptism and Christian instruction are both of vital concern to God's people, the Church, which hands on and nourishes the faith received from the apostles. Through the ministry of the Church, adults are called to the Gospel by the Holy Spirit and infants are baptized in the faith of the Church and brought up in that faith. Therefore, it is most important that catechists and other laypersons should work with priests and deacons in the preparation for baptism. In the actual celebration, the people of God (represented not only by the parents, godparents, and relatives, but also, as far as possible, by friends, neighbors, and some members of the local Church) should take an active part. Thus they will show their common faith and the shared joy with which the newly baptized are received into the community of the Church.

8.   It is a very ancient custom of the Church that adults are not admitted to baptism without godparents, members of the Christian community who will assist the candidates at least in the final preparation for baptism and after baptism will help them persevere in the faith and in their lives as Christians. In the baptism of children, as well, godparents are to be present in order to represent both the expanded spiritual family of the one to be baptized and the role of the Church as a mother. As occasion offers, godparents help the parents so that children will come to profess the faith and live up to it.

9.   At least in the later rites of the catechumenate and in the actual celebration of baptism, the part of godparents is to testify to the faith of adult candidates or, together with the parents, to profess the Church's faith, in which children are baptized.

10.   Therefore godparents, chosen by the catechumens or by the families of children to be baptized, must, in the judgment of the parish priest (pastor), be qualified to carry out the proper liturgical functions mentioned in no. 9.

1. Godparents are persons, other than the parents of the candidates, who are designated by the candidates themselves or by a candidate's parents or whoever stands in the place of parents, or, in the absence of these, by the parish priest (pastor) or the minister of baptism. Each candidate may have either a godmother or a godfather or both a godmother and a godfather.

2. Those designated must have the capability and intention of carrying out the responsibility of a godparent and be mature enough to do so. A person sixteen years of age is presumed to have the requisite maturity, but the diocesan bishop may have stipulated another age or the parish priest (pastor) or the minister may decide that there is a legitimate reason for allowing an exception.

3. Those designated as godparents must have received the three sacraments of initiation, baptism, confirmation, and eucharist, and be living a life consistent with faith and with the responsibility of a godparent.

4. Those designated as godparents must also be members of the Catholic Church and be canonically free to carry out this office. At the request of parents, a baptized and believing Christian not belonging to the Catholic Church may act as a Christian witness along with a Catholic godparent.[20] In the case of separated Eastern Christians with whom we do not have full communion the special discipline for the Eastern Churches is to be respected.

11.   The ordinary ministers of baptism are bishops, priests, and deacons.

1. In every celebration of this sacrament they should be mindful that they act in the Church in the name of Christ and by the power of the Holy Spirit.

2. They should therefore be diligent in the ministry of the word of God and in the manner of celebrating the sacrament. They must avoid any action that the faithful could rightly regard as favoritism.[21]

3. Except in a case of necessity, these ministers are not to confer baptism outside their own territory, even on their own subjects, without the requisite permission.

12.   Bishops are the chief stewards of the mysteries of God and leaders of the entire liturgical life in the Church committed to them.[22] This is why they direct the conferring of baptism, which brings to the recipient a share in the kingly priesthood of Christ.[23] Therefore bishops should personally celebrate baptism, especially at the Easter Vigil. They should have a particular concern for the preparation and baptism of adults.

13.   It is the duty of parish priest (pastors) to assist the bishop in the instruction and baptism of the adults entrusted to their care, unless the bishop makes other provisions. Parish priests (pastors), with the assistance of catechists or other qualified laypersons, have the duty of preparing the parents and godparents of children through appropriate pastoral guidance and of baptizing the children.

14.   Other priests and deacons, since they are co-workers in the ministry of bishops and parish priests (pastors), also prepare candidates for baptism and, by the invitation or consent of the bishop or parish priest (pastor), celebrate the sacrament.

15.   The celebrant of baptism may be assisted by other priests and deacons and also by laypersons in those parts that pertain to them, especially if there are a large number to be baptized. Provision for this is made in various parts of the rituals for adults and for children.

16.   In imminent danger of death and especially at the moment of death, when no priest or deacon is available, any member of the faithful, indeed anyone with the right intention, may and sometimes must administer baptism. In a case simply of danger of death the sacrament should be administered, if possible, by a member of the faithful according to one of the shorter rites provided for this situation.[24] Even in this case a small community should be formed to assist at the rite or, if possible, at least one or two witnesses should be present.

17.   Since they belong to the priestly people, all laypersons, especially parents and, by reason of their work, catechists, midwives, family or social workers or nurses of the sick, as well as physicians and surgeons, should be thoroughly aware, according to their capacities, of the proper method of baptizing in case of emergency. They should be taught by parish priests (pastors), deacons, and catechists, Bishops should provide appropriate means within their diocese for such instructions.

REQUIREMENTS FOR THE CELEBRATION OF BAPTISM

18.   The water used in baptism should be true water and, both for the sake of authentic sacramental symbolism and for hygienic reasons, should be pure and clean.

19.   The baptismal font, or the vessel in which on occasion the water is prepared for celebration of the sacrament in the sanctuary, should be spotlessly clean and of pleasing design.

20.   If the climate requires, provision should be made for the water to be heated beforehand.

21.   Except in case of necessity, a priest or deacon is to use only water that has been blessed for the rite. The water blessed at the Easter Vigil should, if possible, be kept and used throughout the Easter season to signify more clearly the relationship between the sacrament of baptism and the paschal mystery. Outside the Easter season, it is desirable that the water be blessed for each occasion, in order that the words of blessing may explicitly express the mystery of salvation that the Church remembers and proclaims. If the baptistery is supplied with running water, the blessing is given as the water flows.

22.   As the rite for baptizing, either immersion, which is more suitable as a symbol of participation in the death and resurrection of Christ, or pouring may lawfully be used.

23.   The words for conferring baptism in the Latin Church are: I BAPTIZE YOU IN THE NAME OF THE FATHER, AND OF THE SON, AND OF THE HOLY SPIRIT.

24.   For celebrating the liturgy of the word of God a suitable place should be provided in the baptistery or in the church.

25.   The baptistery or the area where the baptismal font is located should be reserved for the sacrament of baptism and should be worthy to serve as the place where Christians are reborn in the water and the Holy Spirit. The baptistery may be situated in a chapel either inside or outside the church or in some other part of the church easily seen by the faithful; it should be large enough to accommodate a good number of people. After the Easter season, the Easter candle should be kept reverently in the baptistery, in such a way that it can be lighted for the celebration of baptism and so that from it the candles for the newly baptized can easily be lighted.

26.   In the celebration the parts of the rite that are to be celebrated outside the baptistery should be carried out in different areas of the church that most conveniently suit the size of the congregation and the several parts of the baptismal liturgy. When the baptistery cannot accommodate all the catechumens and the congregation, the parts of the rite that are customarily celebrated inside the baptistery may be transferred to some other suitable area of the church.

27.   As far as possible, all recently born babies should be baptized at a common celebration on the same day. Except for a good reason, baptism should not be celebrated more than once on the same day in the same church.

28. Further details concerning the time for baptism of adults and of children will be found in the respective rituals. But at all times the celebration of the sacrament should have a markedly paschal character.

29. Parish priests (pastors) must carefully and without delay record in the baptismal register the names of those baptized, of the minister, parents, and godparents, as well as the place and date of baptism.

ADAPTATIONS BY THE CONFERENCES OF BISHOPS

30. According to the Constitution on the Liturgy (art. 63, b), it is within the competence of the conferences of bishops to compose for their local rituals a section corresponding to this one in the Roman Ritual, adapted to the needs of their respective regions. After it has been reviewed by the Apostolic See, it may be used in the regions for which it was prepared.

In this connection, it is the responsibility of each conference of bishops:

1. to decide on the adaptations mentioned in the Constitution on the Liturgy (art. 39);

2. carefully and prudently to weigh what elements of a people's distinctive traditions and culture may suitably be admitted into divine worship and so to propose to the Apostolic See other adaptations considered useful or necessary that will be introduced with its consent;

3. to retain distinctive elements of any existing local rituals, as long as they conform to the Constitution on the Liturgy and correspond to contemporary needs, or to modify such elements;

4. to prepare translations of the texts that genuinely reflect the characteristics of various languages and cultures and to add, whenever helpful, music suitable for singing;

5. to adapt and augment the Introductions contained in the Roman Ritual, so that the ministers may fully understand the meaning of the rites and carry them out effectively.

6. to arrange the material in the various editions of the liturgical books prepared under the guidance of the conference of bishops, so that these books may better suit pastoral use.

31. Taking into consideration especially the norms in the Constitution on the Liturgy (art. 37–40, 65), the conferences of bishops in mission countries have the responsibility of judging whether the elements of initiation in use among some peoples can be adapted for the rite of Christian baptism and of deciding whether such elements are to be incorporated into the rite.

32. When the Roman Ritual for baptism provides several optional formularies, local rituals may add other formularies of the same kind.

33.   The celebration of baptism is greatly enhanced by the use of song, which stimulates in the participants a sense of their unity, fosters their praying together, and expresses the joy of Easter that should permeate the whole rite. The conference of bishops should therefore encourage and help specialists in music to compose settings for those liturgical texts particularly suited to congregational singing.

ADAPTATIONS BY THE MINISTER OF BAPTISM

34.   Taking into account existing circumstances and other needs, as well as the wishes of the faithful, the minister should make full use of the various options allowed in the rite.

35.   In addition to the adaptations that are provided in the Roman Ritual for the dialogue and blessings, the minister may make other adaptations for special circumstances. These adaptations will be indicated more fully in the Introductions to the rites of baptism for adults and for children.

NOTES

1. See Vatican Council II, Decree on the Church's Missionary Activity *Ad gentes*, no. 14.

2. See Colossians 1:13; Romans 8:15; Galatians 4:5. See also Council of Trent, sess. 6., *Decr. de justificatione*, cap. 4: Denz.-Schön. 1524.

3. See 1 John 3:a.

4. See Vatican Council II, Decree on the Church's Missionary Activity *Ad gentes*, no. 36

5. See John 6:55.

6. See Augustine, *De civitate Dei* 10,6: PL 41, 284. Vatican Council II, Dogmatic Constitution on the Church *Lumen gentium*, no 11; Decree on the Ministry and Life of Priest *Presbyterorum Ordinis*, no. 2.

7. See Vatican Council II, Dogmatic Constitution on the Church *Lumen gentium*, no. 28.

8. See ibid., no. 31.

9. See John 3:5.

10. Matthew 28:19

11. See Ephesians 2:22.

12. See 1 Peter 2:9.

13. See Vatican Council II, Decree on Ecumenism *Unitatis redintegratio*, no. 22.

14. See Ephesians 5:26.

15. See 2 Peter 1:4.

16. See Romans 8:15; Galatians 4:5.

17. See Titus 3:5.

18. See Romans 6:4–5.

19. See Ephesians 2:5–6.

20. See *Codex Iuris Canonici*, can. 873 and 874, §§ 1 and 2.

21. See Vatican Council II, Constitution on the Liturgy *Sacrosanctum Concilium*, art. 32; Pastoral Constitution on the Church in the Modern World *Gaudium et spes*, no. 29.

22. See Vatican Council II, Decree on the Pastoral Office of Bishops *Christus Dominus*, no. 15.

23. See Vatican Council II, Dogmatic Constitution on the Church *Lumen gentium*, no. 26.

24. See *Rite of Christian Initiation of Adults*, nos. 375–399; *Rite of Baptism for Children*, nos. 157–164.

RITE OF CHRISTIAN INITIATION
OF ADULTS
INTRODUCTION

CONGREGATION FOR DIVINE WORSHIP
6 JANUARY 1972; EMENDED 23 SEPTEMBER 1974

ADAPTATIONS FOR U.S. DIOCESES
NATIONAL CONFERENCE OF CATHOLIC BISHOPS
13 MARCH 1988

OUTLINE

RITE OF CHRISTIAN INITIATION OF ADULTS

INTRODUCTION

1.   The rite of Christian initiation presented here is designed for adults who, after hearing the mystery of Christ proclaimed, consciously and freely seek the living God and enter the way of faith and conversion as the Holy Spirit opens their hearts. By God's help they will be strengthened spiritually during their preparation and at the proper time will receive the sacraments fruitfully.

2.   This rite includes not simply the celebration of the sacraments of baptism, confirmation, and eucharist, but also all the rites belonging to the catechumenate. Endorsed by the ancient practice of the Church, a catechumenate that would be suited to contemporary missionary activity in all regions was so widely requested that the Second Vatican Council decreed its restoration, revision, and adaptation to local traditions.[1]

3.   So that the rite of initiation will be more useful for the work of the Church and for individual, parochial, and missionary circumstances, the rite is first presented in Part I of the book in its complete and usual form (nos. 36 251). This is designed for the preparation of a group of candidates, but by simple adaptation pastors can devise a form suited to one person.

Part II provides rites for special circumstances: the Christian initiation of children (nos. 252–330), a simple form of the rite for adults to be carried out in exceptional circumstances (nos. 331–369), and a short form of the rite for these in danger of death (nos. 370–399). Part II also includes guidelines for preparing uncatechized adults for confirmation and eucharist (nos. 400–410) along with four (4) optional rites which may be used with such candidates, and the rite of reception of baptized Christians into the full communion of the Catholic Church (nos. 473–504).

Rites for catechumens and baptized but previously uncatechized adults celebrated in combination, along with a rite combining the reception of baptized Christians into the full communion of the Catholic Church with the celebration of Christian initiation at the Easter Vigil (nos. 562–594), are contained in Appendix I. The two additional appendices contain acclamations, hymns, and songs, and the National Statutes for the Catechumenate in the Dioceses of the United States of America.

STRUCTURE OF THE INITIATION OF ADULTS

4.   The initiation of catechumens is a gradual process that takes place within the community of the faithful. By joining the catechumens in reflection on the value of the paschal mystery and by renewing their own conversion, the faithful provide an example that will help the catechumens to obey the Holy Spirit more generously.

5.   The rite of initiation is suited to a spiritual journey of adults that varies according to the many forms of God's grace, the free cooperation of the individuals, the action of the Church, and the circumstances of time and place.

6.   The journey includes not only the periods for making inquiry and for maturing (see no. 7), but also the steps marking the catechumens' progress, as they pass, so to speak, through another doorway or ascent to the next level.

> 1. The first step: reaching the point of initial conversion and wishing to become Christians, they are accepted as catechumens by the Church.
>
> 2. The second step: having progressed in faith and nearly completed the catechumenate, they are accepted into a more intense preparation for the sacraments of initiation.
>
> 3. The third step: having completed their spiritual preparation, they receive the sacraments of Christian initiation.

These three steps are to be regarded as the major, more intense moments of initiation and are marked by three liturgical rites: the first by the rite of acceptance into the order of catechumens (nos. 41–74); the second by the rite of election or enrollment of names (nos. 118–137); and the third by the celebration of the sacraments of Christian initiation (nos. 206–243).

7.   The steps lead to periods of inquiry and growth; alternatively the periods may also be seen as preparing for the ensuing step.

> 1. The first period consists of inquiry on the party of the candidates and of evangelization and the precatechumenate on the part of the Church. It ends with the rite of acceptance into the order of catechumens.
>
> 2. The second period, which begins with the rite of acceptance into the order of catechumens and may last for several years, includes catechesis and the rites connected with catechesis. It comes to an end on the day of election.
>
> 3. The third and much shorter period, which follows the rite of election, ordinarily coincides with the Lenten preparation for the Easter celebration and the sacraments of initiation. It is a time of purification and enlightenment and includes the celebration of the rites belonging to this period.
>
> 4. The final period extends through the whole Easter season and is devoted to the postbaptismal catechesis or mystagogy. It is a time for deepening the Christian experience, for spiritual growth, and for entering more fully into the life and unity of the community.

Thus there are four continuous periods: the precatechumenate, the period for hearing the first preaching of the Gospel (nos. 36–40); the period of the catechumenate, set aside for a thorough catechesis and for the rites belonging to this period (nos. 75–117); the period of purification and enlightenment (Lenten preparation), designed for a more intense spiritual preparation, which is assisted by the celebration of the scrutinizes and presentations (nos. 138–205); and the period of postbaptismal catechesis or mystagogy, marked by the new experience of sacraments and community (nos. 244–251).

8.   The whole initiation must bear a markedly paschal character, since the initiation of Christians is the first sacramental sharing in Christ's dying and rising and since, in addition, the period of purification and enlightenment ordinarily coincides with Lent[2] and the period of postbaptismal catechesis or mystagogy with the Easter season. All the resources of Lent should be brought to bear as a more intense preparation of the elect and the Easter Vigil should be regarded as the proper time for the sacraments of initiation. Because of pastoral needs, however, the sacraments of initiation may be celebrated at other times (see nos. 26–30).

MINISTRIES AND OFFICES

9.   In the light of what is said in *Christian Initiation*, General Introduction (no. 7), the people of God, as represented by the local Church, should understand and show by their concern that the initiation of adults is the responsibility of all the baptized.[3] Therefore, the community must always be fully prepared in the pursuit of its apostolic vocation to give help to those who are searching for Christ. In the various circumstances of daily life, even as in the apostolate, all the followers of Christ have the obligation of spreading the faith according to their abilities.[4] Hence, the entire community must help the candidates and the catechumens throughout the process of initiation: during the period of the precatechumenate, the period of the catechumenate, the period of purification and enlightenment, and the period of postbaptismal catechesis of mystagogy. In particular:

1. During the period of evangelization and precatechumenate, the faithful should remember that for the Church and its members the supreme purpose of the apostolate is that Christ's message is made known to the world by word and deed and that his grace is communicated.[5] They should therefore show themselves ready to give the candidates evidence of the spirit of the Christian community and to welcome them into their homes, into personal conversation, and into community gatherings.

2. At the celebrations belonging to the period of the catechumenate, the faithful should seek to be present whenever possible and should take an active part in the responses, prayers, singing, and acclamations.

3. On the day of election, because it is a day of growth for the community, the faithful, when called upon, should be sure to give honest and carefully considered testimony about the catechumens.

4. During Lent, the period of purification and enlightenment, the faithful should take care to participate in the rites of the scrutinies and presentations and give the elect the example of their own renewal in the spirit of penance, faith, and charity. At the Easter Vigil, they should attach great importance to renewing their own baptismal promises.

5. During the period immediately after baptism, the faithful should take part in the Masses for neophytes, that is, the Sunday Masses of the Easter season (see no. 25), welcome the neophytes with open arms in charity, and help them to feel more at home in the community of the baptized.

10. A sponsor accompanies any candidate seeking admission as a catechumen. Sponsors are persons who have known and assisted the candidates and stand as witnesses to the candidates' moral character, faith, and intention. It may happen that it is not the sponsor for the rite of acceptance and the period of the catechumenate but another person who serves as godparent for the periods of purification and enlightenment and of mystagogy.

11. Their godparents (for each a godmother or godfather, or both) accompany the candidates of the day of election, at the celebration of the sacraments of initiation, and during the period of mystagogy.[6] Godparents are persons chosen by the candidates on the basis of example, good qualities, and friendship, delegated by the local Christian community, and approved by the priest. It is the responsibility of godparents to show the candidates how to practice the Gospel in personal and social life, to sustain the candidates in moments of hesitancy and anxiety, to bear witness, and to guide the candidates' progress in the baptismal life. Chosen before the candidates' election, godparents fulfill this office publicly from the day of the rite of election, when they give testimony to the community about the candidates. They continue to be important during the time after reception of the sacraments when the neophytes need to be assisted so that they remain true to their baptismal promises.

12. The bishop,[7] in person or through his delegate, sets up, regulates, and promotes the program of pastoral formation for catechumens and admits the candidates to their election and to the sacraments. It is hoped that, presiding if possible at the Lenten liturgy, he will himself celebrate the rite of election and, at the Easter Vigil, the sacraments of initiation, at least for the initiation of those who are fourteen years old or older. Finally, when pastoral care requires, to celebrate the minor exorcisms (nos. 94–94) and the blessings of the catechumens (nos. 95–97).

13. Priests, in addition to their usual ministry for any celebration of baptism, confirmation, and the eucharist,[8] have the responsibility of attending to the pastoral and personal care of the catechumens,[9] especially those who seem hesitant and discouraged. With the help of deacons and catechists, they are to provide instruction for the catechumens; they are also to approve the choice of godparents and willingly listen to and help them; they are to be diligent in the correct celebration and adaptation of the rites throughout the entire course of Christian initiation (see no. 35).

14.   The priest who baptizes an adult or child of catechetical age should, when the bishop is absent, also confer confirmation,[10] unless this sacrament is to be given at another time (see no. 24). When there are a large number of candidates to be confirmed, the minister of confirmation may associate priests with himself to administer the sacrament. It if preferable that the priests who are so invited:

1. either have a particular function or office in the diocese, being, namely, either vicars general, episcopal vicars, or district or regional vicars;

2. or be the parish priests (pastors) of the places where confirmation is conferred, parish priests (pastors) of the places where the candidates belong, or priests who have had a special part in the catechetical preparation of the candidates.[11]

15.   Deacons should be ready to assist in the ministry to catechumens. Conferences of bishops that have decided in favor of the permanent diaconate should ensure that the number and distribution of permanent deacons are adequate for the carrying out of the steps, periods, and formation programs of the catechumenate wherever pastoral needs require.[12]

16.   Catechists, who have an important office for the progress of the catechumens and for the growth of the community, should, whenever possible, have an active part in the rites. When deputed by the bishop (see no. 12), they may perform the minor exorcisms and blessings contained in the ritual.[13] When they are teaching, catechists should see that their instruction is filled with the spirit of the Gospel, adapted to the liturgical signs and the cycle of the Church's year, suited to the needs of the catechumens, and as far as possible enriched by local traditions.

TIME AND PLACE OF INITIATION

17.   As a general rule, parish priests (pastors) should make use of the rite of initiation in such a way that the sacraments themselves are celebrated at the Easter Vigil and the rite of election takes place on the First Sunday of Lent. The rest of the rites are spaced on the basis of the structure and arrangement of the catechumenate as described previously (nos. 6–8). For pastoral needs of a more serious nature, however, it is lawful to arrange the schedule for the entire rite of initiation differently, as will be detailed later (nos. 26–30).

PROPER OR USUAL TIMES

18.   The following should be noted about the time of celebrating the rite of acceptance into the order of catechumens (nos. 41–74).

1. It should not be too early, but should be delayed until the candidates, according to their own dispositions and situation, have had sufficient time to conceive an initial faith and to show the first signs of conversion (see no. 42).

2. In places where the number of candidates is smaller than usual, the rite of acceptance should be delayed until a group is formed that is sufficiently large for catechesis and the liturgical rites.

3. Two dates in the year, or three if necessary, are to be fixed as the usual times for carrying out this rite.

19. The rite of election or enrollment of names (nos. 118–137) should as a rule be celebrated on the First Sunday of Lent. As circumstances suggest or require, it may be anticipated somewhat or even celebrated on a weekday.

20. The scrutinies (nos. 150–156, 164–177) should take place on the Third, Fourth, and Fifth Sundays of Lent, or, if necessary, on the other Sundays of Lent, or even on convenient weekdays. Three scrutinies should be celebrated. The bishop may dispense from one of them for serious reasons, or, in extraordinary circumstances, even from two (see nos. 34.3, 331). When, for lack of time, the election is held early, the first scrutiny is also to be held early; but in this case care is to be taken not to prolong the period of purification and enlightenment beyond eight weeks.

21. By ancient usage, the presentations, since they take place after the scrutinies, are part of the same period of purification and enlightenment. They are celebrated during the week. The presentation of the Creed to the catechumens (nos. 157–163) takes place during the week after the first scrutiny; the presentation of the Lord's Prayer (nos. 178–184) during the week after the third scrutiny. For pastoral reasons, however, to enrich the liturgy in the period of the catechumenate, each presentation may be transferred and celebrated during the period if the catechumenate as a kind of "rite of passage" (see nos. 79, 104–105).

22. On Holy Saturday, when the elect refrain from work and spend their time in recollection, the various preparation rites may be celebrated: the recitation or "return" of the Creed by the elect, the ephphetha rite, and the choosing of a Christian name (nos. 185–205).

23. The celebration of the sacraments of Christian initiation (nos. 206–243) should take place at the Easter Vigil itself (see nos. 8, 17). But if there are a great many catechumens, the sacraments are given to the majority that night and reception of the sacraments by the rest may be transferred to days within the Easter octave, whether at the principal church or at a mission station. In this case either the Mass of the day or one of the ritual Masses "Christian Initiation: Baptism" may be used and the readings are chosen from those of the Easter Vigil.

24. In certain cases when there is a serious reason, confirmation may be postponed until near the end of the period of postbaptismal catechesis, for example, Pentecost Sunday (see no 249).

25. On all the Sundays of the Easter season after Easter Sunday, the so-called Masses for neophytes are to be scheduled. The entire community and the newly baptized with their godparents should be encouraged to participate (see nos. 247–248).

26.   The entire rite of Christian initiation is normally arranged so that the sacraments will be celebrated during the Easter Vigil. Because of unusual circumstances and pastoral needs, however, the rite of election and the rites belonging to the period of purification, and enlightenment may be held outside Lent and the sacraments of initiation may be celebrated at a time other than the Easter Vigil or Easter Sunday.

Even when the usual time has otherwise been observed, it is permissible, but only for serious pastoral needs (for example, if there are a great many people to be baptized), to choose a day other than the Easter Vigil or Easter Sunday, but preferably one during the Easter season, to celebrate the sacraments of initiation; the program of initiation during Lent, however, must be maintained.

When the time is changed in either way, even though the rite of Christian initiation occurs as a different point in the liturgical year, the structure of the entire rite, with its properly spaced intervals, remains the same. But the following adjustments are made.

27.   As far as possible, the sacraments of initiation are to be celebrated on a Sunday, using, as occasion suggests, the Sunday Mass or one of the ritual Masses "Christian Initiation: Baptism" (see nos. 23, 208).

28.   The rite of acceptance into the order of catechumens is to take place when the time is right (see no. 18).

29.   The rite of election is to be celebrated about six weeks before the sacraments of initiation, so that there is sufficient time for the scrutinies and the presentations. Care should be taken not to schedule the celebration of the rite of election on a solemnity of the liturgical year.

30.   The scrutinies should not be celebrated on solemnities, but on Sundays or even on weekdays, with the usual intervals.

PLACE OF CELEBRATION

31.   The rites should be celebrated in the places appropriate to them as indicated in the ritual. Consideration should be given to special needs that arise in secondary stations of missionary territories.

ADAPTATIONS BY THE CONFERENCES OF BISHOPS IN THE USE OF THE ROMAN RITUAL

32.   In addition to the adaptations envisioned in *Christian Initiation*, General Introduction (nos. 30–33), the rite of Christian initiation of adults allows for other adaptations that will be decided by the conference of bishops.

33. The conference of bishops has discretionary power to make the following decisions:

1. to establish for the precatechumenate, where it seems advisable, some way of receiving inquirers who are interested in the catechumenate (see no. 39);

2. to insert into the rite of acceptance into the order of catechumens a first exorcism and renunciation of false worship, in regions where paganism is widespread (see nos. 69–72) [The National Conference of Catholic Bishops has approved leaving to the discretion of the diocesan bishop this inclusion of a first exorcism and a renunciation of false worship in the rite of acceptance into the order of catechumens];

3. to decide that in the same rite the tracing of the sign of the cross upon the forehead (nos. 54–55) be replaced by making the sign in front of the forehead, in regions where the act of touching may not seem proper [The National Conference of Catholic Bishops has established as the norm in the dioceses of the United States the tracing of the cross on the forehead. It leaves to the discretion of the diocesan bishop the substitution of making the sign of the cross in front of the forehead for those persons in whose culture the act of touching may not seem proper];

4. to decide that in the same rite candidates receive a new name in regions where it is the practice of non-Christian religions to give a new name to initiates immediately (no. 73) [The National Conference of Catholic Bishops establishes as the norm in the dioceses of the United States that there is to be no giving of a new name. It also approves leaving to the discretion of the diocesan bishop the giving of a new name to persons from those cultures in which it is the practice of non-Christian religions to give a new name];

5. to allow within the same rite, according to local customs, additional rites that symbolize reception into the community (no. 74) [The National Conference of Catholic Bishops has approved the inclusion of an optional presentation of a cross (no. 74) while leaving to the discretion of the diocesan bishop the inclusion of additional rites that symbolize reception into the community];

6. to establish during the period of the catechumenate, in addition to the usual rites (nos. 81–97), "rites of passage": for example, early celebration of the presentations (nos. 157–163, 178–184), the ephpheta rite, the catechumens' recitation of the Creed, or even an anointing of the catechumens (nos. 98–103) [The National Conference of Catholic Bishops approves the use of the anointing with the oil of catechumens during the period of the catechumenate as a kind of "rite of passage" (see no. 33.7). In addition it approves, when appropriate in the circumstance, the early celebration of the presentations (nos. 157–163, 178–184), the ephpheta rite (nos. 197–199, and the catechumens' recitation of the Creed (nos. 193–196)];

7. to decide on the omission of the anointing with the oil of catechumens or its transferral to the preparation rites for Holy Saturday or its use during

the period of the catechumenate as a kind of "rite of passage" (nos. 98–103) [The National Conference of Catholic Bishops approves the omission of the anointing with the oil of catechumens both in the celebration of baptism and in the optional preparation rites for Holy Saturday. Thus, anointing with the oil of catechumens is reserved for use in the period of the catechumenate and in the period of purification and enlightenment and is not to be included in the preparation rites on Holy Saturday or in the celebration of initiation at the Easter Vigil or at another time];

8. to make more specific and detailed the formularies of renunciation for the rite of acceptance into the order of catechumens (nos. 70–72) and for the celebration of baptism (no. 224) [The National Conference of Catholic Bishops has established as the norm in the dioceses of the United States that the formularies of renunciation should not be adapted. But for those cases where certain catechumens may be from cultures in which false worship is widespread it has approved leaving to the discretion of the diocesan bishop this matter of making more specific and detailed the formularies of renunciation in the rite of acceptance into the order of catechumens and in the celebration of baptism].

ADAPTATIONS BY THE BISHOP

34. It pertains to the bishop for his own diocese:

1. to set up the formation program of the catechumenate and to lay down norms according to local needs (see no. 12);

2. to decide whether and when, as circumstances warrant, the entire rite of Christian initiation may be celebrated outside the usual times (see no. 26);

3. to dispense, on the basis of some serious obstacle, from one scrutiny or, in extraordinary circumstances, even from two (see no 331);

4. to permit the simple rite to be used in whole or in part (see no. 3310);

5. to depute catechists, truly worthy and properly prepared, to give the exorcisms and blessings (see nos. 12, 16);

6. to preside at the rite of election and to ratify, personally or through a delegate, the admission of the elect (see no. 12);

7. in keeping with the provisions of law,[14] to stipulate the requisite age for sponsors (see *Christian Initiation*, General Introduction, no. 10.2).

ADAPTATIONS BY THE MINISTER

35. Celebrants should make full and intelligent use of the freedom given to them either in *Christian Initiation*, General Introduction (no. 34) or in the rubrics of the rite itself. In many places the manner of acting or praying is intentionally left undetermined or two alternatives are offered, so that ministers, according to their prudent pastoral judgment, may accommodate to the circumstances of the candidates and others who are present. In all the rites the greatest

freedom is left in the invitations and instructions, and the intercessions may always be shortened, changed, or even expanded with new intentions, in order to fit the circumstances or special situation of the candidates (for example, a sad or joyful event occurring in the family) or of the others present (for example, sorrow or joy common to the parish or civic community).

The minister will also adapt the texts by changing the gender and number as required.

PART I: CHRISTIAN INITIATION OF ADULTS

PERIOD OF EVANGELIZATION AND PRECATECHUMENATE

I, the light, have come into the world, so that whoever believes in me need not remain in the dark any more

36.   Although the rite of initiation begins with admission to the catechumenate, the preceding period or precatechumenate is of great importance and as a rule should not be omitted. It is a time of evangelization: faithfully and constantly the living God is proclaimed and Jesus Christ whom he has sent for the salvation of all. Thus those who are not yet Christians, their hearts opened by the Holy Spirit, may believe and be freely converted to the Lord and commit themselves sincerely to him. For he who is the way, the truth, and the life fulfills all their spiritual expectations, indeed infinitely surpasses them.[15]

37.   From evangelization, completed with the help of God, come the faith and initial conversion that cause a person to feel called away from sin and drawn into the mystery of God's love. The whole period of the precatechumenate is set aside for this evangelization, so that the genuine will to follow Christ and seek baptism may mature.

38.   During this period, priests and deacons, catechists and other laypersons are to give the candidates a suitable explanation of the Gospel (see no. 42). The candidates are to receive help and attention so that with a purified and clearer intention they may cooperate with God's grace. Opportunities should be provided for them to meet families and other groups of Christians.

39.   It belongs to the conference of bishops to provide for evangelization proper to this period. The conference may also provide, if circumstances suggest and in keeping with a local custom, a preliminary manner of receiving those interested in the precatechumenate, that is, those inquirers who, even though they do not fully believe, show some leaning toward the Christian faith (and who may be called "sympathizers").

1. Such a reception, if it takes place, will be carried out without any ritual celebration; it is the expression not yet of faith, but of a right intention.

2. The reception will be adapted to local conditions and to the pastoral situation. Some candidates may need to see evidence of the spirit of Christians that they are striving to understand and experience. For others, however, whose catechumenate will be delayed for one reason or another, some initial act of the candidates or the community that expresses their reception may be appropriate.

3. The reception will be held at a meeting or gathering of the local community, on an occasion that will permit friendly conversation. An inquirer or "sympathizer" is introduced by a friend and then welcomed and received by the priest or some other representative member of the community.

During the precatechumenate period, parish priests (pastors) should help those taking part in it with prayers suited to them, for example, by celebrating for their spiritual well-being the prayers of exorcism and the blessings given in the ritual (nos. 94, 97).

FIRST STEP: ACCEPTANCE INTO THE ORDERS OF CATECHUMENS

Lord, let your mercy be on us, as we place our trust in you

41. The rite that is called the rite of acceptance into the order of catechumens is of the utmost importance. Assembling publicly for the first time, the candidates who have completed the period of the precatechumenate declare their intention to the Church and the Church in turn, carrying out its apostolic mission, accepts them as persons who intend to become its members. God showers his grace on the candidates, since the celebration manifests their desire publicly and marks their reception and first consecration by the Church.

42. The prerequisite for making this first step is that the beginning of the spiritual life and the fundamentals of Christian teaching have taken root in the candidates.[16] Thus there must be evidence of the first faith that was conceived during the period of evangelization and precatechumenate and of an initial conversion and intention to change their lives and to enter into a relationship with God in Christ. Consequently, there must also be evidence of the first stirrings of repentance, a start to the practice of calling upon God in prayer, a sense of the Church, and some experience of the company and spirit of Christians through contact with a priest or with members of the community. The candidates should also be instructed about the celebration of the liturgical rite of acceptance.

43. Before the rite is celebrated, therefore, sufficient and necessary time, as required in each case, should be set aside to evaluate and, if necessary, to purify the candidates' motives and dispositions. With the help of the sponsors (see no. 10), catechists, and deacons, parish priests (pastors) have the responsibility for judging the outward indications of such dispositions.[17] Because of the effect of baptism once validly received (see *Christian Initiation*, General Introduction, no. 4), it is the duty of parish priests (pastors) to see to it that no baptized person seeks for any reason whatever to be baptized a second time.

44.   The rite will take place on specified days during the year (see no. 18) that are suited to local conditions. The rite consists in the reception of the candidates, the celebration of the word of God, and the dismissal of the candidates; celebration of the eucharist may follow.

By decision of the conference of bishops, the following may be incorporated into this rite: a first exorcism and renunciation of false worship (nos. 70–72), the giving of a new name (no. 73), and additional rites signifying reception into the community (no. 74). [See no. 33 for the decisions made by the National Conference of Catholic Bishops regarding these matters.]

45.   It is desirable that the entire Christian community or some part of it, consisting of friends and acquaintances, catechists and priests, take an active part in the celebration. The presiding celebrant is a priest or a deacon. The sponsors should also attend in order to present to the Church the candidates they have brought.

46.   After the celebration of the rite of acceptance, the names of the catechumens are to be duly inscribed in the register of catechumens, along with the names of the sponsors and the minister and the date and place of the celebration.

47.   From this time on the Church embraces the catechumens as its own with a mother's love and concern. Joined to the Church, the catechumens are now part of the household of Christ,[18] since the Church nourishes them with the word of God and sustains them by means of liturgical celebrations. The catechumens should be eager, then, to take part in the celebrations of the word of God and to receive blessings and other sacramentals. When two catechumens marry or when a catechumen marries an unbaptized person, the appropriate rite is to be used.[19] One who dies during the catechumenate receives a Christian burial.

OPTIONAL RITES

69.   By decision of the National Conference of Catholic Bishops the presentation of a cross (no. 74) may be included as a symbol of reception into the community. At the discretion of the diocesan bishop, one or more additional rites may be incorporated in to the "Rite of Acceptance into the Order of Catechumens": a first exorcism and renunciation of false worship, the giving of a new name, as well as additional rites that symbolize acceptance into the community. (see no. 33.2, 33.4, 33.5, 33.8).

PERIOD OF THE CATECHUMENATE

Leave your country, and come into the land I will show you

75.   The catechumenate is an extended period during which the candidates are given suitable pastoral formation and guidance, aimed at training them in

the Christian life.[20] In this way, the dispositions manifested at their acceptance into the catechumenate are brought to maturity. This is achieved in four ways.

1. A suitable catechesis is provided by priests or deacons, or by catechists and others of the faithful, planned to be gradual and complete in its coverage, accommodated to the liturgical year, and solidly supported by celebrations of the word. This catechesis leads the catechumens not only to an appropriate acquaintance with dogmas and precepts but also to a profound sense of the mystery of salvation in which they desire to participate.

2. As they become familiar with the Christian way of life and are helped by the example and support of sponsors, godparents, and the entire Christian community, the catechumens learn to turn more readily to God in prayer, to bear witness to the faith, in all things to keep their hopes set on Christ, to follow supernatural inspiration in their deeds, and to practice love of neighbor, even at the cost of self-renunciation. Thus formed, "the newly converted set out on a spiritual journey. Already sharing through faith in the mystery of Christ's death and resurrection, they pass from the old to a new nature made perfect in Christ. Since this transition brings with it a progressive change of outlook and conduct, it should become manifest by means of its social consequences and it should develop gradually during the period of the catechumenate. Since the Lord in whom they believe is a sign of contradiction, the newly converted often experience divisions and separations, but they also taste the joy that God gives without measure."[21]

3. The Church, like a mother, helps the catechumens on their journey by means of suitable liturgical rites, which purify the catechumens little by little and strengthen them with God's blessing. Celebrations of the word of God are arranged for their benefit, and at Mass they may also take part with the faithful in the liturgy of the word, thus better preparing themselves for their eventual participation in the liturgy of the eucharist. Ordinarily, however, when they are present in the assembly of the faithful they should be kindly dismissed before the liturgy of the eucharist begins (unless their dismissal would present practical or pastoral problems). For they must await their baptism, which will join them to God's priestly people and empower them to participate in Christ's new worship (see no. 67 for formularies of dismissal).

4. Since the Church's life is apostolic, catechumens should also learn how to work actively with others to spread the Gospel and build up the Church by the witness of their lives and by professing their faith.[22]

76. The duration of the catechumenate will depend on the grace of God and on various circumstances, such as the program of instruction for the catechumenate, the number of catechists, deacons, and priests, the cooperation of the individual catechumens, the means necessary for them to come to the site of the catechumenate and spend time there, the help of the local community. Nothing, therefore, can be settled a priori.

The time spent in the catechumenate should be long enough—several years if necessary—for the conversion and faith of the catechumens to become strong. By their formation in the entire Christian life and a sufficiently prolonged probation the catechumens are properly initiated into the mysteries of salvation and the practice of an evangelical way of life. By means of sacred rites celebrated at successive times they are led into the life of faith, worship, and charity belonging to the people of God.

77.   It is the responsibility of the bishop to fix the duration and to direct the program of the catechumenate. The conference of bishops, after considering the condition of its people and region,[23] may also wish to provide specific guidelines. At the discretion of the bishop, on the basis of the spiritual preparation of the candidate, the period of the catechumenate may in particular cases be shortened (see nos. 331–335); in altogether extraordinary cases the catechumenate may be completed all at once (see nos. 332, 336–369).

78.   The instruction that the catechumens receive during this period should be of a kind that while presenting Catholic teaching in its entirety also enlightens faith, directs the heart toward God, fosters participation in the liturgy, inspires apostolic activity, and nurtures a life completely in accord with the spirit of Christ.

79.   Among the rites belonging to the period of the catechumenate, then, celebrations of the word of God (nos. 81–89) are foremost. The minor exorcisms (nos. 90–94) and the blessings of the catechumens (nos. 95–97) are ordinarily celebrated in conjunction with a celebration of the word. In addition, other rites may be celebrated to mark the passage of the catechumens from one level of catechesis to another: for example, an anointing of the catechumens may be celebrated (nos. 98–103) and the presentations of the Creed and the Lord's Prayer may be anticipated (see nos. 104–105).

80.   During the period of the catechumenate, the catechumens should give thought to choosing the godparents who will present them to the Church on the day of their election (see No. 11; also *Christian Initiation*, General Introduction, nos. 8–10).

Provision should also be made for the entire community involved in the formation of the catechumens—priest, deacons, catechists, sponsors, godparent, friends and neighbors—to participate in some of the celebrations belonging to the catechumenate, including any of the optional "rites of passage" (nos. 98–105).

RITES BELONGING TO THE PERIOD OF THE CATECHUMENATE

CELEBRATIONS OF THE WORD OF GOD

81.   During the period of the catechumenate there should be celebrations of the word of God that accord with the liturgical season and that contribute to the instruction of the catechumens and the needs of the community. These

celebrations of the word are: first, celebrations held specially for the catechumens; second, participation in the liturgy of the word at the Sunday Mass; third, celebrations held in connection with catechetical instruction.

82.   The special celebrations of the word of God arranged for the benefit of the catechumens have as their main purpose:

1. to implant in their hearts the teachings they are receiving: for example, the morality characteristic of the New Testament, the forgiving of injuries and insults, a sense of sin and repentance, the duties Christians must carry out in the world;

2. to give them instruction and experience in the different aspects and ways of prayer;

3. to explain to them the signs, celebrations, and seasons of the liturgy;

4. to prepare them gradually to enter the worship assembly of the entire community.

83.   From the very beginning of the period of the catechumenate the catechumens should be taught to keep holy the Lord's Day.

1. Care should be taken that some of the special celebrations of the word just mentioned (no. 82) are held on Sunday, so that the catechumens will become accustomed to taking an active and practiced part in these celebrations.

2. Gradually the catechumens should be admitted to the first part of the celebration of the Sunday Mass. After the liturgy of the word they should, if possible, be dismissed, but an intention for them is included in the general intercessions (see no. 67 for formularies of dismissal).

84.   Celebrations of the word may also be held in connection with catechetical or instructional meetings of the catechumens, so that these will occur in a context of prayer.

MODEL FOR A CELEBRATION OF THE WORD OF GOD

85.   For the celebrations of the word of God that are held specially for the benefit of the catechumens (see no. 82), the following structure (nos. 86–89) may be used as a model.

86.   Song: An appropriate song may be sung to open the celebration.

87.   Readings and Responsorial Psalms: One or more readings from Scripture, chosen for their relevance to the formation of the catechumens, are proclaimed by a baptized member of the community. A sung responsorial psalm should ordinarily follow each reading.

88.   Homily: A brief homily that explains and applies the readings should be given.

89. Concluding Rites: The celebration of the word may conclude with a minor exorcism (no. 94) or with a blessing of the catechumens (no. 97). When the minor exorcism is used, it may be followed by one of the blessings (no. 97) or, on occasion, by the rite of anointing (nos. 102–103).*

MINOR EXORCISMS

90. The first or minor exorcisms have been composed in the form of petitions directly addressed to God. They draw the attention of the catechumens to the real nature of Christian life, the struggle between flesh and spirit, the importance of self-denial for reaching the blessedness of God's kingdom, and the unending need for God's help.

91. The presiding celebrant for the minor exorcisms is a priest, a deacon, or a qualified catechist appointed by the bishop for this ministry (see no. 16).

92. The minor exorcisms take place within a celebration of the word of God held in a church, a chapel, or in a center for the catechumenate. A minor exorcism may also be held at the beginning or end of a meeting for catechists. When there is some special need, one of these prayers of exorcism may be said privately for individual catechumens.

93. The formularies for the minor exorcisms may be used on several occasions, as different situations may suggest.

BLESSINGS OF THE CATECHUMENS

95. The blessings of the catechumens are a sign of God's love and of the Church's tender care. They are bestowed on the catechumens so that, even though they do not as yet have the grace of the sacraments, they may still receive from the Church courage, joy, and peace as they proceed along the difficult journey they have begun.

96. The blessings may be given by a priest, a deacon, or a qualified catechist appointed by the bishop (see no. 16). The blessings are usually given at the end of a celebration of the word; they may also be given at the end of a meeting for catechesis. When there is some special need, the blessings may be given privately to individual catechumens.

----

* Celebrations of the word that are held in connection with instructional sessions may include, along with an appropriate reading, a minor exorcism (no. 94) or a blessing of the catechumens (no. 97). When the minor exorcism is used, it may be followed by one of the blessings (no. 97) or, on occasion, by the rite of anointing (nos. 102–103).

The meetings of the catechumens after the liturgy of the word of the Sunday Mass may also include a minor exorcism (no. 94) or a blessing (no. 97). Likewise, when the minor exorcism is used, it may be followed by one of the blessings (no. 97) or, on occasion, by the rite of anointing (nos. 102–103).

ANOINTING OF THE CATECHUMENS

98. During the period of the catechumenate, a rite of anointing the catechumens, through use of the oil of catechumens, may be celebrated wherever this seem beneficial or desirable. The presiding celebrant for such a first anointing of the catechumens is a priest or a deacon.

99. Care is to be taken that the catechumens understand the significance of the anointing with oil. The anointing with oil symbolizes their need for God's help and strength so that, undeterred by the bonds of the past and overcoming the opposition of the devil, they will forthrightly take the step of professing their faith and will hold fast to it unfalteringly throughout their lives.

100. The anointing ordinarily takes place after the homily in a celebration of the word of God (see no. 89), and is conferred on each of the catechumens; this rite of anointing may be celebrated several times during the course of the catechumenate. Further, for particular reasons, a priest or a deacon may confer the anointing privately on individual catechumens.

101. The oil used for this rite is to be the oil blessed by the bishop at the chrism Mass, but for pastoral reasons a priest celebrant may bless oil for the rite immediately before the anointing.[24]

PRESENTATIONS [OPTIONAL]

104. The presentations normally take place during Lent, the period of purification and enlightenment, after the first and third scrutinies. But for pastoral advantage and because the period of purification and enlightenment is rather short, the presentations may be held during the period of the catechumenate, rather than at the regular times. But the presentations are not to take place until a point during the catechumenate when the catechumens are judged ready for these celebrations.

105. Both the presentation of the Creed and the presentation of the Lord's Prayer may be anticipated; each may be concluded with the ephphetha rite.[25] When the presentations are anticipated, care is to be taken to substitute the term "catechumens' for the term "elect" in all formularies.

SENDING OF THE CATECHUMENS FOR ELECTION [OPTIONAL]

106. At the conclusion of the period of the catechumenate, a rite of sending the catechumens to their election by the bishop may be celebrated in parishes wherever this seems beneficial or desirable. When election will take place in the parish, this rite is not used.

107. As the focal point of the Church's concern for the catechumens, admission to election belongs to the bishop who is usually its presiding celebrant. It is within the parish community, however, that the preliminary judgment is made concerning the catechumens' state of formation and progress.

This rite offers the local community the opportunity to express its approval of the catechumens and to send them forth to the celebration of election assured of the parish's care and support.

108. The rite is celebrated in the parish church at a suitable time prior to the rite of election.

109. The rite takes place after the homily in a celebration of the word of God (see no. 89) or at Mass.

110. When the Rite of Sending Catechumens for Election is combined with the rite of sending for recognition by the bishop the (already baptized) adult candidates for the sacraments of confirmation and eucharist (or: for reception into the full communion of the Catholic Church), the alternate rite found on page 289 (Appendix I, 2) is used.

SECOND STEP: ELECTION OR ENROLLMENT OF NAMES

Your ways, O Lord, are love and truth to those who keep your covenant

118. The second step in Christian initiation is the liturgical rite called both election and the enrollment of names, which closes the period of the catechumenate proper, that is, the lengthy period of formation of the catechumens' minds and hearts. The celebration of the rite of election, which usually coincides with the opening of Lent, also marks the beginning of the period of final, more intense preparation for the sacraments of initiation, during which the elect will be encouraged to follow Christ with greater generosity.

119. At this second step, on the basis of the testimony of godparents and catechists and of the catechumens' reaffirmation of their intention, the Church judges their state of readiness and decides on their advancement toward the sacraments of initiation. Thus the Church makes its "election," that is, the choice and admission of those catechumens who have the dispositions that make them fit to take part, at the next major celebration, in the sacraments of initiation.

This step is called election because the acceptance made by the Church is founded on the election by God, in whose name the Church acts. The step is also called the enrollment of names because as a pledge of fidelity the candidates inscribe their names in the book that lists those who have been chosen for initiation.

120. Before the rite of election is celebrated, the catechumens are expected to have undergone a conversion in mind and in action and to have developed a sufficient acquaintance with Christian teaching as well as a spirit of faith and charity. With deliberate will and an enlightened faith they must have the intention to receive the sacraments of the Church, a resolve they will express publicly in the actual celebration of the rite.

121. The election, marked with a rite of such solemnity, is the focal point of the Church's concern for the catechumens. Admission to election therefore belongs to the bishop, and the presiding celebrant for the rite of election is the bishop himself or a priest or a deacon who acts as the bishop's delegate (see no. 12).

Before the rite of election the bishop, priests, deacons, catechists, godparents, and the entire community, in accord with their respective responsibilities and in their own way, should, after considering the matter carefully, arrive at a judgment about the catechumens' state of formation and progress. After the election, they should surround the elect with prayer, so that the entire Church will accompany and lead them to encounter Christ.

122. Within the rite of election the bishop celebrant or his delegate declares in the presence of the community the Church's approval of the candidates. Therefore to exclude any semblance of mere formality from the rite, there should be a deliberation prior to its celebration to decide on the catechumens' suitableness. This deliberation is carried out by the priests, deacons, and catechists involved in the formation of the catechumens, and by the godparents and representatives of the local community. If circumstances suggest, the group of catechumens may also take part. The deliberation may take various forms, depending on local conditions and pastoral needs. During the celebration of election, the assembly is informed of the decision approving the catechumens.

123. Before the rite of election godparents are chosen by the catechumens; the choice should be made with the consent of the priest, and the persons chosen should, as far as possible, be approved for their role by the local community (see no. 11). In the rite of election the godparents exercise their ministry publicly for the first time. They are called by name at the beginning of the rite to come forward with the catechumens (no. 130); they give testimony on behalf of the catechumens before the community (no. 131); they may also write their names along with the catechumens in the book of the elect (no. 132).

124. From the day of their election and admission, the catechumens are called "the elect." They are also described as *competentes* ("co-petitioners"), because they are joined together in asking for and aspiring to receive the three sacraments of Christ and the gift of the Holy Spirit. They are also called *illuminandi* ("those who will be enlightened"), because baptism itself has been called *illuminatio* ("enlightenment") and it fills the newly baptized with the light of faith. In our own times, other names may be applied to the elect that, depending on regions and cultures, are better suited to the people's understanding and the idiom of the language.

125. The bishop celebrant or his delegate, however much or little he was involved in the deliberation prior to the rite, has the responsibility of showing in the homily or elsewhere during the celebration of the religious and ecclesial significance of the election. The celebrant also declares before all present the Church's decision and, if appropriate in the circumstances, asks the community to express its approval of the candidates. He also asks the catechumens to give

a personal expression of their intention and, in the name of the Church, he carries out the act of admitting them as elect. The celebrant should open to all the divine mystery expressed in the call of the Church and in the liturgical celebration of this mystery. He should remind the faithful to give good example to the elect and along with the elect to prepare themselves for the Easter solemnities.

126. The sacraments of initiation are celebrated during the Easter solemnities, and preparation for these sacraments is part of the distinctive character of Lent. Accordingly, the rite of election should normally take place on the First Sunday of Lent and the period of final preparation of the elect should coincide with the Lenten season. The plan arranged for the Lenten season will benefit the elect by reason of both its liturgical structure and the participation of the community. For urgent pastoral reasons, especially in secondary mission stations, it is permitted to celebrate the rite of election during the week preceding or following the First Sunday of Lent.

When, because of unusual circumstances and pastoral needs, the rite of election is celebrated outside Lent, it is to be celebrated about six weeks before the sacraments of initiation, in order to allow sufficient time for the scrutinies and presentations. The rite is not be be celebrated on a solemnity of the liturgical year (see no. 29).

127. The rite should take place in the cathedral church, in a parish church or, if necessary, in some other suitable and fitting place.

128. The rite is celebrated within Mass, after the homily, and should be celebrated within the Mass of the First Sunday of Lent. If, for pastoral reasons, the rite is celebrated on a different day, the texts and the readings of the ritual Mass "Christian Initiation: Election or Enrollment of Names" may always be used. When the Mass of the day is celebrated and its readings are not suitable, the readings are those given for the First Sunday of Lent or others may be chosen from elsewhere in the Lectionary.

When celebrated outside Mass, the rite takes place after the readings and the homily and is concluded with the dismissal of both the elect and the faithful.

[An optional parish rite to send catechumens for election by the bishops precedes the rite of election as is found at no. 106.]

PERIOD OF PURIFICATION AND ENLIGHTENMENT

The water that I shall give will turn into a spring of eternal life

138. The period of purification and enlightenment, which the rite of election begins, customarily coincides with Lent. In the liturgy and liturgical catechesis of Lent the reminder of baptism already received or the preparation for its reception, as well as the theme of repentance, renew the entire community along with those being prepared to celebrate the paschal mystery, in which each of the elect will share through the sacraments of initiation.[26] For both the elect and the

local community, therefore, the Lenten season is a time for spiritual recollection in preparation for the celebration of the paschal mystery.

139. This is a period of more intense spiritual preparation, consisting more in interior reflection than in catechetical instruction, and is intended to purify the minds and hearts of the elect as they search their own consciences and do penance. This period is intended as well to enlighten the minds and hearts of the elect with a deeper knowledge of Christ the Savior. The celebration of certain rites, particularly the scrutinies (see nos. 141–146) and the presentations (see nos. 147–149), brings about this process of purification and enlightenment and extends it over the course of the entire Lenten season.

140. Holy Saturday is the day of proximate preparation for the celebration of the sacraments of initiation and on that day the rites of preparation (see nos. 185–192) may be celebrated.

RITES BELONGING TO THE PERIOD OF PURIFICATION AND ENLIGHTENMENT

SCRUTINIES

141. The scrutinies, which are solemnly celebrated on Sundays and are reinforced by an exorcism, are rites for self-searching and repentance and have above all a spiritual purpose. The scrutinies are meant to uncover, then heal all that is weak, defective, or sinful in the hearts of the elect; to bring out, then strengthen all that is upright, strong, and good. For the scrutinies are celebrated in order to deliver the elect from the power of sin and Satan, to protect them against temptation, and to give them strength in Christ, who is the way, the truth, and the life. These rites, therefore, should complete the conversion of the elect and deepen their resolve to hold fast to Christ and to carry out their decision to love God above all.

142. Because they are asking for the three sacraments of initiation, the elect must have the intention of achieving an intimate knowledge of Christ and his Church, and they are expected particularly to progress in genuine self-knowledge through serious examination of their lives and true repentance.

143. In order to inspire in the elect a desire for purification and redemption by Christ, three scrutinies are celebrated. By this means, first of all, the elect are instructed gradually about the mystery of sin, from which the whole world and every person longs to be delivered and thus saved from its present and future consequences. Second, their spirit is filled with Christ the Redeemer, who is the living water (gospel of the Samaritan woman in the first scrutiny), the light of the world (gospel of the man born blind in the second scrutiny), the resurrection and the life (gospel of Lazarus in the third scrutiny). From the first to the final scrutiny the elect should progress in their perception of sin and their desire for salvation.

144. In the rite of exorcism (nos. 154, 168, 175), which is celebrated by a priest or a deacon, the elect, who have already learned from the Church as their mother the mystery of deliverance from sin by Christ, are freed from the effects of sin and from the influence of the devil. They receive new strength in the midst of their spiritual journey and they open their hearts to receive the gifts of the Savior.

145. The priest or deacon who is the presiding celebrant should carry out the celebration in such a way that the faithful in the assembly will also derive benefit from the liturgy of the scrutinies and join in the intercessions for the elect.

146. The scrutinies should take place within the ritual Masses "Christian Initiation: The Scrutinies," which are celebrated on the Third, Fourth, and Fifth Sundays of Lent; the readings with their chants are those given for these Sundays in the Lectionary for Mass, Year A. When, for pastoral reasons, these ritual Masses cannot be celebrated on their proper Sundays, they are celebrated on other Sundays of Lent or even convenient days during the week.

When, because of unusual circumstances and pastoral needs, the period of purification and enlightenment takes place outside Lent, the scrutinies are celebrated on Sundays or even on weekdays, with the usual intervals between celebrations. They are not celebrated on solemnities of the liturgical year (see no. 30).

In every case the ritual Masses "Christian Initiation: The Scrutinies" are celebrated and in this sequence: for the first scrutiny the Mass with the gospel of the Samaritan woman; for the second, the Mass with the gospel of the man born blind; for the third, the Mass with the gospel of Lazarus.

PRESENTATIONS

147. The presentations take place after the celebration of the scrutinies, unless, for pastoral reasons, they have been anticipated during the period of the catechumenate (see nos. 79, 104–105). Thus, with the catechumenal formation of the elect completed, the Church lovingly entrusts to them the Creed and the Lord's Prayer, the ancient texts that have always been regarded as expressing the heart of the Church's faith and prayer. These texts are presented in order to enlighten the elect. The Creed, as it recalls the wonderful deeds of God for the salvation of the human race, suffuses the vision of the elect with the sure light of faith. The Lord's Prayer fills them with a deeper realization of the new sprit of adoption by which they will call God their Father, especially in the midst of the eucharistic assembly.

148. The first presentation to the elect is the presentation of the Creed, during the week following the first scrutiny. The elect are to commit the Creed to memory and they will recite it publicly (nos. 193–196) prior to professing their faith in accordance with that Creed on the day of their baptism.

149. The second presentation to the elect is the presentation of the Lord's Prayer, during the week following the third scrutiny (but, if necessary, this presentation may be deferred for inclusion in the preparation rites of Holy Saturday; see no. 185). From antiquity the Lord's Prayer has been the prayer proper

to those who in baptism have received the spirit of adoption. When the elect have been baptized and take part in their first celebration of the eucharist, they will join the rest of the faithful in saying the Lord's Prayer.

PREPARATION RITES ON HOLY SUNDAY

185. In proximate preparation for the celebration of the sacraments of initiation:

1. The elect are to be advised that on Holy Saturday they should refrain from their usual activities, spend their time in prayer and reflection, and, as far as they can, observe a fast.

2. When it is possible to bring the elect together on Holy Saturday for reflection and prayer, some or all of the following rites may be celebrated as an immediate preparation for the sacraments: the presentation of the Lord's Prayer, if it has been deferred (see nos. 149, 178–180), the "return" or recitation of the Creed (nos. 193–196), the ephphetha rite (nos. 197–199), and the choosing of a baptismal name (nos. 200–202).

186. The choice and arrangement of these rites should be guided by what best suits the particular circumstances of the elect, but the following should be observed with regard to their celebration:

1. In cases where celebration of the presentation of the Creed was not possible, the recitation of the Creed is not celebrated.

2. When both the recitation of the Creed and the ephphetha rite are celebrated, the ephphetha rite immediately precedes the "Prayer before the Recitation" (no. 194).

MODEL FOR A CELEBRATION OF THE PREPARATION RITES

187. Song: When the elect have gathered, the celebration begins with a suitable song.

188. Greeting: After the singing, the celebrant greets the elect and any of the faithful who are present, using one of the greetings for Mass or other suitable words.

189. Reading of the Word of God: Where indicated in the particular rites, the read of the word of God follows; the readings may be chosen from those suggested for each rite. If more than one reading is used, a suitable psalm or hymn may be sung between the readings.

190. Homily: Where indicated in the particular rites, a brief homily or an explanation of the text follows the reading of the word of God.

191. Celebration of the Rites Chosen: See nos. 193–202.

192. Concluding Rites: The celebration may be concluded with a prayer of blessing and dismissal given in nos. 204–205.

RECITATION OF THE CREED

193. The rite of recitation of the Creed prepares the elect for the profession of faith they will make immediately before they are baptized (no. 225); the rite also instructs them in their duty to proclaim the message of the Gospel.

EPHPHETHA RITE

197. By the power of its symbolism the ephphetha rite, or rite of opening the ears and mouth, impresses on the elect their need of grace in order that they may hear the word of God and profess it for their salvation.

CHOOSING A BAPTISMAL NAME

200. The rite of choosing a baptismal name may be celebrated on Holy Saturday, unless it was included in the rite of acceptance into the order of catechumens (see nos. 33.4, 74). The elect may choose a new name, which is either a traditional Christian name or a name of regional usage that is not incompatible with Christian beliefs. Where it seems better suited to the circumstances and the elect are not too numerous, the naming may consist simply in an explanation of the given name of each of the elect.

THIRD STEP: CELEBRATION OF THE SACRAMENTS OF INITIATION

When we were baptized we joined Jesus in death so that we might walk in the newness of life

206. The third step in the Christian initiation of adults is the celebration of the sacraments of baptism, confirmation, and eucharist. Through this final step the elect, receiving pardon for their sins, are admitted into the people of God. They are graced with adoption as children of God and are led by the Holy Spirit into the promised fullness of time begun in Christ[27] and, as they share in the eucharistic sacrifice and meal, even to a foretaste of the kingdom of God.

207. The usual time for the celebration of the sacraments of initiation is the Easter Vigil (see no. 23), at which preferably the bishop himself presides as celebrant, at least for the initiation of those who are fourteen years old or older (see no. 12). As indicated in the Roman Missal, "Easter Vigil" (no. 44), the conferral of the sacraments follows the blessing of the water.

208. When the celebration takes place outside the usual time (see nos. 26–27), care should be taken to ensure that it has a markedly paschal character (see *Christian Initiation*, General Introduction, no. 6). Thus the texts for one of the ritual Masses "Christian Initiation: Baptism" given in the Roman Missal are used, and the readings are chosen from those given in the Lectionary for Mass, "Celebration of the Sacraments of Initiation apart from the Easter Vigil."

209. The celebration of baptism has as its center and high point the baptismal washing and the invocation of the Holy Trinity. Beforehand there are rites that have an inherent relationship to the baptismal washing: first, the blessing of water, then the renunciation of sin by the elect, and their profession of faith. Following the baptismal washing, the effects received through this sacrament are given expression in the explanatory rites: the anointing with chrism (when confirmation does not immediately follow baptism), the clothing with a white garment, and the presentation of a lighted candle.

210. Prayer over the Water: The celebration of baptism begins with the blessing of water, even when the sacraments of initiation are received outside the Easter Season. Should the sacraments be celebrated outside the Easter Vigil but during the Easter Season (see no. 26), the water blessed at the Vigil is used, but a prayer of thanksgiving, having the same themes as the blessing, is included. The blessing declares the religious meaning of water as God's creation and the sacramental use of water in the unfolding of the paschal mystery, and the blessing is also a remembrance of God's wonderful works in the history of salvation.

The blessing thus introduces an invocation of the Trinity at the very outset of the celebration of baptism. For it calls to mind the mystery of God's love from the beginning of the world and the creation of the human race; by invoking the Holy Spirit and proclaiming Christ's death and resurrection, it impresses on the mind the newness of Christian baptism, by which we share in his own death and resurrection and receive the holiness of God himself.

211. Renunciation of Sin and Profession of Faith: In their renunciation of sin and profession of faith those to be baptized express their explicit faith in the paschal mystery that has already been recalled in the blessing of water and that will be connoted by the words of the sacrament soon to be spoken by the baptizing minister. Adults are not saved unless they come forward of their own accord and with the will to accept God's gift through their own belief. The faith of those to be baptized is not simply the faith of the Church, but the personal faith of each one of them and each one of them is expected to keep it a living faith.

Therefore the renunciation of sin and the profession of faith are an apt prelude to baptism, the sacrament of that faith by which the elect hold fast to God and receive new birth from him. Because of the renunciation of sin and the profession of faith, which form the one rite, the elect will not be baptized merely passively but will receive this great sacrament with the active resolve to renounce error and to hold fast to God. By their own personal act in the rite of renouncing sin and professing their faith, the elect, as was prefigured in the first covenant with the patriarch, renounce sin and Satan in order to commit themselves for ever to the promise of the Savior and to the mystery of the Trinity. By professing their faith before the celebrant and the entire community, the elect express the intention, developed to maturity during the preceding periods of initiation, to enter into a new covenant with Christ. Thus these adults embrace the faith that through divine help the Church has handed down, and are baptized in that faith.

212. Baptism: Immediately after their profession of living faith in Christ's paschal mystery, the elect come forward and receive that mystery as expressed in the washing with water; thus once the elect have professed faith in the Father, Son, and Holy Spirit, invoked by the celebrant, the divine persons act so that those they have chosen receive divine adoption and become members of the people of God.

213. Therefore in the celebration of baptism the washing with water should take on its full importance as the sign of that mystical sharing in Christ's death and resurrection through which those who believe in his name die to sin and rise to eternal life. Either immersion or the pouring of water should be chosen for the rite, whichever will serve in individual cases and in the various traditions and circumstances to ensure the clear understanding that this washing is not a mere purification rite but the sacrament of being joined to Christ.

214. Explanatory Rites: The baptismal washing is followed by rites that give expression to the effects of the sacrament just received. The anointing with chrism is a sign of the royal priesthood of the baptized and that they are now numbered in the company of the people of God. The clothing with the baptismal garment signifies the new dignity they have received. The presentation of a lighted candle shows that they are called to walk as befits the children of light.

CELEBRATION OF CONFIRMATION

215. In accord with the ancient practice followed in the Roman liturgy, adults are not to be baptized without receiving confirmation immediately afterward, unless some serious reason stands in the way. The conjunction of the two celebrations signifies the unity of the paschal mystery, the close link between the mission of the Son and the outpouring of the Holy Spirit, and the connection between the two sacraments through which the Son and the Holy Spirit come with the Father to those who are baptized.

216. Accordingly, confirmation is conferred after the explanatory rites of baptism, the anointing after baptism (no. 228) being omitted.

THE NEOPHYTES' FIRST SHARING IN THE CELEBRATION OF THE EUCHARIST

217. Finally in the celebration of the eucharist, as they take part for the first time and with full right, the newly baptized reach the culminating point in their Christian initiation. In this eucharist the neophytes, now raised to the ranks of the royal priesthood, have an active part both in the general intercessions and, to the extent possible, in bringing the gifts to the altar. With the entire community they share in the offering of the sacrifice and say the Lord's Prayer, giving expression to the sprit of adoption as God's children that they have received in baptism. When in communion they receive the body that was

given for us and the blood that was shed, the neophytes are strengthened in the gifts they have already received and are given a foretaste of the eternal banquet.

PERIOD OF POSTBAPTISMAL CATECHESIS OR MYSTAGOGY

You are a chosen race, a royal priesthood, a holy people; praise God who called you out of darkness and into his marvelous light

244. The third step of Christian initiation, the celebration of the sacraments, is followed by the final period, the period of postbaptismal catechesis or mystagogy. This is a time for the community and the neophytes together to grow in deepening their grasp of the paschal mystery and in making it part of their lives through meditation on the Gospel, sharing in the eucharist, and doing the works of charity. To strengthen the neophytes as they begin to walk in newness of life, the community of the faithful, their godparents, and their parish priests (pastors) should give them thoughtful and friendly help.

245. The neophytes are, as the term "mystagogy" suggests, introduced into a fuller and more effective understanding of the mysteries through the Gospel message they have learned and above all through their experience of the sacraments they have received. For they have truly been renewed in mind, tasted more deeply the sweetness of God's word, received the fellowship of the Holy Spirit, and grown to know the goodness of the Lord. Out of this experience, which belongs to Christians and increases as it is lived, they derive a new perception of the faith, of the Church, and of the world.

246. Just as their new participation in the sacraments enlightens the neophytes' understanding of the Scriptures, so too it increases their contact with the rest of the faithful and has an impact on the experience of the community. As a result, interaction between the neophytes and the faithful is made easier and more beneficial. The period of postbaptismal catechesis is of great significance for both the neophytes and the rest of the faithful. Through it the neophytes, with the help of their godparents, should experience a full and joyful welcome into the community and enter into closer ties with the other faithful. The faithful, in turn, should derive from it a renewal of inspiration and of outlook.

247. Since the distinctive spirit and power of the period of postbaptismal catechesis or mystagogy derive from the new, personal experience of the sacraments and of the community, its main setting is the so-called Masses for neophytes, that is, the Sunday Masses of the Easter season. Besides being occasions for the newly baptized to gather with the community and share in the mysteries, these celebrations include particularly suitable readings from the Lectionary, especially the readings for Year A. Even when Christian initiation has been celebrated outside the usual times, the texts for these Sunday Masses of the Easter season may be used.

248. All the neophytes and their godparents should make an effort to take part in the Masses for the neophytes and the entire local community should be

invited to participate with them. Special places in the congregation are to be reserved for the neophytes and their godparents. The homily and, as circumstance suggest, the general intercessions should take into account the presence and needs of the neophytes.

249. To close the period of the postbaptismal catechesis, some sort of celebration should be held at the end of the Easter season near Pentecost Sunday; festivities in keeping with local custom may accompany the occasion.

250. On the anniversary of their baptism the neophytes should be brought together in order to give thanks to God, to share with one another their spiritual experiences, and to renew their commitment.

251. To show his pastoral concern for these new members of the Church, the bishop, particularly if he was unable to preside at the sacraments of initiation himself, should arrange, if possible, to meet the recently baptized at least once in the year and to preside at a celebration of the eucharist with them. At this Mass they may receive holy communion under both kinds.

PART II: RITES FOR PARTICULAR CIRCUMSTANCES

1 CHRISTIAN INITIATION OF CHILDREN WHO HAVE REACHED CATECHETICAL AGE

Do not keep the children from me

252. This form of the rite of Christian initiation is intended for children, not baptized as infants, who have attained the use of reason and are of catechetical age. They seek Christian initiation either at the direction of their parents or guardians or, with parental permission, on their own initiative. Such children are capable of receiving and nurturing a personal faith and of recognizing an obligation in conscience. But they cannot yet be treated as adults because, at this stage of their lives, they are dependent on their parents or guardians and are still strongly influenced by their companions and their social surroundings.

253. The Christian initiation of these children requires both a conversion that is personal and somewhat developed, in proportion to their age, and the assistance of the education they need. The process of initiation thus must be adapted both to their spiritual progress, that is, to the children's growth in faith, and to the catechetical instruction they receive. Accordingly, as with adults, their initiation is to be extended over several years, if need be, before they receive the sacraments. Also as with adults, their initiation is marked by several steps, the liturgical rites of acceptance into the order of catechumens (nos. 260–275), the optional rite of election (nos. 277–290), penitential rites or scrutinies (nos. 291–303), and the celebration of the sacraments of initiation (nos. 304–329); corresponding to the periods of adult initiation are the periods of the children's catechetical formation that lead up to and follow the steps of their initiation.

254. The children's progress in the formation they receive depends on the help and example of their companions and on the influence of their parents. Both of these factors should therefore be taken into account.

1. Since the children to be initiated often belong to a group of children of the same age who are already baptized and are preparing for confirmation and eucharist, their initiation progresses gradually and with the supportive setting of this group of companions.

2. It is to be hoped that the children will also receive as much help and example as possible from the parents, whose permission is required for the children to be initiated and to live the Christian life. The period of initiation will also provide a good opportunity for the family to have contact with priests and catechists.

255. For the celebrations proper to this form of Christian initiation, it is advantageous, as circumstances allow, to form a group of several children who are in this same situation, in order that by example they may help one another in their progress as catechumens.

256. In regard to the time for the celebration of the steps of initiation, it is preferable that, if possible, the final period of preparation, begun by the second step, the penitential rites (or by the optional rite of election), coincide with Lent and that the final step, celebration of the sacraments of initiation, take place at the Easter Vigil (see no. 8). Nevertheless before the children are admitted to the sacraments at Easter, it should be established that they are ready for the sacraments. Celebration at this time must also be consistent with the program of catechetical instruction they are receiving, since the candidates should, if possible, come to the sacraments of initiation at the time that their baptized companions are to receive confirmation or eucharist.

257. For children of this age, at the rites during the process of initiation, it is generally preferable not to have the whole parish community present, but simply represented. Thus these rites should be celebrated with the active participation of a congregation that consists of a suitable number of the faithful, the parents, family, members of the catechetical group, and a few adult friends.

258. Each conference of bishops may adapt and add to the form of the rite given here in order that the rite will more effectively satisfy local needs, conditions, and pastoral requirements. [The National Conference of Catholic Bishops has done this by providing an optional "Rite of Election" before "Second Step: Penitential Rites (Scrutinies)." The rites for the presentation of the Creed (nos. 157–162) and the Lord's Prayer (nos. 178–183), adapted to the age of the children, may be incorporated. When the form of the rite of initiation for children is translated, the instructions and prayers should be adapted to their understanding. Furthermore, in addition to any liturgical text translated from the Latin *editio typica*, the conference of bishops may also approve an original, alternative text that says the same thing in a way more suited to children (see *Christian Initiation*, General Introduction, no. 32).

259. In following this form of the rite of Christian initiation the celebrant should make full and wise use of the options mentioned in *Christian Initiation*, General Introduction (nos. 34–35), in the *Rite of Baptism for Children*, Introduction (no. 31), and in the *Rite of Christian Initiation of Adults*, Introduction (no. 35).

FIRST STEP: ACCEPTANCE INTO THE ORDER OF CATECHUMENS

Happy the people the Lord has chosen to be his own

260. It is important that this rite be celebrated with an actively participating but small congregation, since the presence of a large group might make the children uncomfortable (see no. 257). When possible, the children's parents or guardians should be present. If they cannot come, they should indicate that they have given consent to their children and their place should be taken by "sponsors" (see no. 10), that is, suitable members of the Church who act on this occasion for the parents and present the children. The presiding celebrant is a priest or deacon.

261. The celebration takes place in the church or in a place that, according to the age and understanding of the children, can help them to experience a warm welcome. As circumstances suggest, the first part of the rite, "Receiving the Children," is carried out at the entrance of the place chosen for the celebration, and the second part of the rite, "Liturgy of the Word," takes place inside.

The celebration is not normally combined with celebration of the eucharist.

RITE OF ENROLLMENT OR ENROLLMENT OF NAMES [OPTIONAL]

To just such as these the Kingdom of God belongs

277. The (optional) liturgical rite called both election and the enrollment of names may be celebrated with children of catechetical age, especially those whose catechumenate has extended over a long period of time. This celebration, which usually coincides with the beginning of Lent, marks the beginning of the period of final preparation for the sacraments of initiation, during which the children will be encouraged to follow Christ with greater generosity.

278. In the rite of election, on the basis of the testimony of parents, godparents and catechists and of the children's reaffirmation of their intention, the Church judges their state of readiness and decides on their advancement toward the sacraments of initiation. Thus the Church makes its "election," that is, the choice and admission of those children who have the dispositions that make them fit to take part, at the next major celebration, in the sacraments of initiation.

279. The rite should take place in the cathedral church, in a parish church or, if necessary, in some other suitable and fitting place. If the election of children of catechetical age is to take place within a celebration in which older catechumens

are also to receive the Church's election, the rite for adults (nos. 129–137) should be used, with appropriate adaptation of the texts to be made by the celebrant.

280. The rite is celebrated within Mass, after the homily, and should be celebrated within the Mass of the First Sunday of Lent. If, for pastoral reasons, the rite is celebrated on a different day, the texts and the readings of the ritual Mass "Christian Initiation: Election or Enrollment of Names" may always be used. When the Mass of the day is celebrated and its readings are not suitable, the readings are those given for the First Sunday of Lent or others may be chosen from elsewhere in the Lectionary.

When celebrated outside Mass, the rite takes place after the readings and the homily and is concluded with the dismissal of both the elect and the faithful.

SECOND STEP: PENITENTIAL RITES (SCRUTINIES)

Create in me a new heart and a new spirit

291. These penitential rites, which mark the second step in the children's Christian initiation, are major occasions in their catechumenate. They are held within a celebration of the word of God as a kind of scrutiny, similar to the scrutinies in the adult rite. Thus the guidelines given for the adult rite (nos. 41–46) may be followed and adapted, since the children's penitential rites have a similar purpose.

292. Because the penitential rites normally belong to the period of final preparation for baptism, the condition for their celebration is that the children are approaching the maturity of faith and understanding requisite for baptism.

293. Along with the children, their godparents and their baptized companions from the catechetical group participate in the celebration of these penitential rites. Therefore the rites are to be adapted in such a way that they also benefit the participants who are not catechumens. In particular, these penitential rites are a proper occasion for baptized children of the catechetical group to celebrate the sacrament of penance for the first time. When this is the case, care should be taken to include explanations, prayers, and ritual acts that relate to the celebration of the sacrament with these children.

294. The penitential rites are celebrated during Lent, if the catechumens are to be initiated at Easter; if not, at the most suitable time. At least one penitential rite is to be celebrated, and, if this can be arranged conveniently a second should follow after an appropriate interval. The texts for a second celebration are to be composed on the model of the first given here, but the texts for the intercessions and prayer of exorcism given in the adult rite (nos. 153–154, 167–168, 174–175) are used, with the requisite modifications.

THIRD STEP: CELEBRATION OF THE SACRAMENTS OF INITIATION

Wake up and rise from death: Christ will shine upon you

304. In order to bring out the paschal character of baptism, celebration of the sacraments of initiation should preferably take place at the Easter Vigil or on a Sunday, the day that the Church devotes to the remembrance of Christ's resurrection (see *Rite of Baptism for Children,* Introduction, no. 9). But the provisions of no. 256 should also guide the choice of time for the celebration of the sacraments of initiation.

305. At this third step of their Christian initiation, the children will receive the sacrament of baptism, the bishop or priest who baptizes them will also confer confirmation, and the children will for the first time participate in the liturgy of the eucharist.

306. If the sacraments of initiation are celebrated at a time other than the Easter Vigil or Easter Sunday, the Mass of the day or one of the ritual Masses in the Roman Missal, "Christian Initiation: Baptism" is used. The readings are chosen from those given in the Lectionary for Mass, "Celebration of the Sacraments of Initiation apart from the Easter Vigil"; but the readings for the Sunday or feast on which the celebration takes place may be used instead.

307. All the children to be baptized are to be accompanied by their own godparent or godparents, chosen by themselves and approved by the priest (see no. 11; *Christian Initiation,* General Introduction, no. 10).

308. Baptized children of the catechetical group may be completing their Christian initiation in the sacraments of confirmation and the eucharist at this same celebration. When the bishop himself will not be the celebrant, he should grant the faculty to confirm such children to the priest who will be the celebrant.[1] For their confirmation, previously baptized children of the catechetical group are to have their own sponsors. If possible, these should be the persons who were godparents for their baptism, but other qualified persons may be chosen.[2]

PERIOD OF POSTBAPTISMAL CATECHESIS
OR MYSTAGOGY

The Father chose us to be his adopted children through Jesus Christ

330. A period of postbaptismal catechesis or mystagogy should be provided to assist the young neophytes and their companions who have completed their Christian initiation. This period can be arranged by an adaptation of the guidelines given for adults (nos. 244–251).

2 CHRISTIAN INITIATION OF ADULTS IN EXCEPTIONAL CIRCUMSTANCES

He gave power to become children of God to all who believe in his name

331. Exceptional circumstances may arise in which the local bishop, in individual cases, can allow the use of a form of Christian initiation that is simpler than the usual, complete rite (see no. 34.4).

The bishop may permit this simpler form to consist in the abbreviated form of the rite (nos. 340–369) that is carried out in one celebration. Or he may permit an expansion of this abbreviated rite, so that there are celebrations not only of the sacraments of initiation but also of one or more of the rites belonging to the period of the catechumenate and to the period of purification and enlightenment (see nos. 332–335).

The extraordinary circumstances in question are either events that prevent the candidate from completing all the steps of the catechumenate or a depth of Christian conversion and a degree of religious maturity that lead the local bishop to decide that the candidate may receive baptism without delay.

EXPANDED FORM

332. Extraordinary circumstances, for example, sickness, old age, change of residence, long absence for travel, may sometimes either prevent a candidate from celebrating the rite of acceptance that leads to the period of the catechumenate or, having begun the catechumenate, from completing it by participation in all the rites belonging to the period. Yet merely to use the abbreviated form of the rite given in nos. 340–369 could mean a spiritual loss for the candidate, who would be deprived of the benefits of a longer preparation for the sacraments of initiation. It is therefore important that, with the bishop's permission, an expanded form of initiation be developed by the incorporation of elements from the complete rite for the Christian initiation of adults.

333. Through such an expansion of the abbreviated rite a new candidate can reach the same level as those who are already advanced in the catechumenate, since some of the earlier elements from the full rite can be added, for example, the rite of acceptance into the order of catechumens (nos. 48–74) or the minor exorcisms (no. 94) and blessings (no. 97) from the period of the catechumenate. The expansion also makes it possible for a candidate who had begun the catechumenate with others, but was forced to interrupt it, to complete the catechumenate alone by celebrating, in addition to the sacraments of initiation (see nos. 206–217), elements from the full rite, for example, the rite of election (see nos. 118-128) and rites belonging to the period of purification and enlightenment (see nos. 141–149).

334. Pastors can arrange this expanded form of initiation by taking the abbreviated form as a basis, then choosing wisely from the full rite to make adaptations in any of the following ways:

1. supplementing the abbreviated form: for example, adding rites belonging to the period of the catechumenate (nos. 81–103) or adding the presentations (nos. 157–162, 178–182);

2. making the rite of "Receiving the Candidate" or the "Liturgy of the Word" in the abbreviated rite separate or expanded celebrations. As to "Receiving the Candidate" (nos. 340–245), this can be expanded by replacing no. 342 and using elements from the rite of acceptance into the order of catechumens (nos. 48–74); or, depending on the candidate's state of preparation, by celebrating the rite of election (nos. 129–137) in place of nos. 343–344. As to the "Liturgy of the Word," after the readings, the intercessions, penitential rite, and prayer of exorcism, nos. 349–351, can be adapted by use of the elements in the scrutinies (nos. 152–154, 166–168, 173–175).

3. replacing elements of the complete rite with elements of the abbreviated form; or combining the rite of acceptance into the order of catechumens (nos. 48–74) and the rite of election (nos. 129–137) at the time of receiving a properly disposed candidate (which is comparable to the time of receiving interested inquirers in the period of the precatechumenate; see no. 39.3).

335. When this expanded form of initiation is arranged, care should be taken to ensure that:

1. the candidate has received a full catechesis;

2. the rite is celebrated with the active participation of an assembly;

3. after receiving the sacraments the neophyte has the benefit of a period of postbaptismal catechesis, if at all possible.

ABBREVIATED FORM

336. Before the abbreviated form of the rite is celebrated the candidate must have gone through an adequate period of instruction and preparation before baptism, in order to purify his or her motives for requesting baptism and to grow stronger in conversion and faith. The candidate should also have chosen godparents or a godparent (see no. 11) and become acquainted with the local Christian community (see nos. 39, 75.2).

337. This rite includes elements that express the presentation and welcoming of the candidate and that also express the candidate's clear and firm resolve to request Christian initiation, as well as the Church's approval of the candidate. A suitable liturgy of the word is also celebrated, then the sacraments of initiation.

338. Normally the rite is celebrated within Mass. The choice of readings should be in keeping with the character of the celebration; they may be either those of the day or those in the Lectionary for Mass, ritual Mass, "Christian Initiation apart from the Easter Vigil." The other Mass texts are those of one of the ritual Masses "Christian Initiation: Baptism" or of another Mass. After receiving

baptism and confirmation, the candidate takes part for the first time in the celebration of the eucharist.

339. If at all possible, the celebration should take place on a Sunday (see no. 27), with the local community taking an active part.

---

3 CHRISTIAN INITIATION OF A PERSON IN DANGER OF DEATH

By becoming coheirs with Christ, we share in his sufferings; we will also share in his glory

370. Persons, whether catechumens or not, who are in danger of death but are not at the point of death and so are able to hear and answer the questions involved may be baptized with this short rite.

371. Persons who have already been accepted as catechumens must make a promise that upon recovery they will complete the usual catechesis. Persons who are not catechumens must give serious indication of their conversion to Christ and renunciation of pagan worship and must not be seen to be attached to anything that conflicts with the moral life (for example, "simultaneous polygamy"). They must also promise that upon recovery they will go through the complete program of initiation as it applies to them.

372. This shorter rite is designed particularly for use by catechists and laypersons; a priest or a deacon may use it in a case of emergency. But normally a priest or a deacon is to use the abbreviated form of Christian initiation given in nos. 340–369, making any changes required by circumstances of place and time.

The minister of baptism who is a priest should, when the chrism is at hand and there is time, confer confirmation after the baptism; in this case there is no postbaptismal anointing.

The minister of baptism who is a priest, a deacon, or a catechist or layperson having permission to distribute communion, should, if this is possible, give the eucharist to the newly baptized person. In this case before the beginning of the celebration of the rite the blessed sacrament is placed reverently on a table covered with a white cloth.

373. In the case of a person who is at the point of death, that is, whose death is imminent, and time is short, the minister, omitting everything else, pours natural water (even if not blessed) on the head of the sick person, while saying the usual sacramental form (see *Christian Initiation*, General Introduction, no. 23).

374. If persons who were baptized when in danger of death or at the point of death recover their health, they are to be given a suitable formation, be welcomed at the church in due time, and there receive the other sacraments of initiation. In such cases the guidelines given in nos. 400–410 for baptized but

uncatechized adults are followed, with the necessary changes. The same guidelines should be applied when sick persons recover after receiving not only baptism but also confirmation and eucharist as viaticum.

---

4 PREPARATION OF UNCATECHIZED ADULTS FOR CONFIRMATION AND EUCHARIST

If then you have been raised with Christ, seek the things that are above, where Christ is seated at the right hand of God

400. The following pastoral guidelines concern adults who were baptized as infants either as Roman Catholics or as members of another Christian community but did not receive further catechetical formation nor, consequently, the sacraments of confirmation and eucharist. These suggestions may also be applied to similar cases, especially that of an adult who recovers after being baptized in danger of death or at the point of death (see no. 374).

Even though uncatechized adults have not yet heard the message of the mystery of Christ, their status differs from that of catechumens, since by baptism they have already become members of the Church and children of God. Hence their conversion is based on the baptism they have already received, the effects of which they must develop.

401. As in the case of catechumens, the preparation of these adults requires a considerable time (see no. 76), during which the faith infused in baptism must grow in them and take deep root through the pastoral formation they receive. A program of training, catechesis suited to their needs, contact with the community of the faithful, and participation in certain liturgical rites are needed in order to strengthen them in the Christian life.

402. For the most part the plan of catechesis corresponds to the one laid down for catechumens (see no. 75.1). But in the process of catechesis the priest, deacon, or catechist should take into account that these adults have a special status because they are already baptized.

403. Just as it helps catechumens, the Christian community should also help these adults by its love and prayer (see nos. 4, 75.2) and by testifying to their suitability when it is time for them to be admitted to the sacraments (see nos. 120, 121).

404. A sponsor presents these adults to the community (see no. 10). During the period of their catechetical formation, they all choose godparents (a godfather, a godmother, or both) approved by the priest. Their godparents work with these adults as the representatives of the community and have the same responsibilities as the godparents have toward catechumens (see no. 11). The same persons who were the godparents at the baptism of these adults may be chosen as godparents at this time, provided they are truly capable of carrying out the responsibilities of godparents.

405. The period of preparation is made holy by means of liturgical celebrations. The first of these is a rite by which the adults are welcomed into the community and acknowledge themselves to be part of it because they have already been marked with the seal of baptism. [The Rite of Welcoming the Candidates, which follows in Part II, 4A is provided for this purpose.]

406. Once a rite of reception has been celebrated, these adults take part in celebrations of the word of God, both those of the entire Christian assembly and those celebrations arranged specially for the benefit of the catechumens (see nos. 81–84).

407. As a sign of God's activity in this work of preparation, some of the rites belonging to the catechumenate, especially suited to the condition and spiritual needs of these baptized adults, can be used to advantage. Among these are the presentation of the Creed (nos. 157–162) and of the Lord's Prayer (nos. 178–182) or also a presentation of a book of the Gospels (no. 64). [The additional rites in Part II, 4B, 4C, and 4D may also be used in accordance with the individual needs and circumstances of the candidates.]

408. The period of catechesis for these adults should be properly coordinated with the liturgical year. This is particularly true of its final phase, which should as a rule coincide with Lent. During the Lenten season penitential services should be arranged in such a way as to prepare these adults for the celebration of the sacrament of penance.

409. The high point of their entire formation will normally be the Easter Vigil. At that time they will make a profession of the faith in which they were baptized, receive the sacrament of confirmation, and take part in the eucharist. If, because neither the bishop nor another authorized minister is present, confirmation cannot be given at the Easter Vigil, it is to be celebrated as soon as possible and, if this can be arranged, during the Easter season.

410. These adults will complete their Christian formation and become fully integrated into the community by going through the period of postbaptismal catechesis or mystagogy with the newly baptized members of the Christian community.

OPTIONAL RITES FOR BAPTIZED BUT UNCATECHIZED ADULTS

4A RITE OF WELCOMING THE CANDIDATES

Teach us your ways, O Lord

411. This optional rite welcomes baptized but previously uncatechized adults who are seeking to complete their Christian initiation through the sacraments of confirmation and eucharist or to be received into the full communion of the Catholic Church.

412. The prayers and ritual gestures acknowledge that such candidates are already part of the community because they have been marked by baptism. Now the Church surrounds them with special care and support as they prepare to be sealed with the gift of the Spirit in confirmation and take their place at the banquet table of Christ's sacrifice.

413. Once formally welcomed into the life of the community, these adults, besides regularly attending Sunday eucharist, take part in celebrations of the word of God in the full Christian assembly and in celebrations arranged especially for the benefit of the candidates.

414. The rite will take place on specified days throughout the year (see no. 18) that are suited to local conditions.

415. When the rite of welcoming candidates for the sacraments of confirmation and eucharist is to be combined with the rite of acceptance into the order of catechumens, the alternate rite found on page 289 (Appendix I, 1) is used.

4B RITE OF SENDING THE CANDIDATES FOR RECOGNITION BY THE BISHOP AND FOR THE CALL TO CONTINUING CONVERSION

My sheep hear my voice and follow me

434. This optional rite is provided for parishes whose candidates seeking to complete their Christian initiation or to be received into the full communion of the Catholic Church will be recognized by the bishop in a subsequent celebration (for example, at the cathedral with the bishop).

435. Because he is the sign of unity within the particular Church, it is fitting for the bishop to recognize these candidates. It is the responsibility of the parish community, however, to prepare the candidates for their fuller life in the Church. Through the experience of worship, daily life, and service in the parish community the candidates deepen their appreciation of the Church's tradition and universal character.

This rite offers that local community the opportunity to express its joy in the candidates' decision and to send them forth to the celebration of recognition assured of the parish's care and support.

436. The rite is celebrated in the parish church at a suitable time prior to the rite of recognition and call to continuing conversion.

437. When the rite of sending candidates for recognition is to be combined with the rite of sending catechumens for election, the alternate rite found on page 305 (Appendix I, 2) is used.

4C RITE OF CALLING THE CANDIDATES TO CONTINUING CONVERSION

As members of one body, you have been called to his peace

446. This rite may be celebrated with baptized but previously uncatechized adults who wish to complete their Christian initiation through the sacraments of confirmation and eucharist or who wish to be received into the full communion of the Catholic Church.

447. The rite is intended for celebrations in communities where there are no catechumens.

448. The rite is celebrated at the beginning of Lent. The presiding celebrant is the pastor of the parish.

449. If the calling of candidates to continuing conversion is to be combined with the rite of election of catechumens (either in a parish celebration or at one in which the bishop is celebrant) the alternate rite given on page 315 (Appendix I, 3) is used.

4D PENITENTIAL RITE (SCRUTINY)

May you all be kept blameless, spirit, soul, and body, for the coming of our Lord Jesus Christ

459. This penitential rite can serve to mark the Lenten purification of baptized but previously uncatechized aults who are preparing to receive the sacraments of confirmation and eucharist or to be received into the full communion of the Catholic Church. It is held within a celebration of the word of God as a kind of scrutiny, similar to the scrutinies for catechumens.

460. Because the penitential rite normally belongs to the period of final preparation for the sacraments, its celebration presumes that the candidates are approaching the maturity of faith and understanding requisite for fuller life in the community.

461. Along with the candidates, their sponsors and the larger liturgical assembly also participate in the celebration of the penitential rite. Therefore the rite is to be adapted in such a way that it benefits all the participants. This penitential rite may also help to prepare the candidates to celebrate the sacrament of penance.

462. This penitential rite may be celebrated on the Second Sunday of Lent or on a Lenten weekday, if the candidates are to receive the sacraments of confirmation and eucharist and/or be received into the full communion of the Catholic Church at Easter; if not, at the most suitable time.

463. This penitential rite is intended solely for celebrations with baptized adults preparing for confirmation and eucharist or reception into the full communion of the Catholic Church. Because the prayer of exorcism in the three scrutinies for catechumens who have received the Church's election properly belongs to the elect and uses numerous images referring to their approaching baptism, those scrutinies of the elect and this penitential rite for those preparing for confirmation and eucharist have been kept separate and distinct. Thus, no combined rite has been included in Appendix I.

---

5 RECEPTION OF BAPTIZED CHRISTIANS INTO THE FULL COMMUNION OF THE CATHOLIC CHURCH

All of you are one, united in Christ Jesus

473. This is the liturgical rite by which a person born and baptized in a separated ecclesial community is received, according to the Latin rite,[3] into the full communion of the Catholic Church. The rite is so arranged that no greater burden than necessary (see Acts 15:28) is required for the establishment of communion and unity.[4]

474. In the case of Eastern Christians who enter into the fullness of Catholic communion, no liturgical rite is required, but simply a profession of Catholic faith, even if such persons are permitted, in virtue of recourse to the Apostolic See, to transfer to the Latin rite.[5]

475. In regard to the manner of celebrating the rite of reception:

1. The rite should appear clearly as a celebration of the Church and have as its high point eucharistic communion. For this reason the rite should normally take place within Mass.

2. Any appearance of triumphalism should be carefully avoided and the manner of celebrating this Mass should be decided beforehand and with a view to the particular circumstances. Both the ecumenical implications and the bond between the candidate and the parish community should be considered. Often it will be preferable to celebrate the Mass with only a few relatives and friends. If for a serious reason Mass cannot be celebrated, the reception should at least take place within a liturgy of the word, whenever this is possible. The person to be received into full communion should be consulted about the form of reception.

476. If the rite of reception is celebrated outside Mass, the Mass in which for the first time the newly received will take part with the Catholic community should be celebrated as soon as possible, in order to make clear the connection between the reception and eucharistic communion.

477. The baptized Christian is to receive both doctrinal and spiritual preparation, adapted to individual pastoral requirements, for reception into the full

communion of the Catholic Church. The candidate should learn to deepen an inner adherence to the Church, where he or she will find the fullness of his or her baptism. During the period of preparation the candidate may share in worship in conformity with the provisions of the *Ecumenical Directory*.

Anything that would equate candidates for reception with those who are catechumens is to be absolutely avoided

478. During the period of their doctrinal and spiritual preparation individual candidates for reception into the full communion of the Catholic Church may benefit from the celebration of liturgical rites marking their progress in formation. Thus for pastoral reasons and in light of the catechesis in the faith which these baptized Christians have received previously, one or several of the rites included in Part II, "4 Preparation of Uncatechized Adults for Confirmation and Eucharist," may be celebrated as they are presented or in similar words. In all cases, however, discernment should be made regarding the length of catechetical formation required for each individual candidate for reception into the full communion of the Catholic Church.

479. One who was born and baptized outside the visible communion of the Catholic Church is not required to make an abjuration of heresy but simply a profession of faith.[6]

480. The sacrament of baptism cannot be repeated and therefore it is not permitted to confer it again conditionally, unless there is a reasonable doubt about the fact or validity of the baptism already conferred. If serious investigation raises such prudent doubt and it seems necessary to confer baptism again conditionally, the minister should explain beforehand the reasons why this is being done and a nonsolemn form of baptism is to be used.[7]

The local Ordinary is to decide in each case what rites are to be included or excluded in conferring conditional baptism.

481. It is the office of the bishop to receive baptized Christians into the full communion of the Catholic Church. But a priest to whom the bishop entrusts the celebration of the rite has the faculty of confirming the candidate within the rite of reception,[8] unless the person received has already been validly confirmed.

482. If the profession of faith and reception take place within Mass, the candidate, according to his or her own conscience, should make a confession of sins beforehand, first informing the confessor that he or she is about to be received into full communion. Any confessor who is lawfully approved may hear the candidate's confession.

483. At the reception, the candidate should be accompanied by a sponsor and may even have two sponsors. If someone has had the principal part in guiding or preparing the candidate, he or she should be the sponsor.

484. In the eucharistic celebration within which reception into full communion takes place or, if the reception takes place outside Mass, in the Mass that follows at a later time, communion under both kinds is permitted for the person received, the sponsor, the parents and spouse who are Catholics, lay catechists who may have instructed the person, and, if the number involved and other circumstances make this feasible, for all Catholics present.

485. The conferences of bishops may, in accord with the provisions of the Constitution on the Liturgy, art. 63, adapt the rite of reception to various circumstances. The local Ordinary, by expanding or shortening the rite, may arrange it to suit the particular circumstances of the persons and place involved.[9]

APPENDIX I
ADDITIONAL (COMBINED) RITES

1 CELEBRATION OF THE RITE OF ACCEPTANCE INTO THE ORDER OF CATECHUMENS AND OF THE RITE OF WELCOMING BAPTIZED BUT PREVIOUSLY UNCATECHIZED ADULTS WHO ARE PREPARING FOR CONFIRMATION AND/OR EUCHARIST OR RECEPTION INTO THE FULL COMMUNION OF THE CATHOLIC CHURCH

I am the good shepherd: I know my sheep and mine know me

505. This rite is for use in communities where catechumens are preparing for initiation and where baptized but previously uncatechized adults are beginning catechetical formation either prior to completing their Christian initiation in the sacraments of confirmation and eucharist or prior to being received into the full communion of the Catholic Church.

506. In the catechesis of the community and in the celebration of these rites, care must be taken to maintain the distinction between the catechumens and the baptized candidates.

---

2 PARISH CELEBRATION FOR SENDING CATECHUMENS FOR ELECTION AND CANDIDATES FOR RECOGNITION BY THE BISHOP (OPTIONAL)

The community was of one mind and one heart

530. This optional rite is provided for parishes whose catechumens will celebrate their election and whose adult candidates for confirmation and eucharist or reception into the full communion of the Catholic Church will celebrate their recognition in a subsequent celebration (for example, at the cathedral with the bishop).

531. As the focal point of the Church's concern for the catechumens, admission to election belongs to the bishop who is usually its presiding celebrant. It is within the parish community, however, that the preliminary judgment is made concerning the catechumens' state of formation and progress.

This rite offers that local community the opportunity to express its approval of the catechumens and to send them forth to the celebration of election assured of the parish's care and support.

532. In addition, those who either are completing their initiation through the sacraments of confirmation and the eucharist or are preparing for reception into the full communion of the Catholic Church are also included in this rite, since they too will be presented to the bishop at the celebration of the rite of election for the catechumens.

533. The rite is celebrated in the parish church at a suitable time prior to the rite of election.

534. The rite takes place after the homily in a celebration of the word of God (see no. 89) or at Mass.

535. In the catechesis of the community and in the celebration of these rites, care must be taken to maintain the distinction between the catechumens and the baptized candidates

---

3 CELEBRATION OF THE RITE OF ELECTION OF CATECHUMENS AND OF THE CALL TO CONTINUING CONVERSION OF CANDIDATES WHO ARE PREPARING FOR CONFIRMATION AND/OR EUCHARIST OR RECEPTION INTO THE FULL COMMUNION OF THE CATHOLIC CHURCH

The body is one and has many members

547. This rite is for use when the election of catechumens and the call to continuing conversion of candidates preparing either for confirmation and/or eucharist or reception into the full communion of the Catholic Church are celebrated together.

548. The rite should normally take place on the First Sunday of Lent, and the presiding celebrant is the bishop or his delegate.

549. In the catechesis of the community and in the celebration of these rites, care must be taken to maintain the distinction between the catechumens and the baptized candidates.

---

4 CELEBRATION AT THE EASTER VIGIL OF THE SACRAMENTS OF INITIATION AND OF THE RITE OF RECEPTION INTO THE FULL COMMUNION OF THE CATHOLIC CHURCH

The Father chose us in Christ to be holy and spotless in love

562. Pastoral considerations may suggest that along with the celebration of the sacraments of Christian initiation the Easter Vigil should include the rite of reception of already baptized Christians into the full communion of the Catholic Church. But such a decision must be guided by the theological and pastoral directives proper to each rite. The model provided here simply arranges the ritual elements belonging to such a combined celebration. But the model can only be used properly in the light of nos. 206–217, regarding celebration of the sacraments of Christian initiation, and of nos. 473–486, regarding the rite of reception into the full communion of the Catholic Church.

563. Inclusion at the Easter Vigil of the rite of reception into full communion may also be opportune liturgically, especially when the candidates have undergone a lengthy period of spiritual formation coinciding with Lent. In the liturgical year the Easter Vigil, the preeminent commemoration of Christ's paschal mystery, is the preferred occasion for the celebration in which the elect will enter the paschal mystery through baptism, confirmation, and eucharist. Candidates for reception, who in baptism have already been justified by faith and incorporated into Christ,[10] are entering fully into a community that is constituted by its communion both in faith and in the sacramental sharing of the paschal mystery. The celebration of their reception at the Easter Vigil provides the candidates with a privileged opportunity to recall and reaffirm their own baptism, "the sacramental bond of unity [and] foundation of communion between all Christians."[11] At the Easter Vigil these candidates can make their profession of faith by joining the community in the renewal of the baptismal promises, and, if they have not yet been confirmed, they can receive the sacrament of confirmation, which is intimately connected with baptism. Since of its nature baptism points to complete entrance into eucharistic communion,[12] the baptismal themes of the Easter Vigil can serve to emphasize why the high point of the candidates' reception is their sharing in the eucharist with the Catholic community for the first time (see no. 475.1).

564. The decision to combine the two celebrations at the Easter Vigil must beguided by the provision in the *Rite of Reception*, Introduction (no. 475.2). The decision should, then, be consistent in the actual situation with respect for ecumenical values and beguided by attentiveness both to local conditions and to personal and family preferences. The person to be received should always be consulted about the form of reception (see no. 475.2).

565. In its actual arrangement the celebration itself must reflect the status of candidates for reception into the full communion of the Catholic Church: such candidates have already been incorporated into Christ in baptism and anything that would equate them with catechumens is to be absolutely avoided (see no. 477).

NOTES

PART I

1. See Vatican Council II, Constitution on the Liturgy *Sacrosanctum Concilium*, art. 64–66; Decree on the Church's Missionary Activity *Ad gentes*, no 14; Decree on the Pastoral Office of Bishops *Christus Dominus*, no. 14.

2. See Vatican Council II, Constitution on the Liturgy *Sacrosanctum Concilium*, art. 109.

3. See Vatican Council II, Decree on the Church's Missionary Activity *Ad gentes*, no. 14.

4. See Vatican Council II, Dogmatic Constitution on the Church *Lumen gentium*, no. 17.

5. See Vatican Council II, Decree on the Apostolate of the Laity *Apostolicam actuositatem*, no. 6.

6. See *Christian Initiation*, General Introduction, nos. 8 and 10.1.

7. See ibid., no. 12.

8. See ibid., nos. 13–15.

9. See Vatican Council II, Decree on the Ministry and Life of Priests *Presbyterorum Ordinis*, no. 6.

10. See *Rite of Confirmation*, Introduction, no. 7.b.

11. See ibid., no. 8.

12. See Vatican Council II, Dogmatic Constitution on the Church *Lumen gentium*, no. 26; Decree on the Church's Missionary Activity *Ad gentes*, no. 16.

13. See Vatican Council II, Constitution on the Liturgy *Sacrosanctum Concilium*, art. 79.

14. See *Codex Iuris Canonici*, can., 874, §1, 2º.

15. See Vatican Council II, Decree on the Church's Missionary Activity *Ad gentes*, no. 13.

16. See Vatican Council II, Decree on the Church's Missionary Activity *Ad gentes*, no. 14.

17. See ibid., no. 13.

18. See Vatican Council II, Dogmatic Constitution on the Church *Lumen gentium*, no. 14; Decree on the Church's Missionary Activity *Ad gentes*, no. 14.

19. See *Rite of Marriage*, nos. 55–66.

20. See Vatican Council II, Decree on the Church's Missionary Activity *Ad gentes*, no. 14.

21. Ibid., no. 13.

22. See Vatican Council II, Decree on the Church's Missionary Activity *Ad gentes*, no. 14.

23. See Vatican Council II, Constitution on the Liturgy *Sacrosanctum Concilium*, art. 64.

24. See *Rite of the Blessing of Oils, Rite of Consecrating the Chrism*, Introduction, no. 7.

25. But if the recitation of the Creed (nos. 193–196) is also anticipated as one of the "rites of passage" (see no. 33.6), the ephpheta rite is used only to begin this rite of recitation and not with the presentations.

26. See Vatican Council II, Decree on the Church's Missionary Activity *Ad gentes*, no. 14.

27. See Vatican Council II, Dogmatic Constitution on the Church *Lumen gentium*, no. 48; also Ephesians 1:10.

PART II

1. See *Rite of Confirmation*, Introduction, no. 7.b.

2. See ibid., nos. 5 and 6.

3. See Vatican Council II, Constitution on the Liturgy *Sacrosanctum Concilium*, art. 69,b; Decree on Ecumenism *Unitatis redintegratio*, no. 3. Secretariat for Christian Unity, *Ecumenical Directory I*, no. 19: AAS 59 (1967), 581.

4. See Vatican Council II, Decree on Ecumenism *Unitatis redintegratio*, no. 18.

5. See Vatican Council II, Decree on the Eastern Catholic Churches *Orientalium Ecclesiarum*, nos. 25 and 4.

6. See Secretariat for Christian Unity, *Ecumenical Directory I*, nos. 19 and 20: AAS 59 (1967), 581.

7. See ibid., nos. 14–15: AAS 59 (1967), 580.

8. See *Rite of Confirmation*, Introduction, no. 7.b.

9. See Secretariat for Christian Unity, *Ecumenical Directory I*, no. 19: AAS 59 (1967), 581.

10. See Secretariat for Christian Unity, *Ecumenical Directory I*, no. 11: AAS 59 (1967). Vatican Council II, Decree on Ecumenism *Unitatis redintegratio*, no. 3.

11. See *Ecumenical Directory I*, no. 11: AAS 59 (1967), 578. Vatican Council II, Decree on Ecumenism *Unitatis redintegratio*, no. 22.

12. See Vatican Council II, Decree on Ecumenism *Unitatis redintegratio*, no. 22.

NATIONAL STATUTES
FOR THE
CATECHUMENATE

APPROVED BY THE NATIONAL CONFERENCE OF CATHOLIC BISHOPS
ON 11 NOVEMBER 1986

CONFIRMED BY THE CONGREGATION FOR DIVINE WORSHIP
ON 26 JUNE 1988 (PROT. 1191/86)

OUTLINE

NATIONAL STATUTES FOR THE CATECHUMENATE

PRECATECHUMENATE

1.   Any reception or service of welcome or prayer for inquirers at the beginning or during a precatechumenate (or in an earlier period of evangelization) must be entirely informal. Such meetings should take into account that the inquirers are not yet catechumens and that the rite of acceptance into the order of catechumens, intended for those who have been converted from unbelief and have initial faith, may not be anticipated.

CATECHUMENATE

2.   The term "catechumen" should be strictly reserved for the unbaptized who have been admitted into the order of catechumens; the term "convert" should be reserved strictly for those converted from unbelief to Christian belief and never used of those baptized Christians who are received into the full communion of the Catholic Church.

3.   This holds true even if elements of catechumenal formation are appropriate for those who are not catechumens, namely, (a) baptized Catholic Christians who have not received catechetical instruction and whose Christian initiation has not been completed by confirmation and eucharist and (b) baptized Christians who have been members of another Church or ecclesial community and seek to be received into the full communion of the Catholic Church.

4.   If the catechumenal preparation takes place in a non-parochial setting such as a center, school, or other institution, the catechumens should be introduced into the Christian life of a parish or similar community from the very beginning of the catechumenate, so that after their initiation and mystagogy they will not find themselves isolated from the ordinary life of the Christian people.

5.   In the celebration of the rite of acceptance into the order of catechumens, it is for the diocesan bishop to determine whether the additional rites listed in no. 74, *Rite of Christian Initiation of Adults,* are to be incorporated (see no. 33.5).

6.   The period of catechumenate, beginning at acceptance into the order of catechumens and including both the catechumenate proper and the period of purification and enlightenment after election or enrollment of names, should extend for at least one year of formation, instruction, and probation. Ordinarily this period should go from at least the Easter season of one year until the next; preferably it should begin before Lent in one year and extend until Easter of the following year.

7.   A thoroughly comprehensive catechesis on the truths of Catholic doctrine and moral life, aided by approved catechetical texts, is to be provided during the period of the catechumenate (see RCIA, no. 75).

CATECHUMENS

8.   Catechumens should be encouraged to seek blessings and other suffrages from the Church, since they are of the household of Christ; they are entitled to Christian burial should they die before the completion of their initiation.

9.   In this case, the funeral liturgy, including the funeral Mass, should be celebrated as usual, omitting only language referring directly to the sacraments which the catechumen has not received. In view of the sensibilities of the immediate family of the deceased catechumen, however, the funeral Mass may be omitted at the discretion of the pastor.

10.   The marriages of catechumens, whether with other catechumens or with baptized Christians or even non-Christians, should be celebrated at a liturgy of the word and never at the eucharistic liturgy. Chapter III of the *Rite of Marriage* is to be followed, but the nuptial blessing in Chapter I, no. 33, may be used, all references to eucharistic sharing being omitted.

MINISTER OF BAPTISM AND CONFIRMATION

11.   The diocesan bishop is the proper minister of the sacraments of initiation for adults, including children of catechetical age, in accord with canon 852:1. If he is unable to celebrate the sacraments of initiation with all the candidates of the local church, he should at least celebrate the rite of election or enrollment of names, ordinarily at the beginning of Lent, for the catechumens of the diocese.

12.   Priests who do not exercise a pastoral office but participate in a catechumenal program require a mandate from the diocesan bishop if they are to baptize adults; they then do not require any additional mandate or authorization in order to confirm, but have the faculty to confirm from the law, as do priests who baptize adults in the exercise of their pastoral office.

13.   Since those who have the faculty to confirm are bound to exercise it in accord with canon 885:2, and may not be prohibited from using the faculty, a diocesan bishop who is desirous of confirming neophytes should reserve to himself the baptism of adults in accord with canon 863.

CELEBRATION OF THE SACRAMENTS OF INITIATION

14.   In order to signify clearly the interrelation or coalescence of the three sacraments which are required for full Christian initiation (canon 842:2), adult candidates, including children of catechetical age, are to receive baptism, confirmation, and eucharist in a single eucharistic celebration, whether at the Easter Vigil or, if necessary, at some other time.

15.   Candidates for initiation, as well as those who assist them and participate in the celebration of the Easter Vigil with them, are encouraged to keep and extend the paschal fast of Good Friday, as determined by canon 1251, throughout the day of Holy Saturday until the end of the Vigil itself, in accord with the Constitution on the Liturgy, *Sacrosanctum Concilium*, art. 110.

16.   The rite of anointing with the oil of catechumens is to be omitted in the baptism of adults at the Easter Vigil.

17.   Baptism by immersion is the fuller and more expressive sign of the sacrament and, therefore, provision should be made for its more frequent use in the baptism of adults. The provision of the *Rite of Christian Initiation of Adults* for partial immersion, namely, immersion of the candidate's head, should be taken into account.

CHILDREN OF CATECHETICAL AGE

18.   Since children who have reached the use of reason are considered, for purposes of Christian initiation, to be adults (canon 852:1), their formation should follow the general pattern of the ordinary catechumenate as far as possible, with the appropriate adaptations permitted by the ritual. They should receive the sacraments of baptism, confirmation, and eucharist at the Easter Vigil, together with the older catechumens.

19.   Some elements of the ordinary catechetical instruction of baptized children before their reception of the sacraments of confirmation and eucharist may be appropriately shared with catechumens of catechetical age. Their condition and status as catechumens, however, should not be compromised or confused, nor should they receive the sacraments of initiation in any sequence other than that determined in the ritual of Christian initiation.

20.   The abbreviated catechumenate, which the diocesan bishop may permit only in individual and exceptional cases, as described in nos. 331–332 of the *Rite of Christian Initiation of Adults*, should always be as limited as possible. It should extend over a substantial and appropriate period of time. The rites prior to sacramental initiation should not be unduly compressed, much less celebrated on a single occasion. The catechumenate of persons who move from one parish to another or from one diocese to another should not on that account alone be abbreviated.

21.   Candidates who have received their formation in an abbreviated catechumenate should receive the sacraments of Christian initiation at the Easter Vigil, if possible, together with candidates who have participated in the more extended catechumenate. They should also participate in the period of mystagogy, to the extent possible.

MYSTAGOGY

22.   After the completion of their Christian initiation in the sacraments of baptism, confirmation, and eucharist, the neophytes should begin the period of

mystagogy by participating in the principal Sunday eucharist of the community throughout the Easter season, which ends on Pentecost Sunday. They should do this as a body in company with their godparents and those who have assisted in their Christian formation.

23. Under the moderation of the diocesan bishop, the mystagogy should embrace a deepened understanding of the mysteries of baptism, confirmation, and the eucharist, and especially of the eucharist as the continuing celebration of faith and conversion.

24. After the immediate mystagogy or postbaptismal catechesis during the Easter season, the program for the neophytes should extend until the anniversary of Christian initiation, with at least monthly assemblies of the neophytes for their deeper Christian formation and incorporation into the full life of the Christian community.

UNCATECHIZED ADULT CATHOLICS

25. Although baptized adult Catholics who have never received catechetical instruction or been admitted to the sacraments of confirmation and eucharist are not catechumens, some elements of the usual catechumenal formation are appropriate to their preparation for the sacraments, in accord with the norms of the ritual, "Preparation of Uncatechized Adults for Confirmation and Eucharist."

26. Although it is not generally recommended, if the sacramental initiation of such candidates is completed with confirmation and eucharist on the same occasion as the celebration of the full Christian initiation of candidates for baptism, the condition and status of those already baptized should be carefully respected and distinguished.

27. The celebration of the sacrament of reconciliation with candidates for confirmation and eucharist is to be carried out at a time prior to and distinct from the celebration of confirmation and the eucharist. As part of the formation of such candidates, they should be encouraged in the frequent celebration of this sacrament.

28. Priests mentioned in canon 883:2 also have the faculty to confirm (a) in the case of the readmission to communion of a baptized Catholic who has been an apostate from the faith and also (b) in the case of a baptized Catholic who has without fault been instructed in a non-Catholic religion or adhered to a non-Catholic religion, but (c) not in the case of a baptized Catholic who without his or her fault never put the faith into practice.

29. In the instance mentioned in No. 28 c, in order to maintain the inter-relationship and sequence of confirmation and eucharist as defined in canon 842:2, priests who lack the faculty to confirm should seek it from the diocesan bishop, who may, in accord with canon 884:1, grant the faculty if he judges it necessary.

30.   Those who have already been baptized in another Church or ecclesial community should not be treated as catechumens or so designated. Their doctrinal and spiritual preparation for reception into full Catholic communion should be determined according to the individual case, that is, it should depend on the extent to which the baptized person has led a Christian life within a community of faith and been appropriately catechized to deepen his or her inner adherence to the Church.

31.   Those who have been baptized but have received relatively little Christian upbringing may participate in the elements of catechumenal formation so far as necessary and appropriate, but should not take part in rites intended for the unbaptized catechumens. They may, however, participate in celebrations of the word together with catechumens. In addition they may be included with uncatechized adult Catholics in such rites as may be appropriate among those included or mentioned in the ritual in Part III, 4, "Preparation of Uncatechized Adults for Confirmation and Eucharist." The rites of presentation of the Creed, the Lord's Prayer, and the book of the Gospels are not proper except for those who have received no Christian instruction and formation. Those baptized persons who have lived as Christians and need only instruction in the Catholic tradition and a degree of probation within the Catholic community should not be asked to undergo a full program parallel to the catechumenate.

32.   The reception of candidates into the communion of the Catholic Church should ordinarily take place at the Sunday Eucharist of the parish community, in such a way that it is understood that they are indeed Christian believers who have already shared in the sacramental life of the Church and are not welcomed into the Catholic eucharistic community upon their profession of faith and confirmation, if they have not been confirmed, before receiving the eucharist.

33.   It is preferable that reception into full communion not take place at the Easter Vigil lest there be any confusion of such baptized Christians with the candidates for baptism, possible misunderstanding of or even reflection upon the sacrament of baptism celebrated in another Church or ecclesial community, or any perceived triumphalism in the liturgical welcome into the Catholic eucharistic community.

34.   Nevertheless if there are both catechumens to be baptized and baptized Christians to be received into full communion at the Vigil, for pastoral reasons and in view of the Vigil's being the principal annual celebration of the Church, the combined rite is to be followed: "Celebration at the Easter Vigil of the Sacraments of Initiation and of the Rite of Reception into the Full Communion of the Catholic Church." A clear distinction should be maintained during the celebration between candidates for sacramental initiation and candidates for reception into full communion, and ecumenical sensitivities should be carefully respected.

35.   The "Rite of Reception into the Full Communion of the Catholic Church" respects the traditional sequence of confirmation before eucharist. When the

bishop, whose office it is to receive adult Christians into the full communion of the Catholic Church (RCIA, no. 481 [R8]) entrusts the celebration of the rite to a presbyter, the priest receives from the law itself (canon 883:2) the faculty to confirm the candidate for reception and is obliged to use it (canon 885:2); he may not be prohibited from exercising the faculty. The confirmation of such candidates for reception should not be deferred, nor should they be admitted to the eucharist until they are confirmed. A diocesan bishop who is desirous of confirming those received into full communion should reserve the rite of reception to himself.

36.   The celebration of the sacrament of reconciliation with candidates for reception into full communion is to be carried out at a time prior to and distinct from the celebration of the rite of reception. As part of the formation of such candidates, they should be encouraged in the frequent celebration of this sacrament.

37.   There may be a reasonable and prudent doubt concerning the baptism of such Christians which cannot be resolved after serious investigation into the fact and/or validity of baptism, namely, to ascertain whether the person who was baptized with water and with the Trinitarian formula, and whether the minister and the recipient of the sacrament had the proper requisite intentions. If conditional baptism then seems necessary, this must be celebrated privately rather than at a public liturgical assembly of the community and with only those limited rites which the diocesan bishop determines. The reception into full communion should take place later at the Sunday Eucharist of the community.

DOCUMENTATION

The *Rite of Christian Initiation of Adults* incorporates the (slight) emendations of the introduction (*praenotanda*) occasioned by the promulgation of the Code of Canon Law in 1983. It does not, however, include the text of pertinent canons or the underlying condiliar decisions and statements on the catechumenate, although the latter are reflected in the introduction to the ritual. In order to have these texts available in one place, this documentary appendix has been compiled.

A. CONCILIAR CONSTITUTIONS AND DECREES

Unless otherwise noted all translations are from: *Documents on the Liturgy, 1963–1979: Conciliar, Papal, and Curial Texts* (Collegeville, MN: The Liturgical Press, 1982)

Constitution on the Liturgy *Sacrosanctum Concilium*, art. 64:

> The catechumenate for adults, divided into several stages, is to be restored and put into use at the discretion of the local Ordinary. By this means the time of the catechumenate, which is intended as a period of well-suited instruction, may be sanctified by sacred rites to be celebrated at successive intervals of time.

Constitution on the Liturgy *Sacrosanctum Concilium*, art. 65:

> With art. 37–40 of this Constitution as the norm, it is lawful in mission lands to allow, besides what is part of Christian tradition, those initiation elements in use among individual peoples, to the extent that such elements are compatible with the Christian rite of initiation.

Constitution on the Liturgy *Sacrosanctum Concilium*, art. 66:

> Both of the rites for the baptism of adults are to be revised: not only the simpler rite, but also the more solemn one, with proper attention to the restored catechumenate. A special Mass "On the Occasion of a Baptism" is to be incorporated into the Roman Missal.

Dogmatic Constitution on the Church *Lumen Gentium*, no.14:

> This holy Council first of all turns its attention to the Catholic faithful. Basing itself on scripture and tradition, it teaches that the Church, a pilgrim now on earth, is necessary for salvation: the one Christ is mediator and the way of salvation; he is present to us in his body which is the Church. He himself explicitly asserted the necessity of faith and baptism (see Mark 16:16; John 3:5), and thereby affirmed at the same time the necessity of the Church which men enter through baptism as through a door. Hence they could not be saved who, knowing that the Catholic church was founded as necessary by God through Christ, would refuse either to enter it, or to remain in it.
>
> Fully incorporated into the Church are those who, possessing the Spirit of Christ, accept all the means of salvation given to the Church together with her entire organization, and who—by the bonds constituted by the profession of faith, the sacraments, ecclesiastical government, and communion— are joined in the visible structure of the Church of Christ, who rules her through the Supreme Pontiff and the bishops. Even though incorporated into the Church, one who does not however persevere in charity is not saved. He remains indeed in the bosom of the Church, but "in body" not "in heart." All children of the Church should nevertheless remember that their exalted condition results, not from their own merits, but from the grace of Christ. If they fail to respond in thought, word and deed to that grace, not only shall they not be saved, but they shall be the more severely judged.
>
> Catechumens who, moved by the Holy Spirit, desire with an explicit intention to be incorporated into the Church, are by that very intention joined to her. With love and solicitude mother Church already embraces them as her own (Flannery translation).

Decree on the Church's Missionary Activity *Ad gentes*, no.13:

> Whenever God opens a door for the word in order to declare the mystery of Christ (see Colossians 4:3) then the living God, and he whom he has sent for the salvation of all, Jesus Christ (see 1 Thessalonians 1:9–10;

1 Corinthians 1:18–21; Galatians 1:31; Acts 14:15–17; 17:22–31), are confidently and perseveringly (see Acts 4:13, 29, 31; 9:27, 28; 13:40; 14:3; 198; 26:26; 28:31; 1 Thessalonians 2:2; 2 Corinthians 3:12; 7:4; Philippians 1:20; Ephesians 3:12; 6:19–20) proclaimed (see 1 Corinthians 9:15; Romans 10:14) to all men (see Mark 16:15). And this is in order that non-Christians, whose heart is being opened by the Holy Spirit (see Acts 16:4), might, while believing, freely turn to the Lord who, since he is the "way, the truth and the life" (John 14:6), will satisfy all their inner hopes, or rather infinitely surpass them.

This conversion is, indeed, only initial; sufficient however to make a man realize that he has been snatched from sin, and is being led into the mystery of God's love, who invites him to establish a personal relationship with him in Christ. Under the movement of divine grace the new convert sets out on a spiritual journey by means of which, while already sharing through faith in the mystery of the death and resurrection, he passes from the old man to the new man who has been made perfect in Christ (see Colossians 3:5–10; Ephesians 4:20–24). This transition, which involves a progressive change of outlook and morals, should be manifested in its social implications and effected gradually during the period of catechumenate. Since the Lord in whom he believes is a sign of contradiction (see Luke 2:34; Matthew 10:34–39) the convert often has to suffer misunderstanding and separation, but he also experience those joys which are generously granted by God.

The Church strictly forbids that anyone should be forced to accept the faith, or be induced or enticed by unworthy devices; as it likewise strongly defends the right that no one should be frightened away from the faith by unjust persecutions.

In accordance with the very ancient practice of the Church, the motives for the conversion should be examined and, if necessary, purified (Flannery translation).

Decree on the Church's Missionary Activity *Ad gentes*, no. 14:

Those who through the Church have accepted from the Father faith in Christ should be admitted to the catechumenate by means of liturgical ceremonies. The catechumenate means not simply a presentation of teachings and precepts, but a formation in the whole of Christian life and a sufficiently prolonged period of training; by these means the disciples will become bound to Christ as their master. Catechumens should therefore be properly initiated into the mystery of salvation and the practices of gospel living; by means of sacred rites celebrated at successive times, they should be led gradually into the life of faith, liturgy, and charity belonging to the people of God.

Next, freed from the power of darkness, dying, buried, and risen again together with Christ through the sacraments of Christian initiation, they receive the Spirit of adoption of children, and with the whole people of God celebrate the memorial of the Lord's death and resurrection.

There is a great need for a reform of the Lenten and Easter liturgy so that it will be a spiritual preparation of the catechumens for the celebration of the paschal mystery, the rites of which will include their being reborn to Christ through baptism.

Christian initiation during the catechumenate is not the concern of catechists or priests alone, but of the whole community of believers and especially of godparents, so that from the outset the catechumens will have a sense of being part of the people of God. Moreover, because the Church's life is apostolic, catechumens should learn to take an active share in the evangelization and the building up of the Church through the witness of their life and the profession of their faith.

Finally, the new code of canon law should set out clearly the juridic status of catechumens; they are already joined to the church, already part of Christ's household, and are in many cases already living a life of faith, hope, and charity.

Decree on the Church's Missionary Activity *Ad gentes*, no. 15:

The Holy Spirit calls all to Christ through the seed of the word and the preaching of the Gospel and inspires in hearts the obedience of faith. When in the womb of the baptismal font the Spirit gives birth into a new life to those who believe in Christ, he gathers them all together into the one people of God, "a chosen race, a royal priesthood, a holy nation, God's own people" (1 Peter 2:9).

As God's co-workers, therefore, missionaries are to create congregations of believers of a kind that, living in a way worthy of their calling, will carry out the divinely appointed offices of priest, prophet, and king. This is how the Christian community becomes a sign of God's presence in the world: by the eucharistic sacrifice it goes constantly with Christ to the Father; strengthened by God's word, it bears witness to Christ; it walks in charity and burns with the apostolic spirit. Right from the beginning the Christian community should be trained to be as far as possible self-sufficient in regard to its own needs.

Decree on the Pastoral Office of Bishops in the Church *Christus Dominus*, no. 14:

[Bishops] should . . . take steps toward restoring the instruction of adult catechumens or toward adapting it more effectively.

Decree on the Ministry and Life of Priests *Presbyterorum ordinis*, no. 5:

God, who alone is holy and the author of holiness, willed to take to himself as companions and helpers men who would humbly dedicate themselves to the work of making others holy. Through the ministry of the bishop God consecrates priests to be sharers by a special title in the priesthood of Christ. In exercising sacred functions they act therefore as the ministers of him who in the liturgy continually fulfills his priestly office on our behalf by the action of his Spirit. By baptism men and women are brought into the people of God and the Church; by the oil of the sick those who are ill find relief; by the celebration of Mass people sacramentally offer the sacrifice of Christ. But in administering all the sacraments, as St. Ignatius the Martyr already attested in the early days of the Church, priests, on various grounds, are linked hierarchically with their bishop and so, in a certain way, bring his presence to every gathering of the faithful.

The other sacraments, like every ministry of the Church and every work of the apostolate, are linked with the holy eucharist and have it as their end. For the eucharist contains the church's entire spiritual wealth, that is, Christ, himself. He is our Passover and living bread; through his flesh, made living and life-giving by the Holy Spirit, he is bringing life to people and thereby inviting them to offer themselves together with him, as well as their labors and all created things. The eucharist therefore stands as the source and apex of all evangelization: catechumens are led gradually toward a share in the eucharist and the faithful who already bear the seal of baptism and confirmation enter through the eucharist more fully into the Body of Christ.

Decree on the Ministry and Life of Priests *Presbyterorum ordinis*, no. 6:

The pastor's task is not limited to individual care of the faithful. It extends by right also to the formation of a genuine Christian community. But if a community spirit is to be properly cultivated it must embrace not only the local church but the universal Church. A local community ought not merely to promote the care of the faithful within itself, but should be imbued with the missionary spirit and smooth the path to Christ for all men. But it must regard as its special charge those under instruction and the newly converted who are gradually educated in knowing and living the Christian life (Flannery translation).

B. CODE OF CANON LAW

Translations are from: *Code of Canon Law: Latin–English Edition* (Washington, DC: The Canon Law Society of America, 1983)

206. 1. Catechumens are in union with the Church in a special manner, that is, under the influence of the Holy Spirit, they ask to be incorporated into the Church by explicit choice and are therefore united with the Church by that choice just as by a life of faith, hope and charity which they lead; the Church already cherishes them as its own.

2. The Church has special care for catechumens; the Church invites them to lead the evangelical life and introduces them to the celebration of sacred rites, and grants them various prerogatives which are proper to Christians.

787. 1. By the witness of their life and words missionaries are to establish a sincere dialogue with those who do not believe in Christ in order that through

methods suited to their characteristics and culture avenues may be open to them by which they can be led to an understanding of the gospel message.

2. Missionaries are to see to that they teach the truths of faith to those whom they judge to be ready to accept the gospel message so that these persons can be admitted to the reception of baptism when they freely request it.

788. 1. After a period of pre-catechumenate has elapsed, persons who have manifested a willingness to embrace faith in Christ are to be admitted to the catechumenate in liturgical ceremonies and their names are to be registered in a book destined for this purpose.

2. Through instruction and an apprenticeship in the Christian life catechumens are suitably to be initiated into the mystery of salvation and introduced to the life of faith, liturgy, charity of the people of God and the apostolate.

3. It is the responsibility of the conference of bishops to issue statutes by which the catechumenate is regulated; these statutes are to determine what things are to be expected of catechumens and define what prerogatives are recognized as theirs.

789. Through a suitable instruction neophytes are to be formed to a more thorough understanding of the gospel truth and the baptismal duties to be fulfilled; they are to be imbued with a love of Christ and of His Church.

842. 2. The sacraments of baptism, confirmation, and the Most Holy Eucharist are so interrelated that they are required for full Christian initiation.

851. 1. An adult who intends to receive baptism is to be admitted to the catechumenate and, to the extent possible, be led through the several stages to sacramental initiation, in accord with the order of initiation adapted by the conference of bishops and the special norms published by it.

852. 1. What is prescribed in the canons on the baptism of an adult is applicable to all who are no longer infants but have attained the use of reason.

863. The baptism of adults, at least those who have completed fourteen years of age is to be referred to the bishop so that it may be conferred by him, if he judges it expedient.

865. 1. To be baptized, it is required that an adult have manifested the will to receive baptism, be sufficiently instructed in the truths and in Christian obligations and be tested in the Christian life by means of the catechumenate; the adult is also to be exhorted to have sorrow for personal sins.

2. An adult in danger of death may be baptized if, having some knowledge of the principal truths of faith, the person has in any way manifested an intention of receiving baptism and promises to observe the commandments of the Christian religion.

866. Unless a grave reason prevents it, an adult who is baptized is to be confirmed immediately after baptism and participate in the celebration of the Eucharist, also receiving Communion.

869. 1. If there is a doubt whether one has been baptized or whether baptism was validly conferred and the doubt remains after serious investigation, baptism is to be conferred conditionally.

2. Those baptized in a non-Catholic ecclesial community are not to be baptized conditionally unless, after an examination of the matter and the form of words used in the conferral of baptism and after a consideration of the intention of an adult baptized person and of the minister of the baptism, a serious reason for doubting the validity of the baptism is present.

3. If the conferral or the validity of the baptism in the cases mentioned in nos. 1 and 2 remains doubtful, baptism is not to be conferred until the doctrine of the sacrament of baptism is explained to the person, if an adult, and the reasons for the doubtful validity of the baptism has been explained to the adult recipient or, in the case of an infant, to the parents.

883. The following have the faculty of administering confirmation by the law itself:

1. within the limits of their territory, those who are equivalent in law to the diocesan bishop;

2. with regard to the person in question, the presbyter who by reason of office or mandate of the diocesan bishop baptizes one who is no longer an infant or one already baptized whom he admits into the full communion of the Catholic Church;

3. with regard to those in danger of death, the pastor or indeed any presbyter.

884. 1. The diocesan bishop is to administer confirmation personally or see that it is administered by another bishop, but if necessity requires he may give the faculty to administer this sacrament to one or more specified presbyters.

2. For a grave cause, a bishop and likewise a presbyter who has the faculty to confirm by virtue of law or special concession of competent authority may in individual cases associate presbyters with themselves to that they may administer the sacrament.

885. 2. A presbyter who has this faculty must use it for those in whose favor the faculty was granted.

1170. Blessings, to be imparted especially to Catholics, can also be given to catechumens and even to non-Catholics unless a church prohibition precludes this.

1183. 1. As regards funeral rites catechumens are to be considered members of the Christian faithful.

ORDER OF
CHRISTIAN FUNERALS

GENERAL INTRODUCTION

NATIONAL CONFERENCE OF CATHOLIC BISHOPS
14 NOVEMBER 1985, 15 AUGUST 1989

OUTLINE

ORDER OF CHRISTIAN FUNERALS

GENERAL INTRODUCTION

1.   In the face of death, the Church confidently proclaims that God has create each person for eternal life and that Jesus, the Son of God, by his death and resurrection, has broken the chains of sin and death that bound humanity. Christ "achieved his task of redeeming humanity and giving perfect glory to God, principally by the paschal mystery of his blessed passion, resurrection from the dead, and glorious ascension."[1]

2.   The proclamation of Jesus Christ "who was put to death for our sins and raised to life to justify us" (Romans 4:25) is at the center of the Church's life. The mystery of the Lord's death and resurrection gives power to all of the Church's activity. "For it was from the side of Christ as he slept the sleep of death upon the cross that there came forth the sublime sacrament of the whole Church."[2] The Church's liturgical and sacramental life and proclamation of the Gospel make this mystery present in the life of the faithful. Through the sacraments of baptism, confirmation, and eucharist, men and women are initiated into this mystery. "You have been taught that when we were baptized in Christ Jesus we were baptized into his death; in other words when we were baptized we went into the tomb with him and joined him in death, so that as Christ was raised from the dead by the Father's glory, we too might live a new life. If in union with Christ we have imitated his death, we shall also imitate him in his resurrection" (Romans 6:3–5).

3.   In the eucharistic sacrifice, the Church's celebration of Christ's Passover from death to life, the faith of the baptized in the paschal mystery is renewed and nourished. Their union with Christ and with each other is strengthened: "Because there is one bread, we who are many are one body, for we all partake of the one bread" (1 Corinthians 10:17).

4.   At the death of a Christian, whose life of faith was begun in the waters of baptism and strengthened at the eucharistic table, The Church intercedes on behalf of the deceased because of its confident belief that death is not the end nor does it break the bonds forged in life. The Church also ministers to the sorrowing and consoles them in the funeral rites with the comforting word of God and the sacrament of the eucharist.

5.   Christians celebrate the funeral rites to offer worship, praise, and thanksgiving to God for the gift of a life which has now been returned to God, the

author of life and the hope of the just. The Mass, the memorial of Christ's death and resurrection, is the principal celebration of the Christian funeral.

6.   The Church through its funeral rites commends the dead to God's merciful love and pleads for the forgiveness of their sins. At the funeral rites, especially at the celebration of the eucharistic sacrifice, the Christian community affirms and expresses the union of the Church on earth with the Church in heaven in the one great communion of saints. Though separated from the living, the dead are still at one with the community of believers on earth and benefit from their prayers and intercession. At the rite of final commendation and farewell, the community acknowledges the reality of separation and commends the deceased to God. In this way, it recognizes the spiritual bond that still exists between the living and the dead and proclaims its belief that all the faithful will be raised up and reunited in the new heavens and a new earth, where death will be no more.

7.   The celebration of the Christian funeral brings hope and consolation to the living. While proclaiming the Gospel of Jesus Christ and witnessing to Christian hope in the resurrection, the funeral rites also recall to all who take part in them God's mercy and judgment and meet the human need to turn always to God in times of crisis.

MINISTRY AND PARTICIPATION

8.   "If one member suffers in the body of Christ which is the Church, all the members suffer with that member" (1 Corinthians 12:26). For this reason, those who are baptized into Christ and nourished at the same table of the Lord are responsible for one another. When Christians are sick, their brothers and sisters share a ministry of mutual charity and "do all that they can to help the sick return to health, by showing love for the sick, and by celebrating the sacraments with them."[3] So too when a member of Christ's Body dies, the faithful are called to a ministry of consolation to those who have suffered the loss of one whom they love. Christian consolation is rooted in that hope that comes from faith in the saving death and resurrection of the Lord Jesus Christ. Christian hope faces the reality of death and the anguish of grief but trusts confidently that the power of sin and death has been vanquished by the risen Lord. The Church calls each member of Christ's Body—priest, deacon, layperson—to participate in the ministry of consolation: to care for the dying, to pray for the dead, to comfort those who mourn.

COMMUNITY

9.   The responsibility for the ministry of consolation rests with the believing community, which heeds the words and example of the Lord Jesus: "Blessed are they who mourn; they shall be consoled" (Matthew 5:3). Each Christian shares in this ministry according to the various gifts and offices in the Church. As part of the pastoral community, pastors, associate pastors, and other ministers should instruct the parish community on the Christian meaning of death and on the purpose and significance of the Church's liturgical rites for the dead. Information

on how the parish community assists families in preparing for funerals should also be provided.

By giving instruction, pastors and associate pastors should lead the community to a deeper appreciation of its role in the ministry of consolation and to a fuller understanding of the significance of the death of a fellow Christian. Often the community must respond to the anguish voiced by Martha, the sister of Lazarus: "Lord, if you had been here, my brother would never have died" (John 11:21) and must console those who mourn, as Jesus himself consoled Martha: "Your brother will rise again. . . . I am the resurrection and the life: those who believe in me, though they should die, will come to life; and those who are alive and believe in me will never die" (John 11:25–26). The faith of the Christian community in the resurrection of the dead brings support and strength to those who suffer the loss of those whom they love.

10.   Members of the community should console the mourners with words of faith and support and with acts of kindness, for example, assisting them with some of the routine tasks of daily living. Such assistance may allow members of the family to devote time to planning the funeral rites with the priest and other ministers and may also give the family time for prayer and mutual comfort.

11.   The community's principal involvement in the ministry of consolation is expressed in its active participation in the celebration of the funeral rites, particularly the vigil for the deceased, the funeral liturgy, and the rite of committal. For this reason these rites should be scheduled at times that permit as many of the community as possible to be present. The assembly's participation can be assisted by the preparation of booklets that contain an outline of the rite, the texts and songs belonging to the people, and directions for posture, gesture, and movement.

12.   At the vigil for the deceased or on another occasion before the eucharistic celebration, the presiding minister should invite all to be present at the funeral liturgy and to take an active part in it. The minister may also describe the funeral liturgy and explain why the community gathers to hear the word of God proclaimed and to celebrate the eucharist when one of the faithful dies.

Pastors, associate pastors, and other ministers should also be mindful of those persons who are not members of the Catholic Church, or Catholics who are not involved in the life of the Church.

13.   As a minister of reconciliation, the priest should be especially sensitive to the possible needs for reconciliation felt by the family and others. Funerals can begin the process of reconciling differences and supporting those ties that can help the bereaved adjust to the loss brought about by death. With attentiveness to each situation, the priest can help to begin the process of reconciliation when needed. In some cases this process may find expression in the celebration of the sacrament of penance, either before the funeral liturgy or at a later time.

Presiding Minister

14.   Priests, as teachers of faith and ministers of comfort, preside at the funeral rites, especially the Mass; the celebration of the funeral liturgy is especially entrusted to pastors and associate pastors. When no priest is available, deacons, as ministers of the word, of the altar, and of charity, preside at funeral rites. When no priest or deacon is available for the vigil and related rites or the rite of committal, a layperson presides.

Other Liturgical Ministers

15.   In the celebration of the funeral rites laymen and laywomen may serve as readers, musicians, ushers, pallbearers, and, according to existing norms, as special ministers of the eucharist. Pastors and other priests should instill in these ministers an appreciation of how much the reverent exercise of their ministries contributes to the celebration of the funeral rites. Family members should be encouraged to take an active part in these ministries, but they should not be asked to assume any role that their grief or sense of loss may make too burdensome.

MINISTRY FOR THE MOURNERS AND THE DECEASED

FAMILY AND FRIENDS

16.   In planning and carrying out the funeral rites the pastor and all other ministers should keep in mind the life of the deceased and the circumstances of death. They should also take into consideration the spiritual and psychological needs of the family and friends of the deceased to express grief and their sense of loss, to accept the reality of death, and to comfort one another.

17.   Whenever possible, ministers should involve the family in planning the funeral rites: in the choice of texts and rites provided in the ritual, in the selection of music for the rites, and in the designation of liturgical ministers.

Planning of the funeral rites may take place during the visit of the pastor or other minister at some appropriate time after the death and before the vigil service. Ministers should explain to the family the meaning and significance of each of the funeral rites, especially the vigil, the funeral liturgy, and the rite of committal.

If pastoral and personal considerations allow, the period before death may be an appropriate time to plan the funeral rites with the family and even with the family member who is dying. Although planning the funeral before death should be approached with sensitivity and care, it can have the effect of helping the one who is dying and the family face the reality of death with Christian hope. It can also help relieve the family of numerous details after the death and may allow them to benefit more fully from the celebration of the funeral rites.

18.   Through the celebration of the funeral rites, the Church manifests its care for the dead, both baptized members and catechumens. In keeping with the provisions of *Codex Iuris Canonici,* can. 1183, the Church's funeral rites may be celebrated for a child who died before baptism and whose parents intended to have the child baptized.

At the discretion of the local Ordinary, the Church's funeral rites may be celebrated for baptized member of another Church or ecclesial community provided this would not be contrary to the wishes of the deceased person and provided the minister of the Church or ecclesial community in which the deceased person was a regular member of communicant is unavailable.

19.   Since in baptism the body was marked with the seal of the Trinity and became the temple of the Holy Spirit, Christians respect and honor the bodies of the dead and the places where they rest. Any customs associated with the preparation of the body of the deceased should always be marked with dignity and reverence and never with the despair of those who have no hope. Preparation of the body should include prayer, especially at those intimate moments reserved for family members. For the final disposition of the body, it is the ancient Christian custom to bury or entomb the bodies of the dead; cremation is permitted, unless it is evident that cremation was chosen for anti-Christian motives.

20.   In countries of regions where an undertaker, and the family or community, carrics out the preparation and transfer of the body, the pastor and other ministers are to ensure that the undertakers appreciate the values and beliefs of the Christian community.

The family and friends of the deceased should not be excluded from taking part in the services sometimes provided by undertakers, for example, the preparation and laying out of the body.

LITURGICAL ELEMENTS

21.   Since liturgical celebration involves the whole person, it requires attentiveness to all that affects the senses. The readings and prayers, psalms and songs should be proclaimed or sung with understanding, conviction, and reverence. Music for the assembly should be truly expressive of the texts and at the same time simple and easily sung. The ritual gestures, processions, and postures should express and foster an attitude of reverence and reflectiveness in those taking part in the funeral rites. The funeral rites should be celebrated in an atmosphere of simple beauty, in a setting that encourages participation. Liturgical signs and symbols affirming Christian belief and hope in the paschal mystery are abundant in the celebration of the funeral rites, but their undue multiplication or repletion should be avoided. Care must be taken that the choice and use of signs and symbols are in accord with the culture of the people.

Readings

22.   In every celebration for the dead, the Church attaches great importance to the reading of the word of God. The readings proclaim to the assembly the paschal mystery, teach remembrance of the dead, convey the hope of being gathered together again in God's kingdom, and encourage the witness of Christian life. Above all, the readings tell of God's designs for a world in which suffering and death will relinquish their hold on all whom God has called his own. A careful selection and use of readings from Scripture for the funeral rites will provide the family and the community with an opportunity to hear God speak to them in their needs, sorrows, fears, and hopes.

23.   In the celebration of the liturgy of the word at the funeral liturgy, the biblical readings may not be replaced by nonbiblical readings. But during prayer services with the family nonbiblical readings may be used in addition to readings from Scripture.

24.   Liturgical tradition assigns the proclamation of the readings in the celebration of the liturgy of the word to readers and the deacon. The presiding minister proclaims the readings only when there are no assisting ministers present. Those designated to proclaim the word of God should prepare themselves to exercise this ministry.[4]

Psalmody

25.   The psalms are rich in imagery, feeling, and symbolism. They powerfully express the suffering and pain, the hope and trust of people of every age and culture. Above all the psalms sing of faith in God, of revelation and redemption. They enable the assembly to pray in the words that Jesus himself used during his life on earth. Jesus, who knew anguish and the fear of death, "offered up prayer and entreaty, aloud and in silent tears, to the one who had the power to save him out of death. . . . Although he was Son, he learned to obey through suffering; but having been made perfect, he became for all who obey him the source of eternal salvation . . ." (Hebrews 5:7–9). In the psalms the members of the assembly pray in the voice of Christ, who intercedes on their behalf before the Father.[5] The Church, like Christ, turns again and again to the psalms as a genuine expression of grief and of praise and as a sure source of trust and hope in ties of trial. Pastors and other ministers are, therefore, to make an earnest effort through an effective catechesis to lead their communities to a clearer and deeper grasp of at least some of the psalms provided for the funeral rites.

26.   The psalms are designated for use in many places in the funeral rites (for example, as responses to the readings, for the processions, for use at the vigil for the deceased). Since the psalms are songs, whenever possible, they should be sung.

27.   A brief homily based on the readings is always given after the gospel reading at the funeral liturgy and may also be given after the readings at the vigil service; but there is never to be a eulogy. Attentive to the grief of those present, the homilist should dwell on God's compassionate love and on the paschal mystery of the Lord, as proclaimed in the Scripture readings. The homilist should also help the members of the assembly to understand that the mystery of God's love and the mystery of Jesus' victorious death and resurrection were present in the life and death of the deceased and that these mysteries are active in their own lives as well. Through the homily members of the family and community should receive consolation and strength to face the death of one of their members with a hope nourished by the saving word of God. Laypersons who preside at the funeral rites give an instruction on the readings.

PRAYERS AND INTERCESSIONS

28.   In the presidential prayers of the funeral rites the presiding minister addresses God on behalf of the deceased and the mourners in the name of the entire Church. From the variety of prayers provided the minister in consultation with the family should carefully select texts that truly capture the unspoken prayers and hopes of the assembly and also respond to the needs of the mourners.

29.   Having heard the word of God proclaimed and preached, the assembly responds at the vigil and at the funeral liturgy with prayers of intercession for the deceased and all the dead, for the family and all who mourn, and for all in the assembly. The holy people of God, confident in their belief in the communion of saints, exercise their royal priesthood by joining together in this prayer for all those who have died.[6]

Several models of intercessions are provided within the rites for adaptation to the circumstances.

MUSIC

30.   Music is integral to the funeral rites. It allows the community to express convictions and feelings that words alone may fail to convey. It has the power to console and uplift the mourners and to strengthen the unity of the assembly in faith and love. The texts of the songs chosen for a particular celebration should express the paschal mystery of the Lord's suffering, death, and triumph over death and should be related to the readings from Scripture.

31.   Since music can evoke strong feelings, the music for the celebration of the funeral rites should be chosen with great care. The music at funerals should support, console, and uplift the participants and should help to create in them a spirit of hope in Christ's victory over death and in the Christian's share in that victory.

32.   Music should be provided for the vigil and funeral liturgy and, whenever possible, for the funeral processions and the rite of committal. The specific notes

that precede each of these rites suggest places in the rites where music is appropriate. Many musical settings used by the parish community during the liturgical year may be suitable for use at funerals. Efforts should be made to develop and expand the parish's repertoire for use at funerals.

33.   An organist or other instrumentalist, a cantor, and, whenever possible, even a choir should assist the assembly's full participation in singing the songs, responses, and acclamations of these rites.

SILENCE

34.   Prayerful silence is an element important to the celebration of the funeral rites. Intervals of silence should be observed, for example, after each reading and during the final commendation and farewell, to permit the assembly to reflect upon the word of God and the meaning of the celebration.

SYMBOLS

Easter Candle and Other Candles

35.   The Easter candle reminds the faithful of Christ's undying presence among them, of his victory over sin and death, and of their share in that victory by virtue of their initiation. It recalls the Easter Vigil, the night when the Church awaits the Lord's resurrection and when new light for the living and the dad is kindled. During the funeral liturgy and also during the vigil service, when celebrated in the church, the Easter candle may be placed beforehand near the position the coffin will occupy at the conclusion of the procession.

According to local custom, other candles may also be placed near the coffin during the funeral liturgy as a sign of reverence and solemnity.

Holy Water

36.   Blessed or holy water reminds the assembly of the saving waters of baptism. In the rite of reception of the body at the church, its use calls to mind the deceased's baptism and initiation into the community of faith. In the rite of final commendation the gesture of sprinkling may also signify farewell.

Incense

37.   Incense is used during the funeral rites as a sign of honor to the body of the deceased, which through baptism became the temple of the Holy Spirit. Incense is also used as a sign of the community's prayers for the deceased rising to the throne of God and as a sign of farewell.

Other Symbols

38.   If it is the custom in the local community, a pall may be placed over the coffin when it is received at the church. A reminder of the baptismal garment of the deceased the pall is a sign of the Christian dignity of the person. The use of the pall also signifies that all are equal in the eyes of God (see James 2:1–9).

A Book of the Gospels or a Bible may be placed on the coffin as a sign that Christians live by the word of God and that fidelity to that word leads to eternal life.

A cross may be placed on the coffin as a reminder that the Christian is marked by the cross in baptism and through Jesus' suffering on the cross is brought to the victory of his resurrection.

Fresh flowers, used in moderation, can enhance the setting of the funeral rites.

Only Christian symbols may rest on or be placed near the coffin during the funeral liturgy. Any other symbols, for example national flags, or flags or insignia of associations, have no place in the funeral liturgy (see no. 132).

Liturgical Color

39.   The liturgical color chosen for funerals should express Christian hope but should not be offensive to human grief or sorrow. In the United States, white, violet, or black vestments may be worn at the funeral rites and at other offices and Masses for the dead.

RITUAL GESTURES AND MOVEMENT

40.   The presiding minister or an assisting minister may quietly direct the assembly in the movements, gestures, and posture appropriate to the particular ritual moment or action.

41.   Processions, especially when accompanied with music and singing, can strengthen the bond of communion in the assembly. For processions, ministers of music should give preference to settings of psalms and songs that are responsorial or litanic in style and that allow the people to respond to the verses with an invariable refrain. During the various processions, it is preferable that the pallbearers carry the coffin as a sign of reverence and respect for the deceased.

42.   Processions continue to have special significance in funeral celebrations, as in Christian Rome where funeral rites consisted of three "stages" or "stations" joined by two processions. Christians accompanied the body on its last journey. From the home of the deceased the Christian community proceeded to the church singing psalms. When the service in the church concluded, the body was carried in solemn procession to the grave or tomb. During the final procession the congregation sang psalms praising the God of mercy and redemption and antiphons entrusting the deceased to the care of the angels and saints. The funeral liturgy mirrored the journey of human life, the Christian pilgrimage to the heavenly Jerusalem.

In many places and situations a solemn procession on foot to the church or to the place of committal may not be possible. Nevertheless at the conclusion of the funeral liturgy an antiphon or versicle and response may be sung as the body is taken to the entrance of the church. Psalms, hymns, or liturgical songs may also be sung when the participants gather at the place of committal.

43. The *Order of Christian Funerals* makes provision for the minister, in consultation with the family, to choose those rites and texts that are most suitable to the situation: those that most closely apply to the needs of the mourners, the circumstances of death, and the customs of the local Christian community. The minister and family may be assisted in the choice of a rite or rites by the reflections preceding each rite or group of rites.

44. Part I, "Funeral Rites," of the *Order of Christian Funerals* provides those rites that may be used in the funerals of Christians and is divided into three groups of rites that correspond in general to the three principal ritual moments in Christian funerals: "Vigil and Related Rites and Prayers," "Funeral Liturgy," and "Rite of Committal."

45. The section entitled "Vigil and Related Rites and Prayers" includes rites that may be celebrated between the time of death and the funeral liturgy or, should there be no funeral liturgy, before the rite of committal. The vigil is the principal celebration of the Christian community during the time before the funeral liturgy. It may take the form of a liturgy of the word (see nos. 54–97) or of some part of the office for the dead (see Part IV, nos. 348–395). Two vigil services are provided: "Vigil for the Deceased" and "Vigil for the Deceased with Reception at the Church." The second service is used when the vigil is celebrated in the church and the body is to be received at this time.

"Related Rites and Prayers" includes three brief rites that may be used on occasions of prayer with the family: "Prayers after Death," "Gathering in the Presence of the Body," and "Transfer of the Body to the Church or to the Place of Committal." These rites are examples or models of what can be done and should be adapted to the circumstances.

46. The section entitled "Funeral Liturgy" provides two forms of the funeral liturgy, the central celebration of the Christian community for the deceased: "Funeral Mass" and "Funeral Liturgy outside Mass." When one of its members dies, the Church especially encourages the celebration of the Mass. When Mass cannot be celebrated (see no. 178), the second form of the funeral liturgy may be used and a Mass for the deceased should be celebrated, if possible, at a later time.

47. The section entitled "Rite of Committal" includes two forms of the rite of committal, the concluding rite of the funeral: "Rite of Committal" and "Rite of Committal with Final Commendation." The first form is used when the final commendation is celebrated as part of the conclusion of the funeral liturgy. The second from is used when the final commendation does not take place during the funeral liturgy or when no funeral liturgy precedes the committal.

48. Part II, "Funeral Rites for Children," provides an adaptation of the principal rites in Part I: "Vigil for a Deceased Child," "Funeral Liturgy," and "Rite of Committal." These rites may be used in the funerals of infants and young children,

including those of early school age. The rites in Part II include texts for use in the case of a baptized child and in the case of a child who died before baptism.

In some instances, for example, the death of an infant, the vigil and funeral liturgy may not be appropriate. Only the rite of committal and perhaps one of the forms of prayer with the family as provided in "Related Rites and Prayers' may be desirable. Part II does not contain "Related Rites and Prayers," but the rites from Part I may be adapted.

49.   Part III, "Texts from Sacred Scripture," includes the Scripture readings and psalms for the celebration of the funeral rites. Part IV, "Office for the Dead," includes "Morning Prayer," "Evening Prayer," and "Additional Hymns." Part V, "Additional Texts," contains "Prayers and Texts in Particular Circumstances" and "Holy Communion outside Mass." The texts that appear in the various rites in Parts I, II, and IV may be replaced by corresponding readings and psalms given in Part III and by corresponding prayers and texts given in Part V.

PART I
FUNERAL RITES

50.   Part I of the Order of Christian Funerals is divided into three groups of rites that correspond in general to the three principal ritual moments in the funerals of Christians: "Vigil and Related Rites and Prayers," "Funeral Liturgy," and "Rite of Committal." The minister, in consultation with those concerned, chooses from within these three groups of rites those that best correspond to the particular needs and customs of the mourners. This choice may be assisted by the reflections given in the General Introduction and in the introduction to each rite or group of rites.

VIGIL AND RELATED RITES AND PRAYERS

51.   The rites provided here may be celebrated between the time of death and the funeral liturgy or, should there be no funeral liturgy, before the rite of committal. Two forms of the vigil are presented here: "Vigil for the Deceased," and "Vigil for the Deceased with Reception at the Church," for convenient use in accord with the circumstances.

"Related Rites and Prayers" includes three brief rites that may be used on occasions of prayer with the family: "Prayers after Death," "Gathering in the Presence of the Body," and "Transfer of the Body to the Church or to the Place of Committal." These rites are examples or models of what can be done and should be adapted to the circumstances.

52.   The time immediately following death is often one of bewilderment and may involve shock or heartrending grief for the family and close friends. The ministry of the Church at this time is one of gently accompanying the mourners in their initial adjustment to the fact of death and to the sorrow this entails. Through a careful use of the rites contained in this section, the minister helps

the mourners to express their sorrow and to find strength and consolation through faith in Christ and his resurrection to eternal life. The members of the Christian community offer support to the mourners, especially by praying that the one they have lost may have eternal life.

53.   Ministers should be aware that the experience of death can bring about in the mourners possible needs for reconciliation. With attentiveness to each situation, the minister can help to begin the process of reconciliation. In some cases this process may find expression in the celebration of the sacrament of penance, either before the funeral liturgy or at a later time.

1 VIGIL FOR THE DECEASED

Happy now are the dead who die in the Lord;
they shall find rest from their labors

54.   The vigil for the deceased is the principal rite celebrated by the Christian community in the time following death and before the funeral liturgy, or if there is no funeral liturgy, before the rite of committal. It may take the form either of a liturgy of the word (nos. 69–81, 82–97) or of some part of the office for the dead (see Part IV, p. 296). Two vigil services are provided: "Vigil for the Deceased" and "Vigil for the Deceased with Reception at the Church." The second service is used when the vigil is celebrated in the church and begins with the reception of the body.

55.   The vigil may be celebrated in the home of the deceased, in the funeral home, parlor or chapel of rest, or in some other suitable place. It may also be celebrated in the church, but at a time well before the funeral liturgy, so that the funeral liturgy will not be lengthy and the liturgy of the word repetitious. Adaptations of the vigil will often be suggested by the place in which the celebration occurs. A celebration in the home of the deceased, for example, may be simplified and shortened.

If the reception of the body at church is celebrated apart from the vigil or the funeral liturgy, the "Vigil for the Deceased with Reception at the Church" may be used and simplified.

56.   At the vigil the Christian community keeps watch with the family in prayer to the God of mercy and finds strength in Christ's presence. It is the first occasion among the funeral rites for the solemn reading of the word of God. In this time of loss the family and community turn to God's word as the source of faith and hope, as light and life in the face of darkness and death. Consoled by the redeeming word of God and by the abiding presence of Christ and his Spirit, the assembly at the vigil calls upon the Father of mercy to receive the deceased into the kingdom of light and peace.

57. The vigil in the form of the liturgy of the word consists of the introductory rites, the liturgy of the word, the prayer of intercession, and a concluding rite.

Introductory Rites

58. The introductory rites gather the faithful together to form a community and to prepare all to listen to God's word. The introductory rites of the vigil for the deceased include the greeting, an opening song, an invitation to prayer, a pause for silent prayer, and an opening prayer.

In the vigil for the deceased with reception at the church, the rite of reception forms the introductory rites (nos. 82–86). In this case the family and others who have accompanied the body are greeted at the entrance of the church. The body is then sprinkled with holy water and, if it is the custom, the pall is placed on the coffin by family members, friends, or the minister. The entrance procession follows, during which a hymn or psalm is sung. At the conclusion of the procession a symbol of the Christian life may be placed on the coffin. Then the invitation to prayer, a pause for silent prayer, and an opening prayer conclude the introductory rites.

The opening song or entrance song should be a profound expression of belief in eternal life and the resurrection of the dead, as well as a prayer of intercession for the dead.

Liturgy of the Word

59. The proclamation of the word of God is the high point and central focus of the vigil. The liturgy of the word usually includes a first reading, responsorial psalm, gospel reading, and homily. A reader proclaims the first reading. The responsorial psalm should be sung, whenever possible. If an assisting deacon is present, he proclaims the gospel reading. Otherwise the presiding minister proclaims the gospel reading.

60. The purpose of the readings at the vigil is to proclaim the paschal mystery, teach remembrance of the dead, convey the hope of being gathered together in God's kingdom, and encourage the witness of Christian life. Above all, the readings tell of God's designs for a world in which suffering and death will relinquish their hold on all whom God has called his own. The responsorial psalm enables the community to respond in faith to the reading and to express its grief and its praise of God. In the selection of readings the needs of the mourners and the circumstances of the death should be kept in mind.

61. A homily based on the readings is given at the vigil to help those present find strength and hope in God's saving word.

62.   In the prayer of intercession the community calls upon God to comfort the mourners and to show mercy to the deceased. The prayer of intercession takes the form of a litany, the Lord's Prayer, and a concluding prayer.

After this prayer and before the blessing or at some other suitable time during the vigil, a member of the family or a friend of the deceased may speak in remembrance of the deceased.

Concluding Rite

63.   The vigil concludes with a blessing, which may be followed by a liturgical song or a few moments of silent prayer or both.

MINISTRY AND PARTICIPATION

64.   Members of the local parish community should be encouraged to participate in the vigil as a sign of concern and support for the mourners. In many circumstances the vigil will be the first opportunity for friends, neighbors, and members of the local parish community to show their concern for the family of the deceased by gathering for prayer. The vigil may also serve as an opportunity for participation in the funeral by those who, because of work or other reasons, cannot be present for the funeral liturgy or the rite of committal.

65.   The full participation by all present is to be encouraged. This is best achieved through careful planning of the celebration. Whenever possible, the family of the deceased should take part in the selection of texts and music and in the designation of liturgical ministers.

66.   Besides the presiding minister, other available ministers (a reader, a cantor, an acolyte) should exercise their ministries. Family members may assume some of these liturgical roles, unless their grief prevents them from doing so.

The residing minister and assisting members should vest for the vigil according to local custom. If the vigil is celebrated in the church, a priest or deacon who presides wears an alb or surplice with stole.

67.   As needs require, and especially if the funeral liturgy or rite of committal is not to take place for a few days, the vigil may be celebrated more than once and should be adapted to each occasion.

68.   Music is integral to any vigil, especially the vigil for the deceased. In the difficult circumstances following death, well-chosen music can touch the mourners and others present at levels of human need that words alone often fail to reach. Such music can enliven the faith of the community gathered to support the family and to affirm hope in the resurrection.

Whenever possible, an instrumentalist and a cantor or leader of song should assist the assembly's full participation in the singing.

In the choice of music for the vigil, preference should be given to the singing of the opening song and the responsorial psalm. The litany, the Lord's Prayer, and a closing song may also be sung.

---

2 RELATED RITES AND PRAYERS

If we have died with Christ, we believe we shall also live with him

98. The section entitled "Related Rites and Prayers" contains three brief rites, "Prayers after Death," "Gathering in the Presence of the Body," and "Transfer of the Body to the Church or to the Place of Committal," when the family and friends prepare to accompany the body of the deceased in the procession to the church or to the place of committal.

99. These rites are signs of the concern of the Christian community for the family and close friends of the deceased. The compassionate presence of the minister and others and the familiar elements of these simple rites can have the effect of ressuring the mourners and of providing a consoling and hopeful situation in which to pray and to express their grief.

100. The circumstances for the celebration of these rites may vary from place to place and from culture to culture. The rites as given are only models, for adaptation by the minister according to the circumstances.

PRAYERS AFTER DEATH

Blessed are the sorrowing; they shall be consoled

101. This rite provides a model of prayer that may be used when the minister first meets with the family following death. The rite follows a common pattern of readings, response, prayer, and blessing and may be adapted according to the circumstances.

102. The presence of the minister and the calming effect of familiar prayers can comfort the mourners as they begin to face their loss. When the minister is present with the family at the time death occurs, this rite can be used as a quiet and prayerful response to the death. In other circumstances, for example, in the case of sudden or unexpected death, this form of prayer can be the principal part of the first pastoral visit of the minister.

103. The initial pastoral visit can be important as the first tangible expression of the community's support for the mourners. A minister unfamiliar with the family or the deceased person can learn a great deal on this occasion about the needs of the family and about the life of the deceased. The minister may also be able to form some preliminary judgments to help the family in planning the funeral rites. If circumstances allow, some first steps in the planning may take place at this time.

If we have died with Christ, we believe we shall also live with him

109. This rite provides a model of prayer that may be used when the family first gathers in the presence of the body, when the body is to be prepared for burial, or after it has been prepared. The family members, in assembling in the presence of the body, confront in the most immediate way the fact of their loss and the mystery of death. Because cultural attitudes and practices on such occasions may vary, the minister should adapt the rite.

110. Through the presence of the minister and others and through the celebration of this brief rite, the community seeks to be with the mourners in their need and to provide an atmosphere of sensitive concern and confident faith. In prayer and gesture those present show reverence for the body of the deceased as a temple of the life-giving Spirit and ask, in that same Spirit, for the eternal life promised to the faithful.

111. The minister should try to be as attentive as possible to the particular needs of the mourners. The minister begins the rite at an opportune moment and, as much as possible, in an atmosphere of calm and recollection. The pause for silent prayer after the Scripture verse can be especially helpful in this regard.

TRANSFER OF THE BODY TO THE CHURCH OR TO THE PLACE OF COMMITTAL

Your life is hidden now with Christ in God

119. This rite may be used for prayer with the family and close friends as they prepare to accompany the body of the deceased in the procession to the church or to the place of committal. It is a model, for adaptation by the minister according to the circumstances.

120. The procession to the church is a rite of initial separation of the mourners from the deceased; the procession to the place of committal is the journey to the place of final separation of the mourners from the deceased. Because the transfer of the body may be an occasion of great emotion for the mourners, the minister and other members of the community should make every effort to be present to support them. Reverent celebration of the rite can help reassure the mourners and create an atmosphere of calm preparation before the procession.

FUNERAL LITURGY

128. The funeral liturgy is the central liturgical celebration of the Christian community for the deceased. Two forms of the funeral liturgy are presented here: "Funeral Mass" and "Funeral Liturgy outside Mass."

When one of its members dies, the Church encourages the celebration of the Mass. But when Mass cannot be celebrated (see no. 178), the second form of the funeral liturgy is used. When a the funeral liturgy is celebrated outside Mass before the committal, a Mass for the deceased should be scheduled, if possible, for the family and friends at a convenient time after the funeral.

129. At the funeral liturgy the community gathers with the family and friends of the deceased to give praise and thanks to God for Christ's victory over sin and death, to commend the deceased to God's tender mercy and compassion, and to seek strength in the proclamation of the paschal mystery. Through the Holy Spirit the community is joined together in faith as one Body in Christ to reaffirm in sign and symbol, word and gesture that each believer through baptism shares in Christ's death and resurrection and can look to the day when all the elect will be raised up and united in the kingdom of light and peace.

STRUCTURE AND CONTENT OF THE FUNERAL LITURGY

130. The funeral Mass includes the reception of the body, if this has not already occurred, the celebration of the liturgy of the word, the liturgy of the eucharist, and the final commendation and farewell. The funeral liturgy outside Mass includes all these elements except the liturgy of the eucharist. Both the funeral Mass and the funeral liturgy outside Mass may be followed by the procession to the place of committal.

RECEPTION AT THE CHURCH

131. Since the church is the place where the community of faith assembles for worship, the rite of reception of the body at the church has great significance. The church is the place where the Christian life is begotten in baptism, nourished in the eucharist, and where the community gathers to commend one of its deceased members to the Father. The church is at once a symbol of the community and of the heavenly liturgy that the celebration of the liturgy anticipates. In the act of receiving the body, the members of the community acknowledge the deceased as one of their own, as one who was welcomed in baptism and who held a place in the assembly. Through the use of various baptismal symbols the community shows the reverence due the body, the temple of the Spirit, and in this way prepares for the funeral liturgy in which it asks for a share in the heavenly banquet promised to the deceased and to all who have been washed in the waters of rebirth and marked with the sign of faith.

132. Any national flags or the flags or insignia of associations to which the deceased belonged are to be removed from the coffin at the entrance of the church. They may be replaced after the coffin has been taken from the church.

133. The rite of reception takes place at the beginning of the funeral liturgy usually at the entrance of the church. It begins with a greeting of the family and others who have accompanied the coffin to the door of the church. The minister sprinkles the coffin with holy water in remembrance of the deceased person's initiation and first acceptance into the community of faith. If it is the custom in the local community, a funeral pall, a reminder of the garment given at baptism, and therefore signifying life in Christ, may then be placed on the

coffin by family members, friends, or the minister. The entrance procession follows. The minister precedes the coffin and the mourners into the church. If the Easter candle is used on this occasion, it may be placed beforehand near the position the coffin will occupy at the conclusion of the procession.

134. If in this rite a symbol of the Christian life is to be placed on the coffin, it is carried in the procession and is placed on the coffin by a family member, friend, or the minister at the conclusion of the procession.

135. To draw the community together in prayer at the beginning of the funeral liturgy, the procession should be accompanied, whenever possible, by the singing of the entrance song. This song ought to be a profound expression of belief in eternal life and the resurrection of the dead as well as a prayer of intercession for the deceased (see, for example, no. 403).

136. If the rite of reception has already taken place, the funeral Mass begins in the usual way and the funeral liturgy outside Mass begins with the entrance song, followed by the greeting and an invitation to prayer.

LITURGY OF THE WORD

137. The reading of the word of God is an essential element of the celebration of the funeral liturgy. The readings proclaim the paschal mystery, teach remembrance of the dead, convey the hope of being gathered together again in God's kingdom, and encourage the witness of Christian life. Above all, the readings tell of God's design for a world in which suffering and death will relinquish their hold on all whom God has called his own.

138. Depending on pastoral circumstances, there may be either one or two readings before the gospel reading. When there is a first and second reading before the gospel reading, it is preferable to have a different reader for each.

139. The responsorial psalm enables the community to respond in faith to the first reading. Through the psalms the community expresses its grief and praise, and acknowledges its Creator and Redeemer as the sure source of trust and hope in times of trial. Since the responsorial psalm is a song, whenever possible, it should be sung. Psalms may be sung responsorially, with the response sung by the assembly and all the verses by the cantor or choir, or directly, with no response and all the verses sung by all or by the cantor or choir. When not sung, the responsorial psalm after the reading should be recited in a manner conducive to meditation on the word of God.[7]

140. In the *alleluia*, or the gospel acclamation, the community welcomes the Lord who is about to speak to it. If the *alleluia* is not sung, it is omitted. The cantor or choir sings the *alleluia* or Lenten acclamation first and the people repeat it. The verse is then sung by the cantor or choir and the *alleluia* or Lenten acclamation is then sung once more by all.

141. A brief homily based on the readings should always be given at the funeral liturgy, but never any kind of eulogy. The homilist should dwell on God's compassionate love and on the paschal mystery of the Lord as proclaimed in the Scripture readings. Through the homily, the community should receive the consolation and strength to face the death of one of its members with a hope that has been nourished by the proclamation of the saving word of God.

142. In the intercessions the community responds to the proclamation of the word of God by prayer for the deceased and all the dead, for the bereaved and all who mourn, and for all the assembly. The intercessions provided may be used or adapted to the circumstances, or new intercessions may be composed.

LITURGY OF THE EUCHARIST

143. At the funeral Mass, the community, having been spiritually renewed at the table of God's word, turns for spiritual nourishment to the table of the eucharist. The community with the priest offers to the Father the sacrifice of the New Covenant and shares in the one bread and the one cup. In partaking of the body of Christ, all are given a foretaste of eternal life in Christ and are united with Christ, with each other, and with all the faithful, living and dead: "Because there is one bread, we who are many are one body, for we all partake of the one bread" (1 Corinthians 10:17).

144. The liturgy of the eucharist takes place in the usual manner at the funeral Mass. Members of the family or friends of the deceased should bring the gifts to the altar. Instrumental music or a song (for example, Psalm 118:1–6, Psalm 63, Psalm 66:13–20, or Psalm 138) may accompany the procession with the gifts. Before the priest washes his hands, he may incense the gifts and the altar. Afterward the deacon or other minister may incense the priest and the congregation.

Eucharistic Prayer II and Eucharistic Prayer III are especially appropriate for use at the funeral Mass, because they provide special texts of intercession for the dead. Since music gives greater solemnity to a ritual action, the singing of the people's parts of the eucharistic prayer should be encouraged, that is, the responses of the preface dialogue, the Sanctus, the memorial acclamation, and the Great Amen.

To reinforce and to express more fully the unity of the congregation during the communion rite, the people may sing the Lord's Prayer, the doxology, the Lamb of God, and a song for the communion procession (for example, Psalm 23, Psalm 27, Psalm 34, Psalm 63, or Psalm 121).

FINAL COMMENDATION AND FAREWELL

145. At the conclusion of the funeral liturgy, the rite of final commendation and farewell is celebrated, unless it is to be celebrated later at the place of committal.

146. The final commendation is a final farewell by the members of the community, an act of respect for one of their members, whom they entrust to the

tender and merciful embrace of God. This act of last farewell also acknowledges the reality of separation and affirms that the community and the deceased, baptized into the one Body, share the same destiny, resurrection on the last day. On that day the one Shepherd will call each by name and gather the faithful together in the new and eternal Jerusalem.

147. The rite begins with the minister's opening words and a few moments of silent prayer. The opening words serve as a brief explanation of the rite and as an invitation to pray in silence for the deceased. The pause for silence allows the bereaved and all present to relate their own feelings of loss and grief to the mystery of Christian hope in God's abundant mercy and his promise of eternal life.

Where this is customary, the body may then be sprinkled with holy water and incensed, or this may be done during or after the song of farewell. The sprinkling is a reminder that through baptism the person was marked for eternal life and the incensation signifies respect for the body as the temple of the Holy Spirit.

The song of farewell, which should affirm hope and trust in the paschal mystery, is the climax of the rite of final commendation. It should be sung to a melody simple enough for all to sing. It may take the form of a responsory or even a hymn. When singing is not possible, invocations may be recited by the assembly.

A prayer of commendation concludes the rite. In this prayer the community calls upon God's mercy, commends the deceased into God's hands, and affirms its belief that those who have died in Christ will share in Christ's victory over death.

PROCESSION TO THE PLACE OF COMMITTAL

148. At the conclusion of the funeral liturgy, the procession is formed and the body is accompanied to the place of committal. This final procession of the funeral rite mirrors the journey of human life as a pilgrimage to God's kingdom of peace and light, the new and eternal Jerusalem.

149. Especially when accompanied with music and singing, the procession can help to reinforce the bond of communion between the participants. Whenever possible, psalms or songs may accompany the entire procession from the church to the place of committal. In situations where a solemn procession on foot from the church to the place of committal is not possible, an antiphon or song may be sung as the body is being taken to the entrance of the church. Psalms, hymns, or liturgical songs may also be sung by the participants as they gather at the place of committal.

MINISTRY AND PARTICIPATION

150. Because the funeral liturgy is the central celebration for the deceased, it should be scheduled for a time that permits as many of the Christian community as possible to be present. The full and active participation of the assembly affirms the value of prayer for the dead, gives strength and support to the bereaved,

and is a sure sign of faith and hope in the paschal mystery. Every effort, therefore, should be made by the various liturgical ministers to encourage the active participation of the family and of the entire assembly.

151. The priest is the ordinary presiding minister of the funeral liturgy. Except for Mass, a deacon may conduct the funeral liturgy. If pastoral need requires, the conference of bishops, with the permission of the Apostolic See, may decide that laypersons also preside at the funeral liturgy outside Mass.

152. Whenever possible, ministers should involve the family in the planning of the funeral liturgy: in the choice of readings, prayers, and music for the liturgy and in the designation of ushers, pallbearers, readers, acolytes, special ministers of the eucharist, when needed, and musicians. The family should also be given the opportunity to designate persons who will place the pall or other Christian symbols on the coffin during the rite of reception of the body at the church and who will bring the gifts to the altar at Mass.

153. An organist or other instrumentalist, a cantor, and whenever possible, a choir should be present to assist the congregation in singing the songs, responses, and acclamations of the funeral liturgy.

3 FUNERAL MASS

Until the Lord comes, you are proclaiming his death

154. When one of its members dies, the Church encourages the celebration of the Mass. In the proclamation of the Scriptures, the saving word of God through the power of the Spirit becomes living and active in the minds and hearts of the community. Having been strengthened at the table of God's word, the community calls to mind God's saving deeds and offers the Father in the Spirit the eucharistic sacrifice of Christ's Passover from death to life, a living sacrifice of praise and thanksgiving, of reconciliation and atonement. Communion nourishes the community and expresses its unity. In communion, the participants have a foretaste of the heavenly banquet that awaits them and are reminded of Christ's own words: "Whoever eats my flesh and drinks my blood shall live for ever" (John 6:55). Confident in Jesus' presence among them in the living word, the living sacrifice, the living meal, those present in union with the whole Church offer prayers and petitions for the deceased, whom they entrust to God's merciful love.

155. The funeral Mass is ordinarily celebrated in the parish church.

156. The Mass texts are those of the Roman Missal and the Lectionary for Mass, "Masses for the Dead." The intercessions should be adapted to the circumstances. Models are given in place and in Part V, no. 401.

157. In the choice of music for the funeral Mass, preference should be given to the singing of the acclamations, the responsorial psalm, the entrance and communion songs, and especially the song of farewell at the final commendation.

---

4 FUNERAL LITURGY OUTSIDE MASS

I am the resurrection and the life; whoever believes in me shall never die

177. In the funeral liturgy outside Mass the community gathers to hear the message of Easter hope proclaimed in the liturgy of the word and to commend the deceased to God.

178. This rite may be used for various reasons:

1. when the funeral Mass is not permitted, namely, on solemnities of obligation, on Holy Thursday and the Easter Triduum, and on the Sundays of Advent, Lent, and the Easter Season;[8]

2. when in some places or circumstances it is not possible to celebrate the funeral Mass before the committal, for example, if a priest is not available;

3. when for pastoral reasons the pastor and the family judge that the funeral liturgy outside Mass is a more suitable form of celebration.

179. The funeral liturgy outside Mass is ordinarily celebrated in the parish church, but may also be celebrated in the home of the deceased, a funeral home, parlor, chapel of rest, or cemetery chapel.

180. The readings are those of the Lectionary for Mass, "Masses for the Dead." The intercessions should be adapted to the circumstances. Models are given in place and in Part V, no. 401. The celebration may also include holy communion.

181. In the choice of music for the funeral liturgy, preference should be given to the singing of the entrance song, the responsorial psalm, the gospel acclamation, and especially the song of farewell at the final commendation.

182. The minister who is a priest or deacon wears an alb with stole (a cope may be used, if desired); a layperson who presides wears the liturgical vestments approved for the region.

RITE OF COMMITTAL

204. The rite of committal, the conclusion of the funeral rites, is the final act of the community of faith in caring for the body of its deceased member. It may be celebrated at the grave, tomb, or crematorium and may be used for burial at sea. Whenever possible, the rite of committal is to be celebrated at the site of committal, that is, beside the open grave or place of interment, rather than at a cemetery chapel.

205. Two forms of the rite of committal are provided here: "Rite of Committal" and "Rite of Committal with Final Commendation." The first form is used when the final commendation is celebrated as part of the conclusion of the funeral liturgy. The second form is used when the final commendation does not take place during the funeral liturgy or when no funeral liturgy precedes the committal rite.

206. In committing the body to its resting place, the community expresses the hope that, with all those who have gone before marked with the sign of faith, the deceased awaits the glory of the resurrection. The rite of committal is an expression of the communion that exists between the Church on earth and the Church in heaven: the deceased passes with the farewell prayers of the community of believers into the welcoming company of those who need faith no longer but see God face to face.

STRUCTURE AND CONTENT OF THE RITE OF COMMITTAL

207. Both forms of the committal rite begin with an invitation, Scripture verse, and a prayer over the place of committal. The several alternatives for the prayer over the place of committal take into account whether the grave, tomb, or resting place has already been blessed and situations in which the final disposition of the body will actually take place at a later time (for example, when the body is to be cremated or will remain in a cemetery chapel until burial at a later time).

208. The rite of committal continues with the words of committal, the intercessions, and the Lord's Prayer.

The rite of committal with final commendation continues with an invitation to prayer, a pause for silent prayer, the sprinkling and incensing of the body, where is customary, the song of farewell, and the prayer of commendation (see nos. 227–231).

209. The act of committal takes place after the words of committal (in the rite of committal with final commendation, after the prayer of commendation) or the conclusion of the rite. The act of committal expresses the full significance of this rite. Through this act the community of faith proclaims that the grave or place of interment, once a sign of futility and despair, has been transformed by means of Christ's own death and resurrection into a sign of hope and promise.

210. Both forms of the rite conclude with a prayer over the people, which includes the verse *Eternal rest,* and a blessing. Depending on local custom, a song may then be sung and a gesture of final leave-taking may be made, for example, placing flowers or soil on the coffin.

ADAPTATION

211. If there is pastoral need for a longer committal rite than those provided here, for example, when the funeral liturgy has been celebrated on a previous day or in a different community, the minister may use the appropriate form of the committal rite and adapt it, for example, by adding a greeting, song, one or more

readings, a psalm, and a brief homily. When there has been no funeral liturgy prior to the committal rite, the "Rite of Committal with Final Commendation" may be used and similarly adapted.

212. The rite of committal may be celebrated in circumstances in which the final disposition of the body will not take place for some time, for example, when winter delays burial or when ashes are to be interred at some time after cremation. The rite of committal may then be repeated on the later occasion when the actual burial or interment takes place. On the second occasion the rite may include a longer Scripture reading as well as a homily.

In the case of a body donated to science, the rite of committal may be celebrated whenever interment takes place.

MINISTRY AND PARTICIPATION

213. The community continues to show its concern for the mourners by participating in the rite of committal. The rite marks the separation in this life of the mourners from the deceased, and through it the community assists them as they complete their care for the deceased and lay the body to rest. The act of committal is a stark and powerful expression of this separation. When carried out in the midst of the community of faith, the committal can help the mourners to face the end of one relationship with the deceased and to begin a new one based on prayerful remembrance, gratitude, and hope of resurrection and reunion.

By their presence and prayer members of the community signify their intention to continue to support the mourners in the time following the funeral.

214. The singing of well-chosen music at the rite of committal can help the mourners as they face the reality of the separation. At the rite of committal with final commendation, whenever possible, the song of farewell should be sung. In either form of the committal rite, a hymn or liturgical song that affirms hope in God's mercy and in the resurrection of the dead is desirable at the conclusion of the rite.

215. In the absence of a parish minister, a friend or member of the family should lead those present in the rite of committal.

The minister should vest according to local custom.

PART II
FUNERAL RITES FOR CHILDREN

234. Part II of the *Order of Christian Funerals* provides rites that are used in the funerals of infants and young children, including those of early school age. It includes "Vigil for a Deceased Child," "Funeral Liturgy," and "Rite of Committal."

Part II does not contain "Related Rites and Prayers," nos. 98–127, which are brief rites for prayer with the family and friends before the funeral liturgy. The rites as they are presented in Part I are models and should be adapted by the minister to the circumstances of the funeral for a child.

235. The minister, in consultation with those concerned, chooses those rites that best correspond to the particular needs and customs of the mourners. In some instances, for example, the death of an infant, only the rite of committal and perhaps one of the forms of prayer with the family may be desirable.

236. In the celebration of a the funeral of a child the Church offers worship to God, the author of life, commends the child to God's love, and prayers for the consolation of the family and close friends.

237. Funeral rites may be celebrated for children whose parents intended them to be baptized but who died before baptism.[9] In these celebrations the Christian community entrusts the child to God's all-embracing love and finds strength in this love and in Jesus' affirmation that the kingdom of God belongs to little children (see Matthew 19:14).

238. In its pastoral ministry to the bereaved the Christian community is challenged in a particular way by the death of an infant or child. The bewilderment and pain that death causes can be overwhelming in this situation, especially for the parents and the brothers and sisters of the deceased child. The community seeks to offer support and consolation to the family during and after the time of the funeral rites.

239. Through prayer and words of comfort the minister and others can help the mourners to understand that their child has gone before them into the kingdom of the Lord and that one day they will all be reunited there in joy. The participation of the community in the funeral rites is a sign of the compassionate presence of Christ, who embraced little children, wept at the death of a friend, and endured the pain and separation of death in order to render it powerless over those he loves. Christ still sorrows with those who sorrow and longs with them for the fulfillment of the Father's plan in a new creation where tears and death will have no place.

240. The minister should invite members of the community to use their individual gifts in this ministry of consolation. Those who have lost children of their own may be able in a special way to help the family as they struggle to accept the death of the child.

241. Those involved in planning the funeral rites for a deceased child should take into account the age of the child, the circumstances of death, the grief of the family, and the needs and customs of those taking part in the rites. In choosing the texts and elements of celebration, the minister should bear in mind whether the child was baptized or died before baptism.

242. Special consideration should be given to any sisters, brothers, friends, or classmates of the deceased child who may be present at the funeral rites. Children will be better able to take part in the celebration if the various elements are planned and selected with them in mind: texts, readings, music, gesture, processions, silence. The minister may wish to offer brief remarks for the children's benefit at suitable points during the celebration.

If children will be present at the funeral rites, those with requisite ability should be asked to exercise some of the liturgical roles. During the funeral Mass, for example, children may serve as readers, acolytes, or musicians, or assist in the reading of the general intercessions and in the procession with the gifts. Depending upon the age and number of children taking part, adaptations recommended in the *Directory for Masses with Children* may be appropriate.

7 VIGIL FOR A DECEASED CHILD

243. The vigil for the deceased is the principal celebration of the Christian community during the time before the funeral liturgy or, if there is no funeral liturgy, before the rite of committal. The vigil may take the form of a liturgy of the word, as described in Part I, nos. 57–68, or of some part of the office for the dead (see Part IV).

244. The vigil may be celebrated at a convenient time in the home of the deceased child, in the funeral home, parlor chapel of rest, or in some other suitable place. The vigil may also be celebrated in the church, but at a time well before the funeral liturgy, so that the funeral liturgy will not be lengthy and the liturgy of the word repetitious. When the body is brought to the church for the celebration of the vigil, the vigil begins with the rite of reception (see no. 58). Otherwise the vigil begins with a greeting, followed by an opening song, an invitation to prayer, and an opening prayer.

245. After the opening prayer, the vigil continues with the liturgy of the word, which usually includes a first reading, responsorial psalm, gospel reading, and homily. If there is to be only one reading, however, it should be the gospel reading. The prayer of intercession, which includes a litany, the Lord's Prayer, and a concluding prayer, then follows. Alternative concluding prayers are provided for use in the case of a baptized child or of a child who died before baptism. The vigil concludes with a blessing, which may be followed by a song or a few moments of silent prayer or both.

246. The minister should adapt the vigil to the circumstances. If, for example, a large number of children are present or if the vigil is held in the home of the deceased child, elements of the rite may be simplified or shortened and other elements or symbols that have special meaning for those taking part may be incorporated into the celebration. If custom and circumstances suggest, a member or a friend of the family may speak in remembrance of he deceased child.

FUNERAL LITURGY

264. The funeral liturgy, as described in nos. 128–153, is the central liturgical celebration of the Christian community for the deceased. Two forms of the funeral liturgy are provided: "Funeral Mass" and "Funeral Liturgy outside Mass." If the second form is used, Mass may be celebrated at a later date.

265. The funeral Mass includes the reception of the body, if this has not already occurred, the celebration of the liturgy of the word, the liturgy of the eucharist, and the final commendation and farewell. The funeral liturgy outside Mass includes all these elements except the liturgy of the eucharist. Both the funeral Mass and the funeral liturgy outside Mass may be followed by the procession to the place of committal.

266. The rite of reception of the body begins with a greeting of the family and others who have accompanied the body to the door of the church. The minister may give brief explanations of the symbols in this rite for the benefit of any children who may be present for the celebration. In the case of a baptized child, the minister sprinkles the coffin in remembrance of the deceased child's acceptance into the community of faith. If it is the custom in the local community, a funeral pall, a reminder of the garment given at baptism, and therefore signifying life in Christ, may then be placed on the coffin by family members, friends, or the minister. In the case of a child who died before baptism, the minister addresses the community with a few words. The entrance procession follows. The minister precedes the coffin and the mourners into the church, as all sing an entrance song. If the Easter candle is used on this occasion, it may be placed beforehand near the position the coffin will occupy at the conclusion of the procession.

If in this rite a symbol of the Christian life is to be placed on the coffin, it is carried in the procession and placed on the coffin by a family member, friend, or the minister at the conclusion of the procession.

267. The rite of final commendation and farewell is celebrated at the conclusion of the funeral liturgy unless it is deferred for celebration at the place of committal. The rite begins with the invitation to prayer, followed by a pause for silent prayer. In the case of a baptized child, the body may then be sprinkled with holy water and incensed. Or this may be done during or after the song of farewell. The song of farewell is then sung and the rite concludes with the prayer of commendation.

FUNERAL MASS

268. The funeral Mass is ordinarily celebrated in the parish church.

269. The Mass texts are those of the Roman Missal and the Lectionary for Mass, "Masses for the Dead." The intercessions should be adapted to the circumstances; models are given in place and in Part V, no. 401.

271. The funeral liturgy outside Mass may be celebrated for various reasons:

1. when the funeral Mass is not permitted, namely, on solemnities of obligation, on Holy Thursday and the Easter Triduum, and on the Sundays of Advent, Lent, and the Easter Season;[10]

2. when in some places or circumstances it is not possible to celebrate the funeral Mass before the committal, for example, if a priest is not available;

3. when for pastoral reasons the pastor and the family judge that the funeral liturgy outside Mass is a more suitable form of celebration for the deceased child.

272. The funeral liturgy outside Mass is ordinarily celebrated in the parish church, but may also be celebrated in the home of the deceased, a funeral home, parlor, chapel of rest, or cemetery chapel.

273. The readings are those of the Lectionary for Mass, "Masses for the Dead." The intercessions should be adapted to the circumstances; models are given in place and in Part V, no. 401. The celebration may include holy communion.

274. In the choice of music for the funeral liturgy, preference should be given to the singing of the entrance song, the responsorial psalm, the gospel acclamation, and especially the song of farewell at the final commendation.

275. The minister who is a priest or deacon wears an alb with stole (a cope may be used, if desired); a layperson who presides wears the liturgical vestments approved for the region.

RITE OF COMMITTAL

316. The rite of committal, the conclusion of the funeral rites (see nos. 204–215), is celebrated at the grave, tomb, or crematorium and may be used for burial at sea.

Three forms of the rite of committal are provided for the funeral of a child: "Rite of Committal," "Rite of Committal with Final Commendation," and "Rite of Final Commendation for an Infant."

317. The rite of committal is used when the final commendation and farewell is celebrated within the funeral liturgy. The rite of committal with final commendation is used when the final commendation is not celebrated within the funeral liturgy.

When the funeral liturgy is celebrated on a day prior to the committal or in a different community, the minister may wish to adapt the rite of committal, for example, by adding a song, a greeting, one or more readings, a psalm, and a brief homily. When no funeral liturgy precedes the rite of committal, the rite of committal with the final commendation is used and should be similarly adapted.

318. The "Rite of Final Commendation for an Infant" may be used in the case of a stillborn or a newborn infant who dies shortly after birth. This short rite of prayer with the parents is celebrated to give them comfort and to commend and entrust the infant to God. This rite is a model and the minister should adapt it to the circumstances. It may be used in the hospital or place of birth or at the time of the committal of the body.

PART III
TEXTS OF SACRED SCRIPTURE

343. Part III, "Texts of Sacred Scripture," contains the Scriptural readings and psalms for the celebration of the funeral. It is divided into four sections: "Funerals for Adults," "Funerals for Baptized Children," "Funerals for Children Who Died before Baptism," "Antiphons and Psalms."

344. As a general rule, all corresponding texts from sacred Scripture in the funeral rites are interchangeable. In consultation with the family and close friends, the minister chooses the texts that most closely reflect the particular circumstances and the needs of the mourners.

PART IV
OFFICE FOR THE DEAD

348. The vigil for the deceased may be celebrated in the form of some part of the office for the dead. To encourage this form of the vigil, the chief hours, "Morning Prayer" and "Evening Prayer," are provided here. When the funeral liturgy is celebrated the evening before the committal, it may be appropriate to celebrate morning prayer before the procession to the place of committal.

349. In the celebration of the office for the dead members of the Christian community gather to offer praise and thanks to God especially for the gifts of redemption and resurrection, to intercede for the dead, and to find strength in Christ's victory over death. When the community celebrates the hours, Christ the Mediator and High Priest is truly present through his Spirit in the gathered assembly, in the proclamation of God's word, and in the prayer and song of the Church.[11] The community's celebration of the hours acknowledges that spiritual bond that links the Church on earth with the Church in heaven, for it is in union with the whole Church that this prayer is offered on behalf of the deceased.

350. At morning prayer the Christian community recalls "the resurrection of the Lord Jesus, the true light enlightening all people (see John 1:9) and 'the sun of justice' (Malachi 4:2) 'rising from on high' (Luke 1:78)."[12] The celebration of morning prayer from the office for the dead relates the death of the Christian to Christ's victory over death and affirms the hope that those who have received the light of Christ at baptism will share in that victory.

351. At evening prayer the Christian community gathers to give thanks for the gifts it has received, to recall the sacrifice of Jesus Christ and the saving works of redemption, and to call upon Christ, the evening star and unconquerable light.[13] Through evening prayer from the office for the dead the community gives thanks to God for the gift of life received by the deceased and praises the Father for the redemption brought about by the sacrifice of his Son, who is the joy-giving light and the true source of hope.

STRUCTURE AND CONTENT OF MORNING PRAYER AND EVENING PRAYER

352. Morning prayer and evening prayer from the office for the dead include the introduction (or the reception of the body), hymn, psalmody, reading, response to the word of God, gospel canticle, intercessions, concluding prayer, and dismissal.

INTRODUCTORY VERSE OR RECEPTION OF THE BODY

353. Morning prayer and evening prayer begin with the introductory verse, *God, come to my assistance*, except when the invitatory replaces it, or when the rite of reception of the body is celebrated, since this replaces both the introductory verse and the hymn.

HYMN

354. To set the tone for the hour, a hymn is sung.

PSALMODY

355. In praying the psalms of the office for the dead, the assembly offers God praise and intercedes for the deceased person and the mourners in the words of prayer that Jesus himself used during his life on earth. Through the psalms the assembly prays in the voice of Christ, who intercedes on its behalf before the Father. In the psalms of petition and lament it expresses its sorrow and its firm hope in the redemption won by Christ. In the psalms of praise the assembly has a foretaste of the destiny of its deceased member and its own destiny, participation in the liturgy of heaven, where every tear will be wiped away and the Lord's victory over death will be complete.

356. Since the psalms are songs, whenever possible, they should be sung. The manner of singing them may be:

1. antiphonal, that is, two groups alternate singing the stanzas; the last stanza, the doxology, is sung by both groups;

2. responsorial, that is, the antiphon is sung by all before and after each stanza and the stanzas are sung by a cantor;

3. direct, that is, the stanzas are sung without interruption by all, by a choir, or by a cantor.

The rubrics for each psalm in morning prayer and evening prayer indicate a way for singing it; other ways may be used.

357. The psalmody of morning prayer from the office for the dead consists of Psalm 51, a psalm of lament and petition, Psalm 146 or Psalm 150, a psalm of praise, and an Old Testament canticle from Isaiah.

358. The psalmody of evening prayer consists of Psalm 121 and Psalm 130, two psalms of lament and petition, and New Testament canticle from the letter of Paul to the Philippians.

359. For pastoral reasons, psalms other than those given in the office for the dead may be chosen, provided they are appropriate for the time of day and suitable for use in the office for the dead (see, for example, antiphons and psalms in Part III).[14]

READING

360. The reading of the word of God in the office for the dead proclaims the paschal mystery and conveys the hope of being gathered together again in God's kingdom. The short reading in place in the hour or a longer Scripture reading from Part III may be used.[15] For pastoral reasons and if circumstances allow, a nonbiblical reading may be included at morning or evening prayer in addition to the reading from Scripture, as is the practice in the office of the readings.

RESPONSE TO THE WORD OF GOD

361. A period of silence may follow the reading, then a brief homily based on the reading. After the homily the short responsory or another responsorial song may be sung or recited.

GOSPEL CANTICLE

362. After the response to the word of God, the Canticle of Zechariah is sung at morning prayer and the Canticle of Mary at evening prayer as an expression of praise and thanksgiving for redemption.[16]

363. During the singing of the gospel canticle, the altar, then the presiding minister and the congregation may be incensed.

INTERCESSIONS

364. In the intercessions of the office for the dead, the assembly prays that the deceased and all who die marked with the sign of faith may rise again together in glory with Christ. The intercessions provided in the hour may be used or adapted to the circumstances or new intercessions may be composed.

The presiding minister introduces the intercessions. An assisting minister sings or says the intentions. In keeping with the form of the intentions in the liturgy of the hours, the assembly responds with either the second part of the intention or the response. After a brief introduction by the presiding minister the assembly sings or says the Lord's Prayer.

365. The concluding prayer, proclaimed by the presiding minister, completes the hour.

366. After the concluding prayer and before the dismissal a member of the family or a friend of the deceased may be invited to speak in remembrance of the deceased.

367. When the funeral liturgy is celebrated the evening before the committal, it may be appropriate to celebrate morning prayer before the procession to the place of committal. In such an instance the dismissal is omitted and the rite continues with the procession to the place of committal.

MINISTRY AND PARTICIPATION

368. The celebration of the office for the dead requires careful preparation, especially in the case of communities that may not be familiar with the liturgy of the hours. Pastors and other ministers should provide catechesis on the place and significance of the liturgy of the hours in the life of the Church and the purpose of the celebration of the office for the dead. They should also encourage members of the parish community to participate in the celebration as an effective means of prayer for the deceased, as a sign of their concern and support for the family and close friends, and as a sign of faith and hope in the paschal mystery. This catechesis will help to ensure the full and active participation of the assembly in the celebration of the office for the dead.

369. The office for the dead may be celebrated in the funeral home, parlor, chapel of rest, or in the church. In special circumstances, when the office is combined with the funeral liturgy, care should be taken that the celebration not be too lengthy.[17]

371. A priest or deacon should normally preside whenever the office for the dead is celebrated with a congregation; other ministers (a reader, a cantor, an acolyte) should exercise their proper ministries. In the absence of a priest or deacon, a layperson presides.

Whenever possible, ministers should involve the family of the deceased in the planning of the hour and in the designation of ministers.

The minister vests according to local custom. If morning prayer or evening prayer is celebrated in the church, a priest or a deacon who presides wears an alb or surplice with the stole (a cope may also be worn).

372. The sung celebration of the liturgy of the hours "is more in keeping with the nature of this prayer, and a mark of both higher solemnity and closer union

of hearts in offering praise to God."[18] Whenever possible, therefore, singing at morning or evening prayer should be encouraged.

In the choice of music preference should be given to the singing of the hymn, the psalmody, and gospel canticle. The introductory verse, the responsory, the intercessions, the Lord's Prayer, and dismissal may also be sung.

An organist or other instrumentalist and a cantor should assist the assembly in singing the hymn, psalms, and responses. The parish community should also prepare booklets or participation aids that contain an outline of the hour, the texts and music belonging to the people, and directions for posture, gesture, and movement.

NOTES

1. Vatican Council II, Constitution on the Liturgy *Sacrosanctum Concilium*, art. 5.

2. Ibid.

3. See Roman Ritual, *Pastoral Care of the Sick: Rites of Anointing and Viaticum*, General Introduction, no. 33.

4. See *Lectionary for Mass* (2nd *editio typica*, 1981), General Introduction, nos. 49, 52, and 55.

5. See General Instruction of the Liturgy of the Hours, no. 109.

6. See *De Oratione communi seu fidelium* (2nd ed., Vatican Polyglot Press, 1966), chapter 1, no. 3, p. 7: tr., *Documents on the Liturgy* (The Liturgical Press, 1982), no. 1893.

7. See *Lectionary for Mass* (2nd *editio typica*, 1981), General Introduction, no. 22.

8. See General Instruction of the Roman Missal, no. 336.

9. In the general catechesis of the faithful, pastors and other ministers should explain that the celebration of the funeral rites for children who die before baptism is not intended to weaken the Church's teaching on the necessity of baptism.

10. See General Instruction of the Roman Missal, no. 336.

11. See General Instruction of the Liturgy of the Hours, no. 13.

12. See General Instruction of the Liturgy of the Hours, no. 38.

13. See General Instruction of the Liturgy of the Hours, no. 39.

14. See General Instruction of the Liturgy of the Hours, no. 252.

15. See General Instruction of the Liturgy of the Hours, no. 46.

16. See General Instruction of the Liturgy of the Hours, no. 50.

17. See General Instruction of the Liturgy of the Hours, nos. 93–97.

18. Congregation of Rites, Introduction *Musicam Sacram*, 5 March 1967, no. 37: AAS 59 (1967), 310; DOL 508, no. 4158.

DIRECTORY

FOR

MASSES

WITH

CHILDREN

CONGREGATION FOR DIVINE WORSHIP
1 NOVEMBER 1973

OUTLINE

DIRECTORY FOR MASSES WITH CHILDREN

INTRODUCTION

1.   The Church must show special concern for baptized children who have yet to be fully initiated through the sacraments of confirmation and eucharist as well as for children who have only recently been admitted to holy communion. Today the circumstances in which children grow up are not favorable to their spiritual progress.[1] In addition parents sometimes scarcely fulfill the obligations they accepted at the baptism of their children to bring them up as Christians.

2.   In the upbringing of children in the Church a special difficulty arises from the fact that liturgical celebrations, especially the eucharist, cannot fully exercise their inherent pedagogical force upon children.[2] Although the vernacular may now be used at Mass, still the words and signs have not been sufficiently adapted to the capacity of children.

In fact, even in daily life children do not always understand all their experiences with adults but rather may find them boring. It cannot therefore be expected of the liturgy that everything must always be intelligible to them. Nonetheless, we may fear spiritual harm if over the years children repeatedly experience in the Church things that are barely comprehensible: recent psychological study has established how profoundly children are formed by the religious experience of infancy and early childhood, because of the special religious receptivity proper to those years.[3]

3.   The Church follows its Master, who "put his arms around the children . . . and blessed them" (Mk 10:16). It cannot leave children in the condition described. Vatican Council II had spoken in the Constitution on the Liturgy about the need of liturgical adaptation for various groups.[4] Soon afterwards, especially in the first Synod of Bishops held in Rome in 1967, the Church began to consider how participation by children could be easier. On the occasion of the Synod, the President of the Consilium for the Implementation of the Constitution on the Liturgy said explicitly that it could not be a matter of "creating some entirely special rite but rather of retaining, shortening, or omitting some elements or of making a better selection of texts."[5]

4.   All the details of eucharistic celebration with a congregation were determined in the General Instruction of the revised Roman Missal published in 1969. Then this Congregation began to prepare a special Directory for Masses with Children, as a supplement to the General Instruction. This was done in response

to repeated petitions from the entire Catholic world and with the cooperation of men and women specialists from almost every nation.

5.   Like the *General Instruction of the Roman Missal,* this Directory reserves some adaptations to the conference of bishops or to individual bishops.[6]

Some adaptations of the Mass may be necessary for children in a given country but cannot be included in a general directory. In accord with the *Constitution on the Liturgy* art. 40, the conferences of bishops are to propose such adaptations to the Apostolic See for introduction into the liturgy with its consent.

6.   The Directory is concerned with children who have not yet entered the period of preadolescence. It does not speak directly of children who are physically or mentally handicapped, because a broader adaptation is sometimes necessary for them.[7] Nevertheless, the following norms may also be applied to the handicapped, with the necessary changes.

7.   The first chapter of the Directory (nos. 8–15) gives a kind of foundation by considering the different ways in which children are introduced to the eucharistic liturgy. The second chapter briefly treats Masses with adults in which children also take part (nos. 16–19). Finally, the third chapter (nos. 20–54) treats at greater length Masses with children in which only some adults take part.

CHAPTER I
THE INTRODUCTION OF CHILDREN
TO THE EUCHARISTIC CELEBRATION

8.   A fully Christian life is inconceivable without participation in the liturgical services in which the faithful, gathered into a single assembly, celebrate the paschal mystery. Therefore, the religious initiation of children must be in harmony with this purpose.[8] The Church baptizes children and therefore, relying on the gifts conferred by this sacrament, it must be concerned that once baptized they grow in communion with Christ and each other. The sign and pledge of that communion is participation in the eucharistic table, for which children are being prepared or led to a deeper realization of its meaning. This liturgical and eucharistic formation may not be separated from their general education, both human and Christian; indeed it would be harmful if their liturgical formation lacked such a basis.

9.   For this reason all who have a part in the formation of children should consult and work together toward one objective: that even if children already have some feeling for God and the things of God, they may also experience in proportion to their age and personal development the human values that are present in the eucharistic celebration. These values include the community activity, exchange of greetings, capacity to listen and to seek and grant pardon, expression of gratitude, experience of symbolic actions, a meal of friendship, and festive celebration.[9]

Eucharistic catechesis, dealt with in no. 12, should develop such human values. Then, depending on their age and their psychological and social situation, children will gradually open their minds to the perception of Christian values and the celebration of the mystery of Christ.[10]

10.   The Christian family has the greatest role in instilling these Christian and human values.[11] Thus Christian education, provided by parents and other educators, should be strongly encouraged in relation to the liturgical formation of children as well.

By reason of the duty in conscience freely accepted at the baptism of their children, parents are bound to teach them gradually how to pray. This they do by praying with them each day and by introducing them to prayers said privately.[12] If children, prepared in this way even from their early years, take part in the Mass with their family when they wish, they will easily begin to sing and to pray in the liturgical community and indeed will already have some initial idea of the eucharistic mystery.

If the parents are weak in faith but still wish their children to receive Christian formation, they should be urged at least to communicate to their children the human values mentioned already and, when the occasion arises, to participate in meetings of parents and in noneucharistic celebrations held with children.

11.   The Christian communities to which the individual families belong or in which the children live also have a responsibility toward children baptized in the Church. By giving witness to the Gospel, living communal charity, and actively celebrating the mysteries of Christ, the Christian community is an excellent school of Christian and liturgical formation for the children who live in it.

Within the Christian community, godparents or other persons noted for their dedicated service can, out of apostolic zeal, contribute greatly to the necessary catechesis in the case of families that fail in their obligation toward the children's Christian upbringing.

Preschool programs, Catholic schools, and various kinds of associations for children serve these same ends in a special way.

12.   Even in the case of children, the liturgy itself always exerts its own inherent power to instruct.[13] Yet within religious-education programs in the schools and parishes the necessary importance should be given to catechesis on the Mass.[14] This catechesis should be directed to the child's active, conscious, and authentic participation.[15] "Suited to children's age and capabilities, it should, by means of the main rites and prayers of the Mass, aim at conveying its meaning, including what relates to taking part in the Church's life."[16] This is especially true of the text of the eucharistic prayer and of the acclamations by which the children take part in this prayer.

The catechesis preparing children for first communion calls for special mention. In it they should learn not only the truths of faith regarding the eucharist but also how from first communion on—after being prepared according to their capacity by penance—they can as full members of Christ's Body take part actively with the people of God in the eucharist, sharing in the Lord's table and the community of their brothers and sisters.

13. Various kinds of celebrations may also play a major role in the liturgical formation of children and in their preparation for the Church's liturgical life. By the very fact of such celebrations children easily come to appreciate some liturgical elements, for example, greetings, silence, and common praise (especially when this is sung together). But care must by taken that the instructive element does not become dominant in these celebrations.

14. Depending on the capacity of the children, the word of God should have a greater and greater place in these celebrations. In fact, as the children's spiritual capacity develops, celebrations of the word of God in the strict sense should be held frequently, especially during Advent and Lent.[17] These will help greatly to develop in the children an appreciation of the word of God.

15. While all that has been said remains true, the final purpose of all liturgical and eucharistic formation must be a greater and greater conformity to the Gospel in the daily life of the children.

CHAPTER II
MASSES WITH ADULTS IN WHICH CHILDREN ALSO PARTICIPATE

16. In many places parish Masses are celebrated, especially on Sundays and holy days, at which a good many children take part along with the large number of adults. On such occasions the witness of adult believers can have a great effect upon the children. Adults can in turn benefit spiritually from experiencing the part that the children have within the Christian community. The Christian spirit of the family is greatly fostered when children take part in these Masses together with their parents and other family members.

Infants who as yet are unable or unwilling to take part in the Mass may be brought in at the end of Mass to be blessed together with the rest of the community. This may be done, for example, if parish helpers have been taking care of them in a separate area.

17. Nevertheless, in Masses of this kind it is necessary to take great care that the children present do not feel neglected because of their inability to participate or to understand what happens and what is proclaimed in the celebration. Some account should be taken of their presence: for example, by speaking to them directly in the introductory comments (as at the beginning and the end of Mass) and at some point in the homily.

Sometimes, moreover, if the place itself and the nature of the community permit, it will be appropriate to celebrate the liturgy of the word, including a homily, with the children in a separate, but not too distant, room. Then, before the eucharistic liturgy begins, the children are led to the place where the adults have meanwhile celebrated their own liturgy of the word.

18.   It may also be very helpful to give some tasks to the children. They may, for example, bring forward the gifts or perform one or other of the songs of the Mass.

19.   If the number of children is large, it may at times be suitable to plan the Mass so that it corresponds more closely to the needs of the children. In this case the homily should be directed to them but in such a way that adults may also benefit from it. Wherever the bishop permits, in addition to the adaptations already provided in the Order of Mass, one or other of the particular adaptations described later in the Directory may be employed in a Mass celebrated with adults in which children also participate.

CHAPTER III
MASSES WITH CHILDREN IN WHICH
ONLY A FEW ADULTS PARTICIPATE

20.   In addition to the Masses in which children take part with their parents and other family members (which are not always possible everywhere), Masses with children in which only a few adults take part are recommended, especially during the week. From the beginning of the liturgical reform it has been clear to everyone that some adaptations are necessary in these Masses.[18]

Such adaptations, but only those of a more general kind, will be considered later (nos. 38–54).

21.   It is always necessary to keep in mind that these eucharistic celebrations must lead children toward the celebration of Mass with adults, especially the Masses at which the Christian community must come together on Sundays.[19] Thus, apart from adaptations that are necessary because of the children's age, the result should not be entirely special rites, markedly different from the Order of Mass celebrated with a congregation.[20] The purpose of the various elements should always correspond with what is said in the *General Instruction of the Roman Missal* on individual points, even if at times for pastoral reasons an absolute *identity* cannot be insisted upon.

OFFICES AND MINISTRIES IN THE CELEBRATION

22.   The principles of active and conscious participation are in a sense even more significant for Masses celebrated with children. Every effort should therefore be made to increase this participation and to make it more intense. For this reason as many children as possible should have special parts in the celebration: for example, preparing the place and the altar (see no. 29), acting as cantor (see no. 24), singing in a choir, playing musical instruments (see no. 32), proclaiming the readings (see nos. 24 and 47), responding during the homily (see no. 48), reciting the intentions of the general intercessions, bringing the gifts to the altar, and performing similar activities in accord with the usage of various peoples (see no. 34).

To encourage participation, it will sometimes be helpful to have several additions, for example, the insertion of motives for giving thanks before the priest begins the dialogue of the preface.

In all this, it should be kept in mind that external activities will be fruitless and even harmful if they do not serve the internal participation of the children. Thus religious silence has its importance even in Masses with children (see no. 37). The children should not be allowed to forget that all the forms of participation reach their high point in eucharistic communion, when the body and blood of Christ are received as spiritual nourishment.[21]

23. It is the responsibility of the priest who celebrates with children to make the celebration festive, familial, and meditative.[22] Even more than in Masses with adults, the priest is the one to create this kind of attitude, which depends on his personal preparation and his manner of acting and speaking with others.

The priest should be concerned above all about the dignity, clarity, and simplicity of his actions and gestures. In speaking to the children he should express himself so that he will be easily understood, while avoiding any childish style of speech.

The free use of introductory comments[23] will lead children to a genuine liturgical participation, but these should be more than mere explanatory remarks.

It will help him to reach the hearts of the children if the priest sometimes expresses the invitations in his own words, for example, at the penitential rite, the prayer over the gifts, the Lord's Prayer, the sign of peace, and communion.

24. Since the eucharist is always the action of the entire ecclesial community, the participation of at least some adults is desirable. These should be present not as monitors but as participants, praying with the children and helping them to the extent necessary.

With the consent of the pastor or rector of the church, one of the adults may speak to the children after the gospel, especially if the priest finds it difficult to adapt himself to the mentality of children. In this matter the norms soon to be issued by the Congregation for the Clergy should be observed.

Even in Masses with children attention is to be paid to the diversity of ministries so that the Mass may stand out clearly as the celebration of a community.[24] For example, readers and cantors, whether children or adults, should be employed. In this way a variety of voices will keep the children from becoming bored.

PLACE AND TIME OF CELEBRATION

25. The primary place for the eucharistic celebration for children is the church. Within the church, however, a space should be carefully chosen, if available, that will be suited to the number of participants. It should be a place where the children can act with a feeling of ease according to the requirements of a living liturgy that is suited to their age.

If the church does not satisfy these demands, it will sometimes be suitable to celebrate the eucharist with children outside a place of worship. But in that case the place chosen should be appropriate and worthy of the celebration.[25]

26. The time of day chosen for Masses with children should correspond to the circumstances of their lives so that they may be most open to hearing the word of God and to celebrating the eucharist.

27. Weekday Mass in which children participate can certainly be celebrated with greater effect and less danger of boredom if it does not take place every day (for example, in boarding schools). Moreover, preparation can be more careful if there is a longer interval between diverse celebrations.

Sometimes it will be preferable to have common prayer, to which the children may contribute spontaneously, or else a common meditation, or a celebration of the word of God. These are ways of continuing the eucharistic celebrations already held and of leading to a deeper participation in subsequent celebrations.

28. When the number of children who celebrate the eucharist together is very great, attentive and conscious participation becomes more difficult. Therefore, if possible, several groups should be formed; these should not be set up rigidly according to age but with regard for the children's progress in religious formation and catechetical preparation.

During the week such groups may be invited to the sacrifice of the Mass on different days.

PREPARATION FOR THE CELEBRATION

29. Each eucharistic celebration with children should be carefully prepared beforehand, especially with regard to the prayers, songs, readings, and intentions of the general intercessions. This should be done in discussion with the adults and with the children who will have a special ministry in these Masses. If possible, some of the children should take part in preparing and ornamenting the place of celebration and preparing the chalice with the paten and the cruets. Presupposing the appropriate internal participation, such activity will help to develop the spirit of community celebration.

SINGING AND MUSIC

30. Singing must be given great importance in all celebrations, but it is to be especially encouraged in every way for Masses celebrated with children, in view of their special affinity for music.[26] The culture of various peoples and the capabilities of the children present should be taken into account.

If possible, the acclamations should be sung by the children rather than recited, especially the acclamations that form part of the eucharistic prayer.

31. To facilitate the children's participation in singing the *Gloria*, *Credo*, *Sanctus*, and *Agnus Dei*, it is permissible to use with the melodies appropriate

vernacular texts, accepted by competent authority, even if these do not correspond exactly to the liturgical texts.[27]

32.   The use of "musical instruments can add a great deal" in Masses with children, especially if they are played by the children themselves.[28] The playing of instruments will help to sustain the singing or to encourage the reflection of the children; sometimes in their own fashion instruments express festive joy and the praise of God.

Care should always be taken, however, that the musical accompaniment does not overpower the singing or become a distraction rather than a help to the children. Music should correspond to the purpose intended for the different periods at which it is played during the Mass.

With these precautions and with due and special discretion, recorded music may also be used in Masses with children, in accord with norms established by the conferences of bishops.

GESTURES

33.   In view of the nature of the liturgy as an activity of the entire person and in view of the psychology of children, participation by means of gestures and posture should be strongly encouraged in Masses with children, with due regard for age and local customs. Much depends not only on the actions of the priest,[29] but also on the manner in which the children conduct themselves as a community.

If, in accord with the norms of the *General Instruction of the Roman Missal*,[30] a conference of bishops adapts the congregation's actions at Mass to the mentality of a people, it should take the special condition of children into account or should decide on adaptations that are for children only.

34.   Among the actions that are considered under this heading, processions and other activities that involve physical participation deserve special mention.

The children's entering in procession with the priest can serve to help them to experience a sense of the communion that is thus being created.[31] The participation of at least some children in the procession with the Book of the Gospels makes clear the presence of Christ announcing the word to his people. The procession of children with the chalice and the gifts expresses more clearly the value and meaning of the preparation of the gifts. The communion procession, if properly arranged, helps greatly to develop the children's devotion.

VISUAL ELEMENTS

35.   The liturgy of the Mass contains many visual elements and these should be given great prominence with children. This is especially true of the particular visual elements in the course of the liturgical year, for example, the veneration of the cross, the Easter candle, the lights on the feast of the Presentation of the Lord, and the variety of colors and liturgical appointments.

In addition to the visual elements that belong to the celebration and to the place of celebration, it is appropriate to introduce other elements that will permit children to perceive visually the wonderful works of God in creation and redemption and thus support their prayer. The liturgy should never appear as something dry and merely intellectual.

36. For the same reason, the use of art work prepared by the children themselves may be useful, for example, as illustrations of a homily, as visual expressions of the intentions of the general intercessions, or as inspirations to reflection.

SILENCE

37. Even in Masses with children "silence should be observed at the designated times as part of the celebration"[32] lest too great a place be given to external action. In their own way children are genuinely capable of reflection. They need some guidance, however, so that they will learn how, in keeping with the different moments of the Mass (for example, after the homily or after communion[33]), to recollect themselves, meditate briefly, or praise God and pray to him in their hearts.[34]

Besides this, with even greater care than in Masses with adults, the liturgical texts should be proclaimed intelligibly and unhurriedly, with the necessary pauses.

PARTS OF THE MASS

38. The general structure of the Mass, which "is made up as it were of the liturgy of the word and the liturgy of the eucharist," should always be maintained, as should certain rites to open and conclude the celebration.[35] Within individual parts of the celebration, the adaptations that follow seem necessary if children are truly to experience, in their own way and according to the psychological patterns of childhood, "the mystery of faith . . . by means of rites and prayers."[36]

39. Some rites and texts should never be adapted for children lest the difference between Masses with children and the Masses with adults become too pronounced.[37] These are "the acclamations and the responses to the priest's greeting,"[38] the Lord's Prayer, and the Trinitarian formulary at the end of the blessing with which the priest concludes the Mass. It is urged, moreover, that children should become accustomed to the Nicene Creed little by little, the right to use the Apostles' Creed indicated in no. 49 remaining intact.

A. Introductory Rite

40. The introductory rite of Mass has as its purpose "that the faithful coming together take on the form of a community and prepare themselves to listen to God's word and celebrate the eucharist properly."[39] Therefore every effort should be made to create this disposition in the children and not to jeopardize it by any excess of rites in this part of Mass.

It is sometimes proper to omit one or other element of the introductory rite or perhaps to expand one of the elements. There should always be at least some introductory element, which is completed by the opening prayer. In choosing individual elements, care should be taken that each one be used from time to time and that none be entirely neglected.

B. Reading and Explanation of the Word of God

41.   Since readings taken from holy Scripture "form the main part of the liturgy of the word,"[40] even in Masses celebrated with children biblical reading should never be omitted.

42.   With regard to the number of readings on Sundays and holy days, the decrees of the conferences of bishops are to be observed. If three or even two readings appointed on Sundays or weekdays can be understood by children only with difficulty, it is permissible to read two or only one of them, but the reading of the gospel should never be omitted.

43.   If all the readings assigned to the day seem to be unsuited to the capacity of the children, it is permissible to choose readings or a reading either from the Lectionary of the Roman Missal or directly from the Bible, but taking into account the liturgical seasons. It is recommended, moreover, that the individual conferences of bishops see to the composition of lectionaries for Masses with children.

If, because of the limited capabilities of the children, it seems necessary to omit one or other verse of a biblical reading, this should be done cautiously and in such a way "that the meaning of the text or the intent and, as it were, style of the Scriptures are not distorted."[41]

44.   In the choice of readings the criterion to be followed is the quality rather than the quantity of the texts from the Scriptures. A shorter reading is not as such always more suited to children than a lengthy reading. Everything depends on the spiritual advantage that the reading can bring to the children.

45.   In the biblical texts "God is speaking to his people . . . and Christ is present to the faithful through his own word."[42] Paraphrases of Scripture should therefore be avoided. On the other hand, the use of translations that may already exist for the catechesis of children and that are accepted by the competent authority is recommended.

46.   Verses of psalms, carefully selected in accord with the understanding of children, or singing in the form of psalmody or the *Alleluia* with a simple verse should be sung between the readings. The children should always have a part in this singing, but sometimes a reflective silence may be substituted for the singing.

If only a single reading is chosen, the singing may follow the homily.

47.   All the elements that will help explain the readings should be given great consideration so that the children may make the biblical readings their own and may come more and more to appreciate the value of God's word.

Among such elements are the introductory comments that may precede the readings[43] and that by explaining the context or by introducing the text itself help the children to listen better and more fruitfully. The interpretation and explanation of the readings from the Scriptures in the Mass on a saint's day may include an account of the saint's life, not only in the homily but even before the readings in the form of an introduction.

When the text of the readings lends itself to this, it may be helpful to have the children read it with parts distributed among them, as is provided for the reading of the Lord's passion during Holy Week.

48.   The homily explaining the word of God should be given great prominence in all Masses with children. Sometimes the homily intended for children should become a dialogue with them, unless it is preferred that they should listen in silence.

49.   If the profession of faith occurs at the end of the liturgy of the word, the Apostle's Creed may be used with children, especially because it is part of their catechetical formation.

C. Presidential Prayers

50.   The priest is permitted to choose from the Roman Missal texts of presidential prayers more suited to children, so that he may truly associate the children with himself. But he is to take into account the liturgical season.

51.   Since these prayers were composed for adult Christians, however, the principle simply of choosing from among them does not serve the purpose of having the children regard the prayers as an expression of their own life and religious experience.[44] If this is the case, the text of prayers of the Roman Missal may be adapted to the needs of children, but this should be done in such a way that, preserving the purpose of the prayer and to some extent its substance as well, the priest avoids anything that is foreign to the literary genre of a presidential prayer, such as moral exhortations or a childish manner of speech.

52.   The eucharistic prayer is of the greatest importance in the eucharist celebrated with children because it is the high point of the entire celebration.[45] Much depends on the manner in which the priest proclaims this prayer[46] and on the way the children take part by listening and making their acclamations.

The disposition of mind required for this central part of the celebration and the calm and reverence with which everything is done must make the children as attentive as possible. Their attention should be on the real presence of Christ on the altar under the elements of bread and wine, on his offering, on the thanksgiving through him and with him and in him, and on the Church's offering, which is made during the prayer and by which the faithful offer themselves and their lives with Christ to the eternal Father in the Holy Spirit.

For the present, the four eucharistic prayers approved by the supreme authority for Masses with adults and introduced into liturgical use are to be employed until the Apostolic See makes other provision for Masses with children.

D. Rites before Communion

53. When the eucharistic prayer has ended, the Lord's Prayer, the breaking of bread, and the invitation to communion should always follow,[47] that is, the elements that have the principal significance in the structure of this part of the Mass.

E. Communion and the Following Rites

54. Everything should be done so that the children who are properly disposed and who have already been admitted to the eucharist may go to the holy table calmly and with recollection and thus take part fully in the eucharistic mystery. If possible, there should be singing, suited to the children, during the communion procession.[48]

The comments that precede the final blessing[49] are important in Masses with children. Before they are dismissed they need some repetition and application of what they have heard, but this should be done in a very few words. In particular, this is the appropriate time to express the connection between the liturgy and life.

At least sometimes, depending on the liturgical seasons and different occasions in the children's life, the priest should use more expanded forms of blessing, but at the end should always retain the Trinitarian formulary with the sign of the cross.[50]

*　　*　　*　　*　　*

55. The contents of the Directory have as their purpose to help children readily and joyfully to encounter Christ together in the eucharistic celebration and to stand with him in the presence of the Father.[51] If they are formed by conscious and active participation in the eucharistic sacrifice and meal, they should learn day by day, at home and away from home, to proclaim Christ to others among their family and among their peers, by living the "faith, that works through love" (Gal 5:6).

This Directory was prepared by the Congregation for Divine Worship. On 22 October 1973, Pope Paul VI approved and confirmed it and ordered that it be published.

NOTES

1. See GCD 5.

2. See SC 33.

3. See GCD 78.

4. See SC 38; also AP.

5. First Synod of Bishops, Liturgy: *Notitiae* 3 (1967) 368.

6. See DMC 19, 32, 33.

7. See Order of Mass with deaf and mute children of German-speaking regions approved, that is, confirmed by CDW, 26 June 1970 (Prot. no. 1546/70).

8. See SC 14, 19.

9. See GCD 25.

10. See Vatican Council II, Declaration on Christian Education, *Gravissimum educationis*, no. 2.

11. See ibid, 3.

12. See GCD 78.

13. See SC 33.

14. See EM 14.

15. See GCD 25.

16. See EM 14; GCD 57.

17. See SC 35, 4.

18. See DMC 3.

19. See SC 42, 106.

20. See First Synod of Bishops, Liturgy: *Notitiae* (1967) 368.

21. See GIRM 56.

22. See DMC 37.

23. See GIRM 11.

24. See SC 28.

25. See GIRM 253.

26. See GIRM 19.

27. See MS 55.

28. MS 62.

29. See DMC 23.

30. See GIRM 21.

31. See GIRM 24.

32. GIRM 23.

33. See EM 38.

34. See GIRM 23.

35. GIRM 8.

36. SC 48.

37. See DMC 21.

38. GIRM 15.

39. GIRM 24.

40. GIRM 33.

41. Lectionary for Mass: Introduction, 1969 edition, no. 7d.

42. GIRM 33.

43. See GIRM 11.

44. See Consilium for the Implementation of the Constitution on the Sacred Liturgy, instruction on translations of liturgical texts for celebrations with a congregation, 25 Jan 1969, no. 20: *Notitiae* 5 (1969) 7.

45. GIRM 54.

46. See DMC 23, 37.

47. See DMC 23.

48. See MS 32.

49. See GIRM 11.

50. See DMC 39.

51. See RomM, Eucharistic Prayer II.

CEREMONIAL

OF

BISHOPS

(EXCERPTS)

CONGREGATION FOR DIVINE WORSHIP
14 SEPTEMBER 1984

OUTLINE

*Parts of these sections are reproduced in this volume. For the complete texts,
refer to the Ceremonial of Bishops.

THE CEREMONIAL OF BISHOPS

The following sections have been excerpted from the *Ceremonial of Bishops:*
Most of Part I, containing general considerations; from Part IV, on the liturgical
year, one paragraph from the description of each season or celebration; from
Parts V, VI and VIII, one chapter from each as an example. See the *Ceremonial*
itself for further treatment of all the topics discussed here.

PART I
GENERAL CONSIDERATIONS

CHAPTER 1
CHARACTER AND IMPORTANCE OF A LITURGY
AT WHICH THE BISHOP PRESIDES

I. DIGNITY OF THE PARTICULAR CHURCHES

1.   "The diocese forms that part of the people of God entrusted to the pastoral
care of the bishop with the assistance of the presbyterate. In allegiance to its
pastor and by him gathered together in the Holy Spirit through the Gospel and the
eucharist, the diocese stands as a particular Church, in which Christ's one, holy,
catholic, and apostolic Church is present and at work."[1] Indeed, Christ is present,
since by his power the Church is gathered together in unity.[2] As Saint Ignatius of
Antioch has truly written: "Just as where Christ Jesus is, there also is the Catholic
Church, so also where the bishop is, there also should be the whole assembly of
his people."[3]

2.   Hence the dignity of the Church of Christ is embodied in the particular
Churches. Each such Church is not simply a group of people who on their own
choose to band together for some common endeavor; rather each Church is a
gift that comes down from the Father of lights. Nor are the particular Churches
to be regarded merely as administrative divisions of the people of God. In their
own proper way they contain and manifest the nature of the universal Church,
which issued from the side of Christ crucified, which lives and grows through
the eucharist, which is espoused to Christ, and which, as their mother, cares for
all the faithful. The particular Churches "in their own locality are the new people
called by God in the Holy Spirit and in great fullness (see 1 Thessalonians 1:5)."[4]

3.   But, as the Council also teaches, there is no lawful assembly of the faithful,
no community of the altar except under the sacred ministry of the bishop.[5] The
congregation making up the particular Church is situated and has its life in the

many individual assemblies of the faithful, over which the bishop places his presbyters, in order that under his authority they may sanctify and guide the portion of the Lord's flock that is assigned to them.[6]

4.   Just as the universal Church is present and manifested in the particular Churches,[7] so too each particular Church contributes its own distinctive gifts to the other Churches and to the Church as a whole, "so that from their sharing of gifts with one another and their common effort in unity toward perfection, the church achieves growth as a whole and in its particular parts."[8]

II. THE BISHOP AS FOUNDATION AND SIGN OF COMMUNION IN THE PARTICULAR CHURCH

5.   As Christ's vicar and representative, marked with the fullness of the sacrament of orders, the bishop leads the particular Church in communion with the pope and under his authority.[9]

"Placed there by the Holy Spirit, bishops are the successors of the apostles as shepherds of souls, . . . for Christ gave the apostles and their successors the mandate and the power to teach all nations and to sanctify and to shepherd their people in truth. By the Holy Spirit who has been given to them, therefore, bishops have been made true and authentic teachers of the faith, high priests, and pastors."[10]

6.   Through the preaching of the Gospel and in the power of the Spirit the bishop calls men and women to faith or confirms them in the faith they already have, and he proclaims to them the mystery of Christ in its entirety.[11]

7.   The bishop's authority regulates the orderly and effective celebration of the sacraments and through them he sanctifies the faithful. He supervises the bestowal of baptism, since it brings with it a share in the royal priesthood of Christ. He is the primary minister of confirmation, he alone confers the sacrament of holy orders, and he oversees the penitential discipline in his diocese. He regulates every lawful celebration of the eucharist, from which the Church continually receives life and growth. He never ceases to exhort and to instruct his people to fulfill their part in the liturgy with faith and reverence, and especially in the eucharistic sacrifice.[12]

8.   In the person of the bishop, with the presbyters gathered round him, the Lord Jesus Christ, the High Priest, is present in the midst of the faithful. Seated at the right hand of the Father, Christ is not absent from the gathering of his high priests. They have been chosen to feed the Lord's flock and they are Christ's ministers and the stewards of the mysteries of God.[13] Therefore, "the bishop is to be looked on as the high priest of his flock, the faithful's life in Christ in some way deriving from and depending on him."[14]

9.   The bishop is "the steward of the grace of the supreme priesthood."[15] On him depend both presbyters and deacons in the exercise of their orders. Presbyters, appointed to be prudent co-workers of the order of bishops, are themselves

consecrated as true priests of the New Testament; deacons serve as ministers ordained to service for the people of God in communion with the bishop and his presbyters. The bishop himself is the chief steward of the mysteries of God and the overseer, promoter, and guardian of all liturgical life in the particular Church entrusted to his care.[16] To him "is committed the office of offering to the divine majesty the worship of Christian religion and administering it in accordance with the Lord's commandments and the Church's laws, as further specified by his particular judgment for his diocese."[17]

10.   The bishop rules the particular Church entrusted to him by counsel, persuasion, and example, but also by the authority and sacred power that he received through his ordination as bishop,[18] which he uses only for the building up of his flock in truth and holiness. "The faithful should cling to the bishop as the Church clings to Jesus Christ and as Jesus Christ clings to the Father, so that through such unity there may be harmony in everything and so that everything may conspire to the glory of God."[19]

III. IMPORTANCE OF A LITURGY AT WHICH THE BISHOP PRESIDES

11.   The office of bishop as teacher, sanctifier, and pastor of his Church shines forth most clearly in a liturgy that he celebrates with his people.

"Therefore all should hold in great esteem the liturgical life of the diocese centered around the bishop, especially in his cathedral church; they must be convinced that the preeminent manifestation of the Church is present in the full, active participation of all God's holy people in these liturgical celebrations, especially in the same eucharist, in a single prayer, at one altar at which the bishop presides, surrounded by his college of presbyters and by his ministers."[20]

12.   Hence liturgical celebrations in which the bishop presides manifest the mystery of the Church as that mystery involves Christ's presence; such celebrations, then, are not a mere display of ceremony.

These celebrations should also serve as a model for the entire diocese and be shining examples of active participation by the people. The whole gathered community should thus take part through song, dialogue, prayerful silence, and attentiveness and by sharing in the sacraments.

13.   Provision should be made at appointed times and on the major dates of the liturgical year for the special manifestation of the particular Church that such a celebration means. The faithful from different areas of the diocese should be invited to gather and, as far as possible, the presbyters should join them. To encourage and make more convenient gatherings of the faithful and the presbyters, arrangement should be made for gatherings of this kind at different times in the various parts of the diocese.

14.   These gatherings should be occasions for the faithful to grow in their love for the entire Church and to heighten their desire to serve the Gospel and their neighbor.

IV. THE BISHOP'S FULFILLMENT OF THE OFFICE OF PREACHING

15.   Among the principal duties of a bishop the preaching of the Gospel is pre-eminent. The bishop as herald of the faith leads new followers to Christ. As their authentic teacher, that is, one invested with the authority of Christ, he proclaims to the people entrusted to him the truths of faith they are to believe and to live by. Under the light of the Holy Spirit the bishop explains the teachings of faith, bringing forth from the treasure-house of revelation new things and old. He works to make faith yield its harvest and, like the good shepherd, he is vigilant in protecting his people from the threat of error.[21]

The liturgy is one of the ways in which the bishop discharges this responsibility: he preaches the homily at celebrations of the eucharist, celebrations of the word of God and, as occasion suggests, celebrations of morning and evening prayer; also when he imparts catechesis and in his introductions, invitations, or commentary during celebrations of the sacraments and sacramentals.

16.   This preaching "should draw its content mainly from scriptural and liturgical sources, being a proclamation of God's wonderful works in the history of salvation, the mystery of Christ, ever present and active within us, especially in the celebration of the liturgy."[22]

17.   Since the office of preaching is proper to the bishop, so that other ordained ministers fulfill this office only in his name, he should preach the homily himself whenever he presides at a celebration of the liturgy. Unless he decides that some other way is preferable, the bishop should preach while seated at the chair, wearing the miter and holding the pastoral staff.

CHAPTER 2
OFFICE AND MINISTRIES IN THE LITURGY OF BISHOPS

18.   "Any community of the altar, under the sacred ministry of the bishop, stands out clearly as a symbol of that charity and 'unity of the Mystical Body, without which there can be no salvation.'"[23]

Thus it is very fitting that when the bishop, who is marked by the fullness of the sacrament of orders, is present at a liturgical celebration in which a congregation takes part, he personally preside. The reason for this is not to give added outward solemnity to the rite, but to make the celebration a more striking sign of the mystery of the Church.

For the same reason it is fitting that the bishop associate presbyters with himself as concelebrants.

When a bishop presides at the eucharist but is not the celebrant, he does everything in the liturgy of the word that belongs to the celebrant and he concludes the Mass with the rite of dismissal,[24] following the provisions given in nos. 176–185.

19.   In every liturgical assembly, and especially one at which the bishop presides, all those present have the right and the duty to carry out their parts in the different ways corresponding to their differences in order and office. Each one, therefore, minister or layperson, should do all of, but only, those parts which pertain to that office by the nature of the rite and the principles of liturgy.[25] This way of celebration manifests the Church in its variety of orders and ministries as a body whose individual members form a unity.[26]

Presbyters

20.   Even though they do not possess the fullness of priesthood that belongs to the episcopate and in the exercise of their power depend upon the bishop, presbyters are nevertheless joined to the bishop by the bond of priestly dignity.

Presbyters, prudent co-workers with the episcopal order, its aid and instrument, called to serve the people of God, constitute one college of prebysters with their bishop and, under the bishop's authority, sanctify and govern that portion of the Lord's flock entrusted to them.[27]

21.   It is strongly recommended that in liturgical celebrations the bishop should have presbyters to assist him. In a eucharistic celebration presided over by the bishop, presbyters should concelebrate with him so that the mystery of the unity of the Church may be made manifest through the eucharistic celebration and so that the presbyters may be seen by the entire community to be the presbyterate of the bishop.

22.   Presbyters taking part in a liturgy with the bishop should do only what belongs to the order of presbyter;[28] in the absence of deacons they may perform some of the ministries proper to the deacon, but should never wear diaconal vestments.

Deacons

23.   Deacons hold the highest place among ministers and from the Church's earliest age the diaconate has been held in great honor. As men of good repute and full of wisdom,[29] they should act in such a way that, with the help of God, all may know them to be true disciples[30] of one who came, not to be served but to serve,[31] and who was among his disciples as one who serves.[32]

24.   Strengthened by the gift of the Holy Spirit, deacons assist the bishop and his presbyterate in the ministry of the word, the altar, and of charity. As ministers of the altar they proclaim the gospel reading, help at the celebration of the sacrifice, and serve as eucharistic ministers.

Deacons should therefore look upon the bishop as a father and assist him as they would the Lord Jesus Christ himself, who is the eternal High Priest, present in the midst of his people.

25.   In liturgical celebrations it belongs to the deacon to assist the celebrant, to minister at the altar with the book and the cup, to guide the assembly of

the faithful with suitable directions, to announce the intentions of the general intercessions.

If there is no other minister, the deacon also carries out other ministerial functions as required.[33]

When assisting at an altar that does not face the people, the deacon is always to turn toward the people when he addresses them.

26.   At a liturgical celebration presided over by the bishop there should be at least three deacons, one to proclaim the gospel reading and to minister at the altar, and two to assist the bishop. If more than three deacons are present, they should divide the ministries accordingly,[34] and at least one of them should be charged with assisting the active participation of the faithful.

Acolytes

27.   In the ministry of the altar, acolytes have their own proper functions and should exercise these even though ministers of a higher rank may be present.

28.   Acolytes receive institution so that they may help the deacon and minister to the priest. Their proper ministry is to look after the service of the altar and to assist the deacon and priest in liturgical services, especially the celebration of Mass. In addition, acolytes may serve as special ministers of the eucharist, giving holy communion in accord with the provisions of the law.

When necessary, acolytes should instruct those who serve as ministers in liturgical rites by carrying the book, the cross, candles, or the censer or by performing other similar duties. But in celebrations presided over by the bishop it is fitting that all such ministerial functions be carried out by formally instituted acolytes, and if a number are present, they should divide the ministries accordingly.[35]

29.   So that they may fulfill their responsibilities more worthily, acolytes should take part in the celebration of the eucharist with ever increasing devotion, as the source of their spiritual life and the object of an ever deeper appreciation. They should seek to acquire an interior and spiritual sense of their ministry so that each day they may offer themselves wholly to God and grow in sincere love for the Mystical Body of Christ, the people of God, and especially for the members who are weak and infirm.

Readers

30.   In liturgical celebrations readers have their own proper function and should exercise this, even though ministers of a higher rank may be present.[36]

31.   The office of reader was historically the first of the lesser ministries to emerge. This office exists in all the Churches and has never disappeared. Readers receive institution for an office proper to them: to proclaim the word of God in the liturgical assembly. Hence at Mass and in other rites of the liturgy readers proclaim the readings other than the gospel reading. When there is no cantor of the psalm present, the reader also leads the assembly in the responsorial psalm;

when no deacon is present, the reader announces the intentions of the general intercessions.

Whenever necessary, the reader should see to the preparation of any members of the faithful who may be appointed to proclaim the readings from Sacred Scripture in liturgical celebrations. But in celebrations presided over by the bishop it is fitting that readers formally instituted proclaim the readings and, if several readers are present, they should divide the readings accordingly.[37]

32.   Conscious of the dignity of God's word and the importance of their office, readers should be eager to learn how best to speak and proclaim, in order that those who listen may clearly hear and understand the word of God.

In proclaiming the word of God to others, readers should themselves receive it with docility and meditate on it with devotion so that they may bear witness to that word in their daily lives.

Psalmist or Cantor of the Psalm

33.   The chants between the readings are very important liturgically and pastorally; it is therefore desirable in celebrations presided over by the bishop, especially in the cathedral church, that there be a psalmist or cantor who has the necessary musical ability and devotion to the liturgy. The cantor of the psalm is responsible for singing, either responsorially or directly, the chants between the readings—the psalm or other biblical canticle, the gradual and *Alleluia,* or other chant—in such a way as to assist the faithful to join in the singing and to reflect on the meaning of the texts.[38]

Master of Ceremonies

34.   For a liturgical celebration, especially a celebration presided over by the bishop, to be distinguished by grace, simplicity, and order, a master of ceremonies is needed to prepare and direct the celebration in close cooperation with the bishop and others responsible for planning its several parts, and especially from a pastoral standpoint.

The master of ceremonies should be well-versed in the history and nature of the liturgy and in its laws and precepts. But equally he should be well-versed in pastoral science, so that he knows how to plan liturgical celebrations in a way that encourages fruitful participation by the people and enhances the beauty of the rites.

He should seek to ensure an observance of liturgical laws that is in accord with the true spirit of such laws and with those legitimate traditions of the particular Church that have pastoral value.

35.   In due time he should arrange with the cantors, assistants, ministers, and celebrants the actions to be carried out and the texts to be used, but during the celebration he should exercise the greatest discretion: he is not to speak more than is necessary, nor replace the deacons or assistants at the side of the celebrant. The master of ceremonies should carry out his responsibilities with reverence, patience, and careful attention.

36.   The master of ceremonies wears either an alb or a cassock and surplice. Within a celebration a master of ceremonies who is an ordained deacon may wear a dalmatic and the other diaconal vestments.

Sacristan

37.   Along with the master of ceremonies and under his direction, the sacristan sees to the preparation for a celebration with the bishop. The sacristan should carefully arrange the books needed for the proclamation of the word and for the presidential prayers; he or she should lay out the vestments and have ready whatever else is needed for the celebration. He or she should see to the ringing of bells for celebrations. He or she should ensure the observance of silence and quiet in the sacristy and the vesting room. Vestments, church furnishings, and decorative objects that have been handed down from the past are not to be treated carelessly, but kept in good condition. When anything new needs to be provided, it should be chosen to meet the standards of contemporary art, but not out of a desire simply for novelty.

38.   The first of all the elements belonging to the beauty of the place where the liturgy is celebrated is the spotless condition of the floor and walls and of all the images and articles that will be used or seen during a service. In all the liturgical appurtenances both ostentation and shabbiness are to be avoided; instead the norms of noble simplicity, refinement, gracefulness, and artistic excellence are to be respected. The culture of the people and local tradition should guide the choice of objects and their arrangement, "on condition that they serve the places of worship and the sacred rites with the reverence and honor due to them."[39]

The adornment and decor of a church should be such as to make the church a visible sign of love and reverence toward God, and to remind the people of God of the real meaning of the feasts celebrated there and to inspire in them a sense of joy and devotion.

Choir and Musicians

39.   All who have a special part in the singing and music for the liturgy—choir directors, cantors, organists, and others—should be careful to follow the provisions concerning their functions that are found in the liturgical books and other documents published by the Apostolic See.[40]

40.   Musicians should constantly keep in mind those norms especially that regard the participation of the people in singing. In addition, they should take care that the singing expresses the note of universality belonging to celebrations presided over by the bishop; hence, the faithful should be able to recite or sing together not only in the vernacular but also in Latin the parts of the Order of Mass that pertain to them.

41.   From Ash Wednesday until the singing of the *Gloria* at the Easter Vigil and in celebrations for the dead, the organ and other instruments should be played only to sustain the singing.[41] An exception is made for *Laetare* Sunday (the Fourth Sunday of Lent) and for solemnities and festive days.

From the end of the *Gloria* in the Mass of the Lord's Supper on Holy Thursday until the *Gloria* at the Easter Vigil, the organ and other musical instruments should be played only to sustain the singing.

During Advent musical instruments should be played with a moderation that is in keeping with the spirit of joyful expectation characteristic of this season, but does not anticipate the fullness of joy belonging to the celebration of the nativity of the Lord.

CHAPTER 3
CATHEDRAL CHURCH

42.   The cathedral church is the church that is the site of the bishop's cathedra or chair, the sign of his teaching office and pastoral power in the particular Church and a sign also of the unity of believers in the faith that the bishop proclaims as shepherd of the Lord's flock.

In this church, on the more solemn liturgical days, the bishop presides at the liturgy. There also, unless pastoral considerations suggest otherwise, he consecrates the sacred chrism and confers the sacrament of holy orders.

43.   The diocesan cathedral "in the majesty of its building is a symbol of the spiritual temple that is built up in souls and is resplendent with the glory of divine grace. As Saint Paul says: 'We are the temple of the living God' (2 Corinthians 6:16). The cathedral, furthermore, should be regarded as the express image of Christ's visible Church, praying, singing, and worshiping on earth. The cathedral should be regarded as the image of Christ's Mystical Body, whose members are joined together in an organism of charity that is sustained by the outpouring of God's gifts."[42]

44.   With good reason, then, the cathedral church should be regarded as the center of the liturgical life of the diocese.

45.   Effective measures should be taken to instill esteem and reverence for the cathedral church in the hearts of the faithful. Among such measures are the annual celebration of the dedication of the cathedral and pilgrimages in which the faithful, especially in groups of parishes or sections of the diocese, visit the cathedral in a spirit of devotion.

46.   The cathedral church should be a model for the other churches of the diocese in its conformity to the directives laid down in liturgical documents and books with regard to the arrangement and adornment of churches.[43]

47.   The bishop's *cathedra* or *chair* mentioned in no. 42, should be a chair that stands alone and is permanently installed. Its placement should make it clear that the bishop is presiding over the whole community of the faithful.

Depending on the design of each church, the chair should have enough steps leading up to it for the bishop to be clearly visible to the faithful.

There is to be no baldachin over the bishop's chair; but valuable works of art from the past are to be preserved with utmost care.

Apart from the cases provided by law, only the diocesan bishop, or a bishop he permits to use it, occupies this chair.[44] Seats are to be provided in a convenient place for other bishops or prelates who may be present at a celebration, but such seats are not to be set up in the manner of a cathedra.[45]

The chair for a priest celebrant should be set up in a place separate from the site of the bishop's chair.

48. The *altar* should be constructed and adorned in accordance with the provisions of the law. It should be so placed as to be a focal point on which the attention of the whole congregation centers naturally.[46]

The altar of the cathedral church should normally be a fixed altar that has been dedicated. This altar should be freestanding to allow the ministers to walk around it easily and to permit celebration facing the people.[47] But when the cathedral has an old altar constructed so that it makes participation of the people difficult and cannot be moved without damage to its artistic value, another fixed altar, of artistic merit and duly dedicated, should be erected. Only at this altar are liturgical celebrations to be carried out.

Flowers should not adorn the altar from Ash Wednesday until the *Gloria* at the Easter Vigil, nor in celebrations for the dead. Exceptions to this rule are *Laetare* Sunday (the Fourth Sunday of Lent), solemnities and feasts.

49. It is recommended that the *tabernacle*, in accordance with a very ancient tradition in cathedral churches, should be located in a chapel separate from the main body of the church.[48]

But when, in a particular case, there is a tabernacle on the altar at which the bishop is to celebrate, the blessed sacrament should be transferred to another fitting place.

50. The *sanctuary* or *chancel*, that is, the place where the bishop, presbyters and ministers carry out their ministries, should be set apart from the body of the church in some way—for example, by being at a somewhat higher level or by its distinctive design and ornamentation—in such a way that even the layout of the sanctuary highlights the hierarchic offices of the ministers. The sanctuary should be sufficiently spacious for the rites to be carried out without obstruction to movement or to the view of the assembly.

Seats, benches or stools should be provided in the sanctuary so that concelebrants, or canons and presbyters not concelebrating but assisting in choir dress, as well as the ministers, all have their own places, and in such a way as to facilitate the exercise of their various parts in a celebration.

A minister who is not wearing a vestment, a cassock and surplice or other lawfully approved garb may not enter the sanctuary (chancel) during a celebration.[49]

51.   The cathedral church should have an *ambo* or *lectern* constructed in keeping with liturgical norms currently in force.[50] But the bishop should address the people of God from the bishop's chair (cathedra) unless local conditions suggest otherwise.

The cantor, the commentator or the choirmaster should not normally use the ambo or lectern, but should carry out their functions from another suitable place.

52.   Even when it is not a parochial church, the cathedral should have a *baptistery*, at least for the celebration of baptism at the Easter Vigil. The baptistery should be designed and equipped in keeping with the provisions of The Roman Ritual.[51]

53.   The cathedral church should have a *vesting room*, that is, a suitable place, as close as possible to the church entrance, where the bishop, concelebrants, and ministers can put on their liturgical vestments and from which the entrance procession can begin.

The sacristy, which should normally be separate from the vesting room, is a room where vestments and other liturgical materials are kept. It may also serve as the place where the celebrant and the ministers prepare for a celebration on ordinary occasions.

54.   If at all possible, provision should be made for a *gathering place* of the people near the cathedral church—another church, a suitable hall, a square, or a cloister—where the blessings of candles, of palms, and of fire, as well as other preparatory celebrations, may take place and from which processions to the cathedral church may begin.

CHAPTER 4
GENERAL NORMS
INTRODUCTION

55.   According to the teaching of the Second Vatican Council, care must be taken to ensure that rites are marked by a noble simplicity.[52] This applies also to a liturgy in which the bishop presides, although the respect and reverence owed to a bishop are not to be disregarded. In him the Lord Jesus is present in the midst of those who believe and the faithful's life in Christ in some way depends on and derives from him.[53]

In addition, a liturgy in which the bishop presides is usually marked by the participation of those having the different orders existing in the Church and in this way the mystery of the Church is more clearly made visible. Thus celebrations with the bishop ought to be marked by love and mutual esteem between the members of the Mystical Body of Jesus Christ, so that the liturgy may truly fulfill the precept of Saint Paul: "Be first in showing honor to each other."[54]

Before describing the individual rites, it seems advisable to state some general norms that have proved valid by long use and that should be followed.

I. VESTURE AND INSIGNIA

[See the *Ceremonial* for the norms regarding the vesture and insignia of the bishop.]

Vesture of priests and other ministers

65.   The vestment common to ministers of every rank is the alb, tied at the waist with a cincture, unless it is made to fit without a cincture. An amice should be put on first if the alb does not completely cover the minister's street clothing at the neck. A surplice may not be substituted for the alb when the chasuble or dalmatic is to be worn or when a stole is used instead of the chasuble or dalmatic.[60] When a surplice is worn, it must be worn with the cassock.

Acolytes, readers, and other ministers may wear other lawfully approved vesture in place of the vestments already mentioned.

66.   Unless otherwise indicated, the chasuble, worn over the alb and stole, is the vestment proper to the presbyter who is the celebrant at Mass and other rites immediately connected with Mass.

The priest wears the stole around his neck and hanging down in front.

The cope is worn by the priest in solemn liturgical services outside Mass and in processions; in other liturgical services, in keeping with the rubrics proper to each rite.[61]

Presbyters who take part in a liturgical service but not as concelebrants are to wear choir dress if they are prelates or canons,[62] cassock and surplice if they are not.

67.   The dalmatic, worn over the alb and stole, is the vestment proper to the deacon. The dalmatic may be omitted either out of necessity or for less solemnity. The deacon wears the stole over his left shoulder and drawn across the chest to the right side, where it is fastened.[63]

II. SIGNS OF REVERENCE IN GENERAL

68.   A *bow* signifies reverence and honor toward persons or toward objects that represent persons.

There are two kinds of bows, a bow of the head and a bow of the body:

a. a bow of the head is made at the name of Jesus, the Blessed Virgin Mary, and the saint in whose honor the Mass or the liturgy of the hours is being celebrated;

b. a bow of the body, or deep bow, is made: to the altar if there is no tabernacle with the blessed sacrament on the altar; to the bishop, before and after incensation, as indicated in no. 91; whenever it is expressly called for by the rubrics of the various liturgical books.[64]

69. A *genuflection,* made by bending only the right knee to the ground, signifies adoration, and is therefore reserved for the blessed sacrament, whether exposed or reserved in the tabernacle, and for the holy cross from the time of the solemn adoration in the liturgical celebration of Good Friday until the beginning of the Easter Vigil.

70. Neither a genuflection nor a deep bow is made by those who are carrying articles used in a celebration, for example, the cross, candlesticks, the Book of the Gospels.

Reverence toward the blessed sacrament

71. No one who enters a church should fail to adore the blessed sacrament, either by visiting the blessed sacrament chapel or at least by genuflecting.

Similarly, those who pass before the blessed sacrament genuflect except when they are walking in procession.

Reverence toward the altar

72. A deep bow is made to the altar by all who enter the sanctuary (chancel), leave it, or pass before the altar.

73. In addition, the celebrant and concelebrants at the beginning of Mass kiss the altar as a sign of reverence. The principal celebrant as a rule venerates the altar by kissing it before he leaves, while the other concelebrants, particularly if there are a number of them, venerate the altar by bowing.

When the bishop presides at a solemn celebration of morning or evening prayer, he kisses the altar at the beginning and, as circumstances suggest, at the end.

But if such a sign of reverence as kissing the altar is out of keeping with the traditions or the culture of the region, the conference of bishops may substitute some other sign, after informing the Apostolic See.[65]

Reverence toward the gospel

74. While the gospel reading is being proclaimed at Mass, at a celebration of the word, and at a prolonged vigil, all stand and, as a rule, face the reader.

The deacon solemnly carrying the Book of the Gospels to the ambo is preceded by the censerbearer with the censer[66] and acolytes with lighted candles.[67]

At the ambo the deacon stands facing the people and, with hands joined, says the greeting; then with his right thumb he makes the sign of the cross, first on the book at the beginning of the gospel passage that he is about to read, then on his forehead, lips, and breast, saying, A reading from the holy gospel. The bishop signs himself in the same way on forehead, lips, and breast, and all present do the same. Then, at least at a stational Mass, the deacon incenses the Book of the Gospels three times, that is, in the center, to the left, and to the right. Then he proclaims the gospel reading to its conclusion.

After the reading, the deacon takes the book to the bishop to be kissed, or the deacon himself kisses the book, unless, as mentioned in no. 73, another sign of reverence has been decided on by the conference of bishops.[68]

In the absence of a deacon, a presbyter asks for and receives a blessing from the bishop, and proclaims the gospel reading in the way just described.

75.   All present also stand for the singing or recitation of the gospel canticles, the Canticles of Zechariah, of Mary, and of Simeon, and at the beginning of these canticles sign themselves with the sign of the cross.[69]

Reverence toward the bishop and other persons

76.   The bishop is greeted with a deep bow by the minister or others when they approach to assist him, when they leave after assisting him, or when they pass in front of him.[70]

77.   When the bishop's chair is behind the altar, the ministers should reverence either the altar or the bishop, depending on whether they are approaching the altar or approaching the bishop; out of reverence for both, ministers should, as far as possible, avoid passing between the bishop and the altar.

78.   If several bishops are present in the sanctuary (chancel), a reverence is made only to the one presiding.

79.   When the bishop, vested as indicated in no. 63, proceeds to a church to celebrate some liturgical rite, he may, in accordance with local custom, be escorted publicly to the church by the canons or other presbyters and clerics in choir dress or wearing cassock and surplice, or he may be received by the clergy at the door after proceeding to the church in a less solemn way.

In both cases the bishop goes first: if he is an archbishop he is preceded by an acolyte carrying the archiepiscopal cross with the image of Christ facing forward; behind the bishop follow the canons, presbyters, and clergy, two by two. At the door of the church the senior of the presbyters hands the bishop the sprinkler, unless the blessing and sprinkling of water is to replace the penitential rite. With head uncovered, the bishop sprinkles himself and those around him, then returns the sprinkler. He next goes in procession to the place of reservation of the blessed sacrament and prays there for a short time; finally he goes to the vesting room (sacristy).

The bishop may, however, go directly to the vesting room (sacristy) and be received there by the clergy.

80.   In a procession the bishop who presides at a liturgical celebration always walks vested and alone, following the presbyters, but preceding his assisting ministers, who walk a little behind him.

81.   When the bishop presides at a celebration or only takes part in it wearing choir dress, he has as assistants two canons in choir dress or two presbyters or deacons in cassock and surplice.

82.   A head of state in official attendance at a liturgical celebration is received by the bishop, who waits in vestments at the door of the church. The bishop may offer holy water to a head of state who is a Catholic. After greeting the head of state in a manner that accords with local custom, the bishop, keeping to the left, escorts the head of state to an appointed place reserved in the church outside the sanctuary (chancel). At the end of the celebration the bishop, as he leaves, again greets the head of state.

83.   If such is the practice, other officials holding high position in the government of a nation, region, or city are received at the door of the church in a manner that accords with local custom by an ecclesiastic dignitary, who greets them and escorts them to their appointed place. The bishop may greet such personages during the entrance procession as he goes to the altar, and as he leaves.

III. INCENSATION

84.   The rite of incensation or thurification is a sign of reverence and of prayer, as is clear from Psalm 141 (140):2 and Revelation 8:3.

85.   The substance placed in the censer should be pure sweet-scented incense alone or at least in larger proportion than any additive mixed with the incense.

86.   At the stational Mass of the bishop incense should be used:

   a. during the entrance procession;

   b. at the beginning of Mass to incense the altar;

   c. at the gospel, in the procession and at the proclamation of the gospel reading;

   d. at the presentation of the gifts, to incense the gifts, the altar, the cross, the bishop, the concelebrants, and the people;

   e. at the elevation of the consecrated bread and cup after their consecration.

At other Masses incense may be used as circumstances suggest.[71]

87.   Incense is also to be used as indicated in the liturgical books:

   a. in the rite of dedication of a church or altar;

   b. in the rite of the blessing of oils and consecrating the chrism, as the blessed oils and consecrated chrism are being taken away;

   c. at exposition of the blessed sacrament when the monstrance is used;

   d. at funerals.

88.   In addition, incense should as a rule be used during the processions for the feast of the Presentation of the Lord, Passion Sunday (Palm Sunday), the Mass of the Lord's Supper, the Easter Vigil, the solemnity of the Body and Blood of Christ (Corpus Christi), and the solemn translation of relics and, in general, in any procession of some solemnity.

89.   At the solemn celebration of morning or evening prayer the altar, the bishop, and the people may be incensed during the singing of the gospel canticle.

90.   If the bishop puts incense into the censer at his chair (cathedra) or another chair, he remains seated; otherwise he puts in the incense while standing. The deacon presents the incense boat[72] and the bishop blesses the incense with the sign of the cross, saying nothing.[73]

After the blessing, the deacon takes the censer from the acolyte and hands it to the bishop.[74]

91.   Before and after an incensation, a profound bow is made to the person or object that is incensed, except in the case of the incensation of the altar and the gifts for the eucharistic sacrifice.[75]

92.   The censer is swung back and forth three times for the incensation of: the blessed sacrament, a relic of the true cross and images of the Lord solemnly exposed, the gifts on the altar, the altar cross, the Book of the Gospels, the Easter candle, the bishop or presbyter who is celebrant, a representative of the civil authority in official attendance at a liturgical celebration, the choir and people, the body of a deceased person.

The censer is swung back and forth twice for the incensation of relics and images of the saints exposed for public veneration.

93.   The altar is incensed with a series of single swings of the censer in this way:

a. if the altar is freestanding, the bishop incenses it while walking around it;

b. if the altar is not freestanding, the bishop incenses it while walking first to the right side, then to the left.

If there is a cross on or beside the altar, he incenses it before he incenses the altar. If the cross is behind the altar, the bishop incenses it when he passes in front of it.[76]

The gifts of bread and wine are incensed before the incensation of the altar and the cross.

94.   The blessed sacrament is incensed from a kneeling position.

95.   Relics and images exposed for public veneration are incensed after the incensation of the altar; at Mass they are incensed only at the beginning of the celebration.

96.   Whether he is at the altar or at the chair (cathedra), the bishop receives the incensation standing and without the miter, unless he is already wearing it.

Concelebrants are incensed as a body by the deacon.

Lastly, the deacon incenses the people from the place most convenient. Canons who are not concelebrating or a community assembled in choir are incensed together with the people, unless the spatial arrangement suggests otherwise.

Bishops who may be present are also incensed along with the people.

97. A bishop who presides but does not concelebrate is incensed after the celebrant or concelebrants.

Where such a practice is customary, a head of state in official attendance at a liturgical celebration is incensed after the bishop.

98. The bishop should not begin any invitation, introduction, or prayer meant to be heard by all before the rite of incensation has been completed.

IV. SIGN OF PEACE

99. After the deacon has said, Let us offer each other a sign of peace, the bishop who is celebrant gives the kiss of peace at least to the two concelebrants nearest to him, then to the first deacon.

100. Meanwhile the concelebrants and deacons and the other ministers as well as any bishops present also give each other the kiss of peace.

101. The faithful also exchange a sign of peace in the manner approved by the conference of bishops.

102. The deacon or one of the concelebrants goes to give a head of state in official attendance the sign of peace according to local custom.

103. The exchange of the sign of peace may be accompanied by the words, Peace be with you, and the response, And also with you. But other words may be used in accordance with local custom.

V. POSITION OF THE HANDS

Raised and outstretched hands

104. Customarily in the Church, a bishop or presbyter addresses prayers to God while standing and with hands slightly raised and outstretched.

This practice appears already in the tradition of the Old Testament,[77] and was taken by Christians in memory of the Lord's passion: "Not only do we raise our hands, but also hold them outstretched, so that by imitating the Lord in his passion, we bear witness to him as we pray."[78]

Outstretched hands over persons or objects

105. The bishop holds his hands outstretched over the people when he blesses them solemnly and wherever the liturgical books call for such a gesture in the celebration of the sacraments or sacramentals.

106. The bishop and the concelebrants hold their hands outstretched over the offerings in Mass at the epiclesis before the consecration.

At the consecration, as the bishop holds the host or cup in his hands and says the words of consecration, the concelebrants say the words of institution and, if this seems appropriate, hold the right hand outstretched toward the bread and the cup.[79]

Joined hands

107. Unless the bishop is holding the pastoral staff, he keeps his hands joined:[80] when, vested, he walks in procession for the celebration of a liturgy; when he is kneeling at prayer; when he moves from altar to chair or from chair to altar; when the liturgical books prescribe joined hands.

Similarly, concelebrants and ministers keep their hands joined when walking from place to place or when standing, unless they are holding something.

Other positions for the hands

108. When the bishop signs himself with the sign of the cross or when he gives a blessing,[81] he places his left hand on his breast, unless he is holding something. When he is standing at the altar and blesses the offerings or something else with his right hand, he places his left hand on the altar, unless a rubric indicates otherwise.

109. When the bishop is seated and wearing vestments, he places his palms on his knees, unless he is holding the pastoral staff.

VI. USE OF HOLY WATER

110. It is an old and honored practice for all who enter a church to dip their hand in a font (stoup) of holy water and sign themselves with the sign of the cross as a reminder of their baptism.

111. If holy water is to be offered to the bishop as he enters the church, a senior cleric of the local Church offers it to him, presenting a sprinkler, with which the bishop sprinkles himself and those accompanying him. Then the bishop hands back the sprinkler.

112. All this is omitted if the bishop enters the church already vested, as well as on Sunday whenever the blessing and sprinkling of water replace the penitential rite.

113. The sprinkling of the people with water at the Easter Vigil and at the dedication of a church will be treated in nos. 369 and 892–893 of this *Ceremonial.*

114. Objects being blessed are sprinkled with holy water in keeping with the provisions of the liturgical books.

VII. CARE OF LITURGICAL BOOKS AND WAYS
OF PROCLAIMING VARIOUS LITURGICAL TEXTS

115. The liturgical books are to be treated with care and reverence, since it is from them that the word of God is proclaimed and the prayer of the Church offered. Care must therefore be taken, and especially in liturgical celebrations carried out by a bishop, to have on hand the official liturgical books in an edition that is current and is beautifully printed and bound.

116. In texts that are to be delivered in a clear, audible voice, whether by the bishop or by the ministers or by all, the tone of voice should correspond to the genre of the text, that is, accordingly as it is a reading, a prayer, an instruction, an acclamation, or a song; the tone should also be suited to the form of celebration and to the solemnity of the gathering.

117. Hence, in the rubrics and norms that follow in this *Ceremonial*, the words "say" *(dicere)*, "recite" *(recitare)*, "proclaim" *(proferre)* should be understood of both singing and speaking, in accordance with the principles set out in the respective liturgical books[82] and with the norms given in place in this *Ceremonial*.

118. The phrase "sing or say," which is used frequently in this *Ceremonial*, is to be understood as referring to singing, unless some other consideration rules out singing.

PART IV
CELEBRATIONS OF THE MYSTERY OF THE LORD
THROUGH THE CYCLE OF THE LITURGICAL YEAR

INTRODUCTION

Sunday, the Lord's Day

228. "The Church celebrates the paschal mystery on the first day of the week, known as the Lord's Day or Sunday. This follows a tradition handed down from the apostles and having its origin from the day of Christ's resurrection. Thus Sunday must be ranked as the first holy day of all."

Since Sunday is the nucleus and foundation of the yearly liturgical cycle by which the Church unfolds the entire mystery of Christ, the Sunday celebration gives way only to those solemnities or feasts of the Lord belonging to the General Roman Calendar. By its nature, then, Sunday excludes any other celebrations' being permanently assigned to that day, with these exceptions: the feasts of the Holy Family and the Baptism of the Lord, the solemnities of the Holy Trinity and Christ the King.

The Sundays of Advent, of Lent, and of the Easter season have precedence over all feasts of the Lord and over all solemnities.[2]

CHAPTER 1
ADVENT AND THE CHRISTMAS SEASON

234. Next to the yearly celebration of the paschal mystery, the Church holds most sacred the commemoration of Christ's birth and first manifestations. This is the purpose of the Christmas season.[7]

235. The season of Advent, the preparation for this commemoration, has a twofold character: it is a time to prepare for Christmas, when Christ's First Coming is remembered; it is a time when that remembrance directs the mind and heart to await Christ's Second Coming in the last days. In this way Advent is a period of devout and joyful expectation.[8]

CHAPTER 2
FEAST OF THE PRESENTATION OF THE LORD

241. On this day Christ's faithful people, with candles in their hands, go out to meet the Lord and to acclaim him with Simeon, who recognized Christ as "a light to reveal God to the nations."

They should therefore be taught to walk as children of the light in their entire way of life, because they have a duty to show the light of Christ to all by acting in the works that they do as lighted lamps.

CHAPTER 3
LENT

249. The annual observance of Lent is the special season for the ascent to the holy mountain of Easter.

Through its twofold theme of repentance and baptism, the season of Lent disposes both the catechumens and the faithful to celebrate the paschal mystery. Catechumens are led to the sacraments of initiation by means of the rite of election, the scrutinies, and catechesis. The faithful, listening more intently to the word of God and devoting themselves to prayer, are prepared through a spirit of repentance to renew their baptismal promises.[16]

CHAPTER 4
ASH WEDNESDAY

253. On the Wednesday before the First Sunday of Lent the faithful, by receiving ashes, enter upon the season appointed for spiritual purification. This sign of penance, biblical in origin[20] and preserved among the customs of the Church until our own day, expresses the human condition as affected by sin. In this sign we outwardly profess our guilt before God and thereby, prompted by the hope that the Lord is kind and compassionate, patient and bounding in mercy, express our desire for inward conversion. This sign is also the beginning of the journey of conversion

that will reach its goal in the celebration of the sacrament of reconciliation during the days leading to Easter.

CHAPTER 5
LITURGICAL ASSEMBLIES DURING LENT

260. All the elements of Lenten observance should conspire to manifest more clearly and to promote the life of the local Church. For this reason *The Roman Missal (Sacramentary)* strongly encourages the preservation and development of the traditional form of gathering the local Church after the fashion of the Roman "stations," at least in the larger cities and in a way suited to the particular place. Especially with the chief pastor of the diocese presiding, such assemblies of the faithful can gather on Sunday or on more convenient weekdays, at the tombs of the saints, in the principal churches or shrines of the city, or in other frequently visited places of pilgrimage in the diocese. This may be done on Sundays or weekdays, in parish churches or places of pilgrimage. The manner of celebration will vary according to local needs.[21]

CHAPTER 6
PASSION SUNDAY (PALM SUNDAY)

263. On Passion Sunday (Palm Sunday) the Church enters upon the mystery of its crucified, buried, and risen Lord, who, by his entrance into Jerusalem, gave a glimpse of his own majesty. Christians carry branches as a sign of the royal triumph that Christ won by his acceptance of the cross. Since Saint Paul says: "Provided we suffer with him in order that we may also be glorified with him,"[22] the link between these two aspects of the paschal mystery should stand out clearly in the liturgical celebration and catechesis of Palm Sunday.

CHAPTER 7
CHRISM MASS

274. This Mass, which the bishop concelebrates with his college of presbyters and at which he consecrates the holy chrism and blesses the other oils, manifests the communion of the presbyters with their bishop.[26]

The holy chrism consecrated by the bishop is used to anoint the newly baptized, to seal the candidates for confirmation, and to anoint the hands of presbyters and the heads of bishops at their ordination, as well as in the rites of anointing pertaining to the dedication of churches and altars. The oil of catechumens is used in the preparation of the catechumens for their baptism. The oil of the sick is used to bring comfort and support to the sick in their infirmity.

Presbyters are brought together and concelebrate this Mass as witnesses and cooperators with their bishop in the consecration of the chrism because they share in the sacred office of the bishop in building up, sanctifying, and ruling the people of God.[27] This Mass is therefore a clear expression of the unity of the priesthood and sacrifice of Christ, which continue to be present in the Church.

To show the unity of the college of presbyters, the presbyters who concelebrate with the bishop should come from different parts of the diocese.[28]

Presbyters who take part but for some reason do not celebrate may receive communion under both kinds.

CHAPTER 8
EASTER TRIDUUM

295. "Christ redeemed us all and gave perfect glory to God principally through his paschal mystery: dying he destroyed our death and rising he restored our life. Therefore the Easter Triduum of the Passion and Resurrection of the Lord is the culmination of the entire liturgical year. Thus the solemnity of Easter has the same kind of preeminence in the liturgical year that Sunday has in the week."[40]

Let the paschal fast be kept sacred. Let it be celebrated everywhere on Good Friday and, wherever possible, prolonged throughout Holy Saturday, as a way of coming to the joys of the Sunday of the resurrection with uplifted and welcoming heart.[41]

CHAPTER 9
MASS OF THE LORD'S SUPPER

297. With this Mass, celebrated in the evening of the Thursday in Holy Week, the Church begins the sacred Easter Triduum and devotes itself to the remembrance of the Last Supper. At this supper on the night he was betrayed, the Lord Jesus, loving those who were his own in the world even to the end, offered his body and blood to the father under the appearances of bread and wine, gave them to the apostles to eat and drink, then enjoined the apostles and their successors in the priesthood to offer them in turn.[42]

This Mass is, first of all, the memorial of the institution of the eucharist, that is, of the memorial of the Lord's Passover, by which under sacramental signs he perpetuated among us the sacrifice of the New Law. The Mass of the Lord's Supper is also the memorial of the institution of the priesthood, by which Christ's mission and sacrifice are perpetuated in the world. In addition this Mass is the memorial of that love by which the Lord loved us even to death. The bishop should see to it that all these considerations are suitably presented to the faithful through the ministry of the word so that by their devotion they may be able to deepen their grasp of such great mysteries and reflect them more faithfully in the conduct of their lives.

CHAPTER 10
CELEBRATION OF THE LORD'S PASSION
INTRODUCTION

312. On this day, when "Christ our paschal lamb was sacrificed,"[56] what had long been promised in signs and figures was at last revealed and brought to fulfillment.

The true lamb replaced the symbolic lamb, and the many offerings of the past gave way to the single sacrifice of Christ.[57]

"The wonderful works of God among the people of the Old Testament were a prelude to the work of Christ the Lord. He achieved his task of redeeming humanity and giving perfect glory to God, principally by the paschal mystery of his blessed passion, resurrection from the dead, and glorious ascension, whereby 'dying he destroyed our death and rising he restored our life' (Preface of Easter). For it was from the side of Christ as he slept the sleep of death upon the cross that there came forth the sublime sacrament of the whole Church."[58]

In contemplating the cross of its Lord and Bridegroom, the Church commemorates its own origin and its mission to extend to all peoples the blessed effects of Christ's passion that it celebrates on this day in a spirit of thanksgiving for his marvelous gift.

CHAPTER 11
EASTER VIGIL
INTRODUCTION

332. In accord with ancient tradition, this night is a night of vigil for the Lord,[77] and, as the memorial of the holy night of Christ's resurrection, the Vigil celebrated is "the mother of all holy vigils."[78] The Church this night awaits the Lord's resurrection and celebrates it with the sacrament of Christian initiation.

CHAPTER 12
EASTER SEASON

371. The fifty days from Easter Sunday to Pentecost are celebrated in joyful exultation as one feast day, or better as one "great Sunday."[123]

These above all others are the days for the singing of the *Alleluia*.

On Easter Sunday, wherever it is in force, the custom should be continued of celebrating a "baptismal" evening prayer, that is, a celebration in which the psalms are sung during a procession to the baptismal font.

CHAPTER 13
ORDINARY TIME

377. Apart from those seasons having their own distinctive character, thirty-three or thirty-four weeks remain in the yearly cycle that do not celebrate a particular element of the mystery of Christ. Rather, especially on the Sundays, these weeks are devoted to the mystery of Christ in its entirety. This period is known as Ordinary Time.[128]

378. Ordinary Time begins on Monday after the Sunday following 6 January and continues until Tuesday before Ash Wednesday inclusive. It begins again on

Monday after Pentecost and ends before Evening Prayer I of the First Sunday of Advent.[129]

379. Since Sunday is the first holy day of all, the nucleus and foundation of the liturgical year,[130] the bishop should ensure that, in view of nos. 228–230 of this *Ceremonial*, on the Sundays in Ordinary Time the proper Sunday liturgy is celebrated, even when such Sundays are days to which special themes are assigned.

380. For the pastoral advantage of the people, it is permissible to observe on the Sundays in Ordinary Time those celebrations that fall during the week and have special appeal to the devotion of the faithful, provided these celebrations take precedence over the Sundays in the table of liturgical days. The Mass for such celebrations may be used at all the Masses at which a congregation is present.[131]

CHAPTER 14
ROGATION AND EMBER DAYS

383. It is important that in each diocese, after taking into account local circumstance and customs, the bishop take great care that suitable means are found to preserve the liturgy of the rogation and ember days and to devote the liturgy of these days to the ministry of charity. In this way the devotion of the people of God will be fostered and their perception of the mystery of Christ deepened.

CHAPTER 15
SOLEMNITY OF THE BODY AND BLOOD OF CHRIST
INTRODUCTION

385. The institution of the eucharist has as a special memorial the Mass of the Lord's Supper, when Christ the Lord shared a meal with his disciples and gave them the sacrament of his body and blood to be celebrated in the Church. The solemnity of the Body and Blood of Christ (Corpus Christi) further proposes the cultus of the blessed sacrament to the faithful so that they may celebrate the wonderful works of God, signified by the sacrament and accomplished by the paschal mystery of Christ. This solemnity is also intended to teach the faithful how to share in the eucharistic sacrifice and to have it more profoundly influence their life, to revere the presence of Christ the Lord in this sacrament, and to offer the thanks due for God's gifts.[135]

CHAPTER 16
ALL SOULS

395. The Church offers the eucharistic sacrifice and its own intercession for the dead not only at their funerals and anniversaries but also in the yearly remembrance of all the sons and daughters of the Church who sleep in Christ. The Church seeks to help the faithful departed by earnest prayer to God for their entry into the communion of the saints in heaven. In this way, because of the

communion of all Christ's members with one another, the Church obtains spiritual help for the dead and brings the consolation of hope to the living.[141]

PART V
SACRAMENTS

CHAPTER 3
SACRAMENT OF MARRIAGE

INTRODUCTION

598. Mindful of Christ the Lord's attendance at the wedding feast of Cana, the bishop should make it his concern to bless occasionally the marriages of his people, and particularly those of the poor.

To prevent his participation from bearing the mark of favoritism[147] or from being a mere sign of outward show, it should be the bishop's normal practice not to assist at marriages in a private chapel or home but in the cathedral or parish church. In this way the ecclesial character of the celebration of the sacrament will more surely stand out and the local community will have the opportunity to participate in the celebration.

599. For the celebration of marriage, in addition to the usual requisites for the nuptial blessing imparted by a presbyter, a miter and pastoral staff should be made ready.

600. The bishop should be assisted by at least one presbyter, who as a rule will be the parish priest (pastor), and at least one deacon, along with several ministers.

I. CELEBRATION OF MARRIAGE WITHIN MASS

601. If the bishop himself celebrates the Mass, he wears Mass vestments and uses the miter and pastoral staff. If a presbyter concelebrates, he also wears Mass vestments.

If the bishop presides at the Mass but does not celebrate, he wears an alb, pectoral cross, stole, and white cope, and uses the miter and pastoral staff.

A deacon wears the vestments of his order. The other ministers wear an alb or other lawfully approved vesture.

In addition to the requisites for the celebration of Mass, the following should be provided:

a. *Rite of Marriage*

b. vessel of holy water with sprinkler;

c. rings for the bridegroom and bride;

d. cup large enough for communion under both kinds.

602. At the appointed time the parish priest (pastor) or other presbyter, vested with a stole over a cassock and surplice or over an alb, or if he is to celebrate, vested for Mass, goes with the ministers to receive the bride and bridegroom at the door of the church or, if more suitable, at the altar. He greets them, then leads them to their places.[148]

Then the bishop goes to the altar and reverences it. The bride and bridegroom are presented to him by the parish priest (pastor) or another presbyter. Meanwhile, the entrance song is sung.

603. On days when ritual Masses are permitted[149] one of the wedding Masses (ROMM, Ritual Masses, IV. Wedding Mass, 1. For the Celebration of Marriage) may be celebrated, with its proper readings. The vestments for the Mass are white or of some other festive color.

On the days listed in nos. 1–4 of the table of liturgical days, the Mass of the day is celebrated, with the nuptial blessing included and, as circumstances suggest, the proper solemn blessing.

But if the Mass in which the sacrament of marriage is celebrated is a regular parish Mass, the Mass of the day is celebrated, even on the Sundays of the Christmas season and of Ordinary Time.

When the ritual Mass is not celebrated, one of the readings may be chosen from those provided for this ritual Mass in the *Lectionary for Mass*, except on those days listed in nos. 1–4 of the table of liturgical days.[150]

604. When a marriage is celebrated during Advent or Lent or on other days of penance, the parish priest (pastor) should advise the couple to take into consideration the special nature of these liturgical seasons.[151]

605. The introductory rites and the liturgy of the word take place in the usual way.

606. After the gospel reading, the bishop, seated and with miter and pastoral staff (unless he decides otherwise), gives the homily, drawn from the sacred text. He speaks about the mystery of Christian marriage, the dignity of wedded love, the grace of the sacrament, and the responsibilities of married people.[152]

607. After the homily, the bishop, with miter and pastoral staff, stands before the bride and bridegroom and questions them about their freedom, faithfulness to each other, and the acceptance and upbringing of children. He then invites the couple to declare their consent.[153]

608. Putting aside the pastoral staff (and also the miter if he uses the alternative, deprecatory formulary of blessing), the bishop blesses the rings and, as circumstances suggest, sprinkles them with holy water and hands them to the bridegroom and bride, who place them on each other's ring finger.[154]

609. When called for by the rubrics, the profession of faith is said; the general intercessions take place in the usual way.

610. In Eucharistic Prayer I there is a commemoration of the bride and bridegroom, in the formulary provided in *The Roman Missal (Sacramentary)* among the Ritual Masses (IV. Wedding Mass).

611. After the Lord's Prayer, the embolism Deliver us, Lord is omitted. The bishop, if he is celebrant of the eucharist, otherwise the presbyter who is the celebrant, faces the bride and bridegroom and, with hands joined, invites the assembly to pray: My dear friends, let us turn to the Lord. All pray silently for a short while. Then, with hands outstretched, the bishop pronounces the prayer of blessing, Father, by your power (or one of the other prayers of blessing provided in the *Rite of Marriage*).[155]

612. The married couple, their parents, witnesses, and relatives may receive communion under both kinds.[156]

613. In place of the usual blessing of the people at the end of Mass, the bishop uses one of the blessing formularies provided in the *Rite of Marriage* for this Mass.[157]

With miter and with hands outstretched, the bishop greets the people, saying, The Lord be with you. One of the deacons may then give the invitation before the blessing. With hands outstretched over the people, the bishop says the blessing invocations. Taking the pastoral staff, he then pronounces the blessing, as he makes the sign of the cross three times over the people.

The bishop may also impart the blessing by using one of the formularies given in nos. 1120–1121 of this *Ceremonial*.

II. CELEBRATION OF MARRIAGE OUTSIDE MASS

614. The bishop is vested in the way indicated in no. 176 for a Mass at which he presides but does not celebrate. The presbyter assisting him wears a stole over a cassock and surplice or over an alb; the deacon wears the vestments of his order.

615. The bride and bridegroom and the bishop enter the church in the way already indicated in no. 602, while the entrance song is being sung.

616. After the singing, the bishop greets all present and says the opening prayer from *The Roman Missal (Sacramentary)* among the Ritual Masses (IV. Wedding Mass) or the *Rite of Marriage.* The liturgy of the word follows in the same way as at Mass.

617. The questions about freedom of choice, the expression of consent, and the exchange of rings take place in the manner already indicated in nos. 607–608.

618. The intercessions follow. Then, omitting the prayer that concludes the intercessions, the bishop, with hands outstretched, blesses the bride and bridegroom. He uses the text provided in the *Rite of Marriage* for this blessing within Mass.[158]

The Lord's Prayer is then recited.

619. If communion is to be given within this rite, the deacon takes the ciborium or pyx with the body of the Lord, places it on the altar, and, with the bishop, genuflects. Then the bishop introduces the Lord's Prayer, which all recite together.

Then the bishop genuflects. Taking the host, he raises it slightly over the ciborium or pyx and, facing those who will receive communion, says, This is the Lamb of God.

Communion is distributed as at Mass.

After communion, a period of silence may be observed, or a psalm or song of praise may be sung. Then the prayer Lord, we who have shared the food at your table, provided in the *Rite of Marriage*, or some other suitable prayer is said.[159]

620. The bishop then gives the final blessing in the manner already indicated in no. 613. The deacon says the dismissal formula, Go in peace, and all reply, Thanks be to God, and leave.

PART VI
SACRAMENTALS

CHAPTER 16
BLESSING OF A NEW CROSS FOR PUBLIC VENERATION

INTRODUCTION

1011. Of all sacred images, the "figure of the precious, life-giving cross of Christ"[334] is preeminent, because it is the symbol of the entire paschal mystery. The cross is the image most cherished by the Christian people and the most ancient; it represents Christ's suffering and victory, and at the same time, as the Fathers of the Church have taught, it points to his Second Coming.

1012. The blessing of a new cross may be celebrated at any hour and on any day except Ash Wednesday, the Easter Triduum, and All Souls. But the preferred day is one that permits a large attendance of the faithful; they should receive proper preparation for their active participation in the rite.[335]

1013. The order presented in this chapter is meant for only two situations:

a. the solemn blessing of a cross erected in a public place, separate from a church;

b. the blessing of the principal cross that occupies a central place in the body of the church where the worshiping community assembles; in this case the rite of blessing begins at the point described here in no. 1020.

1014.The following should be prepared for the rite:

a. *Book of Blessings, Lectionary for Mass;*

b. censer and incense boat with spoon;

c. candlesticks for the acolytes;

The vestments for the celebration of the rite are white or some other festive color:

— for the bishop: alb, pectoral cross, stole, cope, miter, pastoral staff;

— for deacons: albs, stoles, and, as circumstances suggest, dalmatics;

— for other ministers: albs or other lawfully approved vesture.

DESCRIPTION OF THE RITE

1015. When feasible, it is preferable for the community of the faithful to go in procession from the church or another location to the site where the cross that is to be blessed has been erected. When a procession either is not feasible or seems inadvisable, the faithful simply assemble at the site of the cross.[336]

When the people have gathered, the bishop, vested in alb, pectoral cross, stole, and cope, and with miter and pastoral staff, goes to them, accompanied by the ministers. Putting aside miter and pastoral staff, he greets the faithful in the words The grace of Jesus Christ or other suitable words. The people reply, And also with you, or make some other suitable reply.

1016. Then, using if he so chooses the words provided in the *Book of Blessings*, the bishop briefly addresses the faithful, in order to prepare them for the celebration and to explain the meaning of the rite.

After his introductory remarks, the bishop invites all to pray. After a period of silent prayer, the bishop, with hands outstretched, says the opening prayer, Lord, your Son reconciled us to you.[337]

1017. After the opening prayer, the bishop again takes the miter and pastoral staff, and the deacon may say, Let us proceed in peace. The procession to the site of the cross is then formed. During the procession Psalm 98 (97), with the antiphon "We should glory in the cross," or some other suitable song is sung.[338]

When there is no procession, the opening prayer is followed immediately by the reading of the word of God.

1018. After the opening prayer, the bishop puts on the miter and sits for the proclamation of the word of God. There may be one or two readings, each followed by a responsorial psalm related to it. The texts may be taken from those given in the *Lectionary for Mass* (Votive Masses, Holy Cross).[339]

1019. The bishop then gives the homily, in which he explains both the biblical texts and the power of the cross of Christ.

1020. After the homily, the bishop, putting aside the miter and standing before the cross, blesses it, saying the prayer Blessed are you, Lord God or the pray Lord God, Father all-holy.

After the prayer, he puts incense into the censer, stands before the cross, and incenses it, as all sing the antiphon We worship you, or the antiphon "Through the sign of the cross," or some other suitable song in honor of the cross.[340]

1021. After the incensation,* the bishop, the ministers, and the faithful venerate the new cross, if this can be done conveniently. One by one in procession all go to the cross and kneel before it or kiss it or offer some other sign of reverence in keeping with local custom.†

   But if this procedure is impossible because of the large number in attendance or for some other good reason, the bishop speaks a few words, inviting the people to venerate the cross either by observing an interval of silent prayer or by some appropriate acclamation.[341]

1022. The veneration of the cross is followed by intercessions, either in the form usual at Mass or in the form provided in the *Book of Blessings.* The intercessions are concluded by the Lord's Prayer, sung or recited by all, and the prayer of the bishop.

   Then, taking the miter and pastoral staff, the bishop blesses the people in the usual way, and the deacon assisting him dismisses them, saying, Go in peace, and all reply, Thanks be to God. Then a song in honor of the cross of Christ may be sung.[342]

PART VIII
LITURGICAL CELEBRATIONS IN CONNECTION WITH OFFICIAL ACTS PERTAINING TO THE GOVERNMENT OF A DIOCESE

CHAPTER 2
PASTORAL VISITATION

1177. The bishop in fulfilling the obligation to visit the parishes or local communities of his diocese should not appear to be satisfying a purely administrative duty. Rather the faithful should see in him the herald of the Gospel, the teacher, shepherd, and high priest of his flock.

1178. To ensure this happening, the visitation of the bishop should take place, if at all possible, on days that permit large numbers of the faithful to gather. Sufficient time should also be devoted to an apt, preparatory catechesis of the people by their presbyters. The visitation itself should be sufficiently long to enable the bishop to preside at celebrations of the liturgy and to evaluate, promote, encourage, and put into effect the apostolate of the clergy and laity and the works of charity.

1179. The bishop, in the vestments indicated in no. 63, should be received in a manner suited to the circumstances of the place and the situation. If this seems appropriate, the bishop may be solemnly received and greeted by the clergy at the door of the church. But the bishop may even be escorted to the church with festive song, when this is feasible and appropriate. A dignified solemnity in receiving the bishop is a sign of the love and devotion of the faithful toward their good shepherd.

1180. At the entrance of the church the parish priest (pastor), vested in cope, meets the bishop, offers him the crucifix to be kissed, and presents the sprinkler, with which the bishop sprinkles himself and those present. After a brief, silent prayer before the blessed sacrament, the bishop goes to the sanctuary (chancel); there the parish priest (pastor), standing before the altar, invites the faithful to join in prayer for the bishop and, after a brief pause for silent prayer, says the prayer God, eternal shepherd or God, our Father, our shepherd and guide, provided in *The Roman Missal (Sacramentary).*[2]

The bishop then greets the people and announces his agenda for the visitation. He then says the collect for the titular of the church or the patron of the place, and, in the usual way, blesses the people. Then the parish priest (pastor) dismisses them.

1181. But when Mass is to follow the reception of the bishop, immediately after the prayer for the bishop has been said, the bishop, at the chair, puts on the vestments for Mass. The presbyters charged with the pastoral care of the parish or presbyters living within the parish confines concelebrate the Mass with the bishop, and the faithful take an active part. Such participation is particularly to be sought in the more remote parts of the diocese where the people rarely or never have the opportunity to take part in a stational Mass celebrated by the bishop in their own area.

1182. It is recommended that during the pastoral visitation the bishop confer not only the sacrament of confirmation but other sacraments as well, particularly in his visits to the sick. In this way he will more clearly appear to the faithful as the chief steward of the mysteries of God and as the overseer and guardian of the entire liturgical life in the Church entrusted to his care.

1183. When there is a lengthy visitation, there should be a celebration of the liturgy of the hours in the church or a celebration of the word of God, with the homily by the bishop and with intercessions for the universal Church and for the local Church.

1184. As circumstance suggest, the bishop should also go to the cemetery with the people and there offer prayers for the dead and sprinkle the graves with holy water, in the manner described already in nos. 399–402.

NOTES

PART I

1. Vatican Council II, Decree on the Pastoral Office of Bishops *Christus Dominus* (hereafter, CD), no. 11: ICEL, *Documents on the Liturgy, 1963–1979: Conciliar, Papal, and Curial Texts* (hereafter, DOL; The Liturgical Press, Collegeville, Minn., 1982), 7, no. 191. See Vatican Council II, Dogmatic Constitution on the Church *Lumen Gentium* (hereafter, LG), no. 23.

2. See LG, no. 26; DOL 4, no. 146.

3. Ignatius of Antioch, *Ad Smyrnaeos*, 8, 2: Funk, ed., *Patres apostolici*, v. 1, p. 283.

4. LG, no. 26: DOL 4, no. 146.

5. See LG, no. 26: DOL 4, no. 146.

6. See LG, nos. 26, 28: DOL 4, nos. 146, 148. See Vatican Council II, Constitution on the Liturgy *Sacrosanctum Concilium* (hereafter, SC), art. 41: DOL 1, no. 41.

7. See LG, no. 23.

8. LG, no. 13.

9. See LG, nos. 26, 27: DOL 4, nos. 146–147. See CD, no. 3.

10. CD, no. 2.

11. See CD, no. 12: DOL 7, no. 192.

12. See LG, no. 26: DOL 4, no. 146. See CD, no. 15: DOL 7, no. 194.

13. See LG, no. 21: DOL 4, no. 145.

14. SC, art. 41: DOL 1, no. 41.

15. Prayer of consecration of a bishop in the Byzantine rite: *Euchologion to mega* (Rome, 1873), 139; LG, no. 26: DOL 4, no. 146.

16. See CD, no. 15: DOL 7, no. 194.

17. LG, no. 26: DOL 4, no. 146.

18. See LG, no. 21: DOL 4, no. 145. See CD, no. 3.

19. LG, no. 27.

20. SC, art. 41: DOL 1, no. 41.

21. See LG, no. 25.

22. SC, art. 35, 2: DOL 1, no. 35.

23. LG, no. 25: DOL 4, no. 146.

24. See Sacred Congregation of Rites (hereafter, SC Rites), Instruction *Pontificales ritus*, on the simplification of pontifical rites and insignia, 21 June 1968 (hereafter, PR), no. 24: AAS 60 (1968), p. 410; DOL 550, no. 4481.

25. See SC, art. 28: DOL 1, no. 28.

26. See SC, art. 26: DOL 1, no. 26.

27. See LG, no. 28: DOL 4, no 148.

28. See SC, art. 28: DOL 1, no. 28.

29. See Acts 6:3.

30. See John 13:35.

31. See Matthew 20:28.

32. See Luke 22:27.

33. See the General Instruction of the Roman Missal, 4th ed., 1975 (hereafter, GIRM), nos. 71, 127: DOL 208, nos. 1461, 1517.

34. See GIRM, no. 71: DOL 208, no. 1461.

35. See Paul VI, Motu Proprio *Ministeria quaedam*, on first tonsure, minor orders, and the subdiaconate, 15 August 1972 (hereafter, MQ), no. VI: AAS 64 (1972), p. 532; DOL 340, no. 2931.

36. GIRM, no. 66: DOL 208, no. 1456.

37. See MQ, no. V: AAS 64 (1972), p. 532; DOL 340, no. 2931. See The Roman Missal, *Lectionary for Mass*, 2nd English ed., 1981 (hereafter, LM), Introduction, nos. 51–55. See General Instruction of the Liturgy of the Hours (hereafter, GILH), no. 259: DOL 426, no. 3689.

38. See LM, Introduction, nos. 19–20, 56.

39. SC, art. 123: DOL 1, no. 123.

40. See GIRM, particularly nos. 12, 19, 22, 63, 64, 272, 274, 275, 313, 324: DOL 208, nos. 1402, 1409, 1412, 1453, 1454, 1662, 1664, 1665, 1703, 1714. See *Ordo cantus Missae*, Introduction: DOL 505, nos. 4276–4302; GILH, nos. 268–284: DOL 426, nos. 3698–3714. See The Roman Ritual, the *Rite of Baptism for Children, Christian Initiation*, General Introduction, no. 33: DOL 294, no. 2282. See The Roman Ritual,

Holy Communion and Worship of the
Eucharist outside Mass, nos. 12 and 104:
DOL 279, nos. 2204 and 2222. See The
Roman Ritual, *Rite of Penance*, nos. 24
and 36: DOL 368, nos. 3089 and 3101. See
The Roman Ritual, *Pastoral Care of the
Sick: Rites of Anointing and Viaticum*,
nos. 38, d: DOL 411, no. 3358. See The
Roman Ritual, *Order of Christian
Funerals*, no. 12: DOL 416, no. 3384 (see
English ed., nos. 30–33). See SC Rites,
Instruction *Musicam sacrum*, 5 March
1967 (hereafter, MS): AAS 69 (1967), pp.
300–320; DOL 508, nos. 4122–4190. See
Sacred Congregation for Bishops, Direc-
tory on the Pastoral Ministry of Bishops
(1970), no. 90, d: DOL 329, no. 2660.

41. See MS, no. 66: AAS 69 (1967), p. 319; DOL
508, no. 4187.

42. Paul VI, Apostolic Constitution *Mirificus
eventus*, declaring the jubilee of 1966, 7
December 1965: AAS 57 (1965), pp. 948–
949; DOL 484, no. 4054.

43. See GIRM, nos. 253–312: DOL 208, nos.
1643–1702. See LM, Introduction, nos. 32–
34. See The Roman Pontifical, *Dedication
of a Church and an Altar*, ch. 2, no. 3, and
ch. 4, nos. 6–11: DOL 547, no. 4371 and
nos. 4403–4408. See The Roman Ritual,
*Holy Communion and Worship of the
Eucharist outside Mass*, General Introduction, nos. 9–11: DOL 279, nos. 2201–2203.

44. See *Codex Iuris Canonici (Code of Canon
Law)*, 1983 (hereafter, CIC), can. 463, §3.
See in this *Ceremonial*, nos. 1171 and
1176.

45. See PR, nos. 10–13: AAS 60 (1968), pp. 408–
409; DOL 550, nos. 4467–4470.

46. See GIRM, no. 262: DOL 208, no. 1652.

47. See GIRM, no. 262: DOL 208, no. 1652.

48. See SC Rites, Instruction *Eucharisticum
mysterium*, on worship of the eucharist,
25 May 1967, no. 53: AAS 59 (1967), p. 568;
DOL 179, no. 1282. See The Roman Ritual,
*Holy Communion and Worship of the
Eucharist outside Mass*, General Introduction, no. 9: DOL 279, no. 2201.

49. See in this *Ceremonial*, nos. 65–67. See
LM, Introduction, no. 54.

50. See GIRM, no. 272: DOL 208, no. 1662. See
LM, Introduction, nos. 32–34.

51. See The Roman Ritual, *Rite of Baptism
for Children, Christian Initiation*, General
Introduction, no. 25: DOL 294, no. 2274.

52. See SC, art. 34: DOL 1, no. 34.

53. See LG, no. 21: DOL 4, no. 145. See SC, art.
41: DOL 1, no. 41.

54. Romans 12:10.

60. See GIRM, no. 298: DOL 208, no. 1688.

61. See GIRM, nos. 299, 302, 303: DOL 208,
nos. 1689, 1692, 1693.

62. See nos. 1207–1209 of this *Ceremonial*.

63. See GIRM, nos. 300, 81, b, 302: DOL 208,
nos. 1690, 1471, 1692.

64. See GIRM, no. 234: DOL 208, no. 1624.

65. See GIRM, nos. 208 and 232: DOL 208, nos.
1598 and 1622.

66. See GIRM, nos. 93–95, 131: DOL 208, nos.
1483–1485, 1521. The Roman manner for
the censer-bearer to walk in procession is
that "he walks with hands somewhat
raised, he should hold the censer with the
right hand, with his thumb in the ring at
the top, and the middle finger holding the
chain, so that the cover of the censer is
somewhat raised; he holds the boat containing incense and spoon with his left
hand." (*Caeremoniale Episcoporum*, ed.
1886, I, XI, 7).

67. See GIRM, nos. 94, 131: DOL 208, nos. 1484,
1521. According to Roman practice acolytes "hold the candlesticks with their
right hand, so that the acolyte walking
on the right puts his left hand at the base of
the candlestick and his right at the middle
knob of the candlestick; the acolyte walking on the left puts his right hand at the
base and his left at the middle knob of the
candlestick" (*Caeremoniale Episcoporum*,
ed 1886, I, XI, 8).

68. See GIRM, nos. 131, 232: DOL 208, nos.
1521, 1622.

69. See GILH, no 266, b: DOL 426, no. 3696.

70. See PR, no. 25: AAS 60 (1968), p. 411; DOL
550, no. 4482.

71. See GIRM, no. 235: DOL 208, no. 1625.

72. Two acolytes may go to the bishop with
the censer and boat or one acolyte carrying both, the censer with burning charcoal
in the left hand and the boat with the
incense and spoon in the right (see *Caeremoniale Episcoporum*, ed. 1886, I, XIII, 1).

73. See GIRM, no. 236: DOL 208, no. 1626. "From the acolyte the deacon takes the boat, half-opened and with the spoon resting in it, and offers the boat to the bishop. The bishop takes the spoon and with it three times scoops out incense, and three times puts the incense into the censer. After doing so, and having returned the spoon to the minister, the bishop with his right hand makes the sign of the cross over the incense that has been deposited in the censer" (see *Caeremoniale Episcoporum*, ed. 1886, I, XXII, 1–2).

74. The deacon "returns the boat to the acolyte and from him takes the censer, which he presents to the bishop, placing the top of the censer chain in the bishop's left hand and the censer itself in the bishop's right hand." (*Caeremoniale Episcoporum*, ed. 1886, I, IX, 1).

75. The one incensing "holds the top of the censer chain in the left hand, the bottom near the censer in the right hand, so that the censer can be swung back and forth easily." "The one incensing should take care to carry out this function with grave and graceful mien, not moving head or body while swinging the censer, holding the left hand with the top of the chains near the chest and moving the right arm back and forth with a measured beat" (See *Caeremoniale Episcoporum*, ed. 1886, I, XXIII, 4 and 8).

76. See GIRM, no. 236: DOL 208, no. 1626.

77. See Exodus 9:29; Psalm 28 (27):2, 63 (62):5, 134 (133):2; Isaiah 1:15.

78. Tertullian, *De oratione*, 14: 1983 CIC 1, 265; PL 1, 1273.

79. See GIRM, nos. 174, a and c, 180, a and c, 184, a and c, 188, a and c: DOL 208, nos. 1564, 1570, 1574, 1578. At the epiclesis preceding the consecration the hands are to be outstretched toward and above the offerings (see *Missale Romanum*, ed. 1962, *Ritus servandus in celebratione Missae*, VIII, 4). At the consecration the palm of the right hand is held sideward (see *Notitiae*, 1, 1965, p. 143: DOL 223, no. 1810, note R8).

80. "Hands joined" means: "Holding the palms sideward and together before the breast, with the right thumb crossed over the left" (*Caeremoniale Episcoporum*, ed. 1886, I, XIX, 1).

81. "When making the sign of the cross, he holds the palm of the right hand turned toward himself, with all the fingers joined and held straight, and makes the sign of the cross by moving this hand from head to chest and from left shoulder to right. If he blesses others or some object, he points the little finger at the person or thing to be blessed and in blessing extends the whole right hand with all the fingers joined and fully extended" (*Missale Romanum*, ed. 1962, *Ritus servandus in celebratione Missae*, III, 5).

82. See, for example, GIRM, nos. 18–19: DOL 208, nos. 1408–1409. See GILH, nos. 267–284: DOL 426, nos. 3697–3714. See MS, nos. 5–12: AAS 59 (1967), pp. 301–303; DOL 508, nos. 4126–4133. See Sacred Congregation for Divine Worship (hereafter, SC Worship), Circular Letter *Eucharistiae participationem*, on the eucharistic prayers, 27 April 1973, no. 17: AAS 65 (1973), pp. 346–347; DOL 248, no. 1991.

PART IV

2. See SC Rites, General Norms for the Liturgical Year and the Calendar, 21 March 1969 (hereafter, GNLYC), nos. 4–6: DOL 442, nos. 3770–3772.

7. Seen GNLYC, no. 32: DOL 442, no. 3798.

8. See GNLYC, nos. 32, 39: DOL 442, nos. 3798, 3805.

16. See SC, art. 109: DOL 1, no. 109. See GNLYC, no. 27: DOL 442, no. 3793.

20. See 2 Samuel 13:19; Esther 4:1; Job 42:6; 1 Maccabees 3:47, 4:39; Lamentations 2:10.

21. See RomM, Proper of Seasons, the rubric printed at the beginning of the Lenten season.

22. Romans 8:17.

26. See GIRM, no 157: DOL 208, no. 1547. See RomM, Proper of Seasons, Holy Thursday, rubrics preceding the text of the Chrism Mass.

27. See Vatican Council II, Decree on the Ministry and Life of Priests *Presbyterorum Ordinis*, no. 2: DOL 18, no. 257.

28. See RomM, Proper of Seasons, Holy Thursday, rubrics preceding text of the Chrism Mass.

40. GNLYC, no. 18: DOL 442, no. 3784.

41. See SC, art. 110: DOL 1, no. 110.

42. See Council of Trent, sess. 22, 17 Sept. 1562, Doctr. *De ss. Missae sacrificio*, ch. 1: *Concilium Tridentinum, Diariorum, Actorum, Epistolarum, Tractatuum nova collectio*, ed. Görres Gesellschaft, vol. 8, *Actorum*, part 5 (Freiburg, Br., 1919), p. 960.

56. 1 Corinthians 5:7.

57. See Leo the Great, *Sermo* 58, *De Passione Domini* 1: PL 54, 332.

58. SC, art. 6: DOL 1, no. 5.

77. See Exodus 12:42.

78. See Augustine, *Sermo* 219: PL 38, 1088.

123. Anthanasius, *Epist. festal.*, 1: PG 26, 1366. See GNLYC, no. 22: DOL 442, no. 3788.

128. See GNLYC, no. 43: DOL 442, no. 3809.

129. See GNLYC, no. 44: DOL 442, no. 3810.

130. See SC, art. 106: DOL 1, no. 106. See GNLYC, no. 4: DOL 442, no. 3770.

131. See GNLYC, no. 58: DOL 442, no. 3809. See the Table of Liturgical Days in Appendix II of this *Ceremonial* (also in DOL 442, no. 3825).

135. See GIRM, no. 3: DOL 208, no. 1378.

141. See The Roman Ritual, *Rite of Funerals* (hereafter, RF), no. 1: DOL 416, no. 3373. In the English edition of 1985, The Roman Ritual, *Order of Christian Funerals* (hereafter, OCF), nos. 1–13.

PART V

147. See SC, art. 32: DOL 1, no. 32.

148. See The Roman Ritual, *Rite of Marriage*, English ed., 1969 (hereafter, RMar), no. 19.

149. See Appendix III of this *Ceremonial*.

150. See Appendix II of this *Ceremonial*; LM, nos. 801–805 (Ritual Masses, IV. Wedding Mass).

151. See RMar, Introduction, no. 11: DOL 349, no. 2979.

152. See RMar, no. 22.

153. See RMar, nos. 24–26.

154. See RMar, nos. 27–28.

155. See RMar, no. 33.

156. See RMar, no. 36

157. See RMar, nos. 125–127.

158. See RMar, nos. 33, 120–121.

159. See RMar, no. 123; HCWE, nos. 50 and 210–222.

PART VI

334. See Council of Nicaea II, Act. 7: Mansi 13, 378; Denzinger-Schönmetzer, *Enchiridion symbolorum, definitionum et declarationum de rebus fidei et morum*, ed. XXXIV, no. 601.

335. See The Roman Ritual, *Book of Blessings*, ch. 28, Order for the Blessing of a New Cross for Public Veneration (hereafter, OBNC), no. 964.

336. See OBNC, no. 966.

337. See OBNC, nos. 967–968.

338. See OBNC, no. 971.

339. See LM, nos. 969–975 (Votive Masses, Holy Cross); OBNC, nos. 973–975.

340. See OBNC, nos. 977–979.

* OBNC, no. 980, begins *Cantu expleto* ("After the singing"), not *Thurificatione completa* ("After the incensation").

† The rubrics for OBNC do not mention kneeling of kissing.

341. See OBNC, no. 980.

342. See OBNC, nos. 981–983.

PART VIII

2. See RomM, Masses and Prayers for Various Needs and Occasions, 1. For the Church, 3. For the Bishop, A.

MUSIC
IN
CATHOLIC WORSHIP

BISHOPS' COMMITTEE ON THE LITURGY

NATIONAL CONFERENCE OF CATHOLIC BISHOPS
15 NOVEMBER 1982

OUTLINE

MUSIC IN CATHOLIC WORSHIP

THE THEOLOGY OF CELEBRATION

1.   We are Christians because through the Christian community we have met Jesus Christ, heard his word in invitation, and responded to him in faith. We gather at Mass that we may hear and express our faith again in this assembly and, by expressing it, renew and deepen it.

2.   We do not come to meet Christ as if he were absent from the rest of our lives. We come together to deepen our awareness of, and commitment to, the action of his Spirit in the whole of our lives at every moment. We come together to acknowledge the love of God poured out among us in the work of the Spirit, to stand in awe and praise.

3.   We are celebrating when we involve ourselves meaningfully in the thoughts, words, songs, and gestures of the worshiping community—when everything we do is wholehearted and authentic for us—when we mean the words and want to do what is done.

4.   People in love make signs of love, not only to express their love but also to deepen it. Love never expressed dies. Christians' love for Christ and for one another and Christians' faith in Christ and in one another must be expressed in the signs and symbols of celebration or they will die.

5.   Celebrations need not fail, even on a particular Sunday when our feelings do not match the invitation of Christ and his Church to worship. Faith does not always permeate our feelings. But the signs and symbols of worship can give bodily expression to faith as we celebrate. Our own faith is stimulated. We become one with others whose faith is similarly expressed. We rise above our own feelings to respond to God in prayer.

6.   Faith grows when it is well expressed in celebration. Good celebrations foster and nourish faith. Poor celebrations may weaken and destroy it.

7.   To celebrate the liturgy means to do the action or perform the sign in such a way that its full meaning and impact shine forth in clear and compelling fashion. Since liturgical signs are vehicles of communication and instruments of faith, they must be simple and comprehensible. Since they are directed to fellow human beings, they must be humanly attractive. They must be meaningful and appealing to the body of worshipers or they will fail to stir up faith and people will fail to worship the Father.

8.   The signs of celebration should be short, clear, and unencumbered by useless repetition; they should be "within the people's powers of comprehension, and normally should not require much explanation."[1]

If the signs need explanation to communicate faith, they will often be watched instead of celebrated.

9.   In true celebration each sign or sacramental action will be invested with the personal and prayerful faith, care, attention, and enthusiasm of those who carry it out.

PASTORAL PLANNING FOR CELEBRATION

10.   The responsibility for effective pastoral celebration in a parish community falls upon all those who exercise major roles in the liturgy. "The practical preparation for each liturgical celebration should be done in a spirit of cooperation by all parties concerned, under the guidance of the rector of the church, whether it be ritual, pastoral, or musical matters."[2] In practice this ordinarily means an organized "planning team" or committee which meets regularly to achieve creative and coordinated worship and a good use of the liturgical and musical options of a flexible liturgy.

11.   The power of a liturgical celebration to share faith will frequently depend upon its unity—a unity drawn from the liturgical feast or season or from the readings appointed in the lectionary as well artistic unity flowing from the skillful and sensitive selection of options, music, and related arts. The sacred scriptures ought to be the source and inspiration of sound planning for it is of the very nature of celebration that people hear the saving words and works of the Lord and then respond in meaningful signs and symbols. Where the readings of the lectionary possess a thematic unity, the other elements ought to be so arranged as to constitute a setting for and response to the message of the Word.

12.   The planning team or committee is headed by the priest (celebrant and homilist) for no congregation can experience the richness of a unified celebration if that unity is not grasped by the one who presides, as well as by those who have special roles. The planning group should include those with the knowledge and artistic skills needed in celebration: men and women trained in music, poetry, and art, and familiar with current resources in these areas; men and women sensitive also to the present day thirst of so many for the riches of scripture, theology, and prayer. It is always good to include some members of the congregation who have not taken special roles in the celebrations so that honest evaluations can be made.

13.   The planning should go beyond the choosing of options, songs, and ministers to the composition of such texts as the brief introduction, general intercessions, and other appropriate comments as provided for in the *General Instruction of the Roman Missal.* How people are invited to join in a particular song may be as important as the choice of the song itself.

14.   In planning pastoral celebrations the congregation, the occasion, and the celebrant must be taken into consideration.

THE CONGREGATION

15.   "The pastoral effectiveness of a celebration will be heightened if the texts of readings, prayers, and songs correspond as closely as possible to the needs, religious dispositions, and aptitude of the participants."[3] A type of celebration suitable for a youth group may not fit in a retirement home; a more formal style effective in a parish church may be inappropriate in a home liturgy. The music used should be within the competence of most of the worshipers. It should suit their age-level, cultural background, and level of faith.

16.   Variations in level of faith raise special problems. Liturgical celebration presupposes a minimum of biblical knowledge and a deep commitment of living faith. If these are lacking, there might arise the tendency to use the liturgy as a tool of evangelization. Greater liberty in the choice of music and style of celebration may be required as the participants are led toward that day when they can share their growing faith as members of the Christian community. Songs like the psalms may create rather than solve problems where faith is weak. Music, chosen with care, can serve as a bridge to faith as well as an expression of it.

17.   The diversity of people present at a parish liturgy gives rise to a further problem. Can the same parish liturgy be an authentic expression for a grade-school girl, her college-age brother, their married sister with her young family, their parents and grandparents? Can it satisfy the theologically and musically educated along with those lacking in training? Can it please those who seek a more informal style of celebration? The planning team must consider the general makeup of the total community. Each Christian must keep in mind that to live and worship in community often demands a personal sacrifice. All must be willing to share likes and dislikes with others whose ideas and experiences may be quite unlike their own.

18.   Often the problem of diversity can be mitigated by supplementing the parish Sunday celebration with special celebrations for smaller homogeneous groups. "The needs of the faithful of a particular cultural background or of a particular age level may often be met by a music that can serve as a congenial, liturgically oriented expression of prayer."[4] The music and other options may then be more easily suited to the particular group celebrating. Celebration in such groups, "in which the genuine sense of community is more readily experienced, can contribute significantly to growth in awareness of the parish as community, especially when all the faithful participate in the parish Mass on the Lord's day."[5] Nevertheless, it would be out of harmony with the Lord's wish for unity in his Church if believers were to worship only in such homogeneous groupings.[6]

THE OCCASION

19.   The same congregation will want to celebrate in a variety of ways. During the course of the year the different mysteries of redemption are recalled in the

Mass so that in some way they are made present.[7] Each feast and season has its own spirit and its own music. The penitential occasions demand more restraint. The great feasts demand more solemnity. Solemnity, however, depends less on the ornateness of song and magnificence of ceremonial than on worthy and religious celebration.[8]

20.   Generally a congregation or choir will want to sing more on the great feasts like Christmas and Easter and less in the season through the year. Important events in family and parish life will suggest fuller programs of song. Sundays will be celebrated with variety but always as befits the day of the Lord. All liturgies, from the very simple to the most ornate, must be truly pastoral and prayerful.

THE CELEBRANT

21.   No other single factor affects the liturgy as much as the attitude, style, and bearing of the celebrant: his sincere faith and warmth as he welcomes the worshiping community; his human naturalness combined with dignity and seriousness as he breaks the Bread of Word and Eucharist.

22.   The style and pattern of song ought to increase the effectiveness of a good celebrant. His role is enhanced when he is capable of rendering some of his parts in song, and he should be encouraged to do so. What he cannot sing well and effectively he ought to recite. If capable of singing, he ought, for the sake of people, to rehearse carefully the sung parts that contribute to their celebration.[9]

THE PLACE OF MUSIC IN THE CELEBRATION

MUSIC SERVES THE EXPRESSION OF FAITH

23.   Among the many signs and symbols used by the Church to celebrate its faith, music is of preeminent importance. As sacred song united to words it forms a necessary or integral part of the solemn liturgy.[10] Yet the function of music is ministerial; it must serve and never dominate. Music should assist the assembled believers to express and share the gift of faith that is within them and to nourish and strengthen their interior commitment of faith. It should heighten the texts so that they speak more fully and more effectively. The quality of joy and enthusiasm which music adds to community worship cannot be gained in any other way. It imparts a sense of unity to the congregation and sets the appropriate tone for a particular celebration.

24.   In addition to expressing texts, music can also unveil a dimension of meaning and feeling, a communication of ideas and intuitions which words alone cannot yield. This dimension is integral to the human personality and to growth in faith. It cannot be ignored if the signs of worship are to speak to the whole person. Ideally, every communal celebration of faith, including funerals and the sacraments of baptism, confirmation, penance, anointing, and matrimony, should include music and singing. Where it is possible to celebrate the Liturgy of the Hours in a community, it, too, should include music.

25.   To determine the value of a given musical element in a liturgical celebration a threefold judgment must be made: musical, liturgical, and pastoral.

THE MUSICAL JUDGMENT

26.   Is the music technically, aesthetically, and expressively good? This judgment is basic and primary and should be made by competent musicians. Only artistically sound music will be effective in the long run. To admit the cheap, the trite, the musical cliché often found in popular songs for the purpose of "instant liturgy" is to cheapen the liturgy, to expose it to ridicule, and to invite failure.

27.   Musicians must search for and create music of quality for worship, especially the new musical settings for the new liturgical texts. They must also do the research needed to find new uses for the best of the old music. They must explore the repertory of good music used in other communions. They must find practical means of preserving and using our rich heritage of Latin chants and motets.[11]

In the meantime, however, the words of St. Augustine should not be forgotten: "Do not allow yourselves to be offended by the imperfect while you strive for the perfect."

28.   We do a disservice to musical values, however, when we confuse the judgment of music with the judgment of musical style. Style and value are two distinct judgments. Good music of new styles is finding a happy home in the celebrations of today. To chant and polyphony we have effectively added the chorale hymn, restored reponsorial singing to some extent, and employed many styles of contemporary composition. Music in folk idiom is finding acceptance in eucharistic celebrations. We must judge value within each style.

"In modern times the Church has consistently recognized and freely admitted the use of various styles of music as an aid to liturgical worship. Since the promulgation of the Constitution on the Liturgy and more especially since the introduction of vernacular languages into the liturgy, there has arisen a more pressing need for musical compositions in idioms that can be sung by the congregation and thus further communal participation."[12]

29.   The musician has every right to insist that the music be good. But although all liturgical music should be good, not all good music is suitable to the liturgy. The musical judgment is basic but not final. There remain the liturgical and pastoral judgments.

THE LITURGICAL JUDGMENT

30.   The nature of the liturgy itself will help to determine what kind of music is called for, what parts are to be preferred for singing, and who is to sing them.

A. Structural Requirements

31.   The choice of sung parts, the balance between them, and the style of musical setting used should reflect the relative importance of the parts of the Mass (or

other service) and the nature of each part. Thus elaborate settings of the entrance song, "Lord have Mercy" and "Glory to God" may make the proclamation of the word seem unimportant; and an overly elaborate offertory song with a spoken "Holy, Holy, Holy Lord" may make the eucharistic prayer seem less important.

B. Textual Requirements

32.   Does the music express and interpret the text correctly and make it more meaningful? Is the form of the text respected? In making these judgments the principal classes of texts must be kept in mind: proclamations, acclamations, psalms and hymns, and prayers. Each has a specific function which must be served by the music chosen for a text.

In most instances there is an official liturgical text approved by the episcopal conference. "Vernacular texts set to music composed in earlier periods," however, "may be used in liturgical texts."[13] As noted elsewhere, criteria have been provided for the texts which may replace the processional chants of Mass. In these cases and in the choice of all supplementary music, the texts "must always be in conformity with Catholic doctrine; indeed they should be drawn chiefly from holy scripture and from liturgical sources."[14]

C. Role Differentiation

33.   "In liturgical celebrations each one, minister or layperson, who has an office to perform, should do all of, but only, those parts which pertain to that office by the nature of the rite and the principles of liturgy."[15] Special musical concern must be given to the role of the congregation, the cantor, the choir, and the instrumentalists.

D. The Congregation

34.   Music for the congregation must be within its members' performance capability. The congregation must be comfortable and secure with what they are doing in order to celebrate well.

E. The Cantor

35.   While there is no place in the liturgy for display of virtuosity for its own sake, artistry is valued, and an individual singer can effectively lead the assembly, attractively proclaim the Word of God in the psalm sung between the readings, and take his or her part in other responsorial singing. "Provision should be made for at least one or two properly trained singers, especially where there is no possibility of setting up even a small choir. The singer will present some simpler musical settings, with the people taking part, and can lead and support the faithful as far as is needed. The presence of such a singer is desirable even in churches which have a choir, for those celebrations in which the choir cannot take part but which may fittingly be performed with some solemnity and therefore with singing."[16] Although a cantor "cannot enhance the service of worship in the same way as a choir, a trained and competent cantor can perform an important ministry by leading the congregation in common sacred song and in responsorial singing."[17]

F. The Choir

36. A well-trained choir adds beauty and solemnity to the liturgy and also assists and encourages the singing of the congregation. The Second Vatican Council, speaking of the choir, stated emphatically: "Choirs must be diligently promoted," provided that "the whole body of the faithful may be able to contribute that active participation which is rightly theirs."[18]

"At times the choir, within the congregation of the faithful and as part of it, will assume the role of leadership, while at other times it will retain its own distinctive ministry. This means that the choir will lead the people in sung prayer, by alternating or reinforcing the sacred song of the congregation, or by enhancing it with the addition of a musical elaboration. At other times in the course of liturgical celebration the choir alone will sing works whose musical demands enlist and challenge its competence."[19]

G. The Organist and Other Instrumentalists

37. Song is not the only kind of music suitable for liturgical celebration. Music performed on the organ and other instruments can stimulate feelings of joy and contemplation at appropriate times.[20] This can be done effectively at the following points: an instrumental prelude, a soft background to a spoken psalm, at the preparation of the gifts in place of singing, during portions of the communion rite, and the recessional.

In the dioceses of the United States, "musical instruments other than the organ may be used in liturgical services, provided they are played in a manner that is suitable to public worship."[21] This decision deliberately refrains from singling out specific instruments. Their use depends on circumstances, the nature of the congregation, etc.

38. The *proper placing* of the organ and choir according to the arrangement and acoustics of the church will facilitate celebration. Practically speaking, the choir must be near the director and the organ (both console and sound). The choir ought to be able to perform without too much distraction; the acoustics ought to give a lively presence of sound in the choir area and allow both tone and word to reach the congregation with clarity. Visually it is desirable that the choir appear to be part of the worshiping community, yet a part which serves in a unique way. Locating the organ console too far from the congregation causes a time lag which tends to make the singing drag unless the organist is trained to cope with it. A location near the front pews will facilitate congregational singing.

THE PASTORAL JUDGMENT

39. The pastoral judgment governs the use and function of every element of celebration. Ideally this judgment is made by the planning team or committee. It is the judgment that must be made in this particular situation, in these concrete circumstances. Does music in the celebration enable these people to express their faith, in this place, in this age, in this culture?

40.   The instruction of the Congregation for Divine Worship, issued September 5, 1970, encourages episcopal conferences to consider not only liturgical music's suitability to the time and circumstances of the celebration, "but also the needs of the faithful who will sing them. All means must be used to promote singing by the people. New forms should be used, which are adapted to the different mentalities and to modern tastes." The document adds that the music and the instruments "should correspond to the sacred character of the celebration and the place of worship."

41.   A musician may judge that a certain composition or style of composition is good music, but this musical judgment really says nothing about whether and how this music is to be used in this celebration. The signs of the celebration must be accepted and received as meaningful for a genuinely human faith experience for these specific worshipers. This pastoral judgment can be aided by sensitivity to the cultural and social characteristics of the people who make up the congregation: their age, culture, and education. These factors influence the effectiveness of the liturgical signs, including music. No set of rubrics or regulations of itself will ever achieve a truly pastoral celebration of the sacramental rites. Such regulations must always be applied with a pastoral concern for the given worshiping community.

GENERAL CONSIDERATIONS OF LITURGICAL STRUCTURE

42.   Those responsible for planning the music for eucharistic celebrations in accord with the three preceding judgments must have a clear understanding of the structure of the liturgy. They must be aware of what is of primary importance. They should know the nature of each of the parts of the liturgy and the relationship of each part to the overall rhythm of the liturgical action.

43.   The Mass is made up of the liturgy of the word and the liturgy of the Eucharist. These two parts are so closely connected as to form one act of worship. The table of the Lord is both the table of God's Word and the table of Christ's Body, and from it the faithful are instructed and refreshed. In addition, the Mass has introductory and concluding rites.[22] The introductory and concluding rites are secondary.

THE INTRODUCTORY RITES

44.   The parts preceding the liturgy of the word, namely, the entrance, greeting, penitential rite, Kyrie, Gloria, and opening prayer or collect, have the character of introduction and preparation. The purpose of these rites is to help the assembled people become a worshiping community and to prepare them for listening to God's Word and celebrating the Eucharist.[23] Of these parts the entrance song and the opening prayer are primary. All else is secondary.

If Mass begins with the sprinkling of the people with blessed water, the penitential rite is omitted; this may be done at all Sunday Masses.[24] Similarly, if the psalms of part of the Liturgy of the Hours precede Mass, the introductory rite is abbreviated in accord with the *General Instruction on The Liturgy of the Hours.*[25]

THE LITURGY OF THE WORD

45.   Readings from scripture are the heart of the liturgy of the word. The homily, responsorial psalms, profession of faith, and general intercessions develop and complete it. In the readings, God speaks to his people and nourishes their spirit; Christ is present through his word. The homily explains the readings. The chants and the profession of faith comprise the people's acceptance of God's Word. It is of primary importance that the people hear God's message of love, digest it with the aid of psalms, silence, and the homily, and respond, involving themselves in the great covenant of love and redemption. All else is secondary.

THE PREPARATION OF THE GIFTS

46.   The eucharistic prayer is preceded by the preparation of the gifts. The purpose of the rite is to prepare bread and wine for the sacrifice. The secondary character of the rite determines the manner of the celebration. It consists very simply of bringing the gifts to the altar, possibly accompanied by song, prayers to be said by the celebrant as he prepares the gifts, and the prayer over the gifts. Of these elements the bringing of the gifts, the placing of the gifts on the altar, and the prayer over the gifts are primary. All else is secondary.

THE EUCHARISTIC PRAYER

47.   The eucharistic prayer, a prayer of thanksgiving and sanctification, is the center of the entire celebration. By an introductory dialogue the priest invites the people to lift their hearts to God in praise and thanks; he unites them with himself in the prayer he addresses in their name to the Father through Jesus Christ. The meaning of the prayer is that the whole congregation joins itself to Christ in acknowledging the works of God and in offering the sacrifice.[26] As a statement of the faith of the local assembly it is affirmed and ratified by all those present through acclamations of faith: the first acclamation or Sanctus, the memorial acclamation, and the Great Amen.

THE COMMUNION RITE

48.   The eating and drinking of the Body and Blood of the Lord in a paschal meal is the climax of our eucharistic celebration. It is prepared for by several rites: the Lord's Prayer with embolism and doxology, the rite of peace, breaking of bread (and commingling) during the "Lamb of God," private preparation of the priest, and showing of the eucharistic bread. The eating and drinking are accompanied by a song expressing the unity of communicants and followed by a time of prayer after communion.[27] Those elements are primary which show forth signs that the first fruit of the Eucharist is the unity of the Body of Christ, Christians being loved by Christ and loving him through their love of one another. The principal texts to

accompany or express the sacred action are the Lord's Prayer, the song during the communion procession, and the prayer after communion.

THE CONCLUDING RITE

49.   The concluding rite consists of the priest's greeting and blessing, which is sometimes expanded by the prayer over the people or another solemn form, and the dismissal which sends forth each member of the congregation to do good works, praising and blessing the Lord.[28]

A recessional song is optional. The greeting, blessing, dismissal, and recessional song or instrumental music ideally form one continuous action which may culminate in the priest's personal greetings and conversations at the church door.

APPLICATION OF THE PRINCIPLES OF CELEBRATION TO MUSIC IN EUCHARISTIC WORSHIP

GENERAL CONSIDERATIONS

50.   Many and varied musical patterns are now possible within the liturgical structure. Musicians and composers need to respond creatively and responsibly to the challenge of developing new music for today's celebrations.

51.   While it is possible to make technical distinctions in the forms of the Mass—all the way from the Mass in which nothing is sung to the Mass in which everything is sung—such distinctions are of little significance in themselves; almost unlimited combinations of sung and recited parts may be chosen. The important decision is whether or not this or that part may be or should be sung in this particular celebration and under these specific circumstances.[29] The former distinction between the ordinary and proper parts of the Mass with regard to musical settings and distribution of roles is no longer retained. For this reason the musical settings of the past are usually not helpful models for composing truly liturgical pieces today.

52.   Two patterns formerly served as the basis for creating and planning liturgy. One was "High Mass" with its five movements, sung Ordinary and fourfold sung Proper. The other was the four-hymn "Low Mass" format that grew out of the *Instruction of Sacred Music* of 1958. The four-hymn pattern developed in the context of a Latin Mass which could accommodate song in the vernacular only at certain points. It is now outdated, and the Mass has more than a dozen parts that may be sung, as well as numerous options for the celebrant. Each of these parts must be understood according to its proper nature and function.

SPECIFIC APPLICATIONS

A. Acclamations

53.   The acclamations are shouts of joy which arise from the whole assembly as forceful and meaningful assents to God's Word and Action. They are important because they make some of the most significant moments of the Mass (gospel, eucharistic prayer, Lord's Prayer) stand out. It is of their nature that they be rhythmically strong, melodically appealing, and affirmative. The people should know the acclamations by heart in order to sing them spontaneously. Some variety is recommended and even imperative. The challenge to the composer and people alike is one of variety without confusion.

54.   In the eucharistic celebration there are five acclamations which ought to be sung even at Masses in which little else is sung: Alleluia; "Holy, Holy, Holy Lord"; Memorial Acclamation; Great Amen; Doxology to the Lord's Prayer.

THE ALLELUIA

55.   This acclamation of paschal joy is both a reflection upon the Word of God proclaimed in the liturgy and a preparation for the gospel. All stand to sing it. After the cantor or choir sings the alleluia(s), the people customarily repeat it. Then a single proper verse is sung by the cantor or choir, and all repeat the alleluia(s). If not sung, the alleluia should be omitted.[30] A moment of silent reflection may be observed in its place. During Lent a brief verse of acclamatory character replaces the alleluia and is sung in the same way.

HOLY, HOLY, HOLY LORD

56.   This is the people's acclamation of praise concluding the preface of the eucharistic prayer. We join the whole communion of saints in acclaiming the Lord. Settings which add harmony or descants on solemn feasts and occasions are appropriate, but since this chant belongs to priest and people, the choir parts must facilitate and make effective the people's parts.

THE MEMORIAL ACCLAMATION

57.   We support one another's faith in the paschal mystery, the central mystery of our belief. This acclamation is properly a memorial of the Lord's suffering and glorification, with an expression of faith in his coming. Variety in text and music is desirable.

THE GREAT AMEN

58.   The worshipers assent to the eucharistic prayer and make it their own in the Great Amen. To be most effective, the Amen may be repeated or augmented. Choirs may harmonize and expand upon the people's acclamation.

59.   These words of praise, "For the Kingdom, the power and the glory are yours, now and forever," are fittingly sung by all, especially when the Lord's Prayer is sung. Here, too, the choir may enhance the acclamation with harmony.

B. Processional Songs

60.   The two processional chants—the entrance song and the communion song—are very important for creating and sustaining an awareness of community. Proper antiphons are given to be used with appropriate psalm verses. These may be replaced by the chants of the *Simple Gradual*, by other psalms and antiphons, or by other fitting songs.[31]

THE ENTRANCE SONG

61.   The entrance song should create an atmosphere of celebration. It helps put the assembly in the proper frame of mind for listening to the Word of God. It helps people to become conscious of themselves as a worshiping community. The choice of texts for the entrance song should not conflict with these purposes. In general, during the most important seasons of the Church year—Easter, Lent, Christmas, and Advent—it is preferable that most songs used at the entrance be seasonal in nature.[32]

THE COMMUNION SONG

62.   The communion song should foster a sense of unity. It should be simple and not demand great effort. It gives expression to the joy of unity in the body of Christ and the fulfillment of the mystery being celebrated. Because they emphasize adoration rather than communion, most benediction hymns are not suitable. In general, during the most important seasons of the Church year— Easter, Lent, Christmas, and Advent—it is preferable that most songs used at the communion be seasonal in nature. For the remainder of the Church year, however, topical songs may be used during the communion procession, provided these texts do not conflict with the paschal character of every Sunday."[33]

C. Responsorial Psalm

63.   This unique and very important song is the response to the first lesson. The new lectionary's determination to match the content of the psalms to the theme of reading is reflected in its listing of 900 refrains. The liturgy of the Word comes more fully to life if between the first two readings a cantor sings the psalm and all sing the response. Since most groups cannot learn a new response every week, seasonal refrains are offered in the lectionary itself and in the *Simple Gradual*. Other psalms and refrains may also be used, including psalms arranged in responsorial form and metrical and similar versions of psalms, provided they are used in accordance with the principles of the *Simple Gradual* and are selected in harmony with the liturgical season, feast or occasion. The choice of the texts which are not from the psalter is not extended to the chants between the readings.[34] To facilitate reflection, there may be a brief period of silence between the first reading and the responsorial psalm.

D. Ordinary Chants

64.   The fourth category is the ordinary chants, which now may be treated as individual choices. One or more may be sung; the others spoken. The pattern may vary according to the circumstances. These chants are the following:

LORD HAVE MERCY

65.   This short litany was traditionally a prayer of praise to the risen Christ. He has been raised and made "Lord," and we beg him to show his loving kindness. The sixfold Kyrie of the new order of Mass may be sung in other ways, for example, as a ninefold chant.[35] It may also be incorporated in the penitential rite, with invocations addressed to Christ. When sung, the setting should be brief and simple in order not to give undue importance to the introductory rites.

GLORY TO GOD

66.   This ancient hymn of praise is now given in a new poetic and singable translation. It may be introduced by celebrant, cantor, or choir. The restricted use of the Gloria, i.e., only on Sundays outside Advent and Lent and on solemnities and feasts,[36] emphasizes its special and solemn character. The new text offers many opportunities for alternation of choir and people in poetic parallelisms. The "Glory to God" also provides an opportunity for the choir to sing alone on festive occasions.

LORD'S PRAYER

67.   This prayer begins our immediate preparation for sharing in the Paschal Banquet. The traditional text is retained and may be set to music by composers with the same freedom as other parts of the Ordinary. All settings must provide for the participation of the priest and all present.

LAMB OF GOD

68.   The Agnus Dei is a litany-song to accompany the breaking of the bread in preparation for communion. The invocation and response may be repeated as the action demands. The final response is always "grant us peace." Unlike the "Holy, Holy, Holy Lord," and the Lord's Prayer, the "Lamb of God" is not necessarily a song of the people. Hence it may be sung by the choir, though the people should generally make the response.

PROFESSION OF FAITH

69.   This is a communal profession of faith in which". . . . the people who have heard the Word of God in the lesson and in the homily may assent and respond to it, and may renew in themselves the rule of faith as they begin to celebrate the Eucharist."[37] It is usually preferable that the Creed be spoken in declamatory fashion rather than sung.[38] If it is sung, it might more effectively take the form of a simple musical declamation rather than an extensive and involved musical structure.

E. Supplementary Songs

70.   This category includes songs for which there are no specified texts nor any requirements that there should be a spoken or sung text. Here the choir may play a fuller role, for there is no question of usurping the people's part. This category includes the following:

THE OFFERTORY SONG

71.   The offertory song may accompany the procession and preparation of the gifts. It is not always necessary or desirable. Organ or instrumental music is also fitting at the time. When song is used, it need not speak of bread and wine or of offering. The proper function of this song is to accompany and celebrate the communal aspects of the procession. The text, therefore, can be any appropriate song of praise or of rejoicing in keeping with the season. The antiphons of the Roman Gradual, not included in the new Roman Missal, may be used with psalm verses. Instrumental interludes can effectively accompany the procession and preparation of the gifts and thus keep this part of the Mass in proper perspective relative to the eucharistic prayer which follows.

THE PSALM OR SONG AFTER COMMUNION

72.   The singing of a psalm or hymn of praise after the distribution of communion is optional. If the organ is played or the choir sings during the distribution of communion, a congregational song may well provide a fitting expression of oneness in the Eucharistic Lord. Since no particular text is specified, there is ample room for creativity.

THE RECESSIONAL SONG

73.   The recessional song has never been an official part of the rite; hence musicians are free to plan music which provides an appropriate closing to the liturgy. A song is one possible choice. However, if the people have sung a song after communion, it may be advisable to use only an instrumental or choir recessional.

F. Litanies

74.   Litanies are often more effective when sung. The repetition of melody and rhythm draws the people together in a strong and unified response. In addition to the "Lamb of God," already mentioned, the general intercessions (prayer of the faithful) offer an opportunity for litanical singing, as do the invocations of Christ in the penitential rite.

PROGRESS AND NEW DIRECTIONS

75.   Many new patterns and combinations of song are emerging in eucharistic celebrations. Congregations most frequently sing an entrance song, alleluia, "Holy, Holy, Holy Lord," memorial acclamation, Great Amen, and a song at communion (or a song after communion). Other parts are added in varying quantities, depending on season, degree of solemnity and musical resources.

Choirs often add one or more of the following: a song before Mass, an Offertory song, the "Glory to God" on special occasions, additional communion songs or a song after communion or a recessional. They may also enhance the congregationally sung entrance song and acclamations with descants, harmony, and antiphonal arrangements. Harmony is desirable when, without confusing the people, it gives breadth and power to their voices in unison.

76. Flexibility is recognized today as an important value in liturgy. The musician with a sense of artistry and a deep knowledge of the rhythm of the liturgical action will be able to combine the many options into an effective whole. For the composer and performer alike there is an unprecedented challenge. They must enhance the liturgy with new creations of variety and richness and with those compositions from the time-honored treasury of liturgical music which can still serve today's celebrations. Like the wise householder in Matthew's Gospel, the church musician must be one "who can produce from his store both the new and the old."

77. The Church in the United States today needs the service of many qualified musicians as song leaders, organists, instrumentalists, cantors, choir directors, and composers. We have been blessed with many generous musicians who have given years of service despite receiving only meager financial compensation. For the art to grow and face the challenges of today and tomorrow, every diocese and parish should establish policies for hiring and paying living wages to competent musicians. Full-time musicians employed by the Church ought to be on the same salary scale as teachers with similar qualifications and workloads.[39]

78. Likewise, to ensure that composers and publishers receive just compensation for their work, those engaged in parish music programs and those responsible for budgets must often be reminded that it is illegal and immoral to reproduce copyrighted texts and music by any means without written permission of the copyright owner. The fact that these duplicated materials are not for sale but for private use does not alter the legal or moral situation of copying without permission.[40]

MUSIC IN SACRAMENTAL CELEBRATIONS

79. While music has traditionally been part of the celebration of weddings, funerals, and confirmation, the communal celebration of baptism, anointing, and penance has only recently been restored. The renewed rituals, following the *Constitution on the Sacred Liturgy*, provide for and encourage communal celebrations, which, according to the capability of the congregation, should involve song.[41]

80. The rite of baptism is best begun by an entrance song;[42] the liturgy of the word is enhanced by a sung psalm and/or alleluia. Where the processions to and from the place of the liturgy of the word and the baptistry take some time, they should be accompanied by music. Above all, the acclamations—the affirmation

of faith by the people, the acclamation immediately after the baptism, the acclamation upon completion of the rite—should be sung by the whole congregation.

81.   Whenever rites like the anointing of the sick or the sacrament of penance are celebrated communally, music is important. The general structure is introductory rite, liturgy of the word, sacrament, and dismissal. The introductory rite and liturgy of the word follow the pattern of the Mass. At the time of the sacrament an acclamation or song by all the people is desirable.

82.   Confirmation and marriage are most often celebrated within a Mass. The norms given above pertain. Great care should be taken, especially at marriages, that all the people are involved at the important moments of the celebration, that the same general principles of planning worship and judging music are employed as at other liturgies, and, above all, that the liturgy is a prayer for all present, not a theatrical production.

83.   Music becomes particularly important in the new burial rites. Without it the themes of hope and resurrection are very difficult to express. The entrance song, the acclamations, and the song of farewell or commendation are of primary importance for the whole congregation. The choral and instrumental music should fit the paschal mystery theme.[43]

CONCLUSION

84.   There is vital interest today in the Mass as prayer, and in this understanding of the Mass lies a principle of synthesis which is essential to good liturgical worship. When all strive with one accord to make the Mass a prayer, a sharing and celebration of Faith, the result is unity. Styles of music, choices of instruments, forms of celebration—all converge in a single purpose: that men and women of faith may proclaim and share that faith in prayer and Christ may grow among us all.

NOTES

1. SC 34.

2. MS 5e; GIRM 73.

3. GIRM 313.

4. BCLN, 18 April 1966.

5. BCLN, 17 Feb 1967.

6. AP.

7. GIRM 1; cf. SC 102.

8. MS 11.

9. MS 8.

10. Cf. SC 112.

11. Cf. SC 114, 116.

12. BCLN, 18 April 1966.

13. National Conference of Catholic Bishops, [NCCB] Nov 1967.

14. SC 121.

15. SC 28.

16. MS 21.

17. BCLN, 18 April 1966.

18. SC 114.

19. BCLN, 18 April 1966.

20. Cf. SC 120; MS 63–65; LI 3c.

21. NCCB, Nov 1967; cf. SC 120.

22. GIRM 8.

23. GIRM 24.

24. Cf. RomM, Blessing and Sprinkling of Holy Water, 1.

25. The Liturgy of the Hours, General Instruction, 93–98.

26. GIRM 54.

27. GIRM 56.

28. GIRM 57.

29. Cf. GIRM 19; MS 28, 36.

30. GIRM 39. The first edition of this document had the word "may" instead of "should." This change has been made in the second edition in light of the norm found in LMI 23.

31. GIRM 56.

32. NCCB, Nov. 1969.

33. Ibid.

34. NCCB, Nov 1968; cf. GIRM 6.

35. Cf. GIRM 30.

36. GIRM 31.

37. GIRM 43.

38. NCCB, Nov 1967.

39. BCLN, 18 April 1966.

40. BCLN, April 1969.

41. Cf. SC 27.

42. RBaptC 5, 32, 35.

43. Rite of Funerals, 1.

LITURGICAL MUSIC
TODAY

BISHOPS' COMMITTEE ON THE LITURGY

NATIONAL CONFERENCE OF CATHOLIC BISHOPS
15 NOVEMBER 1982

OUTLINE

LITURGICAL MUSIC TODAY

INTRODUCTION

1.   Liturgical music today exhibits signs of great vitality and creativity. During the nearly twenty years that have passed since the promulgation of the *Constitution on the Sacred Liturgy* of the Second Vatican Council, the ministerial role of liturgical music has received growing acceptance and greater appreciation by the Christian people. The sung prayer of our assemblies, often timid and weak but a few years ago, has taken on the characteristics of confidence and strength. In the liturgical ministry of music, more and more capable persons are assuming roles of leadership as cantors, instrumentalists and members of choirs. New musical compositions are appearing in great numbers and the quality of their craftsmanship and beauty is improving. All these developments serve as signs of hope for the present and future of liturgical music.

2.   Ten years ago the Bishops' Committee on the Liturgy published *Music in Catholic Worship,* itself the revision of an earlier statement.[1] That document has proven to be very useful in setting out the principles for Church music in the reformed liturgy. It has served well over these years.

3.   Since the Roman liturgical books were still in the process of revision ten years ago, the Committee recognizes that there are subjects that *Music in Catholic Worship* addressed only briefly or not at all, such as music within sacramental rites and in the Liturgy of the Hours. Moreover, the passage of time has raised a number of unforeseen issues in need of clarification and questions revealing new possibilities for liturgical music. We take this opportunity to note these developments. This statement, therefore, should be read as a companion to *Music in Catholic Worship* and *Environment and Art in Catholic Worship.*[2]

4.   The introduction to *Music in Catholic Worship* includes these words: " . . . mere observance of a pattern or rule of sung liturgy will not create a living and authentic celebration of worship in Christian congregations. That is the reason why statements such as this must take the form of recommendation and attempts at guidance."[3] These words continue to be true. Guidelines, far from being absolute, need to be adapted to particular circumstances. But first they must be read, reflected upon, and valued for the insights they contain. And ultimately they will be successful to the extent that they are implemented, to the extent that the context out of which they grow is communicated and understood.

5.   These guidelines concern the Church's liturgy, which is inherently musical. If music is not valued within the liturgy, then this statement will have little to offer. On the other hand, if music is appreciated as a necessarily normal dimension of every experience of communal worship, then what follows may help to promote continued understanding of the liturgy, dialogue among those responsible for its implementation, and music itself as sung prayer.

GENERAL PRINCIPLES

THE STRUCTURE OF THE LITURGY

6.   A sacrament is celebrated either within Mass or with a liturgy of the word. This is the larger context for making judgments about what will be sung. This consideration will help to preserve the integrity of the entire liturgical prayer experience while, at the same time preventing the celebration from being top heavy in one or other part, and ensuring a good flow throughout.

7.   In all liturgical celebrations proper use should be made of the musical elements within the liturgy of the word, i.e., responsorial psalm, gospel acclamation, and sometimes an acclamation after the homily or profession of faith. *Music in Catholic Worship* treated these sung prayers in its discussion of eucharistic celebrations.[4] What was said there is applicable to all other liturgical celebrations which include a liturgy of the word. Further efforts are needed to make the assembly's responses in song the normal pastoral practice in the celebration of God's Word.

THE PLACE OF SONG

8.   The structure of the liturgical unit will disclose the elements to be enhanced by music. For example, the liturgy of baptism or confirmation is placed between the liturgy of the word and the liturgy of the eucharist when celebrated at Mass. Each rite is composed of a number of elements, some of which lend themselves to singing. The first place to look for guidance in the use and choice of music is the rite itself. Often the rubrics contained in the approved liturgical books will indicate the place for song, and will also prescribe or suggest an appropriate text to be set musically. Thus, in confirmation, the ritual recommends singing at the end of the renewal of baptismal promises and during the anointing.[5] In baptism, the acclamations after the profession of faith and after the baptism itself demand song, since they are by nature musical forms.[6]

THE FUNCTION OF SONG

9.   The various functions of sung prayer must be distinguished within liturgical rites. Sometimes song is meant to accompany ritual actions. In such cases the song is not independent but serves, rather, to support the prayer of the assembly when an action requires a longer period of time or when the action is going to be repeated several times. The music enriches the moments and keeps it from becoming burdensome. Ritual actions which employ such use of song include:

the enrollment of names at the Election of Catechumens;[7] the processions in the celebration of baptism;[8] the vesting and sign of peace at an ordination;[9] the presentation of the Bible at the institution of a reader;[10] the anointings with chrism at confirmation[11] and ordination.[12]

10. At other places in the liturgical action the sung prayer itself is a constituent element of the rite. While it is being prayed, no other ritual action is being performed. Such would be: the song of praise, which may be sung after communion;[13] the litany of saints at celebrations of Christian initiation,[14] ordination,[15] religious profession,[16] or the dedication of a church;[17] the proclamation of praise for God's mercy at the conclusion of the rite of reconciliation;[18] acclamations to conclude the baptismal profession of faith,[19] blessing of water,[20] or the thanksgiving over oil.[21] Even more important is the solemn chanting of the prayer of consecration by the bishop at ordinations,[22] or of the prayer of dedication of a church.[23] In each of these cases the music does not serve as a mere accompaniment, but as the integral mode by which the mystery is proclaimed and presented.

THE FORM OF SONG

11. Beyond determining the moments when song is needed, the musical form employed must match its liturgical function. For instance, at the end of the baptismal profession of faith the assembly may express its assent by an acclamation. In place of the text provided ("This is our faith . . .") another appropriate formula or suitable song may be substituted.[24] An acclamation—a short, direct and strong declarative statement of the community's faith—will usually be more suitable for this than the several verses of a metrical hymn. The hymn form, appropriate in other contexts, may not work here because its form is usually less compact, less intense.

PASTORAL CONCERNS

12. The pastoral judgment discussed in *Music in Catholic Worship* must always be applied when choosing music. Sacramental celebrations are significant moments in an individual's life, but just as importantly they are constitutive events of the community's life in Christ. The music selected must express the prayer of those who celebrate, while at the same time guarding against the imposition of private meanings on public rites. Individual preference is not, of itself, a sufficient principle for the choice of music in the liturgy. It must be balanced with liturgical and musical judgments and with the community's needs. Planning is a team undertaking, involving the presider, the musicians and the assembly.

PROGRESSIVE SOLEMNITY

13. Music should be considered a normal and ordinary part of any liturgical celebration. However, this general principle is to be interpreted in the light of another one, namely, the principle of progressive solemnity.[25] This latter principle takes into account the abilities of the assembly, the relative importance of

the individual rites and their constituent parts, and the relative festivity of the liturgical day. With regard to the Liturgy of the Hours, formerly a sung office meant a service in which everything was sung. Today the elements which lend themselves to singing (the psalms and canticles with their antiphons, the hymns, responsories, litanies and prayers, and the acclamations, greetings and responses) should be sung in accordance with the relative solemnity of the celebration. This principle likewise applies to the music sung in all other liturgical celebrations.

LANGUAGE AND MUSICAL IDIOMS

14.   Different languages may be used in the same celebration.[26] This may also be said of mixing different musical idioms and media. For example, pastoral reasons might suggest that in a given liturgical celebration some music reflect classical hymnody, with other music drawn from gospel or "folk" idioms, from contemporary service music, or from the plainsong or polyphonic repertoires. In the same celebration music may be rendered in various ways: unaccompanied; or accompanied by organ, piano, guitar or other instruments.

15.   While this principle upholding musical plurality has pastoral value, it should never be employed as a license for including poor music. At the same time, it needs to be recognized that a certain musical integrity within a liturgical prayer or rite can be achieved only by unity in the musical composition. Thus, it is recommended that for the acclamations in the eucharistic prayer one musical style be employed.

MUSIC IN THE EUCHARIST

16.   The function of the various chants within the Eucharistic Liturgy has already been set out in *Music in Catholic Worship,* as well as above. Additional notes follow regarding specific elements.

ACCLAMATIONS

17.   The acclamations (gospel acclamation, doxology after the Lord's Prayer, and eucharistic acclamations—including the special acclamations of praise in the *Eucharistic Prayers of Masses with Children*[27]) are the preeminent sung prayers of the eucharistic liturgy. Singing these acclamations makes their prayer all the more effective. They should, therefore, be sung, even at weekday celebrations of the Eucharist. The gospel acclamation, moreover, must always be sung.[28]

PROCESSIONAL CHANTS

18.   Processional chants accompany an action. In some cases they have another function. The entrance song serves to gather and unite the assembly and set the tone for the celebration as much as to conduct the ministers into the sanctuary. The communion processional song serves a similiar purpose. Not only does it accompany movement, and thus give order to the assembly, it also assists each

communicant in the realization and achievement of "the joy of all" and the fellowship of those "who join their voices in a single song."[29]

19. While the responsorial form of singing is especially suitable for processions, the metrical hymn can also fulfill the function of the entrance song. If, however, a metrical hymn with several verses is selected, its form should be respected. The progression of text and music must be allowed to play out its course and achieve its purpose musically and poetically. In other words, the hymn should not be ended indiscriminately at the end of the procession. For this same reason, metrical hymns may not be the most suitable choices to accompany the preparation of the gifts and altar at the Eucharist, since the music should not extend past the time necessary for the ritual.

LITANIES

20. The Lamb of God achieves greater significance at Masses when a larger sized eucharistic bread is broken for distribution and, when communion is given under both kinds, chalices must be filled. The litany is prolonged to accompany this action of breaking and pouring.[30] In this case one should not hesitate to add tropes to the litany so that the prayerfulness of the rite may be enriched.

21. The litany of the third form of the penitential rite at Mass increasingly is being set to music for deacon (or cantor) and assembly, with the people's response made in Greek or English. This litany functions as a "general confession made by the entire assembly"[31] and as praise of Christ's compassionate love and mercy. It is appropriately sung at more solemn celebrations and in Advent and Lent when the Gloria is omitted.[32] Similar litanic forms of song could be employed when the rite of sprinkling replaces the penitential rite.

MUSIC IN THE CELEBRATION
OF OTHER SACRAMENTS AND RITES

CHRISTIAN INITIATION

22. As parish communities become more accustomed to initiate adults in stages, the opportunities for sung prayer within the *Rite of Christian Initiation of Adults* should become more apparent. The ritual book gives attention to the following: in the rite of becoming a catechumen, before the invitation to sponsors to present the candidates, and during their subsequent entry into the church building; in the rite of election, during the enrollment of names; in the Lenten scrutinies, after the prayer of exorcism; at the Easter Vigil celebration, an acclamation following baptism, song between the celebration of baptism and confirmation, and an acclamation during the anointing with chrism.[33]

23. In the *Rite of Baptism of Children,* there is even greater emphasis on the sung prayer of the assembly: during the procession to the place where the Word of God will be celebrated; after the homily or after the short litany; during the procession to the place of baptism; an acclamation after the profession of faith

and after each baptism; an acclamation or baptismal song during the procession to the altar.[34]

24.   At confirmation, the *Roman Pontifical* calls for song after the profession of faith and during the anointings with chrism.[35]

25.   Each of the various rites of initiation includes a liturgy of the word and is often followed by the Eucharist. Thus, in planning music for the celebration, proper emphasis should be given to each of the two or three primary liturgical rites. For instance, in the celebration of the baptism of a child, the assembly should not sing only at the times noted in the ritual for that sacrament while singing nothing during the celebration of the Word. Rather, a proper balance would require that singing be an essential element throughout the entire prayer experience.

26.   Composers of church music are encouraged to create musical settings of the acclamations from Sacred Scripture, the hymns in the style of the New Testament, and the songs from ancient liturgies which are included in the approved ritual books.[36] Much service music, set to texts in English, Spanish, and other vernacular languages, is still required for the full experience of these liturgical celebrations of initiation. Simpler musical settings would be especially welcome for use at celebrations where no musical accompanist is present.

RECONCILIATION

27.   Communal celebrations of reconciliation (Forms 2 and 3 of the sacrament, as well as non-sacramental penance services) normally require an entrance song or song of gathering; a responsorial psalm and a gospel acclamation during the liturgy of the word; an optional hymn after the homily; and a hymn of praise for God's mercy following the absolution.[37] The litany within the General Confession of Sins (alternating between the deacon or cantor and the assembly) or another appropriate song may also be sung, as well as the Lord's Prayer. Singing or soft instrumental music may be used during the time of individual confessions, especially when there is a large number of people present for the celebration.

CHRISTIAN MARRIAGE

28.   Weddings present particular challenges and opportunities to planners. It is helpful for a diocese or a parish to have a definite (but flexible) policy regarding wedding music. This policy should be communicated early to couples as a normal part of their preparation in order to avoid last-minute crises and misunderstandings. Both musician and pastor should make every effort to assist couples to understand and share in the planning of their marriage liturgy. Sometimes the only music familiar to the couple is a song heard at a friend's ceremony and one not necessarily suitable to the sacrament. The pastoral musician will make an effort to demonstrate a wider range of possibilities to the couple, particularly in the choice of music to be sung by the entire assembly present for the liturgy.

29.   Particular decisions about choice and placement of wedding music should grow out of the three judgments proposed in *Music in Catholic Worship.* The liturgical judgment: Is the music's text, form, placement and style congruent with the nature of liturgy?[38] The musical judgment: Is the music technically, aesthetically and expressively good irrespective of musical idiom or style?[39] The pastoral judgment: will it help this assembly to pray?[40] Such a process of dialogue may not be as easy to apply as an absolute list of permitted or prohibited music, but in the long run it will be more effective pastorally.

CHRISTIAN BURIAL

30.   Funerals, because of often difficult pastoral situations in which some family members and friends are overburdened with grief, unchurched or otherwise unable to enter into the liturgy, have frequently received little or no attention musically. In this respect, funerals may be the least successfully reformed of our liturgical rites.

31.   It is the pastoral responsibility of parishes to provide liturgical music at all Masses of Christian Burial. Attempts to involve the congregation more actively are to be encouraged. Appropriate participation aids should be prepared and provided for members of the praying assembly.

32.   Many parishes have found it helpful to form choirs of retired parishioners or others who are at home on weekdays, whose unique ministry it is to assist the grieving members of a funeral assembly by leading the sung prayer of the funeral liturgy. Where this is not possible, a cantor is able to perform a similar ministry. In all cases a serious effort should be made to move beyond the practice of employing a "funeral singer" to perform all the sung parts of the liturgy. Reconsideration should be given to the location of the singer, that person's role, and the kind of music that is sung. The cantor ought not individually sing or recite the congregational prayers as a substitute for the assembly. The same norms applicable to music at any Mass apply equally to the Mass of Christian Burial.[41]

33.   The principle of progressive solemnity, already mentioned, applies especially to the rites of Christian Burial. A few things sung well (the acclamations, responsorial psalm, entrance and communion processionals, and song of farewell during the final commendation) should be given priority at funerals and may be drawn from a parish's common musical repertoire.

MUSIC IN THE LITURGY OF THE HOURS

34.   A growing number of parishes celebrate at least some part of the Liturgy of the Hours, usually Evening Prayer, during one or more of the liturgical seasons. The question of singing in the office is treated in the *General Instruction on the Liturgy of the Hours* and should be consulted along with *Study Text VII.*[42] The following observations expand on what is written there.

35.   The psalms and canticles are songs; therefore they are most satisfying when sung. The *General Instruction* lists several ways in which the psalms may be sung: responsorially, antiphonally or straight through *(in directum.)*[43] Music may be of the formula type (e.g., psalm tones) or composed for each psalm or canticle.

A. Responsorial

36.   The responsorial form of psalm singing appears to have been the original style for congregational use and still remains as the easiest method for engaging the congregation in the singing of psalms. In this model the psalmist or choir sings the verses of the psalm and the assembly responds with a brief antiphon (refrain). For pastoral or musical reasons, the *General Instruction* permits the substitution of other approved texts for these refrains.[44]

B. Antiphonal

37.   In the antiphonal style, the praying assembly is divided into two groups. The text of the psalm is shared between them; generally the same musical configuration (e.g., a psalm tone) is used by both. A refrain is ordinarily sung before and after the psalm by the whole body. This method of singing has its roots in the choir and monastic traditions. Today where it is used by the congregation, care must be taken that the latter can be at ease with this form of sung prayer.

C. Through-composed

38.   In a through-composed setting *(in directum)*, the musical material is ordinarily not repeated, unless the psalm calls for it. The music may be for soloist, soloist and choir or choir alone (e.g., an anthem). Only rarely will this form be found in settings designed for congregational use. The purpose of the *in directum* setting should be to complement the literary structure of the psalm and to capture its emotions.

D. Metrical Psalms

39.   The *General Instruction on the Liturgy of the Hours* makes no mention of the practice of singing the psalms in metrical paraphrases. This manner of psalm singing developed with some of the Reformation churches. Due to its four hundred year tradition, a large and important repertoire of metrical psalms in English is available today. Poets and composers continue to add to this resource of psalm settings.

40.   While metrical psalmody may be employed fruitfully in the Church's liturgy (for instance, when a hymn is part of one of the rites), introduction of this musical form into the psalmody of the Liturgy of the Hours profoundly affects and alters the praying of the psalms as a ritual. Thus, metrical psalms should not be used as substitutes either for the responsorial psalm in a liturgy of the word of one of the rites or for the psalms in the Liturgy of the Hours.

FORMULA TONES

41.   Formula tones (Gregorian plainsong tones, Anglican chants, faux-bourdons) are readily available and adaptable to modern use. Care should be taken in setting vernacular texts that the verbal accent pattern is not distorted by the musical cadence. These tones grew out of the paired half-line pattern of the Vulgate psalter. Modern translations of the psalms, however, have restored the Hebrew pattern of strophes (stanzas) of three, four, five or more lines. The sense unit in a strophe will frequently run beyond the musical pattern of the classical formula tone and will often require some repetition and even some accommodation for half-lines.

42.   Another kind of formula tone has more recently been developed (e.g., the Gelineau and Bevenot systems) which is based on the strophe as a unit. These tones are longer and make provisions for irregularities in the number of lines. They more naturally fit the Grail psalter, which is the approved translation of the psalms for the Liturgy of the Hours.

43.   Where formula tones are employed for the hours of the office, especially with a parish congregation, variety should be sought in the use of other forms of sung prayer, particularly the responsorial style. The Old Testament Canticle in Morning Prayer and the New Testament Canticle in Evening Prayer are especially suitable for this latter method of singing.

OTHER ELEMENTS

44.   The principle mentioned earlier concerning the mixing of different musical idioms has special application in a sung celebration of the Liturgy of the Hours. Psalms may be sung in the manners discussed above. Certain psalms, however, might be sung by a choir alone. A few might lend themselves to recitation. The nature and literary form of the psalm itself should suggest the way it is to be prayed. Likewise, in the same office some parts may be rendered unaccompanied, others accompanied by organ, piano, guitar or other instruments.

45.   Naturally, the hymns in the Liturgy of the Hours should be sung.[45] The responsories also lend themselves to singing, but as yet the number of published settings is few.[46] The readings are not usually chanted.[47] The introductory versicles and greetings can be easily learned and sung. The Lord's Prayer and the intercessions at Morning and Evening Prayer, either in the form of a litany with a fixed response (by far the easiest and most effective method for praying the intercessions) or as versicles and responses, are suited to singing.[48]

OTHER MATTERS

MUSIC AND THE LITURGICAL YEAR

46.   The mystery of God's love in Christ is so great that a single celebration cannot exhaust its meaning. Over the course of the centuries the various seasons

and feasts have developed to express the richness of the paschal mystery and of our need to celebrate it. While the liturgy celebrates but one "theme," the dying and rising of Christ, and while Sunday is the original Christian feast, even so the liturgical year shows forth this mystery like so many facets of a resplendent jewel.[49]

47. Music has been a unique means of celebrating this richness and diversity and of communicating the rhythm of the church year to the assembly. Music enhances the power of the readings and prayer to capture the special quality of the liturgical seasons. What would Christmas be without its carols? How diminished would the fifty-day Easter feast be without the solemn, joyful Alleluia song?

48. Great care must be shown in the selection of music for seasons and feasts. Contemporary culture seems increasingly unwilling either to prepare for or to prolong Christian feasts and seasons. The Church's pastors and ministers must be aware of cultural phenomena which run counter to the liturgical year or even devalue our feasts and seasons, especially through consumerism. The season of Advent should be preserved in its integrity, Christmas carols being reserved for the Christmas season alone. Hymns which emphasize the passion and death of Christ should be used only in the last week of the Lenten season. Easter should not be allowed to end in a day, but rather, the fifty days of its celebration should be planned as a unified experience.

MUSIC OF THE PAST

49. The *Constitution on the Sacred Liturgy* sets forth the principles for the recent reform of the liturgy. At the same time it called the heritage of sacred music "a treasure of inestimable value."[50] These purposes, while not opposed to each other, do exist in a certain tension. The restoration of active participation in the liturgy, the simplification of the rites, and the use of the vernacular have meant a massive change in the theory and practice of church music, a shift already detailed in *Music in Catholic Worship* and the present statement.

50. Some have viewed this situation with profound regret. For some, the setting aside of the Latin repertoire of past centuries has been a painful experience, and a cause of bitter alienation. "Now is the time for healing."[51] It is also the time to make realistic assessments of what place the music of the past can still have in the liturgies of today.

51. On the eve of the Council few parishes were performing the authentic repertoire recommended by Saint Pius X in his famous *motu proprio* on music.[52] Rather, most parishes generally used only a few of the simple chant Masses along with modern imitations of Renaissance motets and Masses. Moreover, the great music of the past was seldom the music of the ordinary parish church. Most often it was a product of the cathedrals and court chapels.

52. However, singing and playing the music of the past is a way for Catholics to stay in touch with and preserve their rich heritage. A place can be found for

this music, a place which does not conflict with the assembly's role and the other demands of the rite. Such a practice no longer envisions the performance of "Masses" as set pieces, but looks more to the repertoire of motets, antiphons and anthems which can be harmonized more easily with the nature of the renewed liturgy and with its pastoral celebration.[53]

53.   At Mass that place will typically include the time during the preparation of the gifts and the period after communion. A skillful director will also be able to find suitable choral repertoire to use as a prelude to the Mass, at the end of it, and at the Glory to God. *Jubilate Deo*, the basic collection of simple Gregorian chants, should also be employed as a source for the assembly's participation.

MUSIC AND CULTURAL HERITAGE

54.   Just as the great liturgical music of the past is to be remembered, cherished and used, so also the rich diversity of the cultural heritage of the many peoples of our country today must be recognized, fostered and celebrated. The United States of America is a nation of nations, a country in which people speak many tongues, live their lives in diverse ways, celebrate events in song and music in the folkways of their cultural, ethnic and racial roots.

55.   Liturgical music today must be as diverse and multi-cultural as the members of the assembly. Pastors and musicians must encourage not only the use of traditional music of other languages, but also the composition of new liturgical music appropriate to various cultures. Likewise the great musical gifts of the Hispanic, Black and other ethnic communities in the Church should enrich the whole Church in the United States in a dialogue of cultures.

INSTRUMENTAL MUSIC

56.   The liturgy prefers song to instrumental music. "As a combination of sacred music and words it forms a necessary or integral part of the solemn liturgy."[54] Yet the contribution of instrumentalists is also important, both in accompanying the singing and in playing by themselves.

57.   Church music legislation of the past reflected a culture in which singing was not only primary, but was presumed to be unaccompanied (chant and polyphony). The music of today, as indeed musical culture today, regularly presumes that the song is accompanied. This places instruments in a different light. The song achieves much of its vitality from the rhythm and harmony of its accompaniment. Instrumental accompaniment is a great support to an assembly in learning new music and in giving full voice to its prayer and praise in worship.

58.   Instrumental music can also assist the assembly in preparing for worship, in meditating on the mysteries, and in joyfully progressing in its passage from liturgy to life. Instrumental music, used in this way, must be understood as more than an easily dispensable adornment to the rites, a decoration to dress up a ceremony. It is rather ministerial, helping the assembly to rejoice, to weep, to be of one mind, to

be converted, to pray. There is a large repertoire of organ music which has always been closely associated with the liturgy. Much suitable music can be selected from the repertoires of other appropriate instruments as well.

59.   The proper place of silence must not be neglected, and the temptation must be resisted to cover every moment with music.[55] There are times when an instrumental interlude is able to bridge the gap between two parts of a ceremony and help to unify the liturgical action. But music's function is always ministerial and must never degenerate into idle background music.

RECORDED MUSIC

60.   The liturgy is a complexus of signs expressed by living human beings. Music, being preeminent among those signs, ought to be "live." While recorded music, therefore, might be used to advantage outside the liturgy as an aid in the teaching of new music, it should, as a general norm, never be used within the liturgy to replace the congregation, the choir, the organist or other instrumentalists.

61.   Some exceptions to this principle should be noted, however. Recorded music may be used to accompany the community's song during a procession out-of-doors and, when used carefully, in Masses with children.[56] Occasionally it might be used as an aid to prayer, for example, during long periods of silence in a communal celebration of reconciliation. It may never become a substitute for the community's song, however, as in the case of the responsorial psalm after a reading from Scripture or during the optional hymn of praise after communion.

62.   A prerecorded sound track is sometimes used as a feature of contemporary "electronic music" composition. When combined with live voices and/or instruments, it is an integral part of the performance and, therefore, is a legitimate use of prerecorded music.

MUSIC MINISTRY

63.   The entire worshiping assembly exercises a ministry of music. Some members of the community, however, are recognized for the special gifts they exhibit in leading the musical praise and thanksgiving of Christian assemblies. These are the pastoral musicians, whose ministry is especially cherished by the Church.

64.   What motivates the pastoral musician? Why does he or she give so much time and effort to the service of the church at prayer? The only answer can be that the church musician is first a disciple and then a minister. The musician belongs first of all to the assembly; he or she is a worshiper above all. Like any member of the assembly, the pastoral musician needs to be a believer, needs to experience conversion, needs to hear the Gospel and so proclaim the praise of God. Thus, the pastoral musician is not merely an employee or volunteer. He or she is a minister, someone who shares faith, serves the community, and expresses the love of God and neighbor through music.

65.   Additional efforts are needed to train men and women for the ministry of music. Colleges and universities offering courses of studies in liturgical music, as well as a growing number of regional and diocesan centers for the formation of liturgical ministers, are encouraged to initiate or to continue programs which develop musical skills and impart a thorough understanding of the liturgy of the Church.

66.   The musician's gift must be recognized as a valued part of the pastoral effort, and for which proper compensation must be made.[57] Clergy and musicians should strive for mutual respect and cooperation in the achievement of their common goals.

67.   As the assembly's principal liturgical leaders, priests and deacons must continue to be mindful of their own musical role in the liturgy. Priests should grow more familiar with chanting the presidential prayers of the Mass and other rites. Deacons, too, in the admonitions, exhortations, and especially in the litanies of the third penitential rite and in the general intercessions of the Mass, have a significant musical role to play in worship.

68.   Among music ministers, the cantor has come to be recognized as having a crucial role in the development of congregational singing. Besides being qualified to lead singing, he or she must have the skills to introduce and teach new music, and to encourage the assembly. This must be done with sensitivity so that the cantor does not intrude on the communal prayer or become manipulative. Introductions and announcements should be brief and avoid a homiletic style.

69.   The cantor's role is distinct from that of the psalmist, whose ministry is the singing of the verses of the responsorial psalm and communion psalm. Frequently the two roles will be combined in one person.

70.   A community will not grow in its ability either to appreciate or express its role in musical liturgy if each celebration is thought of as a discrete moment. A long-range plan must be developed which identifies how music will be used in the parish and how new music will be learned. The abilities of the congregation should never be misjudged. Some cannot or will not sing, for whatever reason. Most will take part and will enjoy learning new music if they have effective leaders.

COPYRIGHT

71.   In the last decade pastors and musicians have become more aware of the legal and moral implications of copyright.[58] As a result parishes and institutions are now more sensitive to the need composers, poets and publishers have to receive a just compensation for their creative work. Publishers have cooperated in making their requirements known and their music available to reprint at reasonable rates, an effort for which they deserve the thanks of the Church in the United States.

72.   Additional education regarding copyright needs to continue. At the same time, parishes and other institutions should annually budget sufficient monies for the purchase of music necessary for the proper celebration of the liturgy. The need for much copying would then be lessened.

CONCLUSION

73.   The past decade has shown important signs of growth. The eagerness of many congregations to make a beginning in singing has been matched by a second harvest of musical compositions. As time goes by, new generations will come to accept, as a matter of course, what was brand new and very strange only a few years ago, namely, that all should join in the songs and prayers of the liturgy.

74.   The Church in the United States continues on its journey of liturgical renewal and spiritual growth. It is the hope of the Bishops' Committee on the Liturgy that this statement will be a further encouragement in our progress along that course. The words of Saint Augustine remind us of our pilgrimage: "You should sing as wayfarers do—sing but continue your journey. Do not be lazy, but sing to make your journey more enjoyable. Sing, but keep going."[59]

NOTES

1. Bishops' Committee on the Liturgy (BCL), *Music in Catholic Worship* (MCW), (Washington: USCC, 1972); BCL, "The Place of Music in Eucharistic Celebrations, November 1967.

2. Text appears in this volume.

3. MCW, Introduction, unpaged.

4. Ibid., 45, 55, 63.

5. *Roman Pontifical* (RP): *Rite of Confirmation* (Confirmation), 23, 29.

6. *Roman Ritual* (RomR): *Rite of Baptism for Children* (RBaptC), 59, 60.

7. RR: *Rite of Christian Initiation of Adults* (RCIA), 146.

8. RR: RBaptC, 42, 52, 67.

9. RP: *Ordination of a Deacon* (Deacon), 25; *Ordination of a Priest* (Priest), 27; *Ordination of a Bishop* (Bishop), 35.

10. RP: *Institution of a Reader*, 7.

11. RP: *Confirmation*, 46.

12. RP: Priest, 25.

13. *Roman Missal*, General Instruction (GIRM), 56j.

14. RR: RCIA, 214; RBaptC, 48.

15. RP: Deacon, 18; Priest, 17; Bishop, 21.

16. RP: *Consecration to a life of Virginity*, 20, 59.

17. RP: *Dedication of a Church and an Altar* (Dedication), 58.

18. RR: *Rite of Penance*, 56.

19. RR: RBaptC, 59.

20. RR: RCIA, 389; RBaptC, 223–4.

21. RR: *Pastoral Care of the Sick: Rites of Anointing and Viaticum*, 75b.

22. RP: Deacon, 21; Priest 22; Bishop 26.

23. RP: Dedication 62.

24. RR: RBaptC, 96.

25. *The Liturgy of the Hours*, General Instruction (GILOTH), 273.

26. GILOTH, 276.

27. *Eucharistic Prayers for Masses with Children and for Masses of Reconciliation*, Provisional Text (Washington: USCC, 1975).

28. *The Lectionary for Mass*, Introduction (second typical edition, 1981), 23. "The *Alleluia* or the verse before the gospel must be sung and during it, all stand. It is not to be sung by the cantor who intones it or by the choir, but by the whole congregation together."

29. GIRM, 56i.

30. Ibid., 56e.

31. Ibid., 29.

32. Ibid., 31.

33. RR: RCIA. Becoming Catechumen, 74, 90. Election, 146, 171, 178. Initiation 221, 227, 231.

34. RR: RBaptC. Procession, 42. Song after homily, 47. Procession to place of baptism, 52. Acclamation after profession of faith, 59. Acclamation after baptism, 60. Procession to altar, 67.

35. RP: Confirmation, 23, 29.

36. RR: RCIA, 390. RR: RBaptC, 225–245. See Also "A Letter to Composers of Liturgical Music from the Bishops' Committee on the Liturgy" in BCL *Newsletter* XVI (December 1980), 237–239.

37. RR: *Rite of Penance*, 56. The ritual recommends the Canticle of Mary (Luke 1:46–55), Psalm 136 or another psalm listed in 206 as especially fitting as a song of praise.

38. MCW, 30–38.

39. MCW, 26–29.

40. MCW, 39–41.

41. RR: *Rite of Funerals*, 23–25, especially 25.5.

42. GILOTH, 267–284; BCL, *Study Text VII: The Liturgy of the Hours* (Washington: USCC, 1981).

43. GILOTH, 279, 121–123

44. Ibid., 274.

45. Ibid., 280.

46. Ibid. 281–282.

47. Ibid., 283.

48. Ibid., 284.

49. *Roman Calendar*, General Norms for the Liturgical Year and the Calendar, 4; Second Vatican Council, Constitution on the Liturgy (SC), *Sacrosanctum Concilium* (4 December 1963), 104ff.

50. SC, 112.

51. BCL, *A Commemorative Statement* (November 1978), in BCL *Newsletter* XIV (December 1978), 143.

52. Pius X, Motu Proprio, *Tra Le Sollecitudini* (22 November 1903).

53. Congregation of Rites, Instruction on Music in the Sacred Liturgy, *Musicam Sacram* (5 March 1967), 53.

54. SC, 112.

55. GIRM, 23; GILOTH, 202; Paul VI, Apostolic Exhortation, *Evangelica Testificatio* (29 June 1971), 46.

56. *Notitiae* 127 (February 1977), 94; Congregation for Divine Worship, *Directory for Masses with Children* (1 November 1973), 32.

57. MCW, 77; BCL, *A Commemorative Statement* (November 1978), in BCL *Newsletter* XIV (December 1978), 143–144.

58. BCL *Newsletter* III, 12 (December 1967), 109; Ibid. V, 5 (May 1969), 177; Ibid. XVI (January 1980), 197; FDLC Liturgical Arts Committee, *Copyright Update: Reprint Permissions of Publishers of Liturgical Music and Sacred Scripture* (Washington: FDLC, 1982).

59. St. Augustine, Sermo 256, 3 (PL 38:1193)

FULFILLED
IN
YOUR HEARING

THE HOMILY IN THE SUNDAY ASSEMBLY

BISHOPS' COMMITTEE ON
PRIESTLY LIFE AND MINISTRY

NATIONAL CONFERENCE OF CATHOLIC BISHOPS
15 FEBRUARY 1982

OUTLINE

FULFILLED IN YOUR HEARING
THE HOMILY IN THE SUNDAY ASSEMBLY

INTRODUCTION

"The primary duty of priests is the proclamation of the Gospel of God to all." These clear, straightforward words of the Second Vatican Council (*Decree on the Ministry and Life of Priests*, #4) may still come as something of a surprise to us. We might more spontaneously think that the primary duty of priests is the celebration of the Church's sacraments, or the pastoral care of the People of God or the leadership of a Christian community. Yet the words of the document are clear: the proclamation of the Gospel is primary. The other duties of the priest are to be considered properly presbyteral to the degree that they support the proclamation of the Gospel.

"Proclamation" can cover a wide variety of activities in the church. A life of quiet faith and generous loving deeds is proclamation; the celebration of the Eucharist is the proclamation "of the death of the Lord until he comes." But a key moment in the proclamation of the Gospel is preaching, preaching which is characterized by "proclamation of God's wonderful works in the history of salvation, that is, the mystery of Christ, which is ever made present and active within us, especially in the celebration of the liturgy" (Constitution on the Sacred Liturgy, #35, 2).

The *Decree on the Ministry and Life of Priests* is especially clear in relating the ministry of preaching to that of the celebration of the sacraments. Since these sacraments are sacraments of faith, and since "faith is born of the Word and nourished by it," the preaching of the Word is an essential part of the celebration of the sacraments. This is especially true in the celebration of the Eucharist, the document goes on to note, for "in this celebration the proclamation of the death and resurrection of the Lord is inseparably joined both to the response of the people who hear, and to the very offering whereby Christ ratified the New Testament in His blood."

This intimate link between preaching and the celebration of the sacraments, especially of the Sunday Eucharist, is what we intend to address in this document on preaching. We recognize that preaching is not limited to priests. Deacons are also ordained ministers of the Word. Indeed, the proclamation of the Word of God is the responsibility of the entire Christian community by virtue of the sacrament of baptism. Moreover, we recognize that preaching is not limited to the Eucharist, and we are pleased to support the ways in which more and more Catholics are celebrating the power of God's Word in evangelistic gatherings, in the catechumenate and in groups devoted to the study of the Bible and to prayer. We also recognize that for the vast majority of Catholics the Sunday homily is the normal and frequently the formal way in which they hear the Word of God proclaimed. For these Catholics the Sunday homily may well be the most decisive factor in determining the depth of their faith and strengthening the level of their commitment to the church.

The focus of this document, therefore, will be the Sunday homily, and even more specifically, the homily preached by the bishop or priest who presides at the celebration of the Eucharist. Again, we recognize that there are occasions when the homily may be preached by someone other than the presider, by a deacon serving in the parish or a guest priest preacher, for example. Yet, in terms of common practice and of liturgical norm, the preaching of the homily belongs to the presiding minister. (See *The General Instruction of the Roman Missal*, #42: "The homily should ordinarily be given by the celebrant.") The unity of Word and Sacrament is thus symbolized in the person of the presiding minister of the Eucharist.

While this document is addressed specifically to priests who have a pastoral ministry that involves regular Sunday preaching, we hope that all who are concerned with effective proclamation of the Gospel will find it helpful. This document may also prove useful in the preparation for and continuing formation of permanent deacons as ministers of the Word.

We propose that this document be used as a basis of discussion among priests and bishops, and by priests with members of their congregations. In such sharing of personal experiences, of expectations and frustrations, and by mutual support, we find hope for a renewal of preaching in the church today.

I. THE ASSEMBLY

[1]   Jesus came to Nazareth where he had been reared, and entering the synagogue on the sabbath as he was in the habit of doing, he stood up to do the reading. When the book of the prophet Isaiah was handed him, he unrolled the scroll and found the passage where it was written:

> "The spirit of the Lord is upon me;
>   therefore he has anointed me.
> He has sent me to bring glad tidings to the poor,
>   to proclaim liberty to captives,
> Recovery of sight to the blind
>   and release to prisoners,
> To announce a year of favor from the Lord."

Rolling up the scroll he gave it back to the assistant and sat down. All in the synagogue had their eyes fixed on him. Then he began by saying to them, "Today this Scripture passage is fulfilled in your hearing." All who were present spoke favorably of him; they marveled at the appealing discourse which came from his lips. (Lk 4:14–22a)

[2]   These verses from the fourth chapter of the Gospel of Saint Luke present us with a picture of Jesus as reader and homilist in the synagogue at Nazareth. He

stands up to read the lesson from the prophet which was placed at the end of the service. He then draws on this passage to speak to the here-and-now situation. All who listened to him were favorably impressed.

[3]   The three major elements of liturgical preaching are all here: the preacher, the word drawn from the Scriptures, and the gathered community. Each element is essential and each must be considered carefully if we are to understand the challenge and the possibilities of liturgical preaching.

[4]   We believe that it is appropriate, indeed essential, to begin this treatment of the Sunday homily with the assembly rather than with the preacher or the homily, and this for two principal reasons. First of all we can point to the great emphasis which communication theorists place on an accurate understanding of the audience if communication is to be effective. Unless a preacher knows what a congregation needs, wants, or is able to hear, there is every possibility that the message offered in the homily will not meet the needs of the people who hear it. To say this is by no means to imply that preachers are only to preach what their congregations want to hear. Only when preachers know what their congregations want to hear will they be able to communicate what a congregation needs to hear. Homilists may indeed preach on what they understand to be the real issues, but if they are not in touch with what the people think are the real issues, they will very likely be misunderstood or not heard at all. What is communicated is not what is said, but it is what is heard, and what is heard is determined in large measure by what the hearer needs or wants to hear.[1]

[5]   Contemporary ecclesiology provides a second and even more fundamental reason for beginning with the assembly rather than with the preacher or the homily. *The Dogmatic Constitution on the Church* describes the church as the mystery of God's saving will, given concrete historical expression in the people with whom he has entered into a covenant. This church is the visible sacrament of the saving unity to which God calls all people. "Established by Christ as a fellowship of life, charity, and truth, the church is also used by Him as an instrument for the redemption of all, and is sent forth into the whole world as the light of the world and the salt of the earth" (#9). The church, therefore, is first and foremost a gathering of those whom the Lord has called into a covenant of peace with himself. In this gathering, as in every other, offices and ministries are necessary, but secondary. The primary reality is Christ in the assembly, the People of God.

[6]   This renewed understanding of the church is gradually becoming consciously present in the words and actions of the Catholic people. By means of their involvement in diocesan and parish organizations, their sharing in various forms of ministry, and their active participation in the liturgy, they are beginning to experience what it means to say that the people are the church and the church are people.

[7]   Obviously the development we are speaking of is not uniform. But it is clear that the parish in which the priest acts in an arbitrary manner, in which virtually all active ministry—liturgical, educational, and social—is in the hands of the

clergy and religious, and in which the laity do little more than attend Mass and receive the sacraments, is no longer the norm. Such a drastic change in the practices and self-consciousness of the Catholic congregation is bound to have significant consequences for the content and style of preaching that takes place in the Sunday Eucharistic assembly.

To preach in a way that sounds as if the preacher alone has access to the truth and knows what is best for everyone else, or that gives the impression that there are no unresolved problems or possibility for dialogue, is to preach in a way that may have been acceptable to those who viewed the church primarily in clerical terms. In a church that thinks and speaks of itself as a pilgrim people, gathered together for worship, witness, and work, such preaching will be heard only with great difficulty, if at all.

THE IDENTITY OF THE ASSEMBLY

[8]   The Eucharistic assembly that gathers Sunday after Sunday is a rich and complex phenomenon. Even in parishes that are more or less uniform in ethnic, social, or economic background, there is great diversity: men and women, old and young, the successes and the failures, the joyful and the bereaved, the fervent and the halfhearted, the strong and the weak. Such diversity is a constant challenge to the preacher, for our words can all too easily be heard as excluding one or the other segment of the congregation. We may not mean to ignore the presence of women when we say "Jesus came to save all men," but if exclusion is heard, then exclusion is communicated, whether intended or not.

[9]   While the diversity of every assembly is a factor that needs to be taken seriously by the preacher, and all the more so when the diversity cuts across racial, ethnic, economic, and social lines, this diversity should not blind us to another, even greater reality: the unity of the congregation. This assembly has come together because its members have been baptized into the one body of Christ and share a common faith. This faith, though rooted in a common baptismal identity, is expressed in ways that extend from the highest levels of personal appropriation and intellectual understanding to the most immature forms of ritualism and routine. And yet, to a greater or lesser degree, it is faith in Jesus Christ that is common to all the members of a community gathered for Eucharist.

[10]   To say that a community shares a common faith is to say that its members have a common way of interpreting the world around them. For the Christian community, the world is seen and interpreted as the creation of a loving God. Although this world turned away from God through sin, God reached out again and again to draw the world to himself, finally sending his own Son in human flesh. This Son expressed the fullness of the Father's love by accepting death on the cross. The Father in turn glorified his Son by raising him from the dead and making him the source of eternal life for all who believe. Believers witness to the presence and word of Jesus in the world and are a continuing sign of the Kingdom of God, which is present both in and through Jesus, and still to come to its fullness through the power of the Holy Spirit.

[11] In very broad outline this is the common faith that binds together the Christian community gathering for worship. No individual in the community would very likely express the faith in quite these words. Some might find it difficult to express their faith in any words at all. They do not possess the background of theology to enable them to do so. We might say, therefore, that one of the principal tasks of the preacher is to provide the congregation of the faithful with words to express their faith, and with words to express the human realities to which this faith responds. Through words drawn from the Scriptures, from the church's theological tradition, and from the personal appropriation of that tradition through study and prayer, the preacher joins himself and the congregation in a common vision. We can say, therefore, that the homily is a unifying moment in the celebration of the liturgy, deepening and giving expression to the unity that is already present through the sacrament of baptism.

THE PREACHER AS MEDIATOR OF MEANING

[12] The person who preaches in the context of the liturgical assembly is thus a mediator, representing both the community and the Lord. The assembly gathers for liturgy as a community of faith, believing that God has acted in human history and more particularly, in their own history. The community gathers to respond to this living and active God. They may also gather to question how or whether the God who once acted in human history is still present and acting today. They may wonder how this God, whom the Scriptures present as so powerful and so loving, can be experienced in lives today that seem so broken and meaningless. How can parents believe in a God who raises the dead to life when their daughter has just been killed in a car accident? How can a family hope in a God who leads his people out of slavery into freedom when they are trapped in an inflationary spiral in which costs increase and the buying power of their salaries diminishes? How can young people join with the angels and saints in praise of the glory of God when they are struggling with the challenges of establishing their own identities and their relationship to family and friends?

[13] The preacher represents this community by voicing its concerns, by naming its demons, and thus enabling it to gain some understanding and control of the evil which afflicts it. He represents the Lord by offering the community another word, a word of healing and pardon, of acceptance and love. Like humans everywhere, the people who make up the liturgical assembly are people hungry, sometimes desperately so, for meaning in their lives. For a time they may find meaning in their jobs, their families and friends, their political or social causes. All these concerns, good and valid as they are, fall short of providing ultimate meaning. Without ultimate meaning, we are ultimately unsatisfied. If we are able to hear a word which gives our lives another level of meaning, which interprets them in relation to God, then our response is to turn to this source of meaning in an attitude of praise and thanksgiving.

[14] The community that gathers Sunday after Sunday comes together to offer God praise and thanksgiving, or at least to await a word that will give a meaning to their lives and enable them to celebrate Eucharist. What the preacher can do best of all at this time and in this place is to enable this community to celebrate

by offering them a word in which they can recognize their own concerns and God's concern for them.

[15]   The preacher acts as a mediator, making connections between the real lives of people who believe in Jesus Christ but are not always sure what difference faith can make in their lives, and the God who calls us into ever deeper communion with himself and with one another. Especially in the Eucharistic celebration, the sign of God's saving presence among his people, the preacher is called to point to the signs of God's presence in the lives of his people so that, in joyous recognition of that presence, they may join the angels and saints to proclaim God's glory and sing with them their unending hymn of praise.

II. THE PREACHER

[16]   We began our treatment of the Sunday homily by looking first to the assembly that gathers to celebrate the liturgy of the Eucharist. Such a beginning could be interpreted to mean that the importance of the ordained priesthood is not what it used to be. Nothing could be further from the truth. The priesthood of the faithful and the ordained ministerial priesthood although distinct are not opposed to one another. In fact, they stand or fall together. To the degree that we give full weight to the priesthood of all the baptized, to that degree do we see the full importance and significance of the ordained priesthood. To the degree that we downplay the importance of the priesthood of the faithful, to that degree is the ordained priesthood diminished.

[17]   The community gathered to worship is a priestly people, men and women called to offer God worship. If this community is conscious of its dignity, then those it calls to service in positions of leadership will be able to recognize their dignity as well. We think of the priest as the representative of Christ. This way of thinking is true, as long as we remember that one represents Christ by representing the church, for the church is the fundamental sacrament of Christ. Moreover, it is the church, through its bishops, that calls individuals to presbyteral ministry in the church.

PASTORAL ROLE OF THE PREACHER

[18]   Preachers who are conscious of their representative role strive to preach in a way that indicates they know and identify with the people to whom they are speaking. Their preaching is pastoral, displaying a sensitive and concerned knowledge of the struggles, doubts, concerns, and joys of the members of a local community.

[19]   To be in touch with the cares and concerns, needs and good fortunes of the assembly does not mean that the preacher has to answer questions or solve problems in every homily. There will be occasions when nothing we can say will do anything to change a situation. We cannot raise a dead daughter to life; our words will not stop inflation or lower unemployment. What our words can do is help people make connections between the realities of their lives and the realities

of the Gospel. We can help them see how God in Jesus Christ has entered and identified himself with the human realities of pain and of happiness.

LISTENING AND PRAYING

[20]   In order to make such connections between the lives of the people and the Gospel, the preacher will have to be a listener before he is a speaker. Listening is not an isolated moment. It is a way of life. It means openness to the Lord's voice not only in the Scriptures but in the events of our daily lives and in the experience of our brothers and sisters. It is not just *my* listening but *our* listening together for the Lord's word to the community. We listen to the Scriptures, we listen to the people, and we ask, "What are they saying to one another? What are they asking of one another?" And out of that dialogue between the Word of God in the Scriptures and the Word of God in the lives of his people, the Word of God in preaching begins to take shape.

[21]   Attentive listening to the Scriptures and to the people is, in essence, a form of prayer, perhaps the form of prayer most appropriate to the spirituality of the priest and preacher. There is nothing more essential than prayerful listening for effective preaching, a praying over the texts which seeks the light and fire of the Holy Spirit to kindle the *now* meaning in our hearts. A week of daily meditation on the readings of the following Sunday is not too much time to spend in preparation for the preaching we are called to do on the Lord's Day. Such regular preparation will allow us not only to savor the word in prayer but also to incorporate the experiences of a full week into our preparation.

[22]   Such extended, prayerful preparation is so important for preaching because it helps us reach the moment of inspiration, an inspiration that has affinities to poetic inspiration but is more. We ask for and expect the real movement of the Holy Spirit in us and in the assembly. If the words of Scripture are divinely inspired, as we believe them to be, then divine inspiration must be at work when those words are made alive and contemporary to the believing community in and through our ministry.

[23]   The preacher is thus called, above all, to be prayerful. The prayer we speak of is not prayer alongside of preparation for preaching, or over and above this preparation, but the very heart and center of the preparation itself. Unless the Word of God in the Scriptures is interiorized through prayerful study and reflection, it cannot possibly sustain the life-giving, love-generating words that preachers want to offer their people. Preachers then are called to a prayerful dwelling with their people and to a prayerful dwelling with the texts of Scripture knowing them and allowing themselves to be known by them.

[24]   This dwelling with the Scriptures and with the people which is the necessary prelude to effective preaching points to the necessity for certain pastoral skills and academic knowledge, both of which the modern seminary offers its candidates for priesthood, but which need continual updating and refining. We speak here of the skills of understanding and communicating with people, and of the knowledge required for the accurate and relevant interpretation of Scriptural texts.

[25] Let us begin with the second requirement first, since that is somewhat easier to describe. The interpretation of texts is the science of hermeneutics, and in order to accomplish its end, hermeneutics relies first of all on exegesis. For exegesis to be done at the highest professional level, the exegete must have knowledge of the original languages, access to the tools of textual criticism, extensive historical and archeological background, a comprehensive knowledge of the development of biblical faith, and a familiarity with the history of the theological interpretation of texts in both the synagogue and the Christian churches. Obviously few preachers have the training or access to the resources for exegesis of this kind.

[26] Exegesis for preaching need not always be done at the highest professional level. Our seminary training and our continuing education provide us with tools and resources to tap the best of contemporary exegesis in a fruitful way. Even a smattering of Hebrew and Greek is helpful in capturing the flavor or nuances of certain words. An acquaintance with the methods of scriptural scholarship enables us to understand, for example, why the sayings of Jesus can appear in such different contexts, and therefore with such different meanings, in the Gospels. Or again, knowing how the biblical author used a particular passage as a building block in a larger literary context can help us appreciate how the church of succeeding ages found it important to set the passage in contemporary contexts, a task which is ours in the liturgical celebration today.

[27] It is hard to imagine that a person who has as his primary duty the proclamation of the Gospel to all would be without the basic tools and methods that help to ensure an accurate understanding of this Gospel. Surely every preacher ought to have a basic library to turn to in the preparation of homilies. A good Bible dictionary will help in picturing the background of a passage; a concordance will locate other passages that are related; a "theological" dictionary of Scripture will trace ideas that recur through Old and New Testaments; Gospel parallels will set similar texts that occur in more than one Gospel side by side. Standard commentaries on the major books of the Bible that appear in the lectionary should also be ready at hand, as well as exegetical commentaries based on the lectionary itself.

[28] The texts of Scripture from which our preaching flows are not locked in antiquity. They are texts which have nourished the church's life throughout all its history, sustaining it in times of trial, calling it back to fidelity in times of weakness and opening up new possibilities when it seemed immobilized by the weight of human traditions.

[29] The history of the interpretation of the Scriptures is part of the contemporary meaning of the Scriptures. The way they have been preached, the liturgical expressions they have generated, the prayer they have nourished, the magisterial statements they have inspired, the theological systems they have fostered, even the heresies they have occasioned, expand and deepen the way the Scriptures speak to us today.

[30] It is the faith of the church that the preacher must proclaim, not merely his own. Consequently, the more familiar the preacher is with the history of scriptural interpretation and the development of the church's doctrine, the more capable he is of bringing that word into dialogue with the contemporary situation. Church doctrine is nourished by profound meditation upon the inspired Word, the exegesis of the fathers, conciliar documents and the teaching of the Magisterium. Therefore, the qualified preacher will lead his people to ever greater unity of faith among themselves as well as with prior generations of believers.

[31] It is somewhat more difficult to speak of what is involved in the understanding of people and how the priest/preacher can prepare himself for this demand of his office. Surely part of the rationale of the requirement that students in theological seminaries have a background in the liberal arts, with an emphasis on philosophy, is that familiarity with the leading ideas, movements, and personalities of human civilization (or at least of Western civilization) will enable preachers to engage in a critical dialogue with contemporary culture, recognizing what is conformable with the Gospel, challenging that which is not. The great artistic and literary achievements of a culture are surely a privileged means of access to the heart and mind of a people.

[32] Regular and sustained contact with the world's greatest literature or with its painting, sculpture, and musical achievements can rightfully be regarded by preachers not simply as a leisure-time activity but as part of their ongoing professional development. The same can be said of attention to modern entertainment media — television, film, radio—or to the theater. Dramatic presentations that deal sensitively with significant human issues can provide a wealth of material for our reflection and our preaching, both in its content and in its form.

[33] If preachers are to know and understand their congregations today, some familiarity with popular forms of entertainment may also be necessary. We need not spend whole afternoons watching soap operas, memorizing baseball statistics, or listening to the latest hit albums. Yet if we are totally unaware, or give the impression that we are unaware of the activities and interests to which people devote a good deal of their leisure time, energy, and money, it will be difficult for us to make connections between their lives and the Gospel, or to call them to fuller, richer, and deeper levels of faith response.

[34] Finally, preachers need to devote some time and energy to understanding the complex social, political, and economic forces that are shaping the contemporary world. Watching the evening news on television or scanning the headlines of the daily paper may be a beginning but it is not enough. Preachers need exposure to more serious and sustained commentary on the contemporary world, the kind of exposure that can be gained through a program of reading or through conversation with people who are professionally involved in such areas as business, politics, or medicine. Without this kind of informed understanding of the complex world we live in, preaching too easily degenerates into platitudes of faith, meaningless broadsides against the wickedness of the modern world, or into an uncritical affirmation of the wonderful advances that have taken place in modern times.

[35] To have a comprehensive knowledge of the social, political and economic forces shaping the contemporary world, while at the same time specializing in scriptural exegesis and theology and being pastorally competent may well appear to be an overwhelming, even impossible, expectation to lay on any one person. The point to be made here, however, is not that preachers must know everything, but rather that there is no limit to the sources of knowledge and insight that a preacher can draw upon. There are many avenues which lead toward a deeper understanding of the human condition. Some will travel more easily down the avenue of the social sciences, others down the avenue of literature and the arts, others down the avenue of popular culture. What ultimately matters is not which avenue we take, but what we take with us as we travel.

[36] As long as we carry the Word of God with us, a word that we have allowed to touch on our own lives in prayer and reflection, and as long as we speak that word in language and images that are familiar to the dwellers of the particular avenue we are traveling, the Word of God will be preached, and the possibility of faith and conversion will be present.

THE LIMITATIONS OF THE PREACHER

[37] It may be good to close this section with a word of caution. While preachers, like other people, cannot be expected to know everything, they are easily tempted to give the impression that they do. As one perceptive critic put it, preachers in their pulpits are people who speak ten feet above contradiction. The Word of God which we are called to proclaim is a divinely inspired Word, and therefore an authoritative and unfailing Word. But we who are limited and fallible possess no guarantee that our understanding of this Word—or of the human situation—is without error and therefore relevant and binding.

[38] Preachers accept their limitations not by making the pulpit a sounding board for their personal doubts, anxieties or problems, but by offering people a Word which has spoken to their lives and inviting these people to think and ponder on that Word so that it might speak to their lives as well. A recent poster says it well: "Jesus came to take away our sins, not our minds." What preachers may need to witness to more than anything else is the conviction that authentic, mature faith demands the hard struggle of thinking and choosing. What the Word of God offers us is a way to interpret our human lives, a way to face the ambiguities and challenges of the human condition, not a pat answer to every problem and question that comes along.

[39] Some years ago a survey was taken among a group of parishioners. They were asked what they hoped to experience during a sermon. When the results were in, the answer was clear. What the majority wanted was simply to hear a person of faith speaking. Ultimately, that's what preaching is all about, not lofty theological speculation, not painstaking biblical exegesis, not oratorical flamboyance. The preacher is a person speaking to people about faith and life.

III. THE HOMILY

[40] The Sunday Eucharist is a privileged point of encounter between a local Christian community and its priest. Within this Eucharistic celebration the homily is a moment when this encounter can be especially intense and personal. We want now to look at the nature and function of this form of preaching, to relate it to the issues we have already raised in speaking of the assembly and the preacher, and finally to suggest a method for building and preaching the homily.

THE HOMILY AND FAITH

[41] Like all preaching, the homily is directed to faith. As Paul writes, "But how shall they call on him in whom they have not believed? And how can they believe unless they have heard of him? And how can they hear unless there is someone to preach?" (Romans 10:14). Some preaching is directed to people who have not heard the Gospel and is meant to lead them to an initial acceptance of Jesus Christ as Savior. Other forms of preaching are directed to a deeper understanding of the faith or to its ethical implications.

[42] The homily is preaching of another kind. It may well include evangelization, catechesis, and exhortation, but its primary purpose is to be found in the fact that it is, in the words of the Second Vatican Council, "a part of the liturgy itself" (*Constitution on the Sacred Liturgy*, #52). The very meaning and function of the homily is determined by its relation to the liturgical action of which it is a part. It flows from the Scriptures which are read at that liturgical celebration, or, more broadly, from the Scriptures which undergird its prayers and actions, and it enables the congregation to participate in the celebration with faith.

[43] The fact that the homily is addressed to a congregation of believers who have gathered to worship indicates that its purpose is not conversion from radical unbelief to belief. A homily presupposes faith. Nor does the homily primarily concern itself with a systematic theological understanding of the faith. The liturgical gathering is not primarily an educational assembly. Rather the homily is preached in order that a community of believers who have gathered to celebrate the liturgy may do so more deeply and more fully—more faithfully—and thus be formed for Christian witness in the world.[2]

FAITH AS INTERPRETATION

[44] To say that preaching, the homily included, is directed to faith is another way of saying that preaching is involved in the task of interpretation. "Faith" can be defined as a way of seeing or interpreting the world. The way we interpret the world, in turn, determines the way we relate to it. For example, if we believe that a particular race or class of people are our enemies, we will relate to them with suspicion and hostility. A friendly gesture will be interpreted not as a genuine sign of good will but as a ruse to get us to lower our guard. On the other hand, if we believe that a group of people are our friends, we will tend to excuse even a hostile gesture with the explanation that there must have been some mistake: they didn't recognize us or we have misinterpreted their gesture. Our "faith" in the way

things are has led us to live in the world in a way that corresponds to what we believe about it.

[45] The Christian interprets the world not as a hostile and evil place, but as a creation of a loving God who did not allow it to destroy itself, but sent his Son to rescue it. The Christian response to the world, then, is one of acceptance and affirmation—along with the recognition that it is still awaiting its full redemption.

[46] One of the most important, and most specifically human, ways in which faith is communicated to individuals and communities is through language. The way we speak about our world expresses the way we think about it and interpret it. One of the reasons we speak about our world at all is to share our vision of the world with others. The preacher is a Christian specially charged with sharing the Christian vision of the world as the creation of a loving God. Into this world human beings unleashed the powers of sin and death. These powers have been met, however, by God through his Son Jesus Christ, in whom he is at work not only to restore creation, but to transform it into a new heaven and a new earth.

FAITH LEADING TO A RESPONSE

[47] When one hears and accepts this vision of the world, this way of interpreting reality, a response is required. That response can take many forms. Sometimes it will be appropriate to call people to repentance for the way they have helped to spread the destructive powers of sin in the world. At other times the preacher will invite the congregation to devote themselves to some specific action as a way of sharing in the redemptive and creative word of God. However, the response that is most general and appropriate "at all times and in every place" is the response of praise and thanksgiving (Eucharist).

[48] When we accept the good news that the ultimate root and source of our being is not some faceless Prime Mover, not a merciless judge, but a prodigally loving Father who calls us to share in his love and to spread it to others, we sense that it is indeed right to give him thanks and praise.

Although we have received this good news, believed in it, and sealed our belief in the sacrament of baptism, we need to rediscover the truth of it again and again in our lives. Our faith grows weak, we are deceived by appearances, overwhelmed by suffering, plagued by doubt, anguished by the dreadful silence of God. And yet we gather for Eucharist, awaiting a word that will rekindle the spark of faith and enable us to recognize once again the presence of a loving God in our lives. We come to break bread in the hope that we will be able to do so with hearts burning. We come expecting to hear a Word from the Lord that will again help us to see the meaning of our lives in such a way that we will be able to say, with faith and conviction, "It is right to give him thanks and praise."

[49] The preacher then has a formidable task: to speak from the Scriptures (those inspired documents of our tradition that hand down to us the way the first believers interpreted the world) to a gathered congregation in such a way that those assembled will be able to worship God in spirit and truth, and then go forth

to love and serve the Lord. But while the task is formidable, it is not impossible, especially if one goes about it with purpose and method.

THE HOMILY AND THE LECTIONARY

[50] The homily is not so much *on* the Scriptures as *from* and *through* them. In the Roman Catholic tradition, the selection of texts to be read at the Eucharistic liturgy is normally not left to the preacher, but is determined ahead of time and presented in the form of a lectionary. The basic purpose of a lectionary is twofold: to ensure that the Scripture texts appropriate to a feast or season are read at that time, and to provide for a comprehensive reading of the Scriptures. Thus, we find in the lectionary two principles guiding the selection of texts: the thematic principle (readings chosen to correspond to the "theme" of a feast or season), and the *lectio continua* principle (readings taken in order from a book of the Bible which is being read over a given period of time).

[51] In the section of the lectionary entitled "Masses for Various Occasions," we find the thematic principle at work in a way that corresponds more closely to what some liturgical planners refer to as the theme of a liturgy: e.g., readings appropriate for Christian unity, or for peace and justice. Such thematic liturgies have their place, as the lectionary title indicates, on various or special occasions, rather than at the regular Sunday liturgy.[3]

[52] It is to these given texts that the preacher turns to prepare the homily for a community that will gather for the Sunday liturgy. Since the purpose of the homily is to enable the gathered congregation to celebrate the liturgy with faith, the preacher does not so much attempt to explain the Scriptures as to interpret the human situation through the Scriptures. In other words, the goal of the liturgical preacher is not to interpret a text of the Bible (as would be the case in teaching a Scripture class) as much as to draw on the texts of the Bible as they are presented in the lectionary to interpret peoples' lives. To be even more precise, the preacher's purpose will be to turn to these Scriptures to interpret peoples' lives in such a way that they will be able to celebrate Eucharist—or be reconciled with God and one another, or be baptized into the Body of Christ, depending on the particular liturgy that is being celebrated.[4]

[53] To preach from the Scriptures in this way means that we have to "get behind them," as it were. We have to hear these texts as real words addressed to real people. Scholarly methods of interpreting Scripture can help us do this by putting us in touch with the life situations that originated these texts, or by making us more aware of the different ways language can function as a conveyer of meaning. But scholarly methods are not enough. As we emphasized in the second chapter, the preacher needs to listen to these texts meditatively and prayerfully.

[54] As preachers we go to the Scriptures saying, "What is the human situation to which these texts were originally addressed? To what human concerns and questions might these same texts have spoken through the Church's history? What is the human situation to which they can speak today? How can they help us to understand, to interpret our lives in such a way that we can turn to God with

praise and thanksgiving?" Only when we approach the Scriptures in this way do they have any possibility of becoming a living word for us and for others.

[55]   Such prayerful listening to the text demands time, not just the time of actual reading and praying and studying but, just as importantly, the time of standing back and letting the text dwell in our unconscious mind. This period of "incubation," as it is often called, is essential to all human creative effort. It is especially important for the homilist when reflecting upon texts which have become overly familiar, or which seem inappropriate for a given situation. With the use of a lectionary, the readings assigned for a particular day may seem to have little to say to a specific congregation at a specific time in its life. However, if the text and the actual human situation are allowed to interact with one another, a powerful interpretative word of faith will often emerge. But for this to happen we need to dwell with the text and allow it to dwell with us. Only then will the text reveal new meaning to us, a new and fresh way of interpreting and speaking about our world.[5]

THE HOMILY, THE CONGREGATION, AND HOMILY SERVICES

[56]   If the homily must be faithful to the Scriptures for it to be the living Word of God, it must also be faithful to the congregation to whom this living Word of God is addressed. The homily will be effective in enabling a community to worship God with praise and thanksgiving only if individuals in that community recognize there a word that responds to the implicit or explicit questions of their lives.

[57]   There are many ways in which priests get to know their congregations and allow themselves to be known by them: involvement with parish organizations, individual and family counseling, social contacts, visits to the sick and the bereaved, planning for weddings and baptisms, the sacrament of reconciliation, and, equally as important, simply being with people as a friend and member of the community. The preacher will be able to draw on all these contacts when he turns to the Scriptures to seek there a Word from the Lord for the lives of his people.

[58]   This pastoral dimension of the homily is the principal reason why some homily services, especially those that do little more than provide ready-to-preach homilies, can actually be a hindrance to effective preaching. Since the homily is integrally related to the liturgy, and since liturgy presupposes a community that gathers to celebrate it, the homily is by definition related to a community. Homily services can be helpful in the interpretation of scriptural texts (though generally not as much as some basic exegetical resources) and give some ideas on how these texts can be related to contemporary human concerns. But they cannot provide individual preachers with specific indications of how these texts can be heard by the particular congregations to whom they will preach.

[59]   Homily services can provide valuable assistance to the preacher when they are concerned to relate the interpretation of the lectionary texts to the liturgical season in which they appear, and when they are attentive to the *lectio continua* principle of the lectionary. They may also be helpful in suggesting some possibilities for the development of a homily, or in providing suitable examples and

illustrations. The primary help that a good homily service will offer is to make available to the preacher recent exegetical work on the specific texts that appear in the lectionary and to indicate some ways in which this biblical word can be heard in the present as God's Word to his people. They can never replace the homilist's own prayer, study, and work.

THE HOMILY AND THE LITURGY OF THE EUCHARIST

[60]   A homily is not a talk given on the occasion of a liturgical celebration. It is "a part of the liturgy itself." In the Eucharistic celebration the homily points to the presence of God in people's lives and then leads a congregation into the Eucharist, providing, as it were, the motive for celebrating the Eucharist in this time and place.[6]

[61]   This integral relation of the homily to the liturgy of the Eucharist which follows the liturgy of the word has implications for the way in which the homily is composed and delivered. In the first place, the homily should flow quite naturally out of the readings and into the liturgical action that follows. To set the homily apart by beginning or ending it with a sign of the cross[7], or by delivering it in a style that is totally different from the style used in the rest of the liturgy, might only reinforce the impression that the homily is simply a talk given on the occasion of a liturgical gathering, one that could just as well be given at another time and in another context.

[62]   Although the preaching of the homily properly belongs to the presiding minister of the Eucharistic celebration, there may occasionally be times when it is fitting for someone else, priest or deacon, to preach. On these occasions the integral relation of the homily to the rest of the liturgy will be safeguarded if the preacher is present and actively involved in the whole of the liturgical celebration. The practice of having a preacher slip in to read the Gospel and preach the homily, and then slip out again, does not do justice to the liturgical integrity of the homily.

HOMILETIC STYLE

[63]   As regards the structure and style of the homily, we can take a lead from the use of the Greek word *homileo* in the New Testament.[8] While the etymology of the word suggests communicating with a crowd, its actual use in the New Testament implies a more personal and conversational form of address than that used by the classical Greek orator. The word is employed in reference to the conversation the two disciples engaged in on their way to Emmaus (Luke 24:14) and of the conversation Antonius Felix, Procurator of Judea, had with Paul when the latter was held prisoner in Caesarea (Acts 24:26). The New Testament usage suggests that a homily should sound more like a personal conversation, albeit a conversation on matters of utmost importance, than like a speech or a classroom lecture. What we should strive for is a style that is purposeful and personal, avoiding whatever sounds casual and chatty on the one extreme or impersonal and detached on the other.

[64]   One of the ways we can move toward a more personal style of address in our homilies is by the way we structure them. Many homilies seem to fall into the same three-part pattern: "In today's readings . . . This reminds us . . . Therefore let us . . ." The very structure of such homilies gives the impression that the preacher's principal purpose is to interpret scriptural texts rather than communicate with real people, and that he interprets these texts primarily to extract ethical demands to impose on a congregation. Such preachers may offer good advice, but they are rarely heard as preachers of good news, and this very fact tends to distance them from their listeners.

[65]   Another way of structuring the homily, and one that is more in keeping with its function of enabling people to celebrate the liturgy with deepened faith, is to begin with a description of a contemporary human situation which is evoked by the scriptural texts, rather than with an interpretation or reiteration of the text. After the human situation has been addressed, the homilist can turn to the Scriptures to interpret this situation, showing how the God described therein is also present and active in our lives today. The conclusion of the homily can then be an invitation to praise this God who wills to be lovingly and powerfully present in the lives of his people.[9]

[66]   The point of the preceding paragraph is not to substitute a new straight jacket for an old one. There is no one correct form for the homily. On occasion it may be a dramatic and engaging story, on another a well-reasoned exposition of a biblical theme showing its relevance to the contemporary situation, or the liturgical day, feast or season. It might also take the form of a dialogue between two preachers or involve the approved local use of visual or audio media. Ideally, the form and style will be determined by the form and style of the Scriptures from which it flows, by the character of the liturgy of which it is a part, and by the composition and expectations of the congregation to which it is addressed, and not exclusively by the preference of the preacher.

[67]   Whatever its form, the function of the Eucharistic homily is to enable people to lift up their hearts, to praise and thank the Lord for his presence in their lives. It will do this more effectively if the language it uses is specific, graphic, and imaginative. The more we can turn to the picture language of the poet and the storyteller, the more we will be able to preach in a way that invites people to respond from the heart as well as from the mind.

THE LIMITS AND POSSIBILITIES OF LITURGICAL PREACHING

[68]   But isn't all this too limited a view of preaching? Does it really respond to the needs of the people? Doesn't regular Sunday preaching have to take into account the ignorance of the Scriptures on the part of large numbers of Catholics, even those who participate regularly in the Sunday Eucharist, and deal in some systematic way with the fundamentals of the faith? Is there not a crying need for regular and sustained teaching about the moral imperatives that flow from an acceptance of the Good News? What about all those times when people's lives are shattered, when they simply are psychologically incapable of offering God praise and thanks, when it seems they have nothing to be thankful for? How do we speak

to all the people in our congregations who have yet to hear the basic Gospel message calling them to faith and conversation, or who may even need a form of preaching that heightens their sensitivity to basic human realities and in this way readies them for the hearing of the Gospel?

[69]   In the last analysis the only proper response to these questions is a pastoral one. Priests will have to decide what form of preaching is most suitable for a particular congregation at a particular time. We would simply like to make two points here. First of all, social science research contends that the oral presentation of a single person is not a particularly effective way to impart new information or to bring about a change in attitude or behavior. It is, however, well suited to make explicit or to reinforce attitudes or knowledge previously held. The homily, therefore, which normally is an oral presentation by a single person, will be less effective as a means of instruction and/or exhortation than of interpretation— that is, as a means of enabling people to recognize the implications, in liturgy and in life, of the faith that is already theirs.

[70]   The second point to be made is that the liturgical homily, which draws on the Scriptures to interpret peoples' lives in such a way that they can recognize the saving presence of God and turn to him with praise and thanksgiving, does not exclude doctrinal instruction and moral exhortation. Such instruction and exhortation, however, are here situated in a broader context, namely, in the recognition of God's active presence in the lives of the people and the praise and thanksgiving that this response elicits.[10]

[71]   It may very well be that what God is doing in the life of a congregation at some particular moment is asking them to change in a way that is demanding and disorienting. The homily can be one way of helping to bring about that change, and it can still lead to a response of praise and thanksgiving by showing that our former way of life, comfortable as it may have been, was a way that led to death, while the new way, with all of its demands and difficulties, is a way that leads to life.

[72]   But even though the liturgical homily can incorporate instruction and exhortation, it will not be able to carry the whole weight of the Church's preaching. There will still need to be special times and occasions for preaching that addresses human values in such a way as to dispose the hearers to be open to the Gospel of Jesus Christ, preaching intended to bring the hearers to an inner conversion of heart, and preaching intended to instruct the faithful in matters of doctrine or morality. These three kinds of preaching—sometimes referred to as pre-evangelization, evangelization, and catechesis—can be found today in evangelistic gatherings, the adult catechumenate, youth ministry programs, spiritual renewal programs, Bible study groups and many forms of religious education.

[73]   The homily can complement all these forms of preaching by attending more specifically to what it is to accomplish. Such would be to show how and where the mystery of our faith, focused upon by that day's Scripture readings, is occurring in our lives. This would bring the hearers to a more explicit and deepened faith, to an

expression of that faith in the liturgical celebration and, following the celebration, in their life and work.

[74]   But is it really possible to create this readiness for praise and thanksgiving in congregations as large and diverse as those in which many of us minister? In these congregations some people will be feeling a sense of loss because of a recent bereavement; some facing marital difficulties; some having problems adjusting emotionally to school, job, home or community; some struggling with a deep sense of guilt stemming from their inability to deal maturely with their sexuality, or because of their addiction to drugs or alcohol. Others in our congregations will be struggling with the relevance of the Gospel to oppressive economic structures, to world peace, or to the many forms of discrimination in our society. Is it really possible to say to these people, "Look at the way in which God is present in your lives and turn to him with praise and thanksgiving?"

[75]   Obviously, it will not always be easy to do this. And we will never be able to do it, at least not with any honesty and integrity, if we have not recognized the active presence of God in our own lives, as broken and shattered as they may be, and out of that brokenness affirm that it is still good to praise him and even to give him thanks. We need to remember in situations like this that our celebration of the Eucharist is done in memory of Jesus Christ who, *on the night before he died*, turned to God and praised and thanked him out of the very depths of his distress. Praise and thanksgiving, therefore, do not automatically imply the presence of euphoria.

[76]   We can and must praise God even when we do not feel like it, for praise and thanksgiving are rooted in and grow out of faith, not feeling, a faith which interprets this world by saying that in spite of appearances often to the contrary, our God is a loving God. It is for this reason that even at the time of death, we celebrate a Eucharist, because we believe that for his faithful ones life is changed, not, as appearances would seem to indicate, taken away.

[77]   The challenge to preachers then is to reflect on human life with the aid of the Word of God and to show by their preaching, as by their lives, that in every place and at every time it is indeed right to praise and thank the Lord.

IV. HOMILETIC METHOD

[78]   Every art is based on a theory and a method, and preaching is no exception. Some artists, it is true, work solely from inspiration. They do not know why or how they do what they do. Consequently, they are incapable of passing their insight on to others. But they have a method nonetheless, and if their work is lasting, their method will sooner or later be uncovered by interpreters and critics of their work.

[79]   Artists who are conscious of their method are in a much more advantageous position than those who are not. They are able to channel and direct their work more easily, can work more efficiently within time constraints, and can adapt their method to changed circumstances and demands. They know what they are

doing and how they go about doing it, and they can pass this information on to others who might like to learn from them.

[80] Ultimately, individual preachers will have to develop their own method for moving from the Scriptures to the homily, learning from their own successes and failures, as well as from other preachers through whose words they have heard the Word of God. The description of a method for building the homily that follows is not intended as—nor could it possibly be—a foolproof system for producing outstanding homilies week after week. Rather it provides a model that includes the major components of the creative process (data gathering, incubation, insight, communication) and does so within the framework of a week.

[81] This method also respects the understanding of the homily that is central to this document: a scriptural interpretation of human existence which enables a community to recognize God's active presence, to respond to that presence in faith through liturgical word and gesture, and beyond the liturgical assembly, through a life lived in conformity with the Gospel.

[82] The most important feature of any method is precisely that it be methodical, that is, orderly and regular. In the preparation of the homily, as in other creative endeavors, the total amount of time we spend preparing may be less important than our observance of a regular pattern of activity spread out over a certain period of time. Doing the same thing each day for the same amount of time is often a condition for success, whether this be in study, in prayer, in writing, or in artistic achievement. A regular daily pattern of activity for the preparation of the Sunday homily is likewise often the key factor in effective preaching over the long term.

[83] Each of us called to the regular ministry of preaching needs to determine just what part of each day of the week is going to be devoted to the preparation of the Sunday homily. The time we spend each day need not be lengthy, but it needs to be determined ahead of time and be held sacred. Schedules, of course, are always to be adjusted for emergencies, but unless we determine in advance that a particular time is going to be used for a particular purpose, and stick to it, it is all too easy to have our entire day filled with appointments and meetings which we felt we could not turn down or postpone because "we had nothing special planned."

[84] One final preliminary remark. The method that follows describes a process that extends over a week's time. Some form of "remote preparation" is also in order. Such preparation could take the form of reading a recent work on the theology of the particular Synoptic Gospel that will be the "Gospel of the Year" or spending some time planning a unified sequence of homilies for a particular liturgical season.

[85] One of the reasons our preaching is less effective than it could be is that we have not taken seriously enough the *lectio continua* principle of our lectionary. We preach each Sunday's homily as if it had no connection with what preceded or what will follow. It should be possible, and indeed it would emphasize a sense of continuity and identity in the congregation, if from time to time our homilies would end on a "to be continued" note.

[86]   The preparation for a Sunday homily should begin early in the week whenever possible, even on Sunday evening. The first step is to read and reread the texts for the liturgy. Frequently the texts will be familiar, so it is important for us to do everything we can to make this reading as fresh as possible. Read the texts aloud; read them in several versions; if we read and understand Greek or Hebrew, we might try to read them in the original. Even if our knowledge of these languages is minimal, we may find ourselves becoming aware of nuances and connections that can easily be missed if we rely entirely on translations.

[87]   At this point in the preparation process it is helpful, indeed almost essential, to read the texts in context—that is, to read them from the Bible rather than from the lectionary only. In reading and rereading the texts, continue to read all four of them (Gospel, Old Testament, Psalm, New Testament), even if a decision has been made about which text will become the focus of the homily. It is not necessary for a homily to tie together all the readings. Indeed, for the Sundays throughout the year, when the New Testament lesson is chosen without reference to the Old Testament or the Gospel, attempts to impose some kind of thematic unity can be quite artificial. Nonetheless, the reading of the texts side by side, even if they are unrelated to one another, can often prompt new and rich insights into the "now" meaning of the Scriptures.

[88]   Read the texts with pen in hand, jotting down any and all ideas. Keep in mind that what we are listening for is a Word from the Lord, a Word which can be heard as good news. We will be all the more disposed to hear and receive such a word if our reading is a prayerful, attentive listening to the text of the Scriptures. Try to read the text without asking "What does it mean?" Approach it humbly, dwell with it, and let it speak for itself.

STUDY AND FURTHER REFLECTION

[89]   One of the major temptations of students when they are assigned a paper is immediately to run to the "experts." The same temptation afflicts preachers. All too often our preparation for a homily consists of looking up the lessons, reading them over quickly, and then turning to a commentary or a homily service to find out what they mean and what we might be able to say about them. By so doing we block out the possibility of letting these texts speak to us and to the concerns we share with a congregation.

[90]   Another danger in going to the commentaries too early is that we program ourselves for preaching which, in content and style, is academic rather than existential. We look for information about the texts that we can pass on to our hearers. We think of the text as a container of a hidden meaning that we have to discover and pry loose with the appropriate tools, rather than as a word spoken directly to us by the Lord. This approach to the text leads to preaching that is a word about something rather than a word, God's Word, to someone.

[91]   The process of personal reflection and interpretation, therefore, should go on for a couple of days without the aid of commentaries. We are our own interpreters first of all, and then when we do turn to the professional exegetes, we do so for the purpose of checking out the accuracy of our own interpretation. We will frequently receive new insights and ideas from the professionals, and these will be helpful to us. If we have allowed the texts to speak to us directly, we will be much better prepared to speak a word that is expressive of our own faith and in touch with the concerns of our people. We will also be able to better recognize and use the insights the professional exegetes give us.

LETTING GO

[92]   Sometime in the middle of the preparation process we should allow ourselves to step back from the work we are doing and give free reign to the subconscious processes of our minds. At times we will find that our preparation has brought us to a roadblock. A passage may make no sense to us. It may even scandalize us. We may want to ignore it, but it will not go away. The more we wrestle with it, the more troublesome it becomes. The words of Jesus about love for enemies fly in the face of our natural inclination for retribution; his words about selling possessions and giving them to the poor contradict our instinctive sense of the necessity for prudent stewardship. Paul's teaching that sin and death entered the world through one man seems to contradict everything we hold about individual, personal freedom and responsibility. We sense a real tension between the Word of God and the human situation.

[93]   When this happens we have one of the best signs that we are on to something vital. The Word of God may in fact be challenging our faith, calling us to conversion, to a new vision of the world. This period can be a difficult one, for we can feel that we are being asked to give up a way of looking at and dealing with the world which has served us well and with which we have grown comfortable. At a time like this we need to let go in order to allow the Holy Spirit to work within us and lead us to a deeper and richer faith.

DRAFTING

[94]   A time for writing should be scheduled at least two days before the preaching of the homily in order to provide ample time for alterations. Knowing that there will be opportunity to rework the homily will do much to save us from writer's block. At this stage we need not be concerned with matters of style, or even with making sure that the homily is tightly reasoned and well constructed. The point is simply to begin getting ideas down on paper so that we will have something to work with.

[95]   It is quite possible that we will come to this stage of preparation still not having any idea—any new and fresh idea, that is—of what we are going to say. We may simply feel empty and without inspiration. Begin writing anyway, for the very act of writing often unleashes a flow of ideas that will be new, fresh, and exciting. It is often at this point of initial writing that the difficult text suddenly opens up its meaning and provides a new, a richer understanding of how God is

present in our lives. At this point, too, the two readings which had seemed so totally unrelated may suddenly come together and illuminate one another. When something like this happens (sometimes referred to as the moment of insight, or the "aha" experience), we may well have the central idea for our homily.

[96]   So, at this point, simply write. Jot down words, phrases, unrelated sentences. Think of sketching the homily, or of working on an outline, rather than writing out a text. In fact, it is better not to put the ideas in too fixed a form at this point, for we may find that it then becomes difficult to alter them. Don't stop to think of the best way to say something; don't go back and cross out words and phrases because they don't sound right. There is time for that later. Let the pen or the typewriter simply go, even though we are sure that we will not use anything we are putting down on paper. The very act of writing is a way of calling to the surface the ideas and the words that will in fact be the stuff of which our homilies are made.

REVISING

[97]   The revising stage is one of the most important and the one that is too easily omitted for lack of time. To revise is frequently to cut: the good but extraneous material that surfaced in the jotting down stage of preparation; the technical theological terms and jargony "in" words that creep into our vocabularies; the use of the non-specific "this" or "it" at the beginning of sentences; the moralistic "therefore let us" or "we should" which we so easily resort to in winding up the homily; the references to "he" and "men" when the words are meant to include everyone; the vague generalities that can be replaced with specific incidents or examples.

[98]   The time for revising is also the time to arrange the material in the order best suited to gain, and hold, people's attention and to invite them to a response of faith in God's Word. In the sketching stage a story may have occurred to us which exemplified perfectly the human situation being addressed by the Word of God. Bring that story up front. Use it as the opening so that people are able to identify with the situation right from the beginning. Beginning the homily with "in today's Gospel . . ." or words to that effect, risks losing the attention of the congregation right at the beginning for they will not have been given any indication of why they should be interested in what was said in today's Gospel.

[99]   The time of revising is also the time to make sure that the homily does in fact have a central, unifying idea, and that this idea is clearly stated and repeated throughout the homily. We need not repeat the idea in the same words all the time, but we need to come back to it several times. People will inevitably drift in and out, no matter how good the preacher is. The restatement of the central idea is a way of inviting people back into the homily again if they happen to have been distracted from what we were saying.

[100] Finally, the time for revising is the time to make sure that the homily is fashioned not simply as a freestanding talk, but as an integral part of the liturgical action. Does the conclusion in any way lead people into the liturgy that follows?

Have we spoken the Word of God in such a way that God has become more present in people's lives and they are enabled to be drawn more fully into the act of worship for which they have gathered? Remember that a homily is not a talk given on the occasion of a liturgical celebration, but an integral part of the liturgy. Just as a homily flows out of the Scriptures of the liturgy of the Word, so it should flow into the prayers and actions of the liturgy of the Eucharist which follows.

PRACTICING

[101] After revising the homily, practice it. Repeat it several times to become familiar with what has to be said and how to say it. Practice it aloud and ask if that is really "me" speaking. Does it sound natural, or have I introduced words and phrases that sounded good when I jotted them down but are not suited to oral communication? It may be helpful to preach the homily to a friend or co-worker or to use an audio/video tape recorder. Can I say to that person without embarrassment what I intend to say to the congregation? Do I really believe what I am saying, or have I hidden behind some conventional expression of piety or theology that I would probably not use in any other situation?

PREACHING

[102] Our emphasis on the importance of writing in the preparation of a homily does not in any way imply that homilies should normally be read. Writing is a means to arrive at good organization, clarity of expression, and concreteness. Whether or not we actually take a manuscript to the pulpit with us will depend on a number of things: the nature of the gathering (very formal or more informal); how familiar we are with our own material; how apprehensive we feel about forgetting something essential.

[103] Sometimes we know what we are going to say so well, and are so enthused about it that a manuscript would only get in the way or distract us. On the other hand, there may be times when we are sure that our message will be clearer and more forceful if we have the text with us. As long as we have something to say, as long as we are saying it, and as long as we establish and maintain rapport with the congregation, we may be able to preach quite effectively from a text.

[104] In general, it is much better to speak from notes or an outline—or without any written aids at all, for such a way of preaching enables us to enter more fully into direct, personal contact with a congregation. If we feel we must take the text with us, be familiar enough with the material so that instead of reading it, we can simply have it present as an aid to our memory.

[105] In preaching, as in all forms of communication, remember that it is the whole person who communicates. Facial expression, the tone of voice, the posture of the body are all powerful factors in determining whether a congregation will be receptive to what we have to say. If, as we preach, we remember that in carrying out this ministry we are showing our love, and God's, for the people, we will more easily avoid a delivery that sounds affected ("churchy") or impersonal.

[106] An effective way for preachers to be sure that they are addressing some of the real concerns of the congregation in the homily is to involve members of that congregation in a homily preparation group. One way to begin such a group is for the preachers to invite four or five people they trust and can work with easily to join them for an hour at the beginning of the week. In a parish setting it is advisable to have one of the members drop out after four weeks and invite someone else to take his or her place. Similarly, a second will drop out after the fifth week, so that after eight weeks or so they will be working with a new group of people.

[107] A homily preparation group can also be formed by gathering the priests in the rectory, the parish staff, priests from the area, priest and ministers, or a priests' support group. The presence of members of the congregation in a group is especially helpful in raising issues that are of concern to them and which the homily may be able to address. Groups that involve only clergy or parish staff members can also be a rich source of insight into the ways in which the Scriptures point to the continuing presence of God in human history.

[108] After the group has gathered and spent a few minutes quieting down, the following steps can be followed:

1. *Read the passages* (15 minutes). Begin with the Gospel, then the Old Testament, Psalm, and New Testament. As one of the participants reads the passages slowly, the others listen and jot down images, words or phrases that strike them.

2. *Share the words* (10 minutes). This is not a time for discussion but simply an opportunity for each person to share the words or phrases which resonated and fired the imagination. As this sharing is going on, the homilist may pick up some recurring words and phrases. He may be surprised to hear what parts of the Scriptures are being highlighted. These responses are already a sign of the concerns, questions and interests that are present in the lives of the congregation.

3. *Exegete the texts* (10 minutes). One of the members of the group presents a short exegesis of the texts. The task is not to bring to the discussion everything that could be said, but to make a special effort to determine what concrete human concerns the author was addressing when the text was written. What questions were there to which these words were at least a partial answer? When dealing with the Gospel passage, one way to answer this question is to show how other evangelists treated the same materials.

4. *Share the good news* (10 minutes). What good news did the first listeners hear in these accounts? What good news does the group hear? Where is God's promise, power and influence in our personal story present in the readings?

5. *Share the challenge these words offer us* (10 minutes). What is the doubt, the sin, the pain, the fracturing in our own lives which the passage touches? To what form of conversion do these words call us? In responding to these questions,

the group may resort to generalities. By gentle persuasion and personal example the homilist can encourage the group to speak personally and with examples.

6. *Explore the consequences* (5 minutes). What difference can the good news make in my life? What happens if the scriptural good news is applied to contemporary bad news? Can my life be changed? Can the world be transformed if people believe in the good news and begin acting according to it? These are questions to which final answers cannot be given. They demand prayer and reflection.

7. *Give thanks and praise* (5 minutes). Conclude with a brief prayer of thanksgiving for God`s saving Word .

Working with a homily preparation group will help to ensure two things: that the homilist hears the proclamation of the good news in the Sunday Scripture readings as it is heard by the people in the congregation; and secondly, that the preacher is able to point in concrete and specific ways to the difference that the hearing of this good news can make in the lives of those who hear it. When the preacher spends time with the congregation, struggling with how the Word touches real life, the possibility of this homily striking a listener as "talking to me" increases. The Word of God then achieves that for which it was sent. Preacher and listener, responding together, are nourished by the Word of God and drawn to praise the God who has again given a sign of his presence and power.

THE NON-NEGOTIABLES OF HOMILY PREPARATION

[109] As we mentioned at the beginning of this chapter, there is no one way to prepare a homily, nor does a particular method work the same way all the time for the same person. But no matter what the method, there are certain elements in the preparation of the homily which cannot be omitted if our preaching over the long term is going to be scripturally sound and pastorally relevant. We may be able to "wing it" on occasion, but to try to sustain a weekly ministry of preaching with little more than a glance at the lectionary and the quick consultation of a homily service is to attempt the impossible.

[110] Effective preaching—that is, preaching that enables people to hear the Word of God as good news for their lives and to respond accordingly—requires time and serious work. Unless we are willing to accept the drudgery that is a part of preaching, as it is of all creative work, we will not know the joy of having the Scriptures come alive for us, nor the profoundly satisfying experience of sharing that discovery with others.

[111] To conclude this chapter on homiletic method we would point to what we consider to be the non-negotiable elements of effective preaching:

1. *Time.* The amount of time will vary from preacher to preacher. However, the importance of the ministry of preaching demands that a significant amount of time be devoted to the homily each week, and ideally, that this time be spread out over the entire week.

2. *Prayer.* All preaching flows from faith to faith. It is only through prayer that faith is nourished.

3. *Study.* Without continuing study, stagnation sets in and preaching becomes insipid. Preachers have a professional responsibility to continue their education in the areas of Scripture, theology, and related disciplines. They might well make a book on preaching part of their regular reading program.

4. *Organization.* Much preaching suffers from lack of direction and the absence of a central, controlling idea. The writing and revising of homilies helps to ensure that there is a point to what we preach.

5. *Concreteness.* Another common fault of preachers is their tendency to speak in vague generalities or to use technical theological language. Once again, writing and revising helps to ensure that homilies are concrete and specific.

6. *Evaluation.* In public discourse we easily fall back on familiar ideas and set patterns of speech. More often than not, we are unaware of such tendencies and need the feedback of others to alert us to them.

EPILOGUE: THE POWER OF THE WORD

[112] The pulpit of St. Stephen's Cathedral in Vienna displays an elaborate handrail in which are carved a detailed series of ugly, mythical creatures. The open mouths and oversized snouts of the beasts are there to remind the preacher of his inadequacies as he ascends the stairs. At the very top of the handrail, carved into the pillar that separates the stairs from the open, circular pulpit, stands a dog, jaws open, barking down at the ominous figures. The hellish beasts are not to enter the sacred place. The preacher has been enjoined to leave his sinful self behind as he prepares to speak God's Word.

[113] The medieval artisan has captured in stone the inner tension of all of us who dare to preach. We are aware that the words we speak are human words, formed through reflection both on the Scriptures and on our personal experience of the needs of our community. Looking into the faces of the people who sit before us, we see those who are holier, more intelligent, and more creative. And yet they wait for us to speak, to preach, to proclaim and witness to the presence of God among us. Our theology tells us that the words we speak are also God's Word. "What we utter is God's wisdom, a mysterious, a hidden wisdom" (1 Cor 2:7).

[114] We dare to utter that sacred Word because we once heard the voice of Mystery who spoke to Isaiah: "Whom shall I send? Who will go for us?" And we answered with Isaiah, "Here I am; send me" (Is 6:8). With Jeremiah we trust that the Lord will place his words in our mouths, despite our youth or age, our ignorance and our inadequacies (Jer 1:6–9). Even when we fall on our faces, the promise of Ezechiel is there, that a voice will speak to us and a spirit enter into us and set us again on our feet (Ezek 2:1–3). We believe that the Word we speak is the Word God intends to have an effect upon the world in which we live.

For just as from the heavens the rain and snow come
And do not return there till they have watered the earth, making it fertile and fruitful,
Giving seed to him who sows and bread to him who eats,
So shall my word be that goes forth from my mouth;
It shall not return to me void, but shall do my will, achieving the end for which I sent it. (Is 55:10–11)

[115] We too stand in sacred space, aware of our personal inadequacy, yet willing to share how the scriptural story has become integrated into our thoughts and actions while we walked among those who turn their faces toward us. The words we speak are human words describing how God's action has become apparent to us this week. Is it any wonder then that excitement and tension fill us in the moments before we preach? With a final deep breath may we also breathe in the Spirit of God who will animate our human words with divine power.

APPENDIX

[116] This document on preaching has dealt mainly with what the individual preacher can do to improve the quality of the Sunday homily. In conclusion, we offer some recommendations for steps that can be taken on the national, diocesan, and parish levels to foster more effective preaching.

NATIONAL

[117] 1. A doctoral program in homiletics to prepare teachers of preaching should be established with diocesan support, perhaps at the Catholic University of America.

2. Seminaries, especially at the theologate level, are urged to emphasize preaching as a priority (cf. *Program of Priestly Formation*, 3rd Edition, Chapter III, Art. 2, Homiletics).

DIOCESAN

[118] 1. Programs to improve preaching skills should be established at the diocesan or regional level.

2. Programs for the study and deeper understanding of Scripture and preaching theology should also be established.

3. A Center for Preaching Resources should be founded in each diocese by the diocesan office for worship or continuing education, or by the seminary.

4. The Bishop(s) of the diocese should model the nature and purpose of the homily in preaching. They should not accept more preaching engagements per day than allow for preparation.

5. Criteria for the granting of faculties to preach should be clearly formulated and followed.

6. Continuing development of good preaching should be supported by the diocese through the granting of time and funding.

PARISH

[119] 1. A resource center should be established within each parish to assist preachers and lectors in fulfilling their ministry.

2. Groups to help preachers prepare and evaluate their homilies should be formed.

3. When there are several preachers in a parish, their preparation for preaching should be coordinated.

4. Readers should be trained in the effective proclamation of Scripture and provided opportunities to grow in their understanding of it.

5. Job descriptions for priests should be evaluated in order to highlight the importance and provide adequate time for preparation of the ministry of preaching.

6. Some record should be kept of the themes of each Sunday's homily in order to bring the parish community into contact with the major facets of our faith each year, and to avoid undue emphasis on one truth at the expense of others.

[120] At all levels, national, diocesan and parish, bishops and priests are urged to invite religious and laity to read this document so as to assist, encourage and support priests in efforts toward a renewal of preaching in the church.

NOTES

1. The material on "audience analysis" is voluminous. Access to the most up-to-date studies can be found by consulting the bibliographies of recent books on speech communication. Such materials frequently describe various methods for determining with some accuracy the interest and abilities of an audience.

2. While the homily is not the same as catechetical instruction, as Pope Paul VI makes clear in his apostolic exhortation *Evangelii nuntiandi* (nos. 43 and 44), the homily can certainly be a means of catechesis for Christian communities. The homilist who preaches from the Scriptures as these are arranged in the lectionary over a three-year cycle of Sundays and feasts will certainly deal with all the major truths of the faith. It will still be necessary, however, to provide educational opportunities in and through which the faithful can reflect more deeply on the meaning of these truths and on their concrete contemporary implications for Christian life. In the early church such a systematic presentation of the truths of the faith was given to the newly baptized in the post-baptismal preaching known as mystagogy.

3. A fuller description of the principles guiding the choice of readings can be found in the introduction to the lectionary. These principles should be familiar to all preachers, for a knowledge of how and why passages of Scripture are assigned to certain times and feasts provides an important key to the liturgical interpretation of those readings in preaching.

4. Cf. *Lectionary for Mass.* English translation of the Second *Editio-Typica* (1981) no. 24 prepared by International Commission on English in the Liturgy.

5. Ibid. no. 8–10.

6. Ibid. no. 24.

7. With regard to the sign of the cross before and after the homily, the Congregation for the Sacraments and Divine Worship gave the following official *responsum* in 1973: Query: Is it advisable to invite the faithful to bless themselves before or after the homily, to address a salutation to them, for example, "Praised be Jesus Christ"? Reply: It all depends on lawful local custom. But generally speaking it is inadvisable to continue such customs because they have their origin in preaching *outside Mass.* The homily is *part* of the liturgy; the people have already blessed themselves and received the greeting at the beginning of Mass. It is better, then, not to have a repetition before or after the homily. Source: *Notitiae* 29 (1973) 178.

8. *Keryssein,* "To proclaim," is the word most frequently used for preaching in the New Testament. The word "presupposes that the preachers are heralds who announce simply that which they are commissioned to announce, not in their own name, but by the authority of the one who sends them" (John L. McKenzie, *Dictionary of the Bible,* p. 689). Although the practice of first-century Jewish synagogues may have included explanations and applications of the Scriptures as part of the regular service, the New Testament itself does not use a specific technical word to describe the kind of preaching we refer to as a "homily," that is, the exposition of a text of scripture which takes place in and as a part of a liturgical celebration. The word *homileo* does appear in the New Testament, and its usage there can provide a way to understand a homiletic approach to preaching as distinguished from preaching addressed to unbelievers *(kerygma).*

9. The continuing ability of Scripture texts to speak to situations that are temporally and culturally distinct from those to which they were originally addressed is one way in which the canonicity of the Scriptures continues to be affirmed by the church. The canon is, in fact, composed of those writings which the church considers too important to forget because they address issues which are present in every generation, albeit in different garb and guises.

10. In the Apostolic Exhortation, *On Cate-chesis in Our Time*, 1979, #48, Pope John Paul II observes, "Respecting the specific nature and proper cadence of this setting [i.e., liturgy, especially the Eucharistic assembly], the homily takes up again the journey of faith put forward by catechesis and brings it to its natural fulfillment. At the same time it encourages the Lord's disciples to begin anew each day their spiritual journey in truth, adoration and thanksgiving. Accordingly, one can say that catechetical teaching, too, finds its source and fulfillment in the eucharist, within the whole circle of the liturgical year.

"Preaching, centered upon the Bible texts, must then in its own way make it possible to familiarize the faithful with the whole of the mysteries of the faith and the norms of Christian living. . . ." Cf. also: *Sharing the Light of Faith*, An Official Commentary on the National Cate-chetical Directory for Catholics of the United States, 1981, p. 54, Office of Publishing Services, USCC, Washington, D.C.

BUILT OF LIVING STONES
ART, ARCHITECTURE, AND WORSHIP

GUIDELINES OF THE UNITED STATES CONFERENCE OF
CATHOLIC BISHOPS

UNITED STATES CONFERENCE OF CATHOLIC BISHOPS
WASHINGTON, D.C.
16 NOVEMBER 2000

CONTENTS

BUILT OF LIVING STONES

PREFACE

§ 1 §   One of the most significant and formative experiences in the life of a parish community is the process of building or renovating a church. As part of that process, parish members are called upon to study the Church's teaching and liturgical theology and to reflect upon their personal pieties, their individual tastes, and the parish history. By bringing together these personal and ecclesial elements in faith and in charity, parishioners help to build a new structure and to renew their parish community.

§ 2 §   The decision-making process and the parish education component that are part of the building experience can assist the parish and its individual members to deepen their sense of Catholic identity. This identity is shaped by the history of the particular parish, by its relationship to other parishes in the local Church known as the diocese, and by its relationship within the communion of local Churches known as the Roman Catholic Church.

§ 3 §   *Built of Living Stones: Art, Architecture, and Worship* is presented to assist the faithful involved in the building or renovation of churches, chapels, and oratories of the Latin Church in the United States. In addition, the document is intended for use by architects, liturgical consultants and artists, contractors, and other professionals engaged in the design and/or construction of these places of worship. The text also may be helpful to those who wish to understand the Catholic Church's tradition regarding church buildings, the arts and architecture. While the suggestions and guidelines within the document have been carefully prepared, they are not exhaustive of the subject matter. They are intended to serve as the basis for decision making at the local level and also can become the foundation for the development of diocesan guidelines and legislation governing liturgical art and architecture.[1]

§ 4 §   Catholics who live and worship in the United States in the twenty-first century celebrate a liturgy that is the same as that of earlier generations in all its essentials but significantly different in its language, style and form. Recent shifts in the visual arts and in building styles as well as the development of new materials and sound amplification systems have created both opportunities and challenges for those engaged in the building and renovation of places for worship.

§ 5 §   To be able to make specific recommendations about building and renovation projects, parish members need to understand the nature of the liturgy, the space it requires, and the ways in which the physical building can help or hinder worship. Because of the spectrum of ideas, opinions, spiritualities, and personal preferences present in every parish, the assistance of church documents and teachings and of consultants and facilitators is beneficial in the processes of learning and making decisions. With such assistance, parish leaders and members can develop the skills needed for building consensus and resolving conflicts.

§ 6 §   The challenges of building or renovating church buildings increase as the Church grows. The richness of ethnic and cultural groups in the Church in the United States today presents opportunities as we strive to become truly "catholic." The Church seeks to integrate and utilize each culture's strength in accomplishing Christ's mission to bring the Gospel to every person and to proclaim—through all the concerns of daily life—the abiding love and presence of God in the world.[2]

§ 7 §   In 1962 Pope John XXIII convened the Second Vatican Council to help the Church renew its sense of mission. The first of the conciliar documents, *Sacrosanctum Concilium: Constitution on the Sacred Liturgy*, articulated the goals of the Council and, in keeping with those goals, established general principles for the reform and promotion of the sacred liturgy. In addition to mandating that liturgical books and rites be revised,[3] *Sacrosanctum Concilium* called for the revision of legislation governing the material elements involved in the liturgy, particularly the construction of places of worship and altars, the placement of the tabernacle and the baptistry, and the use of images and decoration.[4]

§ 8 §   In the thirty-five years following the Second Vatican Council, both the Apostolic See and the National Conference of Catholic Bishops have issued documents to implement the provisions of *Sacrosanctum Concilium*, no. 128. In 1977 the Congregation for the Sacraments and Divine Worship issued the revised *Rite of Dedication of a Church and an Altar*. In addition to the norms in the recently revised *General Instruction of the Roman Missal*, pertinent documents have been issued by Vatican congregations concerning the care of the Church's artistic heritage, artists and the arts, and vesture.[5]

§ 9 §   In the United States, the committee statement *Environment and Art in Catholic Worship* was published by the Bishops' Committee on the Liturgy in 1978.[6] This statement has had a profound impact on the building and renovation of parish churches in the United States. Parish communities have studied, discussed and disagreed about the document; many liturgical design consultants have utilized the text in parish education programs; and architects have tried to transform the underlying principles and theology into brick and mortar, stone and glass. Twenty-two years after the publication of *Environment and Art*, the bishops of the United States present a new document on church art and architecture that builds on and replaces *Environment and Art* and addresses the needs of the next generation of parishes engaged in building or renovating churches. *Built of Living Stones* reflects our understanding of the liturgy, of the role and importance of church art and architecture, and of the integral roles of the local parish and the diocese that enter into a building or renovation project.

§ 10 §   This document has been approved by the bishops of the Latin Church of the United States and issued by the authority of the National Conference of Catholic Bishops on November 16, 2000. *Built of Living Stones* contains many of the provisions of universal law governing liturgical art and architecture and offers pastoral suggestions based upon the experience of the last thirty-five years. The document presents guidelines that can serve as the basis for diocesan bishops to issue further guidelines and directives for their dioceses. Where the document quotes or reiterates norms from liturgical books and the *Code of Canon Law*, those prescriptions are binding on local communities and dioceses.

§ 11 §   The document begins with a theological reflection on the liturgy and liturgical art and architecture. Since decisions about church art and architecture should always be based upon the theology of the eucharistic assembly and its liturgical action and the understanding of the Church as the house of God on earth, the first chapter is foundational for the chapters that follow. The second chapter outlines the liturgical principles for parish communities to apply when building or renovating liturgical space, and it reviews the spatial demands of the major liturgical celebrations during the year. The third chapter offers suggestions for including art in places of worship and for choosing artists and artistic consultants. The fourth and final chapter describes the practical elements involved in the building or renovation process, including the development of a master plan, the design process, the development of a site plan, and the role of professionals in the process. A section on the special issues involved in the preservation and restoration of artworks and architecture has been included.

CHAPTER ONE
THE LIVING CHURCH

THE LIVING CHURCH: GOD'S BUILDING

§ 12 §   God created the universe so that all might have a part in his divine life and be joined in communion with him. Thus did he call forth light from darkness, beauty from chaos, and life from the formless void (Genesis 1:1–23). When all was in readiness, he fashioned Adam and Eve in the divine image and breathed life into them (Genesis 1:24–31) in order to gather all men and women into the great and eternal hymn of praise which is the Church. This is why Christians, from the earliest centuries, could believe that "the world was created for the sake of the Church."[7]

§ 13 §   Despite the sin of Adam, God's call to communion perdured. Gradually, he revealed his wish to save humanity "not as individuals without any mutual bonds, but by making them into a people, a people which acknowledges Him in truth and serves Him in holiness."[8] With Abraham and his descendants, God entered into an everlasting covenant. He promised to be their God and claimed them as his own, a holy nation, a people set apart to praise his mighty deeds throughout the ages. Through the waters of death he led his people, Israel, accepting their sacrifices at Sinai through the hands of Aaron and his descendants. "All of these things, however, were done by way of preparation and as a figure of that new and perfect covenant which was to be ratified in Christ. . . . this new covenant in His blood . . . calling together a people made up of Jew and Gentile, making them one, not according to the flesh but in the Spirit."[9]

§ 14 §　From the altar of the cross Christ accomplished our redemption,[10] forming a holy people, a "temple of God built of living stones, where the Father is worshiped in spirit and in truth."[11] The hymn of praise that Christ places within the heart and on the lips of the Church will be sung at the end of time in all its fullness, when all the members gather at the wedding feast of the Lamb in the heavenly Jerusalem.

§ 15 §　That same hymn is sung today by the Church whenever the liturgy is celebrated. For every time the Church gathers for prayer, she is joined to Christ's priesthood and made one with all the saints and angels, transcending time and space. Together the members worship with the whole company of heaven, "venerating the memory of the saints" and hoping "for some part and fellowship with them"; together they eagerly await Christ's coming in glory.[12] The sacred liturgy is a window to eternity and a glimpse of what God calls us to be.

THE CHURCH BUILDING

§ 16 §　Just as the term *Church* refers to the *living temple,* God's People, the term *church* also has been used to describe "the building in which the Christian community gathers to hear the word of God, to pray together, to receive the sacraments, and to celebrate the eucharist."[13] That building is both the house of God on earth (*domus Dei*) and a house fit for the prayers of the saints (*domus ecclesiae*). Such a house of prayer must be expressive of the presence of God and suited for the celebration of the sacrifice of Christ, as well as reflective of the community that celebrates there.

§ 17 §　The church is the proper place for the liturgical prayer of the parish community, especially the celebration of the Eucharist on Sunday. It is also the privileged place for adoration of the Blessed Sacrament and reservation of the Eucharist for Communion for the sick. Whenever communities have built houses for worship, the design of the building has been of critical importance.[14] Churches are never "simply gathering spaces" but signify and make visible the Church living in [a particular] place, the dwelling of God" among us, now "reconciled and united in Christ."[15] As such, the building itself becomes "a sign of the pilgrim Church on earth and reflects the Church dwelling in heaven."[16] Every church building is a gathering place for the assembly, a resting place, a place of encounter with God, as well as a point of departure on the Church's unfinished journey toward the reign of God.

§ 18 §　Churches, therefore, must be places "suited to sacred celebrations," "dignified," and beautiful.[17] Their suitability for worship is determined by their ability through the architectural design of space and the application of artistic gifts to embody God's initiative and the community's faithful response. Church buildings and the religious artworks that beautify them are forms of worship themselves and both inspire and reflect the prayer of the community as well as the inner life of grace.[18] Conversely, church buildings and religious artifacts that are trivial, contrived, or lack beauty can detract from the community's liturgy. Architecture and art become the joint work of the Holy Spirit and the local community, that of preparing human hearts to receive God's word and to enter more fully into communion with God.[19]

WORSHIP IN TIME AND SPACE

§ 19 §   Liturgy is "the participation of the People of God in 'the work of God.'"[20] It is the "exercise of the priestly office of Jesus" in which God is worshiped and adored and people are made holy.[21] God begins the work of sanctifying people in time and space and brings that work to completion. Those who respond to God in worship and in service are given the privilege of becoming coworkers in the divine plan.[22]

§ 20 §   The Church marks *time* as holy by setting aside Sunday and by celebrating the liturgical year with its rhythm and seasons. It demonstrates God's reign over all *space* by dedicating buildings to house the Church and its worship. Each Sunday the baptized are challenged to rest from their daily labors, to contemplate the goodness of God, to make present the victory and triumph of Christ's death (SC, no. 6), to enter the joy of the Risen Lord, to receive the life-giving breath of the Spirit, and to commit themselves to serve those in need. Sunday affirms both the primacy of God and the dignity of the person.[23] While the worship of God is not limited to any one place, Christians build churches to shelter the liturgical assembly that praises God and celebrates the sacraments through which the Church is sanctified.

§ 21 §   The liturgy is the perfect expression of the Church, "the summit toward which [all the Church's] activity . . . is directed" and the source of all her power.[24] In the New Testament, the term *liturgy* is intimately connected with the proclamation of the Good News and with active charity.[25] Through baptism and confirmation, Christians share in Christ's priesthood, which they exercise through their worship of God and their vocation of service to others. At the Eucharist, Christ calls his members to conversion in the proclamation of the word; he invites them to join with him in offering his perfect sacrifice to the Father; and he sends them forth from liturgy to serve the community in charity. Liturgical participation commits a person to a life of faithful discipleship. "Every liturgical celebration, because it is an action of Christ the priest and of His Body the Church, is a sacred action surpassing all others."[26]

CHRIST'S PRESENCE IN SIGN AND SYMBOL

§ 22 §   In the liturgical assembly, Christ's presence is realized[27] in all *the baptized* who gather in his name, in the *word of God* proclaimed in the assembly, in the person of *the priest* through whom Christ offers himself to the Father and gathers the assembly, in *sacramental celebrations*, and especially, in the *Sacrament of his Body and Blood*.[28] In building a house for the Church that is also the house of God on earth, all the expressions of Christ's presence have prominence of place that reflects their proper nature. Among these, the eucharistic species is accorded supreme prominence.[29] From the very beginning of the planning and design process, parishes will want to reflect upon the relationship of the altar, the ambo, the tabernacle, the chair of the priest celebrant, and the space for congregation.

§24§   Gestures, language and actions are the *physical, visible* and *public* expressions by which human beings understand and manifest their inner life. Since human beings on this earth are always made of flesh and blood, they not only will and think, but also speak and sing, move and celebrate. These human actions as well as physical objects are also the signs by which Christians express and deepen their relationship to God.[30]

§ 25 §   Jesus himself used physical signs to manifest his union with the Father and to reveal his mission to the world. Jesus was baptized in the waters of the Jordan River, he fed the multitudes with bread, healed the sick with his touch, and forgave sinners. He was anointed with oil, he shared a Passover meal with his disciples, and he surrendered his body to death on the cross. Christ, the incarnate one, used material signs to show to humanity the invisible God.[31]

§ 25 §   Christ, taking on human flesh, reveals the Father. "No one has ever seen God" (1 John 4:12). The only begotten Son, living in the Father's heart, has revealed him. Indeed, Jesus said, "Whoever sees me sees the one who sent me" (John 12:45). Christ is himself the sacrament of the Father. In his risen glory, he is no longer visible in this world and Leo the Great testifies that "What has been visible of our Savior has passed over into the sacraments": *Quod igitur conspicuum fuit Salvatoris Nostri in sacramenta transivit (Sermo.* 74, 2: PL 54, 398). And so washing and anointing, breaking the bread and sharing the cup, raising arms in blessing and imposing hands are *visible* signs by which Christ manifests and accomplishes our sanctification and salvation in the Church.[32] To the central signs and word, the Church adds gestures and material elements such as incense, ashes, holy water, candles and vestments to dispose us for the heavenly gifts of our crucified and Risen Lord and to deepen our reverence for the unceasing mercy and grace that come to us in the Church through the passion and death of Jesus, our Lord.

§ 26 §   Just as Christ invited those who heard him to share his personal union with the Father through material signs, so Christ leads the Church through these same signs in the liturgy from the visible to the invisible.[33] As a result, effective liturgical signs have a teaching function and encourage full, conscious, and active participation, express and strengthen faith, and lead people to God. Poorly utilized or minimal signs do not enliven the community's faith and can even diminish active participation.[34] It must likewise be kept in mind that the liturgy and its signs and symbols do not exercise merely a teaching function.

They also touch and move a person to conversion of heart and not simply to enlightenment of mind.

LITURGICAL PRINCIPLES FOR BUILDING OR RENOVATING CHURCHES

§ 27 §   The basic liturgical principles for designing and renovating churches today are drawn from the Second Vatican Council and the documents that implemented its decrees.[35] Even though the Church offers no universal blueprint or style for the design of a church, attention to the following principles will ensure that from the beginning, the ritual requirements will receive the priority they deserve in the design process.

§ 28 §   1. *The church building is designed in harmony with church laws and serves the needs of the liturgy.* The liturgical books are the foundational source for those who wish to plan a building well suited for the liturgy. First among these are the prescriptions contained in the fifth chapter of the *General Instruction of the Roman Missal* and the norms in the introduction to the *Rite of Dedication of a Church and an Altar.* Other directives can be found in the various liturgical books and the *Code of Canon Law.*

§ 29 §   Because the church is a house of prayer in which the Eucharist is celebrated and the Blessed Sacrament is reserved, a place where the faithful assemble, and a setting where Christ is worshiped, it should be worthy of prayer and sacred celebration, built in conformity with the laws of the Church, and dignified with noble beauty and intrinsically excellent art.[36] The general plan of the building reflects the Church that Christ gathers there, is expressive of its prayer, fosters the members' participation in sacred realities, and supports the solemn character of the sacred liturgy.

§ 30 §   The general plan of the building should be such that "in some way it conveys the image of the gathered assembly. It should also allow the participants to take the place most appropriate to them and assist all to carry out their function properly."[37]

§ 31 §   2. *The church building fosters participation in the liturgy.* Because liturgical actions by their nature are communal celebrations, they are celebrated with the presence and active participation of the Christian faithful whenever possible.[38] Such participation, both internal and external, is the faithful's "right and duty by reason of their baptism."[39] The building itself can promote or hinder the "full, conscious, and active participation" of the faithful. Parishes making decisions about the design of a church must consider how the various aspects and choices they make will affect the ability of all the members to participate fully in liturgical celebrations.

§ 32 §   *The design of the church building reflects the various roles of the participants.* Since the liturgical celebration is an action of Christ and the Church, it belongs to the whole Body of the Church.[40] While all the members are called to participate in worship, not all have the same role.[41] From the earliest days of the Church, the Holy Spirit has called forth members to serve in a variety of ministries. That same Spirit continues to call the members to various ministries today and to bestow gifts necessary for the good of the community.[42]

§ 33 §   **The Church** is a holy people, a chosen race, a royal priesthood, whose members give thanks to God and offer the sacrifice of Christ. Together, they take part in the liturgy conscious of what they are doing, with reverence and full involvement. They are instructed by God's word and nourished at the Table of the Lord's Body; they are formed day by day into an ever more perfect unity with God and with each other—they are sent forth for the transformation of society, so that finally God may be all in all. And by offering Christ, "the Victim not only through the hands of the priest but also together with him," they "learn to offer themselves."[43]

§ 34 §   **Bishops** "are the high priests, the principal dispensers of the mysteries of God, and the directors, promoters, and guardians of the entire liturgical life" of the particular Church.[44] Therefore, every authentic celebration of the liturgy is directed by the bishop, either in person or through the priests who assist him.[45] Within the process of building or renovating a church, the diocesan bishop has an irreplaceable role and final responsibility. The construction of a new church requires the permission of the bishop, who must consult and determine that the building will contribute to the spiritual welfare of the faithful, and that the parish has the necessary means to build and care for the church.[46]

§ 35 §   **Priests** "are consecrated to celebrate divine worship and to sanctify the people."[47] The priest "stands at the head of the faithful people gathered together, presides over its prayer, proclaims the message of salvation, joins the people to himself in offering the sacrifice to God the Father through Christ in the Spirit, gives his brothers and sisters the bread of eternal life, and shares in it with them."[48] As the one who presides, he always prays in the name of the Church and of the community gathered together. As the leader and representative of the local parish, the pastor takes the lead in the building process, keeps the local parish in communication with the bishop and other diocesan officials, and helps to draw the parishioners together in the decision-making process.

§ 36 §   **A variety of ministries** serve the assembly at the liturgy. First among the ministers is the deacon.[49] Some faithful have been installed in the ministries of lector or acolyte. Others serve as readers, altar servers, extraordinary ministers of Holy Communion, cantors, musicians and sacristans.[50] As members of the Church, each person forms an essential and distinct part of the assembly that is gathered by God in an "organic and hierarchical" way.[51] Each minister, ordained or lay, is called upon to fulfill his or her role and only that role in the celebration of the liturgy.[52]

§ 37 §   By its design and its furnishings, the church reflects this diversity of roles. The one who presides, those who proclaim God's word, the ministers of music, those who assist at the altar, and members of the congregation all play an integral part in the public prayer of the Church. The design of the church should reflect the unity of the entire assembly and at the same time ensure that each person is able to exercise his or her ministry in a space that fully accommodates the ritual action called for by that ministry. Careful attention to the placement of the individuals and groups who comprise the liturgical assembly can manifest and enhance their relationship with one another and with the entire body.

§ 38 §   4. *The church building respects the culture of every time and place.* The Roman rite respects cultural differences and fosters the genius and talents of the various races and peoples.[53] This cultural diversity can be expressed in architectural styles, in art forms, and in some instances in the celebration of liturgical rites with appropriate adaptations.

§ 39 §   Just as each local community is different, styles and forms of churches will vary. The New Testament speaks of the upper room where Christ gathered the apostles for the Last Supper and appeared to them after the resurrection, and where the Holy Spirit descended on the Blessed Virgin and the Twelve at Pentecost. After the Lord's ascension, believers gathered in homes for the celebration of the "breaking of the bread."[54] Such homes evolved into "house churches" and became the Christian community's earliest places for worship. The unique forms and architecture of the Roman and Byzantine world provided the Church with an architectural language in the form of the basilica. With its long nave and an apse for the bishop and clergy, the basilica quickly became a standard architectural form for churches of the West. The effect of these architectural forms is still reflected in the structure of our liturgical life today.

§ 40 §   The rich history of Catholic worship space traces a path through every people and place where the liturgy has been offered. Innumerable monasteries, cathedrals and parish churches stand as witnesses to an organic growth of the liturgical and devotional life of the Church throughout the world. Since the Church is not wedded to a single architectural or artistic form, it seeks to engage the genius of every time and place, to craft the finest praise of God from what is available.[55] The rich dialogue between the Church's liturgy, as a singular expression of divine revelation, and a local culture is an essential ingredient in the evangelization of peoples and the celebration of the Roman Catholic liturgy in a given time and place. The liturgy is proclaimed, celebrated and lived in all cultures in such a way that they themselves are not abolished by it but redeemed and fulfilled.[56]

§ 41 §   Inculturation is the incarnation of the Christian message within particular cultures that have their own sense, artistic expressions, vocabulary and grammar, and conceptual frameworks.[57] All ancient and modern evangelizing strategies in art and architecture are acts of inculturation to enable church buildings to proclaim the creative and redemptive meaning of the Gospel in every time and place.

§ 42 §   When the Gospel was first brought to America, it arrived clothed with expressions of European Christian culture and piety. Grateful for these invaluable gifts, the Church in America slowly, and often reluctantly, developed an appreciation for native music, language and art and accepted them for use in the service of the liturgy. Today the Church in the United States is again exploring how to translate the Gospel and to build churches in conversation with complex, secularized cultures that have sometimes rejected religion and attempted their own forms of human transcendence through intricate electronic modes of communication, art, and architecture.[58] Secular cultures in industrial and post-industrial countries have been particularly difficult to evangelize since they often treat human dignity selectively, attempting to control the mystery that animates the human thirst for meaning and purpose, and ignore those who do not fit their economic or social purpose. The Gospel requires that particular care be taken to welcome into the Church's assembly those often discarded by society—the socially and economically marginalized, the elderly, the sick, those with disabilities, and those with special needs. In building a church, every diocese and parish must wrestle with these and other complex questions raised by the Church's mission to evangelize contemporary cultures.

§ 43 §   Parishes in the United States today often find their places of worship shared by people of varied languages and ethnic backgrounds and experience vast differences in styles of public worship and personal devotion. What can sustain Christian communities in this challenge of hospitality is the realization that a pluralism of symbolic, artistic, and architectural expression enriches the community.[59]

§ 44 §   5. _The church building should be beautiful._ The external and internal structure of the church building should be expressive of the dignified beauty of God's holy people who gather there and of the sacred rites they celebrate. Liturgical art and architecture reflect and announce the presence of the God who calls the community to worship and invite believers to raise their minds and hearts to the One who is the source of all beauty and truth. Art or architecture that draws more attention to its own shape, form, texture, or color than to the sacred realities it seeks to disclose is unworthy of the church building.[60]

§ 45 §   The Church's great treasury of art and architecture helps it to transcend the limitations of any one culture, region or period of time.[61] The Church is not exclusively identified with the forms of the past, but is ever open to embrace newer forms that nonetheless have grown organically from her rich heritage of artistic expression. Great religious art fosters the life of prayer of contemporary assemblies who, while rooted in prior artistic traditions, hear God's unceasing call to proclaim the reign of Christ in the languages of a particular time and place. Every artistic form that is at once capable of faithfully expressing sacred realities and serving the Church's liturgical action with the highest quality of the arts can find a home in the Church's house of prayer.[62]

CHAPTER TWO
THE CHURCH BUILDING AND
THE SACRED RITES CELEBRATED THERE

§ 46 §   The church building houses the community of the baptized as it gathers to celebrate the sacred liturgy. By its practical design and beauty it fosters the full, dignified, and graceful celebration of these rites. The primary concern in the building or renovation of a space for worship must be its suitability for the celebration of the Eucharist and other liturgical rites of the Church. Consequently, the fundamental prerequisite for those engaged in the building or renovation of a church is familiarity with the rites to be celebrated there.

§ 47 §   The prayer life of the Church is richly diverse. The eucharistic liturgy, the other sacraments, and the Liturgy of the Hours are sacred actions surpassing all others. The praise and thanksgiving, which are at the heart of the Eucharist, are continued in the celebration of the Liturgy of the Hours. The Liturgy of the Hours is the Church's daily liturgical prayer that expresses the nature of the praying Church and is, itself, a sign of the Church.[63] In addition to their participation in communal prayer, Christ's followers deepen their relationship with God through private prayer, which flows from the liturgy. Thus, the Church encourages popular devotions that "harmonize with the liturgical seasons" and "lead people to [the liturgy]."[64] Besides its primary role of providing a suitable place for the celebration of the liturgical rites, the church building also offers a place to which individuals may come to pray in the presence of the Blessed Sacrament, and in which groups of the faithful may gather for a rich variety of devotions expressive of the faith life of a given culture, region, or ethnic community.

§ 48 §   This chapter is intended to help a community fulfill its role in designing a place that readily accommodates all these needs. In new construction, parishes usually have several options for various elements of design. Sometimes those options are limited by the space or terrain, or by financial resources. And sometimes, as in the case of renovation, there are additional limits imposed by the existing structure. This chapter reviews the spatial demands of the various liturgical rites and offers principles for choosing among the various options. Many dioceses have developed their own procedures and guidelines for the building and renovation of churches. The principles in this document should guide dioceses in the writing of local directives.

THE EUCHARIST

§ 49 §   The celebration of the Eucharist is the center of the entire Christian life, both for the universal Church and for local faith communities. The other sacraments, like every other ministry of the Church and every work of the apostolate, are linked with the Holy Eucharist and have it as their end.[65] The celebration of the Sunday Eucharist is the appropriate starting point for understanding the demands of space, sound, and visibility made upon a church building. An analysis of these requirements will include attention to the place for the congregation, for the preaching of the word, and for the celebration of the Liturgy of the Eucharist, with special care for the location of the altar, the ambo, and the chairs for the priest celebrant and deacon, as necessary. Considerations about the narthex and the environment of the building flow from the central action of the Eucharist. The celebration of the Easter Vigil and of the Sunday Eucharist are appropriate starting points. In addition, special consideration should be given to the place for the reservation of the Blessed Sacrament.

THE BUILDING: THE PLACE FOR THE LITURGICAL ASSEMBLY GATHERED AS ONE BODY IN CHRIST

§ 50 § The church building is a sign and reminder of the immanence and transcendence of God—who chose to dwell among us and whose presence cannot be contained or limited to any single place. Worship is the loving response of God's People to the mystery of God who is with us and who is yet to come. "As visible constructions, churches are signs of the pilgrim church on earth; they are images that proclaim the heavenly Jerusalem, places in which are actualized the mystery of the communion between man and God."[66] In addition, the church building manifests the baptismal unity of all who gather for the celebration of liturgy and "conveys the image of the gathered assembly."[67] While various places "express a hierarchical arrangement and the diversity of functions," those places "should at the same time form a deep and organic unity, clearly expressive of the unity of the entire holy people."[68]

THE CONGREGATION'S AREA

§ 51 § The space within the church building for the faithful other than the priest celebrant and the ministers is sometimes called the *nave*. This space is critical in the overall plan because it accommodates a variety of ritual actions: processions during the Eucharist, the singing of the prayers, movement during baptismal rites, the sprinkling of the congregation with blessed water, the rites during the wedding and funeral liturgies, and personal devotion. This area is not comparable to the audience's space in a theater or public arena because in the liturgical assembly, there is no audience. Rather, the entire congregation acts. The ministers of music could also be located in the body of the church since they lead the entire assembly in song as well as by the example of their reverent attention and prayer.

§ 52 § Two principles guide architectural decisions about the form and arrangement of the nave: (1) the community worships as a single body united in faith, not simply as individuals who happen to find themselves in one place, and the nature of the liturgy demands that the congregation as well as the priest celebrant and ministers be able to exercise their roles in a full and active way; and (2) the priest celebrant and ministers together with the congregation form the liturgical assembly, which is the Church gathered for worship.

§ 53 § The body of the church is not simply a series of unrelated sections. Rather, each part contributes to the unity of the space by proportion, size, and shape. While various rites are celebrated there, the sense of the nave as a unified whole should not be sacrificed to the need for flexibility.

THE SANCTUARY AREA

§ 54 § The sanctuary is the space where the altar and the ambo stand, and "where the priest, deacon and other ministers exercise their offices." The special character of the sanctuary is emphasized and enhanced by the distinctiveness of its design and furnishings, or by its elevation.[69] The challenge to those responsible for its design is to convey the unique quality of the actions that take place in this area while at the same time expressing the organic relationship between those actions and the prayer and actions of the entire liturgical assembly. The sanctuary must be spacious enough to accommodate the full celebration of the various rituals of word and Eucharist with their accompanying movement, as well as those of the other sacraments celebrated there.

§ 55 § The principal ritual furnishings within the sanctuary are the altar on which the eucharistic sacrifice is offered, the ambo from which God's word is proclaimed, and the chair of the priest celebrant. These furnishings should be constructed of substantial materials that express dignity and stability. Their placement and their design again make it clear that although they are distinct entities, they are related in the one eucharistic celebration.

THE ALTAR

§ 56 § At the Eucharist, the liturgical assembly celebrates the ritual sacrificial meal that recalls and makes present Christ's life, death and resurrection, proclaiming "the death of the Lord until he comes."[70] The altar is "the center of thanksgiving that the Eucharist accomplishes"[71] and the point around which the other rites are in some manner arrayed.[72] Since the Church teaches that "the altar is Christ,"[73] its composition should reflect the nobility, beauty, strength and simplicity of the One it represents. In new churches there is to be only one altar so that it "signifies to the assembly of the faithful the one Christ and the one Eucharist of the Church."[74]

§ 57 § The altar is the natural focal point of the sanctuary and is to be "freestanding to allow the [priest] to walk around it easily and Mass to be celebrated facing the people."[75] Ordinarily, it should be fixed (with the base affixed to the floor) and with a table or mensa made of natural stone,[76] since it represents Christ Jesus, the Living Stone (1 Peter 2:4). The pedestal or support for the table may be fashioned from "any sort of material, as long as it is becoming and solid."[77] In the United States it is permissible to use materials other than natural stone for a fixed altar, provided these materials are worthy, solid, properly constructed, and subject to the further judgment of the local ordinary.[78] Parishes building new churches must follow the directives of the diocesan bishop regarding the kind of altar chosen and suitable materials for new altars.

§ 58 § Although there is no specified size or shape for an altar, it should be in proportion to the church. The shape and size should reflect the nature of the altar as the place of sacrifice and the table around which Christ gathers the community to nourish them. In considering the dimensions of the altar, parishes will also want to ensure that the other major furnishings in the sanctuary are in harmony and proportion to the altar. The mensa should be large enough to accommodate the priest celebrant, the deacon and the acolytes who minister there and should be able to hold *The Sacramentary* (*The Roman Missal*) and the vessels with the bread and wine. Impact and focal quality are not only related to placement, size or shape, but also especially to the quality of the altar's design and worthiness of its construction. The altar should be centrally located in the sanctuary and the center of attention in the church.

§ 59 §   During the Liturgy of the Eucharist, the altar must be visible from all parts of the church but not so elevated that it causes visual or symbolic division from the liturgical assembly. Methods of elevation can be found that still allow access to the altar by ministers who need wheelchairs or who have other disabilities.

§ 60 §   In the Church's history and tradition, the altar was often placed over the tombs of the saints or the relics of saints were deposited *beneath* the altar. The presence of relics of saints in the altar provides a witness to the Church's belief that the Eucharist celebrated on the altar is the source of the grace that won sanctity for the saints.[79] The custom of placing small relics of martyrs or other saints in an altar stone and setting this in the mensa has changed since the Second Vatican Council. Relics of martyrs or other saints may be placed beneath the altar, as long as the relics are of a size sufficient for them to be recognizable as parts of a human body and that they are of undoubted authenticity. Relics are no longer placed *on* the altar or set into the mensa in an altar stone.[80]

THE AMBO

§ 61 §   The central focus of the area in which the word of God is proclaimed during the liturgy is the *ambo*. The design of the ambo and its prominent placement reflects the dignity and nobility of that saving word and draws the attention of those present to the proclamation of the word.[81] Here the Christian community encounters the living Lord in the word of God and prepares itself for the "breaking of the bread" and the mission to live the word that will be proclaimed. An ample area around the ambo is needed to allow a gospel procession with a full complement of ministers bearing candles and incense. The *General Introduction to the Lectionary* recommends that the design of altar and ambo bear a "harmonious and close relationship" to one another[82] in order to emphasize the close relationship between word and Eucharist. Since many people share in the ministry of the word, the ambo should be accessible to everyone, including those with physical disabilities.[83]

§ 62 §   Our reverence for the word of God is expressed not only in an attentive listening to and reflection upon the Scripture, but also by the way we handle and treat the Book of the Gospels. The ambo can be designed not only for reading and preaching, but also for displaying the open Book of the Gospels or a copy of the Scriptures before and after the liturgical celebration.[84]

§ 63 §   The chair of the priest celebrant stands "as a symbol of his [office] of presiding over the assembly and of directing prayer."[85] An appropriate placement of the chair allows the priest celebrant to be visible to all in the congregation. The chair reflects the dignity of the one who leads the community in the person of Christ, but is never intended to be remote or grandiose. The priest celebrant's chair is distinguished from the seating for other ministers by its design and placement. "The seat for the deacon should be placed near that of the celebrant."[86] In the cathedral, in addition to the bishop's chair or *cathedra*, which is permanent, an additional chair will be needed for use by the rector or priest celebrant.[87]

§ 64 §   "The [most appropriate] place for the chair is at the head of the sanctuary and turned toward the people, unless the design of the building or other circumstances [such as distance or the placement of the tabernacle] are an obstacle."[88] This chair is not used by a lay person who presides at a service of the word with Communion or a Sunday celebration in the absence of a priest. (Cf. Congregation for Divine Worship, *Directory for Sunday Celebrations in the Absence of a Priest* [1988], no. 40.)

§ 65 §   Other chairs may be placed in the sanctuary for the priest concelebrants and other priests present for the celebration in choir dress.

THE BAPTISTRY

§ 66 §   The rites of baptism, the first of the sacraments of initiation, require a prominent place for celebration.[89] Initiation into the Church is entrance into a eucharistic community united in Jesus Christ. Because the rites of initiation of the Church begin with baptism and are completed by the reception of the Eucharist, the baptismal font and its location reflect the Christian's journey *through* the waters of baptism *to* the altar. This integral relationship between the baptismal font and the altar can be demonstrated in a variety of ways, such as placing the font and altar on the same architectural axis, using natural or artificial lighting, using the same floor patterns, and using common or similar materials and elements of design.

§ 67 §   The location of the baptismal font, its design, and the materials used for its construction are important considerations in the planning and design of the building. It is customary to locate the baptismal font either in a special area within the main body of the church or in a separate baptistry. Through the waters of baptism the faithful enter the life of Christ.[90] For this reason the font should be visible and accessible to all who enter the church building. While the baptistry is proportioned to the building itself and should be able to hold a good number of people, its actual size will be determined by the needs of the local community.

§ 68 §   Water is the key symbol of baptism and the focal point of the font. In this water believers die to sin and are reborn to new life in Christ. In designing the font and the iconography in the baptismal area, the parish will want to consider the traditional symbolism that has been the inspiration for the font's design throughout history. The font is a symbol of both tomb and womb; its power is the power of the triumphant cross; and baptism sets the Christian on the path to the life that will never end, the "eighth day" of eternity where Christ's reign of peace and justice is celebrated.

§ 69 §   The following criteria can be helpful when choosing the design for the font:

1. *One font that will accommodate the baptism of both infants and adults symbolizes the one faith and one baptism that Christians share.* The size and design of the font can facilitate the dignified celebration for all who are baptized at the one font.

2. *The font should be large enough to supply ample water for the baptism of both adults and infants.* Since baptism in Catholic churches may take place by immersion in the water, or by infusion (pouring), fonts that permit all forms of baptismal practice are encouraged.[91]

3. *Baptism is a sacrament of the whole Church and, in particular, of the local parish community.* Therefore the ability of the congregation to participate in baptisms is an important consideration.

4. *The location of the baptistry will determine how, and how actively, the entire liturgical assembly can participate in the rite of baptism.*

5. *Because of the essential relationship of baptism to the celebration of other sacraments and rituals, the parish will want to choose an area for the baptistry or the font that visually symbolizes that relationship.* Some churches choose to place the baptistry and font near the entrance to the church. Confirmation and the Eucharist complete the initiation begun at baptism; marriage and ordination are ways of living the life of faith begun in baptism; the funeral of a Christian is the final journey of a life in Christ that began in baptism; and the sacrament of penance calls the faithful to conversion and to a renewal of their baptismal commitment. Placing the baptismal font in an area near the entrance or gathering space where the members pass regularly and setting it on an axis with the altar can symbolize the relationship between the various sacraments as well as the importance of the Eucharist within the life and faith development of the members.

6. *With the restoration of the* Rite of Christian Initiation of Adults *that culminates in baptism at the Easter Vigil, churches need private spaces where the newly baptized can go immediately after their baptism to be clothed in their white garments and to prepare for the completion of initiation in the Eucharist.* In some instances, nearby sacristies can serve this purpose.

THE RESERVATION OF THE EUCHARIST

§ 70 §   Christ present in the eucharistic species is a treasure the Church has come to cherish and revere over the centuries. The reservation of the Eucharist was originally intended for the communion of the sick, for those unable to attend the Sunday celebration, and as *Viaticum* for the dying. As the appreciation of Christ's presence in the eucharistic species became more developed, Christians desired through prayer to show reverence for Christ's continuing presence in their midst. For Catholics, eucharistic adoration has "an authentic and solid basis, especially because faith in the real presence of the Lord leads naturally to external, public expression of that faith."[92]

§ 71 §   The Second Vatican Council led the Church to a fuller understanding of the relationship between the presence of the Lord in the liturgical celebration of the Eucharist and in the reserved Sacrament, and of the Christian's responsibility to feed the hungry and to care for the poor. As the baptized grow to understand their active participation in the Eucharist, they will be drawn to spend more time in quiet prayer before the Blessed Sacrament reserved in the tabernacle, and be impelled to live out their relationship in active charity. In reverent prayer before the reserved Eucharist, the faithful give praise and thanksgiving to Christ for the priceless gift of redemption and for the spiritual food that sustains them in their daily lives. Here they learn to appreciate their right and responsibility to join the offering of their own lives to the perfect sacrifice of Christ during the Mass[93] and are led to a greater recognition of Christ in themselves and in others, especially in the poor and needy. Providing a suitable place for the reservation of the Blessed Sacrament is a serious consideration in any building or renovation project.

§ 72 §   The general law of the Church provides norms concerning the tabernacle and the place for the reservation of the Eucharist that express the importance Christians place on the presence of the Blessed Sacrament. The *Code of Canon Law* directs that the Eucharist be reserved in a part of the church that is "distinguished, conspicuous, beautifully decorated, and suitable for prayer."[94] It directs that regularly there be "only one tabernacle" in the church.[95] It should be worthy of the Blessed Sacrament—beautifully designed and in harmony with the overall decor of the rest of the church. To provide for the security of the Blessed Sacrament the tabernacle should be "solid," "immovable," "opaque," and "locked."[96] The tabernacle may be situated on a fixed pillar or stand, or it may be attached to or embedded in one of the walls. A special oil lamp or a lamp with a wax candle burns continuously near the tabernacle as an indication of Christ's presence.[97]

§ 73 §   The place of reservation should be a space that is dedicated to Christ present in the Eucharist and that is designed so that the attention of one praying there is drawn to the tabernacle that houses the presence of the Lord. Iconography can be chosen from the rich treasury of symbolism that is associated with the Eucharist.

THE LOCATION OF THE TABERNACLE

§ 74 §   There is a number of possible spaces suitable for eucharistic reservation. The revised *General Instruction of the Roman Missal* states that it is more appropriate that the tabernacle in which the "Blessed Sacrament is reserved not be on the altar on which Mass is celebrated."[98] The bishop is to determine where the tabernacle will be placed and to give further direction. The bishop may decide that the tabernacle be placed in the sanctuary apart from the altar of celebration or in a separate chapel suitable for adoration and for the private prayer of the faithful. In making his determination, the bishop will consider the importance of the assembly's ability to focus on the eucharistic action, the piety of the people, and the custom of the area.[99] The location also should allow for easy access by people in wheelchairs and by those who have other disabilities.

§ 75 §   In exercising his responsibility for the liturgical life of the diocese, the diocesan bishop may issue further directives regarding the reservation of the Eucharist. Before parishes and their liturgical consultants begin the educational component and the discussion process, it will be important for all those involved to know what specific directives or guidelines the diocesan bishop has issued. Good communication at the first stage of the process will help to avoid confusion or conflict between the parish's expectations, the consultant's experience and diocesan directives.

§ 76 §   The pastor, the parish pastoral council, and the building committee will want to examine the principles that underlie each of the options, consider the liturgical advantages of each possibility, and reflect upon the customs and piety of the parishioners. Many diocesan worship offices assist parishes by facilitating the study and discussion process with the parish. This is also an area where liturgical consultants can be of great assistance to the parish.

THE CHAPEL OF RESERVATION

§ 77 §   The diocesan bishop may direct the parish to reserve the Blessed Sacrament in a chapel separate from the nave and sanctuary but "integrally connected with the church" and "conspicuous to the faithful."[100] The placement and design of the chapel can foster reverence and can provide the quiet and focus needed for personal prayer, and it should provide kneelers and chairs for those who come to pray.

§ 78 §   Some parishes have inaugurated the practice of continuous adoration of the Eucharist. If, for some good reason, perpetual exposition must take place in a parish church, the Congregation for Divine Worship and the Discipline of the Sacraments has directed that this take place in a separate chapel that is "distinct from the body of the church so as not to interfere with the normal activities of the parish or its daily liturgical celebration."[101]

THE TABERNACLE IN THE SANCTUARY

§ 79 § A special area can be designed within the sanctuary. Careful planning is needed so that the placement chosen does not draw the attention of the faithful away from the eucharistic celebration and its components.[102] In addition, the placement must allow for a focus on the tabernacle for those periods of quiet prayer outside the celebration of the Eucharist.

§ 80 § Ordinarily, it is helpful to have a sufficient distance to separate the tabernacle and the altar. When a tabernacle is located directly behind the altar, consideration should be given to using distance, lighting or some other architectural device that separates the tabernacle and reservation area during Mass, but that allows the tabernacle to be fully visible to the entire worship area when the eucharistic liturgy is not being celebrated.

HOLY WEEK AND THE PASCHAL TRIDUUM

§ 81 § Passion (Palm) Sunday marks the final movement of the Lenten season toward the Triduum. The liturgy of Palm Sunday requires space for a procession that recalls Christ's triumphant entry into Jerusalem (Matthew 21:1–11). For the cathedral church, the additional consideration of elements of the stational (i.e., pontifical) liturgies should be part of the planning. The Paschal Triduum is the heart of the liturgical year. When designing the church, the rites of the Triduum should be reviewed to ensure that planning will provide space for the key elements of the Triduum: an area for the washing of the feet, a location for the Altar of Reposition after the Evening Mass of the Lord's Supper, space for the Veneration of the Cross on Good Friday, a site for the Blessing of the Fire and the Lighting of the Paschal Candle, and space for the catechumens to be baptized and for candidates for admission to full membership to stand if they are admitted at the Vigil.

THE ALTAR OF REPOSITION

§ 82 § Following the Mass of the Lord's Supper on Holy Thursday, the Blessed Sacrament is carried to a place of reservation. If the Blessed Sacrament is ordinarily reserved in a chapel separated from the central part of the church, the place of repose and adoration will be there.[103] If there is no reservation chapel, then a space for reposition with a tabernacle should be prepared for the occasion.

THE VENERATION OF THE CROSS ON GOOD FRIDAY

§ 83 § The celebration of the Lord's passion on Good Friday has its particular spatial requirements. After the proclamation of the passion and the General Intercessions, the entire assembly rises to venerate the cross or crucifix.[104] The cross used for the veneration preferably should be of sufficient size to be held easily, carried in procession, and venerated. After the veneration, the cross remains in the sanctuary.

§ 84 §   In some circumstances parishes may be able to create a permanent place for lighting the Easter fire. In others, the rite may be conducted in the gathering area immediately outside the church. While safety is always an important consideration, a flame to "dispel the darkness and light up the night" is needed to achieve the full symbolism of the fire.[105] In climates and circumstances where weather precludes lighting the fire outdoors, a more limited fire can be enkindled indoors with the proper accommodations for ventilation, for heat and smoke detectors, for local fire regulations, and for surrounding the space with non-combustible materials.

ACCOMMODATING THE LITURGICAL POSTURES OF THE CONGREGATION

§ 85 §   The location set aside for the people will convey their role within the liturgical assembly.[106] The members of the congregation should be able to see the ministers at the altar, the ambo and the chair.

§ 86 §   Since the liturgy requires various postures and movements, the space and furniture for the congregation should accommodate them well.[107] Styles of benches, pews, or chairs can be found that comfortably accommodate the human form. Kneelers or kneeling cushions should also be provided so that the whole congregation can easily kneel when the liturgy calls for it. Parishes will want to choose a seating arrangement that calls the congregation to active participation and that avoids any semblance of a theater or an arena. It is also important that the seating plan provide spaces for an unimpeded view of the sanctuary by people in wheelchairs or with walkers. Experience indicates that space in the front or at the sides of the church is better than in the rear where a standing congregation obscures the view of those seated in wheelchairs at the back of the church.

SEATING

§ 87 §   There are no universal norms regarding fixed or flexible seating but the diocesan bishop may issue further directives in this area. Many churches have found that a combination of fixed and flexible seating works best to accommodate the various liturgical actions. Ideally, no seat in the nave would be located beyond a point where distance and the lighting level of the sanctuary severely impede the view of and participation in liturgical actions. In earlier periods churches designed for large congregations were limited by engineering constraints. The latest construction and engineering technologies now allow for cost-effective and flexible approaches to designing churches with greater roof spans.

THE PLACE FOR THE PASTORAL MUSICIANS

§ 88 §   Music is integral to the liturgy. It unifies those gathered to worship, supports the song of the congregation, highlights significant parts of the liturgical action, and helps to set the tone for each celebration.[108]

§ 89 §   It is important to recognize that the building must support the music and song of the entire worshiping assembly. In addition, "some members of the community [have] special gifts [for] leading the [assembly in] musical praise and thanksgiving."[109] The skills and talents of these pastoral musicians, choirs and instrumentalists are especially valued by the Church. Because the roles of the choirs and cantors are exercised within the liturgical community, the space chosen for the musicians should clearly express that they are part of the assembly of worshipers.[110] In addition, cantors and song leaders need visual contact with the music director while they themselves are visible to the rest of the congregation.[111] Apart from the singing of the Responsorial Psalm, which normally occurs at the ambo, the stand for the cantor or song leader is distinct from the ambo, which is reserved for the proclamation of the word of God.

§ 90 §   The directives concerning music found in the *General Instruction of the Roman Missal* and the guidance offered by *Music in Catholic Worship and Liturgical Music Today*[112] can assist the parish in planning appropriate space for musicians. The placement and prayerful decorum of the choir members can help the rest of the community to focus on the liturgical action taking place at the ambo, the altar, and the chair. The ministers of music are most appropriately located in a place where they can be part of the assembly and have the ability to be heard. Occasions or physical situations may necessitate that the choir be placed in or near the sanctuary. In such circumstances, the placement of the choir should never crowd or overshadow the other ministers in the sanctuary nor should it distract from the liturgical action.

OTHER RITUAL FURNISHINGS

THE CROSS

§ 91 §   The cross with the image of Christ crucified is a reminder of Christ's paschal mystery. It draws us into the mystery of suffering and makes tangible our belief that our suffering when united with the passion and death of Christ leads to redemption.[113] There should be a crucifix "positioned either on the altar or near it, and . . . clearly visible to the people gathered there."[114] Since a crucifix placed *on* the altar and large enough to be seen by the congregation might well obstruct the view of the action taking place on the altar, other alternatives may be more appropriate. The crucifix may be suspended over the altar or affixed to the sanctuary wall. A processional cross of sufficient size, placed in a stand visible to the people following the entrance procession, is another option. If the processional cross is to be used for this purpose, the size and weight of the cross should not preclude its being carried in procession. If there is already a cross in the sanctuary, the processional cross is placed out of view of the congregation following the procession.[115]

CANDLES

§ 92 §   Candles, which are signs of reverence and festivity, "are to be used at every liturgical service.[116] The living flame of the candle, symbolic of the risen Christ, reminds people that in baptism they are brought out of darkness into

God's marvelous light.[117] For the celebration of the Eucharist it is appropriate to carry candles in the entrance procession and during the procession with the Book of the Gospels.[118] At least two candles are placed near the altar in the sanctuary area. If there is a lack of space, they may be placed on the altar. Four or six candles may be used for the celebration of Mass and for exposition of the Blessed Sacrament. If the bishop of the diocese celebrates, seven candles may be used. Candles placed in floor-standing bases or on the altar should be arranged so they do not obscure the view of the ritual action in the sanctuary, especially the action at the altar.

§ 93 § Candles for liturgical use should be made of a material that provides "a living flame without being smoky or noxious." To safeguard "authenticity and the full symbolism of light," electric lights as a substitute for candles are not permitted.[119]

THE PASCHAL CANDLE

§ 94 § The paschal candle is the symbol of "the light of Christ, rising in glory," scattering "the darkness of our hearts and minds."[120] Above all, the paschal candle should be a genuine candle, the pre-eminent symbol of the light of Christ. Choices of size, design, and color should be made in relationship to the sanctuary in which it will be placed. During the Easter Vigil and throughout the Easter season, the paschal candle belongs near the ambo or in the middle of the sanctuary. After the Easter season it is moved to a place of honor in the baptistry for use in the celebration of baptisms. During funerals the paschal candle is placed near the coffin as a sign of the Christian's passover from death to life.[121]

THE GATHERING SPACE OR NARTHEX

§ 95 § The narthex is a place of welcome—a threshold space between the congregation's space and the outside environment. In the early days of the Church, it was a "waiting area" for catechumens and penitents. Today it serves as gathering space and as the entrance and exit to the building. The gathering space helps believers to make the transition from everyday life to the celebration of the liturgy, and after the liturgy, it helps them return to daily life to live out the mystery that has been celebrated. In the gathering space, people come together to move in procession and to prepare for the celebration of the liturgy. It is in the gathering space that many important liturgical moments occur: men and women participate in the Rite of Becoming a Catechumen as they move toward later, full initiation into the Church; parents, godparents and infants are greeted for the celebration of baptism; and Christians are greeted for the last time as their mortal remains are received into the church building for the celebration of the funeral rites.

§ 96 § In addition to its religious functions, the gathering space may provide access to the vesting sacristy, rooms for choir rehearsal, storage areas, restrooms, and rooms for ushers and their equipment. Adequate space for other gatherings will be an important consideration in planning the narthex and other adjoining areas.

§ 97 § The doors to the church have both practical and symbolic significance. They function as the secure, steady symbol of Christ, "the Good Shepherd" and "the door through which those who follow him enter and are safe [as they] go in and go out."[122] In construction, design and decoration, they have the ability to remind people of Christ's presence as the Way that leads to the Father.[123] Practically, of course, they secure the building from the weather and exterior dangers, expressing by their solid strength the safe harbor that lies within. The appearance and height of the church doors reflect their dignity and address practical considerations such as the accommodation of the processional cross or banners.

THE AREA SURROUNDING THE CHURCH BUILDING

§ 98 § When constructed and maintained well, the outside of a church can proclaim the Gospel to the city or town in which it is located. Even before the members of the worshiping community enter through the doors of the building, the external environment with its landscaping, artwork, and lighting can contribute to a gracious approach to the place of worship. Creative landscaping that separates the entrance to the church from the parking area as well as well-placed religious art can facilitate the spiritual transition as people move to a sense of communal worship. Appropriate signage can provide information and can offer hospitality and an invitation to enter the space for worship. Walkways with well-designed patterns of stone or other materials subtly contribute to the awareness that believers are about to enter holy ground. When choosing a site for a church, consideration should be given to the possibility of landscaped setback so that the church building is not completely surrounded by the parking lot.

§ 99 § It is an ancient practice to summon the Christian people to the liturgical assembly or to alert them to important happenings in the local community by means of bells. The peal of bells is an expression of the sentiments of the People of God as they rejoice or grieve, offer thanks or petition, gather together and show outwardly the mystery of their oneness in Christ.

THE ROLE OF THE CHURCH BUILDING IN OTHER LITURGICAL RITES

§ 100 § The church building is the space for the celebration of the other sacraments, in addition to the Eucharist. While preserving the primary focus upon the eucharistic assembly and the unity and integrity of the building as a whole, the design of the church must also accommodate the needs of these rites.

THE RITES OF INITIATION

§ 101 § Through the waters of baptism Christians are buried with Christ and rise to a new life with him. They are made sharers of God's own life and members of Christ's Body, the Church, and they are regenerated and cleansed of sin. In confirmation the seal of the Holy Spirit is set upon them, and their initiation is completed through their participation in the Eucharist. The specific spatial needs for the celebration of baptism and the Eucharist are addressed in the earlier sections of this chapter.

§ 102 § In the sacrament of holy orders, the ministry of word and sacrament is established and fulfilled. The sacrament is most often celebrated in the cathedral but may also be celebrated in the parish church. Planning should include space for the prostrations and the key liturgical actions such as the imposition of hands, the anointing, and the handing over of the vessels.

THE RITE OF PENANCE OR RECONCILIATION

§ 103 § In the sacrament of penance, God forgives sins and restores broken relationships through the ministry of the Church. The Rite of Penance does not describe the place for the celebration of the sacrament except to say that it be in the space "prescribed by law."[124] The *Code of Canon Law* designates a church or an oratory as "the proper place" for the celebration of the sacrament of penance[125] and requires a screen or fixed grille between penitent and confessor to ensure the anonymity of those who wish it.[126] Canon 964 further directs conferences of bishops to issue more specific norms. The bishops of the United States have directed that the place for sacramental confession be visible and accessible, that it contain a fixed grille, and that it allow for confession face-to-face for those who wish to do so.[127]

§ 104 § By its design, furnishings, and location within the church building, the place for reconciliation can assist penitents on the path to contrition and sorrow for sin and to proclaim their reconciliation with God and the community of faith.

§ 105 § In planning the reconciliation area, parishes will want to provide for a sound-proof place with a chair for the priest and a kneeler and chair for the penitent. Since the rite includes the reading of Scripture, the space should also include a Bible.[128] Appropriate artwork, a crucifix symbolic of Christ's victory over sin and death, icons or images reflective of baptism and the Eucharist, or Scriptural images of God's reconciling love help to enhance the atmosphere of prayer. Warm, inviting lighting welcomes penitents who seek God's help, and some form of amplification as well as braille signs can aid those with hearing or visual disabilities. Additional rooms or spaces will be needed as confessional areas for communal celebrations of penance, especially in Advent and Lent.

THE RITE OF MARRIAGE

§ 106 § The Rite of Christian Marriage contains no directives about the spatial requirements for the celebration. Instead, the ritual focuses upon the consent given by the bride and the groom, the ambo from which the word of God is proclaimed, and the altar at which the couple share the Body and Blood of Christ within a nuptial Mass.

§ 107 § The options within the Rite of Marriage provide for a procession of the priest and ministers to the door of the church to greet the wedding party, followed by an entrance procession, or the entrance of the wedding party and movement down the aisle to meet the priest celebrant at the altar. Some planners have experimented with seating arrangements that eliminate a center aisle in favor of two side aisles. Although this plan can be very useful by allowing the congregation to face the altar and the priest celebrant directly, it challenges parishes to plan how they will provide for entrance processions and recessionals, especially during wedding processions when all wish to have equal visual access to the wedding party.

§ 108 § If it is the custom to have the bride and groom seated in the sanctuary, then the design of the sanctuary should be spacious enough to allow an arrangement of chairs and kneelers that does not impinge upon the primary furniture in the sanctuary. Many ethnic groups and local churches have additional customs for the celebration of marriage that can be honored and accommodated when they are in keeping with the spirit of the liturgy.

THE RITE OF ANOINTING OF THE SICK

§ 109 § The Rite of Anointing and Pastoral Care of the Sick provides for the communal celebration of the sacrament in a parish church or chapel. As noted earlier[129] the church building must be accessible to those with disabilities, including those in wheelchairs and those who must travel with a breathing apparatus. Since many of those to be anointed may be unable to approach the priest, the parish will want to provide an area where the priest is able to approach persons with disabilities with ease and grace. Often this is possible in a section of the church that has flexible rather than fixed seating.

CHRISTIAN FUNERALS

§ 110 § The *Order of Christian Funerals* rites mark the final stage of the journey begun by the Christian in baptism. The structure of the current rites dates back to "Christian Rome where [there were] three 'stages' or 'stations' [during the funeral rite] joined by two processions": the first from the home of the deceased to the church and the second from the church to the place of burial.[130] While the current rite preserves the procession to the church by the mourners who accompany the deceased, a funeral cortege of automobiles is more common than a procession on foot in most places in the United States.

§ 111 § Because the faith journey of the deceased began in baptism, it is appropriate that there be a physical association between the baptismal font and the space for the funeral ritual. "In the act of receiving the body, the members of the community acknowledge the deceased as one of their own, as one who was welcomed in baptism and who held a place in the assembly."[131] With the baptismal symbols of water, light, and the pall, the mourning community prepares for the "liturgy in which it asks for a share in the heavenly banquet promised to the deceased and to all who have been [baptized in Christ]."[132]

§ 112 § In designing the seating configuration, parishes will want to consider the size and placement of the casket and the paschal candle during funerals as well as the presence of the cremated remains when cremation has taken place before the funeral Mass. Good planning will ensure that doors and aisles are wide enough for pall bearers to carry a coffin easily.

§ 113 § The permission to celebrate the funeral Mass in the presence of the cremated remains necessitates a dignified place on which the remains can rest during the Mass.[133] To avoid ritual use of makeshift carriers or other inappropriate containers, parishes may wish to obtain a well-designed urn or ceremonial vessel and stand to hold the cremated remains during the vigil and funeral.

§ 114 § The funeral rites permit the celebration of the vigil for the deceased in the church.[134] If this is the practice, it is appropriate to wake the body in the baptistry or gathering area or in another dignified area of the church that will not interfere with the normal liturgical life of the parish.

THE LITURGY OF THE HOURS

§ 115 § The Liturgy of the Hours is the public, daily prayer of the Church. Recognizing the importance of the Liturgy of the Hours in the life of the Church,[135] many parishes are rediscovering the spiritual beauty of the Hours and are including Morning or Evening Prayer in their daily liturgical life. Although there are no specific spatial requirements for the celebration of the Hours, the focal points of the celebration are the word of God and the praying assembly. An area of flexible seating can facilitate the prayer of a smaller group divided into alternating choirs. The importance of music in public celebrations of the Hours suggests that the place designated for their celebration should provide access to necessary equipment for musicians, particularly cantors and instrumentalists who accompany the singing community.

SUNDAY CELEBRATIONS IN THE ABSENCE OF A PRIEST

§ 116 § The celebration of the Eucharist is the norm for Sunday assemblies. However, a decrease in the number of priests makes this difficult or impossible on a weekly basis in some communities. When the celebration of Mass on a Sunday is not possible in a given parish and the people have no reasonable alternatives, the diocesan bishop can permit the celebration of the Liturgy of the Word or the Liturgy of the Hours or one of these combined with a communion service.[136] When a community gathers for a Sunday celebration in which a priest is not present, the deacon who presides leads the community's prayer from the presidential chair in the sanctuary.[137] A lay person who presides leads the prayer from a chair placed outside the sanctuary.[138]

THE PLACE FOR THE SACRED OILS

§ 117 § The consecrated oil of chrism for initiation, ordination and the dedication of churches, as well as the blessed oils of the sick and of catechumens, are traditionally housed in a special place called an ambry or repository.[139] These oils consecrated or blessed by the bishop at the Mass of Chrism deserve the special care of the community to which they have been entrusted.[140] The style of the ambry may take different forms. A parish church might choose a simple, dignified, and secure niche in the baptistry or in the wall of the sanctuary or a small case for the oils. Cathedrals responsible for the care of a larger supply of the oils need a larger ambry. Since bright light or high temperatures can hasten spoilage, parishes will want to choose a location that helps to preserve the freshness of the oil.

THE RITE OF DEDICATION OF A CHURCH AND AN ALTAR

§ 118 § In addition to containing the rituals of dedication, the *Rite of Dedication of a Church and an Altar* contains liturgies for laying the cornerstone, for commencing work on the building of a church, for dedication of a church already in use, and for the blessing of a church and an altar.[141] These rituals serve as a foundational resource for those engaged in designing and building churches. Just as the initiation of a person into the Christian community occurs in stages, so the construction of church building unfolds over a period of time. Rites are celebrated at the beginning of the building process "to ask God's blessing for the success of the work and to remind the people that the structure built of stone will be a visible sign of the living Church, God's building which is formed of the people themselves."[142] At the conclusion of the construction, the church is dedicated to God with a solemn rite.[143] Familiarity with this rite and the context of prayer that it offers will help to prevent the building project from degenerating into a purely pragmatic or functional enterprise.

§ 119 § Since the celebration of the Eucharist on the new altar after it has been solemnly anointed, incensed, covered, and lighted, is at the heart of the dedication ritual,[144] a new or renovated church is, as far as possible, not used for the celebration of the sacraments until after the Rite of Dedication has taken place. To celebrate the rite after the altar has been in use is anti-climactic and can reduce the rite to empty symbolism.[145] Use of a temporary altar in the period before the dedication is a viable alternative that can help to heighten anticipation of the day of dedication when the new altar will receive the ritual initiation that solemnly prepares it for the celebration of the central mystery of our faith.

§ 120 § When the people of the parish community gather to dedicate their new church building or to celebrate its renovation, they will have made many decisions, balanced a variety of needs, and overcome a multitude of challenges. As the diocesan bishop celebrates the Rite of Dedication and receives the church from his people,[146] the connection between the diocesan Church and the parish community is particularly evident.

§ 121 § The Rite of Dedication provides that the walls of the church may be anointed with sacred chrism in four or twelve places depending on the size and design of the structure. These points can be marked by crosses made from stone, brass, or another appropriate material or carved into the walls themselves. A bracket for a small candle should be affixed to the wall beneath each of these crosses.[147] The candles in these brackets are then lighted during the ritual lighting at the dedication, on anniversaries of the dedication, and on other solemn occasions.

THE LITURGICAL YEAR: SEASONAL DECORATIONS

§ 122 § During the liturgical year the Church unfolds the whole mystery of Christ, from his incarnation and birth through his passion, death, and resurrection to his ascension, the day of Pentecost, and the expectation of his coming in glory. In its celebration of these mysteries, the Church makes these sacred events present to the people of every age.[148]

§ 123 § The tradition of decorating or not decorating the church for liturgical seasons and feasts heightens the awareness of the festive, solemn, or penitential nature of these seasons. Human minds and hearts are stimulated by the sounds, sights, and fragrances of liturgical seasons, which combine to create powerful, lasting impressions of the rich and abundant graces unique to each of the seasons.

§ 124 § Plans for seasonal decorations should include other areas besides the sanctuary. Decorations are intended to draw people to the true nature of the mystery being celebrated rather than being ends in themselves. Natural flowers, plants, wreaths and fabric hangings, and other seasonal objects can be arranged to enhance the primary liturgical points of focus. The altar should remain clear and free-standing, not walled in by massive floral displays or the Christmas crib, and pathways in the narthex, nave, and sanctuary should remain clear.

§ 125 § These seasonal decorations are maintained throughout the entire liturgical season. Since the Christmas season begins with the Vigil Mass on Christmas Eve and ends with the Baptism of the Lord, the placement and removal of Christmas decorations should coincide with these times. Since the Easter season lasts fifty days, planning will encompass ways to sustain the decor until the fiftieth day of Pentecost.

§ 126 § In the course of the liturgical year, the feasts and memorials of Our Lady and of saints with special significance for the parish afford opportunities to show devotion by adorning their images with tasteful floral arrangements or plants.

§ 127 § Fabric art in the form of processional banners and hangings can be an effective way to convey the spirit of liturgical seasons, especially through the use of color, shape, texture, and symbolic form. The use of images rather than words is more in keeping with this medium.

§ 128 § Objects such as the Advent wreath,[149] the Christmas crib,[150] and other traditional seasonal appointments proportioned to the size of the space and to the other furnishings can enhance the prayer and understanding of the parish community.

§ 129 § The use of living flowers and plants, rather than artificial greens, serves as a reminder of the gift of life God has given to the human community. Planning for plants and flowers should include not only the procurement and placement but also the continuing care needed to sustain living things.

THE CHURCH BUILDING AND POPULAR DEVOTIONS

§ 130 § Throughout history and among widely differing cultures, a rich heritage of popular devotions honoring Christ, the Blessed Virgin Mary, and the saints has developed in the Church. Popular devotions "express and nourish the spirit of prayer"[151] and are to be encouraged when they are in conformity with the norms of the Church and are derived from and lead to the liturgy.[152] Like the liturgy, devotions are rituals. They can involve singing, intercession, thanksgiving, and common postures.

§ 131 § Devotional prayer is another way for people to bring the very personal concerns of life to God and to ask the intercession of the saints and of other members of the Christian community. Sacred images are important not only in liturgical prayer but also in devotional prayer because they are sacramentals that help the faithful to focus their attention and their prayer. The design of the church building can do much to foster devotions and to ensure that they enhance and reinforce rather than compete with the liturgical life of the community.

THE STATIONS OF THE CROSS

§ 132 § The Stations of the Cross originated early in the history of the Church. It was the custom of the faithful to follow the way walked by Christ from Pilate's house in Jerusalem to Calvary. As time went on, pilgrims to the holy city desired to continue this devotion when they returned home. In the fourteenth century when the Franciscans were entrusted with the care of the holy places in Jerusalem they promoted the use of images depicting the Lord's Way of the Cross.

§ 133 § Whether celebrated by a community or by individuals, the Stations of the Cross offers a way for the faithful to enter more fully into the passion and death of the Lord and to serve as another manifestation of the pilgrim Church on its homeward journey. Traditionally the stations have been arranged around the walls of the nave of the church, or, in some instances, around the gathering space or even the exterior of the church, marking the devotion as a true journey.[153]

§ 134 § The Stations enjoy a long tradition. In recent times some parishes have clustered the stations in one place. While such an arrangement may be expedient, it is not desirable because it eliminates space for movement, which characterizes this devotion as a "way" of the cross.

SACRED IMAGES

§ 135 § Reflecting the awareness of the Communion of Saints, the practice of incorporating symbols of the Trinity and images of Christ, the Blessed Mother, the angels, and the saints into the design of a church creates a source of devotion and prayer for a parish community and should be part of the design of the church.[154] Images can be found in stained glass windows, on wall frescoes and murals, and as statues and icons. Often these images depict scenes from the Bible or from the lives of the saints and can be a source of instruction and catechesis as well as devotion. Since the Eucharist unites the Body of Christ, including those who are not physically present, the use of images in the church reminds us that we are joined to all who have gone before us, as well as to those who now surround us.

§ 136 § In choosing images and devotional art, parishes should be respectful of traditional iconography when it comes to the way sacred images are recognized and venerated by the faithful. However, they also should be mindful that the tradition is not limited to literal images. While Mary is the mother of Jesus, she is also an icon of the Church, a disciple of the Lord, a liberated and liberating woman. She is the Immaculate Conception, patroness of the United States, and Our Lady of Guadalupe, patroness of all America. Other symbols such as the crucifix, icons, or images of patron saints depicted in various ways can also draw us into the deeper realities of faith and hope as they connect us to the stories behind the image.[155]

§ 137 § The placement of images can be a challenge, especially when a number of cultural traditions are part of a single parish community and each has its own devotional life and practices. Restraint in the number and prominence of sacred images[156] is encouraged to help people focus on the liturgical action that is celebrated in the church. Separate alcoves for statues or icons can display a variety of images through the year. Some parishes designate an area as the shrine for an image that is being venerated on a given day or for a period of time, such as the image of a saint on his or her feast day.

§ 138 § It is important that the images in the church depict saints for whom devotion currently exists in the parish. It is particularly desirable that a significant image of the patron of the church be fittingly displayed, as well as an image of Mary, the Mother of God, as a fitting tribute to her unique role in the plan of salvation. As time passes and demographics change, saints who were once the object of veneration by many parishioners may at another time be venerated by only a few. When this happens, these images could be removed, provided sensitivity is shown with regard to the piety of the faithful and the impact on the building.

CONCLUSION

§ 139 § In this chapter, the liturgical actions of the Church provide the guidelines for the building of a church. There must be space for the variety of the community's prayer, which extends from the primary worship of the Eucharist to popular devotions. The complex balance of all these factors and of the people who participate in them is the most important dimension for the education, planning, and execution of a building plan for a community. The following chapter will reflect upon the use of the arts and the importance of planning for their proper placement early in the design process.

CHAPTER THREE
THE WORK OF OUR HANDS:
ART AND ARTISTS ASSISTING THE CHURCH AT PRAYER

§ 140 § When God's people gather for prayer, the most intimate and all-embracing aspect of their life together occurs: the moment when they touch, taste, smell, hear, see, and share those hidden realities that would otherwise remain imperceptible. Together they adore the holiness of God and give expression to the unceasing life God has given them. God nourishes them as a community and makes them holy through the use of *ordinary* perceptible signs of water, oil, bread, and wine, transformed by *extraordinary* grace. The *place* where God gathers this people powerfully draws them more deeply into communion and expresses in beauty God's profound holiness. This is the place that prompts them to recognize the divine image in which they have been created, now restored in Christ. "For from the greatness and the beauty of created things their original author, by analogy, is seen."[157]

§ 141 § Throughout the history of the Church, a dynamic tension has existed between the continuity of traditional artistic expression and the need to articulate the faith in ways proper to each age and to diverse cultures. In every age the Church has attempted to engage the best contemporary artists and architects to design places of worship that have sheltered the assembly and disclosed the presence of the living God. In the past, dialogue between the Church and the artist has yielded a marriage of faith and art, producing sublime places of prayer, buildings of awe-inspiring, transcendent beauty, and humble places of worship that, in their simplicity, inspire a sense of the sacred.

THE ROLE OF RELIGIOUS ART

§ 142 § In the Christian community's place of prayer, art evokes and glorifies "the transcendent mystery of God—the surpassing invisible beauty of truth and love visible in Christ."[158] Therefore the "Church entrusts art with a mediating role, analogous, we might say, to the role of the priest or, perhaps better, to that of Jacob's ladder descending and ascending. Art is meant to bring the divine to the human world, to the level of the senses, then, from the spiritual insight gained through the senses and the stirring of the emotions, to raise the human world to God, to his inexpressible kingdom of mystery, beauty, and life."[159]

§ 143 § Art chosen for the place of worship is not simply something pretty or well made, an addition to make the ordinary more pleasant. Nor is the place of worship a museum to house artistic masterpieces or artistic models. Rather, artworks truly belong in the church when they are worthy of the place of worship and when they enhance the liturgical, devotional, and contemplative prayer they are inspired to serve.

§ 144 § The central image of Christianity is the cross, calling to mind the passion, resurrection, and Christ's final coming in glory. Every work of Christian art or architecture shares in this image and embraces the ambiguities of suffering and death, healing and resurrection, recognizing that "by his wounds we are healed." Such art draws from the mystery of redemption a unique power to provoke and invite the world more deeply into the mysteries of our faith.

§ 145 § Likewise, Christian art is also a product of "spontaneous spiritual joy" that challenges believers to complete the reign of God for which they hope.[160] Born from an ecstatic love of God, Christian beauty proclaims something new and original, manifesting itself as an echo of God's own creative act.

THE COMPONENTS OF TRUE AND WORTHY ART

§ 146 § Authentic art is integral to the Church at prayer[161] because these objects and actions are "signs and symbols of the supernatural world"[162] and expressions of the divine presence. While personal tastes will differ, parish committees should utilize the criteria of quality and appropriateness in evaluating art for worship. *Quality* is perceived only by contemplation, by standing back from things and really trying to see them, trying to let them speak to the beholder. *Quality* is evident in the honesty and genuineness of the materials that are used, the nobility of the form embodied in them, the love and care that goes into the creation of a work of art, and the personal stamp of the artist whose special gift produces a harmonious whole, a well-crafted work.

§ 147 § *Quality* art draws the beholder to the Creator, who stands behind the artist sharing his own creative power, for the "divine Artist passes on to the human artist a spark of his own surpassing wisdom."[163] This is true of music, architecture, sculpture, painting, pottery making, textiles, and furniture making, as well as other art forms that serve the liturgical environment. The integrity and energy of a piece of art, produced individually by the labor of an artist, is always to be preferred above objects that are mass-produced. Similarly, in the construction of new church buildings, there is no standard pattern for church art nor should art and architectural styles from any particular time or culture be imposed arbitrarily upon another community. Nonetheless, the patrimony of sacred art and architecture provides a standard by which a parish can judge the worthiness of contemporary forms and styles.

§ 148 § *Appropriateness* for liturgical action is the other criterion for choosing a work of art for church. The quality of *appropriateness* is demonstrated by the work's ability to bear the weight of mystery, awe, reverence, and wonder that the liturgical action expresses and by the way it serves and does not interrupt the ritual actions that have their own structure, rhythm, and movement. Since art is revelatory, a gift from God, a truly beautiful object stretches "beyond what the senses perceive and, reaching beneath reality's surface, strives to interpret its hidden mystery." Nonetheless, there is always the chasm between "the work of [the artist's] hands" and the "dazzling perfection" glimpsed in God's creative moment.[164] Art that is used in worship must therefore evoke wonder at its beauty but lead beyond itself to the invisible God. Beautiful, compelling artworks draw the People of God into a deeper awareness of their lives and of their common goals as a Christian community as well as of their roles and responsibilities in the wider world.[165] Art that fulfills these qualities is art *worthy* of the Christian assembly.

§ 149 § Worthy art is an essential, integral element in the sacred beauty of a church building. Through skilled use of proportion, shape, color, and design, art unifies and helps to integrate the place of worship with the actions of worship. Artistic creations in the place of worship inspire contemplation and devotion. Sculpture, furnishings, art-glass, vesture, paintings, bells, organs, and other musical instruments as well as windows, doors, and every visible and tactile detail of architecture possess the potential to express the wholeness, harmony, and radiance of profound beauty.

THE ARTIST WITHIN THE CHRISTIAN COMMUNITY

§ 150 § When artists are called upon to serve the Christian community, there is an "ethic," a "spirituality of artistic service."[166] Breadth of imagination enables artists to communicate deep meaning and powerful religious sentiment with grace and sensitivity. This gift from God is combined with refined educated talents that execute elegantly crafted objects for the good of the community and the glory of God. Like the gift of prophecy, religious imagination is a power through which the Holy Spirit can move and speak. As a result, artists do not always confirm comfortable piety but, like the prophets of old, they may confront God's people with their faults and sins and they challenge the community's injustice and lack of love. "Even when they explore the darkest depths of the soul or the most unsettling aspects of evil, artists give voice in a way to the universal desire for redemption."[167]

§ 151 § Artists respond to the demands of art, actualizing in aesthetic form their ideas, feelings, and intentions so that when artists activate their imagination, their intentions and inner life are expressed in their work. In working with a parish, artists will also express the intentions, faith, and life of that community. A truly worthy and beautiful artwork can transform the artist and the community for which it is intended. The dialogue with God that an artwork mediates can persuade and invite; however, it does not force its meanings upon individuals or communities.

§ 152 § Artists willing to accept commissions destined for a place of worship must be respectful and supportive of the doctrines, beliefs, and liturgical practices of the Church. They also should be knowledgeable about the traditional iconography and symbolism of Christian art. Artists who are genuinely in search of meaning in their work and in their lives will find a homeland for their souls since, in the realm of Christianity, the most vital personal and social questions are posed. Not only does the Bible provide a rich inventory of themes and ideas, but also artists who have envisioned these stories and images have offered unique perspectives on the heart of revelation itself and "this partnership has been a source of mutual spiritual enrichment."[168]

§ 153 § A commission for a church or for worship affords artists an opportunity to join their creative gifts to those in a long history of artists who have placed their talents at the service of God and who have enriched the Church's treasury of sacred art and architecture. "All artists who, in view of their talents, desire to serve God's glory in holy Church should ever bear in mind that they are engaged in a kind of sacred imitation of God the Creator, and are concerned with works destined for use in Catholic worship and for the edification, devotion, and religious instruction of the faithful."[169]

§ 154 § The Church needs art and artists to communicate Christ's message, and artists need the Church to inspire their investigations of the material world, their own inner lives, and the fabric of the community. Before an artist is selected, the parish will want to carefully consider and evaluate the artist and his or her work with the assistance of those best qualified to advise the community. Once a community has chosen artists to assist them in worship, they should give the necessary direction and then trust those they have selected. Artists deserve the independence appropriate to their gifts.

THE SPECIAL REQUIREMENTS OF LITURGICAL ART

§ 155 § In order to create art that truly serves the liturgy, the artist must have an understanding of and reverence for the liturgy. There is both a distinction and a connection between devotional art and that designed for public liturgy. Liturgical arts are integrally related to the sacraments of the Church while devotional arts are designed to enrich the spiritual life of the community and the personal piety of its members. As the devotions of the Church are derived from the liturgy and lead to it,[170] so devotional art must be in harmony with the liturgy, respect its nature, and draw people to its celebration. "The primary norm is that sacred art be functional, that is, the felicitous expression of what the liturgy is meant to be, the worship of God and the language of the community at prayer."[171] Parishes will want both liturgical and devotional art.

§ 156 § Prominent among Christian devotions is piety directed to Mary, the Mother of God. Since the earliest days of the Church, God's People have grown in their love of Mary as their mother, given to them by Jesus on the cross. Venerated and loved, invoked and imitated, she is a model for Christian faith, a support and refuge in time of need, and an eschatological image of what the Church hopes to become.[172] Although this devotion differs essentially from the prayer of adoration directed to Christ, to the Spirit, and to the Father, it is one that is deeply imbedded in the hearts of Catholics.

§ 157 § The special and unique dignity of the Mother of God has been expressed in the devotional art of the Church. Artists have painted her image in wondrously meditative fashion as a "sign of sure hope and solace for the pilgrim People of God."[173] At the same time, veneration of Mary, like that of all other devotions, leads clearly to the worship of her Son. The location, style, and importance of Marian images in the church demonstrate the intimate connection she has with the eucharistic liturgy of Christ, as well as its distinctions.

THE INTEGRATION OF ART WITHIN THE LITURGICAL SETTING

§ 158 §   The role of the Church is to educate artists in the appropriate relationships between their personal approach to art and the needs of the liturgy. The role of artists is to explore the powerful personal resonances that exist between sacred art, interior devotion, and the public life of the community. An essential ingredient for a successful marriage between the artistic needs of the Church and the creative talent of the artist is the ability to collaborate. Artists must cultivate the capacity to work with the leaders and people of the local community and within the frameworks established by the universal Church if they are to have the opportunity to use their talents to fashion beautiful objects that will enliven the worship of the community.

§ 159 §   Artists who collaborate with architects and liturgical consultants need to make an honest assessment of several key elements, attending to the way the objects will be placed within the building, how the works will be integrated with the architecture of the church and with its local setting, and the ways the Christian community moves within its space.

§ 160 §   Attention should also be given to the way artistic objects influence acoustics and other functional elements within the building and, at the same time, to the ways in which various elements, especially lighting, may affect the objects. In addition, consideration must be given to how easily an object can be cleaned and maintained.

MATERIALS OF THE ARTIST

§ 161 §   Artists bridge the worlds of the visible and the mysterious invisible. They focus upon items with specific shapes, sizes, weights, densities, colors, forms, and textures. At the same time, they utilize materials that struggle to express ideas and concepts, visions and imaginative constructions. Even as they nourish the senses with beauty, they also disclose the "transcendent value" and the "aura of mystery" in the Christian message.[174]

§ 162 §   Artists choose materials with integrity because they will endure from generation to generation, because they are noble enough for holy actions, and because they express what is most respected and beautiful in the lives and cultures of the community. Materials, colors, shapes, and designs that are of short-lived popularity are unworthy. In addition to eliminating unsuitable materials, artists and communities should be cautious and discerning about promoting features closely identified with the values and attitudes of any class, ethnic or age group to the exclusion of others in the community.

§ 163 §   Similarly, artworks consisting of technological and interactive media, such as video and other electronically fabricated images, may also be appropriate for sacred purposes. Subject to the same criteria of suitability as other sacred art, technologically produced works of art can point toward sacred realities even though they do not possess the more enduring form, color, texture, weight, and density found in more traditional sacred art.

§ 164 § As in the case of styles of architecture, there is no particular style for sacred furnishings for the liturgy.[175] Sacred vessels may be in "a shape that is in keeping with the culture of each region, provided each type of vessel is suited to the intended liturgical use and is clearly distinguished from [utensils] designed for every day use."[176] Materials used for sacred vessels such as the chalice and paten should be worthy, solid, and durable, and should not break easily. Chalices and cups used for the distribution of the Precious Blood should have bowls made of nonabsorbent material. Vessels made from metal are gilded on the inside if the metal ordinarily rusts. The vestments worn by ministers symbolize the ministers' functions and add beauty to the celebration of the rites. "In addition to traditional materials, natural fabrics proper to the [local area] may be used for making vestments; . . . The beauty and nobility of a vestment should derive from its material and design rather than from lavish ornamentation."[177]

§ 165 § Conferences of bishops may make further determinations regarding the appropriate style and material for sacred vessels and vestments to be used in the celebration of the liturgy.[178] Likewise, the diocesan bishop can make further determinations regarding the suitability of the materials or the design for vessels and vestments, and, in cases of doubt, he is the judge of what is appropriate in this regard.[179]

THE DISPOSITION OF WORKS OF ART
NO LONGER NEEDED FOR SACRED USE

§ 166 § Sacred art that is no longer useful or needed or that is simply worn out and beyond restoration deserves to be treated with respect. To ensure the protection of worn or used sanctuary furnishings, vessels, vesture, and other liturgical artifacts, many diocesan bishops have issued directives about their proper disposition when they are no longer suitable for worship. In addition, with the closing or merging of parishes, vessels and vestments can be available for the use of other parishes and missions. In disposing of such artifacts pastors should consult the diocesan worship office or chancery to learn what directives or procedures are in effect.

§ 167 § In addition, bishops have exercised their responsibility as stewards of the Church's artistic resources by encouraging pastors and diocesan personnel to consult with experts and to create an inventory of historic churches and of objects in any church that have artistic or historical value. Such inventories are most helpful when they carefully itemize and list each entry's value and note any changes to the objects since they were acquired.[180] Usually two copies are made so that one can be kept at the local parish and the other in the diocesan curia, both as a historical record and for insurance purposes. In some cases, copies are sent to the Vatican library if this is appropriate.

§ 168 § Objects of great artistic or historical value or those donated to the Church through a vow may not be sold without special permission of the Holy See.[181] When such objects are not to be sold but disposed of in some other way, the diocesan bishop should be contacted so that the concerns of donors and the requirements of canon law are fulfilled.

§ 169 § Every community knows that, if its house of prayer is to radiate the beauty of divine presence, effort and sacrifice will be required. Besides appropriate remuneration for the work of its artists, the community must show its respect for these works by maintaining and preserving them as the years pass. In doing so, they encourage those with artistic aptitudes to continue to serve the community and in this way build up and support a local community of artists worthy of liturgical work. A covenant is established linking artists and congregations, an "alliance between art and the life of religion" through which may be heard an artistic voice "that love inspires and that inspires love."[182]

CHAPTER FOUR
BUILDING A CHURCH: PRACTICAL CONSIDERATIONS

§ 170 § Having reflected upon the nature and purpose of a church, having reviewed the activities that take place within the worship space, and having considered the role and importance of the arts as part of the act of worship, we here address the actual task of building. This chapter examines the practical considerations such as who should collaborate in building the church, how to develop a master plan, what kind of educational process will be most helpful for parishes, and how to work with the relevant professionals.

§ 171 § Churches are built to be legacies to a community's faith. Every parish community hopes that its space for worship will endure long after those who now pray there have joined the Messianic Banquet. Liturgical education is primary in the development of any parish's plans for the future, since the building is an embodiment of the Church's transmission of the Gospel. If built wisely and well, the building itself will evangelize the descendants of its builders.

THE MASTER PLAN

§ 172 § As part of its stewardship efforts, each parish should have a master plan for the current and future allocation and augmentation of its resources. The master plan contains the statement of the parish vision and priorities, the long-range general plan for parish buildings and properties, and the outline for the allocation of financial and personnel resources.

§ 173 § The parish mission statement and its list of priorities can serve as the basis for making decisions about resources and projects. In addition to the mission statement, the master plan includes a current inventory of buildings and property; a site plan; an analysis of the current condition of significant items that impact budget, plans, and priorities; and regularly updated reports on the parish's financial assets and projections for future growth, or the amortization of debts as well as maintenance and replacement data on major items such as furnaces, roofs, elevators, and other items of capital outlay.

§ 174 § Since planning is affected by many events, a regularly updated report on area demographics, population trends, and planned growth and development by the municipality's planning office that could affect parish property and the surrounding area is an important part of the data in the plan. The assessment of potential items of major liability or sources of income are also part of this long-range plan. The decision to build a church or to renovate an existing worship space is made within the framework of the master plan.

BEGINNING THE PROCESS

§ 175 § The construction or renovation of a church building is a complex task that demands prayer and reflection, technical expertise and study. A building or renovation project is not the work of the pastor alone, nor is it that of a building committee. Rather, it is an act of faith that belongs to and engages the entire community. To be successful, a building project must be rooted in a proper understanding of the Church and of worship that becomes the point of reference for all future decision making. Creating and articulating this shared vision is a key element of the process.

§ 176 § Deepening a sense of ownership for the project involves taking the time to educate the parish, to listen to the people's concerns, and to discuss the vision and values at stake in such a project. The time devoted to communication and education will help make the later stages of the process move more smoothly and will ensure that the relationships among parish members are strengthened rather than strained by the project.

§ 177 § Since no single pastor or parish possesses the totality of expertise or vision required to execute a project of such great scope, the congregation and clergy will need to recognize the areas of their own competence, the role of the diocesan bishop and diocesan personnel, and their limits beyond which the assistance of experts will be required. Respect and appreciation for the competence of others in their respective fields is essential for good teamwork.

THE ROLE OF THE APOSTOLIC SEE AND THE DIOCESAN CHURCH

§ 178 § The Apostolic See has provided guidance for designing places of worship that is necessary and invaluable for the local community. In constructing or renewing a place of worship, it is the bishop who, in his role of fostering and governing the liturgy, must assume primary responsibility and authority for the regulation and direction of such projects.[183] As the *Code of Canon Law* states, "No church is to be built without the express written consent of the diocesan bishop. . . . after having heard the presbyteral council and the rectors of the neighboring churches."[184] Therefore, the building or renovation of a place for worship is a project that belongs to the local parish and the whole diocesan Church.[185] Care must be exercised by the pastor and parish to consult with diocesan personnel from the earliest stages of the discernment process through the completion of the work. The diocesan liturgical commission or diocesan commission on liturgy and art assists with liturgical education and the development of the liturgical and artistic components of the building's design. Some dioceses have additional building offices or similar agencies to help parishes with the selection of architects, engineers, and building contractors, and to provide valuable information about those who have successfully served the Church in the past. In the early stages of the project, the parish needs to be in communication with the appropriate diocesan office or commission in developing the budget for the project and the financial plan, since these require the approval of the bishop and his financial advisors. This document is designed to assist diocesan bishops in developing local norms and procedures to guide parishes in church design and construction and to provide knowledgeable advisors for the local parish, especially in the complex areas of engineering and construction.

§ 179 § In some dioceses the first step in any building or renovation process is a meeting of the pastor, the architect, and possibly, the liturgical consultant with the diocesan bishop or his representative to discuss any diocesan parameters. Such early consultation can prevent confusion and unrealistic expectations or diversions later.

THE ROLE OF THE PARISH COMMUNITY

THE ASSESSMENT OF NEED

§ 180 § The entire parish is an integral part of the needs assessment and the development of priorities, which are the first steps of a process that will lead to a decision about building, renovating, and expending parish resources. While some decisions in the process will be made by committees, the decision and the design should never become the exclusive project of a small select group.

§ 181 § When a parish is determining the need for a new church or for the renovation of an existing church, a thorough self-study and educational program is part of the needs assessment process. In that study the parish community reflects upon what it is, and what it hopes for in a new or renovated church. This is essential to enable the community to give direction to the architect and other professionals who will design the building.

ROLES WITHIN THE PARISH

THE PASTOR

§ 182 § The pastor is vital to the building or renovation of a parish church. The pastor shepherds the community through the various and often lengthy stages of discernment and planning and works with the finance committee in fulfilling his responsibility for the fiscal dimensions of the project. He must open channels of communication with the entire parish so that all voices may be heard. A clear initial presentation on the scope of the project and frequent updates on the progress of the work, especially any alterations to initial plans, coupled with displays of the architect's renderings, floor plans, and scale models help to involve parishioners as part of the project from beginning to end. With the help of the staff and others in the parish, the pastor arranges for the parish self-study, the liturgical education of parishioners, and the preparation of the building committee as it begins discernment. The pastor is also the connection and communication link with the diocese throughout the process. In the final analysis, decisions concerning every facet of the building program from beginning to end remain with the pastor, in conformity with diocesan regulations. Wisdom, however, requires that the pastor consult broadly with the congregation, the parish staff, the parish pastoral council, the parish liturgy committee, and the parish finance council, as well as with liturgical and architectural experts and experienced diocesan personnel.

THE PARISH BUILDING COMMITTEE

§ 183 § Depending on the organization of the parish, a building committee will be formed that will have significant responsibility for the consultation and educational components as well as for the oversight of the actual building or renovation process. In selecting this committee, the pastor will search for parishioners whose skills and knowledge will contribute to the project. Engineers, architects, artists, interior designers, contractors, and individuals with experience in construction can be of great assistance in overseeing the work to be done. As professionals who have a vested interest in the life of the parish but who are not financially or materially engaged in the process, they can assist with the development of realistic plans and can also provide an ongoing objective evaluation of the work as it progresses.

§ 184 § In addition to having professionals and people with a broad range of experience on the committee, the pastor will want to ensure that the committee is representative of the parish by choosing members of various ages and viewpoints and some liaisons from key parish committees. When all views are heard in the discussion phases, better decisions are likely to be made and a greater sense of ownership will result.

THE PARISH PASTORAL COUNCIL, THE PARISH WORSHIP COMMITTEE, AND THE FINANCE COUNCIL

§ 185 § Each of the key parish committees oversees the various aspects of parish life and continues to work during this major parish activity. As the building or renovation project progresses, these parishioners contribute to its development through membership on existing parish committees or on newly formed committees entrusted with specific tasks. The parish pastoral council can assist the pastor with the general oversight of pastoral activity in the parish and represents the concerns of the parishioners. The parish worship committee can contribute its expertise in keeping the liturgical needs in the forefront of the discussion. The finance council has a significant role with regard to sources and limits of funding, debt amortization, and financial campaigns. Areas that might be addressed by other committees include furnishings, seating arrangements, the chapel of reservation, devotional items, interior and exterior artwork, and landscaping design.

§ 186 § However, it is essential that members of these committees approach their tasks from an informed perspective and stay in constant communication with other committees to ensure a well-informed team and a coordinated project. While the professional experience of people related to a building project is valuable, care must be taken that these professionals familiarize themselves with the special requirements of the liturgy related to their area of competence. In many instances, the initial work of the committees will be to gain knowledge of the church's liturgical practices as they relate to their task. As the project develops, these committees may be called upon to provide an ongoing, informed review of plans from their areas of expertise.

THE PARISH SELF-STUDY

§ 187 § By their design and construction, church buildings serve the rites of the Church and the devotion of the people, fostering their encounter with God who dwells in all holiness,[186] and reflecting the faith of the people and the culture in which they live. Ideally the church building will be designed so that it also responds to the local environment. While the church building belongs to the Church, its visual aspects belong to its neighbors. In addition, there must be a concern for the impact of the building on its natural surroundings; that is, the site on which it will be located and the resources available there.

§ 188 § Parishioners may have some sense of the history of the parish, but it is helpful to sharpen the common knowledge of church members at the beginning of the project. This review can consider the origins of the parish; its evolving identity within the local community; and the social, political, economic, and religious elements that have shaped its life. Among other things, the parish will want to reflect on the cultures represented in its members, the geographical and historical factors that have contributed to its development, significant aspects of the community's liturgical and devotional life, and changes that have already taken place in the building in which its members worship.

§ 189 § During the study it may be helpful to invite parishioners to contribute photographs of weddings, first communions, baptisms, and other sacramental and seasonal events. These photos, arranged chronologically, can provide graphic evidence of the changes that the church building has already undergone. The archives of local and diocesan newspapers also can provide material that will help in piecing together the story of the parish over the years.

LITURGICAL EDUCATION

§ 190 § As part of the self-study, the parish will want to develop a process for liturgical education. While the actual content will vary from one parish to another, parishioners need to learn more about the liturgy, which is the heart of the Church's life, and about their participation in the liturgy, which is the "primary and indispensable source" of the "true Christian spirit."[187] In addition, they need to understand the intrinsic relationships between the Eucharist and the other sacraments, the Liturgy of the Hours, the liturgical year, and the building that houses these celebrations. After reflecting on the basics of liturgy, the assembly can learn about the ways in which architectural elements, the placement and design of liturgical objects, and the choice of floor plans can encourage, control, or hinder liturgical actions. Full and active participation will be greatly affected by the appropriate architectural expression of faith for a particular community. The liturgical consultant chosen by the parish often develops and directs this education process. In other instances diocesan offices can provide assistance and resources in this area.

PRIORITIES AND STEWARDSHIP OF RESOURCES

§ 191 § Since the building of a place of worship has serious financial implications, wise stewardship of resources demands that the parish establish liturgical, spiritual, artistic, and social priorities upon which financial decisions rest. However, the cost of an item is not the only consideration in planning for construction and renovation. Every faith community, even the financially poorest, is called to use all the powers of human ingenuity at its disposal to provide beautiful, uplifting, and enriching places of worship that also serve basic human needs.

§ 192 § Building a beautiful church is itself an act of worship because beauty is a reflection of God and "a call to transcendence."[188] All church buildings and their contents should mirror divine beauty, which is not to be confused with lavish display. Whatever the style of architecture adopted, extravagant expenditures on the construction of a church should be avoided in light of the obligation to share the resources of the earth in an equitable manner. However, compromises in cost should not compromise the durability, stability, and structural soundness of the building. Balancing the social needs of the local faith community with their duty to worship God through beauty affects the equation of design and execution. Beauty also can be found in simplicity of shape; in humble, honest materials; in the creative use of light, water, and sound; in elegant design; and in worthy religious art.

SURVEYING EXISTING CHURCHES

§ 193 § Before people make architectural and liturgical decisions, they need some experience of the broad spectrum of architectural designs already in new and renovated churches. People's preferences are often determined by things with which they are familiar. Visits to a variety of churches can help them to develop a store of images that they can evaluate and consider as potential options for the building project in their own parish.

§ 194 § Although the visits should not be confined to the work of architects or liturgical consultants under consideration for their project, people will want to visit churches that demonstrate the candidates' work. Gaining knowledge of a professional's previous work, whether religious or secular, is indispensable to the process of selecting the architect.

§ 195 § When actual site visits are not possible, slides, videos, and other visual aids can expand the experience of those preparing for the building or renovation of a church. Liturgical and construction offices within the diocese also can be invaluable resources in advising parish building committees of recent or exemplary projects in the local area.

THE ROLE OF PROFESSIONALS

§ 196 § In deciding to employ professionals, and in hiring specific people, the parish must be aware of any diocesan directives and requirements for contracts and licenses and is encouraged to utilize the expertise of diocesan staff with experience in this area. Doing so can help to avert serious financial and legal difficulties for the parish and major time delays. Because the architect is the contracted professional responsible for the development of the building's design, it is appropriate that other professionals serve as consultants to the architect. It is also crucial that all professionals chosen have the expertise to fulfill the particular tasks needed and that a clear description of their roles and responsibilities be developed and agreed upon before they actually begin the work.

§ 197 § Normally, engaging the skills of professionals with experience in the lighting of churches, acoustical design and sound transmission, and design is preferable to selecting vendors of equipment or accepting the "good will" services of individuals who may have some knowledge but who lack the requisite qualifications to design and install elements suitable for a church. Both the scale of the building and the demands of the liturgy require varied solutions that differ from those suitable for domestic or smaller-scale projects.

THE ARCHITECT

§ 198 § The architect, the primary agent of design, has an essential role in the building or renovation project. In choosing an architect, the parish will look for someone whose designs will embody the mysteries of the faith expressed and lived in the liturgical assembly. In addition to having the skills and exercising the appropriate standard of care required of a professional architect, those chosen to design church buildings should be able to

1. *Create an environment by the use of space, sound, and visual aspects that will facilitate and encourage liturgical celebrations and the active participation of the faithful.*[189]

2. *Give visual expression to aspects of doctrine and spirituality that words alone cannot adequately express, employing in their own designs, and requiring in those of others hired by them, the highest artistic standards for the inspiration, devotion, and religious formation of believers.*[190]

3. *Draw attention to and protect the significant treasures of the Church's architectural and artistic heritage, whenever possible.*

4. *Be collaborative and willing to participate in the dialogue essential to the development of a building program that will fulfill the needs of the local Church.*

5. *Be sensitive to the financial realities of the parish and work within its budget.*

THE LITURGICAL CONSULTANTS

§ 199 § The construction of a church building cannot be undertaken without proper professionals in a variety of fields. When a parish begins to undertake the building or renovation of a liturgical space, the parish building committee should obtain the services of specialists in liturgical design. lt is the responsibility of the liturgical consultant to assist the pastor, the staff, and the entire parish with continuing education about the importance, role, and value of worship, and the impact of the church building upon worship.

§ 200 § The liturgical consultant also works with the architect. Some architects are *liturgical* architects. They possess, in addition to their architectural credentials, artistic insights and formal liturgical education that equip them to engage in liturgical design. However, this is not always the case. The liturgical consultant(s) selected by the parish work(s) with the architect and other members of the design team from the earliest stages of the process to help them apply the principles and norms of liturgical design to the practical and liturgical needs of the parish being served. This includes examining the acoustics, the flow and movement for processions, appropriate styles for liturgical celebrations, the interrelationships within the Eucharist as well as the relationship of the Eucharist with the other sacraments, and all the elements required by the Church's liturgy. In addition, the consultant may have expertise in design and can help to coordinate the design and fabrication of appropriate furniture and other objects to be used during liturgical services, as well as the liturgical art to be placed within the church.

THE CONTRACTOR

§ 201 § Parishes will search for contractors who exhibit skills appropriate to the scope and significance of the project and who are properly licensed and insured. Candidates should demonstrate their ability to finance and to fulfill their commitments completely and on time and should exhibit skills in the areas of management, supervision, building technology, and construction methods and procedures. They also should have a record of good labor relations supported by positive benefit practices that are consonant with and reflective of the Church's teachings on social justice. Most dioceses keep careful records of the competence, working methods, completion practices, and fiscal responsibility of the contractors who have worked on church buildings in the diocese to assist parishes with the competitive bidding process. This information can be readily available to the pastor and the parish building committee.

COMPENSATION AND PROFESSIONAL STANDARDS

§ 202 § Excellent designs can be brought to beautiful completion only by competent and trustworthy professionals. These professionals have a right to compensation that matches the expectations of the outstanding competence and expertise demanded of them. A major and continuing educational effort is required among believers in order to restore respect for competence and expertise in all the arts and to cultivate a desire for their best use in public worship. The Church needs in its service professional people with the appropriate qualifications. The community must be willing to budget and expend resources for appropriate professionals so that the criteria for good liturgical art and sound building practices can be met.

§ 203 § The architects, liturgical consultants, artists, contractors, and all others engaged in the project should be held to a high professional standard of care and to the observance of the social teaching of the Church. Because they are, in part, responsible for the stewardship of the resources of the parish, all who are engaged in the project must be worthy of the trust of the community.

§ 204 § Volunteers and donors of contributed services and in-kind gifts are valuable assets in any parish building project. However, these individuals and their contributions must be held to the same standard of skill, quality, and appropriateness that is required of services and objects procured through conventional methods. As a parish utilizes contributed services, it will be important to work with diocesan personnel to ensure that all legal and insurance requirements are met.

COLLABORATION

§ 205 § Collaboration is essential to every architectural project, but it is even more so in architecture at the service of liturgy, for cooperation reflects the very nature of the Body of Christ. The members of the parish community along with their pastor, the liturgical consultant, the artist, the architect, and the contractor are all called to a collaborative effort, whose goal is to summon forth the finest expressions of faith within their means. Mutual trust and openness are central components of the collaborative effort. The parish, represented by its pastor and committees, the architect and liturgical design consultant, the artist, and the contractors should strive to listen to each other with careful attention so that a place of sacred beauty will emerge from their mutual dialogue.

THE DESIGN OF THE CHURCH AND ITS SURROUNDINGS: SPECIAL CONCERNS

THE SITE PLAN

§ 206 § The unity of God's People is both expressed and brought about in the gathering of the eucharistic assembly.[191] Since the church building is fundamentally a place where God and his gathered people meet, care should be exercised in designing the entire complex of site and church building so that it will serve this *gathering* of the faithful that is essential to liturgical worship.[192]

§ 207 § The design of the area surrounding the church can integrate trees, shrubs and flowers with places for outdoor gathering and for quiet meditation. While there is no maintenance-free landscaping, it is possible to keep landscape care at a manageable level by using indigenous and low-maintenance plants that can withstand dry conditions without requiring excessive watering.

§ 208 § The outdoor paths that lead to the church building should be welcoming and free of barriers, especially to persons with disabilities. In the design of these paths, consideration should be given not only to groups and individuals coming to Sunday Eucharist but also to the arrival and departure of special groups such as the wedding party or the mourners who accompany the deceased's body at a funeral.

§ 209 § In suburban and rural parishes, the building approach must ordinarily provide access for pedestrians as well as for those who arrive by automobile. The building site can be designed so that all who approach are helped to make the transition from everyday life to the celebration of the mysteries of faith. Parking lots and passenger drop-off areas can be convenient yet unobtrusive. Sensitive design of vehicular approaches, parking sites, and walkways coupled with appropriate landscaping make it possible to accommodate the automobile without allowing it to dominate the site. Weather considerations will influence the arrangement and the choices made by the local parish.

§ 210 § Paths provided for those approaching on foot, especially paths that lead to the principal gathering space outside the building, should receive special attention. The space at which these paths converge should be welcoming and hospitable, drawing together those who assemble for worship and providing for those who wish to linger in conversation with one another after liturgical services. Pavement patterns, borders, and configurations; shrines containing images in sculpture, mosaic, or other art media; as well as planters and outdoor benches help with the passage from the mundane to the sacred action of worship.

ACCESSIBILITY

§ 211 § Every person should be welcomed into the worshiping assembly with respect and care. It was the prophet Isaiah who announced the Lord's message: "For my house shall be called a house of prayer for all peoples."[193] The bishops of the United States have stated that "it is essential that all forms of the liturgy be completely accessible to persons with disabilities, since these forms are the essence of the spiritual tie that binds the Christian community together."[194] Further direction is given by Pope John Paul II, who has called the Church to the full integration of persons with disabilities into family, community, and Church, and to overcome "the tendency to isolate, segregate and marginalize [those with disabilities]."[195] When buildings present barriers to the full and active participation of all, the Body of Christ is harmed.

§ 212 § Special attention should be given to individuals with visual or hearing impairments, to those who have difficulty walking or who are in wheelchairs, and to the elderly with frailties. In addition to ramps, elevators, braille signs, and special sound systems that can be accessed by those who need assistance, staircases should have at least one railing. If the sanctuary is elevated by steps, an unobtrusively placed ramp with a hand rail should be provided to make it possible for everyone to have access to the sanctuary.[196]

§ 213 § The planning process should include consultation with persons with various disabilities and the use of an accessibility inventory[197] to ensure a careful review of potential or existing architectural barriers. All new construction and renovation work must fully integrate the demands of the liturgy with current laws, codes, and ordinances for persons with disabilities.

§ 214 § Older places of worship can be especially challenging because of the obstacles they present to persons with disabilities. In the renovation of older buildings, special provisions must be made to harmonize the requirements for accessibility with the architectural integrity of the building and with the norms for the proper celebration of liturgy. Adaptations to existing buildings can be expensive, but failure to make the community's places of worship accessible will exact a far more costly human and ecclesial toll. The goal is always to make the entire church building accessible to all of God's People.

THE CHOICE OF BUILDING MATERIALS

§ 215 § A church building is a lasting expression of a faith community's life. Because the church building is destined to endure, parishes and the professionals who assist them should ensure that the components of the building, especially the building materials, are sturdy and substantial enough to stand the test of time. While traditional building materials have served the Church well in the past, more recently developed materials and building techniques might better serve a contemporary structure. In all instances, the building that is designed for an extended life will need fine, durable materials. The use of materials available locally and of designs that are expressive of local culture can be an advantage to parishes.

§ 216 § Faithful stewardship of the earth's resources demands that the Church be a partner in the development of a sustainable architecture. Materials, construction methods, and procedures that are toxic to the environment or that are wasteful of the earth's resources should be avoided. Providing heating, ventilating, air conditioning, and lighting systems that are energy efficient is financially sound practice and, at the same time, environmentally responsible. It is an exercise in parish stewardship.

CHANGE ORDERS AND MODIFICATIONS

§ 217 § During the construction phase of the process, the pastor and building committee may find the need to modify the original plan. Because modifications involve additional costs, parishes will want to anticipate as many situations as possible before plans are finalized and contracts are signed.

§ 218 § If the need for modifications becomes apparent at a later stage, the procedures should be clear to all involved. It is helpful to

1. *Specify that the pastor is to communicate any change orders to the architect, who acknowledges them in writing.*

2. *Specify that the acknowledgment is to state the additional cost involved.*

3. *Specify that the pastor and/or someone specifically authorized by the pastor is/are the only one(s) designated to sign the change orders approving the additional expenditure.*

4. *Specify that the architect is responsible for communicating with the contractor or subcontractors regarding the changes.*

BUILDING MAINTENANCE

§ 219 § The design process will include planning for the long-term and short-term maintenance of the new or renovated building. The beauty and utility of a place of worship can be sustained only by an ongoing, careful attention to its upkeep through regular maintenance. Therefore, funds for both general maintenance and capital improvements should be anticipated in every future parish budget.

§ 220 § Durability and maintenance expenses are critical factors in the selection of building materials and of the mechanical, electrical, and plumbing systems. Decisions made on the basis of short-term economy can be very costly when viewed from the perspective of long-term expenses. A well-thought-out plan for maintenance that includes a financial component is necessary in the case of existing structures. In addition, special attention may be needed when the maintenance of historical buildings is at issue.

SOUND IN THE PLACE OF WORSHIP

§ 221 § Silence is the ground of all prayer. From contemplative silence emerge the sung and spoken prayer of the entire assembly and the prayers and proclamations of the various ministers. Liturgical celebrations call for the clear transmission of the sung and spoken responses of the liturgical assembly, as well as of the words of the individual ministers such as the priest celebrant, the deacon, the readers, and the cantor and leader of song. In addition, the space should provide an environment for instrumental music that supports the assembly's song and worship.

§ 222 § The first consideration in providing quality sound transmission is the acoustic design of the building. The interior surfaces such as the walls, the floor, and the ceiling affect the transmission of sound, as do design features like the ceiling height, the shape and construction of rooms, and the mechanical systems such as heating and cooling units and lighting fixtures. The sound-deadening tiles so vital to noise reduction in gymnasiums and other public buildings will be used rarely in a church and only with professional advice to reduce or eliminate outside noise. Soft surfaces such as carpets, rugs, and large fabric wall hangings absorb sound, while hard surfaces such as stone, tile, glass, and metals reflect it. A combination of sound-absorbing and sound-reflecting surfaces properly applied and used in correct proportion provides the kind of system needed for a worship space.

§ 223 § Acoustical engineers can help parishes design a building capable of the natural transmission of sound; they also can be of great assistance in the renovation of existing buildings.

§ 224 § Another aspect of an effective audio environment is the electronic amplification system, which can augment the natural acoustics and can help to remedy problems that cannot be solved in other ways. Planners also should consider provisions for sound in the nave, in the sanctuary, and in adjacent spaces such as the gathering area and the space around the baptismal font. Accommodations should be made for people with special hearing needs.

§ 225 § Providing for the amplification of the proclaimed and sung word and for instrumental and choral music is a complex task that demands the skills and experience of experts in the field of acoustical design. Choosing local vendors who do not possess the requisite skills to understand the complex needs of the liturgical assembly may prove to be a serious, even costly liability.

THE PLACEMENT OF THE ORGAN AND OTHER MUSICAL INSTRUMENTS

§ 226 § Musical instruments, especially the pipe organ, have long added to the beauty and prayerfulness of Catholic worship.[198] Planning sufficient space for the organ and other instruments that may be used to accompany the assembly's prayer is an important part of the building process. This includes the design of the organ casework, if such is used, or the placement of the pipes of large instruments. An acoustical specialist and musicians working together can arrive at a placement that allows the pipes to be seen and heard well without becoming a distraction or competing with the other artwork and iconography. The placement of the organ also must ensure that the instrumentalists have a clear visual connection with the director of music and, if necessary, with the cantor or leader of song.

§ 227 § Some instruments are used only occasionally for more solemn and festive occasions. For this reason there is need for flexibility in the arrangement of the space allotted for music so that there will be adequate room to accommodate them when they are included in the worship services.

LIGHTING THE PLACE OF WORSHIP

§ 228 § Light is a powerful symbol for the followers of Christ who is the "light shining in the darkness" and whose image is seen in the sun and in the paschal candle whose flame is "divided but undimmed."[199] In addition to its theological symbolism, light takes on pastoral, aesthetic, and practical import in the construction of churches. Careful planning enables parishes to choose options that make maximum use of the natural light, which can be supplemented by artificial sources.

§ 229 § Professionals can make planners aware of the ways in which fixtures shield glare, of the manner in which specific lamp types render color, and of the noise level of ballasts in some fixtures. If a church building is to foster the worship of those who gather there, it must first meet minimum standards of hospitality, which means that those gathered for worship will be able to see as well as to hear one another. In the design of the lighting scheme for a church, the highest priority should be given to the ability of the worshipers to see both the faces of those with whom they gather as the Body of Christ and the faces of those who minister to them.

§ 230 § In addition, lighting can aesthetically enhance the architectural and artistic components of the building and its appointments. Lighting for Sunday Mass differs from lighting required for a baptism or for times when the church is open for private prayer. What is appropriate for the chapel of reservation may not be effective in the nave, and what works in the sanctuary at the priest celebrant's chair may not be helpful for the reader or the priest at the altar. Lighting engineers can suggest appropriate options to ensure the light production that will best serve the liturgy. Additional practical considerations include the cost and efficiency of various types of lamping, the ease or difficulty of replacing burnt-out bulbs, possible computerization, and the ease of use and flexibility of the system to meet the needs of a variety of liturgical situations.[200]

§ 231 § Planning the building's lighting includes both the exterior and the interior of the building. Illumination of pathways and entries is not only a matter of safety but also of aesthetic enhancement. In keeping with good stewardship, using lighting generated by solar power is ecologically responsible, and it is an effective form of exterior lighting to be considered.

§ 232 § Building codes require that exit signs, fire alarm strobes, fire alarm pull boxes, annunciator panels, and fire extinguisher cabinets be located in "conspicuous places." Timely planning can help to reconcile these required elements with liturgical, devotional, and artistic focal points. It is the responsibility of the architect to work with all design and engineering consultants to ensure that conflicts are avoided and that smoke-detecting devices are calibrated so that candle smoke and incense do not set off fire alarms.[201]

§ 233 § Provisions for electronic media should be incorporated into the initial design of a new building. These should fit into the architectural design and should be made inconspicuous. Consideration should be given to the effect of light on projected images.

SACRISTIES

§ 234 § Well-designed, well-equipped, and well-organized sacristies contribute to the smooth function of the liturgy and to the maintenance and preservation of vesture, vessels, linens, and other liturgical appointments. Since the Second Vatican Council, most new churches and some renovated structures provide a vesting sacristy near the entrance to the church adjacent to the gathering space so that the entrance procession can proceed directly from the sacristy into the gathering space and down the aisle to the altar. The vesting sacristy provides storage space for vestments as well as a place where the vestments of the day can be arranged by the sacristan. A restroom, or at least a wash basin with running water, and a full-length mirror can be helpful additions to this area. If the vesting sacristy is located in the rear of the church, it is helpful to have an additional work sacristy that offers easy access to the altar located near the sanctuary. This sacristy would contain the *sacrarium* (see below) and another basin deep enough to fill tall vases with water. It could contain locked cabinets for items of special value and storage for sacred vessels, altar cloths and other linens, candles and candle stands, and vases, containers, and plant stands. In addition, the work sacristy should be equipped for the laundering and care of church linens. If fabric art in the form of hangings or banners is used in the church, it will be desirable to include a storage area with rods over which these fabrics can be hung so that they do not become wrinkled or damaged from improper storage.

SECURITY ISSUES

§ 235 § Distressing though it may be, the contemporary reality compels the Church to be mindful also of security issues for the church building. This is appropriate not only for the sake of securing items and treasures within the church building but it is also equally important for the safety of the faithful. It is unfortunate that so many churches today must be locked, thus preventing the faithful from entering for prayer and meditation except at specific times. Investigation should be made regarding the possibility of securing the items inside the church in such a way as to allow the faithful greater access to this house of prayer.

THE SACRARIUM

§ 236 § The sacristy near the sanctuary will usually contain the *sacrarium*, the special sink used for the reverent disposal of sacred substances. This sink has a cover, a basin, and a special pipe and drain that empty directly into the earth, rather than into the sewer system. After Mass, when the vessels are rinsed and cleansed, the water is poured into the sacrarium so that any remaining particles that might be left will not be poured into the sewer but will go directly into the earth. When the purificators and corporals are rinsed before being washed, the water is disposed of in the sacrarium. The sacrarium also can be used to discard old baptismal water, leftover ashes, and the previous year's oils, if they are not burned.

§ 237 § In addition, if any of the Precious Blood is accidentally spilled during Mass, it is carefully wiped up and the area is washed. The water from this process also should be poured down the sacrarium. Reverence for sacred things continues even after they are no longer useful in the liturgy.

SPECIAL ISSUES IN THE RENOVATION OF CHURCHES

§ 238 § When a parish constructs a new building, there are many options available for responding to the liturgical needs and balancing the values involved.

When a parish is renovating an existing worship space, the building itself may limit some of the design possibilities and constrain the parish to choose between options that are less than ideal. In making compromises demanded by the limits of the existing space, it is important for the parish to continue to work with professionals to consider all the possible options and to make the choice that will best serve the requirements of the liturgy and the other parish priorities.

ALTERATION OF HISTORIC STRUCTURES

§ 239 § Over time, as public expressions of worship change, there is a consequent shift in the demands on the physical space used for the Church's liturgy. In accord with the norms of the liturgical reform, it is sometimes necessary to alter historic structures that pose a challenge.[202] In projects of this kind, a delicate balance can be achieved through a selection of designs and appointments that respect and protect the Church's ancient artistic heritage and, at the same time, effectively serve the requirements of contemporary worship.

RENOVATION OF CHURCHES

§ 240 § When renovation of a church is to be undertaken or when it becomes necessary to raze an old church, special care is needed. A church that has served its people over many years will not easily be relinquished, especially by those with deep roots in the parish. In this type of project, parish involvement in the assessment of need and in subsequent planning is especially critical. Although consultation allows opposition to emerge more quickly than it otherwise might, in the final analysis it is better that all points of view be heard and dealt with in an atmosphere of respect and collaboration than that they be left unvoiced to fester for the future.

§ 241 § There will always be some members of a community who will find it difficult, if not impossible, to relinquish their past church, but an open assessment of the local needs, coupled with education about the liturgical rites, can go far toward drawing a parish together in support of the work to be done. In principle, the community deserves to hear how the renovation will enhance their ability to pray with solemnity, beauty, and dignity.

§ 242 § It is also important in situations such as these for respect to be shown for the existing building and its appointments so as to preserve as much of the original worthy fabric as possible. When the project involves a renovation, materials such as marble and wood paneling, as well as other artifacts or furnishings, often can be refurbished and incorporated into the new design, provided they are of requisite quality. Informing the parish of the efforts being made in this regard may make the adjustment to the new worship space less difficult, if not more appealing.

§ 243 § There are times, however, when the materials are no longer suitable, either because they are worn or because they no longer serve the needs of the liturgy. In such cases, pastors and committees need to consult with the diocesan worship office or the chancery regarding any policies governing the disposal of such items. In recent years there have been examples of religious artifacts and sacred vessels appearing at auctions and on websites for purchase with seemingly no consideration of their purpose or significance.

§ 244 § Finally, when a church interior is to be gutted or torn down, celebrating a final Mass to mark the closing of the church building is appropriate. Perhaps the most appropriate ritual would be the final celebration of Mass in the church, followed by a procession in which the people journey to either the new place of worship or to the place that will serve them temporarily until the necessary work on the new or renewed space for worship is finished.

THE ALTAR

§ 245 § In the construction of new churches, there should be only one altar to signify the one Eucharist and the one Lord, Jesus Christ, who gathers the community at the one Table of his Body and Blood. However, in renovating an existing church, when the position of the old altar hinders the people's participation, or if "it is impossible to move it without detriment to its artistic value, then another fixed altar may be erected" in the church. This new altar is the one on which the liturgy should be celebrated.[203]

§ 246 § It is usually better to avoid attaching individual names to specific appointments, furnishings, or works of art within the church. While allowing people to pay for these objects may be an easy fund-raising solution, it can lead to future problems when there may be need to remove or alter the memorialized object.

THE SPACE FOR THE RESERVATION OF THE BLESSED SACRAMENT

§ 247 § In an earlier chapter, the issue of the location of the tabernacle was covered. The structure of the existing building will determine some of the options the parish is able to consider. In exercising his responsibility for the liturgical life of the diocese, the diocesan bishop may issue specific directives regarding the reservation of the Eucharist and the placement of the tabernacle. Again, the pastor, the parish pastoral council, and the building committee will need to review all existing diocesan norms and then carefully examine the principles that underlie each of the options, weigh the liturgical advantages of each possibility, and reflect upon the customs and piety of the parishioners before making a recommendation on the placement of the tabernacle. The location also should allow for easy access by people in wheelchairs and by those who have other disabilities. Diocesan worship offices can assist parishes by facilitating the study and discussion process regarding the placement of the tabernacle and other significant issues involved in the renovation of a church. This is an area where liturgical consultants also can be of great assistance to the parish.

§ 248 § In most churches built before 1969, the tabernacle was situated on the main altar. At the close of the Second Vatican Council, when parishes were able to celebrate the liturgy facing the congregation, many pastors installed movable altars somewhere in front of the existing altar, and they used the former altar as the place for the reservation of the Blessed Sacrament.

§ 249 § In renovating a church designed in another time period, a parish has an opportunity to consider other locations for the tabernacle. Care must be taken to ensure that the area set aside for the reservation of the Eucharist is worthy and distinguished. The place for eucharistic reservation and its furnishings should never be temporary, makeshift, or difficult to find.

§ 250 § In some renovated churches it is possible to remove older altars and tabernacles. When there are good reasons for not removing the altar, an alternate site for the tabernacle may still be considered. In some churches an area that previously housed a side altar or some devotional space might be an appropriate space for reservation, assuming that it meets the other requirements set forth in the *General Instruction of the Roman Missal.* In other situations, the only appropriate place for reservation will be in the sanctuary itself and on the former main altar. In these instances, a balance must be sought so that the placement of the tabernacle does not draw the attention of the faithful away from the eucharistic celebration and its components.[204] On the other hand, the location must provide for a focus on the tabernacle during those periods of quiet prayer outside the celebration of the Eucharist.

§ 251 § Ordinarily, there should be a sufficient distance to separate the tabernacle and the altar. When a tabernacle is located directly behind the altar, consideration should be given to using distance, lighting, or some other architectural device that separates the tabernacle and reservation area during Mass but that allows the tabernacle to be fully visible to the entire worship area when the eucharistic liturgy is not being celebrated.

§ 252 § When a place is chosen for the tabernacle and the former tabernacle can be removed from an existing altar without damaging the altar or the setting, this will be beneficial and will help to prevent confusion among the faithful.

PRESERVATION OF THE ARTISTIC HERITAGE OF THE CHURCH

§ 253 § The coexistence of past and present called for in renovating and restoring church art and architecture is not without rich, multilayered, and successful precedent. "The Church is intent on keeping the works of art and the treasures handed down from the past and, when necessary, on adapting them to new needs."[205] In many parishes, even those whose churches are not considered historically, architecturally, or artistically significant, it is possible to find worthy works of art such as art-glass, furnishings, wood and marble structures, and musical instruments that are of aesthetic and artistic value. Parishes, therefore, are encouraged to undertake an assessment of their artistic works and furnishings to determine their value. The architect, artist, and liturgical consultant, as well as diocesan personnel, are indispensable collaborators in discerning works that are considered part of the sacred heritage of the Church's art. "Many people have made unwarranted changes in places of worship under the pretext of carrying out the reform of the liturgy and have thus caused the disfigurement or loss of priceless works of art."[206]

§ 254 § "Care should be taken against destroying the treasures of sacred art in the course of remodeling churches." When it is necessary to relocate or remove artistic pieces in the interest of the liturgical reform, they can be appropriately cared for and placed in a location "befitting and worthy of the works themselves."[207] Sacred art that at one time appropriately served liturgy and devotion but that is less capable of functioning in that capacity must still be accorded respect and must never be put to secular or "profane use."[208]

§ 255 § Each diocese is strongly encouraged to record and protect the cultural heritage of the faithful. Where possible, a diocesan repository or museum can properly preserve and make available the rich heritage of the local Church. Every renovation project should include a careful photographic and videographic documentation of the building as it evolves.

§ 256 § As custodians of the Church's sacred heritage, architects, artists, and clergy must be educated in the appreciation of sacred art and in its purposes within liturgy. The priests' leadership often will provide the initial inspiration to communities seeking to build new churches, to design new liturgical art, or to renovate existing worship spaces. The Second Vatican Council was particularly clear in its teaching on this issue:

> "Clerics are to be taught about the history and development of sacred art and about the sound principles on which the productions of its works must be grounded. In consequence they will be able to appreciate and preserve the Church's treasured monuments and be in a position to offer good advice to artists who are engaged in producing works of art."[209]

CONCLUSION

§ 257 § Church architecture embodies the Gospel and awakens true liturgical piety in all believers, drawing them into the life of the Triune God.[210] The eucharistic piety around which churches are built is always Trinitarian, Christological, Scriptural, and communal, and builds upon the Church's liturgical tradition *lex orandi, lex credendi*. Without such well-grounded liturgical piety, the church building will lack the essentials for which it was constructed. The most technically brilliant architecture can lack a Christian soul if it does not house a community with the mind and heart of Christ.

§ 258 § Decisions about what is considered appropriate Christian art, while they should be informed by expert taste and opinion, are best made after consultation with the whole liturgical assembly under the leadership of the pastor. When the Church's buildings and artworks engender a contemplative attitude toward God's creation, Christ's redemption of history, and the gifts of the Holy Spirit, they proclaim her faith in visible signs and evangelize the neighborhood, the city, and the nation. Non-believers point to them as stunning examples of art as well as mysterious, public symbols of Christian piety. Without a meditative dimension, Christian architecture risks reducing the mystery of divine presence to either social action or to a comfortable domesticity.

§ 259 § Prayer and liturgy both arise from communities of faith and, at the same time, help to create those communities. The eucharistic assembly enters into a dialogue initiated by God and continued among brothers and sisters. Without a commitment to the building of community, a parish may create a church building that is architecturally refined but stark and oppressively distant.

§ 260 § The process of building a church calls the People of God to the unfinished business of the community; it alerts the eucharistic assembly to the fact that complacency is destructive and that Christ's redemption of the universe is incomplete until God is truly all in all. Without the prophetic challenge of the Holy Spirit, church buildings could be merely triumphalistic monuments, a confirmation of comfortable opinions. The Spirit's prophetic gift reminds the assembly of the poor in the midst of plenty, of the homeless living on the streets, and of the abused and battered whose faces can be so easily avoided. These members of the Communion of Saints must be welcome at the Table of the Lord, and their concerns and needs must guide all building decisions. "What makes a church different from any other building is not its form or shape but rather how it facilitates for a particular community of believers a regular unfolding of the Christian mystery, the eternal divine plan for humanity as revealed in the person of Jesus Christ."[211] Eucharistic assemblies, housed in church buildings, have Jesus Christ at their center. He is the Word spoken by divine mystery, the beloved Son of the Father, the head of the community of believers, and the prophet who challenges and inspires them to live for God and neighbor. Every church built for the People of God unfolds his presence.

§ 261 § A characteristic of Christians is how they love one another even while they meet the challenge of building a new place for worship. It may be difficult and the fabric of the assembly may fray and even tear. But the Spirit's work in the assembly of God's People encourages cooperation so that each can perform a task for the building up of the Body of Christ. During a building process, the community works together with the diocese and with the universal Church as another way of building up the Church with the "living stones" from which God's assembly is made. If the community looks upon its work with the eyes of faith, then it can be assured that God will bring the good work to completion.

NOTES

1. Second Vatican Council, *Sacrosanctum Concilium: Constitution on the Sacred Liturgy* [SC] (December 4, 1963), nos. 45–46: "Likewise, by way of advancing the liturgical apostolate, every diocese is to have a commission on the sacred liturgy under the direction of the bishop. Sometimes it may be expedient for several dioceses to form between them one single commission which will be able to promote liturgy by common consultation.

   "Besides the commission on the sacred liturgy, every diocese, as far as possible, should have commissions for sacred music and sacred art. These three commissions must harmonize their activities. Indeed it will frequently be advisable to fuse the three of them into a single commission."

2. Second Vatican Council, *Lumen Gentium: Dogmatic Constitution on the Church* [LG] (November 21, 1964), no. 17: "Whatever good lies latent in the religious practices and cultures of diverse peoples, is not only saved from destruction but is also healed, ennobled, and perfected unto the glory of God, the confusion of the devil, and the happiness of man."

   Congregation for Divine Worship and the Discipline of the Sacraments, *Inculturation and the Roman Liturgy* [IRL] (1994), no. 18: "So the Liturgy of the church must not be foreign to any country, people or individual, and at the same time it should transcend the particularity of race and nation. It must be capable of expressing itself in every human culture, all the while maintaining its identity through fidelity to the tradition which comes to it from the Lord."

3. SC, no. 25: "The liturgical books are to be revised as soon as possible; from various parts of the world, experts are to be employed and bishops are to be consulted."

4. SC, no. 128: "Along with the revision of the liturgical books, as laid down in Article 25, there is to be an early revision of the canons and ecclesiastical statutes which govern the disposition of material things involved in sacred worship. These laws refer especially to the worthy and well-planned construction of sacred buildings, the shape and construction of altars, the nobility, location, and security of the Eucharistic tabernacle, the suitability and dignity of the baptistery, the proper use of sacred images, embellishments, and vestments. Laws which seem less suited to the reformed liturgy are to be brought into harmony with it, or else abolished; and any which are helpful are to be retained if already in use, and introduced where they are lacking. According to the norm of Article 22 of the Constitution, the territorial bodies of bishops are empowered to adapt matters to the needs and customs of their different regions; this applies especially to the material and form of sacred furnishings and vestments."

5. Cf. the Circular Letter *Opera Artis: On the Care of the Church's Historical and Artistic Heritage* [OA] (April 11, 1971), from the Congregation for the Clergy to presidents of the episcopal conferences; the decree *Domus Dei* (1968) on the norms for minor basilicas, from the Congregation of Rites (Consilium); the *Rite of Dedication of a Church and an Altar* [RDCA] (1977) from the Congregation for the Sacraments and Divine Worship; the Instruction *Pontificalis Ritus* (1968) on the simplification of pontifical rites and insignia, from the Congregation of Rites; the Instruction *Ut Sive Sollicite* (1969) on vesture, from the Vatican's Secretariat of State; the Motu Proprio *Inter Eximia Episcopalis* (1978) on the use of the pallium, from Pope Paul VI; and Pope John Paul II's *Letter to Artists* [LA] (April 4, 1999).

6. National Conference of Catholic Bishops' Committee on the Liturgy, *Environment and Art in Catholic Worship* [EACW] (Washington, D.C.: United States Catholic Conference, 1978).

7. United States Catholic Conference-Libreria Editrice Vaticana, *Catechism of the Catholic Church* [CCC] (2000), no. 760.

8. LG, no. 9.

9. Ibid.

10. SC, no. 5: "For it was from the side of Christ as He slept the sleep of death upon the cross that there came forth the wondrous sacrament which is the whole Church."

11. RDCA, ch. 2, no. 1 (International Committee on English in the Liturgy, *Documents on the Liturgy: 1963–1979: Conciliar, Papal and Curial Texts* [DOL] [1982] 547, no. 4369): "This holy people, made one as the Father, Son, and Holy Spirit are one, is the Church, that is, the temple of God built of living stones, where the Father is worshiped in spirit and in truth."

12. SC, no. 8: "In the earthly liturgy, by way of foretaste, we share in that heavenly liturgy which is celebrated in the holy city of Jerusalem toward which we journey as pilgrims, and in which Christ is sitting at the right hand of God, a minister of the sanctuaries and of the true tabernacle . . . ; we sing a hymn to the Lord's glory with all the warriors of the heavenly army; venerating the memory of the saints, we hope for some part and fellowship with them; we eagerly await the Savior, our Lord Jesus Christ, until He, our life, shall appear and we too will appear with Him in glory (cf. Phil. 3:20; Col. 3:4)."

13. RDCA, ch. 2, no. 1 (DOL 547, no. 4369): "Rightly, then, from early times 'church' has also been the name given to the building in which the Christian community gathers to hear the word of God, to pray together, to receive the sacraments, and to celebrate the eucharist."

14. Cf. CCC, no. 2691: "The church, the house of God, is the proper place for the liturgical prayer of the parish community. It is also the privileged place for adoration of the real presence of Christ in the Blessed Sacrament. The choice of a favorable place is not a matter of indifference for true prayer."

   Cf. RDCA, *Theological Commentary*, no. 6.

15. CCC, no. 1180: "These visible churches are not simply gathering places but signify and make visible the Church living in this place, the dwelling of God with men reconciled and united in Christ."

16. RDCA, ch. 1, no. 2 (DOL 547, no. 4370): "Because the church is a visible building, it stands as a special sign of the pilgrim Church on earth and reflects the Church dwelling in heaven."

   Cf. Canon Law Society of America, *Code of Canon Law* [CIC] (1998), c. 1214: "By the term *church* is understood a sacred building designated for divine worship to which the faithful have a right of entry for the exercise, especially the public exercise, of divine worship."

17. RDCA, ch. 2, no. 3 (DOL 547, no. 4371): "The very nature of a church demands that it be suited to sacred celebrations, dignified, and evincing a noble beauty, not merely costly display, and it should stand as a sign and symbol of heavenly realities."

18. Cf. LA, no. 12: "Art must make perceptible, and as far as possible attractive, the world of the spirit, of the invisible, of God. It must therefore translate into meaningful terms that which is in itself ineffable. Art has a unique capacity to take one or other facet of the message and translate it into colors, shapes and sounds which nourish the intuition of those who look or listen. It does so without emptying the message itself of its transcendent value and its aura of mystery."

   Cf. LA, no. 16: "Beauty is a key to the mystery and a call to transcendence. It is an invitation to savor life and to dream of the future. That is why the beauty of created things can never fully satisfy. It stirs that hidden nostalgia for God which a lover of beauty like St. Augustine could express in incomparable terms: 'Late have I loved you, beauty so old and so new: Late have I loved you!' (Confessions 10:27)."

19. CCC, no. 1098: "The preparation of hearts is the joint work of the Holy Spirit and the assembly, especially of its ministers. The grace of the Holy Spirit seeks to awaken faith, conversion of heart, and adherence to the Father's will. These dispositions are the precondition both for the reception of other graces conferred in the celebration itself and the fruits of new life which the celebration is intended to produce afterward."

It is for this reason that *Sacrosanctum Concilium* (nos. 14–17, and 129) maintains that a firm education in liturgical theology and in the historical development of the arts is central to seminary education.

20. Ibid., no. 1069: "The word 'liturgy' originally meant a 'public work' or a 'service in the name of/on behalf of the people.' In Christian tradition it means the participation of the People of God in 'the work of God' (cf. John 17:4). Through the liturgy Christ, our redeemer and high priest, continues the work of our redemption in, with, and through his Church."

The ministerial priest, by the sacred power that he has, forms and rules the priestly people; in the person of Christ he effects the eucharistic sacrifice and offers it to God in the name of all the people. The faithful, indeed by virtue of their royal priesthood, participate in the offering of the Eucharist.

21. SC, no. 7: "Rightly, then, the liturgy is considered as an exercise of the priestly office of Jesus Christ. In the liturgy the sanctification of man is manifested by signs perceptible to the senses, and is effected in a way which is proper to each of these signs; in the liturgy full public worship is performed by the Mystical Body of Jesus Christ, that is, by the Head and His members."

Cf. CIC, c. 834.

22. The *Catechism of Catholic Church*, no. 2567, speaks of God's revelation and prayer as a "covenant drama" that engages the heart and unfolds throughout the whole history of salvation.

23. Pope John Paul II, *Dies Domini: Observing and Celebrating the Day of the Lord* [DD] (May 31, 1998), no. 68: "In order that rest may not degenerate into emptiness or boredom, it must offer spiritual enrichment, greater freedom, opportunities for contemplation and fraternal communion. Therefore, among the forms of culture and entertainment which society offers, the faithful should choose those which are most in keeping with a life lived in obedience to the precepts of the Gospel. Sunday rest then becomes 'prophetic,' affirming not only the absolute primacy of God, but also the primacy and dignity of the person with respect to the demands of social and economic life, and anticipating in a certain sense the 'new heavens' and the 'new earth,' in which liberation from slavery to needs will be final and complete. In short, the Lord's Day thus becomes in the truest sense the day of man as well."

24. SC, no. 10: "Nevertheless the liturgy is the summit toward which the activity of the Church is directed; at the same time it is the fountain from which all her power flows."

25. Cf. Luke 1:23; Acts 13:2; Romans 15:16, 27:2; and Philippians 2:14–17, 25, 30.

26. SC, no. 7: "From this it follows that every liturgical celebration, because it is an action of Christ the priest and of His Body the Church, is a sacred action surpassing all others."

CCC, no. 1070: "In the New Testament the word 'liturgy' refers not only to the celebration of divine worship but also the proclamation of the Gospel and to active charity. In all of these situations it is a question of the service of God and neighbor. In a liturgical celebration, the Church is servant in the image of her Lord, the one 'leitourgos'; she shares in Christ's priesthood (worship), which is both prophetic (proclamation) and kingly service (service of charity)."

27. From the creation of the world, God's presence has been mediated through the very works of his hands (Romans 1:20). With the people of Israel, that presence was seen more clearly and even localized at first in the Tent of Meeting and later in the Temple. These were understood as the place or epiphany of God's glory (the *Shekinah*) (Exodus 40:34–35). In the New Testament, Christ comes to be seen as the complete and definitive epiphany of God's glory (John 1:4; Hebrews 1:3, 10:5–7). The Church, the People of God, is the continued sacramental presence of Christ, and the new church building is the privileged place of this continued epiphany in the ongoing history of salvation.

28. Congregation for Divine Worship and the Discipline of the Sacraments, *General Instruction of the Roman Missal* [GIRM] (2000), no. 27: "At Mass or the Lord's Supper, the people of God are called into unity, with a priest presiding and acting in the person of Christ, to celebrate the memorial

of the Lord or Eucharistic sacrifice. For this reason Christ's promise applies supremely to such a local gathering together of the Church: 'Where two or three come together in my name, there am I in their midst' (Matthew 18:20). For at the celebration of Mass, which perpetuates the sacrifice of the cross, Christ is really present in the assembly gathered in his name; he is present in the person of the minister, in his own word, and indeed substantially and permanently under the eucharistic elements."

29. Cf. Pope Paul VI, *Mysterium Fidei: On the Doctrine and Worship of the Eucharist* [MF] (September 3, 1965), no. 39 (DOL 176, no. 1183): "This presence is called the *real presence* not to exclude the other kinds as though they were not real, but because it is real par excellence, since it is substantial, in the sense that Christ whole and entire, God and man, becomes present."

* In the first printing of this text, the paragraph number 23 was missing. However, no text was omitted. To maintain consistency across editions, we are maintaining the original numbering.

30. Cf. CCC, no. 1146: "In human life, signs and symbols occupy an important place. As a being at once body and spirit, man expresses and perceives spiritual realities through physical signs and symbols. As a social being, man needs signs and symbols to communicate with others, through language, gestures, and actions. The same holds true for his relationship with God."

Cf. GIRM, no. 288: "Churches and other places of worship should therefore be suited to celebrating the liturgy and to ensuring the active participation of the faithful. Further, the buildings and requisites for worship should be truly worthy and beautiful, signs and symbols of heavenly realities."

31. Cf. CCC, no. 1151: "In his preaching the Lord Jesus often makes use of the signs of creation to make known the mysteries of the Kingdom of God. He performs healings and illustrates his preaching with physical signs or symbolic gestures."

32. Cf. CCC, no. 1148; cf. no. 1152: "Since Pentecost, it is through the sacramental signs of his Church that the Holy Spirit carries on the work of sanctification. The sacraments of the Church do not abolish but purify and integrate all the richness of the signs and symbols of the cosmos and of social life. Further, they fulfill the types and figures of the Old Covenant, signify and make actively present the salvation wrought by Christ, and prefigure and anticipate the glory of heaven."

33. Cf. SC, no. 59; CCC, no. 1075: "Liturgical catechesis aims to initiate people into the mystery of Christ (It is 'mystagogy.') by proceeding from the visible to the invisible, from the sign to the thing signified, from the 'sacraments' to the 'mysteries.'"

34. Cf. National Conference of Catholic Bishops' Committee on the Liturgy, *Music in Catholic Worship* [MCW] (1983), nos. 6–7.

35. These include the SC, the GIRM, the RDCA, the *Ceremonial of Bishops*, the various sacramental rituals, and the CIC.

36. CCC, no. 1179; Second Vatican Council, *Presbyterorum Ordinis: Decree on the Ministry and Life of Priests* [PO] (December 7, 1965), no. 5; cf. SC, nos. 122–127; GIRM no. 288: "For the celebration of the Eucharist the people of God normally assemble in a church or, if there is none or one that is inadequate for some reason, then in some other place nevertheless worthy of so great a mystery. Churches and other places of worship should therefore be suited to celebrating the liturgy and to ensuring the active participation of the faithful. Further, the buildings and requisites for worship should be truly worthy and beautiful, signs and symbols of heavenly realities."

37. RDCA, ch. 2, no. 3 (DOL, 547, no. 4371): "The very nature of a church demands that it be suited to sacred celebrations, dignified, evincing a noble beauty, not mere costly display, and it should stand as a sign and symbol of heavenly realities. 'The general plan of the sacred edifice should be such that in some way it conveys the image of the gathered assembly. It should also allow the participants to take the place most appropriate to them and assist all to carry out their function properly.'"

38. CIC, c. 837 § 2: "Inasmuch as liturgical actions by their nature entail a common celebration, they are to be celebrated with the presence and active participation of the Christian faithful where possible."

39. SC, no. 14: "[The] Church earnestly desires that all the faithful be led to that full, conscious, and active participation in liturgical celebrations which is demanded by the very nature of the liturgy. Such participation by the Christian people as 'a chosen race, a royal priesthood, a holy nation, a purchased people' (1 Peter 2:9, cf. 2:4–5), is their right and duty by reason of their baptism."

40. GIRM, no. 294: "The people of God assembled at Mass possess an organic and hierarchical structure, expressed by the various ministries and actions for each part of the celebration. The general plan of the sacred building should be such that in some way it conveys the image of the gathered assembly. Thus it should also allow the participants to take the place most appropriate to them and assist all to carry out their individual functions properly.

"The faithful and the choir should have a place that facilitates their active participation.

"The priest celebrant, the deacon and other ministers have their place in the sanctuary. At the same time, seats for the concelebrants should be prepared. If there is truly a great number of concelebrants, then seats should be arranged in another part of the church, but near the altar.

"Even though all these elements must express a hierarchical arrangement and the diversity of functions, they should at the same time form a deep and organic unity, clearly expressive of the unity of the entire holy people. The character and beauty of the place and all its appointments should foster devotion and show the holiness of the mysteries celebrated there."

41. Cf. SC, nos. 14 and 26; PO, no. 2; LG, no. 28; GIRM, nos. 4, 58 and 60.

42. Cf. 1 Cor 12:27–28.

43. GIRM, no. 95: "In the celebration of Mass the faithful are a holy people, a chosen people, a royal priesthood: they give thanks to God and offer the Victim not only through the hands of the priest but also together with him and learn to offer themselves. They should endeavor to make this clear by their deep sense of reverence for God and their charity toward brothers and sisters who share with them in the celebration."

44. CIC, c. 835 § 1: "The bishops in the first place exercise the sanctifying function; they are the high priests, the principal dispensers of the mysteries of God, and the directors, promoters, and guardians of the entire liturgical life in the church entrusted to them."

Ibid, c. 838 § 4: "Within the limits of his competence, it pertains to the diocesan bishop in the Church entrusted to him to issue liturgical norms which bind everyone."

45. Cf. GIRM, no. 22; LG, nos. 26 and 28; SC, no. 42: "Because it is impossible for the bishop always and everywhere to preside over the whole flock in his church, he cannot do other than establish lesser groupings of the faithful. Among these, parishes set up locally under a pastor who takes the place of the bishop are the most important: for in a certain way they represent the visible Church as it is established throughout the world.

"Therefore the liturgical life of the parish and its relationship to the bishop must be fostered in the thinking of and practice of both laity and clergy; efforts also must be made to encourage a sense of community within the parish, above all in the common celebration of the Sunday Mass."

46. CIC, c. 1215 §§ 1 and 2: "No church is to be built without the express written consent of the diocesan bishop.

"The diocesan bishop is not to give consent unless, after having heard the presbyteral council and the rectors of the neighboring churches, he judges that the new church can serve the good of souls and that the means necessary for building the church and for divine worship will not be lacking."

47. Ibid., c. 835 § 2: "Presbyters also exercise this function [the sanctifying function]; sharing in the priesthood of Christ and as his ministers under the authority of the bishop, they are consecrated to celebrate divine worship and to sanctify the people."

48. GIRM, no. 93: "Within the Church the priest also possesses the power of Holy Orders to offer sacrifice in the person of Christ. He therefore stands at the head of

the faithful people gathered together, presides over its prayer, proclaims the message of salvation, joins the people to himself in offering the sacrifice to God the Father through Christ in the Spirit, gives his brothers and sisters the bread of eternal life, and shares in it with them. At the Eucharist he should, then, serve God and the people with dignity and humility; by his bearing and by the way he recites the words of the liturgy he should communicate to the faithful a sense of the living presence of Christ."

49. Ibid., no. 94: "After the priest, in virtue of the sacred ordination he has received, the deacon has first place among those who minister in the celebration of the Eucharist. For the sacred Order of the diaconate has been held in high honor in the Church since the time of the Apostles. At Mass the deacon proclaims the gospel reading, sometimes preaches God's word, announces the intentions of the general intercessions, ministers to the priest, prepares the altar and serves the celebration of the sacrifice, distributes the Eucharist to the faithful, especially under the species of wine, and from time to time gives directions regarding the people's gestures and posture."

50. LG, nos. 26 and 28.

51. GIRM, no. 294: "The people of God assembled at Mass possess an organic and hierarchical structure, expressed by the various ministries and actions for each part of the celebration."

Cf. GIRM, no. 5: "In addition, the nature of the ministerial priesthood puts into its proper light another reality of which much should be made, namely, the royal priesthood of believers. Through the ministry of priests, the people's spiritual sacrifice is brought to completeness in union with the sacrifice of Christ, our one and only Mediator. For the celebration of the Eucharist is the action of the whole Church; in it all should do only, but all of, those parts that belong to them in virtue of their place within the people of God."

52. SC, no. 28: "In liturgical celebrations, whether as a minister or as one of the faithful, each person should perform his role by doing solely and totally what the nature of the things and liturgical norms require of him."

53. SC, nos. 37 and 119; CCC, no. 1158: "The harmony of signs (song, music, words, and actions) is all the more expressive and fruitful when expressed in the cultural richness of the People of God who celebrate."

54. Cf. Mark 14:15; Acts 2:42 and 17:16–34.

55. Cf. SC, no. 123; GIRM, no. 289: "At all times, therefore, the Church seeks out the noble support of the arts and welcomes the artistic expressions of all peoples and regions. Even more, the Church is intent on keeping the works of art and the treasures handed down from the past and, when necessary, on adapting them to new needs. It strives as well to promote new works of art that appeal to the contemporary mentality.

"In commissioning artists and choosing works of art that are to become part of a church, the highest artistic standard is therefore to be set, in order that art may aid faith and devotion and be true to the reality it is to symbolize and the purpose it is to serve."

56. Cf. CCC, nos. 1201–1206; Pope John Paul II, *Catechesi Tradendae: On Catechesis in Our Time* [CT] (October 16, 1979), no. 53.

57. Cf. CT, no. 53: "'The term "acculturation" or "inculturation" may be a neologism, but it expresses very well one factor of the great mystery of the Incarnation.' We can say of catechesis, as well as of evangelization in general, that it is called to bring the power of the Gospel into the very heart of culture and cultures. For this purpose, catechesis will seek to know these cultures and their essential components; it will learn their most significant expressions; it will respect their particular values and riches. In this manner it will be able to offer these cultures the knowledge of the hidden mystery and help them to bring forth from their own living tradition original expressions of Christian life, celebration and thought. Two things must however be kept in mind.

"On the one hand the Gospel message cannot be purely and simply isolated from the culture in which it was first inserted (the Biblical world or, more concretely, the cultural milieu in which Jesus of Nazareth lived), nor, without serious loss, from the cultures in which it has already been expressed down the centuries; it does not spring spontaneously from any cultural soil; it has always been transmitted by means of an apostolic dialogue which inevitably becomes part of a certain dialogue of cultures.

"On the other hand, the power of the Gospel everywhere transforms and regenerates. When that power enters into a culture, it is no surprise that it rectifies many of its elements. There would be no catechesis if it were the Gospel that had to change when it came into contact with the cultures.

"To forget this would simply amount to what Saint Paul very forcefully calls 'emptying the cross of Christ of its power' (1 Corinthians 1:17).

"It is a different matter to take, with wise discernment, certain elements, religious or otherwise, that form part of the cultural heritage of a human group and use them to help its members to understand better the whole of the Christian mystery. Genuine catechists know that catechesis 'takes flesh' in the various cultures and milieux: one has only to think of the peoples with their great differences, of modern youth, of the great variety of circumstances in which people find themselves today. But they refuse to accept an impoverishment of catechesis through a renunciation or obscuring of its message, by adaptations, even in language, that would endanger the 'precious deposit' of the faith, or by concessions in matters of faith or morals. They are convinced that true catechesis eventually enriches these cultures by helping them to go beyond the defective or even inhuman features in them, and by communicating to their legitimate values the fullness of Christ."

58. Cf. Pope Paul VI, *Evangelii Nuntiandi: On Evangelization in the Modern World* (December 8, 1975), no. 42; CT, no. 53; Irish Episcopal Commission for Liturgy, *The Place of Worship: Pastoral Directory on the Building and Reordering of Churches* [PW] (1994), no. 3.7.

59. CCC, nos. 1157–1158; cf. SC, no. 119.

60. Cf. LA, no. 6: "Every genuine artistic intuition goes beyond what the senses perceive and, reaching beneath reality's surface, strives to interpret its hidden mystery. The intuition itself springs from the depths of the human soul, where the desire to give meaning to one's own life is joined by the fleeting vision of beauty and of the mysterious unity of things. All artists experience the unbridgeable gap which lies between the work of their hands, however successful it may be, and the dazzling perfection of the beauty glimpsed in the ardor of the creative moment: What they manage to express in their painting, their sculpting, their creating is no more than a glimmer of the splendor which flared for a moment before the eyes of their spirit. . . .

"Every genuine art form in its own way is a path to the inmost reality of man and of the world. It is therefore a wholly valid approach to the realm of faith, which gives human experience its ultimate meaning. That is why the Gospel fullness of truth was bound from the beginning to stir the interest of artists, who by their very nature are alert to every 'epiphany' of the inner beauty of things."

61. Cf. SC, nos. 123 and 129; Congregation of Rites, *Eucharisticum Mysterium: On Worship of the Eucharist* [EM] (May 25, 1967), no. 24 (DOL 179, no. 1253).

62. Cf. SC, no. 124: "When churches are to be built, let great care be taken that they be suitable for the celebration of liturgical services and for the active participation of the faithful."

Cf. GIRM, no. 292: "Church decor should seek to achieve noble simplicity rather than ostentation. The choice of materials for church appointments must be marked by concern for genuineness and by the intent to foster instruction of the faithful and the dignity of the place of worship."

Cf. GIRM, nos. 295, 306, and 311–312.

63. Pope Paul VI, *Laudis Canticum* (November 1, 1970) (DOL, 424, no. 3427): "The life of Christ in his Mystical Body also perfects and elevates for each member of the faithful his own personal life, any conflict between the prayer of the Church and personal prayer must be entirely rejected, and the relationship between

them strengthened and enlarged. . . . If the prayer of the Divine Office becomes genuine personal prayer, the relation between the liturgy and the whole Christian life also becomes clearer. The whole life of the faithful, hour by hour during the day and night, is a kind of *leitourgia* or public service, in which the faithful give themselves over to the ministry of love toward God and men, identifying themselves with the action of Christ, who by his life and self-offering sanctified the life of all mankind."

64. SC, nos. 12 and 13: "The spiritual life, however, is not confined solely to participation in the liturgy. The Christian is assuredly called to pray with his brethren, but he must also enter into his chamber to pray to the Father in secret (cf. Matthew 6:6); indeed, according to the teaching of the Apostle Paul, he should pray without ceasing (cf. 1 Thessalonians 5:17). . . .

"Popular devotions of the Christian people are warmly commended, provided they accord with the laws and norms of the Church. Such is especially the case with devotions called for by the Apostolic See. . . . Nevertheless these devotions should be so drawn up that they harmonize with the liturgical seasons, accord with the sacred liturgy, are in some fashion derived from it, and lead people to it, since the liturgy by its very nature far surpasses any of them."

65. SC, no. 10: "Nevertheless the liturgy is the summit toward which the activity of the Church is directed; at the same time it is the fountain from which all her power flows. For the goal of apostolic works is that all who are made sons of God by faith and baptism should come together to praise God in the midst of His church, to take part in her sacrifice, and to eat the Lord's supper."

66. Congregation for Divine Worship, *Circular Letter on Concerts in Churches* (November 5, 1987), no. 5: "According to tradition as expressed in the rite for the dedication of a church and altar, churches are primarily places where the people of God gather and are 'made one as the Father, the Son and the Holy Spirit are one, and are the church, the temple of God built with living stones, in which the Father is worshiped in spirit and truth.' . . .

"As visible constructions, churches are signs of the pilgrim church on earth; they are images that proclaim the heavenly Jerusalem, places in which are actualized the mystery of the communion between man and God. Both in urban areas and in the countryside, the church remains the house of God and the sign of his dwelling among men. It remains a sacred place, even when no liturgical celebration is taking place."

67. GIRM, no. 294: "The people of God assembled at Mass possess an organic and hierarchical structure, expressed by the various ministries and actions for each part of the celebration. The general plan of the sacred building should be such that in some way it conveys the image of the gathered assembly. Thus it should also allow the participants to take the place most appropriate to them and assist all to carry out their individual functions properly.

"The faithful and the choir should have a place that facilitates their active participation."

68. Ibid.: "Even though all these elements must express a hierarchical arrangement and the diversity of functions, they should at the same time form a deep and organic unity, clearly expressive of the unity of the entire holy people. The character and beauty of the place and all its appointments should foster devotion and show the holiness of the mysteries celebrated there."

69. Ibid., no. 295: "The sanctuary is the place where the altar stands, the word of God is proclaimed, and the priest, deacon and other ministers exercise their offices. It should clearly be marked off from the body of the church either by being somewhat elevated or by its distinctive design and appointments. It should be large enough to allow for the proper celebration of the Eucharist which should be easily seen."

70. 1 Corinthians 11:26; cf. Revelation 19:9.

71. GIRM, no. 296: "At the altar the sacrifice of the cross is made present under sacramental signs. It is also the table of the Lord, and the people of God are called together to share in it. The altar is, as well, the center of the thanksgiving that the Eucharist accomplishes."

72. Pope Pius XII, *Mediator Dei: On the Sacred Liturgy* (November 20, 1947), no. 21.

73. RDCA, ch. 4, no. 4 (DOL, 547, no. 4401): "Therefore, the Church's writers have seen in the altar a sign of Christ himself. This is the basis for the saying 'the altar is Christ.'"

74. GIRM, no. 303: "In the building of new churches, it is especially important that a single altar be erected which signifies to the assembly of the faithful the one Christ and the one Eucharist of the Church.

"However, in churches already built, when an old altar is already so positioned that it makes the participation of the people difficult, or it is impossible to move it without detriment to its artistic value, then another fixed altar may be erected. It should be artfully made and dedicated according to the rite. The sacred celebrations should be performed upon it alone; and in order that the attention of the faithful not be distracted from the new altar, the old altar should not be decorated in any special way."

75. Ibid., no. 299: "In every church there should ordinarily be a fixed, dedicated altar, which should be freestanding to allow the ministers to walk around it easily and Mass to be celebrated facing the people, which is desirable whenever possible. The altar should occupy its place so that it is truly the center on which the attention of the whole congregation of the faithful naturally focuses. As a rule, the altar is fixed and dedicated."

76. RDCA, ch. 4, no. 9 (DOL, 547, no. 4406): "In accordance with received custom in the Church and the biblical symbolism connected with an altar, the table of a fixed altar should be of stone, indeed of natural stone. But, at the discretion of the conference of bishops, any becoming, solid, and finely wrought material may be used in erecting an altar."

Cf. GIRM, no. 301; CIC, cc. 1235 and 1236a.

77. GIRM, no. 301: "The pedestal or base of the table may be of any sort of material, as long as it is becoming and solid."

Cf. CIC, c. 1236.

78. GIRM, no. 301: "According to the Church's traditional practice and the altar's symbolism, the table of a fixed altar should be of stone and indeed of natural stone. But at the discretion of the Conference of Bishops some other solid, becoming, and well-crafted material may be used. The pedestal or base of the table may be made of any sort of material, as long as it is becoming and solid."

Cf. National Conference of Catholic Bishops, *The Appendix to the General Instruction for the Dioceses of the United States of America* (1975), no. 263.

79. Cf. RDCA, ch. 4, no. 5 (DOL 547, no. 4402): "[In the words of Saint Ambrose] the triumphant victims come to their rest in the place where Christ is victim: he, however, who suffered for all is on the altar; they who have been redeemed by his sufferings are beneath the altar."

80. RDCA, ch. 4, no. 11c (DOL 547, no. 4408): "A reliquary must not be placed on the altar or set into the table of the altar, but placed beneath the table of the altar, as the design of the altar permits."

81. Congregation for Divine Worship and the Discipline of the Sacraments, *General Introduction to the Lectionary for Mass* [GILM] (1998), no. 32: "There must be a place in the church that is somewhat elevated, fixed, and of a suitable design and nobility. It should reflect the dignity of God's word and be a clear reminder to the people that in the Mass the table of God's word and of Christ's body is placed before them. The place for the readings must also truly help the people's listening and attention during the liturgy of the word. Great pains must therefore be taken, in keeping with the design of each church, over the harmonious and close relationship of the ambo with the altar."

Cf. GIRM, no. 309: "The dignity of the word of God requires the church to have a place that is suitable for proclamation of the word and is a natural focal point for the faithful during the liturgy of the word.

"As a rule the ambo should be stationary, not simply a movable stand. In keeping with the structure of each church, it must be so placed that the ordained ministers and readers may be easily seen and heard by the faithful.

"The readings, responsorial psalm and the Easter Proclamation (*Exsultet*) are proclaimed only from the ambo."

82. GILM, no. 32: "Great pains must therefore be taken, in keeping with the design of each church, over the harmonious and close relationship of the ambo with the altar."

83. The elevation of the ambo, an access without steps, and in situations where it seems feasible, an ambo with a top section that is adjustable in height either manually or electrically will enable all to serve as celebrant, lector, and cantor.

84. It has become customary to provide a place for the permanent display of the Scriptures in the sanctuary area. This can be done using the front of the ambo or another kind of pedestal.

85. GIRM, no. 310: "The priest celebrant's chair ought to stand as a symbol of his function of presiding over the assembly and of directing prayer. Thus the best place for the chair is at the head of the sanctuary and turned toward the people, unless the design of the building or other circumstances are an obstacle, for example, if too great a distance would interfere with communication between the priest and the gathered assembly, or if the tabernacle is positioned medially behind the altar. However, anything resembling a throne is to be avoided.

"The seat for the deacon should be placed near that of the celebrant. However the seats for the other ministers should be arranged so that they are clearly distinguished from the seats for clergy and, so that the lay ministers are easily able to fulfill the office assigned to them."

86. Ibid.

87. *Ceremonial of Bishops*, no. 47.

88. GIRM, no. 310.

89. Congregation for Divine Worship, *Rite of Christian Initiation of Adults* [RCIA] (1988), General Introduction, no. 25: "The baptistery or the area where the baptismal font is located should be reserved for the sacrament of baptism and should be worthy to serve as the place where Christians are reborn in water and the Holy Spirit. The baptistery may be situated in a chapel either inside or outside the church or in some other part of the church easily seen by the faithful; it should be large enough to accommodate a good number of people. After the Easter season, the Easter candle should be kept reverently in the baptistery, in such a way that it can be lighted for the celebration of baptism and so that from it the candles for the newly baptized can easily be lighted."

90. Ibid., no. 213: "Therefore in the celebration of baptism the washing with water should take on its full importance as the sign of that mystical sharing in Christ's death and resurrection through which those who believe in his name die to sin and rise to eternal life. Either immersion or the pouring of water should be chosen for the rite, whichever will serve in individual cases and in the various traditions and circumstances to ensure the clear understanding that this washing is not a mere purification rite but the sacrament of being joined to Christ."

91. Ibid.: "Either immersion or the pouring of water should be chosen for the rite, whichever will serve in individual cases and in the various traditions and circumstances to ensure the clear understanding that this washing is not a mere purification rite but the sacrament of being joined to Christ."

Cf. RCIA, *National Statutes for the Catechumenate* (1986), no. 17: "Baptism by immersion is the fuller and more expressive sign of the sacrament and, therefore, provision should be made for its more frequent use in the baptism of adults. The provision of the *Rite of Christian Initiation of Adults* for partial immersion, namely, immersion of the candidate's head, should be taken into account."

92. Congregation for Divine Worship, *Holy Communion and Worship of the Eucharist Outside Mass* [HCWEOM] (1976), no. 5: "The primary and original reason for reservation of the eucharist outside Mass is the administration of viaticum. The secondary reasons are the giving of communion and the adoration of our Lord Jesus Christ present in the sacrament. The reservation of the sacrament for the sick led to the praiseworthy practice of adoring this heavenly food in the churches. This cult of adoration rests upon an authentic and solid basis, especially

because faith in the real presence of the Lord leads naturally to external, public expression of that faith."

93. SC, no. 48: "The Church, therefore, earnestly desires that Christ's faithful, when present at this mystery of faith, should not be there as strangers or silent spectators. On the contrary, through a proper appreciation of the rites and prayers they should participate knowingly, devoutly, and actively. They should be instructed by God's word and be refreshed at the table of the Lord's body; they should give thanks to God; by offering the Immaculate Victim, not only through the hands of the priest, but also with him, they should learn to offer themselves too. Through Christ the Mediator, they should be drawn day by day into ever closer union with God and with each other, so that finally God may be all in all."

94. CIC, c. 938 § 2: "The tabernacle in which the Most Holy Eucharist is reserved is to be situated in some part of the church or oratory which is distinguished, conspicuous, beautifully decorated, and suitable for prayer."

95. Ibid., c. 938 § 1: "The Most Holy Eucharist is to be reserved habitually in only one tabernacle of a church or oratory."

96. Ibid., c. 938 § 3: "The tabernacle in which the Most Holy Eucharist is reserved habitually is to be immovable, made of solid and opaque material, and locked in such a way that the danger of profanation is avoided as much as possible."

Cf. GIRM, no. 314.

97. HCWEOM, no. 11: "According to traditional usage, an oil lamp or lamp with a wax candle is to burn constantly near the tabernacle as a sign of the honor which is shown to the Lord."

98. GIRM, no. 315: "It is more in keeping with its meaning as a sign, that the tabernacle in which the Most Blessed Sacrament is reserved not be on the altar on which Mass is celebrated.

Moreover, the tabernacle should be placed, according to the judgment of the diocesan Bishop:

(a) either in the sanctuary, apart from the altar of celebration, in the most suitable form and place, not excluding on an old altar which is no longer used for celebration;

(b) or even in another chapel suitable for adoration and the private prayer of the faithful, and which is integrally connected with the church and is conspicuous to the faithful."

99. There has been a shift in directives about the placement of the tabernacle over time. The latest edition of the *General Instruction of the Roman Missal* (2000) alters the earlier directive in GIRM, no. 276, which gave a clear preference for reservation in a separate chapel. GIRM, no. 315, now directs the diocesan bishop to determine the appropriate placement either in the sanctuary (including on the old altar which is no longer used for celebration) or in a separate chapel. It may not be reserved on the altar at which the Eucharist is celebrated.

100. GIRM, no. 315.

101. Cf. Response of the Congregation for Divine Worship and the Discipline of the Sacraments Regarding Perpetual Exposition of the Eucharist published in the June 1995 issue of the National Conference of Catholic Bishops' *BCL* [Bishops' Committee on the Liturgy] *Newsletter,* p. 21: "Because perpetual exposition is a devotional practice of a religious community or a pious association, it should normally take place in a chapel of that religious community or association. If for some good reason perpetual exposition must take place in a parish church, it should be in a chapel distinct from the body of the church so as not to interfere with the normal activities of the parish or its daily liturgical celebration. When Mass is celebrated in a chapel where the Blessed Sacrament is exposed, the Eucharist must be replaced in the tabernacle before the celebration of Mass begins."

102. EM, no. 55 (DOL 179, no. 1284): "It is more in keeping with the nature of the celebration [of the Eucharist] that, through reservation of the sacrament in the tabernacle, Christ not be present eucharistically from the beginning on the altar where Mass is celebrated."

103. Congregation for Divine Worship, *Circular Letter Concerning the Preparation and Celebration of the Easter Feasts* [PCEF]

(January 16, 1988), no. 49: "For the reservation of Blessed Sacrament, a place should be prepared and adorned in such a way as to be conducive to prayer and meditation; that sobriety appropriate to the liturgy of these days is enjoined, to the avoidance or suppression of all abuses."

104. Ibid.

105. PCEF, no. 82: "Insofar as possible, a suitable place should be prepared outside the church for the blessing of the new fire, whose flames should be such that they genuinely dispel the darkness and light up the night."

106. GIRM, no. 294: "The people of God assembled at Mass possess an organic and hierarchical structure, expressed by the various ministries and actions for each part of the celebration. The general plan of the sacred building should be such that in some way it conveys the image of the gathered assembly. Thus it should also allow the participants to take the place most appropriate to them and assist all to carry out their individual functions properly.

"The faithful and the choir should have a place that facilitates their active participation.

"The priest celebrant, the deacon and other ministers have their place in the sanctuary. At the same time, seats for the concelebrants should be prepared. If there is truly a great number of concelebrants, then seats should be arranged in another part of the church, but near the altar.

"Even though all these elements must express a hierarchical arrangement and the diversity of functions, they should at the same time form a deep and organic unity, clearly expressive of the unity of the entire holy people. The character and beauty of the place and all its appointments should foster devotion and show the holiness of the mysteries celebrated there."

107. Ibid., no. 311: "The places for the faithful should be arranged with care so that they are able to take their rightful part in the celebration visually and mentally. As a rule, there should be benches or chairs for their use. But the custom of reserving seats for private persons must be abolished. Especially in newly built churches, however, benches or chairs should be set up in such a way that the people can easily take the postures required during various parts of the celebration and have unimpeded access to receive communion."

108. MCW, no. 23; GIRM, no. 103: "The *schola cantorum* or choir exercises its own liturgical function among the faithful. Its task is to ensure that the parts proper to it, in keeping with the different types of chants, are carried out becomingly and to encourage active participation of the people in the singing. What is said about the choir applies in a similar way to other musicians, especially the organist."

109. National Conference of Catholic Bishops' Committee on the Liturgy, *Liturgical Music Today* (1982), no. 63: "The entire worshiping assembly exercises a ministry of music. Some members of the community, however, are recognized for the special gifts they exhibit in leading the musical praise and thanksgiving of Christian assemblies. These are the pastoral musicians, whose ministry is especially cherished by the Church."

110. GIRM, no. 294: "The people of God assembled at Mass possess an organic and hierarchical structure, expressed by the various ministries and actions for each part of the celebration. The general plan of the sacred building should be such that in some way it conveys the image of the gathered assembly. Thus it should also allow the participants to take the place most appropriate to them and assist all to carry out their individual functions properly.

"The faithful and the choir should have a place that facilitates their active participation."

Ibid., no. 312: "In relation to the design of each church, the *schola cantorum* should be so placed that its character as a part of the assembly of the faithful that has a special function stands out clearly. The location should also assist the exercise of the duties of the *schola cantorum* and allow each member of the choir complete, that is, sacramental participation in the Mass."

111. Cf. MCW, nos. 33–38.

112. Cf. the section in chapter four of this document on "The Placement of the Organ and Other Musical Instruments."

113. Cf. Congregation for Divine Worship, National Conference of Catholic Bishops, *Book of Blessings* [BB] (1988), no. 1233: "Of all sacred images, the 'figure of the precious, life-giving cross of Christ' is pre-eminent, because it is the symbol of the entire paschal mystery. The cross is the image most cherished by the Christian people and the most ancient; it represents Christ's suffering and victory and at the same time, as the Fathers of the Church have taught, it points to his Second Coming."

114. GIRM, no. 308: "There is also to be a cross, with the figure of Christ crucified upon it, positioned either on the altar or near it, and which is clearly visible to the people gathered together. It is fitting that a cross of this kind, recalling for the faithful the saving passion of the Lord, remain near the altar even outside of liturgical celebrations."

115. Cf. ibid., no. 122: "The cross adorned with the figure of Christ crucified and which has been carried in procession, is placed near the altar so that it may become the altar cross, which ought then to be the only cross used; otherwise it is set aside."

116. Ibid., no. 307: "Candles are to be used at every liturgical service as a sign of reverence and of the festiveness of the celebration. The candlesticks are to be placed either on or around the altar in a way suited to the design of the altar and the sanctuary. Everything is to be well balanced and must not interfere with the faithful's clear view of what takes place at the altar or is placed on it."

117. 1 Peter 2:9.

118 GIRM, no. 117: "The altar is to be covered with at least one white colored cloth. On or even next to the altar are to be candlesticks with lighted candles, at least two in every celebration, or even four or six, especially if a Sunday Mass or Mass for a holy day of obligation is celebrated, or if the Bishop of the diocese celebrates, then seven candles should be used. There is also to be a cross on or near the altar, with a figure of Christ crucified. However, the candles and the cross adorned with the figure of Christ crucified may be carried in the entrance procession. The *Book of the Gospels*, if distinct from the book of other readings, may be placed on the altar, unless it is carried in the entrance procession."

119. DOL 208, p. 519, note R47, quoting the newsletter of the Congregation for Divine Worship and the Discipline of the Sacraments *Notitiae* 10:80 (1974), no. 4: "Query: Must the lighted candles that are to be placed in candlesticks for the celebration of Mass consist in part of beeswax, olive oil, or other vegetable oil? Reply: The GIRM prescribes candles for Mass 'as a sign of reverence and festiveness' (nos. 79, 269). But it makes no further determination regarding the material of their composition, except in the case of the sanctuary lamp, the fuel for which must be oil or wax (see *Holy Communion and Worship of the Eucharist Outside Mass*, Introduction no. 11). The faculty that the conferences of bishops possess to choose suitable materials for sacred furnishings applies therefore to the candles for Mass. The faculty is limited only by the condition that in the estimation of the people the materials are valued and worthy and that they are appropriate for sacred use. Candles intended for liturgical use should be made of material that can provide a living flame without being smoky or noxious and that does not stain the altar cloths or coverings. Electric bulbs are banned in the interest of safeguarding authenticity and the full symbolism of light."

120. Congregation for Divine Worship, *The Sacramentary* [*The Roman Missal*] (1973, 1985), The Easter Vigil, no. 12.

121. PCEF, no. 99: "In the celebration of funerals, the paschal candle should be placed near the coffin to indicate that the death of a Christian is one's own passover. The paschal candle should not otherwise be lit or placed in the sanctuary outside the Easter season."

122. BB, no. 1229.

123. Ibid., no. 1216: "It is proper, then, that in construction, design, and decoration church doors should stand as a symbol of Christ, who said, 'I am the door, whoever enters through me will be safe,' and of those who have followed the path of holiness that leads to the dwelling place of God."

124. Congregation for Divine Worship, *Rite of Penance* [OP] (1974), no. 12: "The sacrament of penance is celebrated in the place and location prescribed by law."

125. CIC, c. 964 § 1: "The proper place to hear sacramental confessions is a church or oratory."

126. Ibid., c. 964 § 2: "The conference of bishops is to establish norms regarding the confessional: it is to take care, however, that there are always confessionals with a fixed gate between penitent and the confessor in an open place so that the faithful who wish to can use them freely."

127. Complementary legislation approved at the November 1999 meeting of the NCCB: "The National Conference of Catholic Bishops, in accord with the prescriptions of canon 964 and the approved liturgical rite, hereby decrees the following norms governing the place for sacramental confessions: Provision must be made for a place for sacramental confessions which is clearly visible, truly accessible, and which provides a fixed grille between the penitent and confessor. Provision must also be made for those instances when the penitent wishes to confess face-to-face."

128. OP, no. 17: "Then the priest, or the penitent himself, may read a text of holy Scripture, or this may be done as part of the preparation for the sacrament. Through the word of God the Christian receives light to recognize his sins and is called to conversion and to confidence in God's mercy."

129. Cf. additional sections in this document on accessibility, pp. 16, 23, 24, 29, 32, 38, 39, 68, 69 and 76ff.

130. Congregation for Divine Worship, International Committee on English in the Liturgy, *Order of Christian Funerals* [OCF] (1985, 1989), no. 42: "Processions continue to have special significance in funeral celebrations, as in Christian Rome where funeral rites consisted of three 'stages' or 'stations' joined by two processions. Christians accompanied the body on its last journey. From the home of the deceased the Christian community proceed to the church singing psalms. When the service in the church concluded, the body was carried in solemn procession to the grave or tomb. During the final procession the congregation sang psalms praising the God of mercy and redemption and antiphons entrusting the deceased to the care of the angels and saints. The funeral liturgy mirrored the journey of human life, the Christian pilgrimage to the heavenly Jerusalem."

131. Ibid., no. 131: "Since the church is the place where the community of faith assembles for worship, the rite of reception of the body at the church has great significance. The church is the place where the Christian life is begotten in baptism, nourished in the eucharist, and where the community gathers to commend one of its deceased members to the Father. The church is at once a symbol of the community and of the heavenly liturgy that the celebration of the liturgy anticipates. In the act of receiving the body, the members of the community acknowledge the deceased as one of their own, as one who was welcomed in baptism and who held a place in the assembly. Through the use of various baptismal symbols the community shows the reverence due to the body, the temple of the Spirit, and in this way prepares for the funeral liturgy in which it asks for a share in the heavenly banquet promised to the deceased and to all who have been washed in the waters of rebirth and marked with the sign of faith."

132. Ibid.

133. Cf. OCF, Appendix 2, regarding the indult for the United States and the ritual directives governing the presence of the cremated remains at the funeral Mass, and the reverent disposition of the cremated remains.

134. OCF, no. 55: "The vigil may be celebrated in the home of the deceased, in the funeral home, parlor or chapel of rest, or in some other suitable place. It may also be celebrated in the church, but at a time well before the funeral liturgy, so that the funeral liturgy will not be lengthy and the liturgy of the word repetitious."

135. Congregation for Divine Worship, *General Instruction of the Liturgy of the Hours* (February 2, 1971), no. 20 (DOL, 426, no. 3450): "The liturgy of the hours, like other liturgical services, is not a private matter but belongs to the whole Body of the Church, whose life it both expresses and affects."

136. Cf. National Conference of Catholic Bishops' Committee on the Liturgy, *Sunday Celebrations in the Absence of a Priest: Leader's Edition* (1993), no. 14: "It is the

responsibility of the diocesan bishop, after having received the advice of the diocesan presbyteral council and, if appropriate, other consultative bodies, to decide whether Sunday celebrations in the absence of a priest should be held on an occasional or regular basis in his diocese. He is to set out general and particular norms for such celebrations. They are to be held only when and where approved by the bishop and only under the pastoral ministry of a priest who has the responsibility for the particular community."

137. Ibid., no. 19: "When a deacon presides at a Sunday celebration in the absence of a priest, he acts in the usual manner in regard to the greetings, the prayers, the gospel reading and homily, the giving of communion, and the dismissal and blessing. He wears the vestments proper to his ministry, that is, the alb with stole, and, as circumstances suggest, the dalmatic. He uses the presidential chair."

138. Ibid., no. 24: "The layperson wears vesture that is suitable for his or her function or the vesture prescribed by the bishop. A layperson does not use the presidential chair."

Cf. Congregation for Divine Worship, *Directory for Sunday Celebrations in the Absence of a Priest* (1988), no. 40.

139. BB, no. 1125: "The oils used for the celebration of the sacraments of initiation, holy orders, and the anointing of the sick according to ancient tradition are reverently reserved in a special place in the church. This repository should be secure and be protected by a lock."

140. CIC, c. 847 § 2: "The pastor is to obtain the holy oils from his own bishop and is to preserve them diligently with proper care."

141. RDCA, ch. 5, no. 1 (DOL 547, no. 4428): "Since sacred edifices, that is, churches, are permanently set aside for the celebration of the divine mysteries, it is right for them to receive a dedication to God. This is done according to the rite in chapters two and three [of the *Rite of Dedication of a Church and an Altar*] for dedicating a church, a rite impressive for its striking ceremonies and symbols.

"Private oratories, chapels, or other sacred edifices set aside only temporarily for divine worship because of special conditions, more properly receive a blessing, according to the rite [found in chapter 5 of *the Rite of Dedication of a Church and an Altar*]."

142. Ibid., ch. 1, no. 1 (DOL 547, no. 4361): "When the building of a new church begins, it is desirable to celebrate a rite to ask God's blessing for the success of the work and to remind the people that the structure built of stone will be a visible sign of the living Church, God's building that is formed of the people themselves."

143. Ibid., ch. 2, no. 2 (DOL 547, no. 4370): "When a church is erected as a building destined solely and permanently for assembling the people of God and for carrying out sacred functions, it is fitting that it be dedicated to God with a solemn rite, in accordance with the ancient custom of the Church."

144. Ibid., ch. 2, no. 15 (DOL 547, no. 4383): "The celebration of the eucharist is the most important and the one necessary rite for the dedication of a church."

145. Ibid., ch. 3, no. 1 (DOL 547, no. 4396): "In order to bring out fully the symbolism and the significance of the rite, the opening of a new church and its dedication should take place at one and the same time. For this reason, as was said before, care should be taken that, as far as possible, Mass is not celebrated in a new church before it is dedicated (see chapter two, nos. 8, 15, 17).

"Nevertheless in the case of the dedication of a church where the sacred mysteries are already being celebrated regularly, the rite set out in this chapter must be used."

Cf. RDCA, ch. 4, no. 13 (DOL 547, no. 4410): "Since an altar becomes sacred principally by the celebration of the Eucharist, in fidelity to this truth the celebration of Mass on a new altar before it has been dedicated is to be carefully avoided, so that the Mass of dedication may also be the first eucharist celebrated on the altar."

146. Ibid., ch. 2, no. 33: "At the threshold of the church the procession comes to a halt. Representatives of those who have been involved in the building of the church

(members of the parish or of the diocese, contributors, architects, workers) hand over the building to the bishop, offering him according to place and circumstances either the legal documents for possession of the building, or the keys, or the plan of the building, or the book in which the progress of the work is described and the names of those in charge of it and the names of the workers are recorded."

147. Ibid., ch. 2, no. 22 (DOL 547, no. 4390): "Beneath each cross a small bracket should be fitted and in it a small candlestick is placed, with a candle to be lighted."

148. SC, no. 102: "Holy Mother Church is conscious that she must celebrate the saving work of her divine spouse by devoutly recalling it on certain days throughout the course of the year. Every week, on the day which she has called the Lord's Day, she keeps the memory of His resurrection. In the supreme solemnity of Easter she also makes an annual commemoration of the resurrection, along with the Lord's blessed passion.

"Within the cycle of a year, moreover, she unfolds the whole mystery of Christ, not only from his incarnation and birth until his ascension, but also as reflected in the day of Pentecost, and the expectation of a blessed hoped-for return of the Lord.

"Recalling thus the mysteries of redemption, the Church opens to the faithful the riches of the Lord's powers and merits, so that these are in some way made present at all times, and the faithful are enabled to lay hold of them and become filled with saving grace."

149. Cf. BB, no. 1512.

150. Ibid., no. 1544.

151. Congregation for Bishops, *Directory on the Pastoral Ministry of Bishops* (1974), no. 91: "A healthy zeal for promoting liturgical life carries with it the desire to preserve, foster and even spread those exercises of piety which express and nourish the spirit of prayer. This is especially true if they are redolent of holy scripture and the sacred liturgy, have originated in the hearts of saints or have for a long time witnessed to the traditional faith and piety."

152. SC, no. 13: "Popular devotions of the Christian people are to be warmly commended, provided they accord with the laws and norms of the Church. Such is especially the case with devotions called for by the Apostolic See.

"Devotions proper to individual churches also have a special dignity if they are conducted by mandate of the bishops in accord with customs or books lawfully approved.

"Nevertheless these devotions should be so drawn up that they harmonize with the liturgical seasons, accord with the sacred liturgy, are in some fashion derived from it, and lead the people to it, since the liturgy by its very nature far surpasses any of them."

153. Often churches have images as well as the crosses that mark the fourteen or fifteen stations. While the depictions of the passion are desirable, only the crosses are needed. The images that accompany the crosses are optional.

154. Cf. BB, no. 1258: "The Church encourages the devout veneration of sacred images by the faithful, in order that they may see more deeply into the mystery of God's glory. For that glory has shown in the face of Christ and is reflected in his saints, who have become 'light in the Lord.'"

155. Cf. BB, no. 1258, quoting the Second Council of Nicea, Act. 7, as cited in Mansi 13, 378 and Denzinger-Schoenmetzer, no. 601: "For the faithful such images recall our Lord and the saints whom they depict, but they also in some way lead the faithful back to the Lord and the saints themselves. 'The more often we gaze on these images, the quicker we who behold them are led back to their prototypes in memory and in hope.'"

156. SC, no. 125: "The practice of placing sacred images in churches so that they may be venerated by the faithful is to be firmly maintained. Nevertheless their number should be moderate and their relative locations should reflect right order. Otherwise they may create confusion among the Christian people and promote a faulty sense of devotion."

157. Wisdom 13:5; cf. 13:3.

158. CCC, no. 2502; cf. CCC, nos. 1156–1162; SC , no. 122: "The fine arts are considered

to rank among the noblest expressions of human genius. This judgment applies especially to religious art and to its highest achievement, which is sacred art. By their very nature, both of the latter are oriented to God's boundless beauty, for this is the reality which these human efforts are trying to express in some way. To the extent that these works aim exclusively at turning men's thoughts to God persuasively and devoutly, they are dedicated to the cause of His greater honor and glory."

159. Pope Paul VI, Address to the Pontifical Commission for Sacred Art in Italy (December 17, 1969) (DOL 540, no. 4324).

160. Cf. CCC, nos. 2500–2503, 2513.

161. SC, no. 122: "The fine arts are considered to rank among the noblest expressions of human genius. This judgment applies especially to religious art and to its highest achievement, which is sacred art. By their very nature, both of the latter are oriented to God's boundless beauty, for this is the reality which these human efforts are trying to express in some way. To the extent that these works aim exclusively at turning men's thoughts to God persuasively and devoutly, they are dedicated to the cause of His greater honor and glory."

162. OA, no. 1 (DOL 541, no. 4327): "Works of art, the most exalted expressions of the human spirit, bring us closer and closer to the divine Artisan and with good reason are regarded as the heritage of the entire human family.

"The Church has always held the ministry of the arts in the highest esteem and has striven to see that 'all things set apart for use in divine worship are truly worthy, becoming, and beautiful, signs and symbols of the supernatural world.' The Church through the centuries has also safeguarded the artistic treasures belonging to it."

163. LA, no. 1: "God therefore called man into existence, committing to him the craftsman's task. Through his 'artistic creativity' man appears more than ever 'in the image of God,' and he accomplishes this task above all in shaping the wondrous 'material' of his own humanity and then exercising creative dominion over the universe which surrounds him. With loving regard, the divine Artist passes on to the human artist a spark of his own surpassing wisdom, calling him to share in his creative power. Obviously, this is a sharing which leaves intact the infinite distance between the Creator and the creature, as Cardinal Nicholas of Cusa made clear: 'Creative art, which it is the soul's good fortune to entertain, is not to be identified with that essential art which is God himself, but is only a communication of it and a share in it.'"

164. Ibid., no. 6: "Every genuine artistic intuition goes beyond what the senses perceive and, reaching beneath reality's surface, strives to interpret its hidden mystery. The intuition itself springs from the depths of the human soul, where the desire to give meaning to one's own life is joined by the fleeting vision of beauty and of the mysterious unity of things. All artists experience the unbridgeable gap which lies between the work of their hands, however successful it may be, and the dazzling perfection of the beauty glimpsed in the ardour of the creative moment: What they manage to express in their painting, their sculpting, their creating is no more than a glimmer of the splendor which flared for a moment before the eyes of their spirit."

165. Second Vatican Council, *Gaudium et Spes: Pastoral Constitution on the Church in the Modern World* (December 7, 1965), no. 62: "Literature and the arts are also, in their own way, of great importance to the life of the Church. For they strive to probe the unique nature of man, his problems, his experiences as he struggles to know and perfect both himself and the world. . . .

"Let the Church also acknowledge new forms of art which are adapted to our age and are in keeping with the characteristics of various nations and regions. Adjusted in their mode of expression and conformed to liturgical requirements, they may be introduced into the sanctuary when they raise the mind to God.

"In this way the knowledge of God can be better revealed. Also, the preaching of the gospel can become clearer to man's mind and show its relevance to the conditions of human life."

166. LA, no. 4: "The particular vocation of individual artists decides the arena in which they serve and points as well to the tasks they must assume, the hard work they must endure and the responsibility they must accept. Artists who are conscious of all this know too that they must labor without allowing themselves to be driven by the search for empty glory or the craving for cheap popularity, and still less by the calculation of some possible profit for themselves. There is therefore an ethic, even a 'spirituality' of artistic service, which contributes in its way to the life and renewal of a people. It is precisely this to which Cyprian Norwid seems to allude in declaring that 'beauty is to enthuse us for work, and work is to raise us up.'"

167. Ibid., no. 10.

168. Ibid., no. 13: "The church therefore needs art. But can it also be said that art needs the church? The question may seem like a provocation. Yet, rightly understood, it is both legitimate and profound. Artists are constantly in search of the hidden meaning of things, and their torment is to succeed in expressing the world of the ineffable. How then can we fail to see what a great source of inspiration is offered by that kind of homeland of the soul that is religion? Is it not perhaps within the realm of religion that the most vital personal questions are posed, and answers both concrete and definitive are sought?

"In fact, the religious theme has been among those most frequently treated by artists in every age. The church has always appealed to their creative powers in interpreting the Gospel message and discerning its precise application in the life of the Christian community. This partnership has been a source of mutual spiritual enrichment. Ultimately, it has been a great boon for an understanding of man, of the authentic image and truth of the person.

"The special bond between art and Christian revelation has also become evident. . . . It remains true, however, that because of its central doctrine of the incarnation of the Word of God, Christianity offers artists a horizon especially rich in inspiration. What an impoverishment it would be for art to abandon the inexhaustible mine of the Gospel!"

169. SC, no. 127.

170. Ibid., no. 13.

171. Pope Paul VI, Address to participants in a national congress of diocesan liturgical commissions of Italy (January 4, 1967) (DOL 539, no. 4319).

172. LG, no. 66: "The Church has endorsed many forms of piety toward the Mother of God, provided they were within the limits of sound and orthodox doctrine. These forms have varied according to the circumstances of time and place and have reflected the diversity of native characteristics and temperament among the faithful. While honoring Christ's Mother, these devotions cause her Son to be rightly known, loved, and glorified, and all His commands observed."

173. Ibid., no. 68: "In the bodily and spiritual glory which she possesses in heaven, the Mother of Jesus continues in this present world as the image and first flowering of the Church as she is to be perfected in the world to come. Likewise, Mary shines forth on earth, until the day of the Lord shall come (cf. 2 Peter 3:10), as a sign of sure hope and solace for the pilgrim People of God."

174. LA, no. 12: "In order to communicate the message entrusted to her by Christ, the church needs art. Art must make perceptible, and as far as possible attractive, the world of the spirit, of the invisible, of God. It must therefore translate into meaningful terms that which is in itself ineffable. Art has a unique capacity to take one or other facet of the message and translate it into colors, shapes and sounds which nourish the intuition of those who look or listen. It does so without emptying the message itself of its transcendent value and its aura of mystery.

"The church has need especially of those who can do this on the literary and figurative level, using the endless possibilities of images and their symbolic force. Christ himself made extensive use of images in his preaching, fully in keeping with his willingness to become, in the incarnation, the icon of the unseen God.

"The church also needs musicians. How many sacred works have been composed through the centuries by people deeply imbued with the sense of the mystery! The faith of countless believers has been nourished by melodies flowing from the hearts of other believers, either introduced into the liturgy or used as an aid to dignified worship. In song, faith is experienced as vibrant joy, love and confident expectation of the saving intervention of God.

"The church needs architects, because she needs spaces to bring the Christian people together and celebrate the mysteries of salvation. After the terrible destruction of the last world war and the growth of great cities, a new generation of architects showed themselves adept at responding to the exigencies of Christian worship, confirming that the religious theme can still inspire architectural design in our own day. Not infrequently these architects have constructed churches which are both places of prayer and true works of art."

175. GIRM, no. 325: "As in the case of the building of churches, the Church welcomes the artistic style of every region for all sacred furnishings and accepts adaptations in keeping with the genius and traditions of each people, provided they fit the purpose for which the sacred furnishings are intended.

"In this matter as well, the concern is to be for the noble simplicity that is the perfect companion of genuine art."

176. Ibid., no. 332: "The artist may fashion the sacred vessels in a shape that is in keeping with the culture of each region, provided each type of vessel is suited to the intended liturgical use and is clearly distinguished from those designed for every day use."

177. Ibid., nos. 343–344: "In addition to the traditional materials, natural fabrics proper to the region may be used for making vestments; artificial fabrics that are in keeping with the dignity of the liturgical service and the person wearing them may also be used. The Conference of Bishops will be the judge in this matter.

"The beauty and nobility of a vestment should derive from its material and design rather than from lavish ornamentation. Representations on vestments should consist only of symbols, images, or pictures portraying the sacred. Anything out of keeping with the sacred is to be avoided."

178. Ibid., no. 329: "In accord with the judgment of the Conference of Bishops, in acts confirmed by the Apostolic See, sacred vessels may be made even from other solid materials which, in the common estimation of the region are regarded as noble e.g., ebony or other hard woods as long as such materials are suited to sacred use. In such cases, preference is always to be given to materials that do no break easily or deteriorate. Materials intended for all vessels which hold the Eucharistic bread such as the plate, ciborium, theca, monstrance or others of this kind should be likewise suitable to sacred use."

Cf. SC, no. 128.

179. Cf. National Conference of Catholic Bishops, *The Appendix to the General Instruction for the Dioceses of the United States* (1975), nos. 288 and 305.

180. OA, no. 3 (DOL 541, no. 4330): "Each diocesan curia is responsible for measures to ensure that, in conformity with the norms set by the local Ordinary, rectors of churches, after consultation with experts, prepare an inventory of places of worship and of the contents that are of artistic or historical importance. This is to be an itemized inventory that lists the value of each entry. Two copies are to be drawn up, one to be kept by the church and the other by the diocesan curia. It would be well for another copy to be sent by the curia to the Vatican Library. This inventory should include notations on changes that have taken place in the course of time."

Since the publication of *Opera Artis*, the Pontifical Commission for the Cultural Goods of the Church was established in 1993 to oversee the artistic and historic patrimony of the Church. The current president is Archbishop Francesco Marchisano.

181. CIC, c. 1292 § 2: "The permission of the Holy See is also required for the valid alienation of goods whose value exceeds the maximum amount, goods given to the Church by vow, or goods precious for artistic or historical reasons."

182. Pope Paul VI, Address to the Pontifical Commission for Sacred Art in Italy (December 17, 1969) (DOL 540, no. 4326): "This leads us to conclude by encouraging you to act in such a way that, under the aegis of the liturgy, that is, divine worship, a bond of union, an alliance, will be reestablished between modern art and

the life of religion. This should contribute to restore to art its two greatest and most characteristic values. The first is beauty, perceptible beauty (*id quod visum placet*: a beauty grasped in the integrity, proportion, and purity of the work of art; ST 1a, 39.1). The second is that indefinable but vibrant value, the artistic spirit, the lyrical experience in the artist that is reflected in his work. The alliance between art and the life of religion will also succeed in giving again to the Church, the Bride of Christ, a voice that love inspires and that inspires love.

"There is a second concluding point to which Vatican Council II attributes particular importance. Before anticipating a new epiphany for sacred art, as though it could spontaneously give itself a new birth and new creativity, we must take pains with the formation of artists. As always we must begin with the education of the person (see SC art. 127)."

183. Cf. GIRM, no. 387; SC, no. 124: "Ordinaries, by the encouragement and favor they show to art which is truly sacred, should strive after noble beauty rather than mere extravagance. This principle is to apply also in the matter of sacred vestments and appointments.

"Let bishops carefully exclude from the house of God and from other sacred places those works of artists which are repugnant to faith, morals, and Christian piety, and which offend true religious sense either by distortion of forms or by lack of artistic worth, by mediocrity or by pretense.

"When churches are to be built, let great care be taken that they be suitable for the celebration of liturgical services and for the active participation of the faithful."

184. CIC, c. 1215 §§ 1 and 2.

185. GIRM, no. 291: "All who are involved in the construction, restoration, and remodeling of churches are to consult the diocesan commission on liturgy and liturgical art. However, the diocesan Bishop is to use the counsel and help of this commission whenever it comes to laying down norms on this matter, approving plans for new buildings, and making decisions on the more important issues."

186. SC, no. 122: "Very rightly the fine arts are considered to rank among the noblest expressions of human genius. This judgment applies especially to religious art and to its highest achievement, which is sacred art. By their very nature both of the latter are related to God's boundless beauty, for this is the reality which these human efforts are trying to express in some way. To the extent that these works aim exclusively at turning men's thoughts to God persuasively and devoutly, they are dedicated to God and to the cause of His greater honor and glory.

"Holy Mother Church has therefore always been the friend of the fine arts and has continuously sought their noble ministry with the special aim that all things set apart for use in divine worship should be truly worthy, becoming, and beautiful, signs and symbols of heavenly realities. For this purpose, too, she has trained artists. In fact, the Church has, with good reason, always reserved the right to pass judgment upon the arts, deciding which of the works of artists are in accordance with faith, piety, and cherished traditional laws, and thereby suited to sacred use.

"The Church has been particularly careful to see that sacred furnishings worthily and beautifully serve the dignity of worship, and has welcomed those changes in materials, style, or ornamentation which the progress of the technical arts has brought with the passage of time.

"Therefore it has pleased the Fathers to issue the following decrees on these matters."

187. Ibid., no. 14: "In the restoration and promotion of the sacred liturgy, this full and active participation by all the people is the aim to be considered before all else; for it is the primary and indispensable source from which the faithful are to derive the true Christian spirit. Therefore, through the needed program of instruction, pastors must zealously strive to achieve in it all their pastoral work.

"Yet it would be futile to entertain any hopes of realizing this goal unless the pastors themselves, to begin with, become thoroughly penetrated with the spirit and power of the liturgy, and become masters of it. It is vitally necessary, therefore, that attention be directed, above all, to the liturgical instruction of the clergy. Therefore this most sacred Council has decided to enact as follows."

188. LA, no. 16: "Beauty is a key to the mystery and a call to transcendence. It is an invitation to savor life and to dream of the future. That is why the beauty of created things can never fully satisfy. It stirs that hidden nostalgia for God which a lover of beauty like St. Augustine could express in incomparable terms: 'Late have I loved you, beauty so old and so new: late have I loved you!'

"Artists of the world, may your many different paths all lead to that infinite Ocean of beauty where wonder becomes awe, exhilaration, unspeakable joy."

189. GIRM, no. 288: "For the celebration of the Eucharist, the people of God normally assemble in a church or, if there is none or one that is inadequate for some reason, then in some other place nevertheless worthy of so great a mystery. Churches and other places of worship should therefore be suited to celebrating the liturgy and to ensuring the active participation of the faithful. Further, the buildings and requisites for worship should be truly worthy and beautiful, signs and symbols of heavenly realities."

190. Ibid., no. 289; SC, no. 127: "All artists who, in view of their talents, desire to serve God's glory in holy Church, should ever bear in mind that they are engaged in a kind of sacred imitation of God the Creator and are concerned with works destined for use in Catholic worship and for the edification, devotion, and religious instruction of the faithful."

191. LG, no. 11: "Strengthened anew at the holy table by the Body of Christ, they manifest in a practical way that unity of God's People which is suitably signified and wondrously brought about by this most awesome sacrament."

192. SC, no. 10: "Nevertheless the liturgy is the summit toward which the activity of the Church is directed; at the same time it is the fountain from which all her power flows. For the goal of apostolic works is that all who are made sons of God by faith and baptism should come together to praise God in the midst of His Church, to take part in her sacrifice, and to eat the Lord's supper."

193. Isiah 56:7.

194. United States Catholic Conference, *Pastoral Statement of the U.S. Catholic Bishops on Persons with Disabilities* (1978), p. 6.

195. Pope John Paul II, *Devoted to the Handicapped* (March 4, 1981), I, 4. In *The Pope Speaks 26:2* (Summer 1981), p. 160.

196. In addition to eliminating architectural barriers, other forms of assistance should be available to persons with disabilities (for example, providing listening devices, providing places for signing/interpretation, using printed texts and captioned audiovisual materials, installing visual emergency alarms, and making available special telephones for use by persons with hearing difficulties).

197. Cf. *Accessibility Inventory* from the National Office of Persons with Disabilities. This is available also in the January 2000 *Environment and Art Newsletter* from Liturgy Training Publications.

198. SC, no. 120: "In the Latin Church the pipe organ is to be held in high esteem, for it is the traditional musical instrument, and one that adds a wonderful splendor to the Church's ceremonies and powerfully lifts up man's mind to God and to heavenly things.

"But other instruments also may be admitted for use in divine worship, with the knowledge and consent of the competent territorial authority, as laid down in Articles 22, § 2; 37 and 40. This may be done, however, only on condition that the instruments are suitable for sacred use, or can be made so, that they accord with the dignity of the temple, and truly contribute to the edification of the faithful."

199. Cf. Congregation for Divine Worship, *The Sacramentary* [*The Roman Missal*] (1973, 1985), Easter Proclamation (*Exsultet*).

200. A dimmer can provide for flexibility of the lighting fixtures and can help to reduce energy consumption.

201. As with the case of selecting professionals to design and install sound systems, normally the skills of a professional with experience in the lighting of churches should be preferred over the "good will" services of someone who may have some knowledge of electricity and domestic

lighting but who lacks the requisite qualifications to design and install lighting suitable for a church.

202. OA, no. 4 (DOL 541, no. 4331): "Mindful of the legislation of Vatican Council II and of the directives in the documents of the Holy See, bishops are to exercise unfailing vigilance to ensure that the remodeling of places of worship by reason of the reform of the liturgy is carried out with the utmost caution. Any alterations must always be in keeping with the norms of the liturgical reform and may never proceed without the approval of the commissions on sacred art, on liturgy, and, when applicable, on music, or without prior consultation with experts. The civil laws of the various countries protecting valuable works of art are also to be taken into account."

203. GIRM, no. 303: "However, in churches already built, when an old altar is already so positioned that it makes the participation of the people difficult, or it is impossible to move it without detriment to its artistic value, then another fixed altar may be erected. It should be artfully made and dedicated according to the rite. The sacred celebrations should be performed upon it alone; and in order that the attention of the faithful not be distracted from the new altar, the old altar should not be decorated in any special way."

204. EM, no. 55 (DOL 179, no. 1284): "It is more in keeping with the nature of the celebration [of the Eucharist] that, through reservation of the sacrament in the tabernacle, Christ not be present eucharistically from the beginning on the altar where Mass is celebrated. That presence is the effect of the consecration and should appear as such."

205. GIRM, no. 289: "The Church is intent on keeping the works of art and the treasures handed down from the past and, when necessary, on adapting them to new needs. It strives as well to promote new works of art that appeal to the contemporary mentality.

"In commissioning artists and choosing works of art that are to become part of a church, the highest artistic standard is therefore to be set, in order that art may aid faith and devotion and be true to the reality it is to symbolize and the purpose it is to serve."

206. OA, no. 5 (DOL 541, no. 4327).

207. EM, no. 24 (DOL 179, no. 1253): "Care should be taken against destroying treasures of sacred art in the course of remodeling churches. On the judgment of the local Ordinary, after consulting experts and, when applicable, with the consent of other concerned parties, the decision may be made to relocate some of these treasures in the interest of the liturgical reform. In such a case this should be done with good sense and in such a way that even in their new locations they will be set up in a manner befitting and worthy of the works themselves."

208. OA, no. 6 (DOL 541, no. 4333): "When it is judged that any such works are no longer suited to divine worship, they are never to be given over to profane use. Rather they are to be set up in a fitting place, namely, in a diocesan or interdiocesan museum, so that they are accessible to all who wish to look at them. Similarly, ecclesiastical buildings graced by art are not to be treated with neglect even when they no longer are used for their original purpose. If they must be sold, buyers who can take proper care of them are to be given preference (see CIC 1187)."

209. Congregation for Seminaries and Universities, *Doctrina et Exemplo* (December 25, 1965), no. 60 (DOL 332, no. 2731), quoting SC, no. 129.

210. Cf. CCC, nos. 1079–1109.

211. PW, Introduction.

NORMS FOR
THE DISTRIBUTION
AND RECEPTION OF
HOLY COMMUNION
UNDER BOTH KINDS IN THE DIOCESES
OF THE UNITED STATES OF AMERICA

APPROVED BY THE UNITED STATES CONFERENCE OF
CATHOLIC BISHOPS ON JUNE 14, 2001

OUTLINE

NORMS FOR THE DISTRIBUTION AND RECEPTION OF HOLY COMMUNION UNDER BOTH KINDS IN THE DIOCESES OF THE UNITED STATES OF AMERICA

PART I
HOLY COMMUNION:
THE BODY AND BLOOD OF THE LORD JESUS

THE MYSTERY OF THE HOLY EUCHARIST

1.   On the night before he died, Christ gathered his Apostles in the upper room to celebrate the Last Supper and to give us the inestimable gift of his Body and Blood. "He did this in order to perpetuate the sacrifice of the Cross throughout the centuries until He should come again, and so to entrust to His beloved spouse, the Church, a memorial of His death and resurrection. . . ."[1] Thus, in the eucharistic Liturgy we are joined with Christ on the altar of the cross and at the table of the upper room in "the sacrificial memorial in which the sacrifice of the cross is perpetuated and [in] the sacred banquet of communion with the Lord's body and blood."[2]

2.   Like all acts of the sacred Liturgy, the Eucharist uses signs to convey sacred realities. *Sacrosanctum Concilium: Constitution on the Sacred Liturgy* reminds us that "the sanctification of man is manifested by signs perceptible to the senses, and is effected in a way which is proper to each of these signs."[3] In a preeminent way the eucharistic Liturgy uses the signs of bread and wine in obedience to the Lord's command and after their transformation gives them to us as the Body and Blood of Christ in the act of communion. It is by taking and sharing the eucharistic bread and chalice—"signs perceptible to the senses"—that we obey the Lord's command and grow in the likeness of the Lord whose Body and Blood they both signify and contain.

3.   The Eucharist constitutes "the Church's entire spiritual wealth, that is, Christ Himself, our Passover and living bread."[4] It is the "sacrament of sacraments."[5] Through it "the work of our redemption is accomplished."[6] He who is the "living bread that came down from heaven" (Jn 6:51) assures us, "Whoever eats my flesh and drinks my blood has eternal life, and I will raise him on the last day. For my flesh is true food, and my blood is true drink" (Jn 6:54–55).

4.   The eyes of faith enable the believer to recognize the ineffable depths of the mystery that is the Holy Eucharist. The *Catechism of the Catholic Church* offers us a number of images from our tradition to refer to this most sacred reality: Eucharistic assembly (*synaxis*), action of thanksgiving, breaking of the

bread, memorial, holy sacrifice, Lord's Supper, holy and divine Liturgy, Holy Communion, and Holy Mass.[7] The eucharistic species of bread and wine derive from the work of human hands. In the action of the Eucharist this bread and this wine are transformed and become our spiritual food and drink. It is Christ, the true vine, who gives life to the branches (cf. Jn 15:1–6). As bread from heaven (cf. Jn 6:41), bread of angels, the chalice of salvation, and the medicine of immortality,[8] the Eucharist is the promise of eternal life to all who eat and drink it (cf. Jn 6:50–51). The Eucharist is a sacred meal, "a sacrament of love, a sign of unity, a bond of charity"[9] in which Christ calls us as his friends to share in the banquet of the kingdom of heaven (cf. Jn 15:15). This bread and chalice were given to his disciples at the Last Supper. This spiritual food has been the daily bread and sustenance for his disciples throughout the ages. The bread and wine of the Lord's Supper—his Body and Blood—as broken and poured out constitute the irreplaceable food for the journey of the "pilgrim church on earth."[10] The Eucharist perpetuates the sacrifice of Christ, offered once and for all for us and for our salvation, making present the victory and triumph of Christ's death and resurrection.[11] It is strength for those who journey in hope through this life and who desire to dwell with God in the life to come. Our final sharing in the Eucharist is *viaticum*, the food for the final journey of the believer to heaven itself. Through these many images, the Church helps us to see the Eucharist as union with Christ from whom she came, through whom she lives, and towards whom she directs her life.[12]

HOLY COMMUNION

5.   While the heart of the celebration of the Eucharist is the Eucharistic Prayer, the consummation of the Mass is found in Holy Communion, whereby the people purchased for the Father by his beloved Son eat and drink the Body and Blood of Christ. They are thereby joined together as members of Christ's mystical Body, sharing the one life of the Spirit. In the great sacrament of the altar, they are joined to Christ Jesus and to one another.

It was also Christ's will that this sacrament be received as the soul's spiritual food to sustain and build up those who live with his life, as he said, "He who eats me, he also shall live because of me" (Jn 6:57). This sacrament is also to be a remedy to free us from our daily defects and to keep us from mortal sin. It was Christ's will, moreover, that this sacrament be a pledge of our future glory and our everlasting happiness and, likewise, a symbol of that one body of which he is the head (cf. Lk 22:19 and 1 Cor 11:3). He willed that we, as members of this body should be united to it by firm bonds of faith, hope and love, so that we might all say the same thing, and that there might be no dissensions among us (cf. 1 Cor 1:10).[13]

As Catholics, we fully participate in the celebration of the Eucharist when we receive Holy Communion. We are encouraged to receive Communion devoutly and frequently. In order to be properly disposed to receive Communion, participants should not be conscious of grave sin and normally should have fasted for one hour. A person who is conscious of grave sin is not to receive the Body and Blood of the Lord without prior sacramental confession except for a grave reason where there is no opportunity for confession. In this case, the person is to be mindful of the obligation to make an act of perfect contrition, including the intention of confessing as soon as possible (canon 916). A frequent reception of the Sacrament of Penance is encouraged for all. (14)

UNION WITH CHRIST

6.   The Lord himself gave us the Eucharist at the Last Supper. The eucharistic sacrifice "is wholly directed toward the intimate union of the faithful with Christ through communion."[15] It is Christ himself who is received in Holy Communion, who said to his disciples, "Take and eat, this is my body." Giving thanks, he then took the chalice and said: "Take and drink, this is the cup of my blood. Do this in remembrance of me" (Mt 26:26–27; 1 Cor 11:25).

7.   Bread and wine are presented by the faithful and placed upon the altar by the priest. These are simple gifts, but they were foreshadowed in the Old Testament and chosen by Christ himself for the Eucharistic sacrifice. When these gifts of bread and wine are offered by the priest in the name of the Church to the Father in the great Eucharistic Prayer of thanksgiving, they are transformed by the Holy Spirit into the Body and Blood of the only-begotten Son of the Father. Finally, when the one bread is broken, "the unity of the faithful is expressed . . . [and through Communion they] receive from the one bread the Lord's body and blood in the same way the apostles received them from Christ's own hands."[16] Hence the import of the words of the hymn adapted from the *Didache*:

> As grain once scattered on the hillsides
> was in this broken bread made one
> so from all lands your church be gathered
> into your kingdom by your Son.[17]

CHRIST HIMSELF IS PRESENT IN THE EUCHARISTIC SPECIES

8.   Christ is "truly, really, and substantially contained"[18] in Holy Communion. His presence is not momentary nor simply signified, but wholly and permanently real under each of the consecrated species of bread and wine.[19]

9.   The Council of Trent teaches that "the true body and blood of our Lord, together with his soul and divinity, exist under the species of bread and wine. His body exists under the species of bread and his blood under the species of wine, according to the import of his words."[20]

10.   The Church also teaches and believes that "immediately after the consecration the true body of our Lord and his true blood exist along with his soul and divinity under the form of bread and wine. The body is present under the form of bread and the blood under the form of wine, by virtue of the words [of Christ]. The same body, however, is under the form of wine and the blood under the form of bread, and the soul under either form, by virtue of the natural link and concomitance by which the parts of Christ the Lord, who has now risen from the dead and will die no more, are mutually united."[21]

11. Since, however, by reason of the sign value, sharing in both eucharistic species reflects more fully the sacred realities that the Liturgy signifies, the Church in her wisdom has made provisions in recent years so that more frequent eucharistic participation from both the sacred host and the chalice of salvation might be made possible for the laity in the Latin Church.

HOLY COMMUNION AS AN ACT OF FAITH

12. Christ's presence in the Eucharist challenges human understanding, logic, and ultimately reason. His presence cannot be known by the senses, but only through faith[22]—a faith that is continually deepened through that communion which takes place between the Lord and his faithful in the very act of the celebration of the Eucharist. Thus the Fathers frequently warned the faithful that by relying solely on their senses they would see only bread and wine. Rather, they exhorted the members of the Church to recall the word of Christ by whose power the bread and wine have been transformed into his own Body and Blood.[23]

13. The teaching of St. Cyril of Jerusalem assists the Church even today in understanding this great mystery:

We have been instructed in these matters and filled with an unshakable faith that what seems to be bread is not bread, though it tastes like it, but the Body of Christ, and that what seems to be wine is not wine, though it tastes like it, but the Blood of Christ.[24]

14. The act of Communion, therefore, is also an act of faith. For when the minister says, "The Body of Christ" or "The Blood of Christ," the communicant's "Amen" is a profession in the presence of the saving Christ, body and blood, soul and divinity, who now gives life to the believer.

15. The communicant makes this act of faith in the total presence of the Lord Jesus Christ whether in Communion under one form or in Communion under both kinds. It should never be construed, therefore, that Communion under the form of bread alone or Communion under the form of wine alone is somehow an incomplete act or that Christ is not fully present to the communicant. The Church's unchanging teaching from the time of the Fathers through the ages— notably in the ecumenical councils of Lateran IV, Constance, Florence, Trent, and Vatican II—has witnessed to a constant unity of faith in the presence of Christ in both elements.[25] Clearly there are some pastoral circumstances that require eucharistic sharing in one species only, such as when Communion is brought to the sick or when one is unable to receive either the Body of the Lord or the Precious Blood due to an illness. Even in the earliest days of the Church's life, when Communion under both species was the norm, there were always instances when the Eucharist was received under only the form of bread or wine. Those who received Holy Communion at home or who were sick would usually receive under only one species, as would the whole Church during the Good Friday Liturgy.[26] Thus, the Church has always taught the doctrine of concomitance, by which we know that under each species alone, the whole Christ is sacramentally present and we "receive all the fruit of Eucharistic grace."[27]

16.   At the same time an appreciation for reception of "the whole Christ" through one species should not diminish in any way the fuller sign value of reception of Holy Communion under both kinds. For just as Christ offered his whole self, body and blood, as a sacrifice for our sins, so too is our reception of his Body and Blood under both kinds an especially fitting participation in his memorial of eternal life.

17.   From the first days of the Church's celebration of the Eucharist, Holy Communion consisted of the reception of both species in fulfillment of the Lord's command to "take and eat . . . take and drink." The distribution of Holy Communion to the faithful under both kinds was thus the norm for more than a millennium of Catholic liturgical practice.

18.   The practice of Holy Communion under both kinds at Mass continued until the late eleventh century, when the custom of distributing the Eucharist to the faithful under the form of bread alone began to grow. By the twelfth century theologians such as Peter Cantor speak of Communion under one kind as a "custom" of the Church.[28] This practice spread until the Council of Constance in 1415 decreed that Holy Communion under the form of bread alone would be distributed to the faithful.

19.   In 1963, the Fathers of the Second Vatican Council authorized the extension of the faculty for Holy Communion under both kinds in *Sacrosanctum Concilium*:

> The dogmatic principles which were laid down by the Council of Trent remaining intact, Communion under both kinds may be granted when the bishops think fit, not only to clerics and religious, but also to the laity, in cases to be determined by the Apostolic See. . . . [29]

20.   The Council's decision to restore Holy Communion under both kinds at the bishop's discretion took expression in the first edition of the *Missale Romanum* and enjoys an even more generous application in the third typical edition of the *Missale Romanum*:

> Holy Communion has a more complete form as a sign when it is received under both kinds. For in this manner of reception a fuller sign of the Eucharistic banquet shines forth. Moreover there is a clearer expression of that will by which the new and everlasting covenant is ratified in the blood of the Lord and of the relationship of the Eucharistic banquet to the eschatological banquet in the Father's kingdom.[30]

> The *General Instruction* further states that "at the same time the faithful should be guided toward a desire to take part more intensely in a sacred rite in which the sign of the Eucharistic meal stands out more explicitly."[31]

21. The extension of the faculty for the distribution of Holy Communion under both kinds does not represent a change in the Church's immemorial beliefs concerning the Holy Eucharist. Rather, today the Church finds it salutary to restore a practice, when appropriate, that for various reasons was not opportune when the Council of Trent was convened in 1545.[32] But with the passing of time, and under the guidance of the Holy Spirit, the reform of the Second Vatican Council has resulted in the restoration of a practice by which the faithful are again able to experience "a fuller sign of the Eucharistic banquet."[33]

PART II
NORMS FOR THE DISTRIBUTION OF HOLY COMMUNION UNDER BOTH KINDS

THE PURPOSE OF THESE NORMS

22. In response to a provision of the *General Instruction of the Roman Missal,* the National Conference of Catholic Bishops herein describes "the methods of distributing Holy Communion to the faithful under both kinds" and approves the following "norms, with the proper *recognitio* of the Apostolic See."[34] The purpose of these norms is to ensure the reverent and careful distribution of Holy Communion under both kinds.

WHEN COMMUNION UNDER BOTH KINDS MAY BE GIVEN

23. The revised *Missale Romanum,* third typical edition, significantly expands those opportunities when Holy Communion may be offered under both kinds. In addition to those instances specified by individual ritual books, the *General Instruction* states that Communion under both kinds may be permitted as follows:

a. for priests who are not able to celebrate or concelebrate

b. for the deacon and others who perform some role at Mass

c. for community members at their conventual Mass or what in some places is known as the "community" Mass, for seminarians, [and] for all who are on retreat or are participating in a spiritual or pastoral gathering[35]

24. The *General Instruction* then indicates that the diocesan Bishop may lay down norms for the distribution of Communion under both kinds for his own diocese, which must be observed. . . . The diocesan Bishop also has the faculty to allow Communion under both kinds, whenever it seems appropriate to the priest to whom charge of a given community has been entrusted as [its] own pastor, provided that the faithful have been well instructed and there is no danger of the profanation of the Sacrament or that the rite would be difficult to carry out on account of the number of participants or for some other reason.[36]

In practice, the need to avoid obscuring the role of the priest and the deacon as the ordinary ministers of Holy Communion by an excessive use of extraordinary minister might in some circumstances constitute a reason either for limiting the distribution of Holy Communion under both species or for using intinction instead of distributing the Precious Blood from the chalice.

Norms established by the diocesan bishop must be observed wherever the Eucharist is celebrated in the diocese, "even in the churches of religious orders and in celebrations with small groups."[37]

CATECHESIS FOR RECEIVING THE BODY AND BLOOD OF THE LORD

25.   When Communion under both kinds is first introduced by the diocesan bishop and also whenever the opportunity for instruction is present, the faithful should be properly catechized on the following matters in the light of the teaching and directives of the *General Instruction*:

    a. the ecclesial nature of the Eucharist as the common possession of the whole Church;

    b. the Eucharist as the memorial of Christ's sacrifice, his death and resurrection, and as the sacred banquet;

    c. the real presence of Christ in the eucharistic elements, whole and entire—in each element of consecrated bread and wine (the doctrine of concomitance);

    d. the kinds of reverence due at all times to the sacrament, whether within the eucharistic Liturgy or outside the celebration;[38] and

    e. the role that ordinary and, if necessary, extraordinary ministers of the Eucharist are assigned in the eucharistic assembly

THE MINISTER OF HOLY COMMUNION

26.   By virtue of his sacred ordination, the bishop or priest offers the sacrifice in the person of Christ, the Head of the Church. He receives gifts of bread and wine from the faithful, offers the sacrifice to God, and returns to them the very Body and Blood of Christ, as from the hands of Christ himself.[39] Thus bishops and priests are considered the ordinary ministers of Holy Communion. In addition the deacon who assists the bishop or priest in distributing Communion is an ordinary minister of Holy Communion. When the Eucharist is distributed under both forms, "the deacon ministers the chalice."[40]

27.   In every celebration of the Eucharist there should be a sufficient number of ministers for Holy Communion so that it can be distributed in an orderly and reverent manner. Bishops, priests, and deacons distribute Holy Communion by virtue of their office as ordinary ministers of the Body and Blood of the Lord.[41]

EXTRAORDINARY MINISTERS OF HOLY COMMUNION

28.   When the size of the congregation or the incapacity of the bishop, priest, or deacon requires it, the celebrant may be assisted by other bishops, priests, or deacons.[42] If such ordinary ministers of Holy Communion are not present, "the

priest may call upon extraordinary ministers to assist him, i.e., formally instituted acolytes or even some of the faithful who have been commissioned according to the prescribed rite. In case of necessity, the priest may also commission suitable members of the faithful for the occasion."[43] Extraordinary ministers of Holy Communion should receive sufficient spiritual, theological, and practical preparation to fulfill their role with knowledge and reverence. When recourse is had to Extraordinary Minister of Holy Communion, especially in the distribution of Holy Communion under both kinds, their number should not be increased beyond what is required for the orderly and reverent distribution of the Body and Blood of the Lord. In all matters such Extraordinary Ministers of Holy Communion should follow the guidance of the diocesan bishop.

REVERENCE

29.   All ministers of Holy Communion should show the greatest reverence for the Most Holy Eucharist by their demeanor, their attire, and the manner in which they handle the consecrated bread or wine. Should there be any mishap—as when, for example, the consecrated wine is spilled from the chalice—then the affected "area . . . should be washed and the water poured into the sacrarium."[44]

PLANNING

30. When Holy Communion is to be distributed under both species, careful planning should be undertaken so that:

- enough bread and wine are made ready for the communication of the faithful at each Mass.[45] As a general rule, Holy Communion is given from hosts consecrated at the same Mass and not from those reserved in the tabernacle. Precious Blood may not be reserved at one Mass for use at another[46]; and

- a suitable number of ministers of Holy Communion are provided at each Mass. For Communion from the chalice, it is desirable that there be generally two ministers of the Precious Blood for each minister of the Body of Christ, lest the liturgical celebration be unduly prolonged.

31.   Even when Communion will be ministered in the form of bread alone to the congregation, care should be taken that sufficient amounts of the elements are consecrated so that the Precious Blood may be distributed to all concelebrating priests.

PREPARATIONS

32.   Before Mass begins, wine and hosts should be provided in vessels of appropriate size and number. The presence on the altar of a single chalice and one large paten can signify the one bread and one chalice by which we are gathered "into the one Body of Christ, a living sacrifice of praise."[47] When this is not possible, care should be taken that the number of vessels should not exceed the need.

33. The unity of all in the one bread will be better expressed when the bread to be broken is of sufficient size that at least some of the faithful are able to receive a piece broken from it. When the number of the faithful is great, however, a single large bread may be used for the breaking of the bread with small breads provided for the rest of the faithful.[48]

34. Sacred vessels, which "hold a place of honor," should be of noble materials, appropriate to their use, and in conformity to the requirements of liturgical law, as specified in the *General Instruction of the Roman Missal*, nos. 327–332.

35. Before being used, vessels for the celebration must be blessed by the bishop or priest according to the *Rite of Blessing a Chalice and Paten*.[49]

AT THE PREPARATION OF THE GIFTS

36. The altar is prepared with corporal, purificator, *Missal*, and chalice (unless the chalice is prepared at a side table) by the deacon and servers. The gifts of bread and wine are brought forward by the faithful and received by the priest or deacon at a convenient place.[50]

AT THE BREAKING OF THE BREAD

37. As the *Agnus Dei* or *Lamb of God* is begun, the bishop or priest alone, or with the assistance of the deacon, and if necessary of concelebrating priests, breaks the eucharistic bread.

Other empty chalices and ciboria or patens are then brought to the altar is this is necessary. The deacon or priest places the consecrated bread in several ciboria or patens and, if necessary, pours the Precious Blood into enough additional chalices as are required for the distribution of Holy Communion. If it is not possible to accomplish this distribution in a reasonable time, the celebrant may call upon the assistance of other deacons or concelebrating priests. This action is usually carried out at the altar, so that the sharing of all from the one cup is signified; in the case of large assemblies, it may be done at the side table within the sanctuary (*presbyterium*).

38. If extraordinary ministers of Holy Communion are required by pastoral need, they should not approach the altar before the priest has received Communion. After the priest has concluded his own Communion, he distributes Communion to the extraordinary ministers, assisted by the deacon, and then hands the sacred vessels to them for distribution of Holy Communion to the people.

39. All receive Holy Communion in the manner described by the *General Instructin to the Roman Missal*, whether priest concelebrants (cf. GIRM, nos. 159, 242, 243, 246), deacons (cf. GIRM, nos. 182, 244, 246), or extraordinary ministers of Holy Communion (cf. GIRM, no. 284). Neither deacons nor lay ministers may ever receive Holy Communion in the manner of a concelebrating priest. The practice of extraordinary ministers of Holy Communion waiting to receive Holy Communion until after the distribution of Holy Communion is not in accord with liturgical law.

40.   After all eucharistic ministers have received Communion, the bishop or priest celebrant reverently hands vessels containing the Body or the Blood of the Lord to the deacons or extraordinary ministers who will assist with the distribution of Holy Communion. The deacon may assist the priest in handing the vessels containing the Body and Blood of the Lord to the extraordinary ministers of Holy Communion.

DISTRIBUTION OF THE BODY AND BLOOD OF THE LORD

41.   Holy Communion under the form of bread is offered to the communicant with the words "The Body of Christ." The communicant may choose whether to receive the Body of Christ in the hand or on the tongue. When receiving in the hand, the communicant should be guided by the words of St. Cyril of Jerusalem: "When you approach, take care not to do so with your hand stretched out and your fingers open or apart, but rather place your left hand as a throne beneath your right, as befits one who is about to receive the King. Then receive him, taking care that nothing is lost."[51]

42.   Among the ways of ministering the Precious Blood as prescribed by the *General Instruction of the Roman Missal,* Communion from the chalice is generally the preferred form in the Latin Church, provided that it can be carried out properly according to the norms and without any risk of even apparent irreverence toward the Blood of Christ.[52]

43.   The chalice is offered to the communicant with the words "The Blood of Christ," to which the communicant responds, "Amen."

44.   The chalice may never be left on the altar or another place to be picked up by the communicant for self-communication (except in the case of concelebrating bishops or priests), nor may the chalice be passed from one communicant to another. There shall always be a minister of the chalice.

45.   After each communicant has received the Blood of Christ, the minister carefully wipes both sides of the rim of the chalice with a purificator. This action is a matter of both reverence and hygiene. For the same reason, the minister turns the chalice slightly after each communicant has received the Precious Blood.

46.   It is the choice of the communicant, not the minister, to receive from the chalice .

47.   Children are encouraged to receive Communion under both kinds provided that they are properly instructed and that they are old enough to receive from the chalice.

OTHER FORMS OF DISTRIBUTION OF THE PRECIOUS BLOOD

48.   Distribution of the Precious Blood by a spoon or through a straw is not customary in the Latin dioceses of the United States of America.

49.   Holy Communion may be distributed by intinction in the following manner: "the communicant, while holding the paten under the chin, approaches the priest who holds the vessel with the hosts and at whose side stands the minister holding the chalice. The priest takes the host, intincts the particle into the chalice and, showing it, says: 'The Body and Blood of Christ.' The communicant responds, 'Amen,' and receives the Sacrament on the tongue from the priest. Afterwards, the communicant returns to his or her place."[53]

50.   The communicant, including the extraordinary minister, is never allowed to self-communicate, even by means of intinction. Communion under either form, bread or wine, must always be given by an ordinary or extraordinary minister of Holy Communion.

PURIFICATION OF SACRED VESSELS

51.   After Communion the consecrated bread that remains is to be reserved in the tabernacle. Care should be taken with any fragments remaining on the corporal or in the sacred vessels. The deacon returns to the altar with the priest and collects and consumes any remaining fragments.

52.   When more of the Precious Blood remains than was necessary for Communion, and if not consumed by the bishop or priest celebrant, "the deacon immediately and reverently consumes at the altar all of the Blood of Christ which remains; he may be assisted, if needs dictate, by other deacons and priests."[54] When there are extraordinary ministers of Holy Communion, they may consume what remains of the Precious Blood from their chalice of distribution with permission of the diocesan bishop.

53.   The chalice and other vessels may be taken to a side table, where they are cleansed and arranged in the usual way. Other sacred vessels that held the Precious Blood are purified in the same way as chalices. Provided the remaining consecrated bread has been consumed or reserved and the remaining Precious Blood has been consumed, "it is permissible to leave the vessels . . . suitably covered and at a side table on a corporal, to be cleansed immediately after Mass following the dismissal of the people."[55]

54.   The Precious Blood may not be reserved, except for giving Communion to someone who is sick. Only sick people who are unable to receive Communion under the form of bread may receive it under the form of wine alone at the discretion of the priest. If not consecrated at a Mass in the presence of the sick person, the Blood of the Lord is kept in a properly covered vessel and is placed in the tabernacle after Communion. The Precious Blood should be carried to the sick in a vessel that is closed in such a way as to eliminate all danger of spilling. If some of the Precious Blood remains after the sick person has received Communion, it should be consumed by the minister, who should also see to it that the vessel is properly purified.

55.   The reverence due to the Precious Blood of the Lord demands that it be fully consumed after Communion is completed and never be poured into the ground or the sacrarium.

CONCLUSION

56.   The norms and directives established by the Church for the celebration of any liturgical rite always have as their immediate goal the proper and careful celebration of those rites. However, such directives also have as their purpose the fostering of celebrations that glorify God and deepen the faith, hope, and charity of the participants in liturgical worship. The ordered preparation and celebration of the Mass, and of Holy Communion in particular, should always profoundly affect the faith of communicants in all its aspects and dimensions. In the case of the distribution of Holy Communion under both kinds, Christian faith in the real presence of Christ in the Holy Eucharist can only be renewed and deepened in the life of the faithful by this esteemed practice.

57.   In all other matters pertaining to the Rite of Communion under both kinds, the directives of the *General Instruction*, nos. 281–287, are to be consulted.

NOTES

1. Second Vatican Council, *Sacrosanctum Concilium: Constitution on the Sacred Liturgy* [SC] (December 4, 1963), no. 47. (All Vatican II citations here refer to the following edition: Walter M. Abbott, ed., *The Documents of Vatican II* [New York: Guild Press, 1966].)

2. United States Catholic Conference-Libreria Editrice Vaticana, *Catechism of the Catholic Church* [CCC] (2000), no. 1382.

3. SC, no. 7.

4. Second Vatican Council, *Presbyterorum Ordinis: Decree on the Ministry and Life of Priests* [PO] (December 7, 1965), no. 5.

5. Congregation for Divine Worship and the Discipline of the Sacraments, *General Instruction of the Roman Missal* [GIRM] (2000), no. 368.

6. *Sacramentary*, Prayer Over the Gifts, Evening Mass of the Lord's Supper, p. 138.

7. CCC, nos. 1328–1332.

8. Cf. St. Ignatius of Antioch, *Ad. Eph.*, 20, 2.

9. SC, no. 47.

10. *Sacramentary*, Eucharistic Prayer III, p. 554.

11. SC, no. 6.

12. Cf. Second Vatican Council, *Lumen Gentium: Dogmatic Constitution on the Church* (November 21, 1964), no. 3.

13. Council of Trent, Session xiii (October 11, 1551), *De ratione institutionis ss. huius sacramenti.* (Latin text in Henricus Denzinger and Adolfus Schönmetzer, eds., *Enchiridion Symbolorum: Definitionum et Declarationum de Rebus Fidei et Morum* [DS] [Barcinone: Herder, 1976], 1638. English text in John F. Clarkson et al., *The Church Teaches* [TCT] [St. Louis, Mo.: B. Herder, 1955], 720.)

14. National Conference of Catholic Bishops, *Guidelines for the Reception of Communion* (Washington, D.C., 1996).

15. CCC, no. 1382.

16. GIRM, no. 72(3).

17. F. Bland Tucker, trans., "Father, We Thank Thee, Who Hast Planted," a hymn adapted from the *Didache*, c. 110 (The Church Pension Fund, 1940).

18. Council of Trent, Session xiii (October 11, 1551), *Canones de ss. Eucharistiae sacramento*, can. 1 (DS 1651; TCT 728).

19. Cf. Council of Trent, Session xiii (October 11, 1551), *Decretum de ss. Eucharistiae sacramento*, cap. IV, *De transubstantione* (DS 1642; TCT 722): "Because Christ our Redeemer said that it was truly his body that he was offering under the species of bread (see Matthew 26:26ff.; Mark 14:22ff.; Luke 22:19ff.; 1 Corinthians 11:24ff.), it has always been the conviction of the Church, and this holy council now again declares it that, by the consecration of the bread and wine a change takes place in which the whole substance of bread is changed into the substance of the Body of Christ our Lord and the whole substance of the wine into the substance of his blood. This change the holy Catholic Church fittingly and properly names transubstantiation."

20. Council of Trent, Session xiii (October 11, 1551), *Decretum de ss. Eucharistiae sacramento*, cap. III, *De excellentia ss. Eucharistiae super reliqua sacramenta* (DS 1640; TCT 721).

21. Ibid. (DS 1640; Norman P. Tanner, ed., *Decrees of the Ecumenical Councils*, Vol. 2: *Trent to Vatican II* [London: Sheed & Ward, 1990], 695.)

22. Cf. CCC, no. 1381.

23. Cf. Paul VI, *Mysterium Fidei: On the Doctrine and Worship of the Eucharist* (September 3, 1965), no. 47 (in International Committee on English in the Liturgy, *Documents on the Liturgy, 1963–1979: Conciliar, Papal, and Curial Texts* [DOL] [1982] 176, no. 1192).

24. Ibid., no. 48 (DOL 176, no. 1193).

25. Cf. GIRM, no. 281.

26. Cf. St. Cyprian, *De Lapsis*, 25, on Communion of infants and children; on Communion of the sick and dying, cf. *Statuta ecclesiae antiqua*, can. 76.

27. CCC, no. 1390.

28. Cf. Petrus Cantor, *Summa de Sacramentis et Animae Consiliis*, ed. J.-A. Dugauquier, *Analecta Medievalis Namurcensia*, vol. 4 (Louvain/Lille, 1954), I, 144.

29. SC, no. 55.

30. GIRM, no. 281. The GIRM goes on to say, "For the faithful who take part in the rite or are present at it, pastors should take care to call to mind as appropriately as possible Catholic teaching according to the Council of Trent on the manner of Communion. Above all they should instruct the Christian faithful that, according to Catholic faith, Christ, whole and entire, as well as the true Sacrament are received under one kind only; that, therefore, as far as the effects are concerned, those who receive in this manner are not deprived of any grace necessary for salvation.

"Pastors are also to teach that the Church has the power in its stewardship of the sacraments, provided their substance remains intact, to make those rules and changes that, in view of the different conditions, times, and places, it decides to be in the interest of reverence for the sacraments or the well-being of the recipients" (no. 282).

31. Ibid., no. 282.

32. Cf. Council of Trent, Session xxi (July 16, 1562), *De doctrina de communione sub utraque specie et parvulorum* (DS 1725–1734; TCT 739–745).

33. Ibid.

34. GIRM, no. 283.

35. Ibid.

36. Ibid.

37. Ibid.

38. Cf. Congregation of Rites, *Eucharisticum Mysterium: On Worship of the Eucharist* [EM] (May 25, 1967), part I, "General Principles to Be Given Prominence in Catechizing the People on the Eucharistic Mystery" (DOL 179, nos. 1234–1244).

39. Cf. GIRM, no. 93.

40. GIRM, no. 182.

41. Cf. GIRM, no. 108.

42. Cf. GIRM, no. 162.

43. GIRM, no. 162. Cf. also Sacred Congregation for the Discipline of the Sacraments, *Immensae Caritatis: Instruction on Facilitating Reception of Communion in Certain Circumstances*, section 1.I.c (DOL 264, no. 2075).

44. GIRM, no. 280.

45. Cf. EM, no. 31 (DOL 179, no. 1260): "The faithful share more fully in the celebration of the eucharist through sacramental communion. It is strongly recommended that they should receive it as a rule in the Mass itself and at that point in the celebration which is prescribed by the rite, that is, right after the communion of the priest celebrant.

"In order that the communion may stand out more clearly even through signs as a participation in the sacrifice actually being celebrated, steps should be taken that enable the faithful to receive hosts consecrated at that Mass."

46. Cf. GIRM, no. 284b: "Whatever happens to remain of the Blood [after the distribution of Holy Communion] is consumed at the altar by the priest or deacon or instituted acolyte who ministered the chalice. . . ."

47. *Sacramentary*, Eucharistic Prayer IV.

48. Cf. GIRM, no. 321.

49. Cf. GIRM, no. 333.

50. Cf. ibid., no. 73.

51. Cat. Myst. V, 21–22.

52. Cf. Sacred Congregation for Divine Worship, *Sacramentali Communione: Instruction Extending the Practice of Communion Under Both Kinds* (June 29, 1970), no. 6 (DOL 270, no. 2115).

53. GIRM, no. 287.

54. GIRM, no. 182.

55. GIRM, no. 183.

INDEX

References are to paragraph or section numbers of individual documents. For a list of abbreviations of document names, see pages vii–viii.

ACCLAMATIONS
Amen, GIRM 43, 54, 77, 79, 89, 124, 127, 146, 147, 151, 154, 161, 165, 167, 175, 180, 249, 259, 286, 287

during Liturgy of the Eucharist, GIRM 37, 79, 142, 146, 147, 151, 153, 165, 180, 238, 266; MCW 47, 53, 56–57; LMT 17

during Liturgy of the Word, GIRM 59, 62, 130, 134, 175; LM 23, 90–91

music for, GIRM 392, 393; MCW 53–59; LMT 15–17

participation in, SC 30; GIRM 35; DMC 30–31

See also Music, liturgical

ACOLYTES,
SC 29; GIRM 98, 100, 116, 120, 139, 140, 162, 178, 187–93, 247, 249, 279, 284, 339; CB 27–29

ADAPTATIONS, CULTURAL.
See Inculturation

ADVENT,
GIRM 53, 66, 305, 313, 346, 354, 355, 372, 374, 376, 380; LM 25, 60, 67, 69, 74, 93–94; GNLY 39–42; CB 235

ALTAR
arrangement of, GIRM 117, 139, 255, 294–310, 350; CB 48

design and placement of, SC 128; CB 48; BLS 49, 54–60, 118–21, 245–46

veneration of, GIRM 49, 122–23, 132, 169, 186, 195, 211, 256, 272–79, 390; CB 72–73

AMBO,
GIRM 44, 58, 61, 71, 105, 118, 128, 130, 133–38, 175, 177, 196, 197, 260, 309; CB 51; BLS 49, 54–55, 61–62

ANOINTING OF THE SICK, SACRAMENT OF,
SC 73–75; MCW 81; BLS 109

ARCHITECTURE, CHURCH.
See Churches

ART, LITURGICAL
criteria for, SC 125, 129; GIRM 289, 325, 351; BLS 146–69, 253–58

role of in liturgies, SC 127; BLS 140–45

types of, SC 46, 122–28; BLS 155–57

ASH WEDNESDAY,
GIRM 355, 372, 374, 381; GNLY 16, 28–29; CB 253

AUDIOVISUALS,
LMT 60–62; BLS 163, 221–25, 233

BAPTISM, SACRAMENT OF
and Christian initiation process, CI 2–6; RCIA 209–14, 304–8; NSC 11–17

music for, MCW 80; LMT 8, 22–26

offices and ministries in, CI 7–17

requirements for, SC 64–70; CI 18–35; BLS 66–69

BIBLE.
See Scripture

BISHOPS
as diocesan leaders, SC 22, 44–46; GIRM 22, 92, 107, 202–3, 283, 291, 315, 374; GNLY 48–55; CB 1–17, 76–83, 1177–84

liturgical adaptations by, SC 36, 39, 77, 120; GIRM 25, 48, 82, 147, 154, 273, 342, 343, 386, 389–92, 395, 397; GNLY 46; CI 30–35; RCIA 32–34, 258; DMC 5

role of in building and renovation of churches, BLS 34, 76, 178–79

role of in catechesis, RCIA 12, 38

role of in liturgies, SC 41–42; GIRM 4–5, 22, 66, 108, 112, 117, 149, 167, 175, 212; CI 12–14; CB 1–41

BLESSINGS,
GIRM 31, 51, 60, 90, 92, 107, 142, 167, 168, 170, 175, 185, 199, 212, 254, 275, 333, 335; RCIA 95–96

BOOK OF THE GOSPELS,
GIRM 44, 60, 117, 119, 120, 122, 133, 172, 173, 175, 194, 195, 272, 273, 277, 306, 349, 390; BLS 62

CALENDAR, CHURCH,
SC 131; GIRM 155, 353–55, 394; GNLY 48–61; LMT 48.

See also Liturgical year

CANDLES,
GIRM 117, 119, 120, 122, 133, 175, 188, 274, 277, 297, 307; BLS 92–94

CATECHESIS,
SC 14, 16, 18, 25, 35, 109; LM 24–27, 41–43; DMC 8–15; NDR 25.
See also Inculturation; Rite of Christian Initiation of Adults

CATECHUMENATE.
See Rite of Christian Initiation of Adults

CHAIRS,
GIRM 211, 310, 311; BLS 49, 63–65, 85–90

CHALICES,
GIRM 72, 73, 83–85, 118, 139, 142, 143, 150, 151, 155–60, 163, 171, 178–83, 190, 191, 207, 215, 222, 227, 230, 233, 243, 245–49, 267, 268–71, 274, 276, 279, 284–87, 306, 324, 327, 330; NDR 36–55.
See also Vessels

CHRISTMAS,
GIRM 204, 346, 354, 355, 376, 381; LM 95–96; GNLY 32–38; CB 234; BLS 125, 128

CHURCHES
building and renovation of, SC 124, 128; CB 42–54; BLS 1–261
decoration of, SC 125, 128; DMC 29; CB 38, 48; BLS 122–38
functional requirements of, BLS 46–139, 206–56
furnishings for, SC 122–28; CB 37–38, 42–54; BLS 91–94
role of cathedrals, SC 41; GIRM 106, 290; CB 42–46
See also individual component parts by name

CIBORIUM,
GIRM 84, 118, 141, 151, 155, 157, 160, 163, 178, 180, 242, 243, 249, 267, 268, 278, 279, 306, 327, 329, 331; NDR 37

COMMENTATORS,
SC 29; GIRM 105, 352

COMMUNION MINISTERS,
NDR 26–29

COMMUNION UNDER BOTH FORMS,
regulations governing, SC 55; GIRM 14, 182, 248, 281, 283, 285, 387; CB 274; NDR 1–57.

See also Eucharist, sacrament of; Liturgy of the Eucharist

COMMUNITY OF THE CHURCH
composition of, DMC 16–55; MCW 15–20
and liturgical celebrations, SC 2, 6, 41–42, 48; GIRM 12, 35, 50, 56, 61, 129, 146, 147, 154, 249, 252, 392, 393; DMC 11; CB 11–14; FYH 1–15; BLS 31–33
participation in, SC 9–11, 14–20, 28, 30, 114; OCF 9–13; DMC 8, 55; CB 19; BLS 95–99
role of in building and renovation of churches, BLS 1–11, 170–77, 180–205, 240–42

CONCELEBRATION,
SC 57, 58; GIRM 199–203, 206, 212, 387

CONFIRMATION, SACRAMENT OF,
SC 71; CI 2; RCIA 215–16, 305, 400–415, 434–37, 446–49, 459–63, 473–85, 505–6, 530–35, 547–49, 562–65; NSC 11–17; CB 1182; MCW 82; LMT 8

CROSSES,
GIRM, 2, 27, 49, 50, 72, 75, 100, 117, 119–24, 134, 144, 167, 173, 175, 178, 188, 190, 211, 222, 257, 274, 276, 277, 296, 297, 308, 340, 350; CB 1011–22; BLS 91

DEACONS,
SC 35; GIRM 22, 38, 40, 42–44, 47, 49, 50, 59, 66, 71, 73, 75, 83, 90, 94, 98, 100, 107, 109, 112, 116, 118–20, 171, 172, 175–86, 189–94, 197, 208, 212, 215, 239, 240, 244, 246–51, 253, 274, 275, 279, 283, 284, 294, 295, 310, 311, 331, 335, 338, 340, 352, 387; CI 11, 14–16; RCIA 15; CB 23–26; BLS 36

EASTER
relationship of to Sunday observances, SC 102, 131; GIRM 51, 64, 66
season of, GIRM 346, 354–55, 372, 374, 376, 380; LM 25, 33, 60, 67, 69, 74, 99–102; GNLY 22–26; CB 371
Triduum liturgies, GNLY 18–21; CB 295, 297, 312, 332, 371; BLS 81–84
Vigil liturgy, GIRM 199, 204, 274; GNLY 17–21; CI 6; RCIA 7–9, 12, 17–30, 207–8, 249, 562–65; CB 332; BLS 84, 94

ECUMENISM,
GIRM 1, 282, 386.
See also Inculturation

EUCHARIST, SACRAMENT OF
and Christian initiation, CI 2; RCIA 217, 305, 400–415, 434–37, 446–49, 459–63,

473–85, 505–6, 530–35, 547–49, 562–65;
NSC 11–17

and design of churches, BLS 17, 29, 47,
49–65, 70–80, 247–52

nature of, SC 5–9, 48–56, 106; GIRM 1–3,
5, 7, 8, 11, 20–22; GNLY 1, 4, 18–21;
DMC 8–15; CB 297; LMT 46; NDR 1–16

reservation of, GIRM 3, 163, 274, 315,
317; CB 49; BLS 17, 29, 70–80, 247–52

See also Communion under both forms;
Liturgy of the Eucharist

FONT, BAPTISMAL,
SC 128; CI 19; BLS 66–69

FUNERALS
for children, OCF 234–46, 264–75, 316–18

liturgical elements of, GIRM 70, 154, 346;
OCF 1–7, 21–42

music for, OCF 30–33; MCW 80, 83;
LMT 22–26, 30–33

offices and ministries in, OCF 8–20,
64–68, 213–15, 368–72

readings for, OCF 343–44, 348–72

rites for, SC 81–82; GIRM 380–85;
NSC 8–9; OCF 43–68, 98–103, 109–11,
119–20, 154–57, 177–82, 204–15,
234–46, 264–75, 316–18; BLS 110–14

GESTURES, LITURGICAL.
See Postures and gestures, liturgical

GODPARENTS,
CI 7–10; RCIA 11, 307, 404

GOOD FRIDAY,
GIRM 274, 346; GNLY 20; CB 312; BLS 83

HOLY ORDERS, SACRAMENT OF,
SC 76; GIRM 94, 147, 199, 203;
DMC 23–24; BLS 102

HOLY THURSDAY,
GIRM 3, 4, 199, 204, 380; GNLY 19, 28;
CB 297; BLS 82

HOMILIES
character and purpose of, SC 52; GIRM
29, 42, 55, 65–67, 97, 136, 165, 213,
360, 382; LM 24–27, 41; RCIA 125;
DMC 48; FYH 1–15, 40–77, 81, 100

interpretation of, FYH 25–36, 44–46

preparation for, SC 35, 55; FYH 50–55,
78–111, 116–20

variations of for special masses, OCF 27,
61; DMC 17, 24, 47–48

See also Liturgy of the Word; Scripture

INCENSATION,
GIRM 75, 145, 174, 178, 276, 277;
CB 84–98

INCULTURATION,
SC 37–40, 65, 68, 119; GIRM 26, 395,
398; BLS 38–45, 108

INITIATION, CHRISTIAN,
CI 1–2; RCIA 1–3; LMT 22–26; BLS 101

of adults. *See* Rite of Christian Initiation
of Adults

of adults in exceptional circumstances,
RCIA 331–39, 370–74; NSC 25–29

of children, RCIA 252–61, 277–80,
291–94, 304–8, 330; NSC 18–21

See also Baptism, sacrament of;
Confirmation, sacrament of;
Eucharist, sacrament of

LANGUAGE
and inculturation, IRL 13, 28–30, 33,
35–39, 50

and interpretation of Scripture, LM 111,
117, 119

use of vernacular, SC 36, 54, 63, 101;
GIRM 9, 11–13, 41, 320, 387, 389, 392;
DMC 31

See also Scripture; Texts, liturgical

LAY MINISTERS,
SC 28–29; GIRM 43, 50, 95–107, 112,
133, 139, 169, 335, 339; CI 7–10, 16–17;
RCIA 38; OCF 15; DMC 24; CB 18–41;
BLS 36.

*See also individual ministerial roles
by name*

LECTIONARY,
GIRM 61, 62, 118, 120, 128, 349, 355,
358, 359, 362

LECTORS,
SC 29; GIRM 38, 40, 48, 59, 71, 87, 97,
99, 101, 109, 116, 120, 128–30, 135,
138, 176, 194–98, 309, 311, 339, 352;
CB 30–32

LENT
character of, SC 109–10; GNLY 27–31;
CB 249, 253

liturgies of, GIRM 53, 62, 66, 305, 313,
346, 354, 355, 372, 373, 374, 380;
LM 25, 60, 67, 69, 97; CB 260

and Rite of Christian Initiation of Adults,
RCIA 7–9, 17–30, 125–28, 138

See also Ash Wednesday

LIGHTING,
GIRM 316; BLS 228–33

LITURGICAL YEAR
nature of, SC 102, 107–11; GNLY 1–2,
17–44; LMT 46–48; BLS 20, 81

Ordinary Time, GIRM 346, 355, 363, 365, 375, 377, 381; GNLY 43–44; CB 377–80
role of Sunday in, SC 106; GNLY 4–7, 16
role of weekdays in, GIRM 66, 354, 355, 358, 363, 365, 375–77, 381
seasons of, SC 107–10; GNLY 18–42; BLS 122–29
solemnities, feasts, and memorials, GIRM 11, 13, 40, 53, 55, 115, 305, 313, 346, 354, 357; GNLY 8–15, 59
See also individual days and seasons by name

LITURGIES.
See individual liturgical components by name

LITURGY COMMITTEES,
DMC 29; CB 34; MCW 10–14, 42

LITURGY OF THE EUCHARIST
consecration, GIRM 3, 11, 43, 79, 147, 150, 151, 179, 218, 275, 276, 324, 331
offertory and preparation of the gifts, GIRM 2, 5, 30, 33, 43, 55, 72–79, 93, 96, 140, 144, 146, 214, 215, 221, 222, 227, 230, 233, 276, 277, 363, 365; MCW 71; LMT 19
relationship of to Liturgy of the Word, SC 56; FYH 60–62
variations of for special masses, DMC 52–54
See also Acclamations; Communion under both forms; Eucharist, sacrament of; Music, liturgical; Prayers

LITURGY OF THE HOURS,
SC 83–85, 89–101; GNLY 3; LMT 34–45; BLS 115

LITURGY OF THE WORD
elements and nature of, SC 24; LM 1–37; CB 74–75; MCW 45; LMT 7
offices and ministries in, LM 38–57
readings during, GIRM 24, 29, 31, 33, 37, 43, 44, 55–60, 65, 67, 84, 94, 99, 101, 102, 109, 117, 119, 120, 122, 130–35, 171–76, 194–96, 212, 260, 262, 273–77, 306, 309, 349, 352, 355, 357–59, 367, 369, 370, 385, 390, 391, 395; LM 17, 23, 36, 74, 93–110; OCF 22–24
relationship of to Liturgy of the Eucharist, SC 56; FYH 60–62
variations of for special masses, OCF 59–61, 360–64; DMC 17, 41–49
See also Acclamations; Homilies; Music, liturgical; Order of Readings for Mass; Prayers; Scripture

MARRIAGE, SACRAMENT OF,
SC 77–78; NSC 10; CB 598–620; MCW 82; LMT 28–29; BLS 106–8

MARY, SAINT (VIRGIN MARY),
SC 103; GIRM 275, 346, 355, 375, 378; GNLY 8, 15; BLS 126, 130, 135–38, 156–57

MASSES, SPECIAL TYPES OF
Chrism Masses, GIRM 4, 199, 203, 204; GNLY 31; CB 274
Masses for the Dead, GIRM 381, 385; MCW 83; LMT 30–33
Masses for Various Needs, GIRM 347, 355, 371, 373, 376
Ritual Masses, SC 67; GIRM 15, 347, 359, 371, 372, 377
Votive Masses, GIRM 347, 355, 371, 375, 376
See also Funerals

MEMORIALS,
GIRM 354, 355, 357, 363, 376, 381; GNLY 8–15

MISSALS,
GIRM 1, 2, 6–10, 15, 25, 31, 43, 48, 73, 87, 90, 111, 118, 139, 147, 163, 170, 179, 190, 198, 215, 218, 256, 306, 363, 364, 368, 386, 389, 390, 394, 398, 399

MUSIC, LITURGICAL
Alleluia, GIRM 37, 43, 62, 63, 64, 131, 132, 175, 212, 261; GNLY 28; CB 371; MCW 55
chants, SC 116–17; GIRM 24, 37, 41, 43–44, 47, 48, 50, 52, 55, 62, 74, 86, 87, 103, 104, 121, 124, 131–32, 139, 142, 159, 175, 261, 366–67, 370, 390; MCW 64–69
communion song, GIRM 87, 269; MCW 48, 62, 72; LMT 18
composers of, SC 121; MCW 50–51, 70–78; LMT 26
copyright issues, MCW 78; LMT 70–71
entrance and recessional songs, GIRM 48, 256; MCW 44, 49, 60–62, 73; LMT 18–19
at funerals, OCF 30–33; MCW 80, 83; LMT 22–26, 30–33
general principles of, SC 112–14, 118–19, 121; MCW 10–41; LMT 6–15, 54–55
Glory to God, GIRM 37, 46, 53, 126, 134, 258; DMC 31; MCW 66
hymns, GIRM 39, 61, 88, 164
Lamb of God, GIRM 37, 43, 83, 155, 157, 240, 243, 267, 268, 366; DMC 31; MCW 68, 74; LMT 20; NDR 37
litanies, MCW 74; LMT 20

during Liturgy of the Word, LM 14, 17, 20–22, 23, 56, 89–91

Lord Have Mercy, MCW 65; LMT 21

offertory song, MCW 71; LMT 19

responsorial psalms, LM 19–22, 33, 56, 89; DMC 46; MCW 63

See also Acclamations; Liturgy of the Hours; Psalms

MUSICIANS, LITURGICAL

cantors, GIRM 48, 52, 53, 61, 62, 68, 71, 83, 87, 103, 104, 116, 138, 352; MCW 35; LMT 68–69

choirs, SC 14, 29, 114–15; GIRM 48, 52, 53, 62, 68, 83, 87, 103, 104, 114, 155, 216, 294, 310–13, 352; CB 39–41; DMC 22; MCW 36; LMT 32

and design of churches, BLS 88–90, 226–27

instrumentalists, SC 120; GIRM 32, 103, 142, 313, 393; DMC 32; CB 39–41; MCW 37–38; LMT 56–59

training of, LMT 63–70

MYSTERY, EXPERIENCE OF,

SC 115; GIRM 1, 3, 5, 8, 11–14, 22, 47, 50, 55, 65, 79, 89, 92, 142, 151, 178, 288, 359, 364–65, 368; LMT 65

ORDER OF READINGS FOR MASS

principles of, LM 1, 39, 45, 58–125

for saints' days, LM 70–71, 83–84

for Sundays and solemnities, LM 65–68, 93, 95, 97, 99, 100, 102, 105–8

for weekdays, LM 69, 82, 94, 96, 98, 101, 109–10

ORDINARY TIME.

See Liturgical year

PARISHES.

See Community of the church

PASSION (PALM) SUNDAY,

GIRM 346; GNLY 30–31; CB 263

PEACE, SIGN OF,

GIRM 82, 83, 154, 181, 239, 266; CB 99–103

PENANCE.

See Reconciliation, sacrament of

PENTECOST,

GNLY 22, 26; RCIA 24, 249; BLS 125

POSTURES AND GESTURES, LITURGICAL

bowing and genuflecting, GIRM 43, 49, 90, 122, 132, 135, 137, 143, 157, 160, 169, 173, 175, 185, 186, 195, 211, 222, 227, 230, 233, 242, 246, 248–51, 256,

262, 267, 268, 272, 274, 275, 277, 330; CB 68–71

kissing of altar, GIRM, 49, 90, 123, 134, 169, 173, 175, 186, 211, 251, 256, 262, 272, 273; CB 72–74

significance of, SC 30; GIRM 42–44, 96; CB 68–83; BLS 85–90

variations of for special masses, OCF 40–42; DMC 33–34

PRAYERS

after communion, GIRM 89, 90, 165–67, 184, 185, 271, 384

Eucharistic Prayer, GIRM 2, 30–33, 43, 72, 77–79, 147–52, 179, 180, 216–19, 226, 228, 229, 232, 235, 236, 355, 364, 365; DMC 52

general intercessions, SC 53–54; GIRM 36, 43, 55, 69–71, 94, 99, 138, 139, 171, 177, 178, 190, 197, 264, 309, 385; LM 30–31, 53; OCF 62, 364; DMC 22, 29; MCW 74

importance of, SC 12; GIRM 5, 15

Lord's Prayer, GIRM 36, 41, 81, 152, 153, 237, 266; MCW 59, 67

and music, MCW 47, 53, 56–58; LMT 15, 17

opening prayer, GIRM 30, 43, 45, 46, 48, 54, 127, 128, 259, 261, 355, 363

variations of for special masses, OCF 28–29, 62, 98–103, 348–67; DMC 10, 22, 27, 29, 50–52

See also Liturgy of the Hours

PRIESTS

as pastors, SC 11, 14, 19, 42, 56, 100, 114; GIRM 10, 11, 107

as preachers, FYH 1–12, 18–39, 77

as presiders, GIRM 4–5, 24, 30–33, 42–44, 47–54, 59, 66, 68–95, 108, 112–287, 294, 310, 337, 376; OCF 14; DMC 23; MCW 21–22; LMT 67

role of in building and renovation of churches, BLS 35, 76, 170–77

role of in catechesis, RCIA 13–15, 38, 43, 125

training of, SC 14–18, 115, 129

PROCESSIONS,

GIRM 44, 47, 74, 86, 105, 117–22, 160, 186, 188, 193, 210, 274, 276, 341, 350; OCF 120; DMC 34; CB 54; MCW 60–62

PROFESSION OF FAITH,

GIRM 36, 41, 43, 55, 67, 68, 137, 138, 263, 275; LM 29; DMC 39, 49; MCW 69

PSALMS,

SC 90–91; GIRM 39, 48, 61, 87, 391; LM 19–22, 33, 56, 89; OCF 25–26,

355–59; DMC 48; CB 33; MCW 72;
LMT 34–43, 69.
See also Music, liturgical

READERS.
See Lectors

RECONCILIATION, SACRAMENT
OF,
SC 72, 110; GIRM 15, 51, 373; CB 253;
MCW 81; LMT 21, 27; BLS 103–5

RITE OF CHRISTIAN INITIATION
OF ADULTS
offices and ministries in, RCIA 9–16
steps in, SC 64–71; GNLY 27; RCIA 1–8,
17–39, 41–47, 69, 75–93, 95–96, 98–101,
104–10, 118–28, 138–49, 185–93, 197,
200, 206–17, 244–51, 400–415, 434–37,
446–49, 459–63, 473–85, 505–6, 530–35,
547–49, 562–65; NSC 1–37; CB 249

RITES, LITURGICAL
character of, SC 3–4, 21, 34, 50, 62
communion, DMC 54; MCW 48, 62, 72;
LMT 18
concluding, GIRM 31, 90, 163, 170, 183,
272; OCF 63; DMC 54; MCW 49
introductory, GIRM 31, 35, 46, 49, 50, 90,
154, 170, 181, 254, 257; OCF 58;
DMC 40; MCW 44

SACRAMENTS, NATURE OF,
SC 7, 27, 36, 59, 63; CI 1–2; MCW 4–9.
See also individual sacraments by name

SACRISTY,
GIRM 45, 119, 193, 280, 334; CB 53;
BLS 234

SAINTS
feasts of, SC 108, 111; GIRM 11, 13, 40,
53, 55, 115, 305, 313, 346, 354, 357;
GNLY 8–15, 49–61; BLS 126, 130–31,
135–38
relics of, SC 8, 111; GIRM 277, 302; BLS 60

SANCTUARY,
BLS 54–55.
See also Altar; Ambo

SCRIPTURE
adaptation and translation of, DMC 43–46
cycle of readings from, LMT table II,
table III
relationship between Old and
New Testaments, LM 4, 66, 67, 84
study of, SC 16, 35, 51, 53, 90; RCIA 38;
DMC 13; FYH 50–55
See also Liturgy of the Word; Order of
Readings for Mass; Texts, liturgical

SECOND VATICAN COUNCIL,
LM 1, 58–59; RCIA 2; BLS 7–8, 27, 71,
234; NDR 19–21

SERVERS.
See Acolytes
Silence, SC 30; GIRM 43, 45, 51, 54–56,
66, 71, 78, 128, 130, 136, 147, 164–65,
271; OCF 34; DMC 37; LMT 59

STATIONS OF THE CROSS,
BLS 132–34

STATUES AND IMAGES,
SC 125; BLS 135–38

SUNDAY, OBSERVANCE OF,
SC 42, 49, 106, 131; GIRM 11, 13, 40, 51,
53, 64, 66, 68, 113, 115, 117, 119, 204,
305, 313, 346, 354, 357, 361, 363, 365,
372–74, 380; GNLY 1, 4–7; CB 228;
BLS 20, 116

SYMBOLS, NATURE OF,
SC 59; GIRM 67, 288, 301, 344, 349;
OCF 35–39; MCW 7–8; BLS 22–26

TABERNACLE,
SC 128; GIRM 274, 310, 314–16; CB 49;
BLS 70–80, 247–52

TEXTS, LITURGICAL,
SC 25, 31, 38; GIRM 1, 22, 24, 32, 38, 40,
57, 61, 101, 207, 352, 355–63, 390–94;
CB 115–18.
See also Liturgy of the Word; Scripture

THURIBLES,
GIRM 100, 119, 120, 132, 133, 135, 144,
173, 175, 179, 190, 212, 277

TRIDUUM.
See Easter; Good Friday; Holy Thursday

VATICAN II.
See Second Vatican Council

VESSELS,
GIRM 98, 118, 142, 163, 171, 178, 183,
192, 255, 279, 284, 306, 327–34, 348,
390; BLS 164–65; NDR 32–55.
See also Chalices

VESTMENTS,
SC 128; GIRM 92, 105, 114, 119, 120,
171, 209, 336–48, 373, 390; CB 37–38,
65–67; BLS 164–65